The Complete Guide to
Blender Graphics
Computer Modeling
& Animation

3RD EDITION

The Complete Guide to
Blender Graphics
Computer Modeling & Animation
3RD EDITION

JOHN M. BLAIN

CRC Press
Taylor & Francis Group
Boca Raton London New York

CRC Press is an imprint of the
Taylor & Francis Group, an **informa** business

AN A K PETERS BOOK

CRC Press
Taylor & Francis Group
6000 Broken Sound Parkway NW, Suite 300
Boca Raton, FL 33487-2742

© 2016 by Taylor & Francis Group, LLC
CRC Press is an imprint of Taylor & Francis Group, an Informa business

Printed and bound in India by Replika Press Pvt. Ltd.

No claim to original U.S. Government works

Printed on acid-free paper
Version Date: 20151120

International Standard Book Number-13: 978-1-4987-4645-8 (Paperback)

Library of Congress Cataloging-in-Publication Data

Names: Blain, John M., 1942- author.
Title: The complete guide to Blender graphics : computer modeling & animation / John M. Blain.
Description: Third edition. | Boca Raton : Taylor & Francis A CRC title, part of the Taylor & Francis imprint, a member of the Taylor & Francis Group, the academic division of T&F Informa, plc, [2016] | Includes bibliographical references and index.
Identifiers: LCCN 2015037888 | ISBN 9781498746458 (alk. paper)
Subjects: LCSH: Computer animation. | Three-dimensional display systems. | Computer graphics. | Blender (Computer file)
Classification: LCC TR897.7 .B573 2016 | DDC 777/.7--dc23
    LC record available at http://lccn.loc.gov/2015037888

Visit the Taylor & Francis Web site at
http://www.taylorandfrancis.com

and the CRC Press Web site at
http://www.crcpress.com

Contents

Introduction

Blender Platforms
Blender Versions
Graphical User Interface
Content
Evolution

Blender is a 3D Computer Graphics Modeling and Animation program. The program provides all the tools for creating models and scenes that may be made into still images or animated movies. Blender opens a world of creativity, which has been traditionally exclusive to those able to afford high-end graphics software.

The Blender program is maintained by the Blender Foundation and released as "Open Source Software," which is available for download and free to be used for any purpose. The program may be downloaded from: www.blender.org.

Blender is a comprehensive program with limitless possibilities, which will allow you to explore and understand the process of computer modeling and animation.

The Complete Guide to Blender Graphics is a manual designed for those who wish to undertake this learning experience and discover a wonderful creative new world. The book will help you with the basics of computer animation using Blender. My approach has been to introduce the Blender features with examples and diagrams referenced to the Graphical User Interface (GUI).

The GUI is the arrangement of windows and panels containing the controls for operating the program and is the gateway to the Blender world.

Blender has many features that allow you to create and animate models and characters in scenes combined with stunning visual effects. Scenes may be rendered into photo realistic images and animations into video clips. Video may be edited and compiled into movies. There is also the facility to create interactive video games. A comprehensive display of the Blender features is available at: www.blender.org/features/

In this third edition of *The Complete Guide to Blender Graphics* I have provided instruction reflecting the latest version of the program. Blender is continually being improved with new features being added as developments are made. The first edition of the book was prompted by the dramatic change to the GUI, which was implemented when

the transition from version 2.49 to 2.50 occurred. Since that time, further developments have subtlety changed some aspects of the program's interface and new exciting features have been incorporated.

Blender Platforms

Blender is a cross-platform application able to be operated on Windows, Linux, and Mac operating systems. The operation of Blender in this manual is applicable to all platforms but operations ancillary to the program, such as saving work to the computers hard drive, have been described exclusively using Windows.

Blender Versions

Blender has been around for a considerable time. Upon starting the program, the GUI shows a panel with the version number in the center of the screen. On each release, this panel has been changed to identify the version. Blender develops over time and as the development evolves, new releases (versions) of the program are made available.

Graphical User Interface

The **GUI** is the arrangement of windows, panels, and buttons that allow you, the user, to interact with the program. The interaction takes place through inputs via a computer keyboard and mouse.

By giving instructions with reference to keyboard and mouse actions, a series of commands has evolved. The list of commands is extensive and it is not recommended that a new user attempts to memorize the list without understanding the meaning. As you progress through this manual, many of the commands are repeated and you'll soon find that it becomes second nature. Of course, you might forget the obscure commands; therefore, a listing is provided in Appendix A.

Content

Blender is a comprehensive application and this book introduces many of its features. While learning and using Blender you will discover many subjects that have not been included. While it is tempting to add material, there is only so much room between the covers. It is my intention, as I discover new features, to write instruction and make this available as a supplement to the book on my website at: www.silverjb.limewebs.com

Evolution

Blender will continue to evolve and change. New versions of the program will inevitably be released with additions and changes incorporated, but the basic operation of the interface and the majority of the functions will remain. If you care to assist in maintaining this manual, your comments and suggestions are welcome. Please email your comments to silverjb12@gmail.com. Good luck and I am sure you will enjoy the experience.

The Author

John M. Blain was born in 1942 in Swindon, Wiltshire in England and then emigrated to Canada with his family in 1952. He now lives in Coffs Harbour, New South Wales in Australia.

Drawing and painting were skills John developed from an early age and, while attending school on Vancouver Island, he became interested in wood sculpture inspired by the work of the indigenous west coast people. Artistic pursuits were curtailed on graduating from high school when he returned to England to undertake a technical engineering apprenticeship. Following his apprenticeship, he worked for a short period in England then made the decision to return to Vancouver, Canada. On the voyage between Southampton and Vancouver he met his wife-to-be and Vancouver became a stopover for a journey to Sydney, Australia. In this new country he began work as an engineering draughtsman, married, had children, and studied engineering. The magic milestone of 7 years saw John move out of the city to the coastal town of Coffs Harbour, New South Wales, with his young family.

Coffs Harbour was a center for sawmill machinery and John became engaged in machinery design and manufacture. He acquired a sound knowledge of this industry, acting as installation engineer, and then progressing to sales. This work afforded travel throughout Australia and to Canada, the United States, and New Zealand.

On retirement, artistic pursuits returned with additional interests in writing and computers. Writing notes while learning computer animation using Blender resulted in *The Complete Guide to Blender Graphics*. The first edition, published in 2012, was well-received, which encouraged John to compile a second edition and this new book inline with the latest version of the Blender program and with the addition of new material.

Acknowledgments

Many thanks to Neal Hirsig for his encouragement and support, and his grand tour of Tufts and Harvard Universities and The Boston Subway.

Helen's infinite patience continues and without it this book could not be written.

—**John M. Blain**

Download Blender 2.76

Blender can be downloaded from: **www.blender.org**

Download Blender 2.76b

Blender 2.76b is the latest stable release from the Blender Foundation
To download it, please select your platform and location. Blender is Free

Blender 2.76b was released on November 3, 2015

Read about the new features and fixes in the Blender 2.76 Features page.
And here are the bugfixes for 'a' and 'b' updates.

How do I install Blender?

To install Blender, download the appropriate package for your platform. The Windows version comes with an optional self-extracting installer, for other operating systems you can simply unpack the compressed file to the location of your choice.

Provided the Blender binary is in the original extracted directory, Blender will run straight out of the box. No system libraries or system preferences are altered.

Recommended Viewing

Blender 3D Design Course: Tufts University

The Blender 3D Design Course provided by Neal Hirsig of Tufts University is a self-paced online educational facility providing a comprehensive series of video tutorials, PDF tutorials, and learning exercises. It can be found at www.gryllus.net

The video tutorials provide the student with an introduction to the many facets of the Blender program. The tutorials are presented in an ordered structure that lead the student gently into the complex and fascinating world of computer modeling and animation using the Blender program. Where you see this logo throughout the manual gives an approximate reference to the relevant Learning Unit and Video Tutorial provided on the Blender 3D Design Course website.

To access the 3D Design Course video tutorials, go to the website address shown above. Click on the "Lesson Number" heading to open a selection menu for Video Tutorials. Clicking on a Tutorial will play the tutorial. You may download the tutorials creating a video library of the Blender subjects.

Supplements to the Book

The author's website outlining the contents of this book includes supplementary exercises in Blender on a variety of topics. Having studied Blender through *The Complete Guide* to *Blender Graphics* the reader will find the exercises interesting and useful (www.silverjb.limewebs.com).

1

The Blender Interface

1.1 The Graphical User Interface

The graphical user interface (GUI) is the arrangement of windows and panels that allow "you," the operator, to interact with the computer program. In the early days of computing interaction, this took place purely by entering keyboard commands. This type of operation is still in use when DOS applications are used where "Command Line" input is required. With computer graphics, by enlarge, windows type systems are employed, which use a graphical display, hence "Graphical User Interface" (GUI).

To operate Blender you must start by becoming familiar with the array of windows and panels that comprise the GUI. This display is the initial input and output to and from the program. You input commands by clicking the mouse buttons with the mouse cursor positioned at specific locations in the GUI, which then allows you to select actions from menus or enter values either by typing or adjusting sliders. In return, Blender outputs information to you via the display (The Screen) on your computer monitor.

1.2 The Blender Screen

When Blender first opens, the screen displays the GUI windows, as shown in Figure 1.1. On some operating systems, the screen may not display the GUI full size upon start up.

Lesson 01
01-01
Blender
Default Scene

1

Tools panel

Expansion button

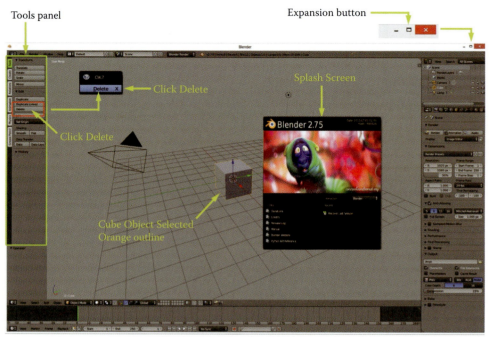

Click Delete

Splash Screen

Click Delete

Cube Object Selected
Orange outline

Figure 1.1

Graphical user interface (GUI)

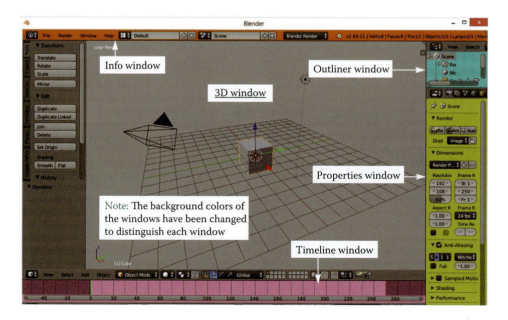

Info window

Outliner window

3D window

Properties window

Note: The background colors of
the windows have been changed
to distinguish each window

Timeline window

Figure 1.2

1. The Blender Interface

Left click on the expansion button in the upper RH corner of the window. The Blender windows open with the "Splash Screen" panel in the middle (there are web page links included here). This panel shows which version of Blender you have opened. Blender is continually being amended and revised and new releases of the program are made available. Check the Blender website to keep up to date with the program. Left click anywhere on the screen to remove the "Splash Screen" panel.

Figure 1.3

Note: You can have more than one Blender version installed at the same time.

The default Blender GUI displays with five different windows opened (Figure 1.2). The main window, the 3D window, shows a view of three-dimensional space with a cube object located at its center. The grid represents the horizontal midplane of the view.

Beside the windows displayed, there are 16 other window types available for selection. Look at the lower LH corner of the 3D window and note the icon (Figure 1.3). This is the icon representing the **3D window**. Each window has an icon displayed in the upper or lower LH corner of the window representing the window type.

Clicking on a window type icon displays a menu for selecting a different type of window (Figure 1.4). Selecting a different window from the menu changes the current window into the type selected.

Here's an example: In the lower LH (left-hand) corner of the 3D window, click on the icon with the mouse cursor. Select "Graph Editor," from the menu and the window changes to the "Graph Editor" window. Click on the "Graph Editor" icon and select "3D View"—the window reverts to the 3D window. Any window may be changed to a different window type in this way.

Editor type:
- Python Console
- File Browser
- Info
- User Preferences
- Outliner
- Properties
- Logic Editor
- Node Editor
- Text Editor
- Movie Clip Editor
- Video Sequence Editor
- UV/Image Editor
- NLA Editor
- DopeSheet
- Graph Editor
- Timeline
- 3D View

Figure 1.4

1.3 Interface Input

The user input to the program is described in this manual using a standard keyboard and a three-button or wheel mouse. Blender is designed to be operated with one hand on the mouse and the other on the keyboard (Laptop users will have to adapt to the instructions provided as notes throughout this manual).

Up to this point I have assumed that you are familiar with the keyboard and mouse and the input of data to the computer via these devices. Blender uses a system of controls employing the keyboard and mouse as follows:

Lesson 01
01-04
Blender
For Laptops

Lesson 01
01-06
Blender Controls

Button Control. Activated by positioning the mouse cursor over the button and clicking the LMB (left mouse button). Button controls either perform a direct action or activate a secondary function. For example:

Click "Delete" in the "Tool Panel" (LHS of window)

Figure 1.5

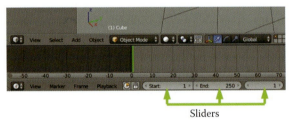

Boxes checked

Properties window—Output tab (RHS of screen)

Figure 1.6

See lower LHS of screen

Sliders

Figure 1.7

With an object selected in the 3D window, clicking on the "Delete" button in the tool panel (Figure 1.5) requires you to click on a "OK-Delete" button to delete the object. Clicking on the "Scale" button in the tool panel requires you to drag the mouse cursor in the 3D window to scale the selected object (click the LMB to cancel the scale action).

Note: An "Object" is a model of something in the 3D window. The default "Cube" object is a model. The "Object" is selected by positioning the mouse cursor over it and clicking the right mouse button (RMB). The "Object" is selected when it has an orange outline. You deselect an "Object" by pressing the A key on your keyboard.

Most button controls are duplicated by keyboard shortcut keys. For example:

Pressing the X key on the keyboard with an object selected prompts the "OK-Delete" button.

Pressing the S key with an object selected and then dragging the mouse cursor scales the object.

Checking (ticking) the button controls requires you to click the LMB in a small square to place a tick, which activates a function (Figure 1.6).

Clicking a menu selection button displays a drop-down menu that requires a selection by clicking the LMB on an option. This activates a function.

Slider Controls. Activated by three separate methods (Figure 1.7):

Click the LMB with the mouse, hold, and drag right or left to change a value.

Click the LMB on the arrows at either side of the slider to incrementally alter a value.

Click the LMB on the value displayed in the slider, press the Delete key, retype a new value, and press Enter.

1.4 Keyboard Shortcuts

Keyboard shortcuts are used extensively in Blender. Some of the most common commands used are listed in "Appendix A" at the back of the book. I would also recommend you to the Keyboard Shortcuts website presented by Waldo Bronchart where you will find an interactive keyboard display showing the shortcuts for different Blender windows (Figure 1.8).

www.waldobronchart.be/blenderkeyboard/

1. The Blender Interface

Blender 2.66a Keyboard Shortcuts
A visual explorer for Blender's default keyboard shortcuts

Press buttons or modifier key on your keyboard to preview underlying shortcuts!

Developed by Waldo Bronchart, Design inspired by Sutherland Boswell and Levi Wintering

Figure 1.8

1.5 Window Arrangements

Lesson 01
01-02
Splitting Joining
Extending
Editor Windows

Every window and panel within a window may be resized. Place the mouse cursor on a window or panel border and it changes to a double-headed arrow (Figure 1.9). Click and hold with the LH mouse button (referred to as LMB from now on) and drag the arrow to resize the panel or window. This works on both horizontal and vertical borders.

Every window may be divided to form a new window. In opposite corners of each window there is a small cross-hatched triangle, which is a **splitter widget** (Figure 1.10). When the mouse cursor is placed on the cross hatching, the cursor changes to a white cross. Click, hold, and drag the cross into the window and the window divides in two, forming an identical copy of the original window. One copy may then be changed to another window type as previously described.

Mouse cursor on the splitter widget

Figure 1.9

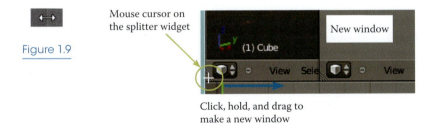

Click, hold, and drag to make a new window

Figure 1.10

To cancel a window, place the mouse cursor on the cross hatching (it changes to a cross), click LMB and drag it out of the window into the window to be canceled (Figure 1.11). A large arrow appears pointing into the window to be canceled. Release the LMB and the

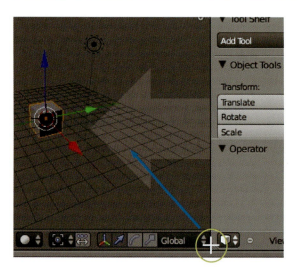

Figure 1.11

window cancels. Before releasing, you can move the cursor from one window to the other and the arrow changes direction accordingly. Releasing the LMB cancels the window into which the arrow is pointing.

The individual windows will be explained as you progress through the book but first you need to understand the components of a window in general terms (Figure 1.12).

One of the great features of Blender is that the GUI may be modified to suit the preferences of individual users. I have mentioned how to resize windows and panels and how to split and cancel windows, but there are many other features that can be changed. At this stage I will demonstrate an example just to show how this is done. The possibilities are endless, so like many things in Blender, you will have to experiment and try these options for yourself. The following example will introduce you to the "User Preferences" window.

Panel (tool panel)   Window (3D window)

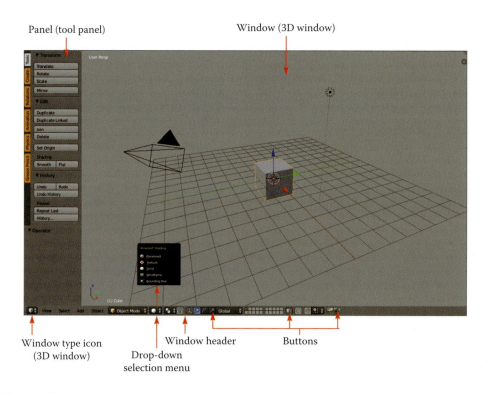

Window type icon   Window header   Buttons
(3D window)
              Drop-down
              selection menu

Figure 1.12

1.6 The User Preferences Window

This example will change the 3D window background. Divide the 3D window in two (see the previous instructions) and make one part the "User Preferences" window by clicking the window type icon; or, you can go to the "Info" window header, click on "File" then click on "User Preferences Window." In the latter scenario, Blender opens an overlapping version of the user preferences window—this is the only time that Blender opens one window over another.

> Note: The "Info" window is at the top of the GUI. Only the window header is shown in this case. The header of any window is the horizontal strip at either the top or the bottom of a window. You may click on the edge of the "Info" window (double-headed arrow displays) and drag to open the window. In the case of the "Info" window you will not see anything until you perform some action in one of the other windows.

Go to the top of the "User Preferences" window (Figure 1.13) and click on "Themes." At the left-hand side (LHS) of the window you will see a list of the different windows. Click on "3D View." You will see a series of colored panels with headings next to them. At the bottom of the second column you will see "Gradient High/Off." This is a gray-colored panel, which is the color of the 3D window background. Click on the panel and a color picker panel will display (Figure 1.14).

Figure 1.13

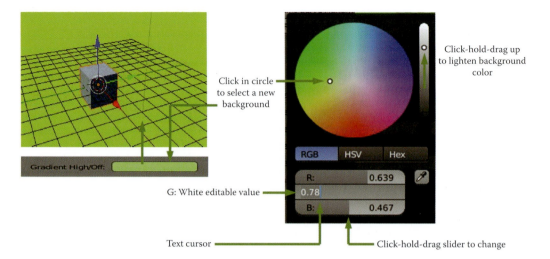

Figure 1.14

At the right-hand side (RHS) of the panel is a vertical bar showing a color gradient from white at the top to black at the bottom with a white dot in the middle. Click the LMB on the dot and drag, while holding the button. Move the dot upward, and you'll see the background color of the 3D window lighten (the color picker also lightens). You can click the LMB anywhere in the colored circle to change the 3D window background to any color you like. You can also change the color by altering the RGB (red-green-blue) values (click the LMB on either the R, G, or B value and the text changes to white, which indicates that it is editable). Press delete to delete the value and retype a new value. A second click before deleting will place a blue text cursor, which allows individual numbers to be edited. You may also click and drag the slider. The background color will remain set for the remainder of the session. You can now close the "User Preferences" window by clicking the red cross in the upper RH corner of the window. Closing the window has set your preference for the remainder of the session. When Blender is closed and then restarted the default settings will be reinstated. If you want to set changes permanently, click on "Save User Settings" at the bottom of the "User Preferences" window; this will change the new setting for the next time you start Blender. Close the window by clicking on the close button (the cross) in the upper RH corner of the window.

If you look around the "User Preferences" window, you will see that there are many options. Feel free to experiment. If you goof up when changing the themes, just press "Reset to Default Theme" at the bottom of the window—this puts everything back to square one.

1.7 Preset Interface Arrangements

While still on the subject of GUIs I will point out that Blender has some preset arrangements for working on different aspects in the program.

In the "Info" window header at the top of the default screen arrangement to the RH of the "Help" button, there is a little window button with "Default" in the panel. "Default" is referring to the default Blender screen arrangement or GUI. Placing the

mouse cursor over the window button displays "Choose Screen layout." Clicking on the button displays a drop-down selection menu with a choice of screen arrangement options. You will see that "Default" is highlighted in blue (Figure 1.15). Clicking on any of the options changes the screen arrangement with window types appropriate for the named function of the program.

Figure 1.15

1.8 The 3D Window

Before you can actually create anything in Blender you should understand the 3D window. First, you should understand the basic concept of creating something with computer graphics. A scene is created; the scene may be static or animated. In either case, the scene is rendered. The render produces a computer image in the case of a static scene or a computer animation in the case of an animated scene. Images are rendered to a number of file formats such as JPEG or PNG while animations are rendered into video files. The scene is set up in the 3D window.

The default 3D window in Blender is shown in Figure 1.16. The window panels have been colored to distinguish them. The 3D window comprises a main window panel and a side "Object Tools" panel. The 3D window header is the strip across the bottom of the window with all the buttons. The default 3D window contains a cube object, a lamp, and a camera. Without the lamp or camera, nothing will render.

The "Object Tools" panel can be hidden from view by pressing the T key on the keyboard. Press the T key again to show the "Object Tool" panel; this process is referred to as toggling. You can also drag the edge of the panel to close it.

Besides the "Object Tools" panel, there is the "Object Properties" panel, which, by default, is hidden. Press the N key with the mouse cursor in the 3D window or click on the expansion icon to show the panel (see note following). Here you will see values pertaining to the object that is selected in the 3D window (Figure 1.17).

Note: With the "Objects Tool" panel and the "Objects Properties" panel hidden, a small tab with a cross is displayed in the upper corners of the 3D window; this is the expansion icon. Clicking the LMB on these will also toggle the display of the panels.

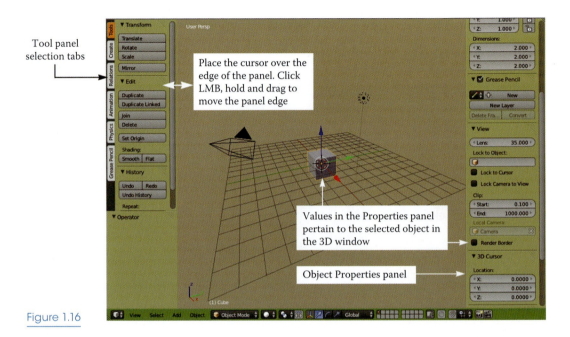

Tool panel selection tabs

Place the cursor over the edge of the panel. Click LMB, hold and drag to move the panel edge

Values in the Properties panel pertain to the selected object in the 3D window

Object Properties panel

Figure 1.16

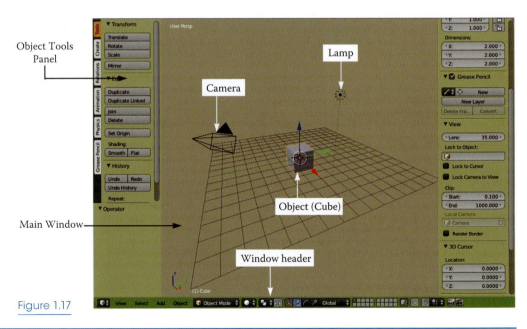

Object Tools Panel

Lamp

Camera

Object (Cube)

Main Window

Window header

Figure 1.17

1. The Blender Interface

By default, the cube is selected as shown by the orange outline around the cube. An object is deselected by pressing the A key and selected by clicking on it with the RMB. Note that if you deselect an object, then press the A key or press the A key a second time, you will select everything in the 3D window.

Try it out: Press the A key to deselect. Click the RMB on the camera. Press the A key to deselect again. Click the RMB on the cube (this selects the cube again).

Note also that with the "Object Properties" panel displayed, the values change according to which object you have selected. At this stage do not be concerned with the values; we are just becoming familiar with the broad outline of the interface.

Remember that in the 3D window you are seeing a three-dimensional representation of a world. The squared grid in the scene represents the horizontal midplane of the world on the X- and Y-axes. The green line on the grid is the Y-axis and the red line is the X-axis. The vertical axis is the Z-axis. If you look at the lower LH corner of the window you see these axes displayed. You also see in white the name of the object selected.

Lesson 01
01-08
Blender Grid
Units and Scale

Lesson 01
01-09
X Y and Z Axis

Figure 1.19

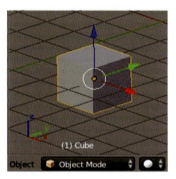

Figure 1.18

The red, green, and blue arrows on the cube object are a 3D manipulator for moving the object around on the scene (Figure 1.18). Click the manipulator button in the window header to toggle the 3D manipulator "On-Off" (Figure 1.19).

This will be discussed in detail later but for now you will use it to move the cube. Click on the green arrow and, while holding the mouse button down, drag the mouse to the right. The cube outline turns white in the process indicating that it is in "Grab" mode and the Y axis is displayed (green line). Release the LMB and the cube will stay where it is placed.

We moved the cube so that you can see the small circle with the cross hairs at the center of the world. This is the 3D cursor, **NOT the mouse cursor** (Figure 1.20).

If you click the LMB anywhere in the scene with the mouse, the 3D cursor relocates to wherever you have clicked. If you were to add another object into the scene, that object would be located at the position of the 3D cursor.

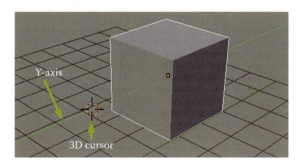

Figure 1.20

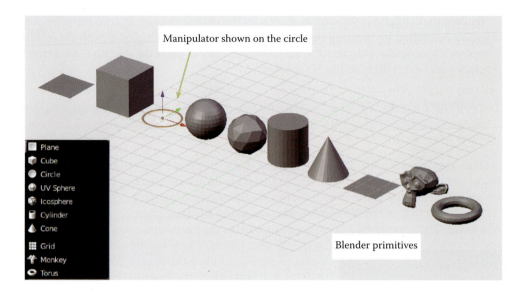

Manipulator shown on the circle

- Plane
- Cube
- Circle
- UV Sphere
- Icosphere
- Cylinder
- Cone
- Grid
- Monkey
- Torus

Blender primitives

Figure 1.21

Lesson 01
01-10
Primitive Mesh
Object

The cube object is called a "Primitive," which is one of ten basic shapes available in Blender from which to commence modeling (Figure 1.21). Click on "Add" in the 3D window header then place the mouse cursor on "Mesh" in the drop-down menu to see the list of primitives. You can click on one to add it to the scene. Another way to do this is to press keyboard Shift + the A key with the mouse cursor in the 3D window to display the same list (Add—Mesh). As you will see there are numerous other options in the selection menu.

1.9 Window Modes

Lesson 01
01-07
Mesh Modeling
Modes and
Viewport
Shading

The 3D window, by default, is opened in "Object" mode. You will see this in the window header. By clicking on the drop-down selection menu you are able to select one of the other modes (Figure 1.22). At this stage, we only need be concerned with the "Edit" mode option.

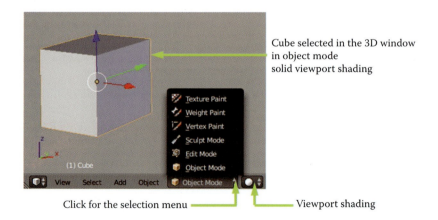

Cube selected in the 3D window
in object mode
solid viewport shading

Click for the selection menu

Viewport shading

Figure 1.22

1. The Blender Interface

"Object" mode allows us to move, rotate, and scale an object in the scene while "Edit" mode allows us to change the shape of the object.

To change between the two modes, you can select the mode from the drop-down menu in the header. Since it is common to switch between "Object" and "Edit" mode, pressing the Tab key toggles between these two modes.

With the cube selected in the 3D window and the mouse cursor positioned in the window, press Tab. You will see the object shown with its edges drawn in orange with dots at each corner; the dots are called vertices (Figure 1.23). The significance of this will be discussed in detail later. For now, toggle back to "Object" mode.

Next to the 3D windows mode selection is the windows display selection button called, "Viewport Shading." You may elect to display the 3D window in five different ways. The default display is "Solid." The alternatives are: "Bounding Box, Wireframe, Texture and Rendered." The significance of these options will be explained as you progress through the book but for now note that the "Rendered" option allows you to view the window as if you had rendered an image of the scene. With the window in "Solid Viewport Shading" mode you would render an image of the scene by pressing F12 on the keyboard.

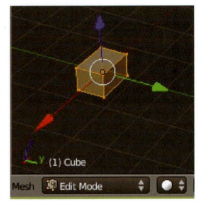

Figure 1.23

Note: Rendering is the process of converting what the camera sees in your scene into an image or into a movie clip if the scene is animated.

1.10 Layers

Like many other graphics programs, Blender uses layers to aid in constructing complex scenes. Note the display in the 3D window header (Figure 1.24); this represents 20 separate layers. Imagine sheets of transparent drawing paper with different items on each sheet being placed one on top of the other. Each square represents one sheet. The orange dot in the first square indicates that an object is on the first layer. The fact that the first square is shaded tells us that we are viewing the first layer.

Lesson 02
02-05
Blender Layers

To move to another layer, click on one of the squares. It becomes shaded indicating that the layer is being seen in the window. If you click on square 2, the screen shows an empty layer. The orange dot remains in square 1 indicating that there is an object in layer 1 (it is not necessarily selected). Go back to square 1.

To move the cube object to layer 2, first select the cube in the 3D window. Press the M key and the "Move to Layer" window appears. Click on square 2 and the cube is moved to layer 2 as indicated by the orange dot displayed in square 2 in the window header (Figure 1.25). Note there is still a dot in square 1. This shows that there are objects on layer 1 (the camera and the lamp).

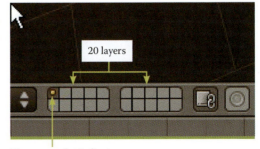

20 layers

The orange dot indicates that an object is in the first layer

Figure 1.24

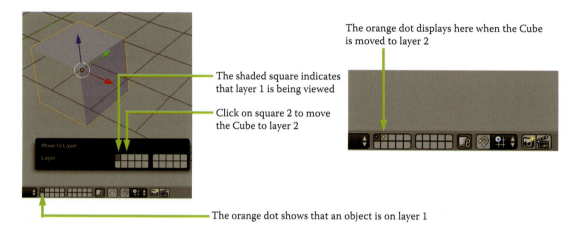

The orange dot displays here when the Cube is moved to layer 2

The shaded square indicates that layer 1 is being viewed

Click on square 2 to move the Cube to layer 2

The orange dot shows that an object is on layer 1

Figure 1.25

To replace the cube in layer 1, click on square 2 in the header, select the cube in the 3D window, press the M key with the cursor in the 3D window, and click on square 1 in the "Move to Layer" window. Click on square 1 to show layer 1 in the 3D window header.

1.11 Object Tools Panel (Tool Shelf Panel)

The "Object Tool Panels" located at the LH side of the 3D window provides quick access to a variety of tools and functions. There are five different display options which are accessed by clicking on the tabs arranged vertically at the LHS of the panel (Figure 1.1). The options are "Create, Relations, Animation, Physics, and Grease Pencil."

By default, the panel is displayed with the "Tools" option active and with the "Transform," "Edit," and "History" tabs shown. The different "Tabs" are opened and closed by clicking on the small triangle next to the name of the tab. The functions are activated by clicking on a panel and using the keyboard or the mouse in the 3D window.

Note: The functions available in the "Tools" panel are relevant to the object that is selected in the 3D window. The functions that are available will vary depending on the type of object.

Note: The "Object Tools Panel" may be hidden from view by pressing the T key on the keyboard. Press the T key again to show the panel.

To demonstrate how the panel works; with the cube selected in the 3D window, in the "Tools" panel option click on "Translate" in the "Transform" tab and move the mouse.

The cube in the 3D window is moved. In the case of the default "Cube" object the orange outline turns white indicating that it is in "Grab" mode and moving the mouse repositions the object. Click LMB to deactivate.

The "Create" option allows you to add mesh objects and other items into your scene the same as pressing Alt + A and selecting from the drop-down menu.

The significance of the other panel options will become obvious as you progress through the book and discover the features of Blender.

Note: When you change from "Object" mode to "Edit" mode the contents of the "Tool Panels" change. This change occurs for all of the panel mode options.

Enter the tool name in the search bar

In earlier versions of Blender there was a search bar at the top of the tool shelf panel where you could enter the name of a tool and it would be added to the shelf. In later versions, since the tool shelf has evolved into a more comprehensive shortcut option, the search bar has disappeared. The search bar is now accessed by pressing the space bar with the cursor in the 3D window. Items may now be found by entering key words much as you would in a search engine (Figure 1.26).

Figure 1.26

1.12 Moving in 3D Space

In a 3D (three dimensional) program, not only do you have to consider where you are in two dimensions (height and width), but you also need to consider depth (how close or far away). Moving around in the 3D window is controlled by the mouse and the keyboard number pad.

Lesson 01
01-05
Maneuvering Around in 3D Space

The Blender default scene opens in the "User Perspective" view showing a cube object located at the center of the scene and with a camera and a lamp positioned relative to the cube. (A perspective view projects parallel lines to a single vanishing point somewhere in the distance. See the midplane grid.)

The center of the scene, in this case, is located at the center of the 3D space therefore the cube, camera, and lamp are all positioned relative to the center. The position of objects relative to each other is important when considering 3D space especially with lamps (lighting) and the camera (seeing). When taking a photograph with a camera, the position of the camera relative to what you want to photograph and where the lighting is located determine what you get in your snapshot. This is the same in a Blender scene.

To see where objects are positioned relative to each other Blender allows you to move objects around in the 3D window. Sometimes it is more convenient and easier to see how far objects are separated by using different orthographic views. Think of a standard three-view orthographic drawing: top, front, and right-side views. These views match up with

the 7, 1, and 3 keys on the number pad. Put your cursor in the 3D window and try pressing those number keys.

Note: When either of the keys are first pressed the view will change to a perspective view. For example, pressing Num Pad 7 opens "Top Perspective" view (see upper LH corner of 3D window). The view shows a square top view of the Cube but note the line pointing from the Lamp toward the Cube. This line is actually a vertical line drawn in perspective. Press Num Pad 5 to go to "Top Orthographic" view. Pressing Num Pad 1 and 3 will now change the view in "Orthographic" projection.

Lesson 01
01-04
Blender
For Laptops

Note: Some laptops do not have number pad keys. In the user preferences window, click on "Input" at the top of the window and then, at the LHS of the window, tick "Emulate Numpad." You can now use the number keys on your laptop to emulate the number pad on a standard keyboard.

Note: To see the four views shown in Figure 1.24 go to the 3D window header and click on "View." From the menu that displays select (click) "Toggle Quad View" or press Ctrl + Alt + Q on the keyboard. Repeat the operation to revert to "User Perspective" view.

When moving from the user perspective view to either of the orthographic views, at first you'll get a top, front, or end **perspective** view (Figure 1.27). Look at the lamp and you should see a line pointing toward the cube. Press on the number pad 5 to get the true orthographic view.

Lesson 02
02-10
Camera View

Pressing the number pad 5 again toggles back to the perspective view. Pressing the number pad 0 will put you into camera view (which is what the camera sees, Figure 1.28). To get back to the user perspective view, press the number pad 5 twice. One press gets a "User Orthographic" view and the second press gets the user perspective view. However, you'll notice that it's not quite the same as what we had in the default scene. We need to rotate the view a bit. Click and hold the middle mouse button and wiggle it slightly; you'll see the scene rotating in the window. Wiggle and practice is the best way to learn. This all sounds a bit complicated, but you will soon get used to it.

When you go to camera view (number pad 0), most of the window becomes shaded leaving a small window in the middle with a dotted line around it (Figure 1.28). This is the part that will actually render to an image. Right click on the outer line and it turns orange—this means you have the camera selected. You can now move and rotate the camera like any object in any view. The shading in the camera view is called "Passepartout" and can be

Lesson 01
01-05
Maneuvering
Around in
3D Space

removed to let you have a clear view of everything in the scene. I will show you how to do that later.

The number pad arrow keys (2, 4, 6, 8) will rotate you in 3D space (not in camera view). The + (Plus) and − (Minus) keys on the number pad will zoom in and out. The **number pad**

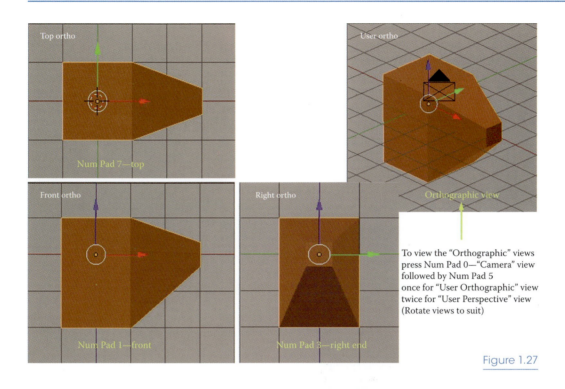

To view the "Orthographic" views
press Num Pad 0—"Camera" view
followed by Num Pad 5
once for "User Orthographic" view
twice for "User Perspective" view
(Rotate views to suit)

Figure 1.27

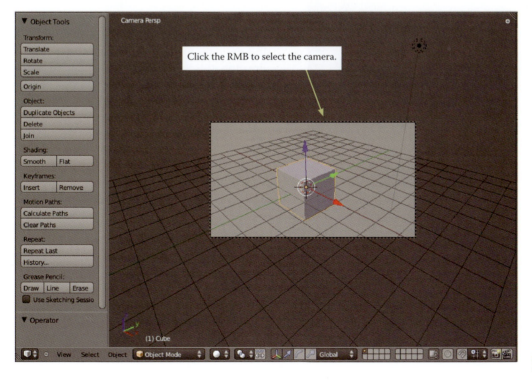

Click the RMB to select the camera.

Figure 1.28

"period—Del" key will center your view on the selected object on your screen. Rotating in 3D space will now use the center of the selected object as the pivot point.

The mouse serves a number of functions. Clicking the LMB in the 3D window repositions the 3D cursor in the scene. Wherever the 3D cursor is positioned is where the next object you add to the scene is located. Clicking the RMB on an object selects that object. Similarly, in edit mode, clicking the RMB on a vertex will select that vertex. Pressing the B key on the keyboard then clicking the LMB and dragging a rectangle over an object will select that object. Click the LMB to cancel. Pressing the C key on the keyboard changes the mouse cursor in the 3D window to a circle. Scroll the mouse wheel to change the size of the circle. Position the circle over an object and click the LMB to select the object. Press the Esc key to cancel the circle selection. Click and hold the middle mouse button or mouse wheel and drag to rotate the 3D view. Scrolling the mouse wheel zooms in and out on the scene.

Don't attempt to memorize all the combinations; they will become second nature with practice since they are used over and over again.

1.13 The Blender View Menu

The Blender view menu shows the full range of options to manipulate the view ports (Figure 1.29).

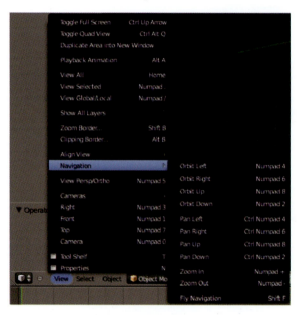

Figure 1.29

Note: Clicking on the "Toggle Quad View" option displays three orthographic views and "User Perspective" view, in separate windows. The keyboard shortcut to select this option is to press Ctrl + Alt + the Q key. Pressing this combination a second time toggles to the front orthographic view. To return to the user perspective view, press the number pad 0 (camera view) then press the number pad 5 twice and rotate the view.

The view menu also shows the shortcut keys for the right, front, and top orthographic views. These are the number pad 1, 3, and 7 keys previously mentioned. Besides these views, the following views are also available:

- Number pad 7: top
- Number pad 1: front
- Number pad 3: right side
- Number pad 0: camera view
- Ctrl + 7: bottom
- Ctrl + 1: rear
- Ctrl + 3: left side
- The number pad 2 and 8 keys rotate the view about the *x*-axis.

- The number pad 4 and 6 keys rotate the view about the *z*-axis
- The number pad period key (.) centers the selected object.
- The number pad forward slash key (/) zooms in on the selected object.
- Hold the Shift + the F key and move the cursor to pan the scene. Click the LMB to stop.

A Fun Way to Navigate: Press the Shift + F key. In the center of the 3D window you will see cross hairs like the centering marks in a telescopic gun sight. Move the mouse and the 3D window pans the view allowing you to see your scene from different perspectives. Click LMB to deactivate. Clicking "View"—"Navigation"—"Fly Navigation" displays the corners of a rectangle in the 3D window. Moving the mouse and using the scroll wheel produces a flying effect. Click LMB to stop.

Warning: Be very gentle with your mouse movements.

Lesson 01
01-04
Blender
For Laptops

Note: The numeric keys at the top of the keyboard change the active layers not the viewports, unless the "Emulate Numpad" function has been set for a laptop computer.

1.14 The Properties Window

The 3D window is the place where you set up your scene to see what you are creating and where you are going. The "Properties" window on the other hand is the engine room with all the controls that drive everything (Figure 1.30). The "Properties" window is the main part of the vertical panel at the RH of the default screen. It controls what you see in the 3D window, how objects move and behave, and finally how the scene renders. It controls how your artificial world is configured, and how everything in the scene appears, moves, and interacts with everything else.

To get an insight into the "Properties" window in practical terms, look at the row of buttons displayed in the window header (Figure 1.31). These buttons are the starting point for everything that happens.

Note: In the 3D window, the default cube object is selected as seen by the orange outline. Buttons available in the properties window header vary depending on what is selected in the 3D window. Try clicking the RMB on the camera then the lamp and back on the cube: You will see the buttons in the header change.

Direction Nomenclature Example : Go to the:

"Properties" window
"Render" button
"Dimensions" tab

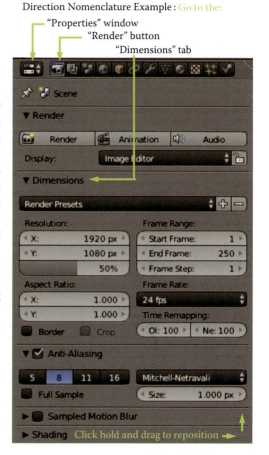

Figure 1.30

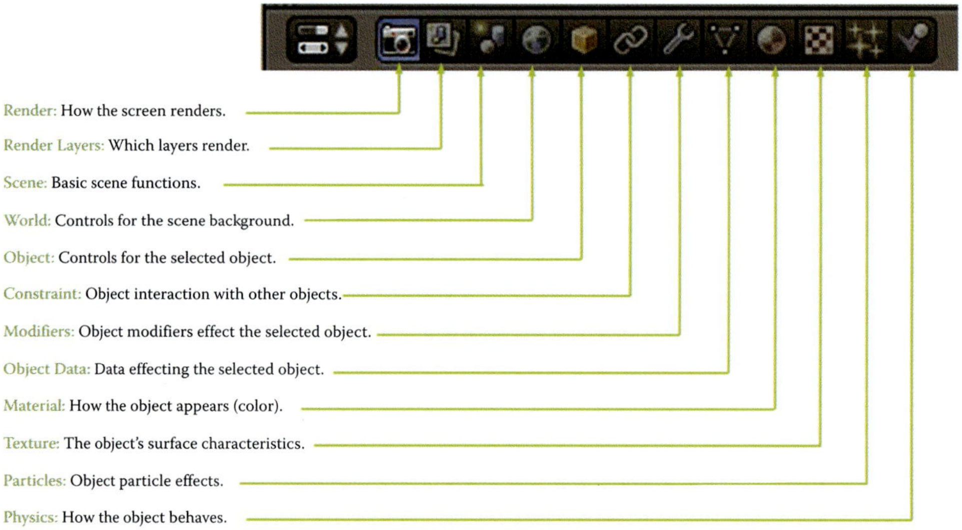

Render: How the screen renders.

Render Layers: Which layers render.

Scene: Basic scene functions.

World: Controls for the scene background.

Object: Controls for the selected object.

Constraint: Object interaction with other objects.

Modifiers: Object modifiers effect the selected object.

Object Data: Data effecting the selected object.

Material: How the object appears (color).

Texture: The object's surface characteristics.

Particles: Object particle effects.

Physics: How the object behaves.

Figure 1.31

Note: Direction to the components of the "Properties" window is given per the following nomenclature (Figure 1.30):

Go to the "Properties" window, "Render" button, "Dimensions" tab.

By default, Blender opens the "Properties" window in the default screen arrangement with the "Render" button active and with the window containing all the render buttons and values. The render button is seen highlighted in blue. Figure 1.31 shows the default "Properties" window header.

It is not my intention to describe the function of every button and value in the properties window. The specific operation of buttons and controls will be demonstrated as you progress through this book and even then it will be up to you to experiment and record as you go.

Clicking on each of the buttons in the header changes the display of buttons and controls in the window. The buttons and controls are separated into panels called tabs arranged in a stack. Some tabs are open and some are closed. Clicking on the little triangle in front of the tab name toggles the tab open or closed. With some buttons selected there are too many tabs to fit in the window. When this happens, a scroll bar appears at the RHS of the window.

The "Properties" window may be resized by dragging the border and may be changed to another window type if required. The location of the tabs in the properties window can be rearranged by clicking and holding the dimpled (dots arranged in a rectangle) area at the upper RHS of the tab and dragging it up or down in the stack.

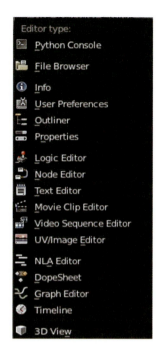

Editor type:

- Python Console
- File Browser
- Info
- User Preferences
- Outliner
- Properties
- Logic Editor
- Node Editor
- Text Editor
- Movie Clip Editor
- Video Sequence Editor
- UV/Image Editor
- NLA Editor
- DopeSheet
- Graph Editor
- Timeline
- 3D View

1.15 Blender Windows

The application of the Blender windows will be explained as you progress through the different sections of the manual (Figure 1.32). There are some windows, however, that require special mention since they have a more general application rather than applying to a specific topic. For that reason, when sticking to the basics, they can be overlooked. They are worth mentioning here to make you aware.

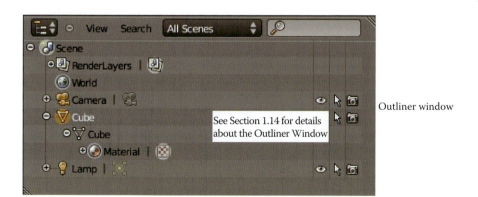

Figure 1.32

Figure 1.33

1.15.1 Python Console Window

The "Python Console" window is where you go if you want to modify the Blender program using Python script (Figure 1.33). Python is the programming language of Blender.

1.15.2 Outliner Window

The "Outliner" window gives you a visual display in the form of a file tree of everything in your scene and shows how the different items are connected (Figure 1.34). For example, if you click on the little cross next to "Cube" you get "Cube" and if you click again you see that it has a material. For more details, see Section 1.17 "The Outliner Window."

Lesson 02
02-09
Outliner Editor

View   Search   All Scenes

- Scene
  - RenderLayers |
  - World
  - Camera |
  - Cube
    - Cube
      - Material |
  - Lamp |

See Section 1.14 for details about the Outliner Window

Outliner window

Figure 1.34

1.15.3 Text Editor Window

The "Text Editor" is just that: a text editor (Figure 1.35). When you create something in Blender and save the .blend file to use later, you can write yourself notes in the "Text Editor" and what you write will be saved in the .blend file. "Python Script" (code) may be entered in the "Text Editor" window to add functionality to Blender.

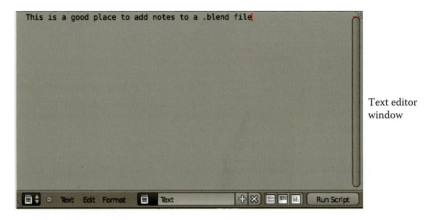

Text editor window

Figure 1.35

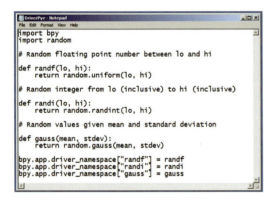

Figure 1.36

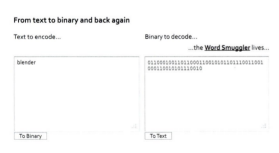

Figure 1.37

1.16 Python Script

Figure 1.36 is a sample of python script. The script is entered (Typed) in the "Notepad" text editor.

Python is a programming language which is written in simple text format. It does not require an interpreter to convert it into binary code which is what a computer uses.

Binary code is a numeric language consisting of only "0" and "1" placed in sequences.

Figure 1.37 shows the word "blender" written in binary.

To use Python on your computer you must have "Python" installed on your computer but for convenience sake Blender comes with an inbuilt version allowing you to use python scripts as additional Blender functions. In the example shown (Figure 1.36) a script named "rand.py" is shown. (This script is used later in the book when randomizing property values using drivers.)

Having Python installed is like having a box full of tools to use which you can select, depending on what you want to do. The tools are called modules which are pre-written pieces of code. You don't need to see them or understand them to use them. Figure 1.38 shows a very simplistic explanation of the code to help in understanding how a python script is used.

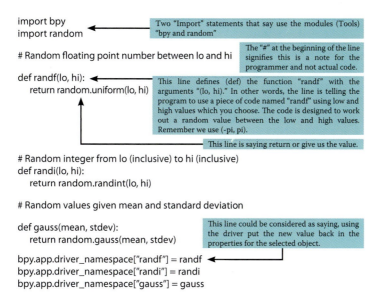

```
import bpy
import random
```
Two "Import" statements that say use the modules (Tools) "bpy and random"

`# Random floating point number between lo and hi`
The "#" at the beginning of the line signifies this is a note for the programmer and not actual code.

```
def randf(lo, hi):
    return random.uniform(lo, hi)
```
This line defines (def) the function "randf" with the arguments "(lo, hi)." In other words, the line is telling the program to use a piece of code named "randf" using low and high values which you choose. The code is designed to work out a random value between the low and high values. Remember we use (-pi, pi).

This line is saying return or give us the value.

```
# Random integer from lo (inclusive) to hi (inclusive)
def randi(lo, hi):
    return random.randint(lo, hi)

# Random values given mean and standard deviation

def gauss(mean, stdev):
    return random.gauss(mean, stdev)
```
This line could be considered as saying, using the driver put the new value back in the properties for the selected object.

```
bpy.app.driver_namespace["randf"] = randf
bpy.app.driver_namespace["randi"] = randi
bpy.app.driver_namespace["gauss"] = gauss
```

Figure 1.38

1.17 The Outliner Window

The "Outliner" window mentioned previously (see Section 1.15.2) gives you a display of everything in your scene. Follow this procedure to discover a little about how the window is arranged and how you can use it.

Lesson 02 02-09 Outliner Editor

Step 1. Start with the default Blender screen showing the five default windows. The "Outliner" window is displayed in the upper right-hand corner of the screen (Figure 1.39).

Step 2. To make life a little easier, divide the 3D window in two and change the left-hand window into a copy of the "Outliner" window (Figure 1.40). The "Outliner" window

The outliner window

Figure 1.39

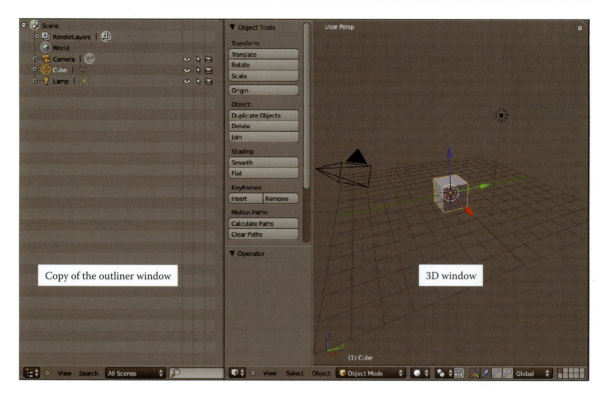

Figure 1.40

contains information about the current scene, which in this case is what is shown in the default 3D window. You can see a list in the "Outliner" window of what the default scene comprises; "Render Layers," "World," "Camera," "Cube," and "Lamp." Each line of information represents a "Data Block," which is a group of data pertaining to something in the scene. The default "Outliner" window shows the five groupings that have just been named. Note that before each line there is a small circle with a + sign in it; this is showing that some information is hidden. After the data block name, you can see a vertical bar followed by an icon; the icon represents a sub-data block. Click on the + sign to reveal the sub-data.

In the case of our default scene, instead of clicking on each + sign, place the cursor in the "Outliner" window and press the number pad + key three times; you will see all the data blocks and sub-data blocks revealed (Figure 1.41).

Step 3. Examine the data block for the cube object in the scene (Figure 1.42). The first line represents the cube object, the second line the cube mesh, the third line the material, and the last line the texture. Each successive line or data block is linked to the next. When you open Blender, the cube object in the scene is selected (as shown in Figure 1.43) by the orange outline in the 3D window. With your mouse cursor in the 3D window, press the A key to deselect the cube.

Step 4. In the "Outliner" window, click on the cube line with the LMB and you will observe that the cube is again selected in the 3D window. Sometimes objects in the 3D window are obscured by other objects or they may even be inside other objects, making

Figure 1.41

them difficult to select with the mouse, you can therefore select them in the "Outliner" window.

With the cursor in the 3D window, press the A key to deselect the cube. In the "Outliner" window, click on the cube mesh data block (the second line) with the LMB. The cube in the 3D window

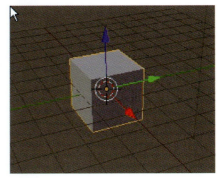

Figure 1.42

Figure 1.43

Figure 1.44

is now selected in "Edit" mode. With the cursor in the 3D window, press the Tab key to go back to "Object" mode. Note that the cube is **not** selected.

Step 5. In the "Outliner" window, look at the three icons at the right end of the data block line (Figure 1.44). Click the eyeball to toggle between visible and invisible in the 3D window, click the white arrow to toggle between allow selection and deselection in the 3D window, and click the camera to cancel render of an object. The three icons are grayed out if they are disengaged.

Step 6. In the "Properties" window at the RHS of the screen, click on the "Material" button with the cube selected in the 3D window (Figure 1.45). You will see that the default cube has a material applied to it, which is named "Material." While still in the "Properties" window, click on the "Textures" button and you will see that a texture is applied; note that the texture type is "None" (Figure 1.46). In other words, there is a texture data block without any texture data in it. Blender is made up of data blocks and sometimes these data blocks do nothing until such time as you modify them. This is the case here.

The "Outliner" window shows data blocks linked in a chain as demonstrated by the cube data block. In the "Outliner" window, right click on the cube texture data block line. In the pop-up panel that displays, select "Unlink." You will see in the Properties window

Figure 1.45

Figure 1.46

1. The Blender Interface

that the cube's texture data is deleted. To reinstate the texture, go to the "Properties" window, "Textures" button and click on the texture drop-down icon (Figure 1.47). In the drop-down panel, select "Tex." If you right click on the cube's material data block in the Outliner window and select "Unlink," both the material and texture are deleted. This occurs because a material must first be in place before a texture can be applied.

Step 7. In the 3D window, press the A key, deselect the cube, then press Shift + the A key and add a UV sphere (Figure 1.48). You will see that a sphere data block is added into the "Outliner" window (Figure 1.49). Click on the + sign at the beginning of the line to display the sphere's mesh data block; note that there is no material and no texture.

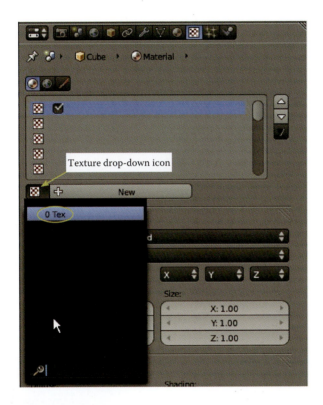

Figure 1.47

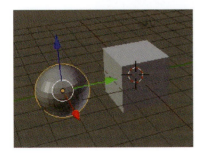

Figure 1.48

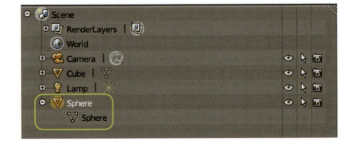

Figure 1.49

Go to the "Info" (information) window header at the top of the screen and click on the "Scene" icon. In the drop-down panel, you can see that the Blender file contains one scene named "Scene" (Figure 1.50). Now press the + sign and select "New" to add a new scene to the file. You will then see "Scene.001" added to the "Outliner" window. With the cursor in the new scene 3D window, press Shift + the A key and add a "Monkey" object (Figure 1.51). The monkey data block is added into the "Outliner" window. By clicking on the + sign, you can expand the links and you will see "Suzanne" (the monkey) listed. As with the "UV Sphere," the "Monkey" has no material or texture. When you click on the "Scene" icon in the "Info" window header, you will see the two scenes in the file.

Step 8. In the "Outliner" window header, there is an "All Scenes" drop-down selection button. If you select "Current Scene" in the drop-down menu, only the data block for the scene showing in the 3D window is displayed (Figure 1.52). This is very handy when you have a complicated file with many different scenes.

Click on the icon to display a drop-down panel

Figure 1.50

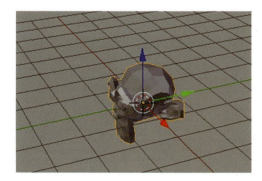

Figure 1.51

Figure 1.52

1.18 Add-Ons

To minimize some of the selection options in various parts of the Blender interface, some features have been put aside in a repository. You could say they have been hidden away, so I will tell you where to look if you can't find something. These features are listed in the Add-ons directory in the "User Preferences" window and may be activated and deactivated depending on what you are doing (Figure 1.53).

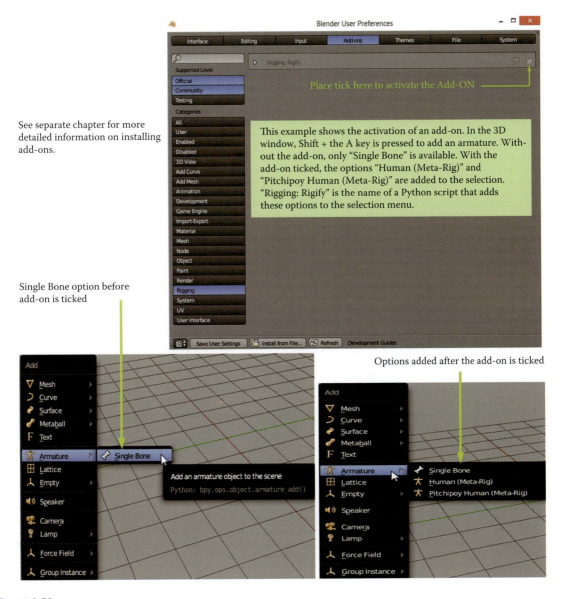

See separate chapter for more detailed information on installing add-ons.

Place tick here to activate the Add-ON

This example shows the activation of an add-on. In the 3D window, Shift + the A key is pressed to add an armature. Without the add-on, only "Single Bone" is available. With the add-on ticked, the options "Human (Meta-Rig)" and "Pitchipoy Human (Meta-Rig)" are added to the selection. "Rigging: Rigify" is the name of a Python script that adds these options to the selection menu.

Single Bone option before add-on is ticked

Options added after the add-on is ticked

Figure 1.53

The following describes the activation of an Add-On.

The Add-On that will be activated adds an option to a function. The function places what is called an "Armature" in the scene. Armatures are used to animate figures. For the time being consider them as the bones in a skeleton.

In the 3D window, Shift + the A key is pressed to display the drop-down menu with the option to add an armature. Without the Add-On activated, only the option "Single Bone" is available for selection. With the Add-On activated the option "Human (Meta-Rig)" is added to the selection. "Single Bone" is just a single bone, "Human (Meta-Rig)" is a full skeleton.

To make the full skeleton option available go to the "User Preference" window (Section 1.6). Click on "Add-ons" at the top of the window to open the "Add-ons" listing. At the LH side of the window is a list which will show all the Add-Ons that are installed in the program. To see the full list you click on "All" in the list but to simplify selection you click on one of the categories. In this case you click on "Rigging." (Rigging is the term used for placing a skeleton [Armature] inside a figure for animation.) There is one single option under this category which is named "Rigging: Rigify." Rigging: Rigify is the name of the Python script which provides the "Human (Meta-Rig)" armature (Skeleton). To activate this Add-on click on the small square button at the extreme RHS of the "Rigging: Rigify" line in the window to place a tick. Close the "User Preference" window.

In the 3D window press Shift + A key and in the selection menu that displays select "Add," "Armature" and you will now see three options available "Single Bone," "Human (Meta-Rig)," and "Pitchipay Human (Meta-Rig)."

To deactivate an Add-on go back to the "User Preference" window and click on the activation button, described previously, to remove the tick.

(See Chapter 24 for more detailed information on installing Add-Ons.)

1.19 Multiple Scenes

Lesson 09
09-02
Multiple
Blender Scenes

Lesson 09
09-01
Multiple Cameras

The objective in Blender is to create models of objects and characters, to place them in a scene, perhaps create an animation sequence and then render the scene to an image or video file. In doing this you may want to take camera shots from different angles for effect, especially when making movies. Movies are constructed from short video files placed in a timeline. In Blender you can have multiple scenes in the same Blender (.blend) file which allow you to have different objects, different animation sequences and different camera positions in each scene (Figures 1.54 and 1.55).

Figure 1.54

To understand the concept of multiple scenes view the 3D window in conjunction with the "Outliner" window and the "Info" window header.

In the "Info" window header at the top of the screen you will see the "Scene" button with "Scene" displayed as the default name. This refers to the display in the 3D window. You may click on the name "Scene" to highlight it (turns white) delete it and retype a new name.

To demonstrate change "Scene" to "Scene01." Note that in the "Outliner" window the name of the scene changes accordingly (Figure 1.56).

Go back to the "Info" window header and click on the "Scene" icon next to where you typed the new name to see the scene drop-down list. At this point it will contain only one scene with the name you have just typed (Scene01).

Click on the plus sign and select "New" from the drop-down selection menu. The name in the scene button reverts to "Scene" (The default name). Click on this and change it to "Scene02."

Outliner window

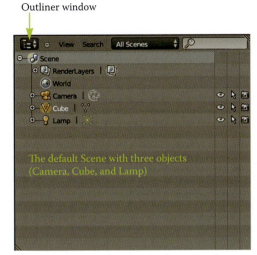

The Outliner window shows information about everything in the scene

Figure 1.55

Note: The 3D window is now empty (No object, no lamp, no camera) (Figure 1.57).

Outliner window with the default 'Scene' renamed 'Scene01'

Click the scene icon to display the drop-down selection list

Scene drop-down selection list

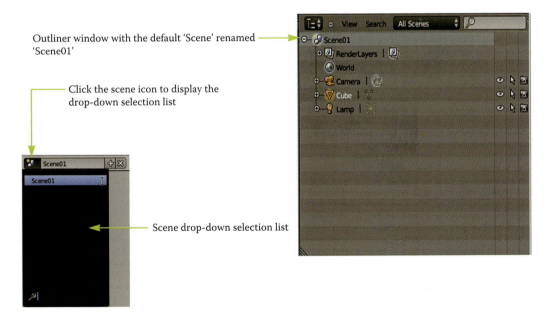

Figure 1.56

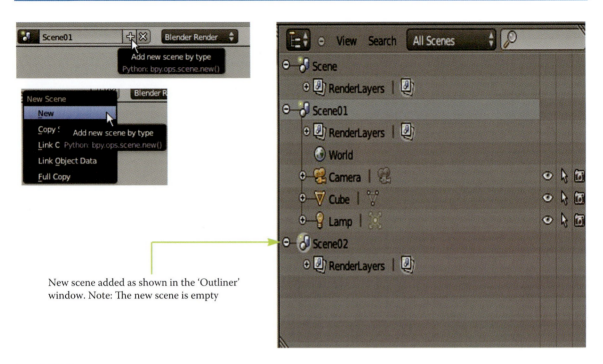

New scene added as shown in the 'Outliner' window. Note: The new scene is empty

Figure 1.57

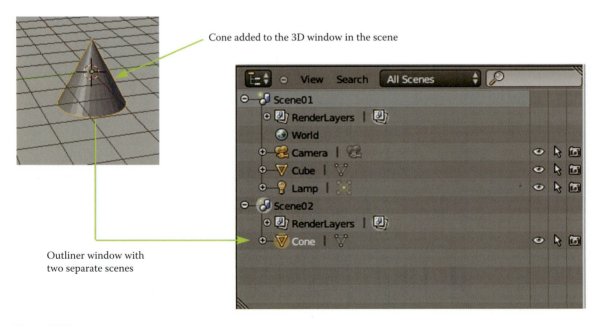

Cone added to the 3D window in the scene

Outliner window with two separate scenes

Figure 1.58

1. The Blender Interface

On clicking the plus sign and selecting "New" you tell Blender to create a new scene. The new scene is created devoid of any objects, that is, No camera, No lamp.

It doesn't matter what you name the different scenes as long as they are relevant to what you are doing and you keep a record.

Go ahead and add objects to the new scene but unless you add a camera and a lamp you will not be able to get "Camera View" (Num Pad 0) or render anything. Note also, when you do add a "Camera" you will have to position it and orientate it to point at your objects. Remember, without a lamp there is no illumination so you will not see anything if you render. You will also have to position the lamp.

There are now two separate scenes in the same Blender file (Scene01 and Scene02) and you can select either one from the scene selection button in the "Info" window header or in the "Outliner" window. The "Outliner" window lists the new scene and everything in the scene (Figure 1.58).

With "Scene02" selected, press the plus sign again and select "New." A new scene is created and is named "Scene" by default. Press the plus sign again and select "New" again. A new scene is created and this time named "Scene.001." Repeating the process will cause Blender to name scenes Scene.002, Scene.003, etc. If you select "Scene01" and create a new scene, Blender names the new scene with the next number in the sequence. If you named all your scenes "Apples," "Oranges," "Lemons," etc., then a new scene would be named "Scene," the default name in the numbering sequence.

2

Navigation

2.1 Navigation

Navigation is the science of finding the way from one place to another. If you can see where you are going it's an easy process to head over to the place but sometimes where you want to go is hidden from view. In Blender you create files and store them away for future use. You can reuse files and build on to them and then save the new material. Saved files are your library of information from which you can extract elements and insert them into future work. The saying is, "There is no point reinventing the wheel." If you have created something that works use it again. But where did I put the wheel? That's where navigation comes in. I need to find the place where I safely stored that wheel or, in the case of Blender, where I saved a file containing the wheel.

Lesson 01
01-15
Opening
Saving
Auto Saving

2.2 Navigate and Save

We will discuss how you navigate in the Blender file browser and save your work to a location of your choice on your computer's hard drive.

　　We will begin by creating a new Blender file. You could simply save a copy of the default file with the default scene containing the "Cube" object but then you wouldn't be able to distinguish between the two. Follow these instructions to create a new file:

Lesson 09
09-04
Blender
Display Speed
and File Size

Open Blender and the default scene is displayed with the "Cube" object selected as shown by the orange outline. Press the A key on the keyboard to deselect the "Cube." Press Alt + A key on your keyboard click on "Mesh" then "Monkey" to place a "Monkey" object in the scene. Press the G key. The outline of the "Monkey" turns white. Drag your mouse to move the "Monkey" away from the default "Cube" and click LMB. This has created a new Blender scene containing a "Cube" object and a "Monkey" object. Make note that this has modified the default Blender file.

To save the file go to the "Info" window header and click on "File." A drop down menu displays and you will see the options (Figure 2.1):

Save: This option will save the default Blender file with the modifications as a new file with a new name. When saved the file remains open (active) in Blender.

Save As: This saves a copy of the file that is opened. You can give the file a new name which will distinguish it from the original. When saved this file is opened (active) in Blender.

Save a Copy: This saves a copy of the file but the file will not be active. The file is saved but the original file is the file which remains opened in Blender.

Figure 2.1

In our case, we will use the "**Save**" option.

With our new scene opened, click on "Save." The Blender file browser window opens with the option "Save Blender File" in the top RH corner of the window. Where you see "untitled.blend" is the name of your file (Figure 2.2). Blender automatically names the file "untitled.blend." Click on the name to highlight it, press Delete on the keyboard, then type in a new name and hit Enter. I have named my file Blenderdemo.blend. It is good practice to add the ".blend" suffix—older versions of Blender did not automatically add this.

Just above where you typed the new name you will see the file path to where your file will be saved. On my computer this is "C:\Users\pc1\Documents\" (Figure 2.2). Blender has

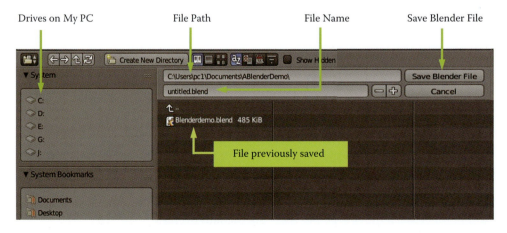

Figure 2.2

automatically decided that if I do not say otherwise my file will be saved in the "Documents" folder on the "C:" drive. The "Documents" or "My Documents" folders would appear to be the default location for saving on a Windows operating system. The "Documents" folder is not where I want my file to go. It would be OK to save Blender files here but then they would become mixed up with everything else that gets put into that folder. To prevent this happening it is better to make a new designated folder for Blender files. One way to do this is to use Blenders "Create New Directory" feature.

With the "File Browser" window open you will see the "Create New Directory" button in the window header at the top LHS of the screen.

I want to create a new subfolder under my "Documents." To do this on my computer I must first navigate to my "Documents" folder. I would click on "C:" in the "File Browser" "Systems tab," click on "Users" in the main "File Browser" window, then click on "pc1" and finally click on "Documents". I can now click on the "Create New Directory" button and a new subfolder will be created in the "Documents" folder. When a new folder is entered you can press "Delete" on your keyboard and type in a new name for the folder. I have named my folder "ABlenderDemo." Putting "A" at the beginning of the name positions the new folder at the top of the list in the "Documents" folder (Figure 2.3). If I began the folder name with a Z the folder would be way down at the bottom of the list. Creating a new folder in this way enters the filepath for the folder ready for saving Blender files.

Remember, in the foregoing procedure I started with a new scene created in the Blender 3D window. Having set up the filepath to my new folder (ABlenderDemo) and having named my Blender file, I simply click "Save Blender File" to save the file.

Figure 2.3

So! I have made a new folder named "ABlenderDemo" on my C: drive for saving new Blender files (Figure 2.3). When I have another (.blend) file created and ready to be saved I will have to find (navigate to) this folder. If I have remembered where the folder is located or written down the file path it isn't too difficult.

C:\Users\pc1\Documents\ABlenderDemo\

The "File Browser" window displays when "Save" is clicked. To navigate to the folder, I go into the system panel at the top LHS of the screen. In the panel there is a list of all the drives on my computer, the top one being the C: drive.

When I click on the "C:" in the panel all the folders on my C: drive display in the main browser window. Remember "ABlenderDemo" is a sub directory in my "Documents" folder. To get to my "AblenderDemo" folder on my computer, having clicked on "C:" in the "Systems" panel, I now click on "Users" in the main window, then "pc1" and then "Documents." At each click the different directories are displayed. The final click on "Documents" shows "ABlenderDemo" at the top of the list. I now click on "ABlenderDemo" to open the folder then, with the Blender file named, I can click on "Save Blender File" in the RH corner of the screen to save my file.

Yes this is the same procedure followed when setting up a new folder.

If you have followed these directions on your computer and have returned to the 3D window scene and want to prove that you have saved your file, change the window type to the "File Browser" window. Click on the 3D window header icon and choose "File Browser." And there's Demo.blend in the C:\ABlenderDemo\ folder (Figure 2.4).

Figure 2.4

Note: In the Blender default 3D window, the 3D window button/icon is in the lower LH corner of the window in the window header. In the file browser window, the button is in the header at the top of the window at the LHS.

That should keep us out of trouble for the time being as far as saving our work, but it is a good idea to play around and find out what all the buttons in the file browser window do.

This has been a brief insight into navigating in the "File Browser" window as well as showing how to save your work. Of course you can use the file browser to find other stuff

Choose how the
files are displayed

Thumbnails

Figure 2.5

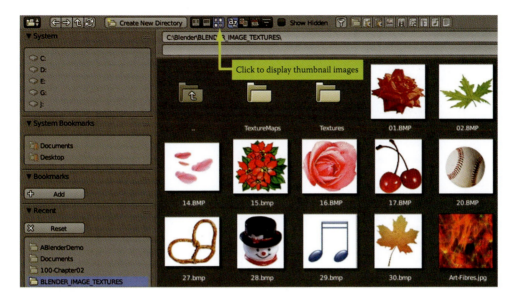

Figure 2.6

as well. Just click on a folder in the window and it opens showing what's inside. There are some buttons at the top of the window that let you choose how the contents of the folders are displayed (Figure 2.5). One helpful button lets you see files as thumbnails (pictures) so if you have photo images you can see them from within Blender (Figure 2.6).

2.3 Windows File Explorer (Windows Explorer)

Let's make a folder where we can save our stuff using **Windows File Explorer** or **Windows Explorer**. Open either of these applications. There are several ways of opening **Explorer** depending on what version of Windows you are using. You can usually find the application in pre-Window 8 by clicking the "Start" button, clicking open "All Programs" and going to "Accessories." Windows Explorer is usually in Accessories. You could have a quick start icon somewhere else.

In Windows 8, Windows Explorer is named "File Explorer" and can be found by doing a search in "Apps." (Type "File Explorer" in the search window while in "Apps.")

If your computer is like mine it persists in opening Widows Explorer showing my "Documents" folder. As explained you can save your stuff there but it will soon accumulate and get all mixed in with your letters to Grandma and the Tax Man. This is not a good thing.

Figure 2.7 shown here displays "File Explorer" with directories opened showing the file "Blenderdemo.blend" saved in the subfolder "ABlenderDemo" in "My Documents" directory. As you see, the file path is somewhat convoluted and it would be better to work to somewhere more convenient.

We will make a new folder in the C:\ drive. Close the folder lists by clicking on the triangles (or crosses) in front of the directory names and get back to the basic "C:\" directory

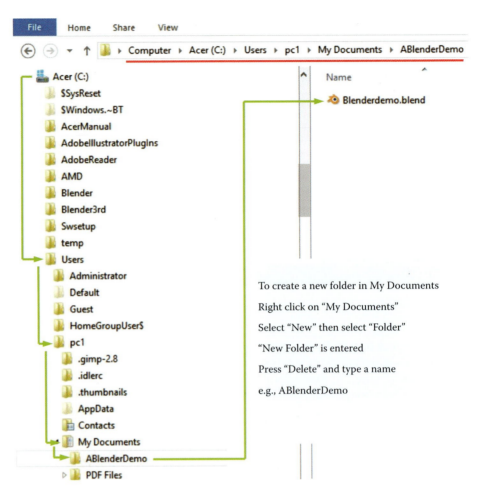

To create a new folder in My Documents

Right click on "My Documents"

Select "New" then select "Folder"

"New Folder" is entered

Press "Delete" and type a name

e.g., ABlenderDemo

Figure 2.7

(Figure 2.8 shows "Acer (C:)" on my Acer PC). Right click on your C:\ drive and in the drop down that displays, click on "New" and then click on "Folder" (Figure 2.9). Windows enters a new folder and names it "New Folder." At this stage you can edit the name. Press Delete to delete "New Folder" and type in your new name.

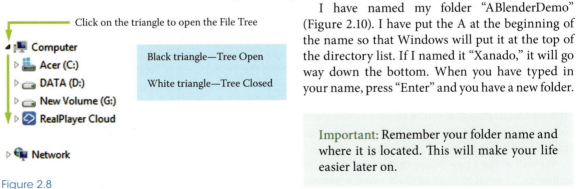

Figure 2.8

I have named my folder "ABlenderDemo" (Figure 2.10). I have put the A at the beginning of the name so that Windows will put it at the top of the directory list. If I named it "Xanado," it will go way down the bottom. When you have typed in your name, press "Enter" and you have a new folder.

Important: Remember your folder name and where it is located. This will make your life easier later on.

2. Navigation

Right click

Figure 2.9

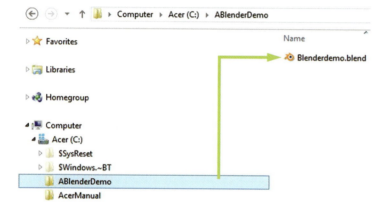

Figure 2.10

Figure 2.11

2.4 The Append or Link Command

When you want to insert elements from one Blender (.blend) file into another, you select the "Append" or "Link" commands from the file pull-down menu in the info window header (Figure 2.11).

"Append" takes data from an existing file and adds it to the current file. "Link" allows you to use data from an existing file in the current file but the data remain in the existing file. The data cannot be edited in the current file—if the data are changed in the existing file, the changes show in the current file the next time it is opened.

Selecting "Append" or "Link" opens the file browser window allowing you to navigate to the Blender file you wish to select elements from. You can append anything from cameras, lights, meshes, materials, textures, scenes, and objects. For most purposes, use the object option. By appending objects, any materials, textures, and animations that are

Lesson 05
05-12

Appending and
Linking Files

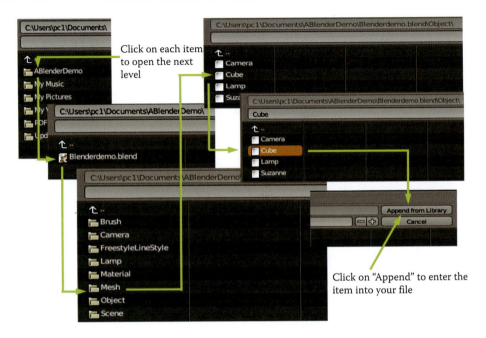

Figure 2.12

linked to that object will automatically be imported with the object. Clicking the LMB on an object will select it. Pressing the A key will deselect. After you select your objects to append, click the "Link/Append from Library" button in the upper right corner of the screen (Figure 2.12).

2.5 Packing Data

Lesson 05
05-15
Packing Image
Texture Files

If you plan to open a Blender file on other computers, you will need to select the "Pack All into .blend file" option in the file menu under "External Data" (Figure 2.13). Textures and sounds are not automatically included in your Blender file in order to keep the file size down. Every time your file opens, the textures and sounds are placed into your file. If the files can't be found, you won't have any textures and sounds. If you pack the data, those files are included with the .blend file so they can be opened anywhere. Remember, your file size may become very large. When data are packed, a message displays in the "Info" window header at the top of your screen letting you know that the file is packed. You can also unpack data to bring the file size back down.

Figure 2.13

2.6 Importing Objects

One of Blender's strong points is its ability to accept several generic types of 3D files from other programs. Two examples are:

- The .mxh file format used by the Make Human program, which creates models of the human figure
- The .dxf file format used by the Elefont program, which creates 3D solid text models

Both the Make Human and Elefont programs are freely available.

Other programs save files in one format but also give the option to export in another format. You will have to find the "Export" command in the program and match up the file type with one of the file types in Blender's import add-ons. With every new release of Blender, the import/export format options list changes. This makes Blender compatible with a variety of other 3D modeling and animation software programs.

> Note: There are only a few file type options shown in the default selection menu. MXH and DXF are not shown. To conserve space in the GUI, Blender has limited the file type display. MXH and DXF as well as other file types are available as Add-ons in the user preferences window in the "Import-Export" category.

To import an MXH or DXF file into a Blender scene, open the "User Preferences" window and click on "Add-ons" at the top of the window. In the list at the LHS of the window, select "Import-Export." A short list of the import/export file types will display (Figure 2.14).

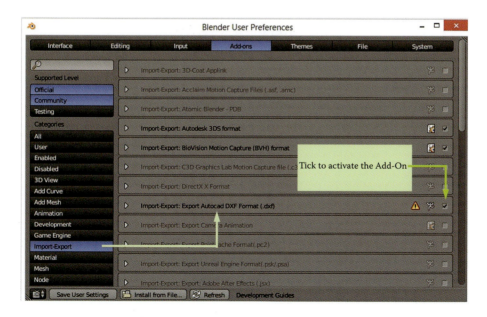

Figure 2.14

Figure 2.15

Find the file type you require and place a tick in the box at the RHS of the panel. The ticked file type will now be available in the "Info Window, File, Import" selection drop down menu (Figure 2.15).

Note: When importing Blender files into other Blender files, remember to use the "Append" command instead of "Import." In the "Append" command, select the file, then select what you would like to bring into the current file. You will usually want the objects option.

3

Creating and Editing Objects

3.1 Working with Basic Meshes

Lesson 01
01-07
Mesh Modeling Modes and Viewport Shading

Now that we know how to move around in Blender, let's start doing some basic building and shaping. In this section we will talk about creating basic shapes and using modifiers to form them. There are a lot of different types of things to make in Blender; right now we will only discuss meshes.

Lesson 02
02-04
Undo - Redo

In Blender you begin modeling something by adding a simple 3D shape to your scene and then shaping it to make a model. The simple shape is called a "Primitive" of which there are several to choose. When the primitive shape is entered into the scene it is referred to as an "Object." Blender automatically names objects according to the shape, that is, "Cube," "Sphere," "Cone," etc. When you reshape (modify) the primitive object to make a model you

will rename it. Primitives are entered in the 3D window in "Object" mode and reshaped (Edited) in "Edit" mode. All primitives are "Mesh Objects" in that the surface of an object is formed from a mesh like a fishing net with knots (Vertices) at the intersection of the strands (Edges). The spaces between the strands (holes in the net) are filled in and called "Faces."

> Note: If you make a mistake Blender has an "Undo" function. Press Ctrl + Z key to undo your last actions. This feature operates for a set number of backward "Steps" (Actions). The number of steps is set in the "User Preferences" window in the "Editing" section, "Undo" category.

Start a new scene in Blender and save it in your "Blender" folder. Name it something meaningful and write down the name. You can save your work wherever you like as long as you remember what you named the file and where you saved it. Be familiar with saving and creating files and folders, so go back and read the section on that subject if necessary.

> Note: Blender may not prompt you to save your file when exiting the program. Remember to always save your work often and don't forget the .blend suffix!

3.2 Placing Objects in the Scene

Lesson 01
01-11

Selecting in
Object Mode

The 3D cursor's location is used to place new objects. Click with the LMB where you want your object located and the 3D cursor locates to that position. When you have the cursor in a good location, press Shift + the A key to bring up the "Add" menu. As an example select "Mesh," and select "UV Sphere." You may select any of the "Mesh" types listed but just for now I will refer to the "Sphere" type mesh.

> Note: A Sphere object is added to the scene and is selected as shown by the orange outline. Being selected means that it may be moved and have its shape altered (Edited). The object can be deselected by pressing the A Key and selected by clicking it with the RMB. Multiple objects can be selected by pressing and holding "Shift" and clicking RMB.

Lesson 02
02-03

Deleting
Objects

If you want to remove an object from a scene you delete it by first selecting, then press the X key and click "OK Delete."

> Note: I previously stated that we were discussing meshes. An object in Blender is a mesh object. Think of a sphere made out of chicken wire or fishing net and you get the idea. A sphere in Blender has a mesh with vertical and horizontal divisions called segments and rings: vertical segments like the inside of an orange and horizontal rings (Figure 3.1). The default UV sphere has 32 segments and 16 rings. You can change these by altering the values in the panel at the bottom of the "Tool Shelf," which displays when you add the sphere to the scene. For now you can keep it at 32 segments and 16 rings.

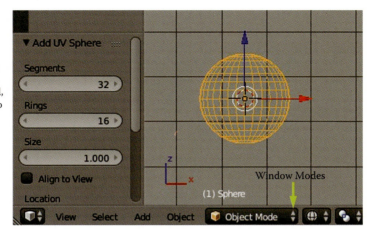

Note: Once the sphere object is deselected in the window, translated, or scaled, the option to change the rings and segments in the tool panel is lost

Figure 3.1

Note: Once the sphere object is deselected in the window, translated, or scaled, the options to change the rings and segments in the tool panel disappear.

3.2.1 Naming Objects

When you add an object to a scene Blender automatically gives it a name. For example, the default cube object is named "Cube." If you **deselect** "Cube" and add a second cube mesh object it will be named "Cube.001." A third cube will be named "Cube.002," etc. This is all very well but inevitably you will model these cubes into something else and the automatic names will be meaningless and confusing when your scene progresses. You can rename them to something meaningful by pressing the N key to display the "Object Properties" panel at the RHS of the 3D window (Figure 3.2). In the "Item" tab you will see "Cube" next

Lesson 02
02-02

Naming Objects

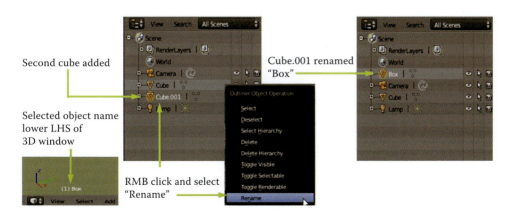

Figure 3.2

to a little orange cube icon. Click LMB on the name, press delete, and retype a new name. Press Enter to change the name. Note that the name change is made in the "Outliner" window automatically (Figure 3.2).

Alternatively you can RMB click on the name in the "Outliner" window and select "Rename" from the menu that displays then delete and type a new name in the "Outliner" window. This will be reflected in the 3D window, "Object Properties" panel and note the name is also shown in the lower RH corner of the 3D window. The name shown here is for the object you have selected in the 3D window (Figure 3.2).

Lesson 01
01-07
Mesh Modeling
Modes and
Viewport Shading

3.3 Edit Mode and Object Mode

Lesson 01
01-11
Selecting in
Object Mode

Lesson 02
02-01
Adding
Mesh Objects
in Edit Mode

When you place an object in Blender, it enters the scene in "Object" mode and is selected as shown by its orange outline. At this stage consider the two states in Blender: "Edit" mode and "Object" mode (Figure 3.3). "Edit" mode is used when modifying the shape of the object by selecting vertices on the object's surface (vertices are the joining points of the mesh). "Object" mode affects the object as a whole. The Tab key toggles you between the two modes.

Before entering a new object into your scene, make sure other objects are in "Object" mode, **not in "Edit" mode**, otherwise when you return to "Object" mode the objects will be joined.

Note: Sometimes you may want to purposely add an object in "Edit" mode so that it becomes part of the selected object.

Another way to switch between modes is to use the mode selection drop down menu in the window header. You will see that besides "Object" and "Edit," there are other modes available (Figure 3.3).

Objects may be displayed in a window in different ways. The display options are called "Viewport Shading." The default "Viewport Shading" is "Solid." In Figure 3.1, which shows the UV sphere with segments and rings, the sphere was drawn in "Wireframe" display mode (Figure 3.4).

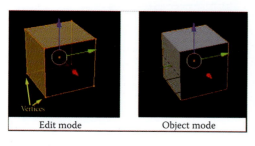

Edit mode   Object mode

Texture Paint
Weight Paint
Vertex Paint
Sculpt Mode
Edit Mode
Object Mode
Object Mode

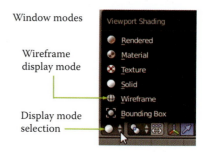

Window modes

Wireframe
display mode

Display mode
selection

Viewport Shading
Rendered
Material
Texture
Solid
Wireframe
Bounding Box

Figure 3.3

Figure 3.4

3.4 Mesh Types

With the mouse cursor in the 3D window press Shift + the A key to reveal the mesh types selection menu. The available mesh types (or primitives) are shown in Figure 3.5. Primitives are basic shapes from which you can begin modeling. Click on one of the mesh types in the menu and it will be added to your scene. Note it is positioned at the location of the 3D window cursor (**not the mouse cursor**).

Lesson 01
01-10
Primitive Mesh
Object

3D manipulation widget shown on the circle primitive

Plane
Cube
Circle
UV Sphere
Ico Sphere
Cylinder
Cone
Torus
Grid
Monkey

Mesh object primitive selection menu (Press Shift + A key)

Figure 3.5

After adding an object to your scene you can duplicate it by pressing Shift + D. The duplicate is shown in white indicating that it is in grab mode. Move your mouse cursor to position it in the scene then LMB click to set it in position.

Lesson 02
02-11
Duplication

3.4.1 Other Types of Objects

In discussing "Objects" we have only considered "Mesh Objects." When you press Shift + A key to display the "Add" menu the list contains other types of objects which can be introduced into a scene. These will be explained as you progress through the book but it is worth making you aware of the "Empty" object. As you see in the list this object can be displayed in a variety of ways but its main attribute is, it will not render in an image or movie. As the name implies it is empty. Having this type of object allows you link other objects to it for such things as camera tracking and following animation paths.

Lesson 04
04-01
Empty Objects

Figure 3.6

3.5 Cursor Placement

To precisely place the 3D cursor, use Shift + the S key for options to move the cursor to objects, grids, etc. (Figure 3.6).

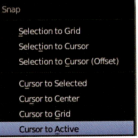

Snap

Selection to Grid
Selection to Cursor
Selection to Cursor (Offset)

Cursor to Selected
Cursor to Center
Cursor to Grid
Cursor to Active

3.6 Moving Objects

The three basic controls for manipulating an object are: G key (grab), S key (scale), and R key (rotate). To move (Translate) an object freely in the plane of the view, press the G key with the object selected and drag the mouse. To lock the move-

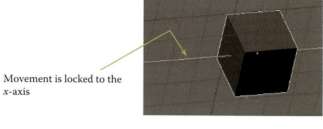

Movement is locked to the x-axis

Figure 3.7

ment to a particular axis, press the G key + X, Y, or Z (Figure 3.7).

3.7 Scaling Objects

To scale an object freely, press the S key and drag the mouse. To lock the scale to a particular axis, press S key + X, Y, or Z (Figure 3.8). To scale by a specific value press S key + Number key (S + 2 + X = Scale two times on the X axis).

Figure 3.8

Scale is locked to the x-axis

By default the size of an object is expressed in "Blender Units." You may elect to change this to "Metric" or "Imperial" units. In the "Properties" window, "Scene" buttons, "Units" tab you will see "None" highlighted in blue. This designates Blender units. Click on either "Metric" or "Imperial" to change this. When selecting either unit system you will see "Meters" or "Feet" displayed in the upper LH corner of the 3D window. When scrolling the mouse to zoom in this changes to centimeters or inches. Scrolling further in metric units displays millimeters. Scrolling out in imperial displays yards.

Note: The units only display in the "Orthographic" window views.

3.8 Rotating Objects

To rotate an object, press the R key and move the mouse about the object's center. To lock the rotation to an axis, press the R key + X, Y, or Z. To rotate a set number of degrees, press R + The number of degrees of rotation, R + 30 rotates the object 30°. R + X + 30 rotates the object 30° about the x-axis.

By default rotation values are in "Degrees." You may change this to "Radians" in the "Properties" window, "Scene" buttons, "Units" tab.

3. Creating and Editing Objects

3.9 Precision Manipulation

To manipulate an object in the scene to a precise location, scale, or angle of rotation, alter the values in the object data numeric panel. By default, the panel is hidden in the 3D window. The N key toggles between hide and display. The panel displays at the RH side of the 3D window and the values therein pertain to the object selected in the window (Figure 3.9). To change a value in the numeric panel

- Click on the value with the LMB, press Delete, retype the value, and press Enter, or
- Repeatedly click on one of the little arrows on either side of the value, or
- Click and hold the LMB in the value box and drag the mouse right or left.

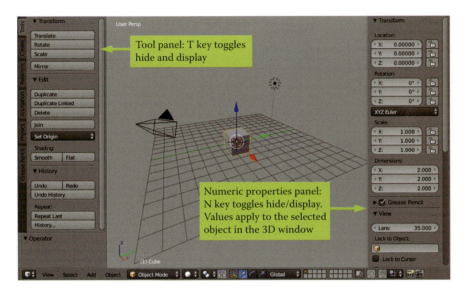

Figure 3.9

3.9.1 Snap and Align Tool

Sometimes it is desirable or essential to accurately position the object or your cursor to a center or grid location. Blender provides a quick shortcut tool for performing these operations. You can view the options from a drop down menu in the 3D window header. Click on "Object, Snap" (Figure 3.10). Alternatively, you can press Shift + the S key to display a selection panel. The selection menu is self-explanatory.

Lesson 04
04-11
Snap and Align Tool

Figure 3.10

3.10 The Transformation Widget

The transformation widget is a handy way of performing the manipulation operations of the G, S, and R keys described previously. By default, the widget is displayed in the 3D window in grab mode (Figure 3.11).

Clicking on the red, green, or blue handles with the LMB and holding while dragging the mouse moves the object in the window. The widget sometimes obstructs the view but it can be toggled off and on in the window header by clicking LMB on the widget icon. The rotate and scale modes are also accessed in the window header (Figure 3.12).

Toggle widget on/off

Scale
Rotate
Translate

Figure 3.11

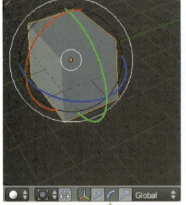

R key = rotate mode

S key = scale mode

Figure 3.12

3.11 Selecting Vertices, Edges, and Faces

Lesson 03
03-01
Vertices Edges
and Faces

Lesson 03
03-02
Selecting Vertices

Lesson 03
03-03
Selecting Edges

While in "Edit" mode, to select a single vertex, first press the A key to deselect all the vertices. In "Edit" mode this does not deselect the object, only the vertices. Click with the RMB on a single vertex to select it. To select multiple vertices, hold down the Shift key while using the RMB to click on them. You can also drag a window around the vertices. Press the B key, hold and drag a window (Rectangle) to select a group of vertices. Pressing the C key will bring up a circular selection tool. Holding the LMB and dragging the circle selects vertices on the move. The circle can be sized by pressing the + or – keys on the number pad or scrolling the center mouse wheel. Pressing Esc will get you out of the circular selection tool. In order to select all vertices or deselect currently selected ones, press the A key once or twice.

Note: See 3.13 Edit Mode selection Options.

After selecting vertices, edges, or faces, you can use the basic tools we talked about earlier to manipulate them (G to grab or move, S to scale, and R to rotate) (Figures 3.13 and 3.14).

3. Creating and Editing Objects

Widget handle: red, green, or blue arrow

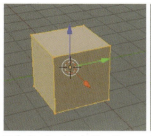 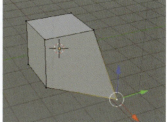 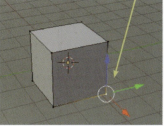

Lesson 03
03-04
Selecting Faces

Lesson 03
03-05
Vertices Edge
Face Menus
and Search

Figure 3.13

Lesson 03
03-15
Box - Circle
Select

Default cube object: all vertices are selected

Single vertex selected: click the RMB on the vertex

Single vertex translated: press the G key + drag the mouse or click and drag the widget handles

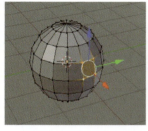 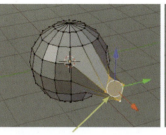 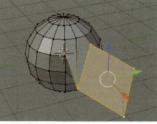

Four vertices selected in a UV sphere: hold Shift + click the RMB

Vertices translated: G key + drag the mouse, or click on the translation widget

Vertices rotated: R key + move the mouse

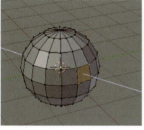 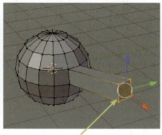 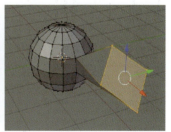

Vertices are extruded along an axis normal to the plane of the selected vertex group

Four vertices selected: E key to extrude + drag the mouse

Vertices rotated: R key + move the mouse

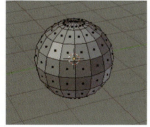 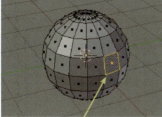 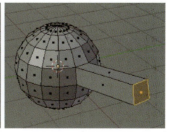

UV sphere in face select mode

Single face selected: click the RMB

Face extruded: E key + drag the mouse

Note: The transformation widget is turned off in this face select mode example.

Figure 3.14

3.11 Selecting Vertices, Edges, and Faces

Note: An alternative to the G key + mouse drag is to click on one of the transformation widget handles, hold the mouse button, and move the mouse (Figure 3.13).

Note: The transformation widget is turned off in this face select mode example (Figure 3.14).

3.12 Mesh Vertex Editing

After you have added a mesh to your scene in "Object" mode, you can enter "Edit" mode (by using the Tab key) and change its shape. In "Edit" mode, you can work with the shape's individual vertices (mesh intersections) to create the shape you want. You know you're in "Edit" mode when you see orange lines and dots on the selected object (Figure 3.15). When you tab into "Edit" mode, the whole of your selected object is in "Edit" mode with all the vertices selected. By default, "Edit" mode is in vertex select mode.

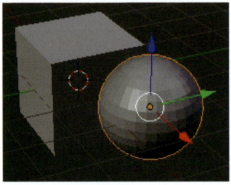 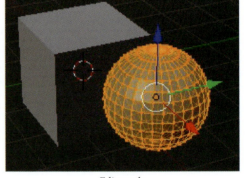

Object mode   Edit mode

Lesson 03
03-03
Selecting Edges

Lesson 03
03-04
Selecting Faces

Figure 3.15

3.13 Edit Mode Selection Options

In "Edit" mode, the default selection mode is "Vertex which means you may select vertices." You can also elect to select "Edge" or "Face" select mode (Figure 3.16). These options are available in the window header.

Also, by default, only visible vertices or faces are available for selection. This means that you can only select the vertices or faces that you actually see in the window. Blender has a "Limit Selection to Visible" function, which allows you to only see the front surface and only select vertices or faces on the front (that or are visible) (Figure 3.17). This function is toggled on and off in the window header.

Lesson 03
03-05
Vertex Edge
Face Menus
and Search

3. Creating and Editing Objects

Vertex selected   Edge selected   Face selected

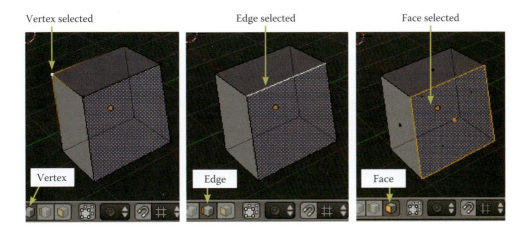

Figure 3.16

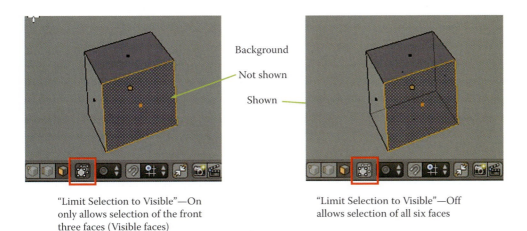

Background

Not shown

Shown

"Limit Selection to Visible"—On only allows selection of the front three faces (Visible faces)

"Limit Selection to Visible"—Off allows selection of all six faces

Figure 3.17

3.14 Creating Vertices

Sometimes you need to add more vertices to part or all of the mesh in order to create detail. To do this, you must first select the vertices in the area that you wish to add detail, then go to the tool shelf at the LH side of the screen (Using the T key toggles between hide and display) and find the "Subdivide" button (Figure 3.18). Click it as many times as you need to divide the area selected. You can of course subdivide the whole mesh object in this way.

To add individual vertices to a mesh, in "Edit" mode simply click the LMB while holding Ctrl. Adding vertices in this way places them on the vertical midplane of the 3D window.

Lesson 03
03-06

Subdivide

Figure 3.18

Subdivide	
Subdivide Smooth	
Merge...	Alt M
Remove Doubles	
Hide	H
Reveal	Alt H
Select Inverse	Ctrl I
Flip Normals	
Smooth	
Laplacian Smooth	
Inset Faces	I
Bevel	Ctrl B
Bridge Edge Loops	
Shade Smooth	
Shade Flat	
Blend From Shape	
Shape Propagate	
Select Shortest Path	
Sort Mesh Elements	
Symmetrize	
Snap to Symmetry	

Figure 3.19

3.14.1 Specials Menu

In edit mode, pressing the W key will bring up a "Specials" menu that will give you a variety of editing options (Figure 3.19). Most of these options can also be selected in the tool shelf.

3.14.2 Creating Vertex Groups

Sometimes you will want to manipulate a group of vertices. You can select multiple vertices on an object and manipulate them, but once deselected you could have trouble selecting the exact same group the next time you want them. To assist with this you can assign multiple vertices to a designated group for re-selection. Working through the following example will give you the idea.

Start the default scene and replace the cube with a UV sphere. Zoom in on the scene to give a better view (press the number pad + sign). Tab to "Edit" mode and then press the A key to deselect all the vertices. Press the C key for circle select (scroll the mouse wheel to adjust the circle size) and click, hold, and drag the circle over the sphere to select a group of vertices (Figure 3.20). Press Esc to cancel the circle selection. The vertices remain selected.

In the "Properties" window, "Object Data" button, "Vertex Groups" tab, click on the + sign to create a vertex group data slot. By default, this will be named simply "Group" (Figure 3.21). You can change the name to something meaningful if you wish by clicking on "Group" in the "Name" slot, deleting it, and retyping a new name. With the group of vertices still selected on the sphere, click on the "Assign" button in the "Vertex Groups" tab—this assigns the selected vertices to "Group." By clicking on the "Select" and "Deselect" buttons, you will see the vertices on the sphere being selected or deselected, respectively. Deselect the vertices and repeat the circle select with a different bunch. Click on the + sign again in

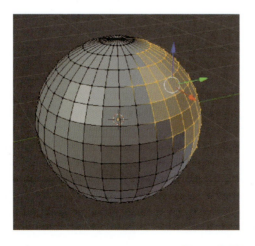

Figure 3.20

Figure 3.21

the "Vertex Groups" tab and you should see a new data block created named "Group.001." Click the "Assign" button to assign the new group of vertices to "Group.001." Deselect the vertices on the sphere in the 3D window, and you can now select "Group" or "Group.001."

3.15 Center Points

Every object you create in Blender has a small dot somewhere in the center (by default, usually in the center geometry of that object). This is the object's center, or pivot point (Figure 3.22). Beginners in Blender often move these center points to locations other than where they want them. This happens because they move all the vertices of the object in "Edit" mode, but the center point fails to move. If you want to move an object maintaining its center, hit Tab to get out of "Edit" mode and into "Object" select mode. Using the G key to move the object in object mode will move the center point along with the object.

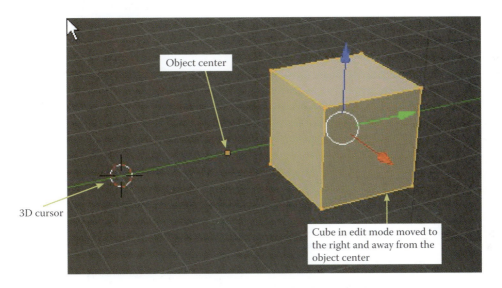

Figure 3.22

If you ever need to relocate an object's center point, move the 3D cursor to the desired center location. In object mode, click on "Object" in the window header, then "Transform," then "Origin to 3D Cursor" (Figure 3.23). This will move the center point

Figure 3.23

to the cursor. Now repeat the process selecting "Geometry to Origin," which moves the vertices to the center.

3.16 Object Display

Figure 3.24

By default, the selected object in the window is set to "Solid Viewport Shading." Many times, you will need to work with your objects in "Wireframe" mode. All shading does is change the way you see your objects. Shading also affects the way you can select vertices in "Edit" mode. In solid shading, only visible vertices can be selected. In "Wireframe," all vertices can be selected. To change between solid and wire modes, press the Z key or select the shading mode from the header toolbar (Figure 3.24). You will notice several other shading options in the menu; experiment with the other options.

Lesson 02
02-12

Mesh Smoothing

3.17 Smooth and Flat Shading Options

As you add objects and view them in "Solid Viewport Shading," you will notice that circular and spherical objects are not displayed smoothly. In the "Tool Panel," "Tools" option, "Shading" tab you will see two buttons under the heading "Shading" labeled "Smooth" and "Flat." Clicking these buttons either smooths the object or reverts it to flat shading (Figure 3.25). These buttons not only affect the way things look on the screen, but how they will be rendered in a final image. Be aware that the appearance of objects on the screen is not displayed at the same quality as a final rendered image. The computer needs to conserve memory because 3D applications can be very memory intensive.

Lesson 09
09-05

Smoothing
Problems

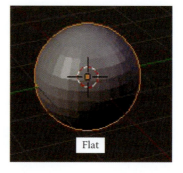

Figure 3.25

3.18 Proportional Vertex Editing

Lesson 04
04-12

Proportional
Editing

Proportional vertex editing is used to create a flow in the shape when editing vertices. To turn proportional vertex editing on, in "Edit" mode, click the "Proportional Editing" button in the 3D window header (Figure 3.26) or with the mouse cursor in the 3D window press the O key while in "Edit mode".

3. Creating and Editing Objects

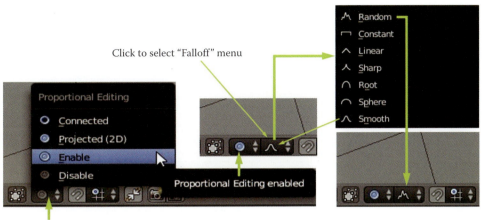

Click to select "Falloff" menu

Proportional Editing enabled

Click to turn on and select "Enable" to activate "Proportional Vertex Editing"

Figure 3.26

Note: You can only select "Proportional Editing" while in edit mode.

You have several options for affecting vertices in "Proportional Editing" mode. With the mode enabled a selection menu button displays in the 3D window header (Figure 3.26).

Experiment with the different types of "Falloff" by adding a "Plane" to your scene. In "Edit" mode subdivide the plane several times, select a single vertex, and translate the vertex on the Z axis. Try the falloff options and see the difference.

3.19 Extruding Shapes

Shapes can be altered by selecting either a single vertex (click RMB) or a group of vertices (press B key—drag rectangle or C key for circle select), then clicking the G key to move the vertices. Press the S key to scale, or the R key to rotate a group of vertices. Click the LMB to leave the vertices in position. Scaling and rotating are relative to the object's center. The G key, R key, and S key are the basic modifiers for manipulating.

A more refined method of altering a shape is by "Extrusion." Select the vertices as in Figure 3.27 and press the E key while in "Edit" mode. The selected vertices are duplicated and by default placed into "Grab" mode, ready to be moved. Also by default, the movement is confined to a line normal to a plane defined by the selected vertices. This line displays on the screen. Moving the mouse moves the vertices along the line. If you want to freely extrude vertices press the E key (do not touch the mouse) then press Enter (the vertices are duplicated) now press the G key, and move the mouse. Clicking the MMB after pressing the E key and then moving the mouse allows you to direct the extrusion to the X, Y, or Z axis. The vertices will follow wherever you go. You can also constrain the extrusion to the X, Y, or Z axis of the scene by pressing the E key + X, Y, or Z. Clicking the LMB when you have finished moving releases the vertices from grab mode, but they remain selected. You

Lesson 03
03-10
Extrude—Part 1

Lesson 03
03-11
Extrude—Part 2

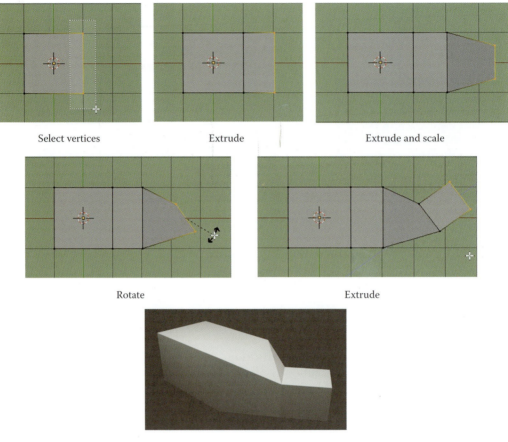

Select vertices   Extrude   Extrude and scale

Rotate   Extrude

Rendered image

Figure 3.27

can now rotate and scale the group; but, in this case, the rotation and scaling takes place about the midpoint of the selected vertex group.

Figure 3.27 is an example of a cube, extruded from the right side several times using scale and rotate. "Basic Extrude" is a great command for making long tubes and tunnels. It is also good when you don't want to subdivide an object too much in order to add detail.

3.20 Creating Ground

Proportional vertex editing described in Section 3.18 may be used to create a landscape (Figure 3.28). The first thing you need to do is create a plane in the top view (number pad 7). In "Edit" mode, make sure all four vertices are selected (the vertices and edges should be orange)—you can use the A key to select them. Press the W key for specials menu, then select "Subdivide" or "Subdivide Smooth" or "click Subdivide" in the tool panel. "Subdivide Smooth" adds vertices and smooths the surface at the same time. Do this a few times. Deselect all vertices (A Key) then select a single vertex somewhere near the center.

Ground terrain can be created by subdividing a plane, then selecting a single vertex and moving it up the *z*-axis with the proportional editing tool on with random falloff

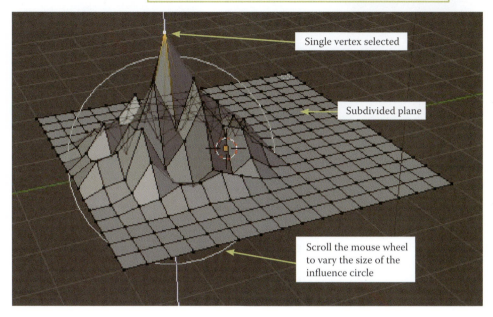

Single vertex selected

Subdivided plane

Scroll the mouse wheel to vary the size of the influence circle

Figure 3.28

Next, switch to a front view (number pad 1) and press the O key to enter "Proportional Vertex Editing" mode. Select sharp or smooth fall off depending on what effect you want. Press the G key to grab (move) the vertex or drag the arrows on the manipulation widget. Use the scroll mouse wheel to change the size of the proportional selection if you have used the G key. Experiment with different size selections and different fall offs.

Figure 3.29

Click Alt + RMB

Lesson 03
03-07
Loop Cut
and Slide

3.21 Edge Loop Selection

When working with vertices, it is sometimes useful to select a group of vertices which form an edge loop. To demonstrate this procedure you will have to create an object like the one shown in Figure 3.29.

Add a "Circle" mesh object to the 3D window and tab to "Edit" mode—the mouse cursor will change to a white cross. Press the E key to extrude (**do not move the mouse cursor**), immediately press the S key. You have created a duplicate set of vertices. Now move the

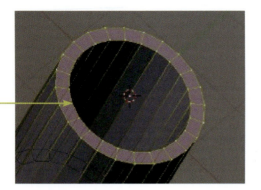
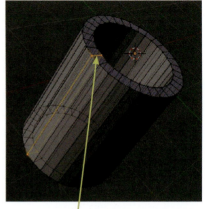

Press Shift + Alt + the RMB to add the inner circle of vertices to the selection

Figure 3.30

Click on the edge with Alt + the RMB to select the loop

mouse cursor toward the center of the circle. This produces an inner circle. Press the A key twice to deselect the inner circle then select all the vertices. With both circles selected, press the E key (extrude) and move the mouse cursor away from or toward the mesh. By default, an extrusion takes place normal to (at right angles to) the plane of the selected vertices, which in this case is along the Z-axis. You should have a mesh object similar to the one shown in Figure 3.30.

Lesson 09
09-06
Cutting a Hole
in a Flat Surface

To select a circular edge loop from this object, perform the following steps in "Edit" mode: click on the outer ring with Alt + the RMB to select the outer ring (Edge Loop); press Shift + Alt + the RMB to add the inner circle of vertices to the selection. To select a longitudinal edge loop, click on the edge with Alt + the RMB to select the loop, as seen in Figure 3.30.

Lesson 09
09-07
Cutting a Hole in
a Curve Surface

3.22 Inset Faces

The "Inset Faces" command causes faces to be created inside or outside a selected geometry.

To demonstrate, delete the default cube in the 3D window and add a "Plane" object. Zoom in (scroll MMB), Tab into "Edit" mode and subdivide the plane twice. Deselect (A key) the vertices. Change from "Vertex" select mode to "Face" select mode.

Select a single face and with the mouse cursor in the 3D window press the W key to bring up the "Specials" menu and select "Inset Faces" (Figure 3.31) (Alternatively press the I key or press "Inset Faces" in the "Tool Panel"). You will see black dots appear at the center of the edges of the selected face. These are new face centers. Move the mouse cursor toward the center of the selected face and you see that new faces have been created (Figure 3.32). Click LMB to set the new faces in position.

Note, when you set the new faces the original face remains selected. The "Inset Faces" tab displays in the "Last Operator" panel of the "Tool Shelf" (Figure 3.33). While this tab is displayed you can make adjustments. The "Thickness" slider controls the size of the original selected face. The "Depth" slider displaces the face normal to the plane. Positive values are above the plane, negative values are below the plane. Repeat the process but this time shift selects two adjoining faces (Figure 3.34).

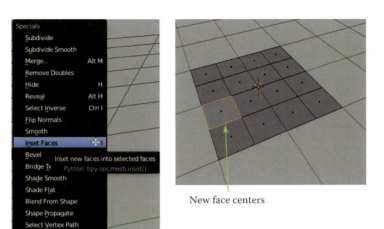

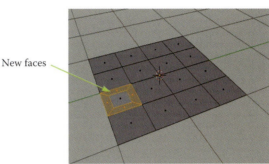

Figure 3.31

New face centers

Note: The procedure can be processed in both "Vertex" select mode and "Edge" select mode by selecting the perimeter of an area on the surface of the plane. The principle can be applied to the surface of any mesh object.

New faces

Figure 3.32

Figure 3.33

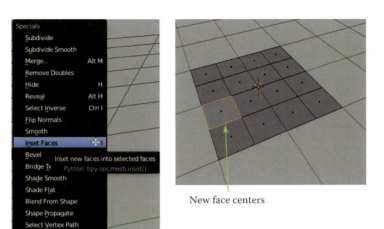

Figure 3.34

3.23 Joining and Separating Meshes

Lesson 04
04-04
Joining Objects

In Blender, "Objects" (Models) are constructed from a Mesh. Different "Mesh Objects" can be joined together to form a single object. The objects can be separated under certain conditions or parts of a mesh can be separated from the main object.

3.23.1 Joining in Object Mode

With two objects selected (Shift—Click RMB) press Ctrl + J key. The objects are joined becoming a single object. Pay attention to the location of the manipulation widget after joining. The widget locates at the center of the last object selected. This center point becomes the center of rotation and manipulation for the new combined object.

Objects can have materials assigned to them in Object mode. At this stage materials may be considered as color. When objects are joined together in "Object" mode the materials remain assigned to the individual parts of the combined object. To demonstrate "Object" mode joining perform the following:

In the default Blender scene add a UV Sphere and position as shown in Figure 3.35 with the meshes of the two objects overlapping. Deselect the sphere and select the default cube.

Note the names of the objects in the "Outliner" window (Cube and Sphere).

At this point the subject of "Materials" has not been covered but we must make note that the default Cube has a material pre-applied as shown by the presence of materials buttons and values in the "Properties" window (Figure 3.36). The Cube's material is named simply "Material." The UV Sphere, being a new object does not have a material applied.

Figure 3.35

Click on "New" to add a material

Note: The preview does not reflect the shape of the object in this case the "Cube"

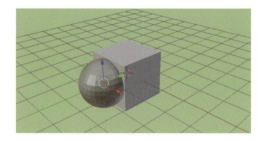

Figure 3.36

3. Creating and Editing Objects

For our demonstration remedy this by selecting the Sphere and clicking on "New" button which adds a material. In the buttons that display the new material is named "Material.001." Blender sees both materials as separate identities despite the fact that they are both identical, that is, the default gray color.

Change the material colors for both the Cube and the Sphere. In "Object" mode select the Cube. In the "Properties" window, "Materials" buttons, "Diffuse" tab, click on the white color bar and select a color in the color picker circle that displays. The Cube in the 3D window will display in the chosen color. Select the Sphere and repeat the process selecting a different color.

In the 3D window the Sphere is selected as shown by the orange outline around the object. Press Shift and select the Cube to have both objects selected. With the manipulator widget active you will see it relocate to a point midway between the two objects. To join the Cube to the Sphere press Ctrl + J key. Both objects have an orange outline and the manipulator widget locates at the center of the Cube (Figure 3.37). The Cube was the last object to be selected before joining.

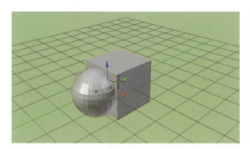 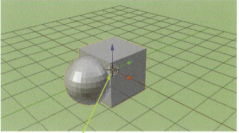

Manipulator widget located at centre of "Cube" after joining

Figure 3.37

Note the object names in the "Outliner" window. "Sphere" is no longer showing since it is part of the combined object and "Cube" was the last object selected before joining.

3.23.2 Joining in Edit Mode

Objects added to a scene in "Edit" mode are automatically joined to the last object that was selected while it was in "Object" mode.

3.23.3 Separating

The separation of joined objects or the parts of a mesh takes place in "Edit" mode. With a part to be separated press the P key to display the separation menu. Select the appropriate option as follows.

Lesson 04
04-05
Separating
Objects

3.23.4 Separating by Materials

Objects which have materials applied before being joined together in "Object" mode can be separated in "Edit" mode. With the joined objects selected in "Object" mode tab to

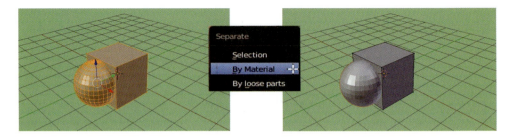

Figure 3.38

"Edit" mode (Figure 3.38). Press the P key and select "Separate by Material." The 3D window will show the Sphere with an orange outline but by pressing the A key you will see that the Cube is selected. The cube is also shown selected in the "Outliner" window and note: you now have "Cube" and "Cube.001." In separating Blender has renamed "Sphere" as "Cube.001."

Tab to "Object" mode where the Cube and the Sphere are now two separate objects, **but they are both selected**. Deselect and then select either the cube or the sphere.

3.23.5 Separating by Loose Parts

An object which is entered in "Edit" mode is automatically joined to the last object that was selected in "Object" mode. To separate them, first select the joined objects in "Object" mode then Tab to "Edit" mode. Press the P key and select the "Loose Parts" option. Figure 3.39 shows a UV Sphere object added to the scene and repositioned in "Edit" mode.

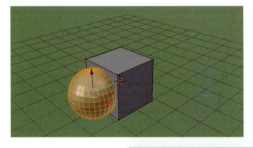

Sphere selected in "Edit Mode"

A key pressed twice selects both objects

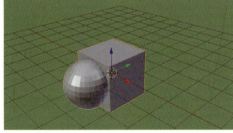

Sphere and cube joined in "Edit Mode"

Figure 3.39

3. Creating and Editing Objects

Tab to "Object" mode. **Both objects will be selected.** Press the A key to deselect then select either object to manipulate.

To separate the objects, in "Edit" mode, press the A key to select then P key to display the separation options (Figure 3.40) and click on "By loose parts." Figure 3.41 shows the objects separated in "Edit" mode. Tab to "Object" mode where there are now two separate objects. Note the center point of the Sphere which remains located outside of the mesh in the relative position that it was located when joined to the Cube. To correct this press Ctrl + S key and select "Centre to Selected" from the menu that displays.

Figure 3.40

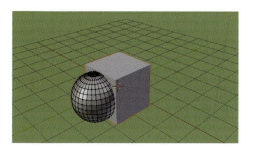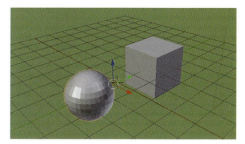

Figure 3.41

3.23.6 Separating by Selection

In "Edit" mode parts of a mesh are separated from an object by selecting groups of vertices. In order to break up a mesh, you need to be in "Edit" mode (Tab key) and select the vertices you wish to separate from the rest of the mesh. With the vertices selected, press the P key (Separate) and click on "By Selection." Press the A key to select vertices and drag the manipulation widget to move the selection. In "Object" mode the selections are treated as separate objects (Figure 3.42).

Lesson 03
03-09
Rip Tool

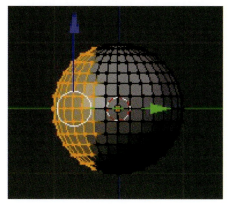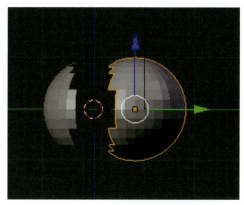

Vertices selected   Separated: P key + "By Selection"

Figure 3.42

3.24 Object Groups

Objects may be linked together into groups which can then be imported into other Blender files.

To demonstrate grouping begin with the default Blender scene containing a cube object. Add a UV sphere object and a cone as shown in Figure 3.43.

At this point each object in the scene may be individually selected then translated, rotated, or scaled. You can "Tab" into "Edit" mode and remodel each object.

In the "Properties" window, "Object" buttons, "Group" tab click on the plus sign next to the "Add to Group" button (Figure 3.44). This creates a group cache which by default is simply named "Group."

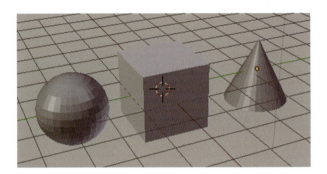

Figure 3.43

Figure 3.44

In the group name panel change this to something more meaningful such as "Object Group."

Select the UV sphere object and then click on the "Add to Group" button and then, in the selection drop down menu that displays click on "Object Group" (Figure 3.45). We will add the objects in the scene to this group.

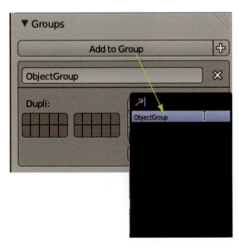

Figure 3.45

Repeat this procedure for the cube and the cone. The three objects have been added to the group named "Object Group," however, there is no indication to show this has occurred. Save the Blender file to a folder on your hard drive. Name the file something like "ObjectGroup.blend." You may name the file anything you like but do not forget what you name it or the location where you save it.

Open a new Blender file and delete the default cube object. Add a "Monkey" object. Adding the "Monkey" is done to distinguish between the files. We will now bring the "Object Group" created into this new Blender file. In the "Info" window header click on "File" then select "Link." The "File Browser" window will display where you navigate to the "ObjectGroup. blend" file you have just saved. Having found it, click LMB and the file contents will display where you will see a folder listed named "Group." Click on this "Group" folder and "Object

Group" displays. Click LMB to select it then click on "Link from Library" in the upper right-hand side of the "File Browser" window (Figure 3.46).

The group containing the sphere, cube, and cone are entered into the new Blender file where it may be translated, rotated, and scaled in the 3D window (Figure 3.47). With the group selected you will **not** be able to enter "Edit" mode and remodel the group or add

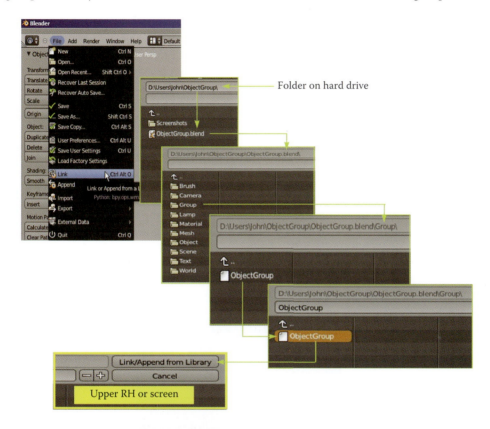

Folder on hard drive

Figure 3.46

The new scene with group linked and translated along the *x*-axis

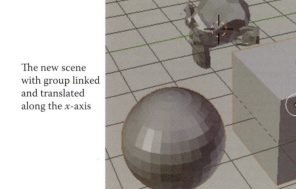

Figure 3.47

color or texture or apply any modifiers. To do that you will have to go back to your original Blender file. You can however animate the translation, rotation, and scale of the group. Don't forget to save the new file with the group and the monkey.

To edit objects go to the original file (ObjectGroup.blend). Here you can select the individual objects, "Tab" to "Edit" mode and remodel. Whatever you do here will be replicated in your new file (Group + Monkey).

Also in the new file you can create instances (Duplicates) of the group by selecting the group and then pressing Shift + A key, select "Group Instances" and select the name of the group. The duplicate is entered in grab mode and can be translated much like duplicating an object.

3.25 Deleting Vertices, Edges, or Faces

If you want to make a hole in a mesh, enter "Edit" mode and select the vertices, edges, or faces you wish to remove, then hit the Delete key. Select the item from the menu that displays.

3.26 Adding Faces

Sometimes you need to fill in holes in a mesh by creating your own faces. To do this, go into "Edit" mode and select the vertices you wish to face together. With vertices selected, hit the F key; a face will be formed. Figure 3.48 is an example. A simple plane object has been added to the scene. In "Edit" mode, a single vertex is added. Deselect the Plane (A key) then press Ctrl + click the LMB where you want the vertex to be placed. Shift select or box select two vertices on the plane and the new vertex and press the F key (face).

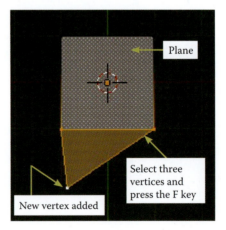

Figure 3.48

3.27 Spin and Spin Duplicate

Blender has tools for creating circular objects and circular arrays of object by spinning about a center point. The "Spin" operation takes place about the axis which is normal to (at 90° to) the view. For "Top Orthographic" view this is the Z axis. For "Front Orthographic" view it will be the Y axis. If you rotate the view somewhere in between it is at right angles to your screen. The rotation axis is located through the center of the 3D window cursor.

3.27.1 The Spin Tool

Lesson 03
03-12

Spin

To demonstrate the "Spin" tool add a "Circle" object to a scene in "Top Orthographic" view. Rotate the circle so that it is vertically on edge (press the R key + X key + 90 = Rotate on the X axis 90°). Click LMB to place the 3D window cursor as shown in Figure 3.49.

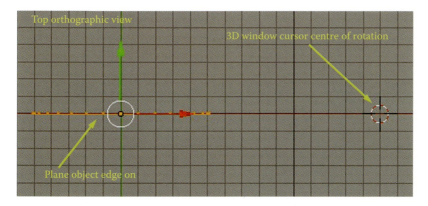

Figure 3.49

To accurately place the cursor on the grid press Shift + S key and select "Cursor to Grid". This will be the center of rotation. Tab to "Edit" mode and in the "Tools" panel press "Spin." The circle's vertices are extruded, by default for 90° (Figure 3.50).

Note that "Spin" tab has displayed in the "Tools" panel (Figure 3.51). In this panel you will see the default angle of rotation (90°) and the number of "Steps" (9). Increase the angle to 360° and the steps to 32. The extruded circle has formed a "Torus." In "Edit" mode you will

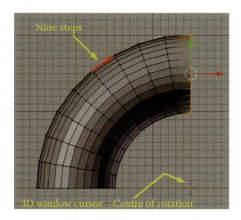

Figure 3.50

Figure 3.51

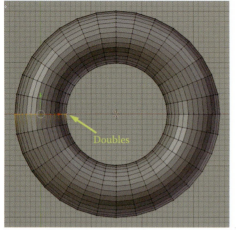

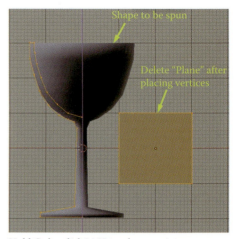

Rotation angle 360—Steps 32

Hold Ctrl + click LMB to place vertices

Figure 3.52

Figure 3.53

see the original set of circle vertices highlighted (Figure 3.52). This set has been positioned over the last set in the extrusion thus they are duplicated. Press Ctrl + V key and select "Remove Doubles." Tab to "Object" mode.

Another example of "Spin" is to spin a freehand shape. In a new scene, in "Front Orthographic" view, delete the "Cube" object and add a "Plane." Turn off the "Transformation Widget." Tab to "Edit" mode relocate the vertices of the "Plane." **Deselect** the "Plane" (A key); (Deselect NOT Delete). Hold Ctrl down and LMB click placing vertices to create one-half of the cross section profile of the shape you wish to create (Figure 3.53).

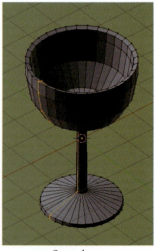

Spun shape

Figure 3.54

Figure 3.55

3. Creating and Editing Objects

Note: Before you can add vertices you must have an object selected in "Edit" mode. You are adding vertices to the object. The "Plane" consists of a minimal number of vertices (4) which will be superfluous to the shape being generated.

Deselect all vertices (A key) then select (B key drag rectangle) to select the original vertices of the "Plane." With the plane's vertices selected press X key to delete them. Press the A key to select the remaining vertices of the cross section profile.

Place the scene in "Top Orthographic" view. Remember the 3D window cursor remains at the center of the 3D World and note that in this case it is also the center of our rotation (Spin). With the new vertices selected press "Spin" in the "Tool" panel.

Increase "Steps" to 32 and change "Angle" to 360° (Figure 3.54). Remove the "Doubles." Rotate the view to see your shape (Figure 3.55).

3.27.2 Spin Duplication

Spin duplication does what it says, that is, duplicates an object around a circular path. The spin is about an axis normal to the view plane at the location of the 3D window cursor.

Lesson 03
03-13
Spin Duplication

In a new scene in "Right Orthographic" view, with the default "Cube" object selected Tab to "Edit" mode, place the 3D window cursor off to one side and hit "Spin" in the "Tools" panel. Make "Steps" the number of duplications you require then change "Angle" to 360° for a full circle. Just to show you the duplication, use the transformation widget and drag to one side, moving the original cube, revealing the number of duplications equal to the "Steps" value. Simply press the X key to delete the original cube (Figure 3.56).

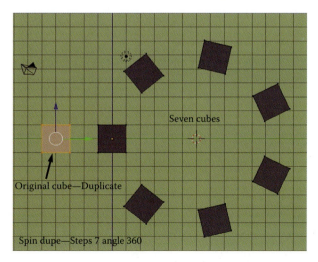

Figure 3.56

3.27.3 Screw

The "Screw" tool spins a spiral shape such as a coil spring. To use the tool in an example be in "Front Orthographic" view. Like the "Spin" tool, "Screw" revolves an extrusion of a cross-sectional shape about an axis but in this case the axis is vertically parallel to the view. The pitch of the screw is determined by a pollyline placed in the view.

Lesson 03
03-14
Screw

Vertically Parallel? In "Front Orthographic" view the Z axis. In "Top Orthographic" view the Y axis.

To demonstrate, place a "Circle" object facing you in "Front Orthographic" view. When you add a circle in "Front" view you will have to rotate it 90° about the X axis. With the "Circle" selected Tab to "Edit" mode and with the circle still selected add a "Plane" to the scene and position as shown in Figure 3.57. Delete one side of the "Plane." In doing this you leave a pollyline consisting of two vertices connected by an edge. The length of the line is scaled to represent the pitch of the screw (Figure 3.58). Place the 3D window cursor as shown. This is the point about which the shape will be spun. With all vertices

Front orthographic view—Edit mode

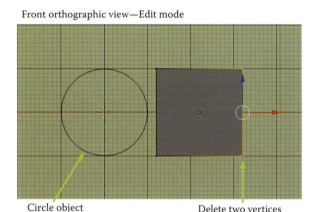

Circle object   Delete two vertices

Figure 3.57

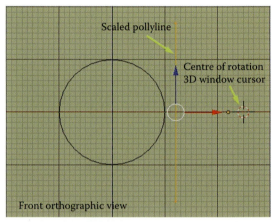

Scaled pollyline

Centre of rotation
3D window cursor

Front orthographic view

Figure 3.58

▼ Screw

Steps	
◄	32 ►

Turns	
◄	1 ►

Center	
◄ X:	2.500 ►
◄ Y:	0.000 ►
◄ Z:	0.000 ►

Axis	
◄ X:	0.000 ►
◄ Y:	-0.0000001 ►
◄ Z:	1.000 ►

Figure 3.59

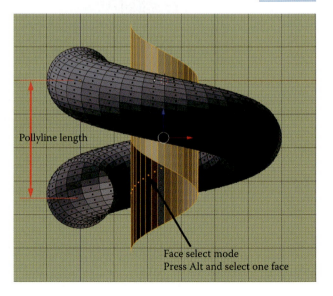

Pollyline length

Face select mode
Press Alt and select one face

Figure 3.60

3. Creating and Editing Objects

selected press the "Screw" button in the "Tools" panel. Adjust "Steps" and "Turns" values to smooth and extend the revolutions of the screw (Figure 3.59). You will see your screw generated with a central column (Figure 3.60).

Finally go into "Face" select mode. Press and hold Alt and select one face of the central column which will select all faces of the column. Press X, select "Faces" to delete the column.

> Note: The "Screw" tool may be used in any view provided you orientate the vertices with the plane of the view. "Top Orthographic" view was used in the example since a circle object is always entered flat on the XY axis.

For fun screw shapes angle the pollyline slightly by selecting the end vertices and rotating.

3.28 Modifiers

Modifiers are predefined functions for modifying, generating, and deforming object meshes and for simulating actions.

Mesh objects can have their shape modified by using Blender's modifiers. Modifiers are accessed from the properties window on the RH side of the screen. With the object selected in the 3D window, go to the "Properties" window, "Object Modifiers" button and click on "Add Modifier" to display the modifier selection menu (Figure 3.61).

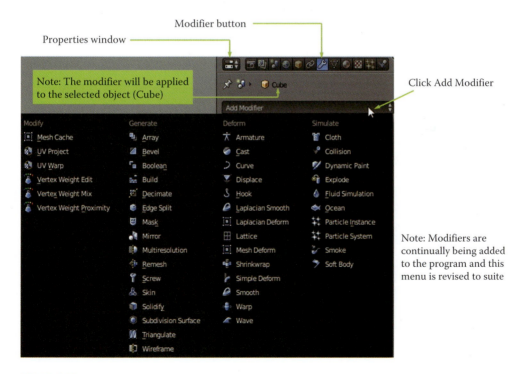

Figure 3.61

A modifier may be selected from the menu to change the shape of an object. As you can see, there are a number of modifiers to choose from. At this stage we will demonstrate a few by applying them to the default Cube object in the 3D window; for more on modifiers, see Chapter 12.

Note: Adding a "Modifier" links it to the object which is selected in the 3D window.

Note: After selecting a modifier and adjusting values to produce the desired effect, clicking on the "Apply" button permanently applies the modification to the object. When the "Apply" button is clicked the modifier panel in the properties windows cancels.

Note: Modifiers are continually being added to the program and the selection options are revised accordingly.

3.28.1 Bevel Modifier

The bevel modifier subdivides edges and/or corners producing a bevel or rounding (Figure 3.62). In "Object" mode, select the cube. In the "Properties" window, "modifier" buttons, click "Add Modifier" and select "Bevel." In the modifier panel adjust the "Width" and "Segments" values.

Properties window—Modifiers button

Add Modifier—Bevel

Applied to the cube object

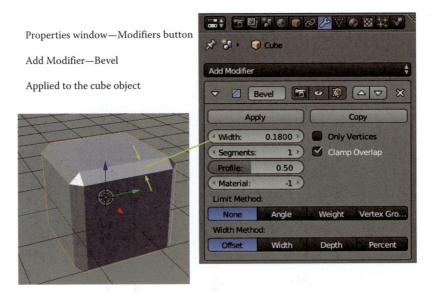

Figure 3.62

As an alternative to using the bevel modifier, Blender provides the "Bevel/Bevel Subdivide" keystroke command.

To demonstrate select the cube object and Tab into "Edit" mode. All vertices and edges are selected by default. Press Ctrl + B Key and drag the mouse to bevel all the edges and corners of the cube. Scroll the mouse wheel up to subdivide the bevel and down to reverse the subdivision. You may select a single edge in "Edge" select mode or by selecting two vertices. The bevel process applies to single edge or multiple edge selections. Press Shift + Ctrl + B key to bevel corners only. Scrolling the mouse wheel subdivides the new corner bevel producing a rounding effect (Figures 3.63 through 3.65)

Figure 3.63

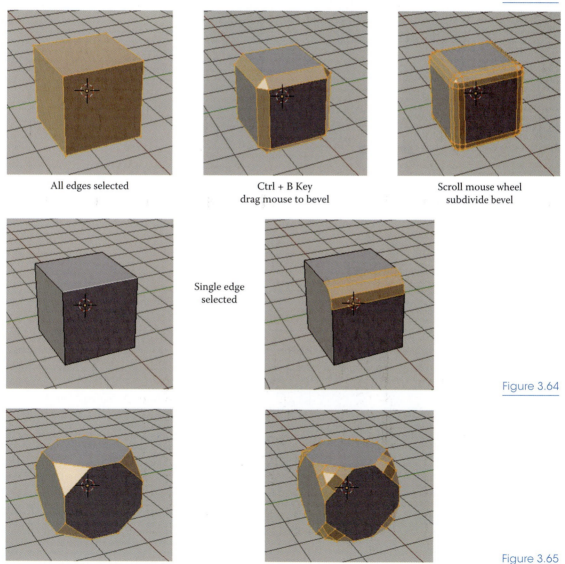

All edges selected

Ctrl + B Key
drag mouse to bevel

Scroll mouse wheel
subdivide bevel

Single edge
selected

Figure 3.64

Figure 3.65

3.28.2 Subdivision Surface Modifier

The "Subdivision Surface," or subsurf for short, modifier subdivides the faces of an object to make it appear smoother/rounder (Figure 3.66).

Cube with a subsurf modifier added

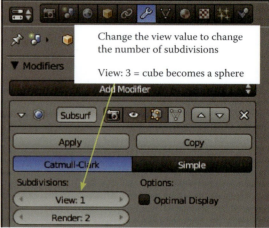

Change the view value to change the number of subdivisions

View: 3 = cube becomes a sphere

View: 1 = 4 divisions

View: 0 = cube

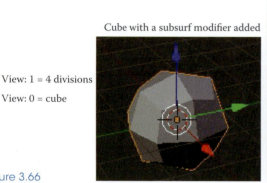

Figure 3.66

3.28.3 Mirror Modifier

Lesson 08
08-06
Mirror Modifier

When creating a complex shape, you sometimes want the shape to be symmetrical on either side of a center line. The mirror modifier is a very useful tool for achieving this.

Start a new scene and place the default cube in the "Front Orthographic" view (number pad 1 followed by number pad 5). Tab into "Edit" mode and in the tool shelf click on "Subdivide" once. The surfaces of the cube have been subdivided into four (Figure 3.67). It is important to note that only the surfaces of the cube are subdivided, not the cube itself. Still in "Edit" mode, deselect all vertices (press A key). Turn off "Limit Selection to Visible." Box-select (press B key + drag a rectangle) over one side of the cube (Figure 3.68) and delete the selected vertices (press X key) so that you are left with half of the cube. Tab to object mode.

If you rotate the scene (click and hold the center mouse wheel and drag) you will see that you have half an empty box with one side missing. Hit the number pad 1 to get back to "Front" view. Remain in "Object" mode and go to the "Properties" window, "Object Modifiers" button. Click on "Add Modifier" and select "Mirror" in the drop-down menu (Figure 3.69). You have the solid cube back again! In "Edit" mode you will have vertices on one side of the cube only. Any modifications you make to that side of the cube will be duplicated on the other side (Figures 3.69 through 3.71).

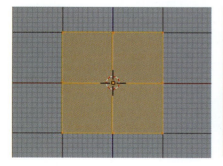

Figure 3.67

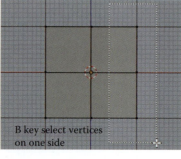

B key select vertices on one side

Figure 3.68

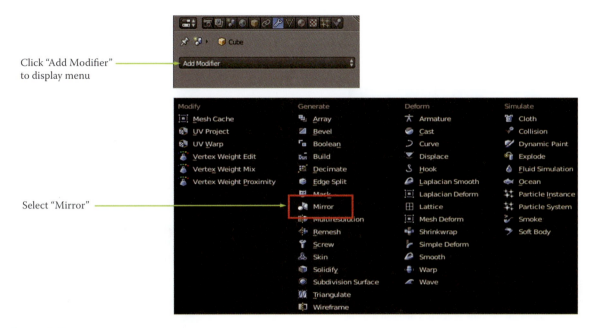

Click "Add Modifier"
to display menu

Select "Mirror"

Figure 3.69

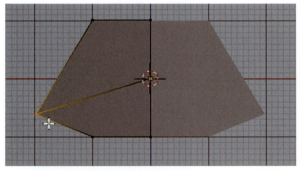

Cube deformed in edit mode by moving vertices on
one side is duplicated on the opposite side

Figure 3.70

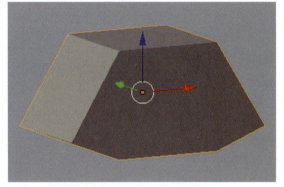

Deformed cube rotated in object mode

Figure 3.71

3.28.4 Boolean Modifier

Boolean operations allow you to cut and join meshes by using other meshes. The operations are implemented by employing "Boolean" modifiers.

An object selected in the 3D window has a modifier applied to it and the modifier is given the instruction to use another mesh to perform an operation. The operations

Lesson 08
08-03
Boolean Modifier

performed are described as intersection (Figure 3.72), union (Figure 3.73), and difference (Figure 3.74).

3.28.4.1 Intersection

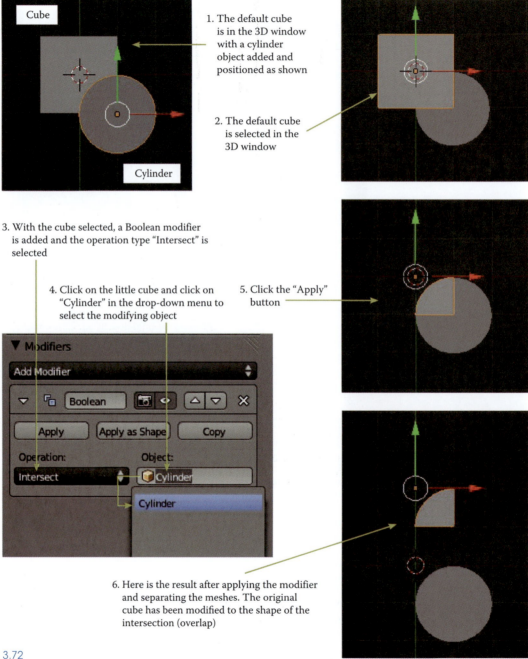

1. The default cube is in the 3D window with a cylinder object added and positioned as shown

2. The default cube is selected in the 3D window

3. With the cube selected, a Boolean modifier is added and the operation type "Intersect" is selected

4. Click on the little cube and click on "Cylinder" in the drop-down menu to select the modifying object

5. Click the "Apply" button

6. Here is the result after applying the modifier and separating the meshes. The original cube has been modified to the shape of the intersection (overlap)

Figure 3.72

3.28.4.2 Union

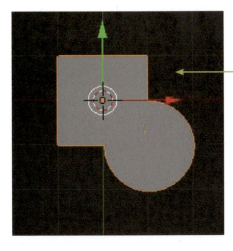

Here is the result after applying the modifier

Here is the result after applying the modifier and separating the meshes. The two meshes are joined together

Figure 3.73

3.28.4.3 Difference

Here is the result after applying the Boolean difference modifier

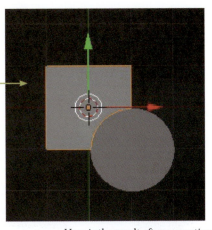

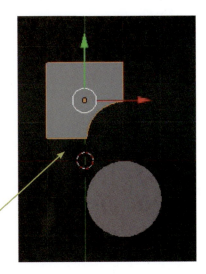

Here is the result after separating the meshes. The overlap of the meshes is subtracted

Figure 3.74

3.29 The Knife Tool

The "Knife" tool allows you to cut across edges on the surface of a mesh object and insert vertices at the intersection of the cut and the edge. The addition of vertices also creates new faces and edges in the division of the mesh. The new vertices, edges, and faces can then be manipulated to remodel the mesh. Pressing Shift + K key allows you to cut through the whole mesh object not just the visible vertices.

Lesson 03
03-08
Knife Cut

As an example using the default cube, tab into "Edit" mode and leave all the vertices selected. (The vertices and edges should be colored orange.)

With the mouse cursor in the 3D window adjacent to an edge, where you wish to commence a cut, press the K key. The mouse cursor turns into a neat little knife tool and when you place it over the edge a green dot appears. LMB click to set a cutting point on the edge. You can move the knife tool to the next edge to be cut and click again to set another cutting point or you can hold Ctrl and drag the knife tool across edges. When you finally LMB click on an edge cutting points are set on all edges that have been crossed. Press the Space Bar to enter the cut and place new vertices at all the cutting points (Figure 3.75).

Knife tool placed over an edge
(Green dot)

Click LMB to set cutting points
(Red dots)

Press space bar to enter the cut,
creating new vertices

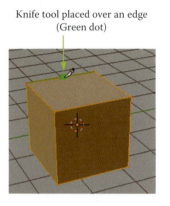 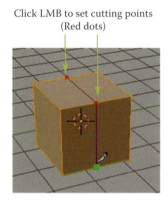 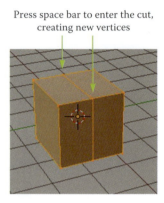

Figure 3.75

3.30 Bezier Curves and Circles

Lesson 04
04-07
Bezier Curves and
Circles Handles

Lesson 04
04-08
Bezier Curves and
Circles Extrusion

Lesson 04
04-09
Bezier Curve
Circle Loft
Bevel Along Path

Lesson 04
04-10
Bezier Curve
Circle Lathe
Bevel Along Path

Blender uses "Curves"—or, to be precise—"Curve Paths" in a variety of ways. Objects can be made to follow a curve path in an animation, they can be extruded following the shape of a curve path, or they can be duplicated in a scene and placed along a path. The speed of an object in an animation can be manipulated by altering the shape of a curve in a graph.

There are many applications for curves and in particular "Bezier" curves. The "Bezier" circle is simply a circular curve joined at the ends.

Curves are added to a scene by pressing Shift + the A key in object mode and selecting "Add – Curves" (Figure 3.76). "Bezier" curves and circles are of particular importance since they have control handles attached, which facilitate the reshaping of the curve. At first, the method of controlling the

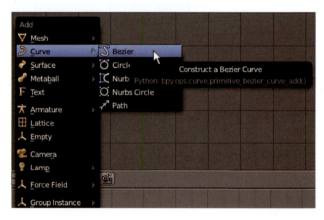

Figure 3.76

3. Creating and Editing Objects

shape of the curve can be tricky to grasp especially without some instruction. Run through the following tutorial to get the idea.

In the default Blender scene press the X key followed by "OK – Delete" to delete the cube object. Change to the top orthographic view (number pad 7 followed by number pad 5). Press Shift + the A key and select "Add – Curve – Bezier" to add a Bezier curve to the scene. Bezier curves are always added to a scene drawn on the *x, y*-plane—that is, in top view. If you add a curve in front view, all you will see is a straight line. As it is, in top view you see a curved orange line (Figure 3.77); you will have to zoom in to see it properly (press the number pad + key two or three times). As with any object in Blender, the line is selected as shown by the orange color and the transformation widget is active by default. Turn the widget off (Figure 3.78).

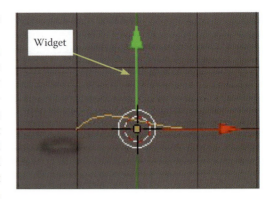

Figure 3.77

To fully appreciate the "Bezier" curve, we need to be in "Edit" mode; press the Tab key. The curve is now displayed as a black line with a series of chevrons along its length and colored straight lines located at either end (Figure 3.79). These colored lines are control

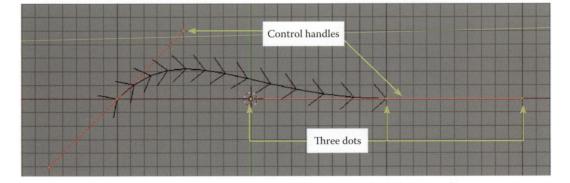

Figure 3.78

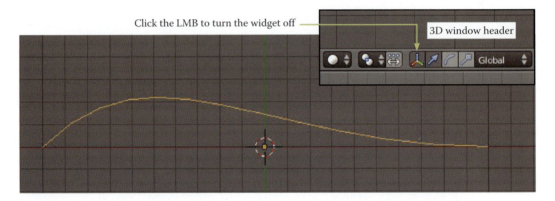

Figure 3.79

handles and they are drawn tangential to the curve. The handles are selected as shown by the bright color. Note that each handle has three dots: one at the center and one at either end. The chevrons indicate the direction of movement when the curve is used as an animation path. The direction may be reversed by pressing W Key for the specials menu and selecting "Switch Direction."

Press the A key to deselect the handles then press the A key again to select. In "Edit" mode, you are selecting and deselecting the handles only, not the curve. Press the A key to deselect the handles and right click on the center dot of the left handle. The whole handle is selected as indicated by the bright color (make note of the white dots). Press the G key and drag the mouse—the handle is moved, reshaping the curve (Figure 3.80). Click the LMB to cancel the movement.

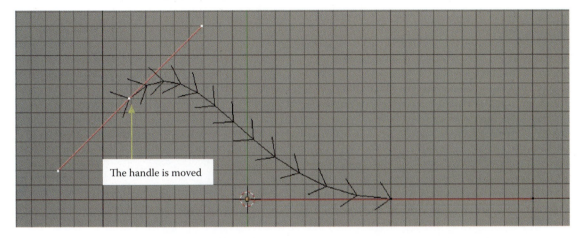

The handle is moved

Figure 3.80

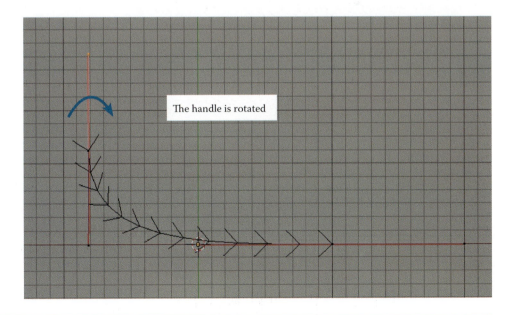

The handle is rotated

Figure 3.81

3. Creating and Editing Objects

Press the A key to deselect the handle. Right click on the dot at the end of the handle; only one half of the handle is selected as indicated by the bright color. Press the G key + drag the mouse to move the end of the handle rotating about the handle's midpoint and reshaping the curve (Figure 3.81). Click the LMB to cancel the operation.

Right click on the handle's midpoint to select. Press the E key (extrude) and drag the mouse, moving the handle away from the curve (Figure 3.82). The curve is extruded, producing a curve with three control handles. Press the A key twice to select all handles (the whole curve). In the tool panel at the left side of the window, click on "Subdivide." The curve is subdivided and control handles are added (Figure 3.83).

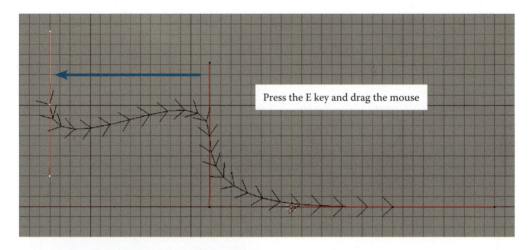

Press the E key and drag the mouse

Figure 3.82

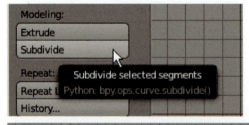

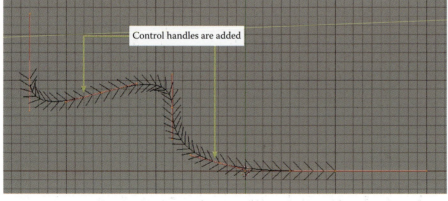

Control handles are added

Figure 3.83

Any of the handles may be selected and manipulated to change the shape of the curve. Tab to object mode and the whole curve may be translated, scaled, and rotated in the scene.

3.31 Sculpt Mode

Lesson 12
12-04
Sculpt Mode

The 3D window "Sculpt" mode allows you to deform an object's surface. Object surfaces are constructed from a mesh of vertices; by pulling and pushing the mesh, you modify the surface. It's a bit like modeling a piece of clay or Plasticine, only there's no inside to the lump. "Sculpt Mode" has numerous options for modeling a mesh surface.

To get you started, let's consider a UV sphere. Add a UV sphere object to your scene. Tab into "Edit" mode and in the "Tool Panel" at the LHS of the window, click "Subdivide" three times. This will provide plenty of vertices on the surface of the mesh to manipulate. Tab back to object mode.

Change the 3D window from "Object" mode to "Sculpt" mode and change the "Viewport Shading" to "Textured" (Figure 3.84). To enter "Sculpt Mode" click on "Object" or "Edit"

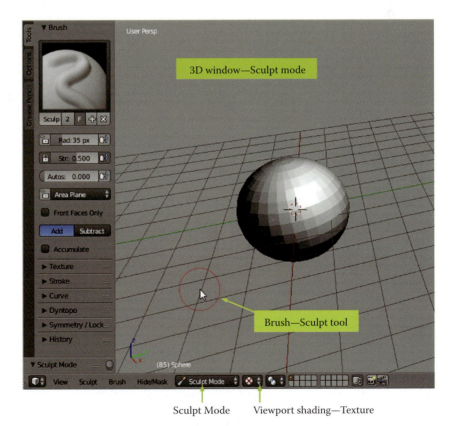

Figure 3.84

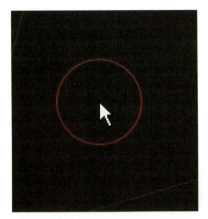

Figure 3.85

Figure 3.86

Welt on the surface

Figure 3.87

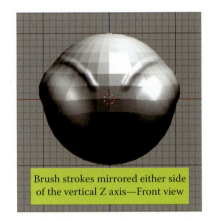

Brush strokes mirrored either side of the vertical Z axis—Front view

Figure 3.88

mode in the 3D window header to display the mode options menu and select "Sculpt Mode." The "Textured Viewport Shading" let's see the effect of your sculpting a little better; it has nothing to do with applying a texture. Zoom in to get a nice big view of the sphere (number pad + key).

Take a look at the 3D window in "Sculpt" mode. The difference between "Object" mode and "Sculpt" mode is that the tool panel at the LHS of the window has changed and the cursor has become a circle (Figure 3.85). The circle is called the "Brush." It is in fact one of several types of sculpting tools available.

The tool panel contains a series of tabs with buttons and sliders for controlling the brush (Figure 3.86). By default, the "Brush Tab" is open. Clicking on the little triangles adjacent to each tab name toggles the tab open or closed. This is purely a space-saving mechanism. If there is too much information to display in a tab, a scroll bar will display at the RHS of the tool panel.

Before attempting to figure out what all the tool panel controls are for, let's see what the "Brush" does. Click the LMB, hold, and drag the cursor circle (the brush) across the surface of the UV sphere (be sure to drag slowly; the computer is working hard here). The mesh surface deforms, producing a welt on the surface (Figure 3.87).

If you rotate the screen (click RMB, hold and drag the mouse) you will see that the surface has been deformed. A welt has been produced on the surface. You will observe that the deformation has been mirrored on either side of the Z axis (Figure 3.88). You will see a

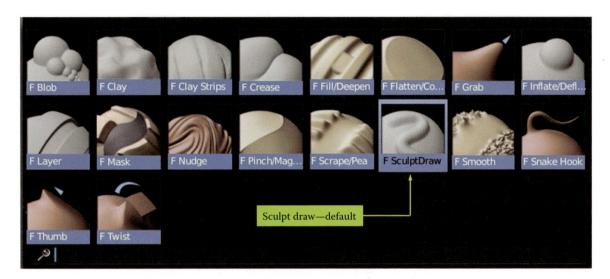

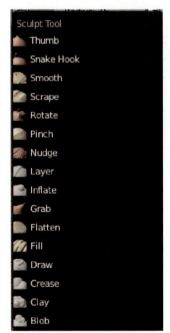

Figure 3.89

Figure 3.90

better view of this in "Front Orthographic" view (press Num Pad 1 then Num Pad 5). This will be explained later.

At the top of the "Brush" tab there is a small window showing part of a sphere with a welt on the surface. By clicking the LMB on the window, a second panel displays showing 18 brush options (Figure 3.89). You will see that type "F Sculpt Draw" is highlighted in blue, which is the default brush type. Clicking on any of the different types selects that particular type, making it active.

Go to the tool panel and open the "Tool" tab. You should see that the tool type "Sculpt Draw" is shown as being active. The tool type "Draw" is the same as "F Sculpt Draw." In the 3D window header click "Brush" then "Sculpt" and you will see a drop down menu that lists the same 18 brush-type options as before (Figure 3.90). You can also select a brush type here.

I will attempt to explain some of the control options for the brush. To do this, we will use the default tool type "Draw." There are many combinations of control options for the brush. Experimenting is the only way to achieve proficiency.

3.31.1 The Brush Tab

The radius slider in the "Brush" tab (Figure 3.86) controls the size of the brush circle. Another way to change the size of the brush circle is to press the F key, click, hold, and drag the mouse (Figure 3.91). Click with the LMB when you have finished dragging (Figure 3.92).

The strength slider controls the strength of the brush influence on the vertices, the "Add" button pulls vertices away from the surface, and the "Subtract" button pushes vertices into the surface (see Section 3.31.2 and Figure 3.93). To see the options try each on

3. Creating and Editing Objects

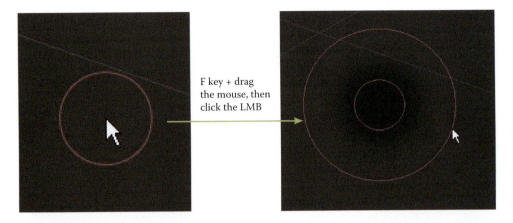

F key + drag the mouse, then click the LMB

Figure 3.91

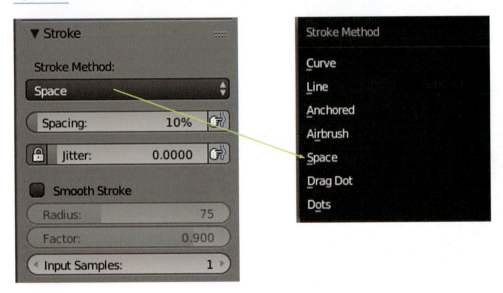

Figure 3.92

the surface of a "Plane" object (Don't forget to subdivide the surface several times in "Edit" mode).

3.31.2 The Stroke Tab

The "Stroke" method drop down menu provides different options for brush effects (Figure 3.92). Remove the UV sphere and add a plane object to the scene. Subdivide seven times to produce vertices. You must be in "Object" mode to delete the sphere and then tab to "Edit" mode to subdivide the plane. After subdividing, change back to "Sculpt" mode—make sure you have "Viewport Shading" type "Textured" selected.

Clicking the LMB and dragging the brush across the surface of the mesh with "Add" selected in the brush tab deforms the mesh in the positive direction as the brush is moved

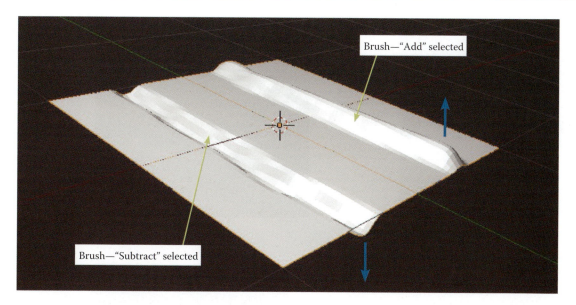

Brush—"Add" selected

Brush—"Subtract" selected

Figure 3.93

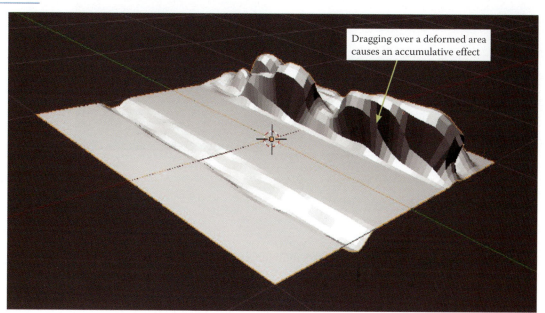

Dragging over a deformed area causes an accumulative effect

Figure 3.94

(Figure 3.93). This applies to all stroke methods. In most cases, dragging over a deformed area produces an accumulative effect even though the "Accumulate" box in the brush tab is not ticked (Figure 3.94). In these screen shots, the brush strength value is 0.963.

As previously mentioned the mesh deformation is mirrored (Figure 3.88). This occurs since a symmetry lock is applied. Look at the "Symmetry/Lock" tab in the "Tools Panel."

Under the "Mirror" heading the X value is highlighted. With X highlighted the deformation is mirrored along the X axis. Note, this means that the deformation is on either side of the Z axis. Click on the X to cancel the lock and deformation will take place only on the vertices that the Brush covers.

Clicking the LMB and dragging with any stroke method produces a deformation with the exception of the "Drag Dot" and "Anchored" methods. With "Drag Dot," the initial deformation upon clicking is duplicated wherever the mouse is positioned and clicked (Figure 3.95). With "Anchored," the deformation is produced (increased) on the same spot (Figure 3.96).

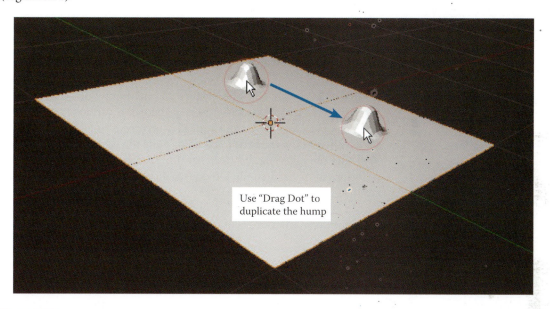

Use "Drag Dot" to duplicate the hump

Figure 3.95

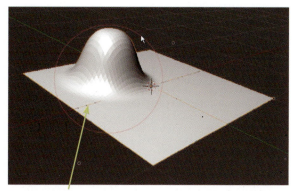

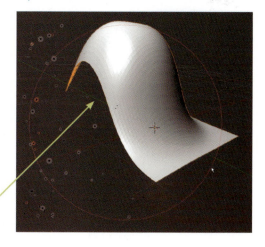

Anchored: click and drag the mouse to produce a hump

Continue dragging the mouse to deform the entire plane object

Figure 3.96

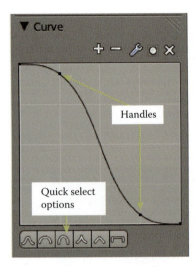

Figure 3.97

Figure 3.98

3.31.3 The Curve Tab

The "Curve" tab is a graphical method of controlling the brush effect. Click and drag the handles (dots) on the curve to reshape the curve or select from the array of quick select options displayed below the curve window (Figure 3.97).

3.31.4 The Dyntopo Tab

"Dyntopo" stands for "Dynamic Topology." Click "Enable" to activate and experiment to understand the effect.

3.31.5 The Texture Tab

Texture in Blender is the appearance of an object's surface other than its material color. A surface could have a red material color but it could also be rough or smooth. Texture is covered in a separate chapter but at this stage simply consider texture as how lumpy or bumpy a surface appears. Textures can be used to deform a surface in regular or irregular patterns. In "Sculpt Mode" a texture is assigned to a brush which affects how the brush pushes or pulls the vertices of the surface. Consider the difference between brushing newly laid cement with a soft paint brush or hard comb. Obviously there will be two very different results.

See Figure 3.98 for the "Texture" tab menu. How to assign a texture to a brush and an example of its effect will be covered in the chapter on textures.

3.31.6 The Symmetry/Lock Tab

Ticking X, Y, or Z under "Mirror" results in a deformation produced on one side of an object's axis being reproduced on the other side of the selected axis (Figure 3.99). At the time of writing X Mirror is activated by default. Click on the X to cancel.

3.31.7 The Options Tab

Up to this point the "Sculpt" mode tabs have been listed under the "Tools" section. Further tabs are located under the "Options Tab" at the LHS of the "Tools" panel.

See Figure 3.100 for the options tab drop down menu, which you can explore on your own.

3.31.8 The Appearance Tab

Clicking either of the two color bars displays color pickers for changing the appearance of the brush circle in the 3D window (Figure 3.89). This depends on whether you have "Add" or "Subtract" selected in the brush tab (Figure 3.101).

Ticking "Custom Icon" allows you to select an image to display for the tool-type icon instead of Blender's default icon (Figure 3.90).

Selecting "Mirror" displays the Mirror modifier panel and immediately the 3D window shows the previously deleted half of the Cube reinstated

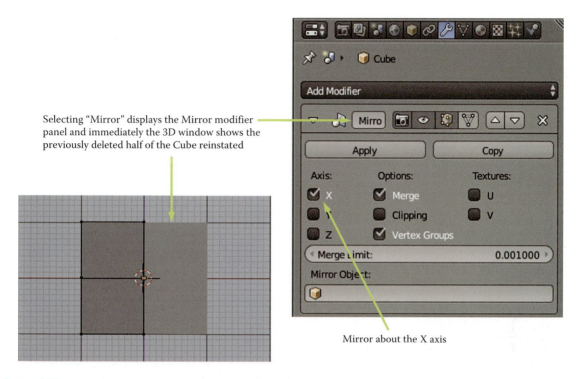

Mirror about the X axis

Figure 3.99

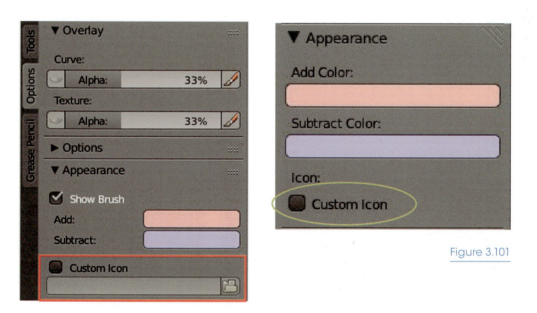

Figure 3.101

Figure 3.100

Figure 3.102

This will add a new icon to the brush-type options panel shown in Figure 3.77. Note the default icons give an indication of the brush effect. Using a Koala as an icon does not reproduce the marsupial when sculpting (Figure 3.102).

3.32 Extruding a Cup

The objective of this exercise will be to give you practice in creating a shape. The shape (a Cup) will be used in Chapter 17. The cup is produced by extruding a circle in "Edit" mode.

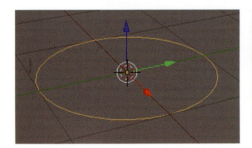

Figure 3.103

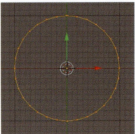

Figure 3.104

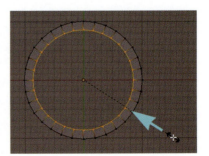

Figure 3.105

3. Creating and Editing Objects

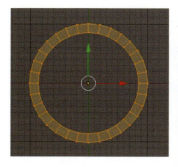

Figure 3.106

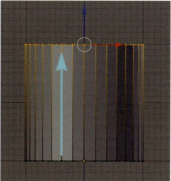

Figure 3.107

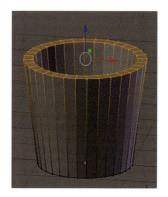

Figure 3.108

In a new Blender scene delete the default "Cube" object (X key—Delete).

Add a mesh "Circle" object (Alt + A key—Add—Mesh—Circle). Zoom in. Note that the "Circle" is in "Object" mode (Figure 3.103).

Tab into "Edit" mode (press the Tab key). Leave the circle with the default 32 vertices and a radius of 1.000.

Change the 3D view to "Top Orthographic" view (Num Pad 7 top perspective—Num Pad 5 top orthographic) (Figure 3.104).

Note: Num Pad 5 toggles between "Perspective" and "Orthographic."

With all the vertices selected press the E key (Extrude). Do not move the mouse. Immediately click LMB then press the S key (Scale) and move the mouse cursor toward the center of the circle forming an inner ring of vertices. Click LMB (Figure 3.105).

Press the A key twice to select both rings of vertices (Figure 3.106).

Change the 3D view to "Front Orthographic" view (Num pad 1).

With all vertices in the circle selected, press the E key and drag the mouse up to extrude the vertices up. The extrusion will be confined to the Z axis as shown by the vertical blue line. If the blue line does not display press the Z key (Figures 3.107 and 3.108).

Note: If you make a mistake at any stage in the process press Ctrl + Z to go back one step. You can repeat Ctrl + Z a number of times as set in the "User Preferences" window.

Note: With the double circle extruded and scaled in top view then changed to "Front Orthographic" view, the second extrusion by default is confined to the vertical axis (the blue line). Extrusions may be confined to any axis by pressing the E key followed by the X, Y, or Z keys.

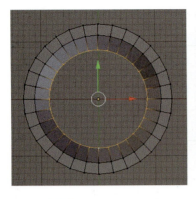

Figure 3.109

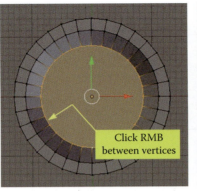

Click RMB
between vertices

Figure 3.110

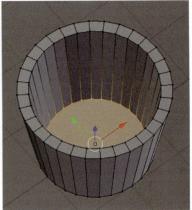

Figure 3.111

Keep the top vertices selected and scale (S key) out to form a tapered cylinder (Figure 3.109).

Deselect all vertices (A key).

Change to "Top Orthographic" view (Num Pad 7).

Select the lower (Innermost circle) of vertices (press Alt—click RMB on a part of the inner circle in-between vertices—not on a vertex). (See Section 3.21.) (Figure 3.110).

With the inner circle selected press the F key (Face) to create a bottom for the cup (Figure 3.111).

Figure 3.112

Figure 3.113

Tab back to object mode and add a "Subdivision Surface" modifier to make a fancy cup ("Properties" window—"Object Modifiers" button—Add Modifier—Select "Subdivision Surface") (Figures 3.112 and 3.113).

3.33 Extruding a Trough Method 1

In this exercise we will extrude a trough shape from a circle which we will use in Chapter 17.

Start with the default Blender scene and delete the "Cube" object (X key—Delete). Add a "Circle" object (Alt + A key—Add—Mesh—Circle). Zoom in (MMB scroll in).

The circle is entered in "Object" mode and is selected as indicated by the orange outline. Press the Tab key to change to "Edit" mode. The default circle is made up of 32 vertices and since it is selected all vertices are displayed as orange dots. Leave all vertices selected (Figures 3.114 and 3.115).

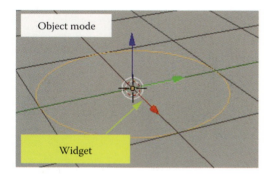

Figure 3.114

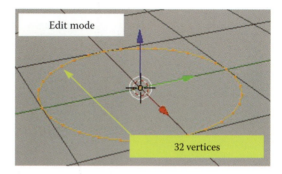

Figure 3.115

Note the default scene is shown in "User Perspective" view as shown by the notation in the upper left hand of the 3D window. Also note that the "Manipulation Widget" is active as indicated by the red, green, and blue arrows at the center of the circle.

With all vertices selected press the E key (Extrude) and immediately LMB click. Do not move the mouse. Pressing the E key has extruded the vertices and created a duplicate set. By not moving the mouse the duplicate set is located in the same location as the original set. The new vertices are selected. Press the S key (Scale) and move the mouse cursor toward the center of the circle scaling the new circle down in size as shown in Figure 3.116. LMB click. If you make a mistake at any stage press Ctrl + Z key to go back a step. The scaling takes place on the xy plane.

Press the A key twice to select both the inner and outer circles of vertices. Zoom out (MMB scroll). Press E key (Extrude) and drag the mouse upward extruding a tube. The extrusion will be confined to the z axis by default as indicated by the vertical white line.

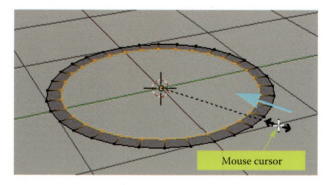

Figure 3.116

Change to top orthographic view (Num Pad 7—Num Pad 5). Zoom in on the window. Press the A key to deselect all vertices.

Note: Num Pad 5 toggles between orthographic and perspective.

In the 3D window header click on the "Limit Selection to Visible" to enable all vertices to be selected.

Press B key (Box select)—click LMB and drag a rectangle around the vertices as shown in Figure 3.107 press X key (Delete)—Delete Vertices (Figures 3.117 through 3.120).

Figure 3.118

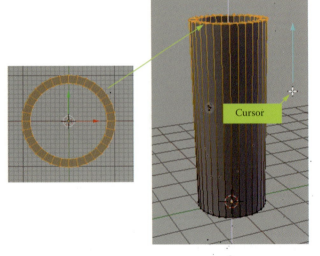

Figure 3.117

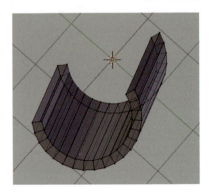

Figure 3.120

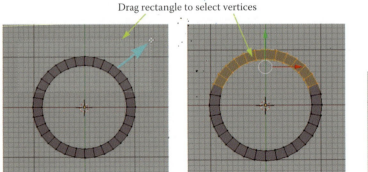

Figure 3.119

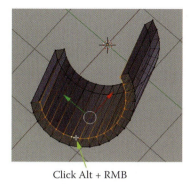

Click Alt + RMB   F Key – Face

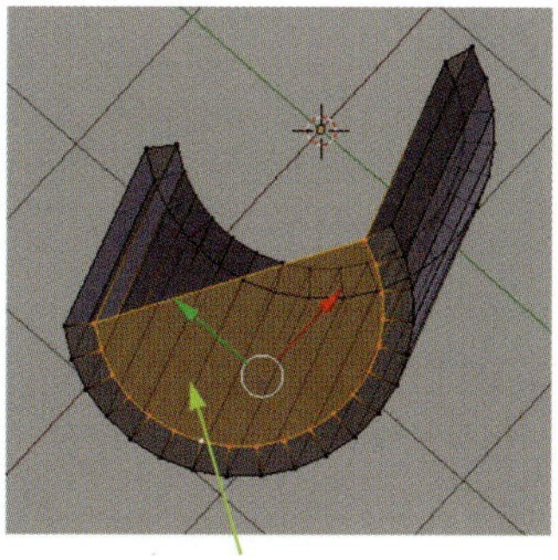

Figure 3.121

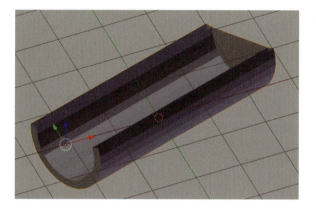

Figure 3.122

Rotate the view (MMB click hold and drag the mouse) to see a U-shaped trough.

Press the Tab key to view in "Object" mode. Tab back to "Edit" mode.

With the trough positioned approximately as shown (Figure 3.121) press Alt and RMB click (Edge Loop Selection) on an edge in the inner ring of vertices. With the ring selected press the F key (Face) to fill in the end of the trough.

Tab to "Object" mode (Figure 3.122).

3.33.1 Extruding a Trough Method 2

There are always more than one way to achieve something. Perhaps this is a simpler way to create a trough.

Figure 3.123

Start a new Blender scene. Delete the default "Cube" object and add a "UV Sphere" object. With the "Cube" selected press the X key (Delete) and select "Delete." Press Alt + A key and from the "Add" menu select, "Mesh," "UV Sphere."

Place the 3D window in "Right Orthographic" view (Num Pad 3 + Num Pad 5) and zoom in on the window (Scroll MMB or Num Pad Plus). Press Tab to enter

3D window header

Click to toggle "Limit Selection to Visible" on-off

"Edit" mode. Press A key to deselect the vertices on the surface of the "Sphere." In the 3D window header turn off "Limit Selection to Visible" (Figure 3.123). Failing to do this will

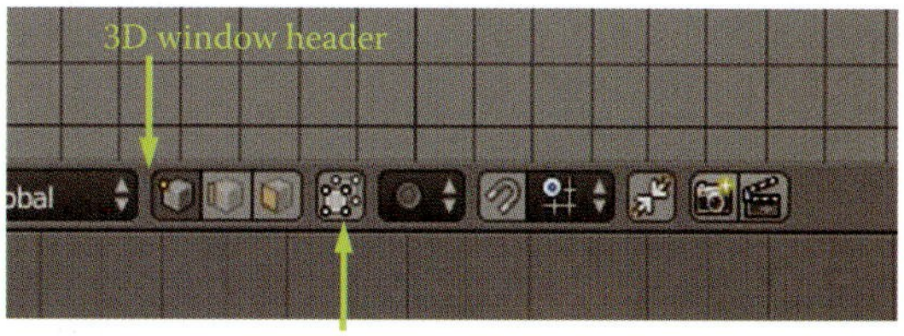

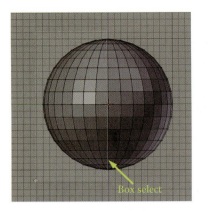

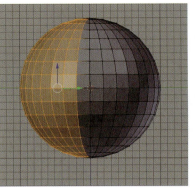

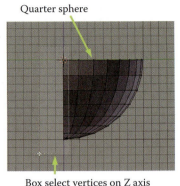
Quarter sphere

Box select

Box select vertices on Z axis

Figure 3.124

Figure 3.125

Figure 3.126

allow you to only select vertices, edges, or faces that you can actually see in the view. Press the B key (Box Select) and drag a rectangle over the LH side of the sphere in the window to select one of the LH half of the sphere's vertices (Figures 3.124 and 3.125). Press X (Delete) and select "Vertices" from the menu that displays. Repeat the process this time selecting the top quarter of the sphere.

Still in "Edit" mode select the remaining vertices on the Z axis. (The vertical LH side of the quarter.) (Figure 3.126). Press the E key (Extrude) and immediately press the Y key to confine the extrusion to the Y axis of the scene. Drag the mouse to the left and the selected vertices follow. When you have extruded the vertices keep them selected and press the S key (Scale) and scale the selection down (Figure 3.127).

You have constructed a trough (Figure 3.128). Save the Blender (.blend) file. In the "Info" winder header press "File," select "Save As," enter a name, press "Enter" then click "Save As Blender File" in the top RH corner of the screen. Make a note of where the file is saved for future.

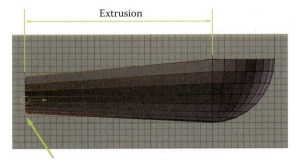
Extrusion

With the vertices selected scale down

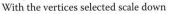
Simple trough extrusion

Figure 3.127

Figure 3.128

3. Creating and Editing Objects

3.34 Using Dupliverts

"Dupliverts" refer to the process of duplicating an object at the position of each vertex of another object. We will demonstrate this by duplicating a "UV Sphere" object at each vertex of a subdivided "Plane" object.

Delete the default "Cube" object in the default Blender scene and in the 3D window add a "Plane" object. Scale the plane up four times the original size then subdivide a number of times. In "Object" mode deselect the plane.

Add a "UV Sphere" object to the scene, scale it down (Figure 3.129).

Shift select the "UV Sphere" then the "Plane." Press CTRL + P key and select "Set Parent to Object" to parent the sphere to the plane (Figure 3.130).

With the plane selected go to the "Properties" window "Object" buttons, "Duplication" tab and select "Verts." The sphere is duplicated at the location of each vertex on the plane (Figure 3.131).

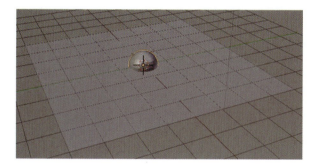

Figure 3.129

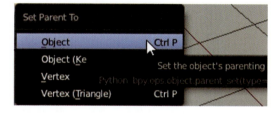

Figure 3.130

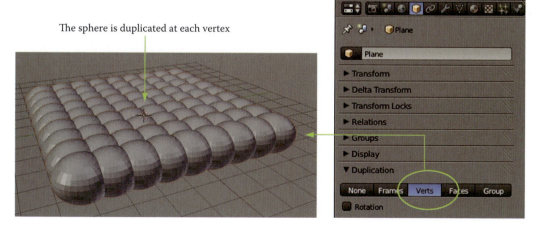

The sphere is duplicated at each vertex

Figure 3.131

Deselect the plane.

We will probably require to scale the sphere to adjust its size but since we entered the sphere into the scene on the center of the plane it is more than likely hidden among the duplications and difficult to select.

Go to the "Outliner" window and locate the sphere. It will be found under "Plane" in the file tree since it is parented to the plane. Select the sphere in the "Outliner" window (click LMB) then in the 3D window scale the sphere as desired (Figure 3.132).

With the plane in "Edit" mode a group of vertices may be selected and with "Proportional Editing" turned on, translated moving the duplicated spheres (Figure 3.133).

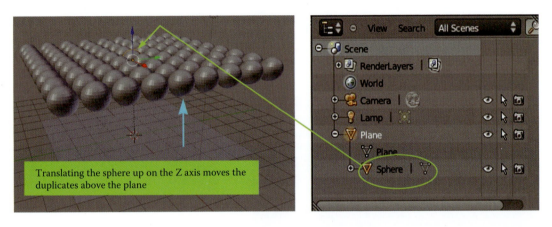

Translating the sphere up on the Z axis moves the duplicates above the plane

Figure 3.132

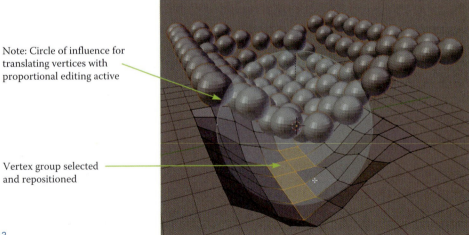

Note: Circle of influence for translating vertices with proportional editing active

Vertex group selected and repositioned

Figure 3.133

3. Creating and Editing Objects

4

Materials

4.1 Introduction to Materials

In Blender a "Material" is the way in which the surface of an object displays. In simplistic terms it could be considered as color but it is much more than that. Consider the color red and think of all the possible shades of red you could image and how the different shades could be applied over a surface. The red could be shiny or dull or the red surface could be partially transparent or translucent. These possibilities are what is meant by a "Material."

Lesson 05
05-01
Colored Materials

4.2 Material Settings

The default Blender scene has a cube object that displays as a dull gray color. Color is the way your eyes interpret the reflected light from an object's surface. If there is no light, you see nothing, so Blender has placed a white-light lamp in the default scene and assigned data to the cube that shows the cube as being gray in this color light. You add a material in the properties window with the "Material" button activated (Figure 4.1).

Properties window   Material button

Figure 4.1

103

Note: In the default Blender scene, the default cube object has been assigned a material as seen by the gray color of the cube object and the fact that the "Material" buttons are displayed in the "Properties" window. Subsequent objects added to the scene also display with this same color although the "Material" buttons for a new object do **not** display. Clicking on the "New" button will display "Material" options. For now, consider an object as *not* having a material unless the "Material" button displays all the tabs shown in Figure 4.2. Remember, the values in the properties window only apply to the object that is selected in the 3D window.

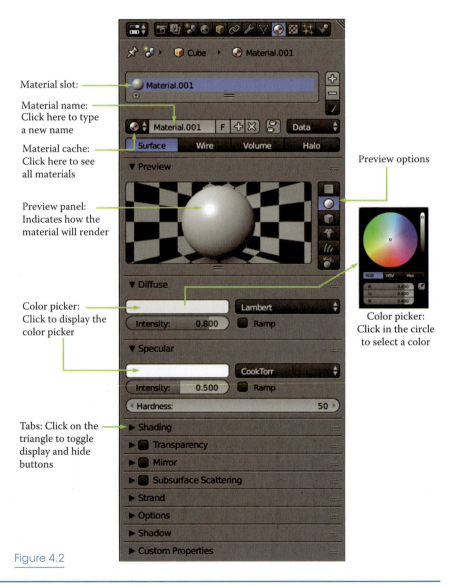

Material slot:

Material name:
Click here to type
a new name

Material cache:
Click here to see
all materials

Preview options

Preview panel:
Indicates how the
material will render

Color picker:
Click in the circle
to select a color

Color picker:
Click to display the
color picker

Tabs: Click on the
triangle to toggle
display and hide
buttons

Figure 4.2

When you click on the Material button for a new object, the "Properties" window only displays the information in Figure 4.1. To add a material to an object, first select the object you want to work with (the default cube comes with a material added). In the "Properties" window header, click the "Material" button, then click the "New" button. You will see the Material Properties tabs open up. The values will be the same as those for the default cube.

Note: When you click "New," Blender assigns a default set of data for the material color, which produces the gray color. You then modify this block of data (datablock) to produce the material to suit your requirements.

4.3 Material Buttons

The "Properties" window, "Material" buttons panel is used to apply material color to an object's surface (Figure 4.2). This panel is where you also set other properties such as shading, transparency, glossy or flat, reflective, halo effect, etc. A brief example of setting a material will follow.

4.4 Material Colors

Each material can exhibit three colors:

- The basic "Diffuse" overall color, which is seen when a surface reflects light
- The "Specular" color, which gives a surface highlights or a shiny appearance
- The "Mirror" color, which is the color used to fake mirror reflections

It is important to remember that the material color is only one element in the rendering process that determines an object's appearance. The rendered color of an object is a product of the material color and the emitting light color. An object may have a yellow material color, but put it under a blue light or a red light and you'll see something else altogether.

Note: The rendering process is the conversion of data, which shows the display in the 3D window as an image.

4.5 Adding a New Material

Adding a material will be demonstrated by the following example.

Start a new Blender scene and add a "Monkey" object (Figure 4.3). Hit the number pad + key and zoom in a bit. Go to the "Tools" panel and under "Shading" click

Figure 4.3

Figure 4.4

on "Smooth." Make sure the monkey is selected then go to the "Properties" window "Material" button (Figure 4.4).

Click on the "New" button to display the Material Properties buttons. When the monkey is added to the scene, Blender assigns it the properties for the gray color even though the material properties are not displayed. After clicking "New," you can modify the properties to achieve appearance you want.

> Note: We selected the smooth option from the tool panel to better display the modifications to the material. Some of the effects are very subtle, so a nice smooth surface is best for this demonstration.

4.6 The Preview Tab

Take a look at the "Preview" tab in the "Properties" window, "Materials" buttons (Figure 4.5). This preview gives an indication of how you will see your material in a render of the 3D window. To save computer memory, Blender does not display everything in the 3D window. On the left-hand (LH) side of the "Preview" tab, there are options for viewing the preview in different formats. One of the options is "Monkey," but for simplicity, I have left the preview as the default sphere.

4.7 The Diffuse Tab

As previously stated the Monkey object has been assigned a gray color. This is the diffuse overall color of the material. Click the gray bar (appears white) to display the color picker and note the R: 0.800, G: 0.800, and B: 0.800 values (Figure 4.6). These are the numeric

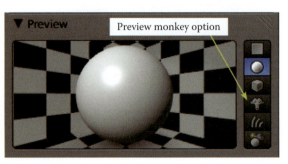

Figure 4.5

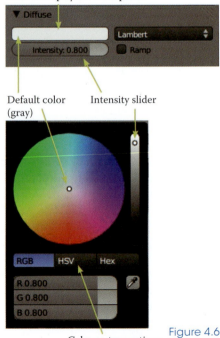

Figure 4.6

Color system options

values that denote the gray color in the RGB color system. RGB stands for "red, green, and blue," the primary colors. Mixing the three 0.800 values produces the gray color. There are three color system options available: RGB, HSV, and Hex.

The intensity of a color is the shade of the color going through a range from absolutely no light to maximum light. Figure 4.7, demonstrates intensity, also serves to show that light has a major effect on

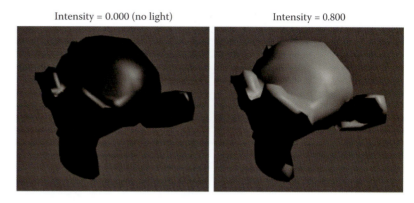

Intensity = 0.000 (no light)   Intensity = 0.800

Figure 4.7

a rendered image. When the monkey was added to the scene, it was located at the center of the world. This means that the position of the default lamp is above and behind the monkey's head, which explains why the monkey's face is in shadow. So how come we see the monkey when the intensity is 0.000 (no light)? We will come back to that a bit later. For now, let's make the monkey more colorful.

Open the color picker again and select a color you like. If you want to match my example exactly, enter the RGB values R: 0.800, G: 0.430, and B: 0.000—we now have a

pretty golden monkey. The difference between what you see in the 3D window and the rendered image is shown in Figure 4.8 (press F12 to see a rendered image—press Esc to cancel). The 3D window has some shadowing effect so that you can see 3D features. This shadowing is evident in the render, but in addition you can see some shiny highlights. The shiny highlights are there because, by default, Blender has added "Specular" color (discussed next) to the monkey; that's why we could see the monkey when we turned the diffuse color intensity down to 0.000 in Figure 4.7. In effect, we canceled the "Diffuse" light reflection but there was still "Specular" light reflection.

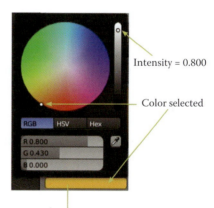

Intensity = 0.800

Color selected

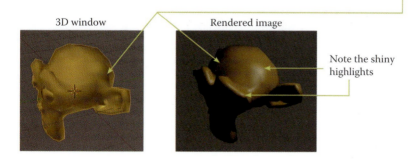

3D window   Rendered image   Note the shiny highlights

Figure 4.8

Intensity = 0.000 (no light)   Intensity = 0.500   Intensity = 1.000

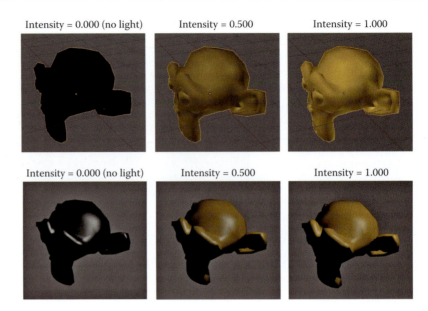

Figure 4.9

Intensity = 0.000 (no light)   Intensity = 0.500   Intensity = 1.000

Figure 4.10

See Figure 4.9 (monkey as seen in the 3D window) and Figure 4.10 (rendered images of monkey) for comparisons when the intensity changes.

4.8 The Specular Tab

The "Specular" tab is similar to the "Diffuse" tab with a color bar that, when clicked, displays a color picker. The difference between the two tabs is that the specular tab has a hardness value (Figure 4.11).

Click to select "Specular" color ⟶

Hardness value

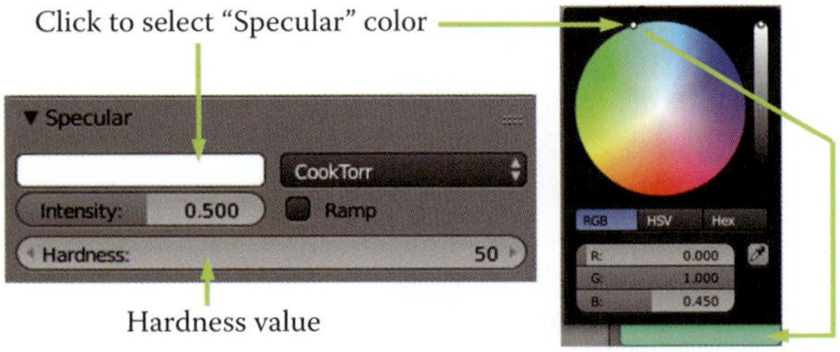

Figure 4.11

Click on the "Specular" color bar and then select the green color with R: 0.000, G: 1.000, and B: 0.450. Set the diffuse color intensity to 0.800. When you add a specular color to an object's material, there is no dramatic effect in the 3D window—the difference will be the specular highlights, which are more evident in the rendered image. Figures 4.12

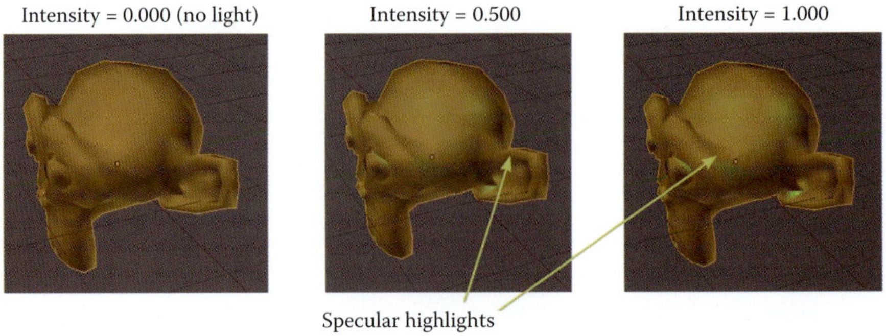

Intensity = 0.000 (no light)   Intensity = 0.500   Intensity = 1.000

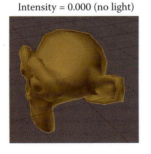
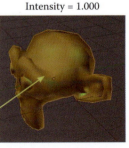

Specular highlights

Figure 4.12

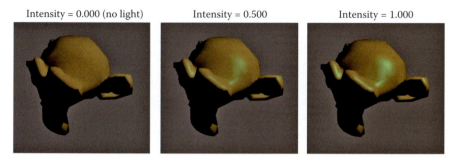

Intensity = 0.000 (no light) Intensity = 0.500 Intensity = 1.000

Figure 4.13

and 4.13 demonstrate the differences with varying intensity values for 3D window objects and rendered images, respectively.

> Note: As an alternative to rendering an image by pressing F12 on the keyboard you may change the 3D window "Viewport Display" mode to "Rendered." Any change to object properties will display automatically with the window in this mode.

4.9 The Hardness Value

The best way to describe the effect of the hardness value is to say that the effect spreads the "Specular" color across the surface of the object (known as "soft light") or focuses it (known as "hard light"). The default hardness value is 50 and the value range is 1–511. The most visible effect when altering the value occurs in the lower region of the range. Figures 4.14 and 4.15 demonstrate this effect for 3D window and rendered images, respectively. Set both diffuse and specular color intensities to 0.800.

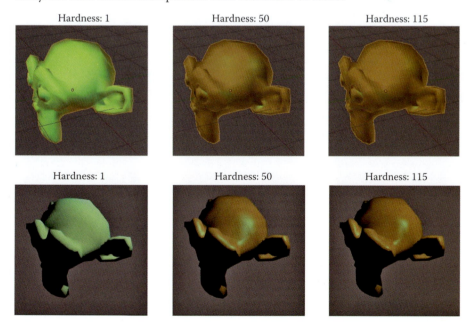

Hardness: 1 Hardness: 50 Hardness: 115

Figure 4.14

Hardness: 1 Hardness: 50 Hardness: 115

Figure 4.15

4.10 Ramp Shaders

Lesson 05
05-06
Blender Materials
Ramps

Lesson 05
05-03
Blender Materials
Shaders

The "Ramp Shader" system in Blender integrates a color shading over a surface, also known as gradient. The following demonstration provides instruction in the use of the Blender interface in implementing the "Ramp Shader."

Ramp shaders are provided for both diffuse and specular colors. They allow the introduction of subtle color mixing on an object's surface. It must be remembered that the ramp shaders are used in conjunction with lighting, therefore, the type of lamp, its strength (energy), and its location in the scene relative to the object all influence the final result and provide a vast array of possibilities in color application.

We will demonstrate "Ramp Shaders" by setting a scene as shown in the diagram with a "UV Sphere" object, the default "Point" lamp, and the default "Camera." The "UV Sphere" and the "Point" lamp are located on the midplane of the scene and translated three Blender units along the *Y*- and *X*-axes, respectively (Figure 4.16).

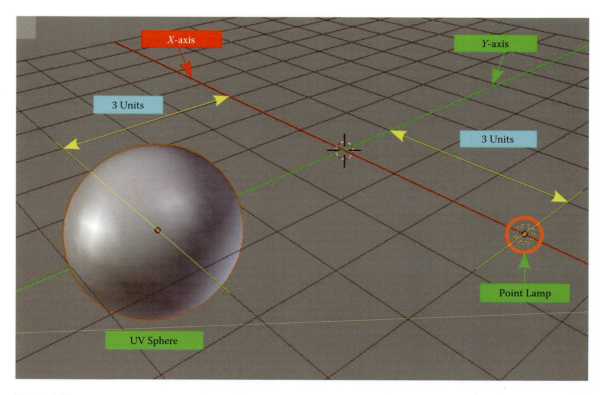

Figure 4.16

4.10.1 Set the Scene

In the 3D window select the sphere and in the "Object Tools" panel at the LH side click on "Smooth" under "Shading." This sets the sphere with a nice smooth surface. In the

"Properties" window, "Material" buttons add a new material. An object entered in a scene displays with a default gray color. Blender automatically assigns hidden material settings; otherwise, the object would not display at all. When you click "New" to add a material you simply display those settings that you then modify to your requirements.

By default the "Diffuse" color is gray with RGB values all 0.800. We can leave the default gray set for the demonstration since the "Ramp Shader" settings will override the default material setting. The default color shaders for an object are the "Diffuse" and "Specular" colors. The diffuse color is the overall color of the object while the specular color is the shiny highlights or reflections on a surface.

The effects of ramp shaders will not display in the default 3D window unless we change the 3D window "Viewport Shading" option to "Rendered" or the 3D window is in "Texture Viewport Shading" mode with GLSL set (explanation following). While in "Solid Viewport Shading" the effects will only show in a rendered image (press F12).

4.10.2 Window Display Settings (GLSL)

With the mouse cursor in the 3D window and the "Sphere" object selected press the N Key to display the "Object Properties" panel (Figure 4.17).

In the "Shading" tab change the "Shading" type from "Multitexture" to "GLSL."

GLSL allows you to see "Ramp Shader" colors in the 3D window when "Texture" display mode is selected.

In the 3D window header change the "Viewport Shading" from "Solid" to "Texture" (Figure 4.18).

When you change the "Viewport Shading" to "Texture" there is an immediate difference in how the surface of the sphere displays.

Figure 4.17

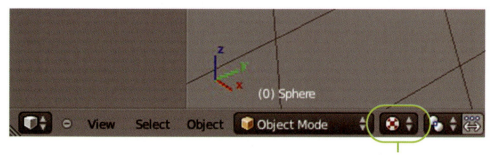

Change "Solid" to "Texture"

Figure 4.18

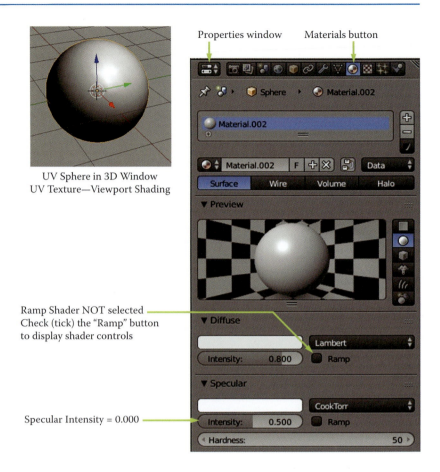

Properties window   Materials button

UV Sphere in 3D Window
UV Texture—Viewport Shading

Ramp Shader NOT selected
Check (tick) the "Ramp" button
to display shader controls

Specular Intensity = 0.000

Figure 4.19

Note: At this point we have not activated the "Ramp Shader" (Figure 4.19). Note also that "Ramp Shaders" are included with both "Diffuse" and "Specular" colors. To make the demonstration as simple as possible we will negate the specular effect by reducing the diffuse specular "Intensity" value to 0.000. We can then concentrate on the "Diffuse" color.

Why the change in display on activating "Texture" shading mode?

The "Diffuse" and "Specular" shaders are applied to materials in the 3D window to allow you to view objects in 3D. These shaders do not display true shading with respect to the light source in the 3D window unless GLSL is activated and the viewport is in "Texture" viewport shading mode.

Lesson 05
05-06

Blender Materials
Ramps

4.10.3 The Ramp Shader

In the "Properties" window, "Material" buttons, "Diffuse" tab, check (tick) the "Ramp" button to display the shader controls (Figure 4.20). Remember these controls are only

applicable to the selected object in the 3D window.

The shading effect is previewed in the chequered horizontal bar. Look closely at the LH end of the bar and observe that there is a vertical **dotted** line with a slider handle underneath. This line is a "Color Stop" which indicates a point in the shader bar. There is also another vertical line and slider handle (Color Stop) at the opposite end of the bar where the bar is white. This stop is not selected. The shader bar is previewing a graduated color range between the two stops. The selected stop (LH end) in the shader bar is shown as "Position: 0.000" in the panel immediately below the LH end of the bar. The color at this location is shown in the panel to the right of the position indicator. The black colored panel is a color picker for selecting colors. Click on the black area to display the picker. You bet! It shows the color black (RGB values all 0.000). It also shows that the "Alpha" (A) value as 0.000 which means that the color is completely transparent; hence, you see the chequered background in the shader bar at position 0.000. This is also indicated by half the color picker showing a chequered pattern. Click on the Color Stop at the RH end of shader bar. The position is now 1.000 and the color picker displays white (RGB values all 1.000) (Figure 4.21).

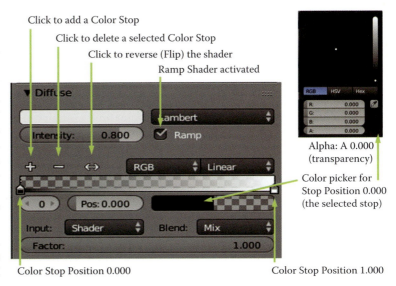

Click to add a Color Stop
Click to delete a selected Color Stop
Click to reverse (Flip) the shader
Ramp Shader activated

Alpha: A 0.000 (transparency)

Color picker for Stop Position 0.000 (the selected stop)

Color Stop Position 0.000   Color Stop Position 1.000

Figure 4.20

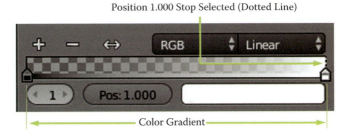

Position 1.000 Stop Selected (Dotted Line)

Color Gradient

Figure 4.21

The "Alpha" value is also 1.000, which means that the color is completely opaque (Solid Color). With these settings, the shader bar shows a color gradient starting at position 0.000 with a completely transparent black and gradually changing to a completely opaque white at position 1.000.

Note: The three panels, Lambert, Shader and Mix. "Lambert" is one of five shader models available in Blender. The "Input—Shader" is one of four methods of mapping the color ramp to the surface of the selected object. The "Blend—Mix" is one of 18 methods of blending the diffuse color with the color ramp. With these method combinations, the effects that can be created for a surface color are endless.

4.10.4 How the Color Shader Displays

How the colors display in the 3D window on the surface of the selected object is highly dependent on lamp settings and the location of lamps and camera relative to the object. The scene setup we have created will allow us to demonstrate basic principles.

Place the scene in top orthographic view (Figure 4.22) by pressing "Num Pad 7." The sphere is positioned at 45° relative to the single point lamp with the highest energy point of light from the lamp at a point on the surface of the sphere immediately adjacent to the lamp. The color in the "Color Ramp" at the stop "Position 1.000" is mapped to the point of highest light energy on the surface of the selected object (the Sphere). The color at stop "Position 0.000" is mapped to the point of lowest light energy on the sphere. The black surface of the sphere is showing that there is no light energy, that is, it is in shadow. We, therefore, have a color gradient equivalent to the "Ramp Shader" mapped from the point on the spheres surface closest to the lamp to the shadow line. The fact that the black color in the ramp is transparent produces the gray shading effect. By changing the "Alpha" value at stop "Position 0.000" to 1.000 (opaque) you will see a true gradient in color from white to black from the high-energy point to the shadow line.

To add a new "Color Stop" to the "Color Ramp" click the "Add" button. To delete a "Color Stop," select the stop and click the "Delete" button (Figures 4.20 and 4.23). To reverse (Flip)

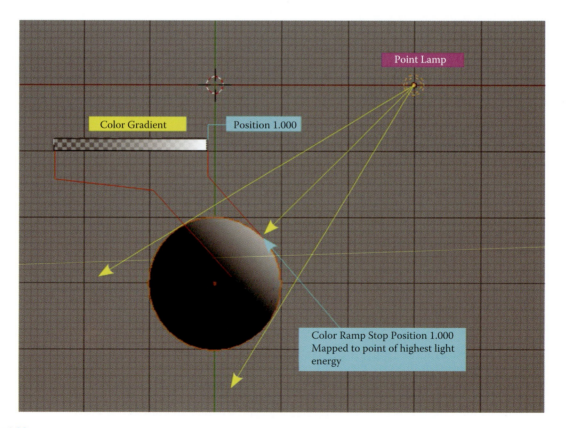

Figure 4.22

the gradient click the double-headed arrow. Adding a stop displays a new dotted line in the ramp. The stop is selected when it displays as a dotted line. The color at the new position takes whatever the color in the ramp is at that location; in this case midway between white and black, gray (Figure 4.23).

Let us brighten things up a little with some bright colors. Select "Stop Position 0.000," click on the color picker bar and move the intensity slider all the way (Figure 4.24) to the top then select a nice bright red color. Select "Stop Position 0.5000" (the new stop in the middle) and repeat the process this time selecting a bright green color. Repeat the process again for "Stop Position 1.000" selecting a bright yellow. At all stop positions set the "Alpha" value to 1.000 (opaque). On the sphere in the 3D window the ramp color is mapped across the surface where light energy strikes the surface (Figure 4.25).

New Stop added at Position 0.500

Figure 4.23

Note: Don't forget to be in "Texture Viewport Shading" mode with the 3D window shading type to GLSL (Section 4.10.2).

To see the effect of using one of the different "Input" mapping methods change "Input—Shader" to "Input—Result." Press the "F" (Flip) button to reverse the direction of the "Ramp Shader" for another effect (Figure 4.26).

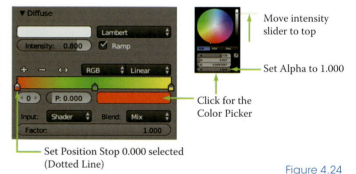

Move intensity slider to top

Set Alpha to 1.000

Click for the Color Picker

Set Position Stop 0.000 selected (Dotted Line)

Figure 4.24

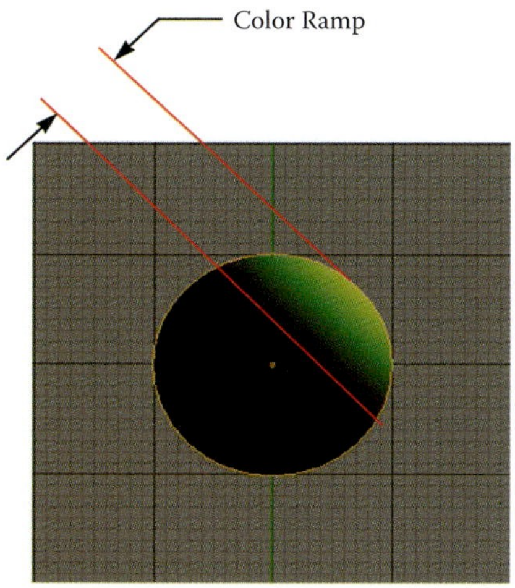

Color Ramp

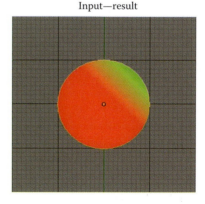

Input—result

Figure 4.25

Figure 4.26

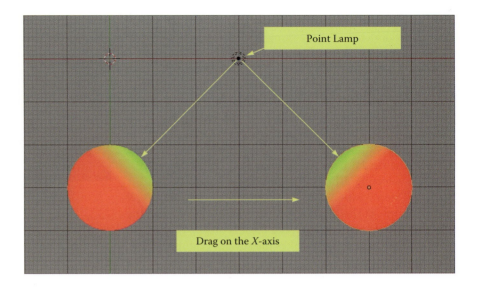

Figure 4.27

Click on the center stop position, drag to one end of the ramp shader to the other, and observe the change in color gradient on the surface of the sphere.

To emphasize the relevance of the objects position relative to the light source drag the sphere along the *X*-axis and see the color map move on the surface (Figure 4.27).

4.10.5 Overlay on Base Diffuse Color

The "Color Ramp" materials are mapped over the base "Diffuse" color (Replaces the "Diffuse" color). In the "Diffuse" color picker select a bright blue color. In the diffuse "Ramp Shader" select "Stop Position 1.000" and make the color completely transparent (Alpha 0.000). You will immediately see a blue strip display on the surface of the sphere at the point of maximum light energy. Drag the stop to the left and observe the blue stripe widening. You are widening the transparency and therefore exposing the base diffuse color (Figures 4.28 and 4.29).

Figure 4.28

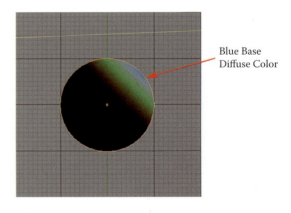

Figure 4.29

Figure 4.30

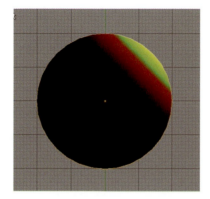

Figure 4.31

Selecting and moving any of the "Stop Positions" in the "Color Ramp" will affect the color bands on the sphere (Figures 4.30 and 4.31).

4.10.6 Summary

As you can see there are a multitude of effects that can be created and only by experimentation and recording will you become proficient in the use of ramp shaders (Figure 4.32).

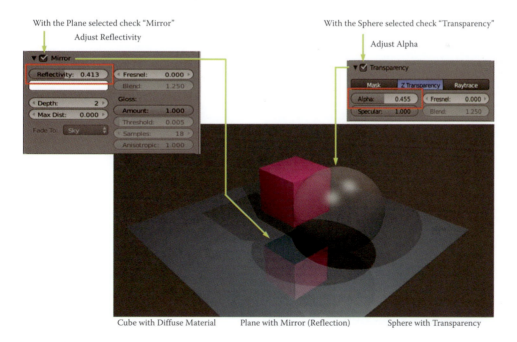

Figure 4.32

4.11 Halo Settings

By using halo settings, only the vertices of a mesh object will be visible when rendered (Figure 4.33). The vertices will display as points of light, which look like rings, lines, or stars, or a combination of all three.

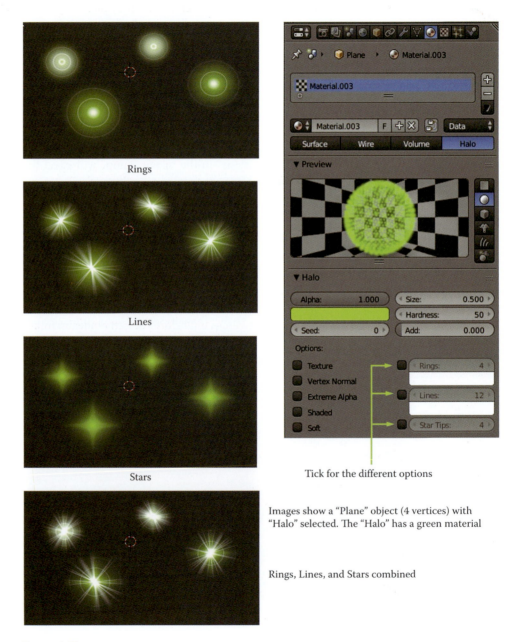

Rings

Lines

Stars

Tick for the different options

Images show a "Plane" object (4 vertices) with "Halo" selected. The "Halo" has a green material

Rings, Lines, and Stars combined

Figure 4.33

4.12 Transparency and Reflection

4.12.1 Transparency

To make an object transparent, add a material, then in the "Properties" window, "Material" buttons, "Transparency" tab check (tick) the "transparency" button. By default "Z Transparency" is set. Adjust the "Alpha" slider to set the amount of transparency (Alpha: 0.000—fully transparent, Alpha: 1.000—fully opaque).

Lesson 05
05-04
Blender Materials
Transparency

Note: To see transparency "Viewport Shading" must be in "Render" mode or you have to render an image (F12).

4.12.2 Reflection (Mirror)

To have an object's surface reflect light as a mirror, add a material then in the "Properties" window, "Materials" buttons, "Mirror" tab, check the "Mirror" button. Adjust the "Reflectivity" slider value (0.000 no reflection—1.000 maximum reflection). To see the effect you must be in "Viewport Shading," Render mode or render an image.

Lesson 05
05-05
Blender Materials
Mirror

4.13 Vertex Painting

In addition to the options for adding materials to an object as described so far in this chapter, Blender also provides the "Vertex Paint" tool, which allows you to manually paint a material onto the surface of an object (Figure 4.34).

You can paint by changing the 3D window from object mode to "Vertex Paint" mode. You will be able to paint a selected object immediately, but before you can render an image with the paint showing, you must have a material added. A new object added to the 3D window displays with the default gray color, but, as you can see in the "Properties" window, "Material" button, there are no control tabs displayed. With the new object selected in the 3D window, in the "Properties" window, "Material" button, press "Add Material." The new

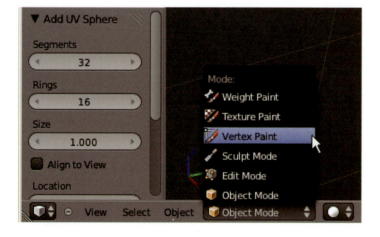

Figure 4.34

object still displays in the 3D window as the same gray color but now the "Material" button contains control tabs.

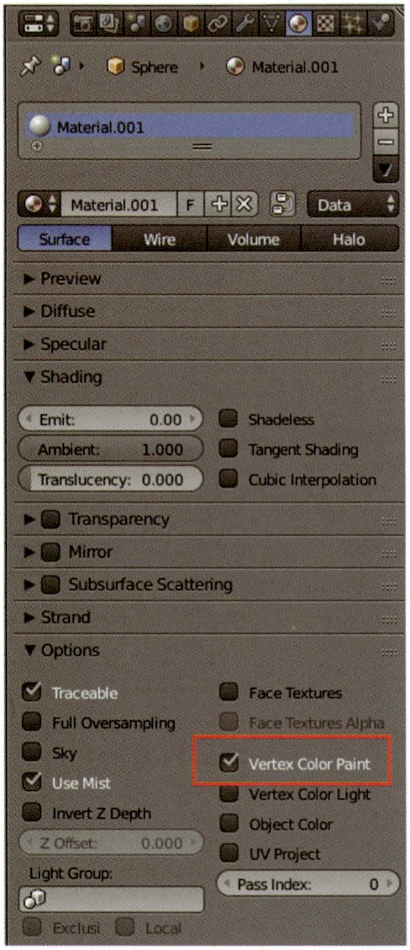

Go to the "Material" button—"Options" tab and tick "Vertex Color Paint" (Figure 4.35). "Vertex Color Paint" tells Blender to use the painted material instead of the base color when you render an image. **It must be ticked before the paint color will render.**

As "Vertex Paint" suggests, the process involves painting vertices. The default cube in the 3D window only has eight vertices, therefore, it doesn't provide much scope for a demonstration. Delete the cube and add a UV sphere. The default UV sphere has 32 segments and 16 rings, which provides a vertex at each intersection point of the mesh. If you would care to count the intersections, you will find there are a lot more vertices in the sphere than the cube. For the demonstration subdivide in "Edit" mode to add more vertices.

Change the 3D window to "Vertex Paint Mode"—your 3D cursor changes to an orange circle (Figure 4.36). The circle is called the "Brush."

4.13.1 The Tools Panel Tabs

The tool panel at the left of the window displays with the "Tools," "Brush" tab open. By default the "Brush Type" is type "Draw." By clicking on the window icon immediately below the heading "Brush" in the tab, you will see there are seven alternative quickset brush options to choose (Figure 4.37). This selection is the default "Pallet." You can add your own brush selections to the pallet by clicking on the white plus sign.

In the "Brush" tab, you have a circular color picker for selecting the paint color with a bar across the bottom that shows the color selected (Figure 4.37). By default, the selected color is white. To paint, click in the colored circle to select a color, then adjust the intensity with the vertical slider at the right, then in the 3D window, click, hold, and drag the brush across the UV sphere.

Figure 4.35

Clicking on the color bar below the circle enlarges the color circle and provides sliders and options to change color values.

Immediately below the color bar are two sliders. "Radius" controls the size of the brush (the circular 3D cursor) and "Strength"

Figure 4.36

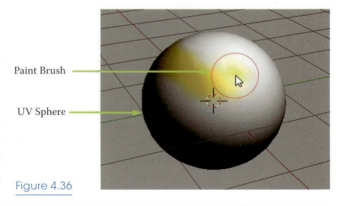

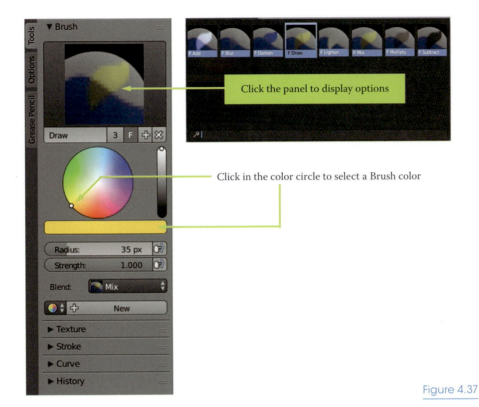

Click the panel to display options

Click in the color circle to select a Brush color

Figure 4.37

controls how much paint color is applied. Another way of controlling the size of the brush is to press the F key and click, hold, and drag the cursor toward or away from the center of the brush circle (Figure 4.38). Click the LMB when finished. The size of the brush circle changes and the slider value in the tool shelf is reset.

The "Blend" drop down. Is a menu for selecting how the paint is applied? The default option is "Mix" (Figure 4.39).

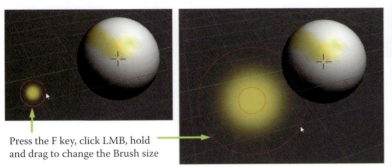

Press the F key, click LMB, hold and drag to change the Brush size

Figure 4.38

Figure 4.39

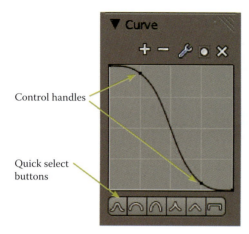

Control handles

Quick select buttons

Figure 4.40

The "New" button. Allows you to create your own specialized pallet.

In the "Tools" panel below the "Brush" tab, there are five other tabs.

The "Texture" tab. Allows you to use a texture to influence the brush stroke.

The "Stroke" tab. Provides options for stroke methods the default method is "Space."

The "Curve" tab. This tab provides a graphical method for controlling how the brush applies paint. A small graph is displayed with a curve containing control handles (Figure 4.40). The handles may be manipulated, altering the curve shape and changing the brush paint application. There are also quick select buttons for changing the shape of the curve.

The "History" tab. Has the facilities to undo and redo stroke actions and select recently used strokes.

4.13.2 The Options Panel Tabs

The "Tools," "Options" tab has more settings for controlling the brush in the "Overlay," "Appearance," and "Options" tabs.

Remember that when painting is in fact a 3D sphere, you will have to rotate it to paint on its entire surface. When painting, you can only paint the visible surface of the object. You have to pan the 3D view or rotate the object to paint the hidden surfaces (Figure 4.41). At some time you will only want to paint a specific selected area of a surface. To do this use the "Face Selection Mask."

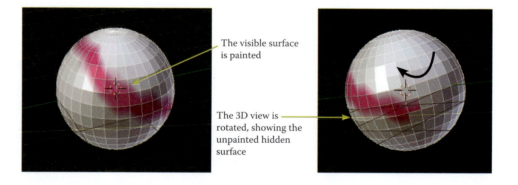

The visible surface is painted

The 3D view is rotated, showing the unpainted hidden surface

Figure 4.41

4.13.3 Vertex Paint: Face Selection Mask

The "Face Selection Mask" allows the selection of specific areas of a surface for painting.

Follow this example: Start a new Blender scene, delete the default Cube object and add a UV sphere. Remember that a new object entered in a scene does not have a material applied and that you cannot Vertex Paint without first applying a material.

Apply a material. The default diffuse gray color will do.

In edit mode, subdivide the Sphere twice to increase the number of vertices forming the mesh surface. Tab back to object mode then change to Vertex Paint mode. Select a nice bright red color from the "Brush" tab color picker. With the default "Brush" settings paint a red stripe on the surface of the Sphere (Figure 4.42). At this stage you could continue painting the entire surface if you wished. To limit painting to a specific area of the surface we will activate "Face Selection Masking" in the 3D window header (Figures 4.43 and 4.44).

Activating "Masking" displays a white mesh grid over the surface of the Sphere (Figure 4.45). The grid mesh coincides with the selected vertices

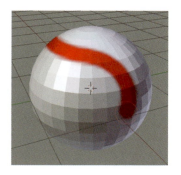

Figure 4.42

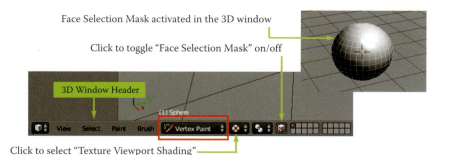

Face Selection Mask activated in the 3D window

Click to toggle "Face Selection Mask" on/off

3D Window Header

Click to select "Texture Viewport Shading"

Figure 4.43

and faces which make up the surface. Tab to edit mode and you will see all vertices selected. Change "Vertex Select" to "Face Select." Deselect all faces (press A key). Now shift select some specific faces (Figure 4.46). Tab back to Vertex Paint mode and you will see the "Face Select Mask" represents only the faces that you selected (Figure 4.47). With the Brush paint over the surface, you will observe that the material color is only applied to the mask area (Figure 4.48).

Figure 4.44

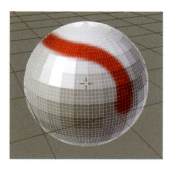

Figure 4.45

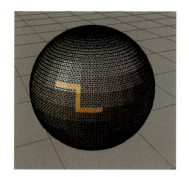

Figure 4.46

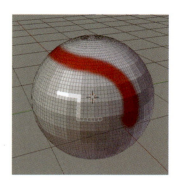

Figure 4.47

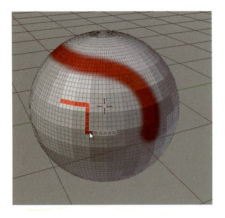

In the Properties window, Material buttons, Options tab check (tick) in the "Vertex Color Paint" box (Figure 4.49). Press F12 to render an image to see the paint displayed on the image of the Sphere (Figure 4.50).

Remember you must have a material applied to the Sphere before painting and you must have "Vertex Color Paint" ticked in the Properties window to see a rendered image.

There is plenty to experiment regarding this topic and, now that you have grasped some of the basics, it's a good idea to look at some tutorials on the Internet (see Bibliography section of this manual for a starting point). Video tutorials pack in a lot of information and there are some good tips to be found.

Figure 4.48

Figure 4.49

Tips:
- Click on the icon in the "Brush" tab for the quickset brush options in the "Tool" tab (Figure 4.37).
- If you want to paint the entire surface of the mesh, go to the 3D window header (while in vertex paint mode) and select "Paint—Set Vertex Colors." Whatever color has been selected in the brush color picker will be applied to the whole mesh surface.
- Sometimes it is difficult to see what is being painted in the 3D window. Remember the default 3D scene only has a single point lamp in place. Therefore, you are going to have shadow that obstructs the paint view. Add some more light with additional point lamps or spot lamps (see Chapter 7 for more information).

Figure 4.50

4.14 Materials and the GUI

To further understand the application of "Materials" in Blender in relation to the GUI the following is offered.

For the moment consider "Materials" as being color which include its "Diffuse" and "Specular" properties and in fact, its properties in general. These properties are the values entered by using the color picker, manually entering RGB values and by moving sliders. A Blender scene may have multiple materials assigned to numerous objects and there may be several scenes within any one Blender file. A single material may be assigned to several objects.

A material's properties are stored in a "Datablock" (a block of data).

To understand this methodology we will work through an exercise starting with the default Blender scene containing the default "Cube" object. Without having entered any values the cube displays as a dull gray color in the 3D window. To understand this, go to the "Properties" window, "Material" buttons and you will see the material properties tabs (Figure 4.51). Components of the upper portion of the "Material" buttons "Properties" window are labeled for clarity.

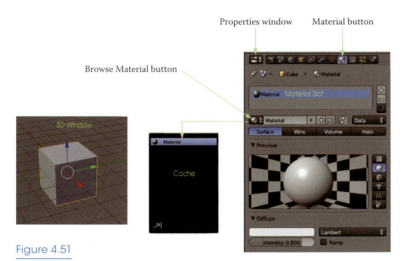

Figure 4.51

Blender has named the "Datablock" (Properties) for the default gray color "Material" and assigned the properties to the cube object in the 3D window.

By clicking on the "Browse Material" button a drop down selection menu is displayed that shows all the "Material Datablocks" available for selection. At this stage there is only one which is the datablock named "Material." The drop down is called the "Material Cache."

An analysis of the relationship between the datablock and the selected object in the 3D window is as follows: (1) Click on the "Browse Material button" to display the "Material Cache." (2) Click on a datablock in the cache drop down to select it. (3) The datablock name is entered in the "Unique Datablock ID Name" panel. (4) The "Material Datablock" is entered in the "Material Slot." (5) The properties of the material are assigned to the object selected in the 3D window (Figure 4.52).

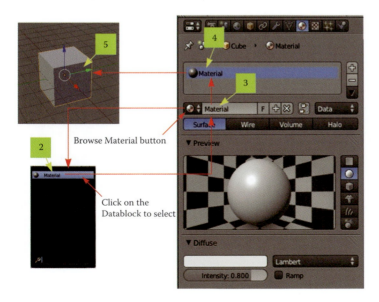

Figure 4.52

4.15 The Outliner Window

The "Outliner" window was explained in Chapter 1—Blender Windows section. This window allows you to see a record of everything that exists in a Blender file and accordingly you will see the "Material Datablocks."

Change the 3D window to the "Outliner" window and in the window header change from the "All Scenes" mode to "Datablock" mode (Figure 4.53). In the window that displays, from the listing at the LH side you will find the heading "Material." Click on the little cross next to this heading and you will see "Material" again. This is the datablock named "Material" that was selected in the previous analysis. Click on the little cross next to this name and all the properties of the material color are displayed (Figure 4.54).

OK! You may consider this is where the material properties are stored. To continue we will have to take a few steps backward.

Start a new Blender scene (in the "Info" window header at the top of the screen click on "File"—"New"—"Reload Start Up File") (Figure 4.55).

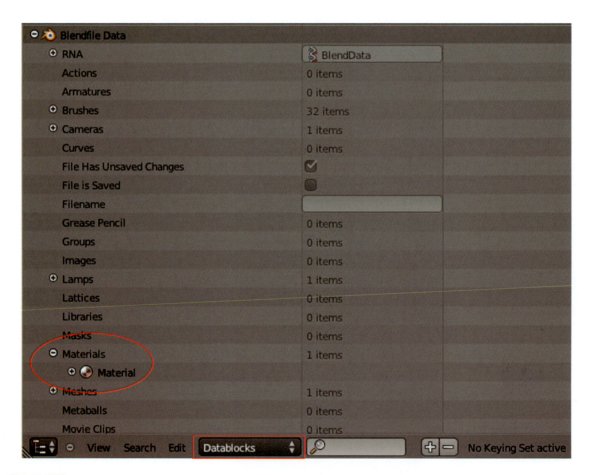

Figure 4.53

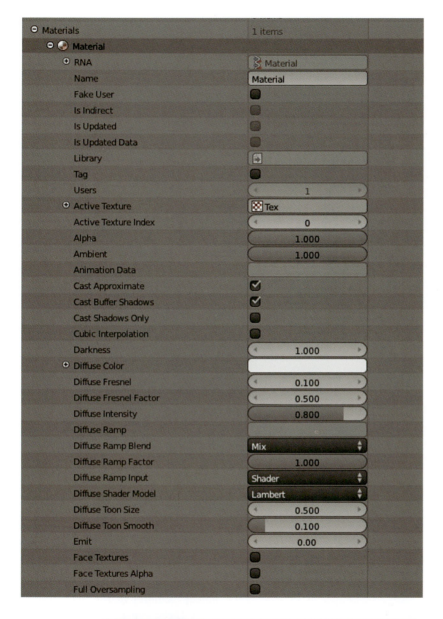

Figure 4.54

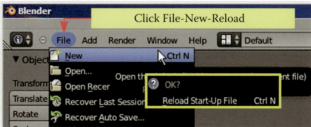

Figure 4.55

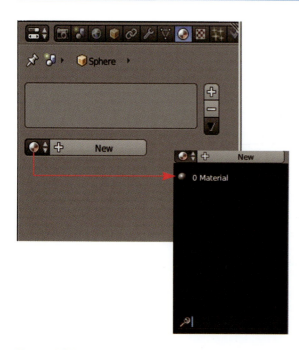

Figure 4.56

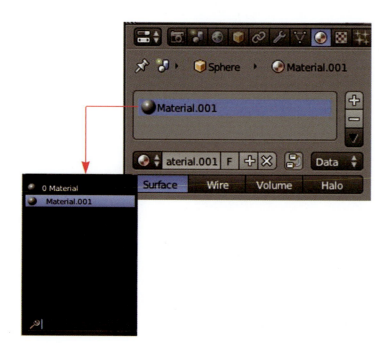

Figure 4.57

Delete the default cube (X key) then add a "UV Sphere" object.

In the "Properties" window, "Material" buttons there is nothing displayed except for the "New" button. This would conclude that there is no "Material Datablock" assigned to the sphere yet the sphere displays in the 3D window as the default gray color.

By clicking on the "Browse Material" button you will see that our old friend "Material," now named "0 Material," is sitting in the cache. Blender has assigned this datablock to the sphere by default. The "0" prefix may be considered to say that this datablock has not been referenced to anything (Figure 4.56).

When we select and assign a material to an object, we are in fact selecting a preconstructed datablock and modifying its properties to produce the effect we require. Starting at this point, we click the "New" button to display the material tabs (the controls for modifying the datablock) (Figure 4.57).

Having clicked on the "New" button you will see that a new datablock has been created and named "Material.001." You will see the name in the "Unique Datablock ID Name" panel and you will also see this in the "Outliner" window.

Clicking on the "Browse Material" button also shows you that "0 Material" is still in the cache.

Blender has created a copy of the original "Material" and automatically renamed it "Material.001." The new datablock has been entered in the active material slot and assigned to the selected object (Sphere) in the 3D window (note there can be more than one "Material slot").

You can modify the new datablock. Click on the "Diffuse" color bar and change the color with the color picker. If you look in the cache you see "0 Material" is the original gray and "Material.001" is the

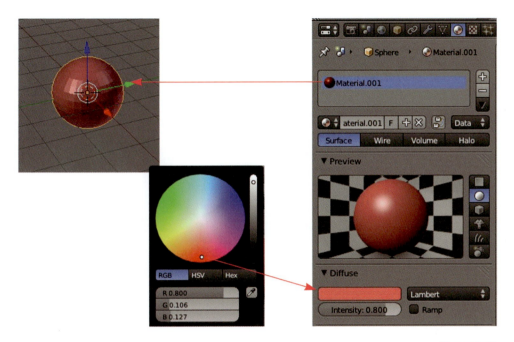

Figure 4.58

new color. The sphere shows the new color. You have modified the new datablock independently of the original (Figure 4.58).

You can manually create a new datablock by clicking on the plus sign at the end of the "Unique Datablock ID Name" panel. This is the same as clicking on "New" button previously. This new datablock will be a copy of whatever datablock you had previously selected. Blender will automatically name it with the next consecutive number, that is, "Material.002." Again you can modify the properties independently (Figure 4.59).

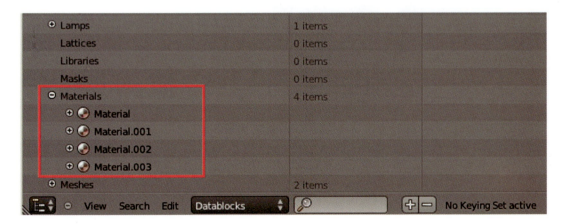

Figure 4.59

Figure 4.60

If you click on the "2" a new datablock is created and named "Material.003". This is useful if you have assigned a material datablock to more than one object and you wish to change a property, say change the diffuse color on one object only.

Once a datablock has been created and saved, the datablock may be retrieved from the cache and assigned to any object selected in the 3D window.

Follow this exercise.

Figure 4.61

Figure 4.62

Start a new scene, delete the default cube, and add three "UV Spheres." Make sure all the spheres are deselected (not selected—press A Key).

In the "Properties" window, "Material" button click on the "Browse Material" button to display the cache (Figures 4.61 and 4.62).

You will see the "0 Material" is the only datablock listed. Click the "New" button still with no objects selected. Blender displays the material buttons, created a new material datablock and names it "Material.001."

Click on the diffuse color bar and pick a color. The color is applied to the last sphere that you entered in the 3D window.

If you click on the "F" button you will see "2" as the number of users. This is somewhat confusing since only one sphere is displaying the color chosen. Select each

of the other spheres in turn and select "Material.001" from the cache (click the "Browse Material" button and click on "Material.001" in the cache). All three spheres display the color chosen, which indicates that they all have the same material datablock assigned. You now see "4" as the number of users. Again this is somewhat confusing. In the "Outliner" window, "Datablocks" mode "Material.001" shows "Users 4" as the number of times the datablock is referenced. I will leave you to draw your own conclusion.

4.16 Multiple Material Slots

Multiple material slots may be introduced for each individual object in the scene. The application of multiple material slots can be demonstrated by showing how a single mesh object can have multiple colors. Follow this procedure, leaving the default cube in the scene. In the default scene Blender has automatically assigned a material to the cube object (Figure 4.63). The material is named "Material."

Add a UV sphere mesh object to the default scene. The sphere will be in object mode and selected in the 3D view. Have the properties window with the "Material" buttons active. The sphere will be the default dull gray color and the materials properties window will be blank. Remember the cache is available for selecting materials if you wish.

Material Datablock ID Name   Material Slot

Click to see the
Material cache

Figure 4.63

Click on the "New" button to create a new material (Figure 4.64). By default, it is the dull gray color but note its data block ID name in the window "Material.001" (Figure 5.60). Click on the "Browse Material" button and you will see the new name has been added to the cache. The name is "Material.001."

Figure 4.64

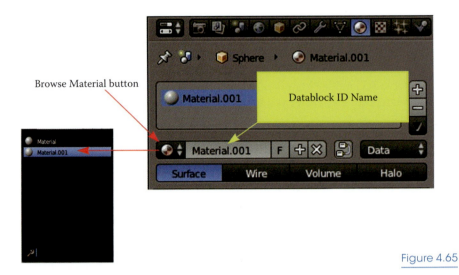

Browse Material button

Datablock ID Name

Figure 4.65

Now click on the "Add Materials Slot" button (Figures 4.65 and 4.66). A new slot is created but note that there is no material linked and the new slot is not assigned to the object selected in the 3D view. At this point, you can click on the "Browse Material" button and link a material to the new slot or you may click on "New" to create a new material data block. Remember, a new datablock will be a duplication of the last datablock selected, which in this case was "Material.001." Click on "New."

Since "Material.001" was the last in the list, Blender names the new material datablock "Material.002" and it is identical to "Material.001" (Figure 4.67). Change the color of "Material.002" (Figure 4.68). Note that the sphere does not change color. There are now two color slots: one is linked to the sphere and the other is not linked. Remember, the information in the properties material window is only relevant to the object that is selected in the 3D view. If the sphere were deselected, the first slot remains assigned to the sphere since it was the last object selected. As a demonstration of the foregoing, select the cube then the sphere and note the change to the properties window.

Click add Material Slot button

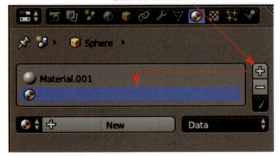

Figure 4.66

Figure 4.67

Figure 4.68

We now have two slots assigned to the sphere: one is assigned and the other is not. To change the assignment, make sure the sphere is selected in the 3D window and tab to edit mode. All the vertices will be selected. Click on the new material slot (in this case, the slot with "Material.002" linked) and click on "Assign." Tab back to object mode and you will see that the sphere has changed color, showing that the material slot with "Material.002" linked is assigned to the sphere object. The material datablock has also been assigned to the sphere since, in edit mode, you had all the vertices selected.

Change the 3D view to a side view (number pad 1 or 3) so the sphere is visible. Enlarge the view with the number pad + key. Tab to edit mode with the sphere selected (in edit mode, the sphere will have all its vertices selected). Press the A key to deselect the vertices. Press the B key and drag a rectangle around part of the sphere, selecting some of the vertices (a vertex group, Figure 4.69). Select "Material.001 slot" and click on the "Assign" button. Blender assigns the slot and thus links the material to the selected group of vertices in this case the default gray (Figure 4.70). Tab to object mode in the 3D view to see the sphere with two colors (Figure 4.71).

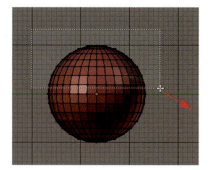

Figure 4.69

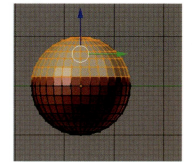

Figure 4.70

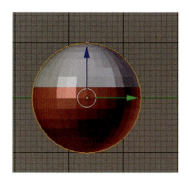

Figure 4.71

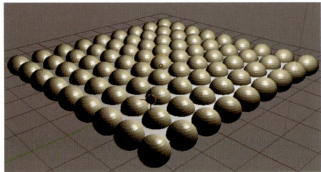

Figure 4.72

4.17 Assigning Texture Color

Image textures may be used to assign multiple colors to dupliverts.

Refer to Chapter 3 Section 3.34.

In the "Outliner" window select the sphere object. Add a material (you must have a material color assigned to an object before you can apply a texture). Add an image texture (you may use any still image as a texture or you can use an animated texture or a movie file) (Figures 4.72 and 4.73).

JPEG Image used as a Texture

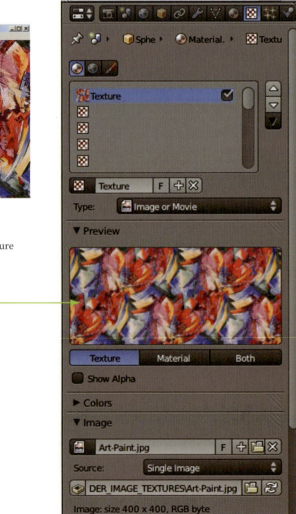

Figure 4.73

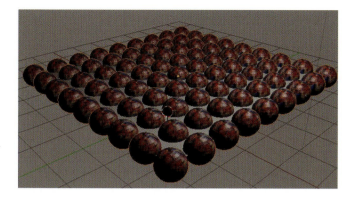

Figure 4.74

Figure 4.75

You can now display the texture in the 3D window as demonstrated in Chapter 3 Section 3.34 but Blender allows every duplivert to be a pixel (Figure 4.74).

With the sphere selected, in the "Properties" window "Texture" buttons, "Mapping" tab tick "From Dupliverts." In the "Properties" window "World" buttons tick "Ambient Occlusion." Render an image (Figure 4.75).

Since each duplivert is considered a pixel, each of the duplicated spheres is assigned a different color as determined by the texture.

5

Textures

5.1 Introduction to Textures

In Chapter 4, consideration was given to the effect of light reflecting on a smooth surface producing a material color. Textures are the physical characteristics or imperfections of a surface such as the grainy surface of bricks, the fibrous pile of carpet, wood grain, etc. Textures may be used in conjunction with materials or used separately.

Lesson 05
05-07
Procedural
Textures
Gradient Blend

In Blender, these types of surface characteristics are created by mapping data blocks or images on to the surface of a model in the 3D window. The data or images are called "Textures." In Blender, there are three texture modes: World Textures, Material Textures, and Other Data Textures. World Texture is used to create scene background. Material Texture is applied to an objects surface material producing the allusion of surface characteristics or deforming the mesh. Other Data Textures are used to affect the characteristics of tools such as the Vertex Paint brush and the Sculpt mode tools. Textures are also used by several of the Blender modifiers.

It should be noted that textures applied to an object do not display in the 3D window unless the window is set to "Rendered Viewport Shading" or an image of the scene is rendered by pressing F12.

It should also be noted that by default, Blender is set to use "Blender Render" which is the Blender internal render engine. Pressing F12 will render an image in a separate window where the texture is displayed (see Chapter 8—Rendering and Raytracing).

Also be aware that rendering produces an image of what is seen in "Camera" view (Num Pad 0). It follows that an object or the camera must be positioned to encompass the object to which a texture is applied.

5.2 Material Textures

Before you can add a texture to a surface you must first add a material since, by default, Blender textures are set to influence the material. Textures are applied to an object's surface using the options in the properties window—"Textures" button. Clicking the "Textures" button displays a panel where you can add a new texture. Blender comes with a series of built-in textures (Procedural Textures) from which to choose or you can use a photo or image stored on your computer. Blender can also place movies on a surface and you can animate the textures.

> Note: In the default scene at start up, the cube object has a material and a texture pre-assigned. The material is the gray color with RGB values of 0.800. The texture is named "Tex" and is Type "None" which means in reality, there is no texture or that this texture data displays the same as the flat gray material.

When a new object is introduced into a scene there is no material or texture applied. In the "Properties" window, in both "Material" and "Texture" buttons you are required to click in the "New" button to add materials and textures. When you click the "New" button properties are displayed for the selected object. If you have entered several objects the new properties are assigned to the last object entered into the scene whether it is selected or not.

To demonstrate the placing of a texture on an objects surface, follow this example: open a new Blender scene, replace the default cube with a plane, and scale the plane up by 5. Add a diffuse material with R: 0.800, G: 0.767, and B: 0.495 values. Go to the properties window—"Textures" button and click "New" (Figure 5.1).

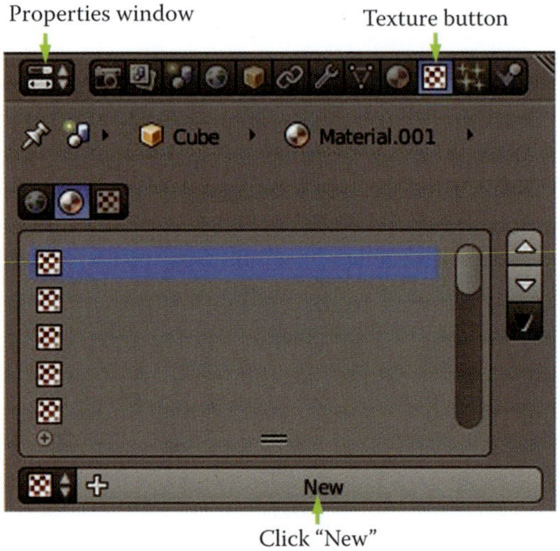

Properties window   Texture button

Click "New"

Figure 5.1

> Note: Textures are superimposed over the underlying material color therefore the material can have an effect on the final render.

> Note: By default, material texture mode is active.

The texture buttons display with a default texture type "Image or Movie" named "Texture." The "Preview" tab shows the texture as a black panel which in reality means there is no texture since an image or movie file has yet to be selected. A rendered view shows the plane with the diffuse material color only.

Click on the texture-type drop down menu and select the "Magic" which is one of the "Procedural" textures. The "Image or Movie" type texture is replaced by the magic

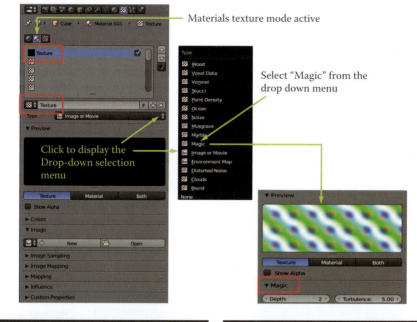

Materials texture mode active

Select "Magic" from the drop down menu

Click to display the Drop-down selection menu

Figure 5.2

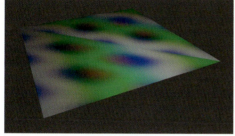

Mapping coordinates: UV

Mapping coordinates: generated

Figure 5.3

texture and the "Image" tab is replaced by the "Magic" tab (Figure 5.2). This tab contains only two values for altering the characteristics of the texture: depth and turbulence. Note that the 3D window does not show the texture on the object. With the 3D window in "Rendered Viewport Shading" mode or by pressing F12 to render an image you will see the texture on the surface of the plane. Observe that the texture appears as if it has been placed on two triangles. This has occurred due to the default mapping coordinates. Look at the "Mapping" tab and note the "Coordinates" are UV and the "Projection" is "Flat." Flat is OK for the flat plane but you have to change UV to "Global," "Generated," or "Object" to see something representing the preview (Figure 5.3). Change the "Coordinates" to "Generated." In the "Magic" tab change the depth value to 4 and render again to see the alteration (Figure 5.4). Change the "Turbulence" value for some interesting effects.

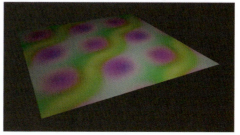

Depth value: 4

Figure 5.4

Lesson 05
05-08
Image Textures

Lesson 05
05-09
Decal Image
Textures

Go back to the texture-type drop down selection and select "Image or Movie." An "Image" tab displays instead of the "Magic" tab, the preview shows a black window and there is no longer a texture on the plane in the 3D window. We haven't told Blender what image to use.

In the "Image" tab, click "Open." The file browser window displays. Navigate to a file containing a picture (I have a picture named "Flower.bmp" in my "Documents" folder). Click on the picture then click "Open" at the top RHS of the screen (Figure 5.5).

Figure 5.5

File browser window showing file names

Flowers.jpg

Note: The File Browser Window can display image files as thumbnail images.

You will see your picture in the preview panel (probably multiple images) and in the 3D window in "Rendered Viewport Shading," the image will be shown on the surface of the plane (Figure 5.6).

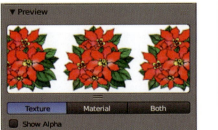

Flowers.jpg in Preview tab.

Rendered image

Figure 5.6

5.3 Texture Display in the 3D Window

Blender displays a texture on the surface of the selected object in the 3D window in "Rendered Viewport Shading" mode or if an image is rendered by pressing F12.

An **image** texture can be displayed in "Texture Viewport Shading" in a limited way by the following.

We will use a plane object in a new Blender scene. Apply an image texture. Press the N Key to display the "Object Properties" panel. In the "Shading" tab change "Multitexture" to "GLSL." With the 3D window in "Texture Viewport Shading" the texture displays on the surface of the cube (Figures 5.7 and 5.8).

Note: The forgoing technique is applicable to image textures only and the "Mapping" settings are limited. To see other types of texture applied to the surface of an object in the 3D window press F12 on the keyboard to render an image or change the "Viewport Shading" to "Rendered."

Figure 5.7

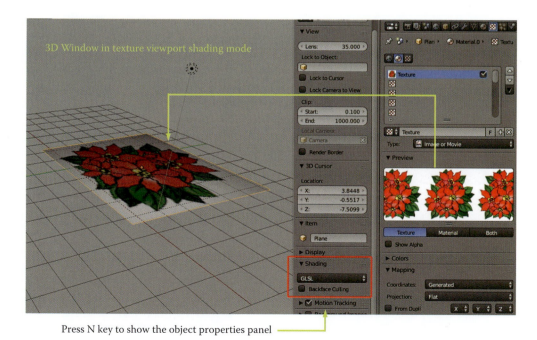

Press N key to show the object properties panel

Figure 5.8

5.4 Texture Mapping

Whether you use one of Blender's built-in textures or an image, you may want to adjust how the texture is positioned on the object. The "Properties" window, "Texture" buttons, "Mapping" tab is the place to do this (Figure 5.9). "Offset" and "Size" are self-explanatory, and can be controlled on either the *x*-, *y*-, or *z*-axis. The "Coordinates" drop down menu gives you a selection of coordinate systems, and the "Projection" drop down menu has a choice of mapping options to suit the shape of your object (Figure 5.10). The defaults are "Coordinates: Generated" and "Projection: Flat." With the Flower image texture "Projection:Flat" places the image

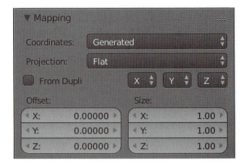

Figure 5.9

Figure 5.10

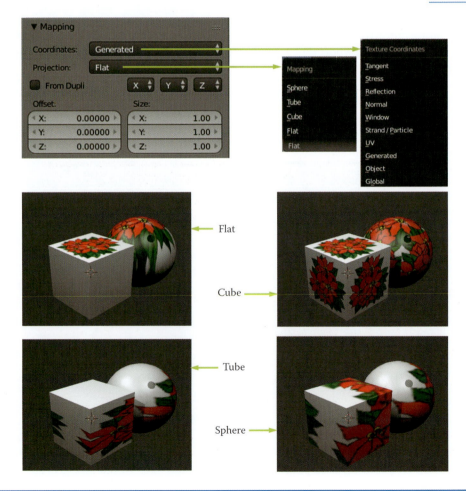

texture on the top face of the cube. "Projection: Cube" places the image texture on each of the cube's six surfaces. "Projection: Tube" attempts to place the image texture as if the object were a tube and "Projection: Sphere" tries to emulate placing the image texture on a spherical object. There are numerous mapping combinations in the "Mapping" tab. Experiment and record results to fully understand the process.

5.5 Displacement Mapping

Texture mapping places data or an image on the surface of an object to create surface characteristics. On a flat surface it is like sticking a 2D picture on the surface. Displacement mapping is using a texture to create the illusion of deforming the mesh surface. You can make a cube or a sphere look wrinkled without having to move vertices around.

Lesson 05
05-10
Bump Textures

Note: The procedure creates the illusion of mesh deformation. The mesh is not actually changed.

Start a new Blender scene with the default cube. Make sure the cube has a material, then in edit mode, subdivide the cube six times. The texture is going to make it look as if the mesh is deformed relative to the vertices forming the surface of the object.

Put a cloud texture on the cube then go to the "Influence" tab. Leave the "Diffuse: Color" ticked. Under the "Geometry" heading, tick "Displace" and alter the value as shown in Figure 5.11. Render to see the effect.

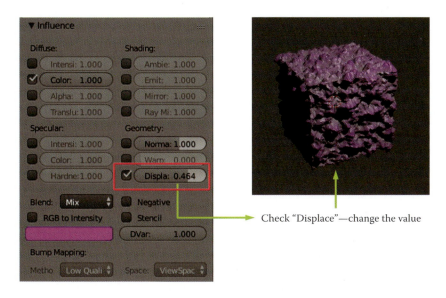

Check "Displace"—change the value

Figure 5.11

Moving the slider next to the "Displacement" box varies the amount of displacement. The "Blend" drop down menu displays options that influence the material by blending the material color and the texture color. Try "Add" and "Subtract" and render to see the

Black-and-white image

Figure 5.12

Rendered image with a negative displacement value

difference. Another example is shown in Figure 5.12. This time, a black-and-white image texture has been used on a plane. Don't forget to subdivide the plane. Negative displacement values raise the surface up, and positive values depress the surface. Experiment with other features and record the outcomes for future reference.

5.6 Texture Surface Displacement

Textures may be used to displace the surface of an object creating interesting effects. We demonstrated how a texture could make the surface of a cube wrinkled and an example using a black and white image texture was given. To better understand this concept we will demonstrate how a simple black and white image texture in conjunction with a displace modifier will affect a plane object. Any texture could be used but for simplicity we will use an image of a black circle on a white background (Figure 5.13).

Figure 5.13

> Note: This image must be saved on your computer.

5.6.1 Displacement Using the Texture Buttons

In a new Blender scene delete the default cube object and add a plane. Scale up the plane three times or zoom in, then in "Edit mode" subdivide six times. The greater number of vertices on the surface the better the displacement effect.

Add a material to the plane then add the image texture (the image of the black circle on the white background saved on your computer). Change the 3D window "Viewport Shading" to "Rendered." In the "Image Mapping" tab ensure "Extension" is set as "Repeat." In the "Mapping" tab change "Coordinates" to "Generated" and "Projection" to "Flat." In the "Influence" tab "Geometry" tick "Displace." With the default "Displace" value of 0.200 the surface of the plane appears to form a depression in the black circle (**Only displays in "Rendered Viewport Shading"**). Increase the "Displace" value to 0.700 to see the deformation with the default 3D window view. If you have not moved the plane or the 3D window cursor, the cursor is located at the center of the scene and the center of the plane. The deformation appears to be above and below the center (Figure 5.14). Placing the plane in edit mode shows that the vertices have not been moved. Increasing or decreasing the "Displace" value alters the deformation in the rendered view.

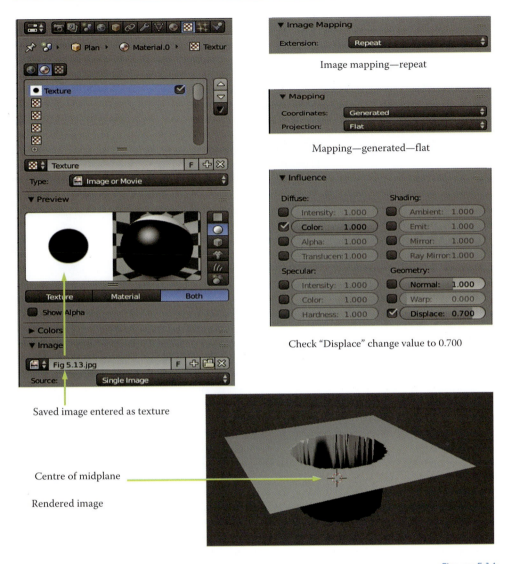

Image mapping—repeat

Mapping—generated—flat

Check "Displace" change value to 0.700

Saved image entered as texture

Centre of midplane

Rendered image

Figure 5.14

5.6.2 Displacement Using a Modifier

The forgoing method is cumbersome but it demonstrates the method. A better method for displacement is to use a "Displacement Modifier." As before add a plane to the scene scale and subdivide. Add a material (the default material settings will be OK). Leave the 3D window in "Solid" "Viewport Shading" mode. Add a "Image or Movie Texture" selecting the saved image of the black circle on the white background.

In the "Properties" window, "Modifier" buttons, click "Add Modifier" and from the selection panel add a "Displace" modifier.

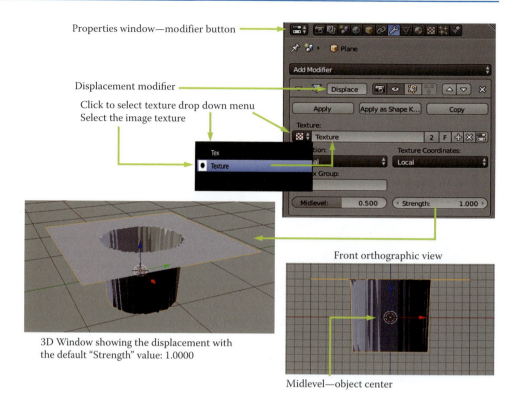

Properties window—modifier button

Displacement modifier

Click to select texture drop down menu
Select the image texture

3D Window showing the displacement with
the default "Strength" value: 1.0000

Front orthographic view

Midlevel—object center

Figure 5.15

Note: In the 3D window the plane locates above the midplane of the scene by 0.500 Blender units. This is the default "Midlevel" value in the modifier panel.

In the modifier panel click on the "Texture" drop down and you will see the image texture that you added named Texture. Click on the name to assign it to the modifier. You will see the deformation in the 3D window in "Object" mode, "Solid Viewport Shading." Placing the 3D window

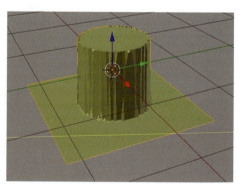

Negative displacement—strength: Minus 1.000

Figure 5.16

in front orthographic view shows the deformation above and below the object's center which is located at the midplane of the scene. Tab to "Edit" mode and see that the vertices remain on the midplane. In the modifier panel you can alter the "Midlevel" to move the deformation and change the "Strength" value to increase, decrease or with a minus value reverse the deformation (Figures 5.15 through 5.17).

5.6.3 Examples of Surface Displacement

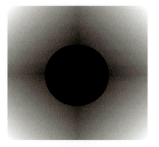

Image

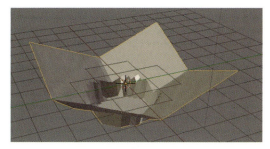

Displacement

Figure 5.17

5.7 UV Mapping

For complex models, regular flat, cubic, cylindrical, or spherical texture mapping are not sufficient to accurately place the texture on the surface. This is where UV mapping is applied. The coordinates u and v are used simply to distinguish from the x, y, z-coordinates used in the 3D window. UV mapping is the process of placing an image on the surface of an object to give the surface texture.

Lesson 12
12-01

UV Texture
Unwrapping UVs

UV mapping is accomplished by taking the surface of an object (the model), peeling it off as you would a skin from an orange, and laying it out flat on a 2D surface. An image is then superimposed as a texture over the flattened surface (this is known as mapping). The window for laying out the flattened object is the "UV/Image Editor" window. As with every basic instruction in Blender, it is best to begin with something simple. Although the process we are describing is for complex surfaces, anything other than simple will be confusing.

Lesson 12
12-02

UV Texture
Rendering

To demonstrate the basic principal of the process start with the Blender's default 3D scene; delete the cube that is loaded automatically and add a plane object. The default cube comes pre-loaded with a material and a texture channel. In our previous discussion on material and textures, it was stated that before a texture could be applied, an object had to

New plane added to scene

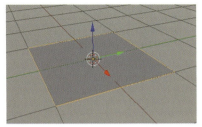

Properties window—material button

With a new plane added to the scene there is no material or texture applied

Properties window—texture button

Figure 5.18

have a material. Adding a new plane that does not have a material or a texture will demonstrate that neither is necessary to apply UV texture mapping (Figure 5.18).

With the new plane added, split the 3D window in two and change one half to the "UV/Image Editor." In the 3D window, zoom in on the plane—when you split the window, the plane is a little too small to see this process clearly. Change the 3D window to "Edit" mode and select "Textured" as the viewport shading type; this will allow you to see the superimposed image texture (Figure 5.19).

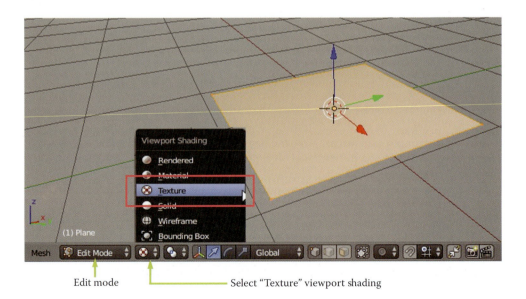

Figure 5.19

Edit mode   Select "Texture" viewport shading

In the 3D window tools panel in the "Shading/UVs" tab, click on "Unwrap" to display the menu for selecting the UV unwrapping type (Figure 5.20). These options allow you to unwrap the surface of the selected object in a variety of ways. Some of the unwrapping methods are difficult to visualize, so the only way to learn is to experiment and record your findings.

Click on the "Unwrap" drop down menu and select (click) the "Unwrap" option. In the "UV Image Editor" window you will see an orange square with vertices at each corner. This is showing the plane's surface unwrapped. Since the plane consists of only one surface, that is what you see in the UV Image Editor window. The orange outline with vertices at the corners shows that the plane is selected. With the mouse cursor in the window, pressing the A key toggles deselect and select. Clicking RMB on a vertex selects that vertex. Pressing the A key deselects the vertex.

Figure 5.20

In the UV/image editor window header, click on "Image" and select "Open Image" (Figure 5.21). This will display the file browser window where you can navigate and find an image saved on your computer, to use as a texture. Once you have located your image file, click on it to select it and then click on "Open Image."

The image will display in the UV Image editor window. With "Texture Viewport Shading" selected in the 3D window the image is also displayed on the surface of the plane in the 3D window (Figure 5.22). In the "UV Image Editor" window, press the A key to deselect then right click on the lower right corner vertex. Press the G key and drag the corner into the

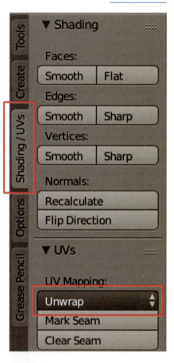

Click "Image" in UV/image editor window

Figure 5.21

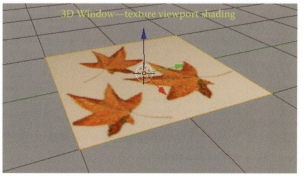

Figure 5.22

Figure 5.23

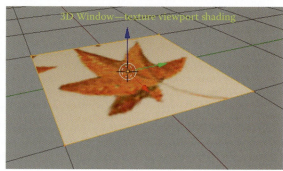

Figure 5.24

square. As you drag the vertex you will see the projection of the image on the plane in the 3D window relocate (Figure 5.23). By moving vertices the unwrapped plane can be reshaped positioning the image in the 3D window to suit your application. Selecting the whole plane in the "UV Image editor" allows you to translate, rotate and scale which also prepositions the image on the surface (Figure 5.24).

This has been a simple demonstration of texture placement using UV unwrapping.

To further demonstrate UV unwrapping and texture placement start a new scene with the default cube selected in the 3D window in Edit mode. Split the screen opening the UV/ image editor in one half as before.

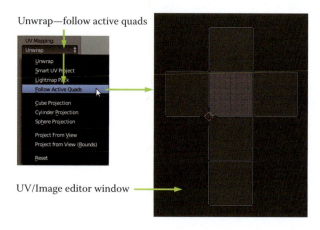

Figure 5.25

Unwrap the cube selecting the "Follow Active Quads—Edge Length Mode—Length Average" method for unwrapping. Press "OK."

This method will lay out the surface of the cube as if you had unfolded a post office mailing box. The surface will consist of six squares. The UV/image editor window will probably require you to zoom out to see the whole arrangement (use the number pad minus key, the same as you do in the 3D window). Now that the flattened surface is displayed, it's time to load an image texture (Figure 5.25).

In the UV/image editor window header click "Image"—"Open Image." In the "File Browser" window find an image to use as a texture, select it and click "Open Image" (Figure 5.26).

File browser window   Click to show images as thumbnails

Select image

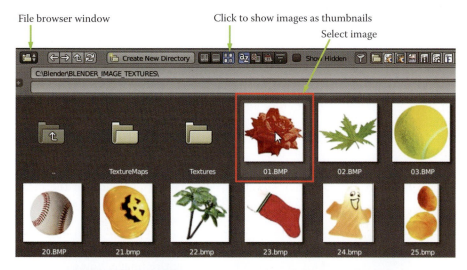

Figure 5.26

 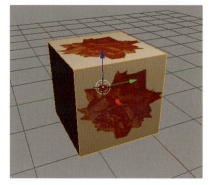

Figure 5.27

The selected image displays in the center face of the unwrapped cube in the "UV/Image Editor" window and on each face of the "Cube" in the 3D window. Remember the 3D window should be in "Edit" mode with "Textured Viewport Shading." The unwrapped cube may now be manipulated in the image editor to position the image on the surface of the cube (Figure 5.27).

The outline of the surfaces in the UV/image editor can be scaled and rotated the same as you would edit a mesh in the 3D window. Individual vertices on the mesh may be selected then grabbed and moved also. As you see by manipulating the surface outline in the UV/image editor, you can accurately position the texture image.

If you were to render an image of the object (by pressing F12) at this stage, you would be disappointed to see that the image texture does not render. To render the image texture, make sure a material has been applied (Default gray is OK) then in the "Properties" window activate "Face Textures" in the "Options" tab of the "Material" buttons (Figure 5.28).

Figure 5.28

5.8 Selective UV Texture Mapping

So far, the image texture has been mapped to all the surfaces of the object, but suppose you wish to place the texture only on one face of the object. Create a new scene and leave the default cube selected. Split the 3D window as before and set up the UV/ image editor window. The 3D window should be in "Edit" mode. Remember that you must have a material added before adding a texture. The default cube object has material pre-loaded but if you are working with a new cube you will have to add a material. In the 3D window, tab to edit mode and select the "Textured Viewport Shading."

In the 3D window, change from "Vertex Select" mode to "Face Select" mode (Figure 5.29). Deselect all faces then select only one face (right click on the face).

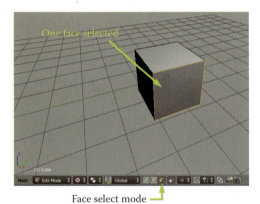

Face select mode

Figure 5.29

In the 3D window "Tool" panel, "Shading/UVs" tab click "Unwrap" and select "Unwrap" which opens the face in the "UV/Image Editor" window. In the UV/image editor window, select and enter an image for your texture as before, zoom out to see the entire image. You will see the image mapped to the face you selected in the 3D window (Figure 5.30).

With the cursor in the UV/image editor window, press the A key to select the face map. The white outline turns orange. You can then manipulate the face map to position your image the way you want. Remember, use the G key to grab, the R key to rotate, and the S key to scale (Figure 5.31). Note that the face map in the UV/image editor is in vertex select mode. There are also the options to select edge and face modes similar to the selections in edit mode in the 3D window. There is also a fourth option, which is island select mode (Figure 5.32). Some unwrapping operations divide the face mesh into separate parts, and island select allows you to select these parts.

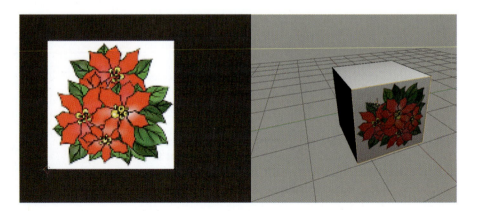

Figure 5.30

Rotated and scaled down

Figure 5.31

By selecting different faces on the cube in the 3D window "Edit" mode, unwrapping the individual face and adding different images to the UV/image editor, you can place the different image textures on the individual faces. You can also shift select multiple faces or shift select edges or vertices to tell Blender on which part of an object's surface you want the image texture placed.

Figure 5.32

5.9 Unwrapping with Seams

Let's go back and consider mesh unwrapping. Pressing the "Unwrap" button gives you different options. In a new Blender scene, add an "IcoSphere." An "IcoSphere" is chosen since, by default, it comes with just enough faces to play with.

Set up the UV/image editor window as we did previously. In the 3D window with the sphere selected, tab to edit mode then press the A key to deselect all vertices. Change to "Edge" select mode and shift select edges, dividing the surface of the IcoSphere into three parts. It's best to zoom in and rotate the view while selecting the edges. With the edges selected, press "Mark Seam" in the tools panel; the selected edges will turn orange showing that a seam has been marked (Figure 5.33).

Lesson 12
12-03

UV Texture
Part 3—Seams

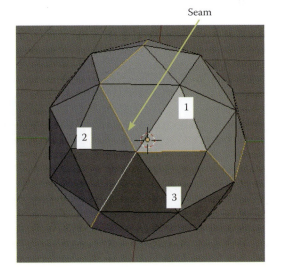

Seam

Figure 5.33

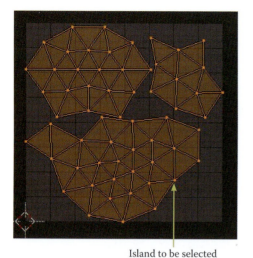

Island to be selected
(part 3 of the icosphere)

Figure 5.35

Figure 5.34

Lesson 05
05-16
Image Texture
Generated
Mapping

The next trick is to select all the edges of the faces, not just the edges marked as the seam. Use the A key to deselect the seam edges then the A key again to select all the edges. Having selected all the edges, press "Unwrap" in the tools panel then select "Unwrap" in the drop down menu. The separated parts of the IcoSphere's surface will be mapped in the UV/image editor window (Figure 5.34).

You can now open an image as a texture. In the 3D window in edit mode with "Textured" viewport shading selected, you will see the image on the surface of the IcoSphere mapped to the three parts you set up with the seam (Figure 5.35). In the UV/image editor window, select island select mode in the header. This will allow you to select separately each of the surface parts. With a part selected, you can manipulate to position the texture on that part (Figure 5.36).

The selected island is scaled down
and positioned over the koala's ear

The selected island has been
moved and rotated

Figure 5.36

5.10 Texture Paint

Texture paint is a built-in painting mode which allows you to paint texture color on to the surface of a model or to edit UV image textures. A UV image texture is a picture that is mapped to the surface of an object, providing color and surface definition (see Section 5.4). Before you can texture paint, the surface of an object the mesh must first be unwrapped to the UV/image editor window and material and texture slots must be created.

To demonstrate the very basic principle of texture paint, use the default Blender scene and delete the default cube object. Add an "IcoSphere" object. The IcoSphere has reasonable number of edges and faces to work with.

5.10.1 Set Up the Screen

Divide the 3D window in two and change the left-hand side to the "UV/Image Editor" window. Change the 3D window to "Texture Viewport Shading" then change the 3D window from "Object" mode to "Texture Paint" mode. The 3D window shows the sphere as a flat white silhouette and in the UV/image editor you see an empty grid square.

In the 3D window Tools Panel for "Texture Paint" you will see the entry "Missing Data"—Missing UVs and Missing Materials. These messages are telling you that the object's surface has not been unwrapped and that material and texture slots have not been created. At this point Blender allows you to add the missing data. In a following example it will be shown how to add the data negating the reminder.

> Note: In the "Properties" window, "Material" and "Texture" buttons no materials or textures have been applied.

5.10.2 Unwrap the Mesh

In the "Tools Panel" click on the "Add simple UVs" button. This unwraps the sphere's mesh as shown in the "UV/Image editor" window (Figure 5.37). In the 3D window the white silhouette turns magenta (Figure 5.38).

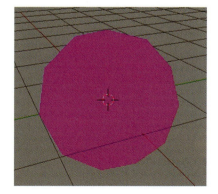

Figure 5.37   Figure 5.38

Figure 5.39

5.10.3 Add Material and Texture Slots

In the 3D window click on the "Add Paint Slot" button selecting the "Diffuse Color" option. In the panel that displays note the name "Material.001 Diffuse Color." Where you see "Color" click on the button and select a light bright color. Click OK (Figure 5.39).

Immediately the sphere in the 3D window displays with the chosen color and a "Tools Brush Panel" opens (Figure 5.40). In the "Properties" window material and texture buttons are opened. If you click on the "Material" button in the "Properties" window you will also see that a material has been added (Material.001—diffuse color RGB 0.800 which is the default gray color). But the sphere is shown with the color you selected a moment ago? In performing these operations you have unwrapped the mesh surface of the sphere and added a material and a texture. The color you selected was a texture color and textures supersede material colors. At this point you could commence painting on the sphere.

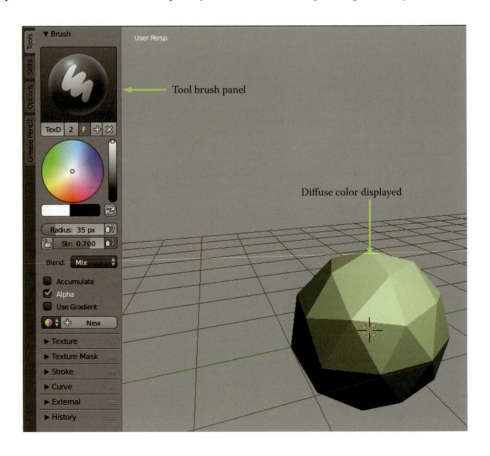

Figure 5.40

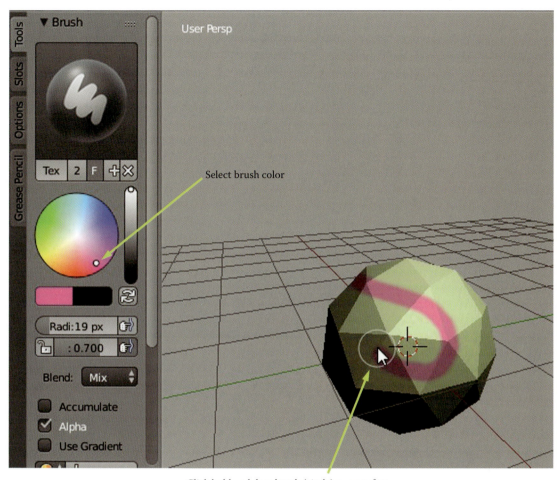

Select brush color

Click hold and drag brush (circle) over surface

Figure 5.41

Go ahead and paint—Reference Image painting (Figure 5.41).

The method for texture painting is very similar to that used in vertex painting described in Chapter 4. I would also recommend the Blender Manual for this topic since it describes the Brush strokes and settings in detail.

The forgoing has been as basic as it gets in texture painting. There are numerous mesh unwrapping methods to use depending on the particular application and different ways of introducing material textures. Some of the unwrapping methods are difficult to visualize and you will have to try them out on different shaped objects to get a feel for them. "Unwrapping with Seams" discussed in Section 5.9 is perhaps the most practical and easily understood.

This next example will show you how to use the seams method with texture paint.

5.10.4 Set Up the Screen and Unwrap the Mesh

Start a Blender scene with the screen arrangement as before and with a new IcoSphere object. Mark seams on the sphere (Figure 5.33 reference Section 5.9) and then unwrap the mesh to the "UV/Image Editor" window (click "Unwrap" then the "Unwrap" option). Using seems gives you control of what parts of the mesh are separated from the object and allow you to texture parts individually (Figure 5.42).

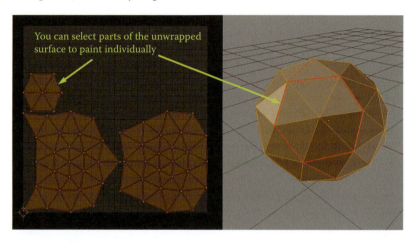

You can select parts of the unwrapped surface to paint individually

Figure 5.42

Since the surface of the sphere has been unwrapped the reminder to unwrap will not show when "Texture Paint" mode is entered.

As before, at this stage, "Material and texture Slots" have not been added. The "Properties" window "Material" and "Texture" buttons tabs will be empty. To add this missing data we will create a "Texture Image."

Select a color

Figure 5.43

5.10.5 Add Material and Texture Slots

In this example we will create a "Texture Image" to enter data in the slots.

In the "UV/Image Editor" window header click on "Image" then "New Image." The same panel displays as in the first example. Give the image a name. Leave the image sizes as the default settings (sizes may be altered to adjust the detail in texture mapping). Click on the "Color" bar and select a color (something bright and soft) (Figure 5.43). Click on OK and the "Color texture Image" is entered in the "UV/Image" editor. You will have to zoom out (scroll MMB or hit Num Pad minus) since the default image size is larger than the original empty display (Figure 5.44).

At this point it is a good idea to save the "texture Image." Note in the header that an asterisk has appeared next to "Image" (Figure 5.45). This is a reminder from Blender that data have been modified and should be saved. Click on

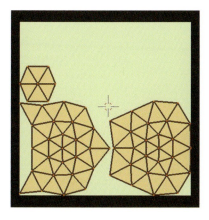

Figure 5.44

Figure 5.45

"Image" in the header and then select "Save As Image." The file browser window displays where you can navigate to a folder and save the image texture. Note that in the UV/image editor window header the "Browse Image to be Linked" is showing the image as "Untitled." Rename the same as your saved image.

5.10.6 Enter Data in the Material and Texture Slots

In the "Properties" window, "Material" buttons, click on "New." Leave the default settings. Remember a material must be added before applying a texture (the texture image). In the "Texture" buttons, click on "New." Note a texture slot is opened named "Texture" and the preview displays a black window. Scroll down to the "Image" tab and click on the "Browse Image to be Linked" icon (Figure 5.46). Select the texture image that you saved from the drop down menu. The preview window will show the texture image and if you change to "Texture Viewport Shading," you will see your texture on the sphere. Having fulfilled the requirements of unwrapping the mesh and applying a texture in a texture slot you are good to go for "Texture Paint."

Figure 5.46

Change the 3D window to "Texture Paint" mode. No missing data this time and the "Brush" tab is open showing the paint tools.

OK, to select one particular area of the mesh to paint go back to "Edit" mode (press Tab). Deselect the edges. Change to "Face" select mode. Select one face within the required area (RMB click) then press Ctrl + L key (select linked). At first the one face clicked shows in the "UV/Image Editor" then the selected area displays (Figures 5.47 and 5.48). Change to

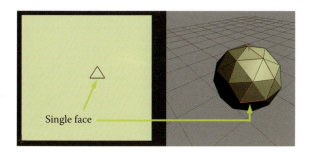

Figure 5.47

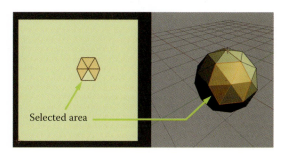

Figure 5.48

Click face selection masking

Figure 5.49

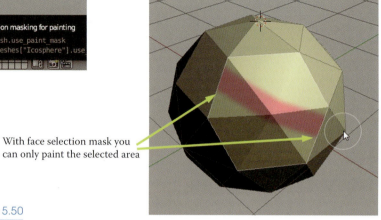

With face selection mask you can only paint the selected area

Figure 5.50

"Texture Paint" mode. In the 3D window header click on "Face Selection Masking" (Figure 5.49). A dotted white outline displays around your selected area. With "Masking" selected you can only paint on the selected area which is fabulous for detailed painting (Figure 5.50).

5.10.7 Painting a Texture

Up to this point we have only painted a flat base texture color but you can paint directly from an image texture. To demonstrate I will use a texture image named "Art-Paint.jpg" which is

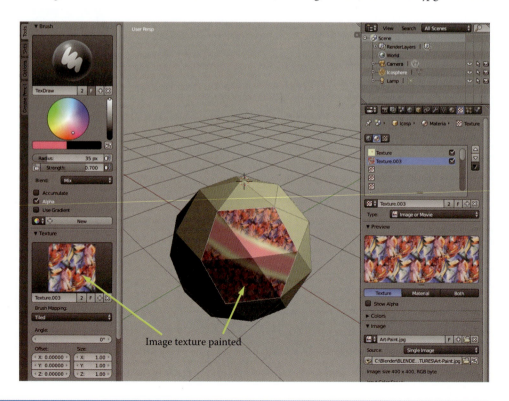

Image texture painted

Figure 5.51

saved on my computer. If we continue on using the previous arrangement, in the "Properties" window, "Texture" buttons click on a new texture slot and with texture type "Image or Movie" open the texture file. With the 3D window in "Texture Paint" mode, in the "Tools" "Texture" tab click on the "Image to be Linked" icon and select the new texture slot. When you paint the detail of the texture image is reproduced on the surface of your object (Figure 5.51).

6

World Settings

6.1 Introduction to World Settings

The "World Settings" are where you set the background for your scene. The default world background is the dull gray color, which displays when an image is rendered. Note: The background in the render is not the same as the background in the 3D window. The "Properties" window, "World" button shows the settings tabs, the first one being a preview panel (Figure 6.1). Click on the color bars in the world tab to display color pickers for setting the background color. Note that you only see the colored background when you render an image of your scene or when the 3D window, "Viewport Shading" is set to "Rendered" mode.

- *Horizon color.* Color at the horizon.
- *Zenith color.* Color at the top of the scene.
- *Ambient color.* Provides an overall lighting effect; an object in the scene will reflect this color regardless of its own material color.
- *Sky.* Paper, blend, real—these options provide combinations of color gradient across the rendered image.

Figure 6.1

163

Vertical pole object   Wall object with horizontal slats

 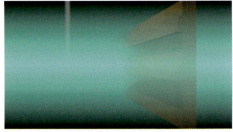

Figure 6.2   Paper sky + Blend sky   Paper sky + Blend sky + Real sky

The examples of sky background combinations in Figure 6.2 have a mist effect added. They are rendered images of a 3D view.

6.2 Mist

Lesson 06
06-11
World Editor
Mist

Mist settings allow you to introduce a mist or fog effect to your scene (Figure 6.3). To see the mist effect, "Mist" must be checked in the "World" button—"Mist" tab and the "Intensity" value must be set.

- *Start.* Distance from the camera where the mist starts.
- *Depth.* Distance over which the mist increases from 0% to 100%.
- *Height.* Height of the mist (Figure 6.4).

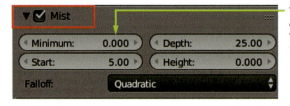

To see the mist effect "Mist" must be checked in the "World setting" tab and the "Minimum (Intensity) value set

Figure 6.3

6.3 Stars

Lesson 06
06-10
World Editor
Stars

Earlier versions of Blender had a "Stars" tab which allowed you to introduce stars to your background (Figure 6.5). Stars are now created using "Particles."

6.4 Texture as Background

Lesson 06
06-08
World Editor
Background Sky

Blender's built-in textures can be used to create a background for your scene. The following demonstration will show you how, but you will soon realize that there are many combinations of settings to experiment with. It is a good idea to search the internet and find tutorials showing how to achieve specific effects, but remember that the effects have probably been derived by experimentation.

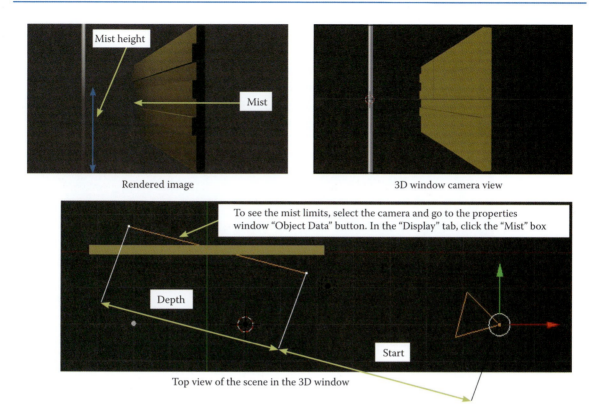

Mist height

Mist

Rendered image

3D window camera view

To see the mist limits, select the camera and go to the properties window "Object Data" button. In the "Display" tab, click the "Mist" box

Depth

Start

Top view of the scene in the 3D window

Figure 6.4

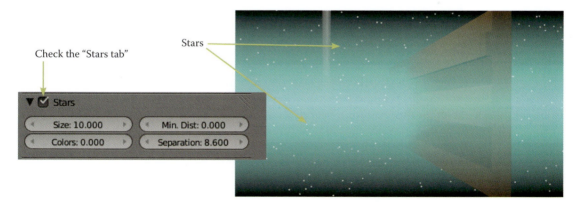

Check the "Stars tab"

Stars

▼ ☑ Stars

◄   Size: 10.000   ►   ◄   Min. Dist: 0.000   ►
◄   Colors: 0.000   ►   ◄   Separation: 8.600   ►

Figure 6.5

Begin with the default Blender scene containing the cube object. You can leave the cube since the texture we will be applying will affect the scene background and not the cube. Make sure the cube is deselected NOT selected. Remember that textures do not display in the 3D window unless "Viewport Shading" is set to "Rendered" or you render

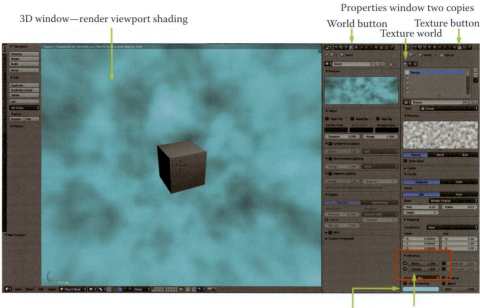

3D window—render viewport shading

Properties window two copies

World button   Texture button

Texture world

Figure 6.6

Select color   Check "Horizon"

an image. To make life a little simpler, divide the screen as shown in Figure 6.6 with two "Properties" windows.

By default, the properties window displays with the "Render" buttons active. In your setup, make one copy of the properties with the "World" buttons active and the other with the "Texture" buttons active. The "Texture" buttons should be in world texture mode. This setup will allow you to see your background texture in the 3D window when you change a setting. The preview in the "Properties" window, "World" buttons only gives an indication of the render.

Now, how do we get the background? In the "Properties" window, "Textures" buttons, click on "New" to display the buttons tabs. By default, the texture type "Image or Movie" opens. Click on the selection menu and select "Clouds." You see the clouds texture in the preview panel, but it is a black-and-white image. There is no display in the properties window "World" buttons, or in a render of the 3D window, there is only the dull gray background. At this stage, you haven't told Blender what to influence with the texture.

In the "Properties" window, "Textures" buttons (in world texture mode)—"Influence" tab, check (tick) the "Horizon" button (which controls the amount the texture affects the color of the horizon). You will now see the texture as a background in the "World" buttons preview tab. The clouds are pink because of the color in the color bar in the "Influence" tab. Click on the color bar and select a nice pale blue color and the clouds in the preview should look more realistic. A render in the 3D window will give you a precise image of your scene background (Figure 6.7).

The rendered image is not the same as the preview, so you have to adjust the values in the "Properties" window to get the desired effect. In the "Properties" window, "World Texture" mode—"Mapping" tab, adjust the "Offset" and "Size" settings and change

"Coordinates" in the drop down menu. In the "Influence" tab, try changing the "Blend: Mix" to something else.

In the "Properties" window, "World" button, "World" tab, checking the different "Sky" settings and choosing different colors from the color bars in the horizon, zenith, and ambient settings produce different effects. In the 3D window, select the lamp. In the "Properties" window, try different lamp settings. In the "Lamp" tab, change the lamp type (Point, Sun, Spot, Hemi, and Area). Adjust the "Energy" value and change the light color by clicking on the color bar to reveal a color picker. Render an image at each change to see the different results. Don't forget to try out all the different texture types.

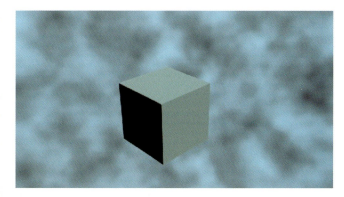

Figure 6.7

As previously stated, there are many combinations. You just have to experiment and record your settings. When you find something you like that suits your purpose, save it in a .blend file for future use; in this way, you can create your own library.

6.5 Image as Background

You can use any image stored on your computer as a background. Deselect objects in the scene and click the "World" texture type button. In the "Properties" window, "Textures" button, click "New" to add a texture. With the texture type "Image or Movie" in the "Image" tab, click "Open" then navigate and select your image. In the "Textures" button— "Influence" tab, click "Horizon." The image will display as the background to your scene when you render (Figure 6.8).

Lesson 04
04-02
Background
Image

Lesson 06
06-09
World Editor
Background
Image

Image displayed as background

Figure 6.8

6.6 Image as Template

An image can be displayed in a scene as a template to aid in modeling. With the mouse cursor in the 3D window, press the N key on the keyboard and follow the steps in Figure 6.9.

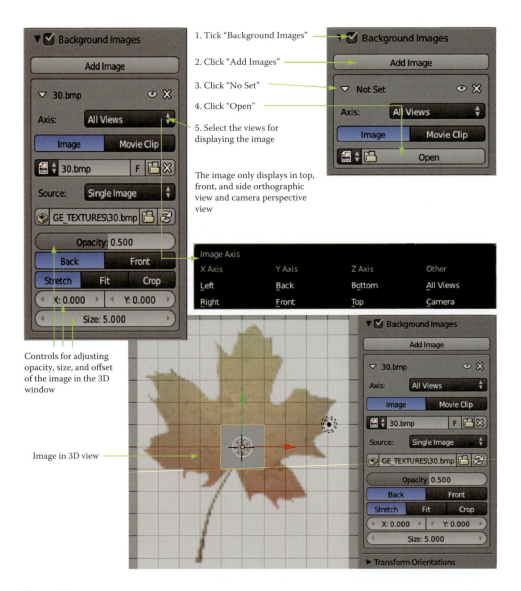

Figure 6.9

7

Lighting and Cameras

Lesson 06
06-01
Blender Lighting
Point Lamps

Lesson 06
06-02
Blender Lighting
Sun Lamp

Lesson 06
06-03
Blender Lighting
Sun Lamp Sky
and Atmosphere

Lesson 06
06-04
Blender Lighting
Hemi Lamp

Lesson 06
06-05
Blender Lighting
Area Lamp

Lesson 06
06-06
Blender Lighting
Spot Lamp

Lesson 06
06-07
Blender Lighting
Ambient Occlusion

7.1 Lighting Types and Settings

The default scene in Blender starts with a cube object, a camera, and a lamp. What the camera sees is what will render as a picture or movie depending on the settings you make. To see a simple rendered view, have the 3D window in "Rendered Viewport Shading" mode or press the F12 key to open a window that displays the rendered output of what the camera is focused on. If the picture shows the cube object as a black silhouette, you do not have a lamp or the lamp settings or placement is incorrect. To exit the render window, press the Esc key.

In most cases, you will need more than one lamp in order to properly illuminate your scene. Most scenes usually require three to four lamps, but be careful not to use too many. Instead of adding lamps, experiment with the distance and energy settings.

7.2 Lamp Settings

To create or add a lamp to the scene, position the 3D window cursor in a desired location and press Shift + the A key and select "Lamp" from the drop down menu. You can choose your type of lamp (Point, Sun, Spot, Hemi, or Area) and that type of lamp will be placed in the scene. With the lamp selected, go to the "Properties" window, "Object Data" button to display the setting options (Figure 7.1). The options displayed vary depending on what type of lamp you select. The diagrammatic representation of the lamp in the 3D window also varies depending on the type (Figure 7.2).

Figure 7.1

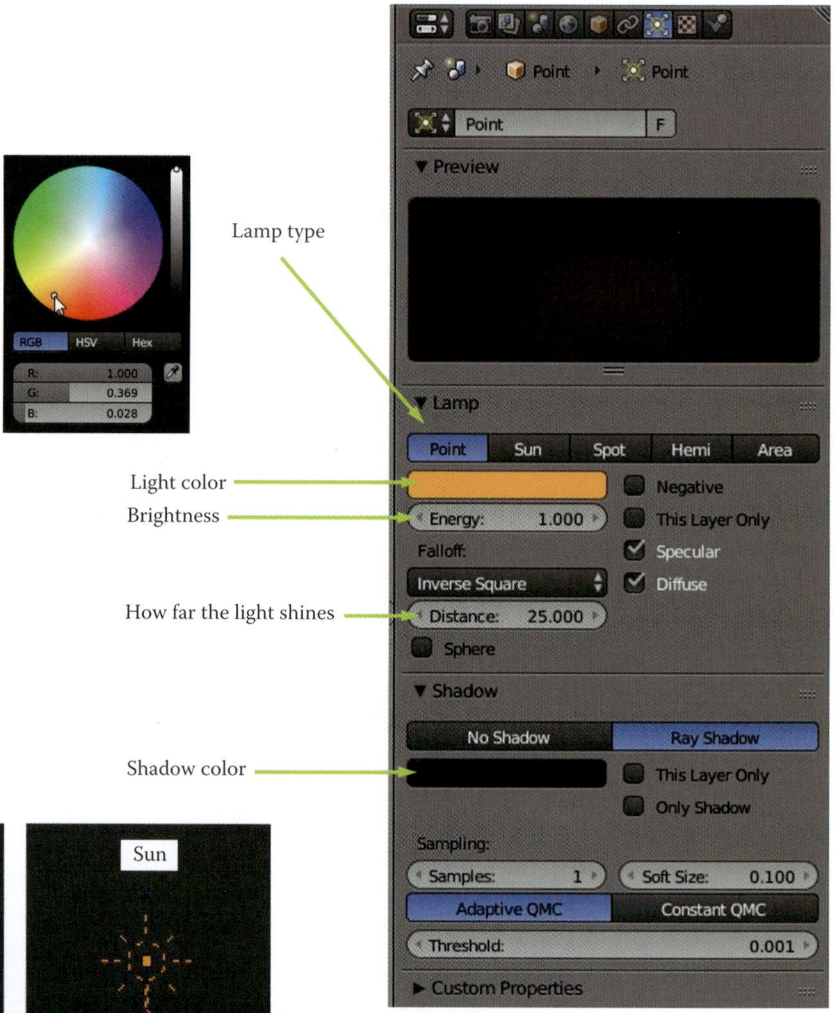

Lamp type

Light color

Brightness

How far the light shines

Figure 7.2

Shadow color

Point

Sun

Spot

Hemi

Area

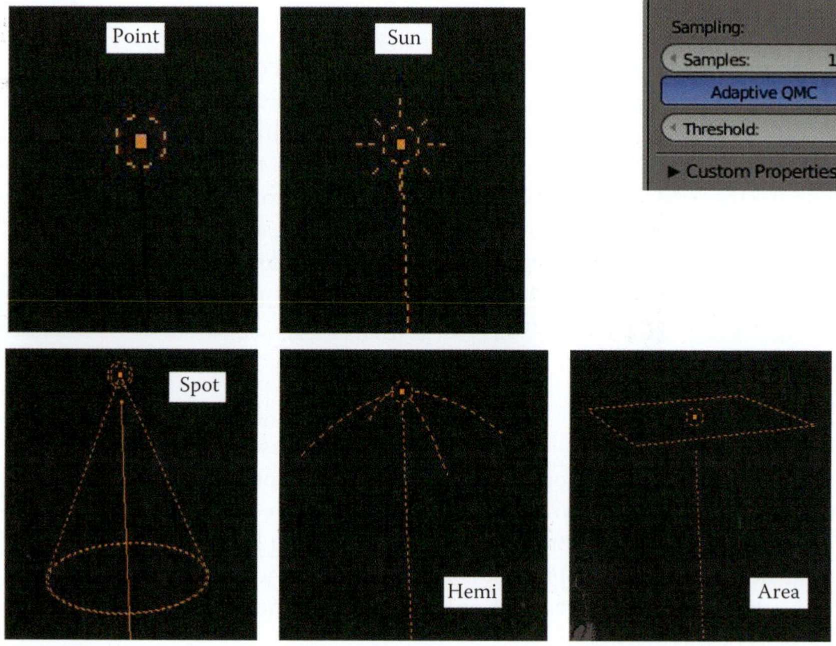

If you decide that the lamp you have selected is not correct for what you want to achieve, you can change the type in the properties window. Click on the different lamp types in the "Lamp" tab.

Spot lamps or spotlights are particularly useful in creating great effects. They can be scaled, rotated, and positioned to cast shadows and they can also be used with a halo effect to provide a simulation of a light shining through a fog (Figure 7.3). For this and other lamps, experiment with the settings and record your results.

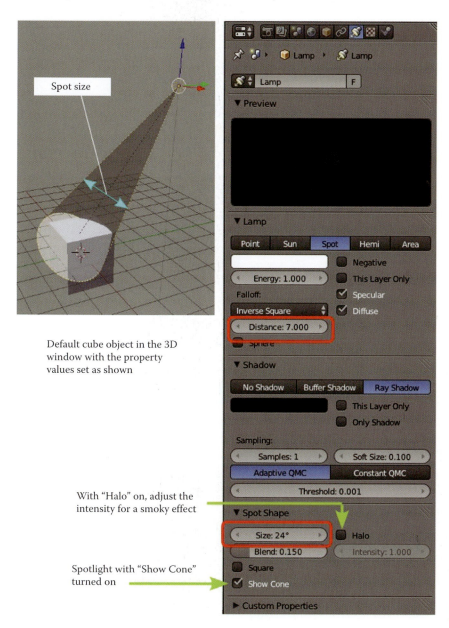

Spot size

Default cube object in the 3D window with the property values set as shown

With "Halo" on, adjust the intensity for a smoky effect

Spotlight with "Show Cone" turned on

Figure 7.3

Lesson 02
02-13
Camera
Lock to View

Lesson 05
05-11
Camera
Constraints

Lesson 09
09-01
Multiple
Cameras

Lesson 09
09-09
Binding Cameras
to the Limeline

7.3 Cameras

By default, your scene already has one camera but you may wish to add more cameras. You can add more cameras by pressing Shift + the A key and selecting "Camera." The new camera will be located where your 3D cursor is positioned and you will have to orientate the camera. To change which camera is active, you need to select that camera and press Ctrl + Num Pad 0. Figure 7.4 shows the "Properties" window, "Camera" button.

7.4 Camera Settings Options

- *Perspective, orthographic, or panoramic.* Used to change the camera from showing a true-life perspective view to an orthographic view.
- *Focal length.* Sets up a lens length much like a real camera; 35 mm is a good, safe setting, but wide and tight angle settings work for different needs.
- *Shift.* Pushes the camera's view in a direction, without changing perspective.
- *Clipping start.* How close an object can get to the camera and still be seen (Figure 7.5).

Figure 7.4

Figure 7.5

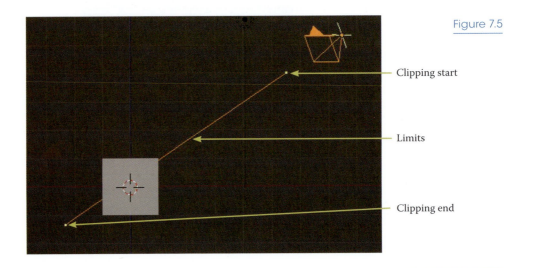

Clipping start

Limits

Clipping end

- *Clipping end.* How far away objects can be seen by the camera; in very large scenes, this needs to be set higher or things "disappear" from view (Figure 7.5).
- *Depth of field.* Used with nodes to blur foreground and background objects; working with nodes will be discussed in Chapter 19.
- *Limits.* Draws a line in the scene to help you visualize the camera's range (Figure 7.5).
- *Mist.* Gives you a visual display of how far the camera sees if you are adding mist.
- *Title safe.* Displays the inner dashed box to help with placement of objects and text.
- *Name.* Displays the name of the active camera in camera view (number pad 0).
- *Size.* How big to draw the camera on the screen; you can also control the size with scale.
- *Passepartout.* Shades the area on the screen outside of the camera's view (Figure 7.6).
- *Alpha.* Controls the darkness of the shaded area with the slider.
- *Sensor.* Show sensor size in camera view.

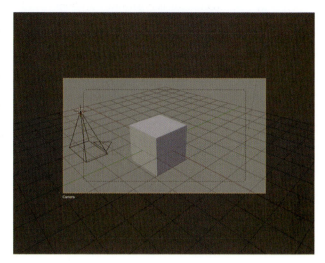

Figure 7.6

7.5 Camera Switching

In "7.3 Cameras," we have shown that you can have more than one camera in a scene and that you can switch between cameras by selecting one, then pressing Ctrl + Num Pad 0. This makes the selected camera active and opens camera view showing what is seen by that camera. This is fine for rendering single images of an object from different viewing perspectives but you may want to animate the switching so that in rendering an animation you switch between cameras as the animation plays.

Chapter 9 describes the basics of animation but the inclusion of a prelude in the following demonstration will do no harm.

Set up a scene similar to that shown in the diagram with three cameras pointed at Susan (Monkey) from different locations. You can use the default camera and add two others (Figure 7.7).

In the 3D window select the default cameras. In the "Timeline" window with the vertical green cursor line at frame 1 and the mouse cursor in the "Timeline" window press the

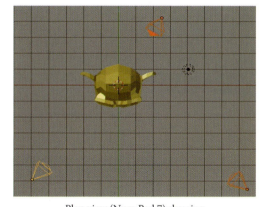

Plan view (Num Pad 7) showing
"Susan" (monkey) with three cameras

Figure 7.7

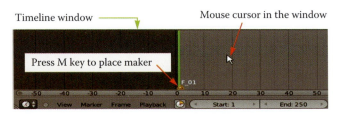

Timeline window

Mouse cursor in the window

Press M key to place maker

Figure 7.8

Figure 7.9

M Key to place a "Marker" at frame 1. Note: You can only place the marker when the 3D window cursor is positioned in the "Timeline" (Figure 7.8).

The selected "Camera" now has to be parented to the "Marker."

Click on "View" in the "Timeline" window header and select "Bind Camera to Markers" (Figure 7.9). The camera view opens (Num Pad 0) showing the view from the default camera.

Select one of the other cameras. In the "Timeline" window move the green cursor line to another frame. With the 3D cursor in the "Timeline" window press the M key to place a second marker. In the "Timeline" header, click on "View" and select "Bind Camera to Marker." Change back to the 3D window plan view (Num Pad 7).

Repeat the process for the third camera. Remember select a different frame in the "Timeline" and when you place a marker have your mouse cursor in the "Timeline" window.

When you press "Play" in the "Timeline" header an animation will play switching from one camera to the other.

7.6 Camera Tracking

Camera tracking is a technique that imitates the real camera motion which occurs when taking a video with a camera. This allows a realistic effect when a 3D model in a Blender scene is superimposed over a video background. Without this effect the Blender 3D camera would track to a stable imaginary point or to a predetermined curve track in the scene. This would be fine for the superimposed 3D object but the actual video used as a background would move differently and produce an unrealistic effect.

The essence of the technique is to plot the movement of multiple points in the video scene and feed that information to the motion of the Blender 3D camera.

At this point the technique is mentioned to make you aware of its existence. For the detailed application you will have to research the excellent video tutorials on the internet. I will decline to direct you to any particular tutorial since at the time of writing the technique is under development and is constantly being revised.

8

Rendering and Ray Tracing

8.1 Rendering an Image or Movie

Rendering is the process of converting the Blender file information into an image file or a movie file. In practice this entails taking what you see in "Camera View" in Blender and converting it into an image or movie file format. The conversion may then be played on a variety of media devices depending on the format chosen. The conversion is performed in the "Properties" window—"Render" buttons.

Note: There are two different rendering processes in Blender. One is the Blender Internal Render Engine and the other is the Cycles Render Engine. Neither engine is better than the other since they both have strengths and weakness. This chapter discusses the render process in the Blender Internal system. Cycles is discussed in Chapter 20.

Figure 8.1

Lesson 05
05-13
Rendering an
Image File

Lesson 05
05-14
Render Slots

Lesson 07
07-09
Rendering to
Video Files

Lesson 09
09-08
Creating an
Animated GIF

8.1.1 The Render Tab

The "Render" tab (Figure 8.1) contains two buttons for activating the render process, a button for mixing audio to a sound file and a drop down menu for selecting where you want your render displayed in Blender.

- *Render.* Pressing "Render" converts the data from the "Camera" view in the 3D window to a still image. This is the same as pressing F12 on the keyboard. The still image is displayed in whatever option you have selected in the "Display" drop down menu. The default selection is the "Image Editor" window; therefore, pressing "Render" or pressing F12 on the keyboard opens the "Image Editor" window (to cancel the "Image Editor" window, press Esc). With an image rendered, it may be saved as a folder (see "Output" tab) by pressing the F3 button. Pressing F3 opens the "File Browser" window where you select where you want to save the file.
- *Animation.* Pressing "Animation" commences rendering of an animation sequence which has been set up in the 3D window. Again the output file is saved to a folder but in this case you select the folder prior to rendering in the "Properties" window, "Render" buttons, "Output" tab. The default output file location is C:/tmp\.
- *Audio.* Pressing "Audio" opens the "File Browser" window allowing you to select a folder where the sound from an animation may be saved.
- *Display.* Clicking on the "Display" button shows the drop down menu for selecting how you want Blender to display a rendered file. The default selection is the "Image Editor" window; therefore, pressing "Render" or pressing F12 on the keyboard opens the "Image Editor" window.

Before you can perform any of the above procedures, you have to tell Blender how and what and where you want to render. To do this you set up options in the "Dimensions" and "Output" tabs.

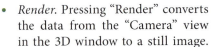

8.1.2 The Dimensions Tab

The "Dimensions" tab (Figure 8.2) is where you tell Blender how big to make your image, the shape of the image, the quality of the image and in the case of an animation where to start and stop rendering and how fast you want it to play back when finished.

- *Render Presets.* The "Render Presets" selection menu provides options for video output to suite a variety of television formats. With the default "Render Presets" in the panel the video will be rendered to play back on your computer.
- *Resolution*
  - X: The number of pixels wide in the display
  - Y: The number of pixels high in the display

Figure 8.2

Pixels are the tiny little rectangles which display on the computer or television screen which make up what you see.

Note: The default "Resolution" 1920 × 1080 equates to the HDTV 1080p "Preset."

The percentage slider sets the quality of the render. The default is 50% which scales the resolution. This means that although the resolution is set at 1920 × 1080, the render will be a preview at 960 × 540. Since rendering takes time this is a way of seeing your image or movie as a preview prior to a final render and, therefore, saving time. For the final render you set the slider to 100%.

- *Frame range.* This is fairly self-explanatory and shows the start frame and end frame of the animation and the "Steps" which means which frames to render. "Frame Steps: 1" means render every frame, "Frame Steps: 2" would mean render every other frame 3 would mean render every third frame, etc.

Note: Pressing F12 with an animation paused renders an image of the single frame in the animation where it paused.

- *Aspect ratio.* The aspect ratio refers to the shape of the pixels. The 1:1 default ratio is for computer monitors which have square pixels. TV screens have rectangular pixels so you have to set a ratio for the appropriate format, that is, HDV NTSC 1080p for America the ratio is 4:3 and HDV PAL 1080p for Europe is also 4:3 but TV PAL 16.9 the ratio is 16:11.

Aspect ratios are very confusing but selecting a "Render Preset" option for different video outputs automatically sets the "Resolution," "Aspect Ratio," and "Frame Rate" for the particular video output selected.

- *Frame rate.* The playback speed of the animation expressed in frames per second (FPS). The drop down menu provides options for a variety of formats (25 FPS for PAL TV European format and 30 FPS for NTSC TV US format—these frame rates are approximate and vary with the actual "Render Preset" selected).
- *Border.* Tick "Border," press Shift + B, drag the mouse to define a portion of the view to render instead of the whole "Camera" view frame.
- *Crop.* Enabling "Crop" will crop the rendered image instead of rendering a black region around it.
- *Time remapping.* Used to remap the length of an animation.

8.1.3 The Antialiasing Tab

Antialiasing—The output quality setting. The default values give a nice output without loss of render time. Video rendering can take a considerable time depending on the content of the animation and computer speed. For that reason, "Render Farms" are available on the Internet which will perform the video rendering for you (at a price).

Figure 8.3

8.1.4 The Output Tab

In the "Output" tab (Figure 8.3) you set options to tell Blender where to save your render and the file format you require.

By default Blender will save your render to the "tmp" folder on your hard drive as seen by the "/tmp\" notation in the output file address bar. You can choose a different location by clicking on the folder icon at the end of the bar and navigating in the file browser that opens. Blender will save your render in a variety of file formats. The default format is "Portable Network Graphics" (PNG). Where you see this in the "Output" tab is a drop down menu for selecting alternative formats. In the menu you will see that the options are in two categories, that is, image and movie. Image types such as PNG or JPEG produce a render of a still image in that particular file type. Selecting one of the "Movie" options produces a render of an animation in a compressed movie file such as "AVI Raw" or "MPEG."

Note: With an "Image" file type selected, a render of an animation will consist of a series of images of each frame of the animation. Although this takes up a lot of room in a folder it is an acceptable method of producing a video file (see Section 8.3).

Note the default "Image" type PNG with the RGB color scheme and "Compression" ratio of 90%. Some formats can compress images to use less disc space for instance, Lossless PNG or JPEG.

8.2 Rendering a JPEG Image

When you have created a scene in the 3D window and decide that you wish to save an image of what you see in the "Camera" view, go to the "Properties" window, "Render" buttons. For the time being leave all the default settings just as they are except in the "Output" tab click on the drop down selection menu where you see "PNG" and change to "JPEG."

With your mouse cursor back in the 3D window, press F12 on the keyboard to render the camera view. Now press F3 to save the rendered image. A file browser window displays (Figure 8.4) which allows you to name your image file and navigate to a folder on your hard drive where you wish to save the JPEG image.

In Figure 8.4, I have named my image file "Test.jpg" and I am saving it to D:\Users\john\Pictures on my hard drive. With this information entered as shown click "Save As Image" in the upper right corner of the window.

Note: If you have an animation sequence paused you can render and save an image of the animation frame.

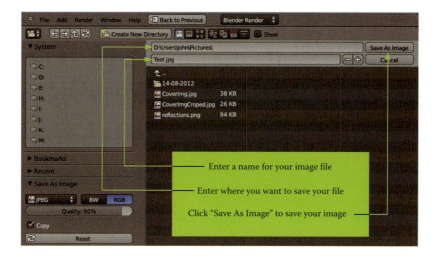

Figure 8.4

8.3 Rendering a Movie File

"Rendering a Movie file" should possibly be, "Rendering a Video clip." Movies are made by combining a series of video clips (short sections of video).

Before you can render a video file you must have an animation sequence. We will create an animation and render it to a video to demonstrate the process. Animation is covered in the next chapter so assuming you are working your way through the book chapter by chapter you will not have covered the topic at this stage.

In the 3D window go into "Camera" view (Num Pad 0) and translate the default cube back along the X-axis keeping it just inside the center rectangle. Press the I key and in the drop down menu select "Location." In the "Timeline" window at the bottom of the screen, click LMB on the vertical green line, hold and drag the line to frame 10. In the 3D window, translate the cube along the X-axis to the lower right corner of the center rectangle. Press I key again and select "Location." In the "Timeline" window header change the "End: 250" value to "End: 10." You have just made an animation consisting of 10 frames. In the "Timeline" window, click on the reverse double arrows to set the animation at frame 1. Press Alt + A or click the start button to play the animation in the 3D window. The cube just zips across the "Camera" view and repeats the 10 frame animation over and over. Press Esc to quit.

OK! Now for the render.

In this demonstration we will use the default settings in the "Properties" window "Render" buttons. The "Output" tab is set to render a PNG file format and save it to the "tmp" folder on the hard drive. If you haven't been messing with your hard drive and repartitioning the "tmp" folder should be in "C:\tmp."

Before you do any rendering to the "tmp" folder give it a clean out so you have a clean slate for this demo.

To render the animation, simply press the "Animation" button in "Render" buttons "Render" tab. Blender will start making an image for each frame of the animation and save it to the "tmp" folder. The reason for rendering an image for each frame is that the default output file type is PNG which is an image file. The same thing would happen if you had JPEG selected. A render progress bar displays at the top of the screen in the "Information"

window header. When the render is finished, press "Esc" to quit the render view. If you look in the "tmp" folder when the render is finished you should see 10 image files.

8.4 Playback

To playback your rendered animation from within Blender you go to the "Info" window header and click on "Render" and select "Play Rendered Animation."

This is telling Blender to use the inbuilt player. There are other options available. If you have one of the other players installed on your computer you can save it as the default player for future use.

To use a different player you have to change a setting in the "User Preference" window.

Click on "File" in the "Information" window header and select "User Preferences." Click on "File" in the row of buttons at the top of the window. In the window that displays look for "Animation Player" in the list at the left of the window and you will see "Internal." Click on the drop down menu and make your selection (Figure 8.5).

Figure 8.5

Note: Although options are listed in the menu they have to be installed on your computer and the file path to the application entered in the "User Preferences" window.

8.5 More Movie File Rendering

Rendering an animation as a series of image files uses up a large chunk of hard

Figure 8.6

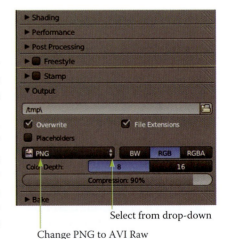

Select from drop-down

Change PNG to AVI Raw

drive space when you have a substantial animation or a series of animations. To save space you can render your animation to a movie file instead.

As an example take the same 10 frame animation previously created and in the "Properties" window, "Render" buttons, "Output tab, (Figure 8.6) change the default "PNG" to one of the other "Movie" options, for example, "AVI Raw" which is a video file format. Video file formats compress the data from the rendered animation into a single file instead of the series of image files.

Before you press "Animation" to render with the video file format clean out the "tmp" folder again.

OK! With a clean slate go ahead and press the "Animation" button so start rendering. When Blender is finished rendering, press "Esc" to exit the render window.

Go look in your "tmp" folder and you will find a single video file. Press the "Play" button to replay the rendered animation in the inbuilt player. Since this is a video file you could also play it in some external application such as "VLC media Player." If you try this with our 10 frame animation pay attention since 10 frames plays pretty quickly at 24 FPS and an external player only plays the file once (less than half a second of video).

8.6 Video Codecs

In the preceding example, in changing the default "PNG" file format to "AVI Raw," you were in fact electing to use the "AVI Raw" video codec which tells the computer how you want your animation data encoded. There are many video codecs to choose from and simply selecting a codec type in Blender doesn't necessarily mean that you will get the result that you want. You must have the "Codec" installed on your computer.

A codec is a little routine that compresses the video so that it will fit on a DVD, or be able to be streamed over the Internet, or over cable, or just be a reasonable file size.

Simply put, using a codec you encode the Blender animation data to a video file which suits a particular output media such as PAL TV or NTSC TV then when you have used the encoded data to create a video CD or DVD, the CD or DVD is played in a device (CD/DVD Player) which decodes the data for display, that is, Television Screen.

As previously stated, you must have the codec installed on your computer.

"Codec Packs" are available for download on the Internet and come in self-installing packages, that is, Codecs.for.windows.7.pack.v4.0.5.setup and K-Lite_Codec_Pack_970_Mega.

Most modern video players will handle a wide range of codecs.

8.7 Making a Movie

In the preceding information, we have briefly explained the procedure for rendering an image or an animation sequence. In rendering the animation, we first created a series of image files and then repeated the process creating a video file. The video file does not constitute a movie. In our case the video was a mere 10 frames but even if it were a thousand frames it would not be a movie. It is merely a render of one animation sequence from one scene into a video file. Movies are made by combining many video files and then rendering the combination to a movie file. At the same time as this combination is compiled sound effects are added and synchronized with the video.

This combining, synchronizing, and editing takes place in a VSE. Blender has its own VSE which is explained in Chapter 22.

The video clip (movie file) will take some time to compile depending on the length of the animation. Each frame of the animation has to be rendered and saved. Depending on the complexity of the scene, a frame can take from a few seconds to several minutes to render. To begin, it is best to keep everything very basic and simple. If you get to the stage where you have created a wonderful movie, you can send the animation files to a "Render Farm" on the Internet to have them rendered—it saves you time but it costs you money.

Figure 8.7

8.8 Ray Tracing

Ray tracing is used to produce mirrored and reflective surfaces. It is also used to create transparency and refraction (bending of images through transparent surfaces like a magnifying glass or lens). Ray tracing can create

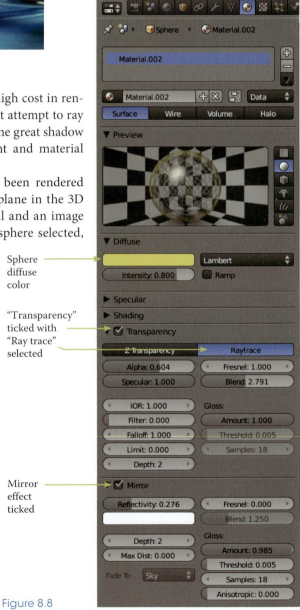

stunning effects but can incur a high cost in render time, so use it sparingly. Don't attempt to ray trace everything—you can get some great shadow and texture effects with spotlight and material settings.

The image in Figure 8.7 has been rendered by positioning a sphere above a plane in the 3D window. The plane has a material and an image texture assigned to it. With the sphere selected, subdivided in edit mode, and set smooth, values have been set in the "Properties" window, "Material" button, as shown in Figure 8.8. Note that the camera in the scene has been positioned close to the horizontal midplane and close to the plane and sphere.

Sphere diffuse color

"Transparency" ticked with "Ray trace" selected

Mirror effect ticked

8.9 Cycles Ray Trace Rendering

In the preceding discussion on rendering and render settings, we have limited the subject to the use of the Blender internal render engine. There are external render engines which can be used to render Blender files but Blender incorporates "Cycles Render."

Figure 8.8

The "Cycles Render" engine is a ray tracing-based engine with support for interactive rendering. It incorporates a shading node system, a different material and texture work flow and it utilizes GPU acceleration.

To simplify this definition of "Cycles," consider it as a rendering process which allows you to see the render as you manipulate and edit the scene in the 3D window.

Note: Since "Cycles Render" employs the Blender "Node" system, described in Chapter 19, it has been assigned a separate chapter. See Chapter 20.

9

Animation Basics

9.1 Introduction to Animation

In this chapter, I will explain how to make objects move about in the scene. This is a big section in Blender with many features. The features will become easier to understand with practice, which will then allow progress beyond the basics. This is a highly developed section and new features are being added all the time so it is likely that before this manual is published, new features will be available. We will therefore only attempt the basics.

Lesson 07
07-01
Basic Keyframe
Animation

Before you start, make sure you understand Chapter 8 and the section on rendering.

What is an animation? In the simplest form an animation is a series of still images each one slightly different to the next, which when viewed in quick succession produces the illusion of motion. This is similar to the early movie films where images or frames were taken with a camera and assembled on a celluloid strip. Animations were created in the same way. In Blender this is accomplished by creating data which displays as a series of still images. Each still image is a single frame of the animation. Each frame (image) is rendered, which means the data you enter in the Blender program are correlated and turned into the digital image; this, by default, is in a PNG format. Finally, all the images are compiled into one video file.

To create an animation you begin by setting up your scene with the object that you wish to animate (the actor). You have to think about what the actor is required to do and how long it should take to do it. Also consider what format you will use in the final render.

The render format determines how many frames per second the animation should run (for playing in a television format, NTSC for the United States at 30 fps and PAL for Australia at 25 fps). One of the problems that beginner animators experience is trying to make the motion occur in an appropriate time. Remember to look at the frames per second and relate it to time. For example, if you want a movement to take 3 seconds and you are running at 25 frames per second, then the animation has to occur in 75 frames.

In Blender you do not have to create every single frame of the animation. You set up single frames ("Keyframes") at specific points and the program works out all the in-between frames.

Think of a 10-second animation that, when running at 25 frames per second, would consist of 250 frames. If you want your actor to go from points A to B and then to point C in the scene within the 250-frame animation, you first insert a "Keyframe" at frame 1 with the actor at position A. This is giving Blender data that says at the frame 1, locate the actor at location A. Then at another frame, midway in the animation, insert a second "Keyframe" with the actor at location B. Finally, insert a third "Keyframe" at frame 250 with the actor at location C. These are the "Keyframes" for the animation. Blender will work out all the in-between frames. The "Keyframes" will also include the data for other features such as scale and rotation.

9.2 Moving, Rotating, and Scaling

Moving, rotating, and scaling are the three basic modifiers to use in an animation. Besides entering data specifying the position of the actor in a scene at different locations (the "Keyframes") you also specify any other changes that take place such as rotation and change in size. When you create "Keyframes" in Blender with these changes Blender will work out all the data for the changes at the in-between frames.

Determining the in-between data is called "Interpolation." There are different methods of interpolation. By default, Blender uses "Bezier"-type interpolation, which for motion gives a nice acceleration and deceleration between "Keyframes." Remember, at the moment we are only considering the movement of an object. When an object moves from points A to B in a given time, it is said to move at a certain velocity (speed). In theory, the speed could be represented as a straight line graph, but in practice an object at rest (motionless) has to go from being motionless to moving at a certain velocity. The rate at which it attains the velocity is called acceleration. Blender's "Bezier" interpolation draws curves at the beginning and end of the straight line graph (acceleration and deceleration). You have the options to choose "Constant" or "Linear"-type interpolation if appropriate. Selection of interpolation types will be discussed later in this chapter.

Using the term "Bezier" to describe interpolation is in fact an anomaly. Bezier actually describes a type of line (the line on a graph described in the previous paragraph). A Bezier line or curve in Blender is a line that has control points on it that allow the shape of the line to be altered or edited. In Blender, the control points are located at the position of the "Keyframes." Interpolation is done according to a mathematical formula that determines the shape of the line. When the data for the frames in the animation are drawn as a line on a graph, the line conforms to that mathematical formula.

For the moment, we will accept the default Bezier-type interpolation and demonstrate the insertion of key frames and the creation of a simple animation. We will use the default

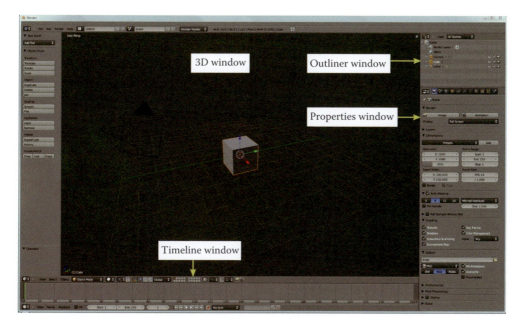

Figure 9.1

Blender screen with the three-dimensional (3D) window containing the default cube object as the actor. The default screen also displays the "Outliner" window and the "Properties" window at the RHS of the screen and the "Timeline" window across the bottom (Figure 9.1).

To set up our animation, first change the 3D window to top view with "Orthographic" projection (with the cursor in the 3D window press number pad 7—number pad 5). This just keeps the view simple so we can see where we are going (Figure 9.2).

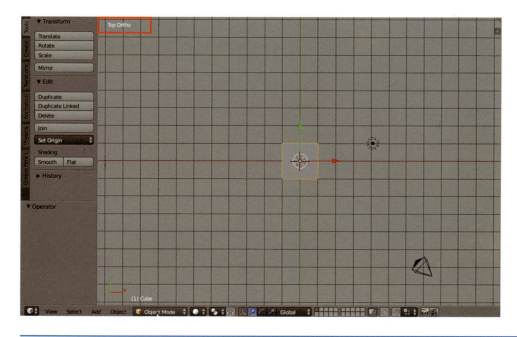

Figure 9.2

9.2 Moving, Rotating, and Scaling

The first step in an animation is to decide what you want your actor to do in a given time. In this case, the actor is the cube object. How long it takes your actor to do something will depend on how many frames per second your animation is run and this is determined by what format your final render will be in.

Let's set our animation to run at 25 frames per second, which would be suitable for PAL format. Go to the "Properties" window, "Render" button, "Dimensions" tab—"Frame Rate" (Figure 9.3). Note that in the "Timeline" window the frame range settings are "Start: 1" and "End: 250" (Figure 9.5); this says that our animation will begin at frame 1 and end at frame 250. Running at the rate of 25 frames per second will give an animation time of 10 seconds. If you think about it, 10 seconds is quite a long time for a single action to take place in a video clip. Also in the "Timeline" window, make note of the lighter grayed area beginning at frame 1 and ending at frame 250. Changing the "Start Frame" and "End Frame" values in the header panel will move the end positions of the lighter grayed area. Note the vertical green line at frame 1. This is the "Timeline Cursor."

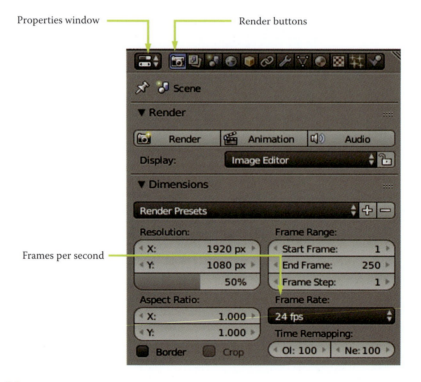

Figure 9.3

To make things relatively simple, we will only make our actor (the cube) move in a straight line across the screen along the *x*-axis and at the same time increase in size. Make sure the cube is selected in the 3D window. We will only insert two "Keyframes" to begin with, just to keep it simple.

In the default scene, by default, the actor (the selected object—the cube) is considered to be at frame 1 in the animation. In the lower LH corner of the window, you will see

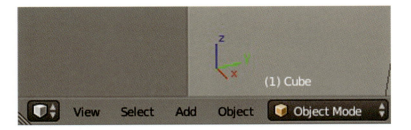

Figure 9.4

"(1) Cube" in white lettering (Figure 9.4). This indicates that you have the cube selected at frame 1. If you had 10 objects in the scene, all of which were actors with maybe some hidden, it's nice to know which one is selected.

Before we insert a "Keyframe," change to frame 25.

Observe the "Timeline" window at the bottom of the screen. The buttons labeled "Start: 1," "End: 250," and "1" show the start frame and end frame that was set by default for the animation and the current frame of the animation. Above the header you will see a scale ranging from −40 to +280. Click LMB on the scale hold and drag the mouse re-positions the scale. At either end of the scale there is a gray dot. Clicking on either dot LMB hold and drag the mouse left or right zooms the scale. With the mouse cursor in the "Timeline" window, pressing Num Pad + or − also zooms the scale.

Next to the 0 point on the scale, the vertical green line is the "Timeline" cursor. The cursor is located at frame 1. Click on the cursor with the LMB, hold and drag it across to frame 25 (Figure 9.5). Note the number change next to the cube at the lower LH side of the window and in the header bar of the "Timeline" window. Other ways to change the frame are to click on the little arrows on either end of the "Start" button in the "Timeline" window header or click LMB on the button, hold and drag to change the frame number or click on the "1," hit delete, and retype the required frame number. *There is always more than one way to skin a cat.*

Now that you are at frame 25 place the **mouse cursor** in the 3D window and press the I key to insert a "Keyframe." In the selection list that displays, select (click) "LocRotScale," which covers moving, rotating, and changing the size of the object (Figure 9.6).

Figure 9.6

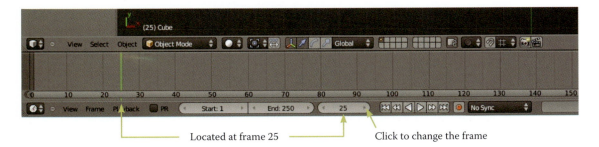

Located at frame 25   Click to change the frame

Figure 9.5

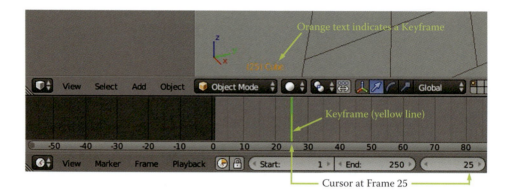

Figure 9.7

You have just inserted a key frame. You will see a short vertical yellow line at frame 25, which indicates a key frame (Figure 9.7).

So far, we have only inserted one key frame and our actor hasn't done anything.

If you click on the "Timeline" window cursor (green line), hold and drag the mouse from frame 1 along the timeline the cube remains stationary. Clicking and dragging the green line in the "Timeline" is called scrubbing the animation, which is actually manually playing the animation. You can play the animation by clicking the "Play" button in the "Timeline" window header, but since we haven't told our actor to do anything yet, nothing happens.

Note that going from frames 1 to 25 at 25 frames per second equals 1 second.

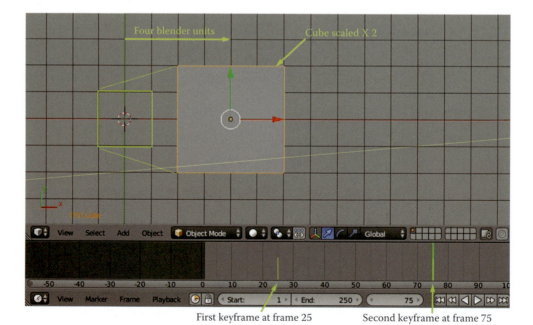

First keyframe at frame 25   Second keyframe at frame 75

Figure 9.8

Continue by moving the cursor to frame 75 (drag the green line). In the 3D window, grab and move the cube 4 Blender units to the right along the *X*-axis and scale it up to twice its original size. With the cursor in the 3D window, press the I key and select "LocRotScale" to insert a second key frame. You will see another yellow key frame line (Figure 9.8). When you scrub the animation between frames 25 and 75, you will see the cube move and change in size—you are manually playing the animation. Note that the action only takes place between frames 25 and 75, which is the location of our key frames; no action takes place on either side of the key frames.

9.3 Viewing Your Animation

To actually play a preview of the animation, move the green line in the "Timeline" to frame 1 then press Alt + the A key with the cursor in the 3D window. Say "one thousand" to yourself slowly (counting 1 second, while the green line in the "Timeline" moves across to frame 25). You will see the cube remain stationary until the green line reaches frame 25, then it will move and increase in size. At frame 75, it stops moving and changing size. The green line in the "Timeline" continues on to frame 250, then jumps back to frame 1 and the preview of the animation plays again. Press Esc to stop playing. Another way to skin this cat is to press the play button in the "Timeline" window (Figure 9.9). This button is much like the play button on any video or audio player.

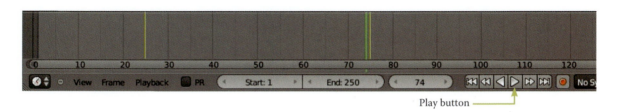

Play button

Figure 9.9

You can add more key frames to your animation to move, scale, and rotate your actor around the screen. For the most part, location and size keys work flawlessly but care needs to be taken with rotation keys. If you try to rotate an object too far in one set of keys, the object may not rotate in the direction you want it to and it may rotate oddly. Try small angular movements between keys while rotating. There are ways to control this better and tools to simplify the process, which will all be discussed later. Besides rotation, the movement of your actor may not be exactly as planned. Blender automatically defaults to trying to create a smooth flow through the key frames.

9.4 The Graph Editor Window

The "Graph Editor" window shows a graphical display of the animation. The graphs can be edited to refine and control the actions. Split the 3D window vertically and change one part to the "Graph Editor" window. In the "Graph Editor" window two panels open: on the

Lesson 07
07-02
Graph Editor

RHS is the graphical display panel and to the LHS is the "Dope Sheet" (Figure 9.10). Note: in the "Graph Editor" window header that you are in F-Curve mode. The alternative mode is "Drivers" which will be discussed later.

Examine the dope sheet panel (Figure 9.11). In the 3D window, we entered "Keyframes" and selected "LocRotScale" as the type. The dope sheet shows a file tree with headings for

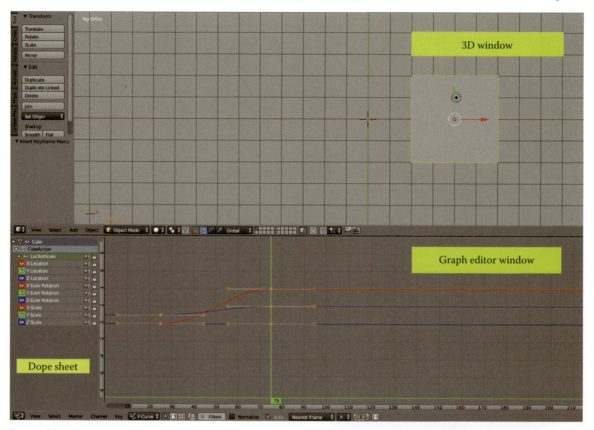

Figure 9.10

Expand/collapse the display

Click the eyeball to toggle on and off

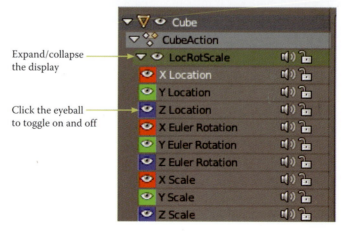

Figure 9.11

9. Animation Basics

"Cube," "CubeAction," and "LocRotScale." At the LHS of each line, there is a small white triangle that, when clicked with the LMB, opens or closes the directory. Click the LMB on the triangle next to "LocRotScale" to display the list of channels (graphs) in the graphical display. Next to the triangle you should see an eye icon. Clicking the eye icon next to "LocRotScale" activates all of the channels. Click again to close the channels. Each line is a channel for an action in the animation. For instance, the top line "X Location" is the channel for the movement of the cube along the X-axis. Clicking the LMB on each of the eye icons will toggle the display on or off. Click all the eye icons except the "X Location" channel. If the name "X Location" turns black and the channel in the graphical display disappears, click the LMB on the name. With only the eye icon for "X Location" active, only the graph for the location of the cube along the X-axis is shown (Figure 9.12). In the "Dope Sheet," X Location is showing with white text indicating that the channel is selected. All other channels are in black text (deselected). If you click on the black "Y Location," it turns white and "X Location" turns black. You have selected the "Y Location" channel. The X Location graph remains displayed, but it is a faint red line graph. The Y Location graph will not display until you click the eye icon.

Note the vertical and horizontal green lines in the graphical display; these are cursors. The vertical green line is the same as the cursor in the "Timeline" window. The horizontal green line cursor provides a visual location for the vertical scale at the LHS. This scale

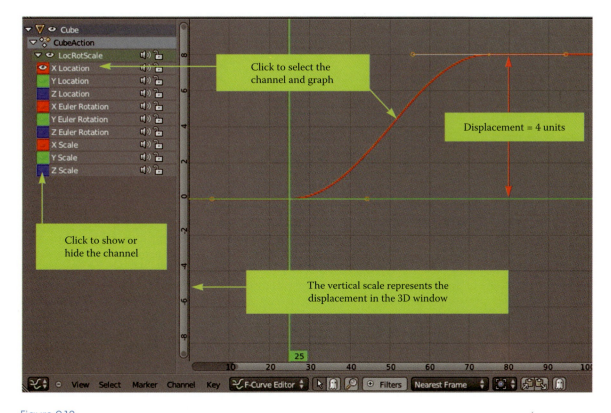

Figure 9.12

represents the value for the action. For instance, with the "X Location" channel displayed, the values represent the displacement along the *X*-axis of the 3D window. Examine the "X Location" channel in the graphical display. The red line has two short orange lines attached to it. Each orange line has a dot at the center and a dot at each end; these orange lines are called handles. We are looking at a Bezier curve and the orange lines are called control handles—the control handles are used to change the shape of the curve. I mentioned this type of curve before (Bezier), and will come back to this topic later.

As previously stated, the location of the vertical green line of the cursor represents the frame number of the animation. You will see it aligns with the frame numbers across the bottom of the window, and at the lower end of the line, a green box holds the frame number. You can click on this line and scrub through the animation the same way as you can in the "Timeline" window. Like all windows in Blender, with the cursor located in that panel, pressing the number pad + and − keys will scale the panel up or down.

Let's get back to the red line ("X Location" channel). The red line shows that from frames 1 to 25, there is no displacement of the actor from the midpoint. From frames 25 to 75, the actor moves from the midpoint of the 3D window to 4 Blender units along the *x*-axis. From frames 75 to 250, the actor remains displaced from the midpoint by 4 Blender units. This is the movement observed when we play the animation. If you now open the eyeball for any one of the "Scale" channels in the dope sheet, you will see a red, green, and blue line representing the fact that the actor changes from 1 Blender unit in size to 2 Blender units in size between frames 25 and 75. The three lines represent the *X*-, *Y*-, and *Z*-axis, respectively.

9.5 Editing the Curve

So far we have introduced "Keyframes" to set up how we want our actor to behave during the animation and we have seen how that action is graphically represented. We will now see how we can alter the behavior of our actor by altering the shape of the curve representing that action. Remember the type of curve being considered is a "Bezier" curve, which is designed to be edited.

Go back to the red line (the X Location channel). With the cursor in the graphical display, press the A key twice to make sure you have the line selected (the control handles turn off and on). If the line shows solid red with the two orange handles, you are in edit mode; if not, press the Tab key. If you are not in edit mode, the line will be a broken red line without handles.

Pressing the A key with the mouse cursor in the graphical display selects and deselects all graphs (the control handles turn on and off). After deselecting all graphs you select an individual graph by clicking the channel in the dope sheet. Remember the graph will not display unless you have clicked the eye icon for that channel. You may also RMB click on one of the control handles in the graphical display to select an individual graph.

It is important to have the line selected (bright red) before additional control points can be added.

Select the X Location graph (red line) with the RMB in the "Dope Sheet" panel and press the A key to deselect the line; you will have a red line with black dots at the location of the handles. Select the handle at frame 75 (click the RMB on the center dot); the handle will be orange and the line will be bright red. Press the G key and drag the mouse and move the handle up 1 unit then click LMB. Now, click on the right-hand dot on the end of the handle with the RMB, and the left-hand half of the handle fades. Then, click on

the right-hand dot on the end of the handle with the RMB and, while holding the mouse button pressed, drag the end of the handle down and to the right. The shape of the curve arches up (Figure 9.13). Note: After starting the movement you can release the RMB and continue dragging. Click LMB to finish the action.

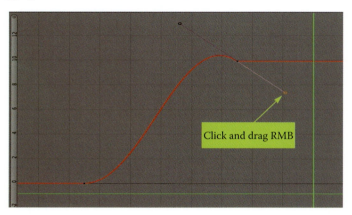

Click and drag RMB

Figure 9.13

Now, if you scrub through your animation between frames 25 and 75, you will see the actor move along the *x*-axis from zero displacement at frame 25 to something more than 5 Blender units, then return to 5 Blender units (Remember we started at 4 units, moved up to 5 units. The arch takes us beyond 5.) at frame 75. The movement of the actor is being dictated by the shape of the curve. This demonstrates that the shape of the curve can be altered by moving the ends of the control handles or by selecting the center point of the control handle thus affecting the movement of the cube.

Another feature of the "Bezier" curve is that control handles may be added anywhere on the curve. In the graphical editor with your "X Location" graph (red line) selected, place your mouse cursor on the line between frames 25 and 75, hold the Ctrl key, and click on the line with the LMB (Figure 9.14). Another control handle is created; this is actually another "Keyframe" as you will see by the yellow line that has been placed in the "Timeline" window. You can enter a new "Keyframe" this way anywhere on the graph.

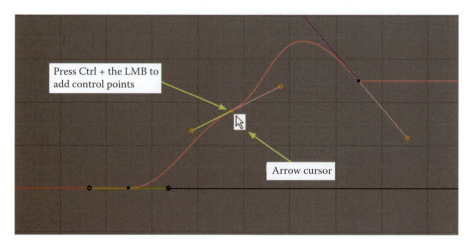

Press Ctrl + the LMB to add control points

Arrow cursor

Figure 9.14

9.6 Other Types of Curves

I had previously made note that, by default, Blender selects the "Bezier"-type interpolation to insert frames between "Keyframes." At this point, it should also be noted that there are two other options. In the "Graph Editor" window, select all the channels in the "Dope Sheet" panel by clicking open the eye icons. All the graphs will display in the graphical editor panel. Now press the A key twice to make sure they are all selected.

Go to the "Graph Editor" window header, "Key" button, "Interpolation Mode" and you will see the option to select "Constant," "Linear," or "Bezier" and a variety of additional options. Clicking on "Constant" or "Linear" will change the type of graph and therefore change the action of the actor. "Constant" results in a dramatic quick change from one state to the other at a given frame, while "Linear" produces a change following a straight line graph between points (Figure 9.15). The choice of these types of graphs and motions depends on how you want your actor to behave in the animation. Both of the alternatives to "Bezier" give the option to grab and move points and to add additional points on the graph, but "Bezier" is by far the most flexible of the three.

Blender interpolates to add frames between the "Keyframes" according to which of the previous graph options were selected. Blender can also figure out what to do with the frames of the animation before the first "Keyframe" and after the last "Keyframe," which

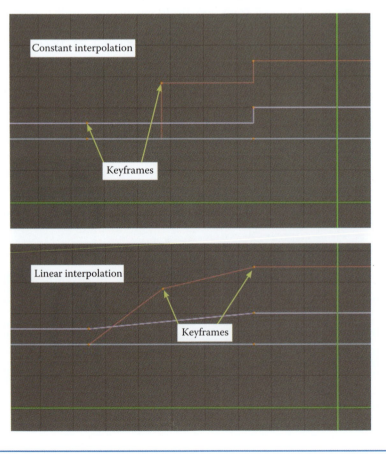

Figure 9.15

is called "Extrapolation." There are two extrapolation options in Blender: "Constant" and "Linear." By default, Blender selects "Constant."

Constant extrapolation can be seen with the "X Location" channel selected in the "Dope Sheet" panel. With "Keyframes" at frames 25 and 75, Blender has interpolated the in-between frames according to the default "Bezier" method. That is, Blender has inserted frames that comply with a "Bezier" curve. On either side of the "Keyframes," you can see horizontal lines that dictate no further change in status. This is constant extrapolation. If you go to the "Graph Editor" window header, "Channel" button, "Extrapolation Mode" and select "Linear Extrapolation," notice what happens to the curve. Blender takes a look at frames 25 and 26 and from the data plots a straight line coming up at an angle. Blender also looks at frames 74 and 75 and plots a straight line curve leaving the curve. The action of the actor before and after the two "Keyframes" will follow these straight line curves.

9.7 Modifying Curves

So far we have discussed creating graphical curves and how to change or modify them, thus changing how our actor behaves in the scene. This has been accomplished by working in the "Graphical Display" panel and the "Dope Sheet" panel. Blender also provides a "Properties" panel which gives precision control over the graphs.

To demonstrate in the "Dope Sheet" panel, deselect all channels. With your mouse cursor in the dope sheet, press the A key until all the channels are grayed out. Click on all the eye icons until they are open. This makes the graph for each channel visible in the graphical display but they are not selected. With the mouse cursor in the graphical display panel press the N key to display the properties panel with a "View Properties" tab (Figure 9.16). Click on the triangle next to the tab name to open the tab. Since all the graphs are deselected the tab is showing properties for the "Graph Editor" window cursors only (vertical and horizontal green lines). Unchecking the "Show Cursor" button (click to remove the tick) hides the horizontal cursor.

The "Cursor" X and Y values give the coordinates for the intersection point of the cursors (X = Frame number and Y = Blender units). If you RMB click a "Keyframe" (Black dot on a graph) you select the "Keyframe" and the graph. Note the channel for that graph is selected in the "Dope Sheet" (text shows white). Clicking on "Cursor from Selection" button in the "Properties" panel, "View Properties" tab centers the intersection point of the cursors on the selected "Keyframe." You will observe that in selecting the "Keyframe," other tabs display in the "Properties" panel (Figure 9.17).

Toggle the green line on and off

Figure 9.16

Figure 9.17

"Active F-Curve"—display color: shows the color of the selected graph. "Auto XYZ to RGB"—shows Blender's automatic color selection for the selected graph. You may click on the selection menu and choose "User Defined" to select your own color.

"Active Keyframe"—displays numeric data panels (sliders) with values pertaining to the selected "Keyframe." You may adjust these values giving very accurate placement of the selected "Keyframe" and therefore precise control.

"Modifiers"—a selection of eight modifiers for effecting the selected graph. For example, selecting the "Noise" modifier changes the straight line of the graph to a jiggled line which in turn jiggles the movement of the object in the 3D window.

At this point, we are interested in modifying our curve, not changing its color. Note the "Modifiers" tab with its "Add Modifier" button. Clicking on this button produces a drop down menu with eight options. We will not attempt to demonstrate all of these options at this time, but several are of particular interest.

Other modifiers of particular interest are demonstrated as follows: Have the "X Location" channel curve selected in the graph editor panel. Now click on "Add Modifier" and select "Cycles" (Figure 9.18). The graph changes rather dramatically. The curve between frames 25 and 75 is the same, but instead of straight lines on either side, Blender has duplicated this curve. By selecting "Cycles," we have made the movement of the curve cycle in 25-frame increments on either side of the 25-to-75 frame block.

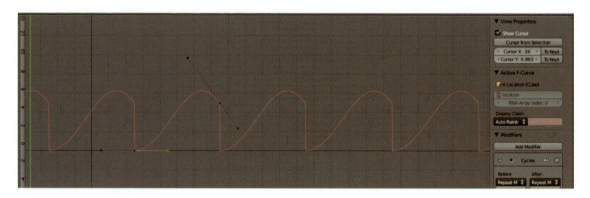

Figure 9.18

Lesson 07
07-03
Cyclic
Animation

We are starting to get into the complexity of Blender and its multiple options. Look at the little "Cycles" panel that has displayed under the "Add Modifier" button. Note the "Before" and "After" options. Each of these has drop down menu buttons that give options for how the cycles are to be repeated before and after the frame block. Click on the "After" button and select "Repeat Mirrored" (Figure 9.19).

Let's have another demonstration. Click on the "X" at the top right-hand corner of the "Cycles" panel to delete the modifier. Click on "Add Modifier" again and this time select the "Noise" modifier we began with (Figure 9.20). This produced a graph with the jitters, and if you scrub your animation, you will see that's exactly what you get in the movement of the actor. Of course, it doesn't stop there; the "Noise" modifier contains

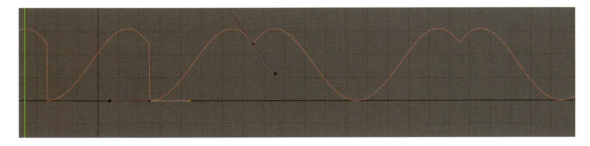

Figure 9.19

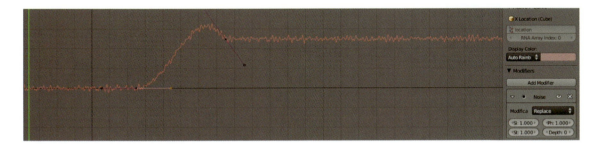

Figure 9.20

a drop down to select suboptions and buttons to alter values for the options. You now have plenty to play with.

For another demonstration, delete the "Noise" modifier and select the "Built In Function" modifier. This produces a straight sinusoidal graph. Check out the drop down menu in this modifier panel for the selection of graphs based on various mathematical functions. All selections have buttons to control values that are introduced, which provides more stuff to play with.

To get more experienced, try adding multiple modifiers to your curve. Just click on the "Add Modifier" button without deleting what you already have.

9.8 Automatic Key Framing

Previously, "Keyframes" have been inserted in our animation by having our cursor in the 3D window, moving the timeline to a particular frame, changing the status of our object, and then pressing the I key and selecting a "Keyframe" option. Besides this method, after the frame has been selected and the object status changed, we can press the "Insert Keyframe" button in the "Animation" tab of the toolbar at the LHS of the 3D window. (The T key toggles between hiding and showing this panel.)

There is another method that makes life a lot easier when multiple key frames are required. In the "Timeline" window header, you will see a red button to the right of the play control buttons. Clicking on this button toggles automatic key framing on and off

Toggle automatic key framing on and off

Figure 9.21

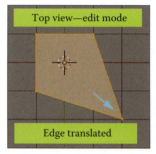

Top view—edit mode

Edge translated

Figure 9.22

Figure 9.23

(Figure 9.21). With auto on, whenever you move, scale, or rotate your actor object in the 3D window, a key frame will be inserted at whatever frame you have selected. Remember to turn this off after you're finished using it.

9.9 Rotation Explained

The simple idea of animating an object to rotate about its center requires a little investigation to understand the concept. Once again an example is the best way to demonstrate what happens in the process.

9.9.1 Rotation Animation Set-Up

Start with the default Blender scene with the "Cube" object at the center of the world. Place the 3D window in top orthographic view (press Num Pad 7, then Num Pad 5).

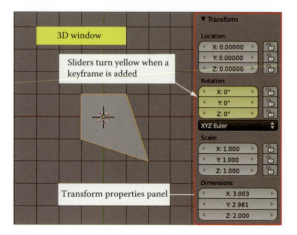

3D window

Sliders turn yellow when a keyframe is added

Transform properties panel

Figure 9.24

Deform the cube as shown in Figure 9.22 to make a pointer for rotation.

In the "Timeline" window with the timeline cursor (the green vertical line) at frame 1 and the mouse cursor in the 3D window, press I key and select "Rotation" to insert a "Keyframe." Move the timeline cursor (the vertical green line) to frame 60 (Figure 9.23).

Press the N key to display the "Transform" properties panel at the RHS of the 3D window (Figure 9.24).

Enter 120 in the Z rotation value slider.

In the 3D window, press I key again to enter a second "Keyframe" (Figure 9.25).

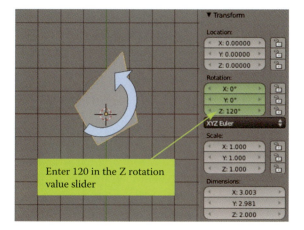

Enter 120 in the Z rotation value slider

Figure 9.25

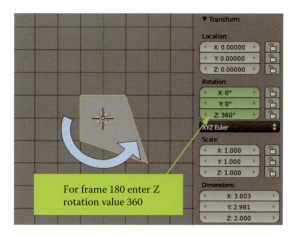

For frame 180 enter Z rotation value 360

Figure 9.27

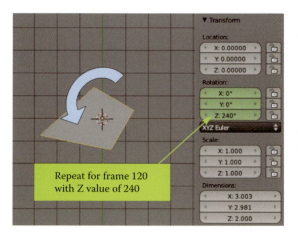

Repeat for frame 120 with Z value of 240

Figure 9.26

Repeat the process for frame 120 with a Z rotation value of 240 (Figure 9.26).

For frame 180, enter Z rotation value 360 (Figure 9.27).

This has set up a 360° rotation of the deformed cube. Change the animation end frame in the timeline to 180. Press the play button in the "Timeline" window to see the result (Figure 9.28).

Note that the animated rotation is not a smooth constant motion.

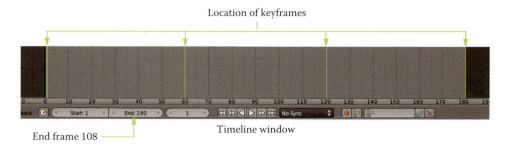

Location of keyframes

End frame 108

Timeline window

Figure 9.28

9.9.2 Examine the F Curve

Divide the 3D window in two and make one half the "Graph Editor" window. Having performed the animation set-up, you will see a graph displayed in this window. It is probably difficult to see since the window requires scaling and positioning.

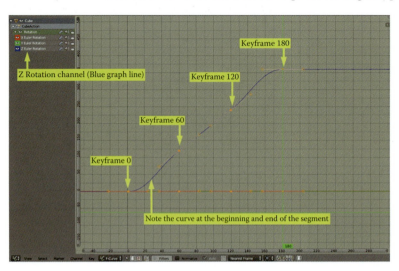

Use the Num Pad + (Plus) and − (Minus) keys or the MMB to zoom the window. Shift key + click and hold MMB to drag and center the graph. Ctrl key + MMB drag right and left to scale the graph on the timeline. Scale and position the graph as shown in the diagram (Figure 9.29).

When inserting "Keyframes," Blender draws "Bezier"-type graphs between the location of the "Keyframes" on the timeline. The graphs represent the motion in the translation. The graphs are curved at the beginning and end of each segment which is indicating an acceleration and deceleration and this is exactly what is observed when playing the animation. There is speeding up and slowing down during the rotation.

Figure 9.29

9.9.3 Correct the Motion

The rotation animation was set up using multiple "Keyframes," since in the past Blender tended to be somewhat erratic in producing a nice smooth rotation when setting one

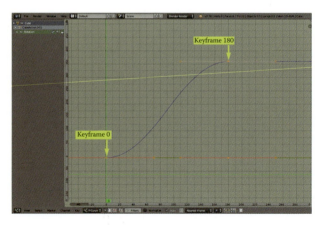

"Keyframe" at frame 1 and another at the last frame for 360°. This however appears to have been corrected in later versions of the program. We can therefore set up an animation by simply inserting two "Keyframes," one at the beginning and one at the end of the rotation. Create the animation as before using only two "Keyframes" (Figure 9.30).

Play the animation and look at the F Curve in the "Graph Editor" window. The motion is smoother but not constant. We still have acceleration and deceleration at the beginning and end of the cycle.

In the "Graph Editor" window header, click on "Key" and select "Interpolation Mode," type "Linear" to produce a straight line "F Curve"

Figure 9.30

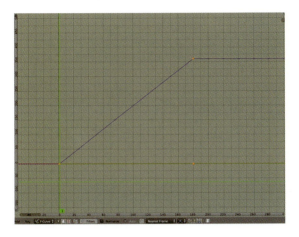

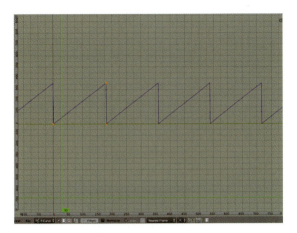

Figure 9.31

Figure 9.32

graph, that is, constant rotation. Having done this, we have produced a single 360° rotation only (Figure 9.31).

Since we set the total animation to rotate 360° in 180 frames, and the animation repeats itself it appears that we have perpetual rotation.

To truly produce perpetual motion in the "Graph Editor" window header, click on "Channel," select "Extrapolation Mode," "Make Cyclic (F Modifier)." This duplicates the F Curve along the timeline to infinity (Figure 9.32). Having done this we have produced a single 360° rotation only. Change the animation end frame to something like 1000 and play the animation to see a smooth constant rotation (Figure 9.32).

9.10 Rotation Using F Curves

In this demonstration we will manipulate "F Curves" to produce a rotation animation.

In Section 9.9, we set an animation to produce a rotation of an object about an axis at its center. In this demonstration, we will have the object rotate about an external center.

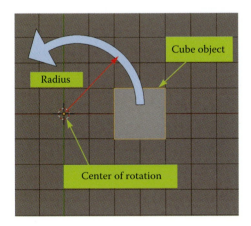

Note: By default no "F Curve Graph" exists in the "Graph Editor" window. An animation has to be created to produce an "F Curve."

The objective of this demonstration is to have a "Cube" object rotate about a center as shown in Figure 9.33.

Figure 9.33

9.10.1 Create an F Curve

The first step is to create an animation which produces an "F Curve" which we can modify.

With a new Blender scene showing the default "Cube" object, change the 3D view to "Top Orthographic" view (Num Pad 7 + Num Pad 5). Set up a translation animation of the cube to move on the *x*-axis from –5 Blender units at frame 1 to +5 Blender units at frame 180. It is best to enter the translation values in the "Translation" properties panel in the 3D window (press N key to display the panel).

Having created the animation an "F Curve Graph" is displayed in the "Graph Editor" window. The graph shows a "Bezier"-type curve (Figure 9.34).

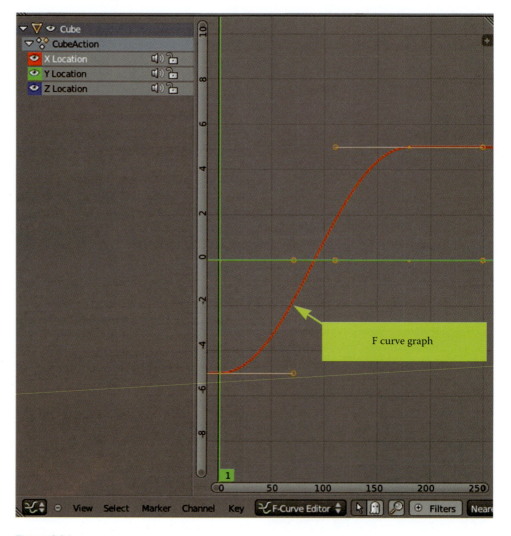

Figure 9.34

9. Animation Basics

9.10.2 *X*-Axis Channel: Add Conversion Modifier

Perform the operations as listed in Figure 9.35.

The "Graph Editor" window may require some adjustment for the graphs to display properly. Here are some tips: with the mouse cursor in the graph editor window, press Ctrl + MMB and drag right or left to scale the curve. Press Shift + MMB and drag the mouse to pan the view.

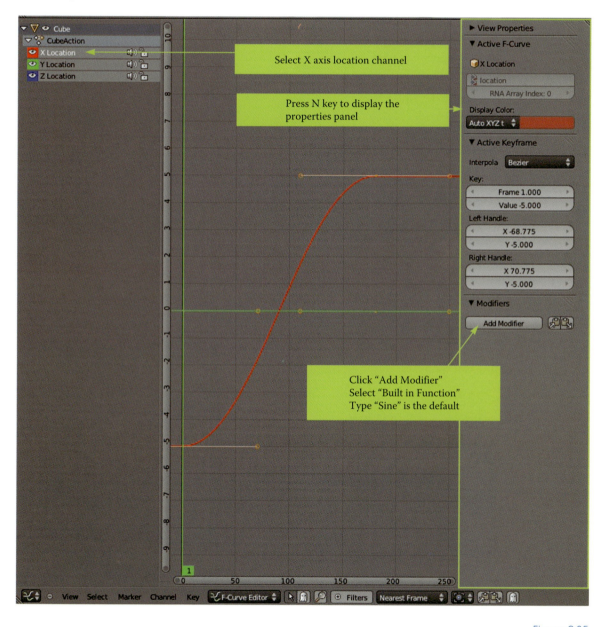

Figure 9.35

Having performed the operations noted in Figure 9.35, the "Bezier" curve will display as a sine curve as shown in Figure 9.36. Note the amplitude of the sine curve −1 to +1. If you play the animation, the cube simply oscillates to the left and right of the center in the 3D window.

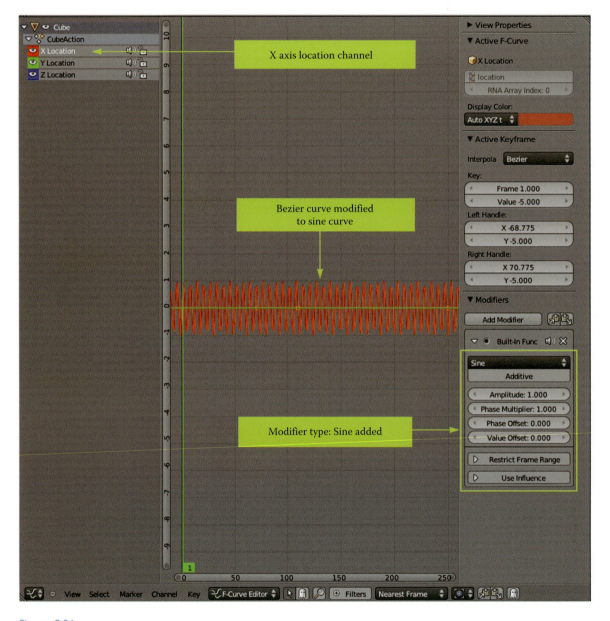

Figure 9.36

9.10.3 *Y*-Axis Channel: Add Conversion Modifier

In the "Graph Editor" window, select the *Y*-axis translation channel. In the "Graph Editor Properties Panel," click "Add Modifier," select "Built in Function." With the modifier displayed change type "Sine" to "Cosine" (Figure 9.37).

In both cases, the translation graphs (F Curves) have been converted from the original "Bezier"-type curves to type sine and cosine curves, respectively. Note: The *Y*-axis curve was a horizontal straight line since we only set up an *X*-axis translation animation.

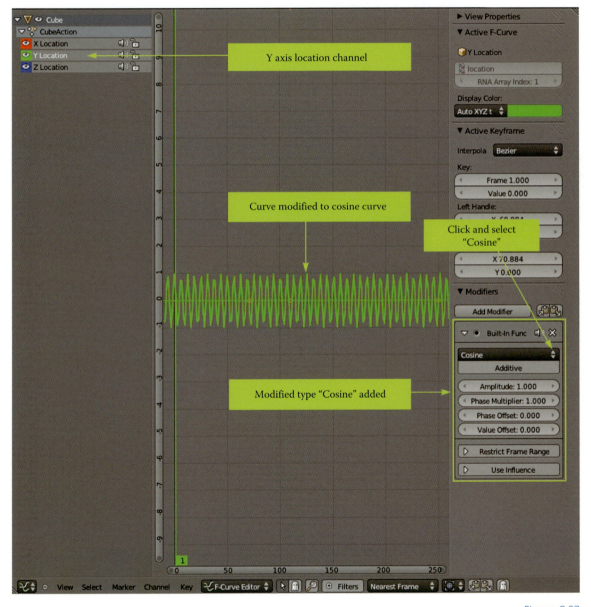

Figure 9.37

9.10.4 Adjust Modifier Values

If you play the animation at this point, the cube will madly spin in a very tight circle.

In the modifier, adjusting the "Amplitude" varies the radius of the rotation. Having different values for the *x*-axis sine amplitude and the *y*-axis cos amplitude will result in an elliptical orbit for the rotation. Adjusting "Phase Multiplier" varies the speed of rotation. A suggested value for starters is 0.181 (Figures 9.38 and 9.39).

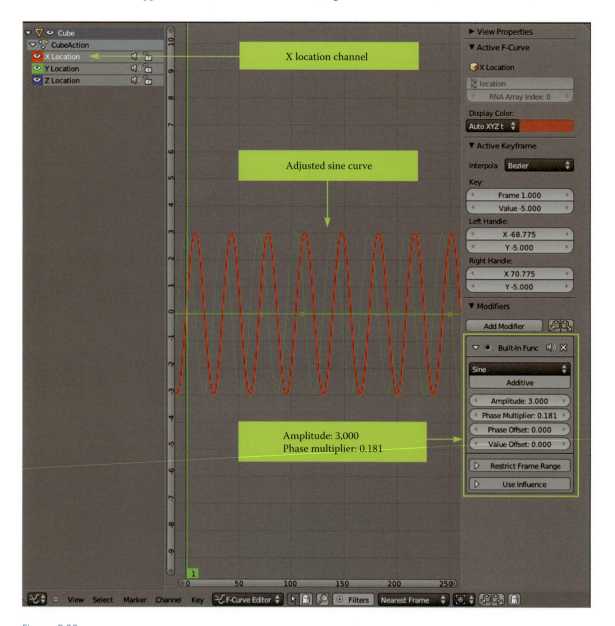

Figure 9.38

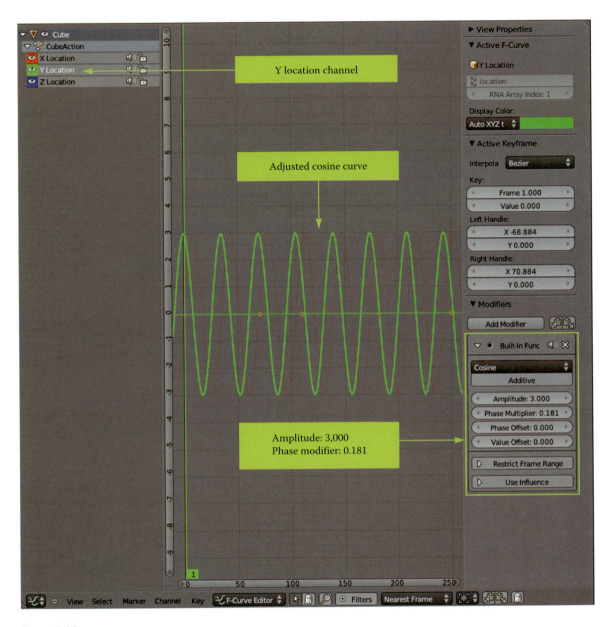

Figure 9.39

9.11 Animating Other Features

Having an understanding of animation basics allows us to look at some of the other things that can be animated in Blender besides the movement, rotation, and size of an object. For example, it is also possible to animate materials, textures, lamps, and world settings.

The following is a list of some of the features that can be animated:

- Material animation options
  - *Material RGB values.* Color can be animated to change.
  - *Alpha.* The transparency of an object can be animated.
  - *Halo size.* A halo can grow or shrink in an animation. Setting a halo to zero will make it disappear.
  - *Texture offset.* Texture applied to an object can be animated. It can move across the face or change in size.
- Lamp animation options
  - *Lamp RGB values.* The color of light can be animated to change.
  - *Energy.* The intensity of light can vary.
  - *Spotlight size.* The angle of the beam can be animated to change.
  - *Texture.* Texture can be applied to a lamp and animated.
- World animation options
  - *Zenith RGB.* Color of the zenith (top) can be animated. This is great for sunsets or sunrises.
  - *Horizon RGB.* Color of the horizon (bottom) can be animated.
  - *Mist.* Fog can be animated for interesting effects.
  - *Stars.* Stars can be made to move.
  - *Texture offset and size.* Texture applied to a world can be made to move.

- Camera animation
  - The camera may be animated to follow a path.

The list above contains only some of the features that can be animated in Blender. To give you an idea how this is possible, we will take a closer look at the following two examples.

9.11.1 Example 1: Color

Let's start with the color of an object. Open up a new scene in Blender (the default scene with the "Cube" object will do). With the "Cube" selected in the 3D window, go to the "Properties window" and click on the "Material" button.

The properties window with the "Material" button activated shows a whole bunch of tabs for controlling how the surface of the object displays in the 3D window. To begin, note the "Preview" tab showing a dull gray sphere and below that the "Diffuse" tab with a button showing the same dull gray color.

Look at the "Timeline" window across the bottom of the screen. The green line cursor is located at frame 1 of a 250-frame animation (the light gray area of the window relating to the scale ranging from 0 to 250 along the bottom of the window above the header). We are going to insert "Keyframes" on the timeline so that we can make the color of our cube object change from gray to red over 50 frames of the animation. You could change the starting color of the cube by clicking on the diffuse color button with the LMB to display a

color picker, and click anywhere in the colored circle to change the color, but let's just leave things alone for the time being and stick with dull old gray.

Instead of clicking with the LMB on the diffuse color button, click with the **RMB** and in the menu that displays click on "Insert Keyframes." You have inserted a "Keyframe" at frame 1 on the timeline. Change to frame 50 (scrub the green line in the "Timeline" window). Now click with the LMB on the diffuse color button and in the color picker that displays, click on the red part of the colored circle. This changes the color of the cube to red. Click on the diffuse color button again, this time with the **RMB** and then click on "Insert Keyframes" to insert a key frame at frame 50. Now when you scrub the timeline, you will see the color of the cube change from gray to red over the 50 frames. Hitting Alt + the A key will play this animation. If you open the graphical editor window, you will see the graphical representation of this animation.

9.11.2 Example 2: Spotlight Size

To show how the spotlight may be animated, we first need to put a spotlight into the Blender scene. Let's start again with the default Blender scene with the cube. Change the 3D window to show the front-side view and deselect the cube with the A key. With the cursor in the 3D window, hit number pad 1, hit Shift + the A key, then select "Add"— "Lamp"—"Spot." You will see some orange lines appear in the 3D window. Hit the G key (grab) then the Z key and move the mouse up. The G key lets you grab the spotlight so you can move it and the Z key confines the movement to the z-axis. You could also have clicked with the LMB on the blue arrow of the 3D manipulator widget and moved the spotlight up the Z-axis. You will see that you have actually moved a cone in the screen. Hit the S key and move the cursor toward the apex of the cone to scale the spotlight down a bit. The light is at the apex of the cone and the circle at the bottom represents the circle of light it would generate.

Now go to the "Properties" window and press the "Object Data" button to display all the buttons that control the properties of the spotlight. Look for the "Spot Shape" tab and you'll notice the button with "Size: 45" in it, which indicates that the angle of the cone is 45°. The "Timeline" window is again across the bottom of the screen and the green line indicates that we are at frame number 1.

Right click on the "Spot Shape Size" button and select "Insert Keyframes" from the menu that displays. The "Size" button will turn yellow indicating that you have inserted a key frame in the timeline. Scrub the green line in the timeline to frame 50. The "Size" button turns green because there is no key frame at frame 50 yet. Left click on the "Size" button and, while holding the mouse button, move the mouse to the left, decreasing the value of the cone angle. The angle of the cone in the 3D window will decrease accordingly. Right click on the "Size" button and select "Insert Keyframes" again, and the button turns yellow. We now have a "Keyframe" at frame 50. Scrub the green line in the "Timeline" window between frames 1 and 50 to see the angle of the cone change. You have animated the spotlight size.

> **Note:** Many properties can be animated this way by inserting "Keyframes" and changing property values. You have lots of experimenting to do.

9.12 Keying Sets

You can add multiple properties to a group called a "Keying Set," which allows you to animate a whole bunch of stuff at one time. You do this by first defining a "Keying Set." We will again look at our cube actor in the default Blender window. Let's say you want to have the cube move along the x-axis and change color at the same time. Not too difficult—just add a bunch of "Keyframes." But consider if you had a lot of property changes. Adding all those key frames one by one could become tedious. It would be nice if you could do the property changes, then hit a button to add all the key frames in one go. Let's do it.

With the cube selected in the 3D window, go to the "Properties" window. We will consider the movement part of the exercise first. Click on the "Object" button in the header and find the "Transform" tab and the "Location" buttons. You will see the values X: 0.000, Y: 0.000, and Z: 0.000. This shows that the cube is at the center of the 3D window in all planes. So, we are concerned with the movement on the X-axis. Right click on "X: 0.000" and in the panel that displays, click "Add Single to Keying Set." If you look at the "Timeline" window header, you will see a button labeled "Buttons Keying Set" and two little key icons next to it. One of them has a red line across it. Note in the timeline that you are at frame 1. You have just entered the information into a "Keying Set," telling Blender that at frame 1 the cube is located on the X-axis at position 0.000.

Now let's consider the color part of the exercise. In the "Properties" window, click on the "Material" button. Right click on the "Diffuse Color" button then click on "Add to Keying Set." The information for the color has been added to the keying set.

In the "Timeline" window header, click on the first of the little key icons (not the one with the red line). You have entered a key frame for the location and color of the cube. You can see this in the graph editor window by opening up all the headings in the dope sheet. Now move to frame 40 or wherever you wish on the "Timeline." Change the value for the "Transform"—"Location"—"X axis" in the "Properties" window, "Object" tab. Right click the new value and click "Add Single to Keying Set." Do the same thing for the "Material"—"Diffuse color" value. Click on "Add to Keying Set." Now click on the first of the key icons again to add the new "Keyframe" at frame 40. Scrub the "Timeline" or play the animation to see the cube move and change color.

9.13 Vertex Animation

Up to now we have considered the animation of an object but no doubt you will, at some stage, want to animate the shape of an object. This entails animating the mesh vertices on the surface of the object. You can select individual vertices or groups of vertices in "Edit" mode and move them about but you will find that you are unable to insert "Keyframes" for this movement in "Edit" mode. Do not despair, there is a way.

We introduced Blender's hidden features, "Add-ons" in Chapter 1 (Section 1.15) and this as an example. In the "User Preferences" window, "Add-ons" tab. In the "Animation" category you will see the "Add-on" named "AnimAll." This tool allows the animation of several features one of them being "Point." Consider "Point" as referring to a vertex or group of vertices.

In the "Users Preferences" window activate "AnimAll" by ticking the little box at the right-hand end of the Add-on line. Close the "User Preferences" window (Figure 9.40).

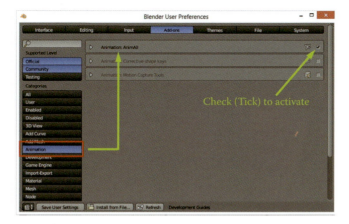

Figure 9.40

Figure 9.41

Figure 9.42

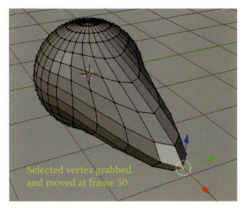

Selected vertex grabbed and moved at frame 50

Figure 9.44

In the 3D window "Tools Panel" (T key toggles display and hide), click on the "Animation" tab at the left-hand side and you will see that the "AnimAll" tab has been added to the panel. Check (tick) "Point" (Figure 9.41).

Figure 9.43

To demonstrate how "Point" is used replace the default "Cube" with a "UV Sphere." Tab into "Edit" mode, deselect all vertices on the sphere (press the A key) and select a single vertex. Enable "Proportional Editing" in the 3D window header (Figure 9.42). With the "Timeline" window cursor at frame 1, click on the "Insert" button in the "AnimAll" tab in the "Tools Panel" (Figure 9.43). This inserts a "Keyframe" for the location of the selected vertex at frame 1.

Move the timeline cursor to frame 50. Grab and move the selected vertex (Figure 9.44) and again press the "Insert" button in the "Tools Panel." This inserts a second "Keyframe" at frame 50 (Figure 9.45).

Timeline cursor moved to reveal the keyframe

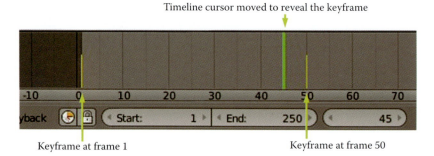

Figure 9.45

Keyframe at frame 1

Keyframe at frame 50

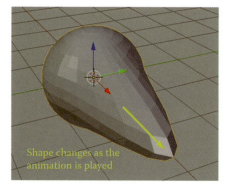

Shape changes as the
animation is played

Figure 9.46

Tab to "Object" mode. Move the timeline cursor to frame 1 and click. Scrub the timeline cursor or play the animation to see the shape of the cube change (Figure 9.46).

9.14 Animation Following Curves

Animating the movement of objects in a scene by inserting "Keyframes" can be very tedious when the movement is complex. To animate the movement of an object that twists and turns in the scene over many frames, you have to insert many "Keyframes." Editing the movement at a later stage after executing this method can be difficult, but there is an easier way.

Actually, there are at least two ways, both of which involve having an object follow a predetermined path. One method requires you to set a child/parent relationship between the object and the path; the other method requires that you place a "Follow Path" constraint on the object.

Lesson 07
07-04
Path Animation

Lesson 11
11-02
Relationship
Constraints Floor
Follow Path

9.14.1 Following a Path: The Child/Parent Relationship Method

Open Blender with the default scene containing the cube object. The scene will be displayed in "User Perspective" view. Change to "Top Orthographic" view (number pad 7 for top perspective view then number pad 5 for top orthographic view). By default, the cube is selected in object mode. Deselect the cube by pressing the A key.

We want the cube to move in the scene following a predetermined path. The path will be a curve path (Shift + the A Key—"Add"—"Curve"—"Path") (Figure 9.47). You can use any of the "Curve" options for your path, but for the time being we will use the "Path" option since it is the simplest.

Adding a curve path places a straight line on your screen in "Object" mode. Do not be confused. In Blender, this particular straight line is considered to be a curve and it is also a path. Scale the line to make it five times as long (S key + number pad 5 and click the LMB). If the line runs off the edge of the window, press the number pad – key to zoom out of the scene. The number pad + key will zoom in.

To start, we will make the cube move along the straight line of the curve path. This isn't very exciting, but it will show you the principles of the operation. Deselect the path with the A key and select the cube (click the RMB with the mouse cursor on the cube). Hold the Shift key and click the RMB on the curve path. The cube and the path will both be selected

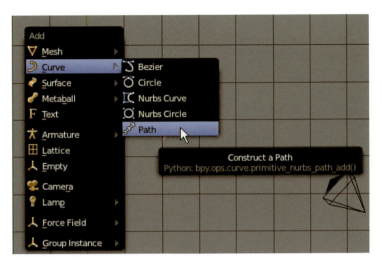

Figure 9.47

at the same time. The outline of the cube turns red. Make sure the cube is selected first followed by the path; it's as if you are pointing to the cube and saying "Cube, follow the path."

We will now apply a specific child/parent relationship. In a normal case, selecting the cube then shift selecting the path and applying an "Object" child/parent relationship would simply make the cube the child of the path. If the path moved, the cube would follow. However, we want the cube to move along the path. With both the cube and the path selected, press Ctrl + the P key and select "Follow Path" from the options displayed (Figure 9.48, the cube has been moved off the path). Remember that in the selection process, the cube must be selected first, followed by the path.

Deselect both the cube and the path with the A key and select only the cube. Move the cube along the Y-axis of the scene (the G key + the Y key and move the mouse). You will see a dotted line drawn from the cube to one end of the path. The line indicates that the child/parent relationship is in place. Move the cube to the end of the path where the dotted line is attached (Figure 9.49). Press Alt + the A key on the keyboard or click on the "Play"

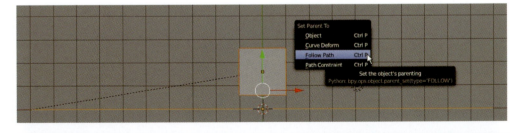

Figure 9.48

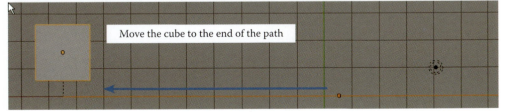

Move the cube to the end of the path

Figure 9.49

Properties window   Object data button

Figure 9.50

arrow in the "Timeline" window—either method will play an animation showing the cube moving along the path.

Blender has created a 100-frame animation. With the path selected, the details of the animation can be seen in the "Properties" window, "Object Data" button, "Path Animation" tab (Figure 9.50). You can also see a graphical display in the graph editor window (Figure 9.51).

Note: In the "Graph Editor" window, the movement of the cube is drawn as a red line inclined rather steeply. Since the line is straight, it shows that the cube moves with constant velocity (speed) along the path.

The scale along the bottom of the window shows frames of the animation and the vertical scale on the LHS shows displacement (how far the object moves). The displacement from one frame to the next is always the same, hence constant velocity. There is no acceleration or deceleration, as would be the case if you had used key frames.

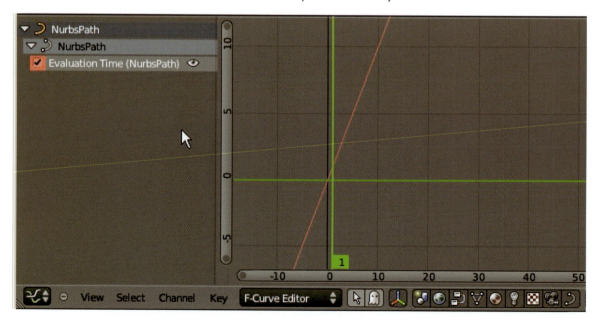

Figure 9.51

Now, if you decide that you want to move in something other than a straight line, the speed, acceleration, and direction of movement may have to be modified. The direction of movement is modified by altering the shape of the path in the 3D window. The variation in velocity and acceleration is altered in the "Graph Editor" window. We will first alter the direction of movement by reshaping the curve path.

In the 3D window, select the path by right clicking on it, and then tab to put the path into "Edit" mode. Remember, in the beginning of this section, we scaled the path to make it longer while it was in object mode. You can do the same thing in "Edit" mode. Just press the S key and drag the mouse or, if you know how many times longer you want the path to be, press the S key followed by a number key (use the number key at the top of the keyboard not a number pad key).

Note that increasing the length of the path does not increase the length of the animation. You still have 100 frames in the animation; therefore, when running the animation at 25 frames per second, your object will move along the path in 4 seconds. If you made the path twice as long, the object would move on the screen twice as fast. Another way to change the speed is to alter the number of frames in the animation in the "Properties" window, "Object Data" button, "Path Animation" tab.

If you increase the number of frames to 200, it will take the object twice as long to move along the same path length. Controlling the speed of the object can also be done in the "Graph Editor" window, but we will come back to that in a moment.

Note: With the path selected in edit mode, there are black chevrons along the path and several orange dots (Figure 9.52). The chevrons indicate the direction of motion and velocity. In this case, they are evenly spaced, indicating constant velocity. The direction may be reversed by pressing the W key for the "Specials" menu and selecting "Change Direction." The orange dots are control handles for shaping the path—there is one at each end and others in between the ends. By default, when you enter edit mode, all the control points are selected. Press the A key to deselect them, then right click on one point to select it alone.

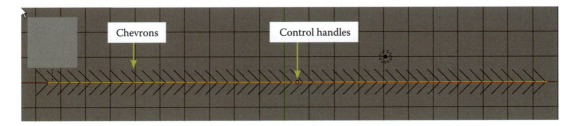

Chevrons   Control handles

Figure 9.52

If you have the manipulation widget turned on, the widget will be located at the selected control point. If you click on the widget handles (with the widget in translate manipulator mode) and drag the mouse, the control point will be moved and the shape of the path will

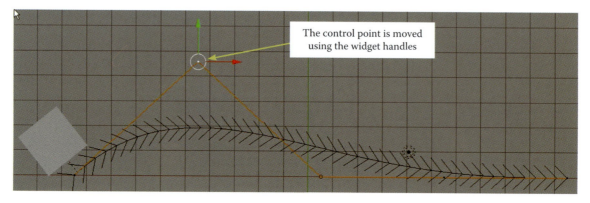

The control point is moved using the widget handles

Figure 9.53

be altered (Figure 9.53). You can select any of the control points and reshape the path in this way. Selecting an end control point and pressing the E key, then dragging the mouse will extrude the end of the path. You can go into front side view or end view and reshape the path in three dimensions, creating any shape you wish.

After reshaping the path, press Alt + the A key to see the cube move along the path. For the cube to follow the path with its axis aligned to the path, you must have "Follow" ticked in the "Properties" window, "Path Animation" tab. Shaping the path gets the cube moving around in the scene, but it moves along the path at a constant speed. In real life, if the cube came to a sharp corner without slowing down, it undoubtedly would suffer an accident. To create a realistic movement, we need to vary the speed.

Varying the speed is performed in the "Graph Editor" window. It helps at this stage if you have both the "Graph Editor" window and the 3D window displayed at the same time. Divide the 3D window in two horizontally and change one half to the "Graph Editor" window. You will probably have to zoom in on the "Graph Editor" window and pan the window into position. At this point, all we have is the red line showing a constant velocity and unfortunately the line is uneditable. The horizontal and vertical green lines are cursor lines; the vertical line is a cursor for positioning along the horizontal timeline measured in frames of the animation, and the horizontal line positions on the vertical displacement scale measured in Blender units.

On the LHS of the "Graph Editor," you will see the "Dope Sheet" panel. With the path selected in the 3D window, the dope sheet shows information associated with the path. Click on the lower white arrow at the LHS of the panel and a channel will display labeled "Evaluation Time." Clicking on the eyeball at the LHS of the channel toggles the display of the red line on and off. Clicking on the little speaker icon at the RHS of the channel toggles between selection and deselection of the channel.

The channel in the "Dope Sheet" panel is a graphical representation of information associated with the display in the "Evaluation Time" button in the "Properties" window, "Object Data" button, "Path Animation" tab (the green bar). The same information is displayed as the red line in the graph editor window.

So what is this "Evaluation Time" business? Let's evaluate what we have at this stage. In the 3D window, we have a cube object parented to a curve path. Blender has set the cube to traverse the path in 100 frames of the animation—this happens to be the first

100 frames of the animation. In the "Timeline" window at the bottom of the screen, the total animation is set at 250 frames starting at frame number 1 and ending at frame 250 (Figure 9.54). Playing the animation shows the cube moving along the path starting at frame 1 and reaching the end of the path at frame 100. The animation continues to play on to frame 250.

Figure 9.54

In the "Properties" window, "Object Data" button, "Path Animation" tab (with the path selected in the 3D window) "Frames: 100" is the number of frames to traverse the path. "Evaluation Time: 1.000" is where the cube is located on the path at frame 1. Increasing the "Evaluation Time" value moves the cube along the path, and increasing the value to 100 places the cube at the end of the path.

Note: At frame 1, the cube is not located exactly at the end of the path. It is in fact positioned 0.01 of the path length from the end (Figure 9.55). The animation starts at frame 1, not from 0. This is evident where the dotted line between the cube and the path is attached. Obviously you can't have zero frames or you wouldn't have an animation.

You may deduce that the "Evaluation Time" is saying, "This is what our cube is doing at this position." We are only considering location here, but if the cube was animated to change scale, rotate, or change color, its state would be evaluated at whatever position was selected. The "Evaluation Time" value is a percentage of the path length. However, we were considering how to change the velocity of the cube as it moved along the path— let's get back to it.

We have established that the "Evaluation Time" data cannot be modified. We will therefore remove it. With the "Evaluation Time" channel selected (highlighted in white) in

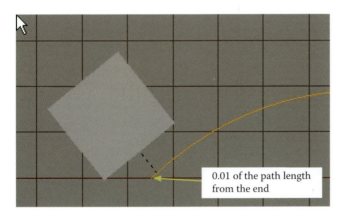

0.01 of the path length from the end

Figure 9.55

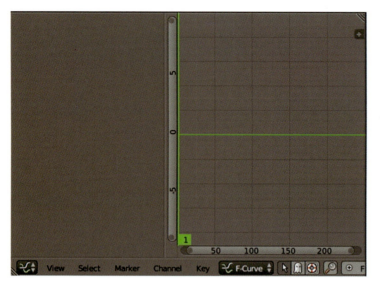

Figure 9.56

the "Dope Sheet" panel of the graph editor, place the mouse cursor in the panel and press the X key. The "Nurbs Path" data are deleted (Figure 9.56). If the animation is played, the cube does not move; the cube remains parented to the path but there is no longer an animation associated with it.

We will now set up a new animation. In the "Timeline" window make sure the cursor (green line) is located at frame 1 and that the cube is at the start of the path in the 3D window. With the path selected in the 3D window, go to the "Properties" window, "Object Data" button, "Path Animation" tab and set the "Evaluation Time" button value to 0.000. Right click on the "Evaluation Time" button and select "Insert Keyframe" from the drop down menu that displays (Figure 9.57).

The "Evaluation Time" button becomes shaded yellow and a "NurbsPath—Evaluation Time" channel is entered in the dope sheet panel (Figure 9.58). An orange dot displays at the intersection of the cursors (Green lines) in the "Graph Editor" window. The cursors are located at frame 1.

In the "Timeline" window, move the cursor to frame 150. We will make the cube move along the path in 150 frames. Change the "Evaluation Time" value to 100 to place the cube at the end of the path—we now have the cube at the end of the path at frame 150

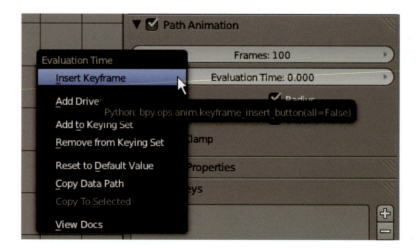

Figure 9.57

Figure 9.58

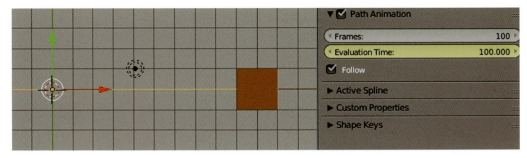

Figure 9.59

(Figure 9.59). Right click on the "Evaluation Time" button and insert another "Keyframe." Zoom in on the "Graph Editor" window and you will see a second "Keyframe" entered

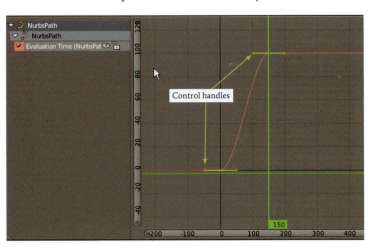

above the first at frame 150. The "Keyframes" now have handles attached showing that the animation curve is a "Bezier"-type curve, which means it is editable (Figure 9.60). In the "Timeline" window, return to frame 1 and press Alt + the A Key or press the "Play" button to play the

Figure 9.60

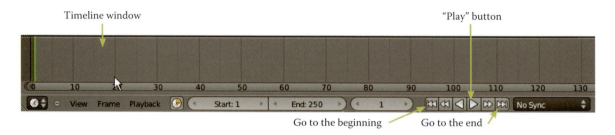

Timeline window   "Play" button

Go to the beginning   Go to the end

Figure 9.61

animation (Figure 9.61). When the cube moves along the path, there is acceleration at the start and deceleration at the end.

    Let's play with the movement of the cube as it traverses the path. To alter the movement of the cube, we will edit the animation curve in the graph editor window. To start, we will make the cube take longer to traverse the length of the path in the 3D window. With the mouse cursor in the "Graph Editor" window, press the A key to deselect the animation curve then right click on the key frame handle at frame 150 (the upper handle). Press the G key and move the mouse, dragging the handle to the right to frame 400 (Figure 9.62). We have told the cube to move along the path in 400 frames instead of 150 frames. Play the animation to see the cube crawl along.

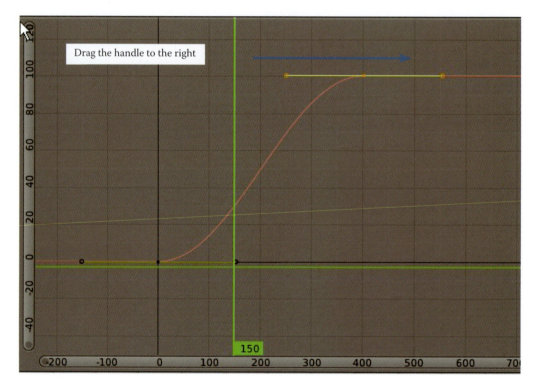

Drag the handle to the right

Figure 9.62

Whoops, the cube doesn't reach the end of the path! In the "Timeline" window, the end frame of the animation is still set at 250, so the animation replays after 250 frames and the cube never reaches the end of the path. In the timeline window, change the "End" value to 400 and replay (Figure 9.63). Now we're right!

Figure 9.63

Since the animation curve in the graph editor window is a "Bezier"-type curve, we can add handles to it to further refine movement. Press Ctrl and click the LMB on the curve to add a handle. Add another handle and then press the G key (grab) and position the handles approximately as shown in Figure 9.64. When the animation is replayed, the cube moves along the path then reverses before continuing on to the end. If the animation curve were horizontal between the two intermediate handles, the cube would simply

Figure 9.64

stop for a rest along the way. By playing with the animation curve in the graph editor and changing the shape of the path in the 3D window, you have full control over the movement of the cube in the 3D window.

9.14.2 Following a Path: The Follow Path Constraint Method

The foregoing tutorial involving the child/parent relationship is akin to following the long and winding road. Now we can take the shortcut, but remember that shortcuts miss out on the detail of the journey.

We will now have the same cube object follow the same path but immediately have an editable "Bezier" curve instated in the "Graph Editor" window. Start with the default scene with the default cube object and leave the 3D window in "User Perspective" view (the default view when Blender opens). Deselect the cube and add a curve path as previously described. Scale the length of the path five times. With the path selected, tab into "Edit" mode and use the handles on the curve to shape the path as shown in Figure 9.65. Tab to "Object" mode; deselect the path and select the cube.

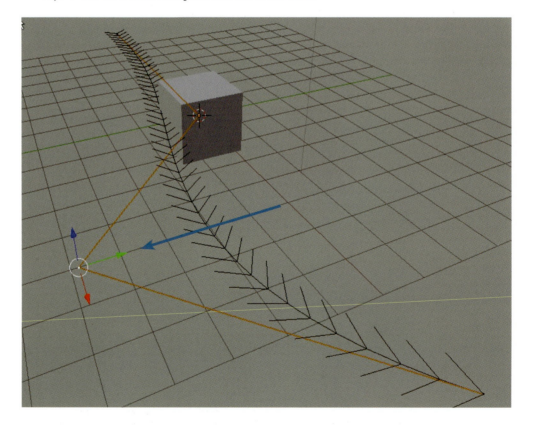

Figure 9.65

In the "Properties" window, "Object Constraints" button, click on "Add Constraint" and select "Follow Path" from the selection menu (Figure 9.66). In the "Object Constraints" tab that opens, enter the target as "Nurbs Path" and tick "Follow Curve" (Figure 9.67). The cube is now positioned at the start of the path.

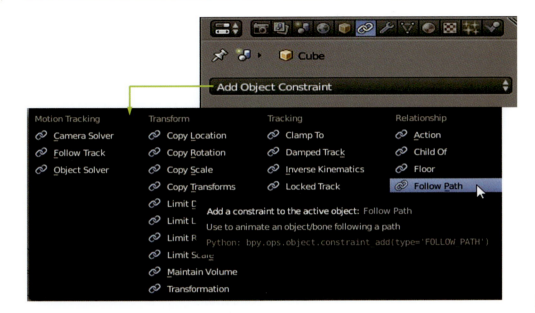

Figure 9.66

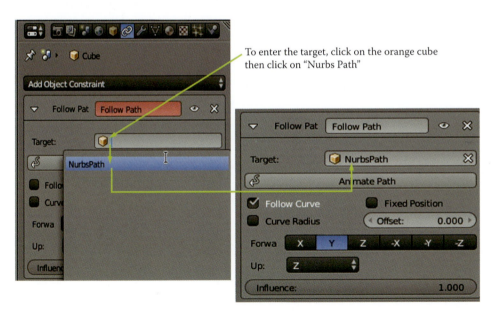

To enter the target, click on the orange cube then click on "Nurbs Path"

Figure 9.67

Deselect the cube and select the path. In the "Properties" window, "Object Data" button, "Path Animation" tab, note that "Frames: 100" and "Evaluation Time: 0.000" (Figure 9.68). This says that there is a 100-frame animation with 0.000 as the start position. Right click on the "Evaluation Time" button and select "Insert Keyframe." Note that in the timeline window, the "Start: 1" and "End: 250" values indicate the animation duration (i.e., 250 frames).

Click on the "Go to End" button in the "Timeline" window to locate the timeline cursor at frame 250 (recall Figure 9.61). In the "Path Animation" tab, change the "Evaluation Time"

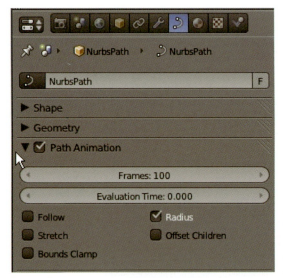

Figure 9.68

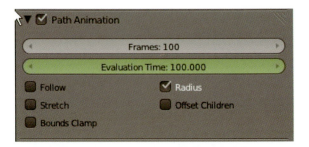

Figure 9.69

value to 100 (Figure 9.69), which positions the cube at the end of the path in the 3D window. Right click on the "Evaluation Time" button and select "Insert Keyframe" again. In the "Timeline" window, click on the "Return to Start" button to go to the start of the animation and click "Play" to see the cube move in the 3D window following the path (Figure 9.70).

In the "Graph Editor" window, you now have an animation curve that is the editable "Bezier" type as discussed in the previous method.

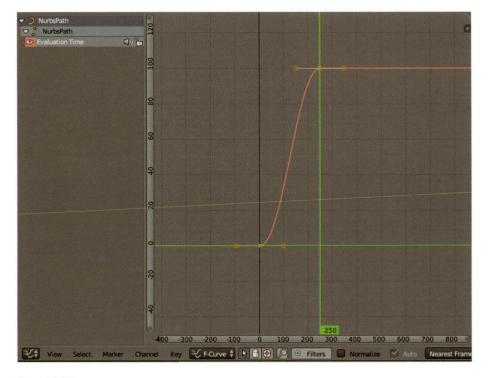

Figure 9.70

9.15 Displacement Sound Animation Control

A sound file (Music) can be used to affect the movement of vertices producing an interesting display effect.

To demonstrate we will set up a plane object with displacement modifier and a texture controlling the displacement as we did in Chapter 5. To make a colorful display we will use the texture image (Figure 9.71).

9.15.1 Add a Sound File

Having completed the setup of the plane object open the "Video Sequence Editor" window and in the header left click on "Add" and select "Sound." Navigate to your sound file, click it to select and in the upper RHS of the window click on "Add Sound Strip." (I am using Windows 7 which comes with the file "Kalimba.mp3" in the Users/Public/Music/Sample Music directory.) Make sure you move the sound file strip to frame 1.

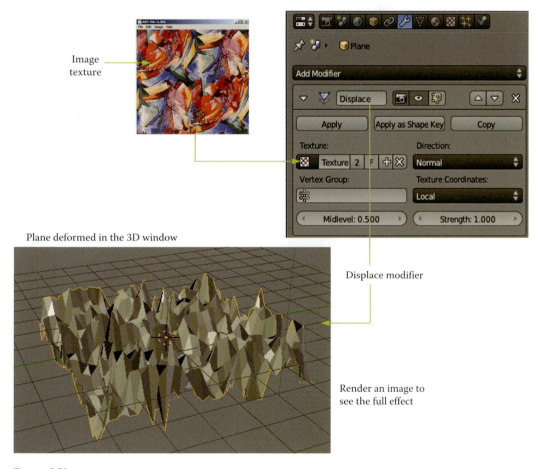

Image texture

Plane deformed in the 3D window

Displace modifier

Render an image to see the full effect

Figure 9.71

9.15.2 Create an F Curve

With the plane selected in the "Displacement" modifier, set the "Strength" vale to 0.000.

In the "Timeline" window, set the cursor at frame 1. Right click on the "Strength" value slider and select "Insert Keyframe" (Figure 9.72).

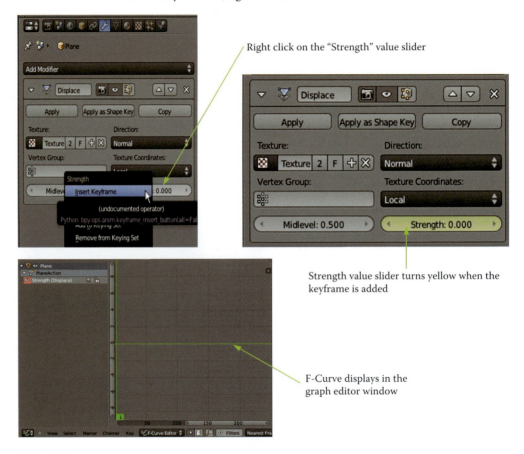

Right click on the "Strength" value slider

Strength value slider turns yellow when the keyframe is added

F-Curve displays in the graph editor window

Figure 9.72

We now have to declare the sound file to affect the "Strength" value, that is, control the deformation of the plane object.

Divide the 3D window in two and change one half to the "Graph Editor" window in "F Curve" mode. In the window header, click on "Key" and select "Bake Sound to F Curve" (Figure 9.73).

Select your sound file again. In the upper RHS of the window click "Bake Sound to F Curve." The sound file will be inserted and a *graph displays* in the window (Figure 9.74).

9.15.3 Play the Animation

In the "Timeline" window, play the animation to see the sound file deforming the plane.

To really see the colorful display you will have to render the animation to a movie file (Figure 9.75).

9.15.4 Modify the F Curve

The amplitude of the sound file "F Curve" may be tweaked to adjust the deformation affect.

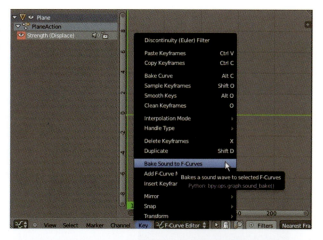

Figure 9.73

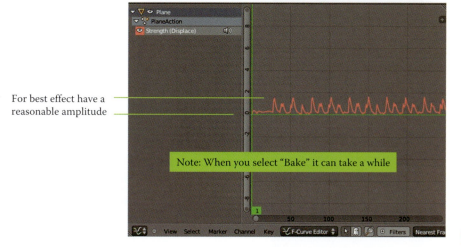

For best effect have a reasonable amplitude

Note: When you select "Bake" it can take a while

Figure 9.74

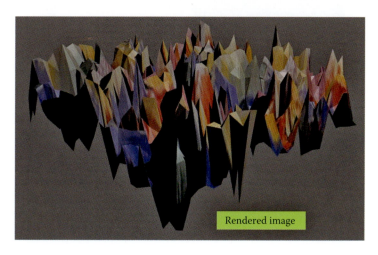

Rendered image

Figure 9.75

In the "Graph Editor" window click on "Key" in the header and select "Add F Curve Modifier" then select "Envelope" (Figure 9.76).

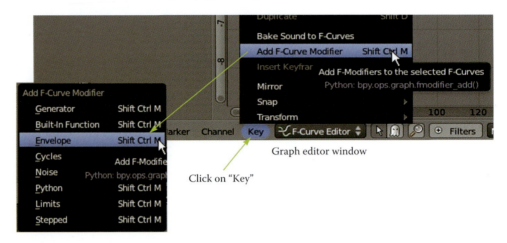

Figure 9.76

Move the cursor in the "Timeline" window to, say, frame 100.

In the "Graph Editor" window, press N key to display the "Envelope" modifier, then in "Control Point" click "Add a Point." Values can be adjusted to effect the amplitude of the sound controls the displacement of the plane's surface (Figure 9.77).

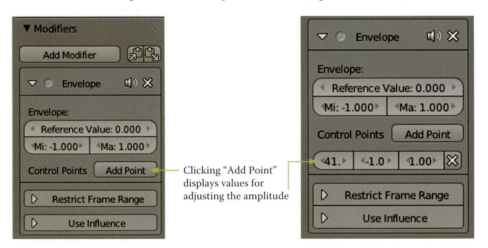

Figure 9.77

9.15.5 Sound Affect and Cast Modifier

The foregoing has used a sound file to affect the "Strength" value of a "Displacement" modifier then "Baked" the sound to an "F Curve" then tweaked the amplitude of the curve. This has been to control the displacement of the plane object's surface.

We can combine a sound file "F Curve" and a "Cast" modifier with an "Empty" control object to produce an animation of the "Plane" surface deformation.

The procedure is as follows:

9.15.6 Combine F Curve and Modifier

Set up the "Plane" object with a "Cast" modifier and an "Empty" control object (Figure 9.78).

Add your sound file to the "Video Sequence Editor" window.

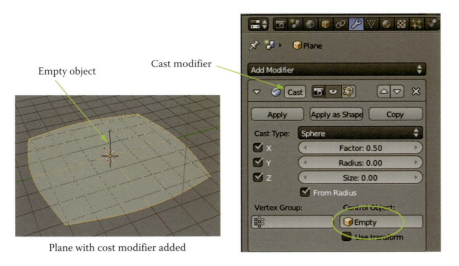

Empty object

Cast modifier

Plane with cost modifier added

Figure 9.78

Figure 9.79

9.15.7 F Curve Factor Value

Create an "F Curve" for the "Factor" value of the "Cast" modifier (Figure 9.79).

In the "Timeline" window, set the cursor at frame 1. With the plane selected in the 3D window, go to the "Properties" window, "Modifier" buttons. In the modifier, set the "Factor" value to 0.000. Right click on the "Factor" slider and select "Insert Keyframe" (Figure 9.80).

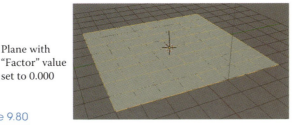

Plane with "Factor" value set to 0.000

Figure 9.80

In the "Graph Editor" window, add "Baked Sound F-Curve" as before. Note: It takes a while to Bake.

You can of course add the modifier envelope and tweak the amplitude at this point.

9.15.8 Automatic Keyframes

We will now select and translate the "Empty" object and automatically insert "Keyframes" in the timeline.

Click to turn "Auto Keyframing" on

Figure 9.81

With the "Empty" object selected in the 3D window (it is easier to select in the "Outliner" window), in the "Timeline" window header turn on "Auto Keyframing" (Figure 9.81).

Play the animation and at the same time, press G key in the 3D window and move the "Empty" object about. "Keyframes" are added to the timeline. Stop the animation and replay to see the effect (Figures 9.82 through 9.84).

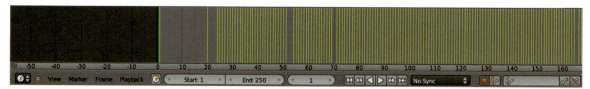

Automatic keyframes added in the "Timeline" window

Figure 9.82

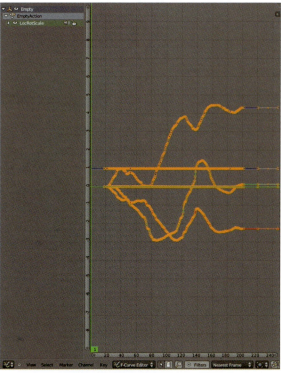

F-Curve added to the "Graph Editor" window
during automatic "Keyframing"

Figure 9.83

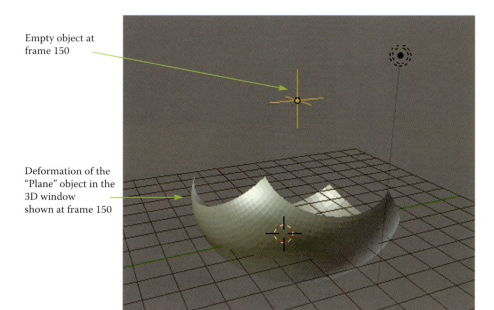

Empty object at
frame 150

Deformation of the
"Plane" object in the
3D window
shown at frame 150

Figure 9.84

3D Text

10.1 Introduction to 3D Text

3D text can be a very important element to add to a scene. Think of all the television advertisements that contain text and how it is animated. There are two ways of adding text to a scene in Blender: one way is to use the built-in text generator and the other is to use an external program. Text made in Blender can be easily edited in the properties window. Text made in an external program like "Elefont" may give you additional options and different fonts.

10.2 Creating 3D Text in Blender

To create text in Blender, put your scene in top view with orthographic projection (number pad 7 and then number pad 5). Text is entered into the scene in the top view. Locate the cursor at the point in the scene where you want your text to go. Press Shift + the A key and select "Add Text" (Figure 10.1). The word "Text" displays in the 3D window in object mode. Tab into edit mode—the word "Text" now has a typing cursor at the end of it (Figure 10.2). You can now backspace to delete letters and type in your own words just like in a text editor. Don't worry about the font style or size at this stage. When you have typed in the words you want, tab back into object mode; this is where you shape and color the text (Figure 10.3).

Figure 10.1

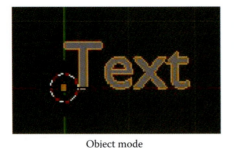

Object mode

Figure 10.2

Edit mode

Typing cursor

The word "Text" has been deleted
and "Edit Mode" typed in its place

Tab to edit mode

Figure 10.3

> Tip: Make sure your 3D window background is a darkish color. Since the default text color is the default gray, it is difficult to see against a light background.

Before you do any shaping or coloring, you can move, rotate, and scale the text just like any object in Blender. Changing the text into something interesting is done in the properties window. Select the text in the 3D window then go to the properties window—"Object Data" button. Note: For text the "Object Data" button is denoted by an "F."

10.3 The Object Data Button "F"

In the "Geometry" tab "Offset, Extrude, and Bevel" depth sliders control exactly what they say:

Figure 10.4

- The offset slider controls the thickness of the text.
- The extrude slider extrudes (Adds Thickness) to the text producing a 3D shape (to see rotate the view or press Num Pad 2 twice).
- The bevel depth slider controls the bevel size.
- The resolution slider rounds the bevel.

Experiment with the settings to modify the shape of the text (Figure 10.4).

10.3.1 Fonts

The default font style is entered as "Bfont" as seen in the "Properties" window, "F" button, "Font" tab. You can change the style to whatever font you have on your system. If you are using a Windows operating system, font styles can be found in C:/Windows/Fonts. To use Windows fonts in Blender they have to be entered in the font slots in the "Properties" window, "F" button, "Font" tab. To enter a font style click on the "Search Folder" icon (Figure 10.5) and in the search window navigate to your fonts folder and select a different font. Blender will

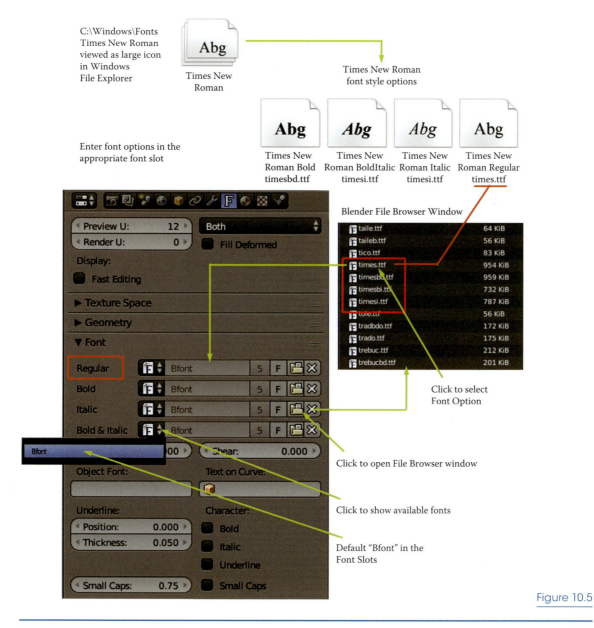

Figure 10.5

accept any of the Windows fonts, but some may be distorted when they are extruded into 3D shapes. Having selected a font click on the "Open Font" button in the upper RH corner of the screen. Do this for each font slot.

The search window lists fonts by file name. For example, the "Times New Roman" font is listed as "times.ttf" which is the "Regular" "Times New Roman" option. The "bold," "italic," and "bold italic" options are listed as timesbd.ttf, timesbi.ttf, and timesi.ttf. To use Times New Roman in Blender each option has to be entered in its respective slot (see Figure 10.5).

Note you can mix and match different font styles and options. For instance you can have one font for regular text and a different font for bold or italic.

By default typing will enter text in the 3D window in "Regular" text. To enter text in one of the alternative options check (tick) one of the "Character" buttons in the "Font" tab. To change text that has already been entered, locate the text cursor using the L and R arrow keys on the keyboard, press and hold shift while using the arrow keys to highlight text, delete the text then check one of the "Character" buttons to change the text option. Retype the text with the new option. Pressing Ctrl plus L or R arrow buttons moves the text cursor to the end of the text line.

Note that the font selected is only applied to the text object selected in the 3D window. The text is treated as an object, therefore, the font style (values) you have assigned are for the selected object only. Entering a second text object will require that you assign a different set of data.

In the "Fonts" tab, the underline position and thickness values only operate when "Underline" is ticked under "Character." Underlining occurs as you type your text in edit mode.

10.4 Creating Text on a Curve

Text in Blender can be made to follow the shape of a curved path. Begin by adding text to your scene as previously described; when it is in object mode, deselect it with the A key. Add a curved path to the scene by pressing Shift + the A key—"Curve"—"Path." Note that by default the path is named "NurbsPath." The curve path is added to the scene in object mode and appears as a straight line (Figure 10.6). You can scale it to make it longer and reposition it in object mode, but you will have to tab to edit mode to extrude or shape it into a curve (Figure 10.7). With the curve shaped however you'd like, tab back to object mode and deselect it.

Select the text object and in the properties window—"Object Data" button—"Font" tab, find the "Text on Curve" panel. Click on the little cube icon and in the drop down

Figure 10.6

Edit mode   Object mode

Figure 10.7

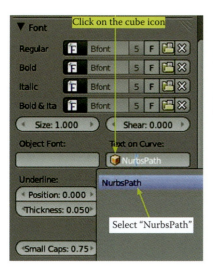

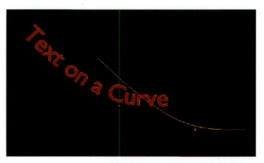

Figure 10.8

menu that displays select "NurbsPath" (Figure 10.8). The text is shaped to follow the profile of the curve.

10.5 Converting Text to a Mesh Object

Figure 10.9

There is only limited functionality in the text "Object Data" button—"Geometry" tab for modifying the text shape. Unless you have extruded the text, it remains a 2D plane object. Entering edit mode only allows you to retype a text change. To perform editing, which actually changes the shape of the text, you have to convert to a mesh object. To do this, select the text in object mode then press Alt + the C key and select "Mesh from Curve/Meta/Surf/Text" in the drop down menu that displays (Figure 10.9). Tab to edit mode and you will see that the text is now a mesh object with vertices that can be moved, rotated, and scaled (Figure 10.10).

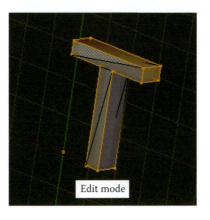

Edit mode

Figure 10.10

10.6 Converting Text to a Curve

If you would like to perform some fancy editing of a single letter, you can convert the letter into a curve. The outline of the letter becomes a curve with handles, which allow you to manipulate the shape into anything you wish. Add text, then in edit mode delete and retype your letter. Scale it up, rotate, and move it where you like then tab to object mode. Press Alt + the C key and select "Curve from Mesh/Text" (Figure 10.11). Now in edit mode you will see the outline of your letter as a curve with manipulating handles (Figure 10.12).

Edit mode   Object mode

Figure 10.11

Figure 10.12

10.7 Elefont 3D Text

Text can be created in an external 3D text editor and imported into Blender. Any program that exports 3D text as .dxf or VRML (.wrl) will work. Elefont is a free to download and use program that exports a .dxf file. The interface is shown in Figure 10.13.

> Note: At the time of writing the .dxf file format produced by Elefont does not appear to import into Blender version 2.74. The following instructions are included for those who are using a previous Blender version. An alternative program to try is StickFont v1.1. This also exports a .dxf file.

After you have created your text in Elefont or an alternative program, save the .dxf file and make note of where you saved it. Open Blender and go into top view in the 3D window. In the information window header, click on "File" then "Open." The Blender file browser window will open. Navigate to the folder where you saved your file.

> Note: By default, Blender does not display all files in the browser window. Go to the header at the top of the window and click on "Enable Filtering" (Figure 10.14). This will display all the files in any folder.

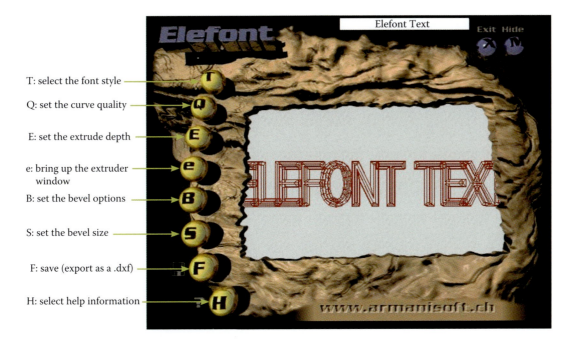

T: select the font style

Q: set the curve quality

E: set the extrude depth

e: bring up the extruder window

B: set the bevel options

S: set the bevel size

F: save (export as a .dxf)

H: select help information

Figure 10.13

Click on "Enable Filtering"

Figure 10.14

Note: In Blender 2.74 you will have to activate a DXF file import Add-on in the "User Preferences" window.

Click on your .dxf file and then click on "Open Blender File" (at the upper LHS of the window). Your text will be displayed in the Blender 3D window but note that each letter is a separate object. Since each letter is a separate object, you can apply a different material color to each letter. To join all the letters into a single object, shift select all the letters then press "Join" in the tool shelf (or press Ctrl + the J key) (Figure 10.15). Tab to edit mode to see the mesh object (Figure 10.16). The text can now be edited as a single object and made to follow the profile of a curve by adding a modifier to the text object—modifiers will be discussed in Chapter 12.

The letters are joined in object mode

Figure 10.15

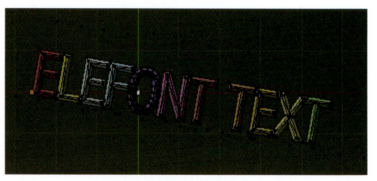

Edit mode showing the mesh object

Figure 10.16

Nurbs and Metashapes

11.1 Using Nurbs

When you press Shift + the A key and select "Add," you will notice other object types besides meshes, cameras, and lights that can be added to the scene. In this chapter, we will look at "Nurbs Curves and Circles" and "Metashapes."

Nurbs stands for "Nonuniform Rational B-Spline," which means it's a type of editable curve or surface that can be converted to a mesh object. "Nurbs" in Blender are found in the "Add" menu under "Curve" and "Surface."

To demonstrate follow the procedure outlined below.

Start a new scene in Blender and delete the default cube. Place the scene in "Top Orthographic" view (Num Pad 7 + 5) and add a Nurbs circle (Shift = A key —"Add"—"Surface"—"Nurbs Circle"). The Nurbs circle will be displayed in the 3D window in "Object" mode (Figure 11.1).

Tab to "Edit" mode and you will see the circle surrounded by manipulation handles, which by default are all selected (Figure 11.2). Deselect the handles using the A key and right click on a handle to select it. If you have the manipulation widget turned on, you can use it to move the handle and deform the circle (Figure 11.3). Alternatively, you can press the G key and drag the mouse.

Figure 11.1

Figure 11.2

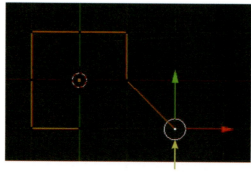

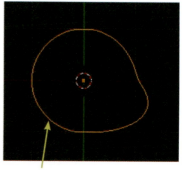

Figure 11.3

Manipulation widget

Deformed circle

Figure 11.4

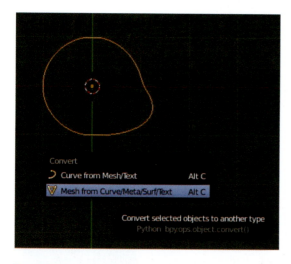

Tab into "Object" mode to see the deformed circle (Figure 11.4). The deformation may be what you want or you may wish to further refine the shape. You can do this by converting the Nurbs shape into a mesh object. With the shape selected in "Object" mode, press Alt + the C key and select "Mesh from Curve/Meta/ Surf/Text" in the drop down menu (Figure 11.5). We are converting "Surface" into a mesh object. Obviously, this same command is applicable to converting "Curve," "Meta," and "Text" into a mesh object.

Tab to "Edit" mode and you will see the shape has vertices applied that you can select and manipulate to further modify the shape (Figure 11.6). The A key will deselect the vertices you have just moved and pressing the A key again will select all the vertices.

Tab to "Object" mode then press Alt + the C key; this time select "Curve from Mesh/Text" (Figure 11.7). This

Figure 11.5

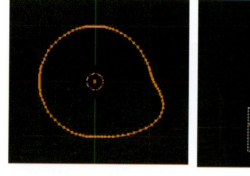

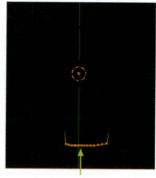

Vertices selected

Vertices moved

Figure 11.6

11. Nurbs and Metashapes

option creates a mesh curve object from the mesh object. Tab back to "Edit" mode and you now have a curve circle object. You can use the "Geometry" values in the "Properties" window, "Object Data" button to manipulate the object's shape or select vertices and move them (Figure 11.8). Since this is a curve circle, it can be used as a path in animation.

Figure 11.7

Nurbs circle modified using geometry tab settings as shown below

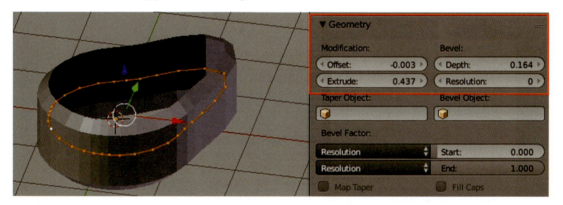

Figure 11.8

This procedure shows that by converting one type of object into another, you have different options for shape manipulation.

11.2 Creating a Lofted Tunnel

This process will take several profiles of a Nurbs circle, which are all manipulated to different profiles, and connect them together to form a hollow object (tunnel).

First, create a Nurbs circle as described in Section 11.1. The circle is entered in the scene in "Object" mode, so you need to tab into "Edit" mode. Select the points and reshape the circle. After shaping, go back into "Object" mode and change your view so you are looking down on the circle (number pad 7). Use Shift + the D key to duplicate the circle several times and position them accordingly, then rotate your view so you can shift

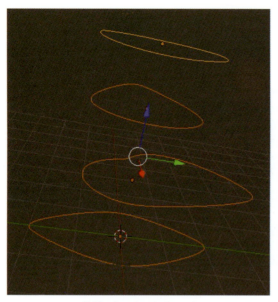

Shift select the circles and
join them together

Figure 11.9

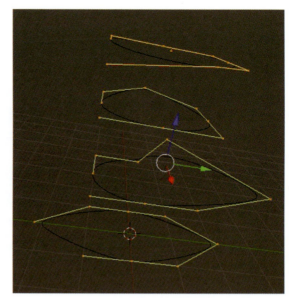

All the vertices are selected

Figure 11.10

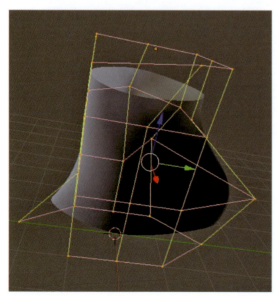

Press the F key to create
the lofted shape

Figure 11.11

select each circle. In "Edit" mode, edit the shapes. After shaping the circles, exit "Edit" mode and select all the circles by RMB clicking on them while holding Shift. Join the circles together, pressing "Join" in the tool shelf (Figure 11.9). For the final step, press Tab for "Edit" mode, press the A key to select all the vertices (Figure 11.10), then press the F key (Face) to create a lofted shape (Figure 11.11).

11.3 Metashapes

There are several "Metashapes" you can use in Blender (Figure 11.12). Metashapes are added to a scene in "Object" mode like any other shape: press Shift + the A key—"Add"—"Metaball" and select either ball, capsule, plane, ellipsoid, or cube. Be sure to deselect one shape before adding another, otherwise the two shapes will be automatically joined. When "Metashapes" get close to one another, they begin to pull and flow together like droplets of liquid (Figure 11.13). The shapes can be animated and textured, and reflection and transparency can be applied to create some stunning effects.

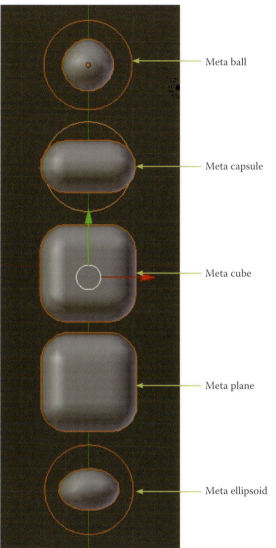

Meta ball

Meta capsule

Meta cube

Meta plane

Meta ellipsoid

Figure 11.12

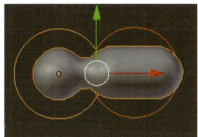

The meta ball and meta capsule
in close proximity

Figure 11.13

Lesson 13
13-01
Nurbs Curves
Basics

Lesson 13
13-02
Nurbs Curves
Surface Basics

Lesson 13
13-03
Nurbs Curves
Circle—Part 1

Lesson 13
13-04
Nurbs Curves
Circle—Part 2
Dupliframes

Lesson 13
13-05
Nurbs Curves
Surface Patch

Lesson 13
13-06
Nurbs Surfaces
Cylinder-Sphere
Torus

Lesson 13
13-07
Nurbs Surfaces
Textures

Lesson 13
13-08
Meta Objects
Object Mode

Lesson 13
13-09
Meta Objects
Edit Mode

12

Modifiers

12.1 Introduction to Modifiers

A "Modifier" in Blender is the application of a process or algorithm to an object. In other words, once you have created an object in the scene you can apply a set of data that will change the shape, the way the object behaves, or how it is seen. The modifiers are designed to take some of the hard work out of shaping objects and controlling their behavior. Applying some of Blender's modifiers has to be performed in conjunction with other processes. The following chapter is offered as a guide. You will have to experiment and record your findings to become proficient in the application of modifiers.

Modifiers are found in the "Properties" window, "Object Modifiers" button (Figure 12.1). The "Object Modifiers" button is only displayed when an object to which a modifier can be applied is in the 3D window. Some objects cannot have modifiers applied to them.

Note: If there are objects in the 3D window to which modifiers may be applied (not necessarily selected), clicking the "Add Modifier" button and selecting a modifier will apply the modifier to the last object that was selected. This occurs even though that object is not selected at the time.

Properties window   "Object Modifiers" button

Figure 12.1

In this section most, but not all, of Blender's modifiers are briefly explained. Those that are not are tending beyond basics will be better understood having studied further. Needless to say, tutorials are available on the Internet, which give practical examples in the use of "Modifiers."

Note: New modifiers are continually being added to the program and the drop down menu changes accordingly.

To demonstrate the very basic procedure for applying a modifier, start with the default Blender scene with the default cube object. Select the cube, go to the "Properties" window, "Object Modifiers" button, and click on "Add Modifier" to display the modifier drop down selection menu (Figure 12.2). The menu is divided into four lists. In the "Generate" list select the "Bevel" modifier. The modifier buttons panel will display. This is where you adjust the values to produce the desired effect. In this example, increase the "Width" value to increase the width of the bevel that has been applied to the edges of the cube. This adjusts the number of "Segments" around the bevel. When you are satisfied with the effect you press the "Apply" button to permanently set the action.

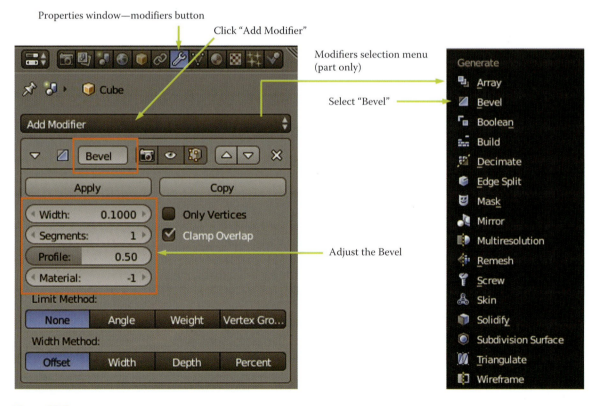

Figure 12.2

12.2 Modifier Stacks

In some cases it is appropriate to apply more than one modifier to an object. When this is done the modifiers are placed in a stack in order of priority. A modifier at the top of the stack takes precedent of modifiers lower down. The priority can be changed by moving a modifier up or down in the stack. Although modifiers are generally applied in object mode, some may be used in edit mode. Figure 12.3 shows an array modifier and a bevel modifier.

The following pages will give a basic insight into how some of the modifiers are employed. The full listing of modifiers available is shown in the modifier selection drop down menu (Figure 12.4). The following modifiers are described in later chapters—Armatures (Chapter 15), Particle Systems (Chapter 13), Fluid Simulation (Chapter 17), and Smoke Simulation (Chapter 18).

Note: The following modifier descriptions are listed generally in the order that they appear in the modifier selection menu. At the time of writing, the "Mesh Cache" modifier listed under "Modify" is the first one in the list. This listing is not the simplest group of modifiers to understand or apply therefore at this stage it will be better if we are selective in attempting to demonstrate the modifiers. It is recommended that you begin experimenting with modifiers by revisiting the "Bevel" modifier previously described. This modifier is also described in Section 12.4.2.

Enable settings in "Edit" mode
Move up/down in stack

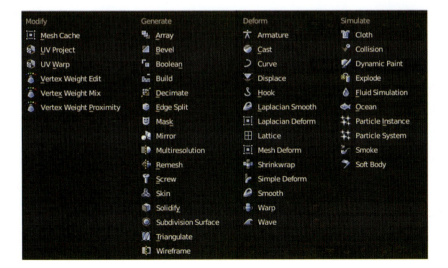

Figure 12.3

Lesson 08
08-14
Multiple Modifiers

Figure 12.4

Figure 12.3 modifier panel screenshot and Figure 12.4 modifier list menu

12.3 Modifiers for Modifying

The "Modify" group of modifiers do not directly affect the shape of an object but rather other data such as vertex groups and appearance. I will not attempt to demonstrate all the modifiers in this group since you would have to understand Blender features that have not been explained. The "UV Project" modifier will serve as an example.

12.3.1 UV Project Modifiers

The "UV Project" modifier projects an image onto the surface of an object much like a slide or movie projector. Before the modifier can be applied, the scene must contain certain items and settings. To demonstrate the very basics of the process we will project an image onto one face of the cube in the default Blender scene. Before beginning, we must have the following items in the scene:

- An object on which to project the image (default cube)
- An image to be projected (know the location of an image saved on your computer)
- A camera to see what is being projected and a light source (lamp)
- A **projector** to do the projecting

A **projector** can be any "Primitive" type (basic object) but it is best to use one that does not render such as an "Empty" or a "Camera." A "Camera" object is easily visualized as a projector so we will use that.

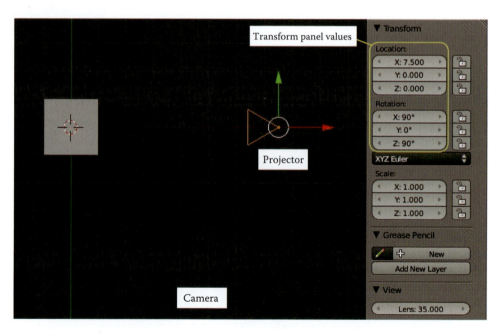

Figure 12.5

Start with the default Blender scene and go to "Top Orthographic" view (number pad 7 + number pad 5). The default scene contains a cube object, a camera, and a lamp.

The first thing to do is to add a projector. Since we already have a camera, it is very simple to duplicate it by pressing Shift + the D key. The duplication will be in "Grab" mode, therefore, move your mouse to relocate it. When the camera is duplicated Blender automatically names it "Camera.001." Go to the "Properties" window, "Object" button, and rename the new camera "Projector" by clicking on the name, deleting it, retyping, then pressing "Enter." In the 3D window move the projector and position it as shown in Figure 12.5. You may position the projector anywhere you like but this demonstration will be easier to follow if you copy the example exactly. To precisely position the projector, use the "Transform" tab in the "Object" properties panel (to show the panel press the N Key). Enter the values as shown in the diagram. This will put the projector squarely pointing at the cube on the X- and Y-axis. Deselect the projector.

Select the "Cube" object. Remember we are applying a modifier to the cube to effect how it displays. In the "Properties" window, "Modifier" button, click on "Add Modifier." From the menu that displays select "UV Project" from the "Modify" list. The "UV Project" modifier panel opens. The panel shows three subpanels for data entry: "Image," "UV Map," and "Projector." In the modifier, you have to tell blender what image you want to project, how and where you want to project (the UV Map), and what to use for projecting (the second camera renamed "Projector").

Change the 3D window to camera view (number pad 0). To perform image projection, the object being projected on must have a material with some unique settings. In the 3D window (while still in camera view), with the cube selected go to the "Properties" window, "Material" tab. The default cube in the default scene comes preloaded with a material, which is the dull gray color that you see. If you have added a new cube object, you will have to add a new material. With a material added, change the following settings in the "Material" tab as shown in Figure 12.6:

Figure 12.6

- In the "Diffuse" tab, set "Intensity: 1.000."
- In the "Shading" tab, tick "Shadeless" and set "Ambient: 0.000."
- In the "Transparency" tab, tick "Transparency" and check that "Alpha: 1.000" is set.
- In the "Options" tab, tick "Face Textures" and leave "Traceable" ticked.

We now have to tell Blender what image we want projected and give some coordinates. Split the 3D window in two and make one-half a "UV/Image Editor" window. In the 3D window with the cube selected, change the viewpoint shading to "Textured" (Figure 12.7). Tab to "Edit" mode and change to "Face select" mode (Figure 12.8). Press the A key to deselect all the faces then right click on the face to which the projector is pointing. With the cursor in the 3D window, press the U key for "UV Mapping" and select "Project From View" (Figure 12.9). You will see the face you have selected appear in the "UV/image Editor" window.

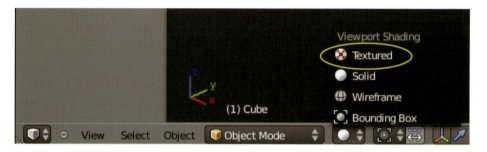

Figure 12.7

Figure 12.8

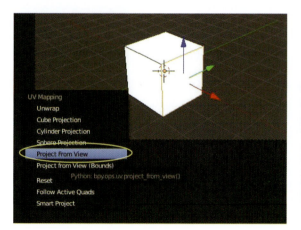

Figure 12.9

Image file location — C:\Users\John Blain\BasicsRewrite\CH14-Modifiers\01-Generate\UV-Project\Screenshots\

File name — Lotus.jpg

01.jpg   02.jpg   03.jpg

Image file selected — Lotus.jpg

Figure 12.10

In the "UV/image Editor" window, load your image by clicking "Image" in the header then select "Open Image." This opens the "File Browser" window where you can navigate to the folder containing your image. Click on the image file and click "Open Image" in the upper RHS of the screen (Figure 12.10). Your image displays in the "UV/image Editor" window, underneath the outline of the face you have selected (Figure 12.11). You will have to zoom in on the window. A portion of the image also shows projected on to the face of the cube in the 3D window. The projection is the portion of the image underneath the outline of the face in the "UV Image Editor" window.

Outline of the selected face

Figure 12.11

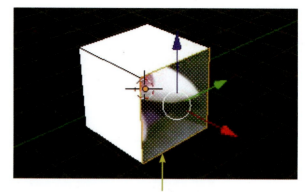

Figure 12.12

Image on the selected face

The face is selected as shown by the orange outline (if not, press the A key). In the "UV Image Editor" window you can translate (G key, grab and move), scale, and rotate the face changing what is projected on the face of the cube in the 3D window (Figure 12.12). If you press F12 with the cursor in the 3D window and render an image, you will see whatever portion of the image that is covered by the face outline in the "UV/image Editor" window rendered onto the selected face of the cube.

This example shows you one method of projection, but that is not where we were heading to begin with. We want to use the "UV Project" modifier.

At this point, we have given Blender the information about our image and have established some mapping coordinates.

Finally, we can use our "UV Project" modifier. The cube remains selected in the 3D window. The "UV Project" modifier is patiently waiting in the "Properties" window, "Object Modifiers" button panel (Figure 12.13). In the modifier panel click on the "Image" panel and select your image from the drop down menu. In the "UV Map" panel select "UVMap" and in the "Projector" panel select "Projector."

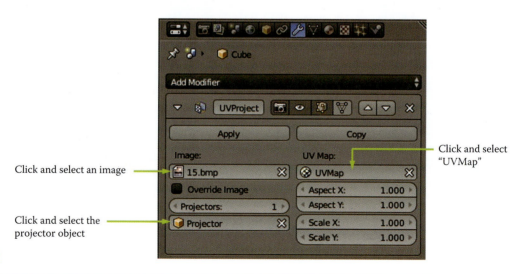

Click and select an image

Click and select the projector object

Click and select "UVMap"

Figure 12.13

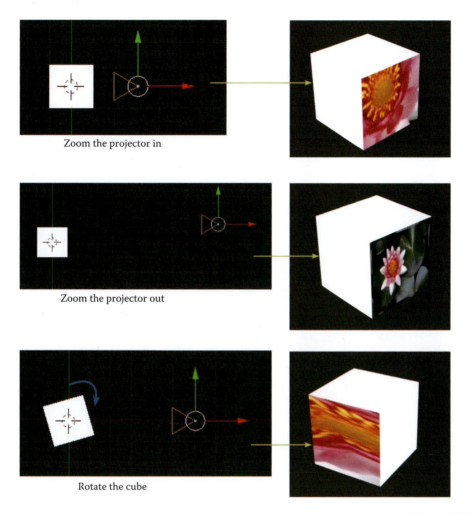

Zoom the projector in

Zoom the projector out

Rotate the cube

Figure 12.14

By moving the projector in the 3D window relative to the cube or moving, rotating, or scaling the cube relative to the projector, the portion of the image displayed can be controlled (Figure 12.14). Altering the "Aspect" and "Scale" values in the modifier panel also controls the projection on to the face of the cube.

Note: If you have used a duplication of the default camera as a projector and haven't renamed it "Projector," then the name of your projector will be "Camera.001."

All the changes in projection may be animated to produce a variety of effects. This has been a very basic introduction to the "UV Project" modifier, which should help in discovering its potential.

12.4 Modifiers for Generating

12.4.1 Array Modifiers

The "Array" modifier creates copies of an object, placing the copies in an array with each copy offset from the original. Figure 12.15 shows a "UV Sphere" object in "Top Orthographic" view duplicated using an array modifier. To add the modifier select the sphere in the 3D window then in the "Properties" window, "Modifier" buttons click on "Add Modifier" and select "Array" from the menu.

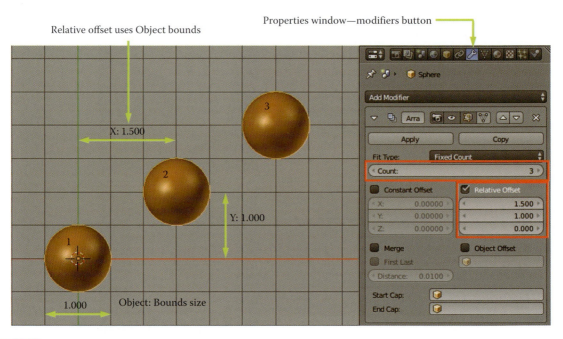

Figure 12.15

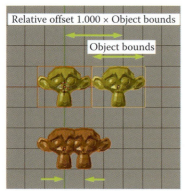

Constant offset 1.000 Blender unit

Figure 12.16

To produce the arrangement shown in Figure 12.15 enter the "Relative Offset" values shown. The "Count: 3" value tells Blender to produce three spheres in the array (the original plus two).

The difference between relative and constant offset is shown in Figure 12.16. Constant offset one (1) means offset one Blender unit irrespective of the objects size. The Monkey's center is offset one blender unit that overlaps the display. Relative offset uses the "Bounds" size (overall size) of the object.

Note: The "Bounds (size)" of an object is displayed by checking "Bounds" in the "Properties" window, "Object Data" buttons, and "Display" tab.

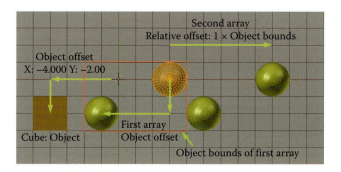

Figure 12.17

The "Object Offset" function is shown in Figure 12.17 and is combined with a second array modifier.

12.4.1.1 Object Offset Using Array Modifiers

The "Object," the cube, is offset from the center of the scene minus two units on the Y-axis and minus four units on the X-axis (Top Orthographic view). A "UV Sphere" object has been added to the scene, at the center of the scene, then in "Edit" mode its vertices have been moved plus three units on the X-axis. This leaves the object center of rotation for the sphere at the center of the scene.

Relocating the sphere's vertices is merely done for clarity to move the final result away from the cube. An "Array" modifier is applied to the sphere with an "Object" offset. An "Object Offset" means offset the objects in the array (spheres) by the offset values applied to another object in the scene (the cube). The cube has been offset from the center of the scene minus Y: 2 and minus X: 4. Therefore, the second sphere in the array is also offset from the first sphere by the same values. The "Count" value is 2, which creates an array consisting of the original sphere plus one other. To apply the "Object" offset values check the "Object Offset" box, click on the orange cube icon and select "Cube" in the drop down menu (Figure 12.18). An array of spheres is created consisting of two spheres (Count 2) with the offset values used by the "Cube" object. The second sphere is offset from the first by minus X = 4 and minus Y = 2.

A second "Array" modifier is added, but this time the modifier is applied to the array that was created by the first modifier. This second array modifier also has a "Count" value of 2, which produces an array consisting of the first array plus an instance of the first array. The second array modifier uses a "Relative Offset" value one (1). Remember "Relative Offset" uses the "Bounds" (size) of the object to which the modifier is added. In this case the bounds of the first array is used.

Figure 12.18

12.4.2 Bevel Modifiers

The bevel modifier was introduced at the beginning of the chapter and simply adds a bevel to the edges of an object; the size of the bevel is controlled by the "Width" button (Figure 12.19).

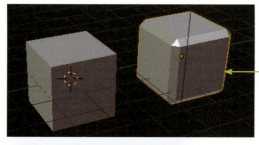

Default cube with a bevel modifier applied

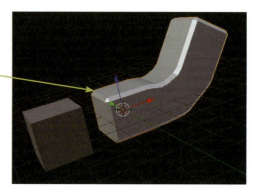

Extruded cube with a bevel modifier applied

Figure 12.19

12.4.3 Boolean Modifiers

Boolean modifiers are used to create shapes by using the "Difference, Intersection, or Union" operations between objects. To demonstrate this, we will use the default cube and a cylinder object. Be warned that, unless you have a reasonably fast computer, some calculations can take several seconds.

Start with the cube and cylinder and position them as shown in Figure 12.20 (this will be the same arrangement for all three "Boolean" operation types). Begin with the Boolean type "Intersect."

Intersect. Intersecting objects creates an object that is the shape of the overlap of two objects. The cube will be the object that is modified, so you must first select the cube. In the "Properties" window, "Object Modifiers" button, click "Add Modifier" and select type "Boolean." The operation type by default is "Intersect." In the "Object" panel click on the little cube icon and select "Cylinder" in the drop down

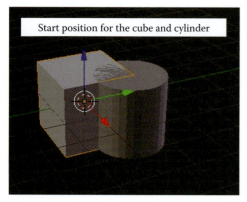

Start position for the cube and cylinder

Figure 12.20

menu (Figure 12.21). Note that this panel always shows a little cube icon despite the shape of the actual object being selected.

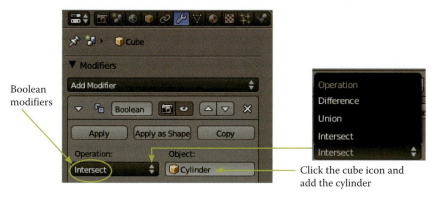

Boolean modifiers

Click the cube icon and add the cylinder

Figure 12.21

In the modifier panel click on "Apply" to apply the modification to the cube. The modifier panel disappears. In the 3D window move the selected object to reveal the new object, which is now the shape of the overlap (Figure 12.22). The cylinder object remains in the scene.

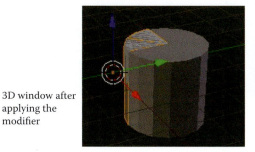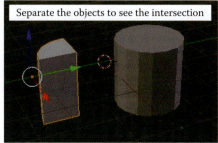

Separate the objects to see the intersection

3D window after applying the modifier

Figure 12.22

Union. Uniting objects creates a shape that is a union of the two objects. Add a "Boolean" modifier to the cube and select operation type "Union." In the "Object" panel click the little cube icon again and select "Cylinder." Click "Apply" and move the selected object in the 3D window; the cube is combined with an instance of the cylinder fused together (Figure 12.23). The original cylinder remains in the scene.

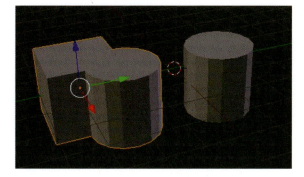

Figure 12.23

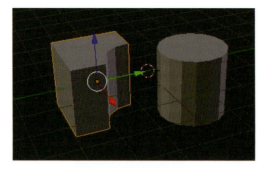

Difference. Differentiating objects creates a shape that is the difference of the two objects. In other words, it subtracts the overlap of the objects from the object being modified. Follow the same procedure as the foregoing examples, but this time select the operation type "Difference" and see the result (Figure 12.24).

Figure 12.24

12.4.4 Build Modifiers

The build modifier creates the effect of something building linearly over a period of time. For example, text can be animated to build across the screen. Any object can have a build modifier, but to see a nice effect, a high vertex count is required.

Add some text to the scene, select the text in the 3D window, and add a "Build" modifier (Figure 12.25). As soon as you add the modifier, the text disappears from

Text in the 3D window selected in object mode

Figure 12.25

Text with the build modifier added

Part of the text is showing.

Figure 12.26

Text building while playing the animation

Build direction

Figure 12.27

the screen (Figure 12.26). Press Alt + the A key to see the animation of the text building (Figure 12.27).

12.4.4.1 Reversing Text Build

Note: This procedure was applicable to Blender versions prior to 2.69.

The "Build" modifier works fine but you will note that it builds the text from right to left. This occurs because the "Build" modifier introduces the data from the mesh object in the order from last to first as it was saved in memory. This means that the build modifier creates the word "Text" in the 3D window starting with the lower case "t" at the end of the word. In many instances, you will want to display your text starting at the beginning of the word.

Here is one method for accomplishing this.

OK! You have your text entered in the 3D window in "Object" mode. In "Edit" mode you enter the text editor mode where you can edit the text, retyping and changing the font, etc. In Chapter 10, Section 10.5, we explained how to convert to a mesh object. To have the "Build" modifier work in reverse we have to convert the text into a mesh object.

With the text in "Object" mode and the "Build" modifier applied press Alt + C key and select "Mesh from Curve/Meta/Surf/Text…"

Press the "Tab" key to go to "Edit" mode. In the 3D window header click on "Mesh"—"Faces"—"Sort Faces" and select "Reverse."

Press "Tab" to go back to "Object" mode.

When you play the animation with the "Build" modifier in place the text will build from left to right.

Note: The individual characters display at different rates depending on the number of vertices that have been generated in converting to a mesh object.

12.4.5 Decimate Modifiers

When a mesh object has been created using complex modeling, with "Proportional Editing," successive refinements, possibly some conversions from "SubSurfed" to "Non-SubSurfed" meshes, you might very well end up with a mesh where lots of vertices and faces are not really necessary.

The "Decimate" modifier allows you to reduce the vertex/face count of a mesh with minimal shape changes. This is not applicable to meshes which have been created by modeling carefully and economically, where all vertices and faces are necessary. The vertex/face count is what Blender uses to calculate such things as shading effects. This should not be confused with the vertices and mesh faces in the actual construction of a model. The vertex/face count is in effect triangulation within mesh faces.

The "Decimate" modifier is a quick and easy way of reducing the vertex/face count of a mesh nondestructively. This modifier demonstrates the advantages of a mesh modifier system because it shows how an operation, which is normally permanent and destroys original mesh data, can be done interactively and safely using a modifier.

Unlike the majority of existing modifiers, the "Decimate" modifier does not allow you to visualize your changes in "Edit" mode.

Decimate only handles triangles, so each quadrilateral face is implicitly split into two triangles for decimation.

To demonstrate decimation start with the default blender scene delete the "Cube" object and add a "Monkey." The "Monkey" is a reasonably complex shape consisting of numerous faces and vertices.

With the "Monkey" selected in "Object" mode, go to the "Properties" window "Modifier" button and add a "Decimate" modifier. Still in "Object" mode, change the 3D window from the "Solid Viewport Shading" display to "Wireframe" display. You will see the "Monkey" drawn as a stick outline of the edges defining the faces, which constitute the shape (Figure 12.29). If you tab into "Edit" mode you will see a similar display of the edges of each face and the vertices at the intersections. The "Monkey" is a complex shape and not all vertices and faces are required in defining the shape. Tab back to "Object" mode.

To reduce unnecessary faces without destroying the shape of the model the "Decimate" modifier is used.

Note the outline of the selected "Monkey" and the "Ratio" value 1.0000 in the "Decimate" modifier panel. This panel is a slider control. Slowly reduce the ratio by clicking on in the slider and dragging to the left (Figure 12.28). You will immediately see

Figure 12.28

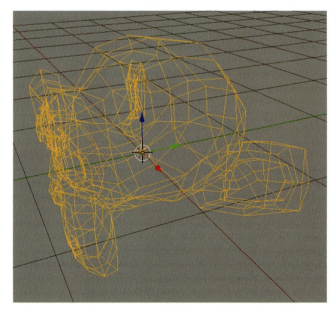

Figure 12.29

12. Modifiers

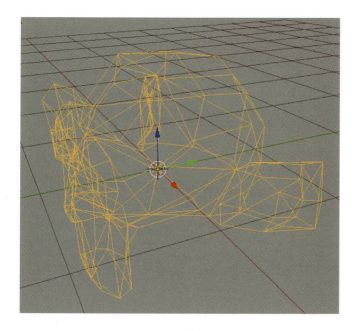

Figure 12.30

changes occurring in the number of faces in the 3D window. Tab to "Edit" mode. The "Monkey" displays with all vertices, edges, and faces (Figure 12.31). Tab back to "Object" mode and reduce the "Ratio" value further to approximately 0.3000. You will observe a substantial reduction in the number of faces. In "Edit" mode there is no change. Compare Figure 12.29 with Figure 12.30.

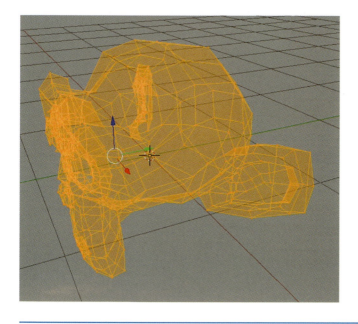

Figure 12.31

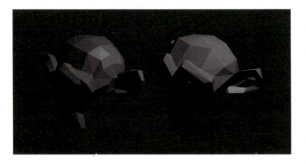

Rendering images of the "Monkey" as you reduce the vertex/face count reveals that there is a minimal change in the render output (Figure 12.32). It is therefore possible to reduce the number of computer calculations that have to be performed in rendering a complex scene.

In a complicated model having many unnecessary vertex/face counts, excessive computer power is consumed and time in performing operations is extended.

Figure 12.33 shows a simple "Plane" subdivided numerous times and having vertices manipulated

Figure 12.32

Rendered image

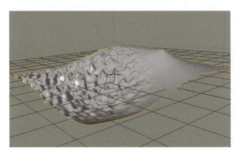

Object mode
ratio reduced to 0.10

Rendered image at reduced ratio value

Subsurf modifier

Decimate modifier—ratio: 1.00

Decimate modifier—ratio: 0.10

Figure 12.33

with "Proportional Editing" active. This could construct a landscape for a scene. A "Subdivision Surface" modifier has been applied.

With a reduced vertex/face count the final image may be perfectly adequate for the requirement. Reducing the vertex/face count will dramatically reduce the file size.

12.4.6 Edge Split Modifiers

The "Edge Split" modifier allows you to split an object apart by selecting vertices, edges, or faces. As an example start with the default scene with the default cube object. In "Object" mode with the cube selected, add an "Edge Split" modifier and click "Apply" (Figure 12.34). Tab to "Edit" mode, select a face and drag the mouse to pull the face away from the cube; the face remains part of the object even though it is separated (Figure 12.35).

Lesson 08
08-12
Edge Split
Modifier

Figure 12.34

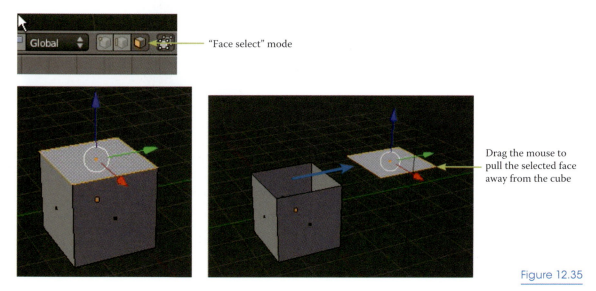

"Face select" mode

Drag the mouse to pull the selected face away from the cube

Figure 12.35

Edge select mode

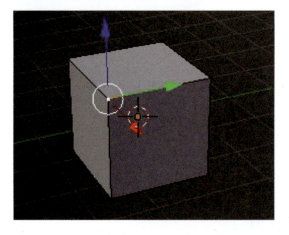

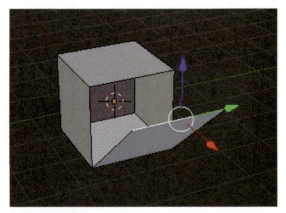

Figure 12.36

Selecting a vertex will allow a corner to be moved. Selecting different vertices will produce some interesting results.

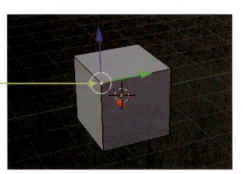

Vertex select mode

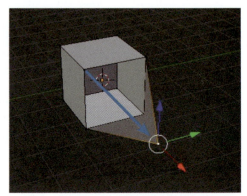

Figure 12.37

Selecting an edge will open a face like the lid on a box (Figure 12.36). Selecting a vertex will allow a corner to be moved (Figure 12.37). Selecting all with the A key and then pressing Ctrl + the V key—"Remove Doubles" will rejoin the faces.

12.4.7 Mask Modifiers

The "Mask" modifier allows portions of a mesh that are defined by vertex groups to be the only part of the mesh that is visible or the only part that displays. Select a few cube vertices in edit mode after subdividing and click "Add Group" (the plus sign) in the "Object Data"

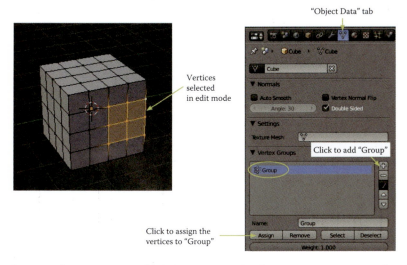

"Object Data" tab

Vertices
selected
in edit mode

Click to add "Group"

Click to assign the
vertices to "Group"

Figure 12.38

buttons, "Vertex Groups" tab (Figure 12.38). The vertices are assigned to the vertex group named "Group." Click "Assign."

Switch to the "Object Modifiers" button and select the "Mask" modifier. The mode should be "Vertex Group" and the vertex group should be "Group." In "Object" mode only the part of the cube defined by the vertex group is displayed. In the "Mask" modifier click the "Invert" button (double-headed arrow) and the complete object less the area defined by the vertex group is displayed (Figure 12.39). By using the modifier, visibility can be controlled without removing any vertices from the cube.

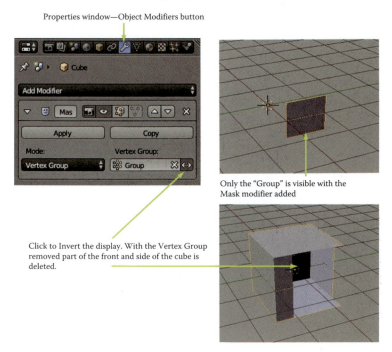

Properties window—Object Modifiers button

Only the "Group" is visible with the
Mask modifier added

Click to Invert the display. With the Vertex Group
removed part of the front and side of the cube is
deleted.

Figure 12.39

12.4.8 Mirror Modifiers

The "Mirror" modifier allows the construction or deformation of a mesh on one side of a center point to be duplicated (mirrored) on the opposite side. Start with a plane in edit mode in top view and subdivide the object into four parts by clicking "Subdivide" on the "Object Tools" panel (Figure 12.40). Select the vertices on one side of the plane and delete them. Add a "Mirror" modifier in the "Object Modifiers" tab, and you'll see the deleted half of the plane mirrored (Figure 12.41). Grab a vertex and deform it; you will observe that the deformation is mirrored (Figure 12.42).

Figure 12.40

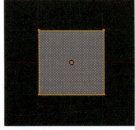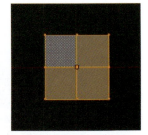

The plane in edit mode   The plane subdivided

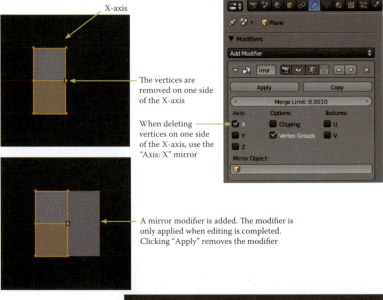

X-axis

The vertices are removed on one side of the X-axis

When deleting vertices on one side of the X-axis, use the "Axis: X" mirror

A mirror modifier is added. The modifier is only applied when editing is completed. Clicking "Apply" removes the modifier

Figure 12.41

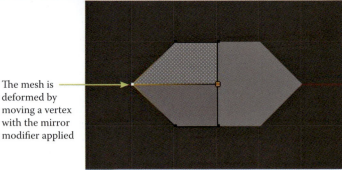

The mesh is deformed by moving a vertex with the mirror modifier applied

Figure 12.42

12. Modifiers

12.4.9 Multiresolution Modifiers

The "Multiresolution" modifier is much like the "Subdivision Surface" modifier. Figure 12.43 is taken from the Blender documentation and perhaps beginners should put it aside for future study. The insert is placed here to make you aware of the modifier's existence.

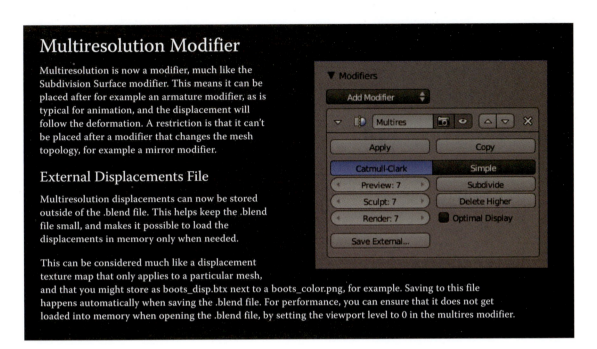

Multiresolution Modifier

Multiresolution is now a modifier, much like the Subdivision Surface modifier. This means it can be placed after for example an armature modifier, as is typical for animation, and the displacement will follow the deformation. A restriction is that it can't be placed after a modifier that changes the mesh topology, for example a mirror modifier.

External Displacements File

Multiresolution displacements can now be stored outside of the .blend file. This helps keep the .blend file small, and makes it possible to load the displacements in memory only when needed.

This can be considered much like a displacement texture map that only applies to a particular mesh, and that you might store as boots_disp.btx next to a boots_color.png, for example. Saving to this file happens automatically when saving the .blend file. For performance, you can ensure that it does not get loaded into memory when opening the .blend file, by setting the viewport level to 0 in the multires modifier.

Figure 12.43

12.4.10 Screw Modifiers

The "Screw" modifier generates a shape by revolving a profile around an axis. To demonstrate this, we will construct a coil spring. All operations are conducted in the default 3D window "User Perspective" view. Follow the steps in the exact order listed below.

Lesson 08
08-13
Screw Modifier

The circle in edit mode

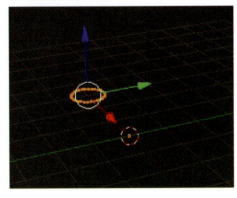

1. Delete the default cube object and add a circle. Scale the circle down by 0.500
2. Tab to edit mode and move the circle along the X-axis to move vertices away from the object center (press the N key to display the "Transform" panel and change the median to "X: minus 6.000") (Figure 12.44)

Figure 12.44

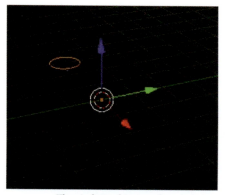

The circle in object mode

Figure 12.45

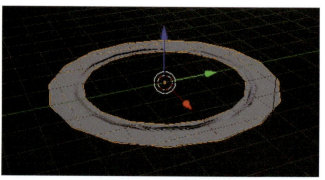

The circle revolved about the default Z-axis
with a screw modifier applied

Figure 12.46

3. Tab to "Object" mode (Figure 12.45)
4. Add a "Screw" modifier to the circle (Figure 12.46)
5. Change the settings in the modifier panel in Figure 12.47 to the ones below
   - Axis: Y (revolve about the Y-axis)
   - Steps: 100 (produces a smooth surface)
   - Screw: 10 (offsets the revolution)
   - Angle: 1000 (number of revolutions)

Default values changed to generate
the screw shown

Y-axis revolved

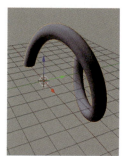

Screw: 10

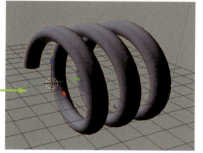

Angle: 1000

Figure 12.47

12.4.11 Skin Modifier

The "Skin" modifier is used for the quick extrusion of rudimentary character shapes, which include a basic armature rig for posing and animating. This modifier may be used in conjunction with a "Subdivision Surface" modifier and a "Mirror" modifier.

Before jumping in and creating a 3D character it is advisable to understand a few fundamentals in the extrusion process. It is also advisable to have an understanding of extrusion covered in Chapter 3, Section 3.18 "Extruding Shapes" and Chapter 15—"Armatures."

Work through the following two procedures and we will explain as we go along.

12.4.11.1 Procedure 1

Begin with a "Plane" object. In "Edit" mode delete two vertices on one side of an axis leaving two vertices connected by one edge (Figure 12.48a).

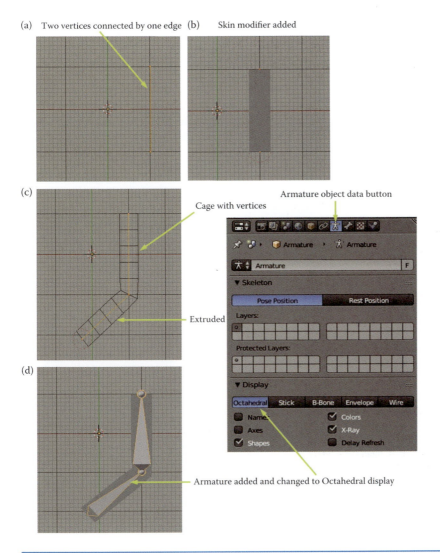

(a) Two vertices connected by one edge (b) Skin modifier added

(c) Armature object data button

Cage with vertices

Extruded

(d) Armature added and changed to Octahedral display

Figure 12.48 (a–d)

In the 3D window, "Solid Display" mode the object is displayed as a single straight line. In the "Properties" window, "Modifiers" button add a "Skin" modifier. With the modifier added the object in the 3D window displays as an elongated cube (Figure 12.48b). In "Edit" mode, "Wireframe Viewport Shading" you will see the original two vertices connected by an edge surrounded by a cage without vertices.

Deselect (A key) then click on one end of the line (vertex). Press the E key and drag the mouse to extrude (Figure 12.48c). Tab to "Object" mode and change to "Solid Viewport Shading." In the "Skin" modifier panel click "Create Armature." An armature comprising two bones created in "Stick" display mode. In the "Armature," "Object Data" buttons change to "Octahedral" display (Figure 12.48d). You can now enter "Pose" mode in the 3D window, select either of the bones and translate, rotate, or scale the bones of the armature.

Note: You may use any of the armature display types. We changed to "Octahedral" since the "Stick" display closely resembles the single straight line we began with.

12.4.11.2 Procedure 2

In the default 3D window delete the "Cube" object and add a "Plane" object. Press the Tab key to enter "Edit" mode (Figure 12.49).

While in "Edit" mode, with the mouse cursor in the 3D window press the W key to display the "Specials" menu and select "Merge" followed by "At Center" (Figure 12.49).

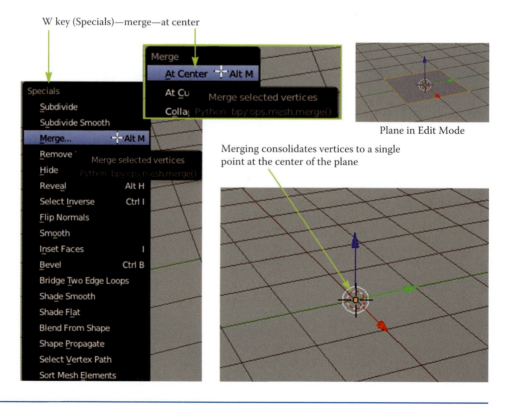

W key (Specials)—merge—at center

Plane in Edit Mode

Merging consolidates vertices to a single point at the center of the plane

Figure 12.49

Modifiers selection panel

Figure 12.50

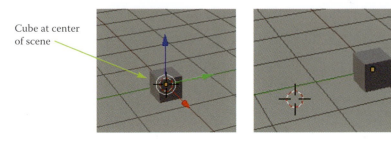

Cube at center of scene

Figure 12.51

The plane appears to disappear leaving the manipulation widget and the 3D window cursor located at the center of the scene.

Note the orange dot at the center of the scene. This is the center of the plane. Merging has consolidated the vertices at the corners of the plane into a single point at the object's center.

Go to the "Properties" window, "Object Modifiers" button and click on "Add Modifier." Select "Skin" (Figure 12.50).

A small cube displays at the center of the scene (Figure 12.51).

Turn the manipulation widget off and click somewhere in the 3D window to relocate the cursor. Now you see the cube with an orange dot at its center indicating that it is selected. Believe it or not the cube is the plane.

If you look at the "Outliner" window in the upper right of the screen you will see "Plane" highlighted in white, which tells you the plane is selected in the 3D window (Figure 12.52).

Zoom in on the cube and change from "Solid Viewport Shading" to "Wireframe Viewport Shading." Note there are

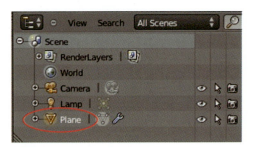

Figure 12.52

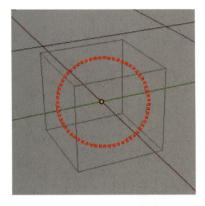

Figure 12.53

no vertices shown and there is a circle at the center drawn in a broken red line. The significance of the circle will be explained a little later (Figure 12.53).

Change back to solid shading and zoom out on the window. Remember the plane (cube) remains selected.

With the mouse cursor in the 3D window press E key—X key (Extrude along the X-axis) and drag the mouse to extrude the cube. LMB click to release the extrusion process. Repeat the procedure extruding the cube further along the X-axis. Zoom in and pan the window to position a close-up of the extrusion (Figure 12.54).

In the 3D window header click on the "Limit Selection to Visible" button.

You will see a thin black line along the centerline of the extrusion. There is an orange dot at the end of the second extrusion and look closely and you will see a small dot somewhere in the middle which

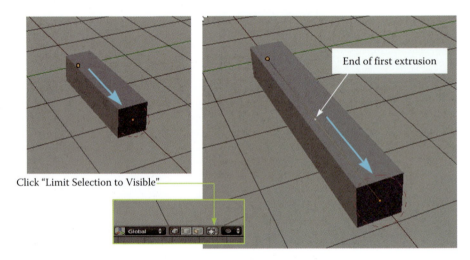

End of first extrusion

Click "Limit Selection to Visible"

Figure 12.54

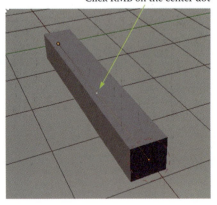

Click RMB on the center dot

Figure 12.55

is the end of the first extruded section. The large orange dot at the LH end is the center of the object (the point of origin). Consider these as control points for manipulation and extrusion.

You RMB click on any of the control points to select and press the A key to deselect, the same as you do when selecting vertices. Press Shift + RMB to select multiple control points.

The control point at the RH end of the extrusion is selected (the end of the last extrusion) as indicated by the small orange dot. Hold the Shift key and RMB click on the middle control point (black dot) to select it. Both the end and the middle points will be selected (Figure 12.55).

Control points added

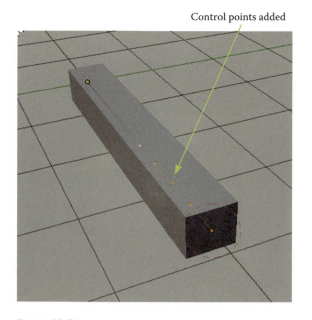

Extrude from any selected point

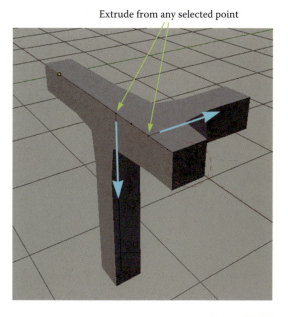

Figure 12.56

Figure 12.58

Figure 12.57

In the "Mesh Tools" panel click on "Subdivide" (Figure 12.57). Another control point is added between the two selected points. Click "Subdivide" again to add more points (Figure 12.56).

Press A key to deselect points, RMB to select any point, and E key to extrude from any selected point. Hold MMB and rotate the scene to see the 3D extrusion (Figure 12.58).

Add a "Subdivision Surface" modifier and tick the "Smooth Shading" button in the "Skin" modifier panel to smooth the extruded shape (Figure 12.57).

You can continue to select control points and extrude branches.

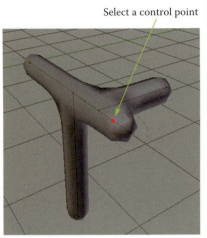

Select a control point

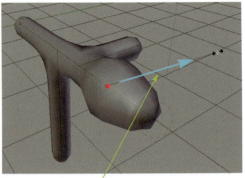

Hold Ctrl + A key and drag mouse to expand area

Figure 12.59

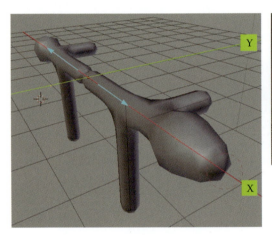

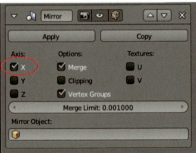

Mirrored along the X-axis

Figure 12.60

By selecting single or multiple control points then pressing and holding Ctrl + A key and dragging the mouse you can scale (enlarge or reduce) the shape adjacent to the selected points. LMB click to cancel the scaling operation (Figure 12.59).

Select two control points and experiment with the scale (S key), rotate (R key), and translate (G key) functions.

After extruding a shape, add a "Mirror" modifier and experiment with the different "Axis" options in "Mirror" modifier panel. Note the mirror effect takes place along the axis selected, not either side of the axis. Experiment in conjunction with the different "Symmetry Axes" options in the "Skin" modifier panel (Figure 12.60).

When you have finished extruding go to "Object" mode and apply the modifiers (click "Apply"). Tab back to "Edit" mode where you will see that a mesh object has been created with vertices, edges, and faces.

12.4.11.3 Extruding a Character

At the beginning of the "Skin Modifier" section we stated that this modifier was used for the quick extrusion of rudimentary character figures. The following is an example:

Extrude the shape as shown in the diagram. Note these are in "Front Orthographic" and "Side Orthographic" views. The red arrows show the direction of extrusion starting at the origin (Figures 12.61 through 12.64).

Side Orthographic View

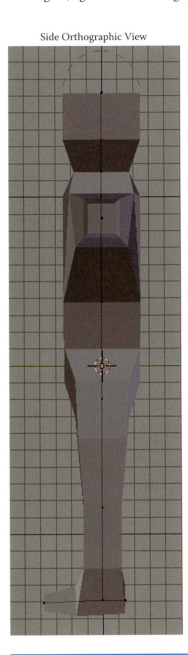

Front Orthographic View

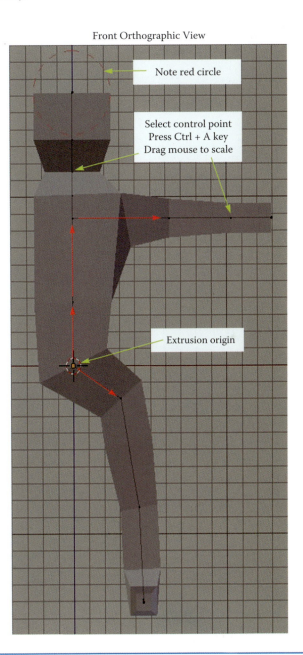

Note red circle

Select control point
Press Ctrl + A key
Drag mouse to scale

Extrusion origin

Figure 12.61

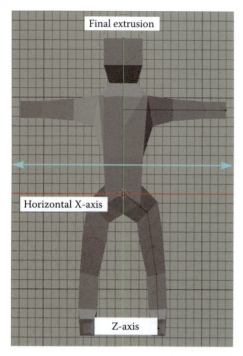

Figure 12.62

Figure 12.63

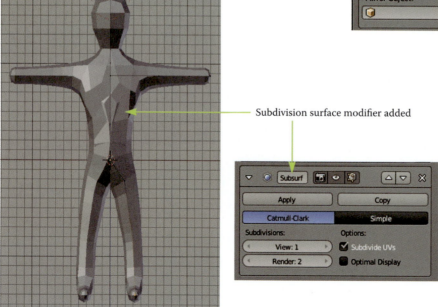

Subdivision surface modifier added

Figure 12.64

Adjusting the topology. Having created the basic figure you will no doubt wish to refine the topology to improve the appearance. The first step would be to tick the "Smooth Shading" button in the "Skin" modifier panel. The next step would be to select control points and tweak their location and use the Ctrl + A scaling function to adjust proportions at the individual points.

Branch smoothing. In the extrusion process, the topology at some points may become distorted. In particular, this can occur where a branch is extruded. In the case of the figure we are creating this would be at the intersection of the spine and the shoulders or at the hips. The topology can be improved at these locations by selecting the control point (in "Edit" mode) at the intersection and then in "Object" mode in the "Skin" modifier panel clicking on the "Branch Smoothing" button and adjusting the numerical value to make the topology fatter or thinner.

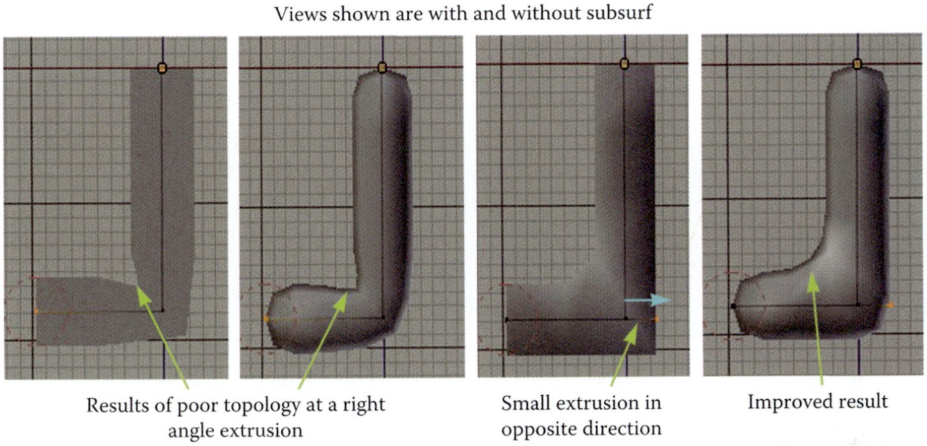

Views shown are with and without subsurf

Results of poor topology at a right angle extrusion

Small extrusion in opposite direction

Improved result

Figure 12.65

Right angles. Another location that can incur topology problems is at a right angle extrusion. In our example this would be at the ankle. A simple solution is to make a short extrusion in the opposite direction (Figure 12.65).

Adding an armature. Up to this point, all operations have taken place in "Edit" mode and as you will see in the "Skin" modifier panel the "Create Armature" button is deactivated.

Before exiting "Edit" mode there is one more operation that explains the significance of the red circle located at the end of the last extrusion. An armature requires a root or generation point to be nominated. Selecting a control point and clicking the "Mark Root" button in the "Skin" modifier panel nominates the root of the armature (Figure 12.66).

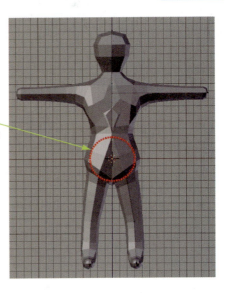

Armature root nominated at the intersection of the spine

Figure 12.66

Figure 12.67

Change from "Edit" mode to "Object" Mode. Before adding an armature click on the "Apply" button in the "Mirror" modifier panel. Failing to do this results in an armature being applied to only one-half of the mirrored model. Modifiers can only be applied in "Object" mode.

Having applied the "Mirror" modifier and nominated the "Armature Root" click the "Create Armature" button in the "Skin" modifier panel. An armature is automatically created and displayed in stick mode. The display may be changed with the "Armature" selected, by selecting the options in the "Properties" window, "Object Data" button (Figures 12.67 and 12.68).

With the "Armature" in place, make sure it is selected and then change from "Object" mode to "Pose" mode. Press the A key to make sure the whole armature is selected. Press

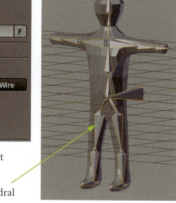

Armature display—stick default

Armature display changed to Octahedral

Figure 12.68

Single Armature Bone selected
and rotated in Pose Mode

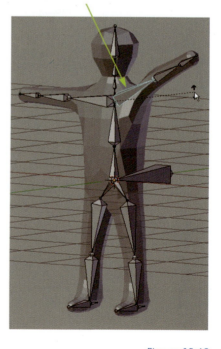

Ctrl + G to bring up the "Bone Groups" menu and click on "Add Bone Group" (Figure 12.69).

Select the figure in "Object" mode and apply the "Skin" modifier.

Add a "Multiresolution" modifier and move it to the top of the modifier stack. You can now remove the "Subdivision Surface" modifier. The figure will display in an ugly block form. Correct this by clicking "Subdivide" a few times in the "Multiresolution" modifier panel. Change to "Sculpt" mode and further refined using the "Sculpt" tools.

Figure 12.69

12.4.12 Solidify Modifiers

The "Solidify" modifier provides a tool for creating solid objects from thin-walled objects. To demonstrate this, begin with a simple plane object selected in the 3D window. Add a "Solidify" modifier in the "Properties" window—look closely at the plane and you will observe that it now has a thickness (Figure 12.70). Note that the "Solidify" modifier by default has two values: "Thickness: 0.0100" (thickness) and "Offset: −1.0000" (offset).

Lesson 08
08-10
Solidify Modifier

To get a better idea of what these values mean, increase them to "Thickness: 0.2000" and "Offset: −2.0000." Change the 3D window to front view (number pad 1); you will see the thickness increased and that it is offset below the midplane of the scene (Figure 12.71).

Tab to "Edit" mode and see that the original vertices of the plane object remain on the midplane of the scene (Figure 12.72). Tab back to "Object" mode and change the 3D window to "User Perspective" view. In the "Object Modifiers" panel untick "Fill Rim"—instead of a single thick plane, there are now two thin planes (Figure 12.73). Tick "Fill Rim" again in the modifier tab and then add a "Subdivision Surface" modifier below the "Solidify" modifier; the thick plane will look like a flattened octagonal shape. This shape can be modified by changing the "Inner," "Outer," and "Rim Crease" values in the "Solidify" modifier panel. Changing all three values to 1.000 produces the thick plane object.

Figure 12.70

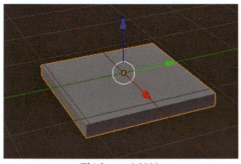

Thickness: 0.2000

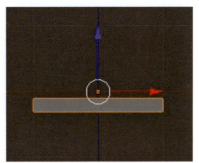

Offset: −2.0000

Figure 12.71

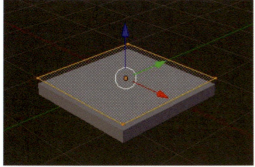

Figure 12.72

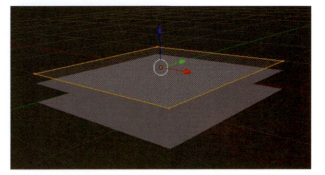

Figure 12.73

With the inner, outer, and rim crease values set back to 0.000, note the value "View: 1" under "Subdivisions" in the "Subdivision Surface" modifier panel. If you change this to "View: 0" you have the thick plane again. Changing the view value from 0 to 1, then to 2, then to 3, and then to 4 changes the thick plane progressively into a smooth flat disc.

For a practical demonstration of the "Solidify" modifier, create a new scene with a cylinder object instead of the default cube. Delete the upper end cap of the cylinder by deleting the single vertex in the center of the cap while in edit mode. You now have a thin-walled container. Add a solidify modifier and increase the thickness value to produce a thicker wall. Play with the offset value to change the size. Add a "Subdivision Surface" modifier and alter the view value to modify the shape. With the "Subdivision Surface" modifier added you can use the inner, outer, and rim crease values to control the shape.

12.4.13 Subdivision Surface Modifiers

Lesson 04
04-06
Subdivision
Surface Modifier

The "Subdivision Surface" modifier is used when the "Smooth" button in the shading section of the tools shelf does not quite do the job, and you do not want to subdivide your mesh by adding more vertices. The following example shows a useful method.

Start with the default cube and switch to front view (number pad 1) and tab to "Edit" mode. Extrude one face of the cube and tab back to "Object" mode in "User Perspective" view (Figure 12.74). Add a "Subdivision Surface" modifier using the default settings (Figure 12.75).

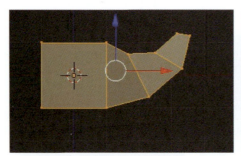
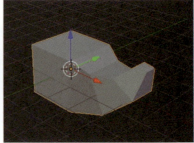

Default cube with one face extruded, rotated, and scaled

Tab back to object mode

Figure 12.74

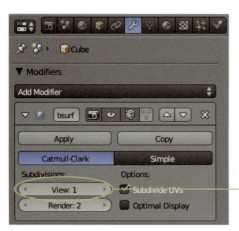

Default settings in the subdivision surface modifier panel

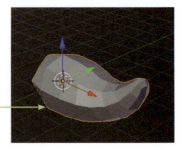

Figure 12.75

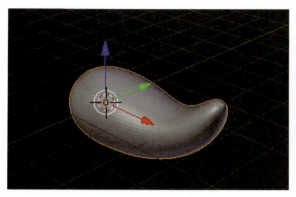 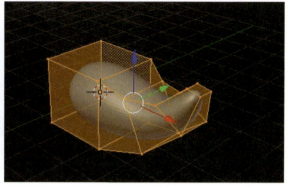

"View" value changed to 4   Tab to edit mode

Figure 12.76

Under "Subdivisions," change the "View" value to 4. Tab to "Edit" mode and see that the original number of vertices has changed (Figure 12.76).

12.4.14 Triangulation Modifier

A "Triangulation" modifier is added when a mesh model has been subdivided and vertices added producing fine detail in a model. The modifier ensures that triangulation will remain consistent when exporting or rendering.

If the model is animated using armatures the modifier should be placed in the modifier stack before (above) the armature modifier.

The "Triangulation" modifier is also used when baking prior to exporting and importing.

12.4.15 Wireframe Modifier

The "Wireframe" modifier converts a solid display as seen in "Solid Viewport Shading" to "Stick" or "Wireframe" display. With the modifier added to a "Cube" object instead of a solid cube you see a frame where the edges of the cube have thickness.

12.5 Modifiers for Deforming

12.5.1 Armature Modifiers

The "Armature" modifier is the mechanism that links a mesh object to a deforming armature. In Chapter 15, armatures are described in detail. The procedure for automatically assigning an armature to a mesh is described by setting up a child/parent relationship. Setting this relationship automatically adds an "Armature" modifier to the mesh being deformed. Instead of setting up a child/parent relationship, the "Armature" modifier can

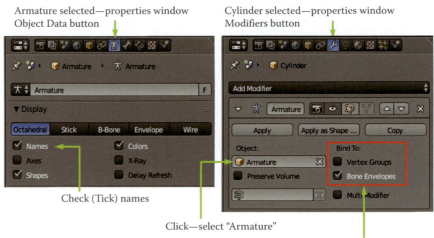

Armature selected—properties window
Object Data button

Cylinder selected—properties window
Modifiers button

Check (Tick) names

Click—select "Armature"

Untick "Vertex Groups"—Tick "Bone Envelopes"

Figure 12.77

be manually added and the deforming armature named as explained in the following procedure (Figure 12.77).

In the default scene, delete the cube and change to front view. Add a single bone armature to the scene (press the Shift key + the A key—"Add"—"Armature"—"Single Bone"). Tab to "Edit" mode, press the E key, and click and hold the LMB, dragging the mouse up to extrude a second bone. Tab back to "Object" mode. In the "Properties" window, "Object Data" button, "Display" tab, check the "Names" button to show the bone names in the 3D window. Deselect the armature by pressing the A key, add a cylinder to the scene, and position it as shown in Figure 12.78. With the cylinder in edit mode, subdivide the mesh once and tab back to object mode.

With the cylinder selected, add an "Armature" modifier and click on the little cube icon in the "Object" panel and select "Armature" from the drop down menu (Figure 12.78). Selecting "Armature" tells the modifier that you will deform the cylinder using the armature object in the 3D window. Still in the "Armature Modifier" panel untick "Vertex Groups" and tick "Bone Envelope." Deselect the cylinder, select the armature, and change to "Pose" mode in the 3D window header. "Pose" mode allows you to manipulate the individual bones in the armature, which in turn deforms the mesh object to which the modifier is applied. Click the RMB on "Bone.001" to select it then press the R key and drag the mouse to the right to rotate the bone (Figure 12.79). Observe how the tube deforms.

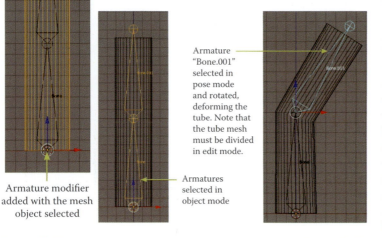

Armature modifier added with the mesh object selected

Armature "Bone.001" selected in pose mode and rotated, deforming the tube. Note that the tube mesh must be divided in edit mode.

Armatures selected in object mode

Figure 12.78

Figure 12.79

12. Modifiers

12.5.2 Cast Modifiers

The "Cast Modifier" may be employed to deform a primitive object.

In the default Blender scene select the default cube object. In "Edit" mode subdivide four times then tab back to "Object" mode.

In the "Properties" window "Modifier" button add a "Cast Modifier" (Figure 12.80).

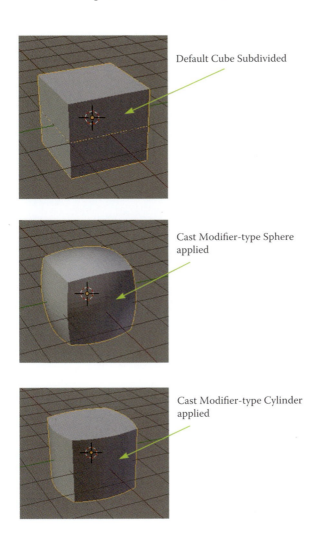

Default Cube Subdivided

Cast Modifier-type Sphere applied

Cast Modifier-type Cylinder applied

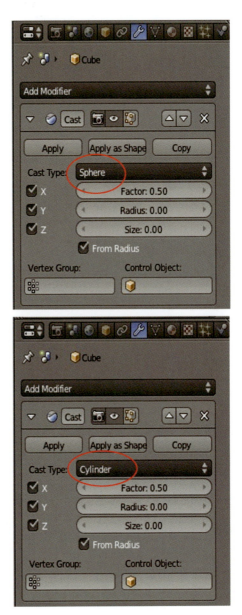

Figure 12.80

By changing the "Cast Type," altering the "Factor," "Radius," and "Size" values and/or limiting the effects to the X-, Y-, and Z-axis the deformation of the cube may be controlled. The deformation may also be controlled by introducing a "Control" object (Figure 12.81).

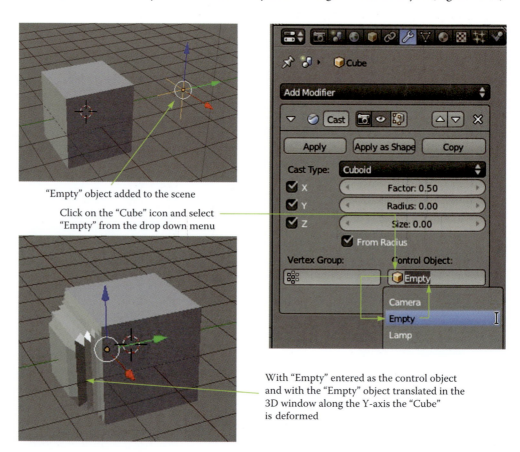

"Empty" object added to the scene

Click on the "Cube" icon and select
"Empty" from the drop down menu

With "Empty" entered as the control object
and with the "Empty" object translated in the
3D window along the Y-axis the "Cube"
is deformed

Figure 12.81

12.5.3 Curve Modifiers

Lesson 08
08-04
Curve Modifier

The "Curve" modifier uses a curve to deform a mesh. Start with the default Blender scene and scale the cube on the X-axis (use the S key + the X key) and subdivide it six times in edit mode (Figure 12.82). Add a "Bezier" curve to the scene and scale up (press the

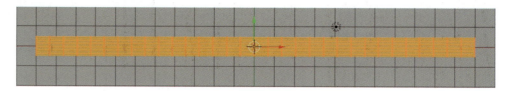

Figure 12.82

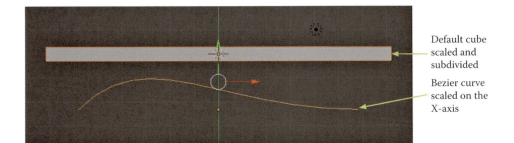

Default cube
scaled and
subdivided

Bezier curve
scaled on the
X-axis

Figure 12.83

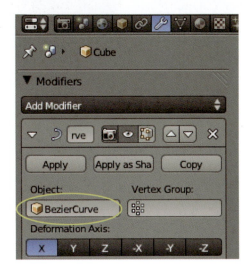

Figure 12.84

S key and drag the mouse, Figure 12.83). Deselect the curve and select the cube. Tab to "Object" mode and add a "Curve" modifier to the scaled cube and enter "BezierCurve" as the name of the "Bezier" curve in the "Object" panel (Figure 12.84). Select the curve in the 3D window and change its shape in edit mode to manipulate the shape of the scaled cube (Figure 12.85).

Scaled cube with a curve modifier added

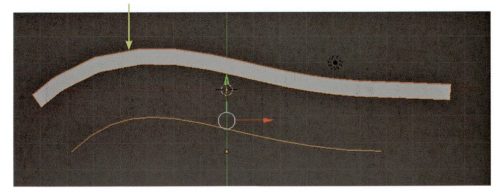

Figure 12.85

12.5.4 Displace Modifiers

Lesson 08
08-08
Displace
Modifier

The "Displace" modifier uses a "Texture" to displace the vertices of a mesh. If vertices are assigned to a vertex group and the group is entered in the modifier, only the vertices belonging to the group will be affected.

Start with the default Blender scene and with the cube selected in "Edit" mode, subdivide it three times (Figure 12.86). Tab back to "Object" mode and in the "Properties" window, "Object Modifiers" button, click "Add Modifier" and select "Displace" (Figure 12.87). We will use a texture to displace the vertices on the cube's surface. Make sure the cube has a "Material" applied and in the "Properties" window, "Textures" button, change the texture type to "Distorted Noise." Go back to

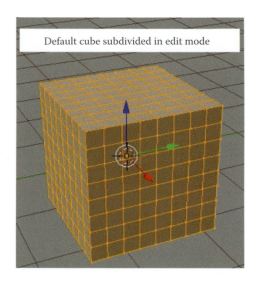

Default cube subdivided in edit mode

Figure 12.86

the "Object Modifiers" button and in the "Modifiers" tab click on the "Browse texture to be linked" button. The default texture data slot to which you assigned the "Distorted Noise" texture is named "Tex." Click on "Tex" and switch to "Object" mode; the vertices on the cube's surface have been displaced according to the intensity of the texture mapped to the

"Textures" tab

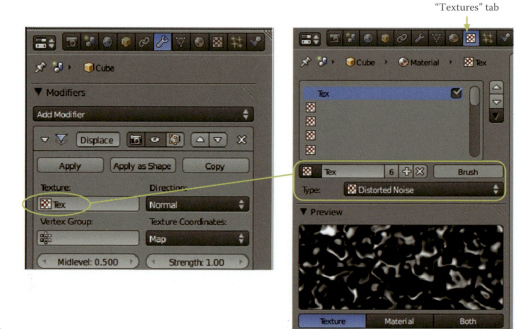

Figure 12.87

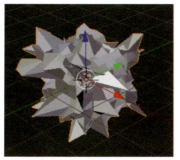
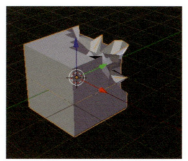

Default cube with a displace
modifier added

Only the vertex group is selected

Figure 12.88

surface of the cube (Figure 12.88, left). You will have to play around with the values in the "Modifiers" tab to establish their effect.

Start over and this time, after subdividing the surface of the cube, deselect all vertices then create a "Vertex Group." Repeat the process, again selecting "Tex" in the "Modifiers" tab, and this time select "Group" in the "Vertex Groups" slot of the modifier. Now, only the vertices in the "Vertex Group" are displaced (Figure 12.60, right).

12.5.5 Hook Modifiers

The "Hook" modifier allows you to manipulate or animate selected vertices of a mesh while in "Object" mode. Vertices are assigned (hooked) to an "Empty" object that can be moved in object mode by pulling the selected vertices with it. This can be used for a static mesh deformation or the movement can be animated.

Let's move one corner of a cube. Start with the default scene with the cube object selected. Tab to "Edit" mode and deselect all vertices with the A key, then select one vertex (corner) by pressing it with the RMB. Press Ctrl + the H key and select "Hook to New Object" (Figure 12.89). An "Empty" object is added to the scene (orange line under

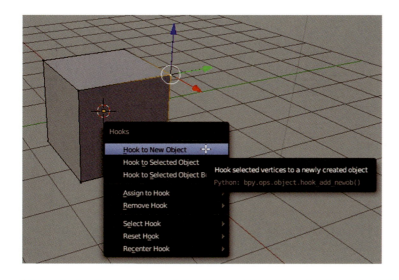

Figure 12.89

Hook modifier with "Empty" added

Figure 12.90

the widget), and by going to the "Properties" window, "Object Modifiers" button, you will see that a "Hook" modifier has been added named "Hook-Empty" (Figure 12.90). Select and move the "Empty" in object mode and you'll see that the cube deforms (Figure 12.91).

Let's do this another way.

With the default "Cube" object in the default scene, tab to "Edit" mode and select one vertex only. In the "Properties" window, "Object Data" buttons, "Vertex Groups" tab click on the plus sign to add a vertex group and click "Assign" which creates a vertex group consisting of the one selected vertex.

In "Object" mode deselect the cube and add an "Empty" object. Reposition the "Empty" away from the "Cube."

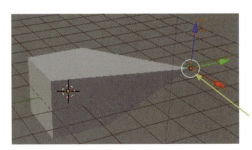

An empty has been added

In edit mode, you can move the corner of the cube away from the empty. However, when the empty is selected and moved in object mode, the corner follows

Figure 12.91

Deselect the "Empty" and select the "Cube." In the "Properties" window, "Modifiers" buttons add a "Hook" modifier. In the "Hook" modifier click on the "Vertex Group" panel and select "Group." This is assigning the vertex group consisting of the one vertex to the modifier. Click on the "Object" panel and select "Empty" to assign the "Empty" object to the modifier.

By selecting the "Empty" object in the 3D window and moving it about the single cube's vertex in the "Vertex Group" will follow the movement.

12.5.6 Lattice Modifiers

Lesson 08
08-07
Lattice Modifier

The "Lattice" modifier is used to deform a mesh object or to control the movement of particles. By using the modifier, it is simple to shape a mesh object that has many vertices. A lattice is a nonrenderable grid of vertices; therefore, it does not render in the scene. You can use the same lattice to deform several objects by giving each object a modifier pointing to the lattice.

Let's deform a UV sphere object with a lattice modifier. Delete the default cube, add a UV sphere to the scene, then add a "Lattice" (Shift + A key—Add—Lattice). Change to "Textured" mode in the "Viewport Shading." Before you can see the lattice mesh, you will have to scale the lattice up (press the S key + drag the mouse); the lattice is entered as a

Figure 12.92   Figure 12.93

simple mesh cube. Select the UV sphere and add a lattice modifier. Enter "Lattice" under the "Object" tab (Figure 12.92). Select the lattice, go to the "Object Data" button in the "Properties" window, and alter the *u*, *v*, and *w* values in the "Lattice" tab to subdivide the lattice mesh (Figure 12.93). In "Edit" mode, select a single lattice vertex and move it to deform the UV sphere mesh (Figure 12.94).

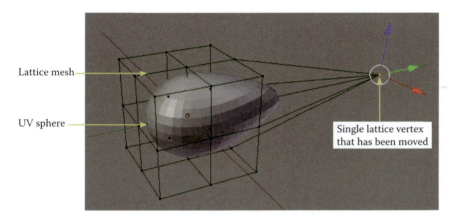

Figure 12.94

12.5.7 Mesh Deform Modifiers

The "Mesh Deform" modifier can deform one mesh with another cage mesh. This is similar to a "Lattice" modifier but instead of being restricted to the regular grid layout of a lattice, the cage can be modeled to fit around the mesh object being deformed. The cage mesh must form a closed cage around the part of the mesh to be deformed, and only vertices within the cage will be deformed. Typically, the cage will have far fewer vertices than the mesh being deformed.

After modeling a UV sphere mesh object, surround it with a simple cage mesh by scaling a cube to fit around the elongated sphere then selecting vertices in "Edit" mode

Click on "Bind" and wait until it changes to "Unbind"

Figure 12.95

and extruding them. Apply a "Mesh Deform" modifier to the scaled UV sphere. Enter the name of the cage mesh and press "Bind" to link the two meshes. The "Bind" operation may take several seconds to calculate depending on the complexity of your model. Wait until "Bind" changes to "Unbind" before selecting vertices on the cage (Figure 12.95). By dragging, scaling, and rotating the selected vertices, the original mesh will be deformed (Figure 12.96). The proximity of the cage to the original object has an influence on how the deformation reacts.

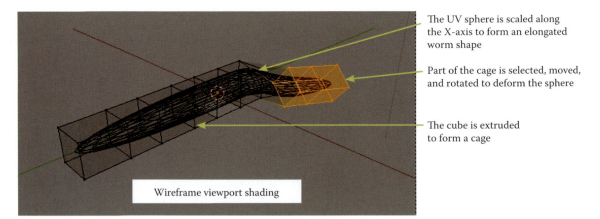

The UV sphere is scaled along the X-axis to form an elongated worm shape

Part of the cage is selected, moved, and rotated to deform the sphere

The cube is extruded to form a cage

Wireframe viewport shading

Figure 12.96

Note: The cage mesh will render in the scene; therefore, with the cage surrounding the elongated sphere, all you will see is the cage. You can select the cage and move it away from the sphere, keeping the deformation, but the cage will still render. To see the elongated sphere deformed without the cage, click on "Apply" in the modifier tab. The modifier is applied to the sphere and removed. You can now delete the cage and the elongated sphere remains deformed.

12.5.8 Shrinkwrap Modifier

The "Shrinkwrap" modifier takes a mesh and shrinks it down, wrapping the mesh around another object. The deformed mesh can then be offset to produce shapes in between the original shape and the deformed shape.

Delete the cube in the default Blender scene and add a UV sphere and a Cone mesh object; the cone should be located inside the UV sphere, which is easy to see when both objects are viewed in "Wireframe" mode (Figure 12.97). Add a "Shrinkwrap" modifier to the UV sphere, and enter "Cone" in the "Target" panel (Figure 12.98). Change the "Offset" value; notice how the shape changes when you increase the value to 1.25 and 3.00 (Figure 12.99).

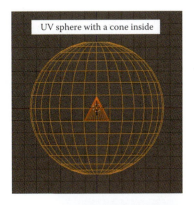

UV sphere with a cone inside

Figure 12.97

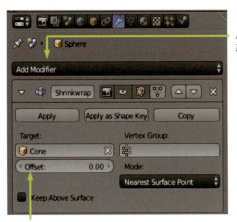

Increase the "Offset" value

Add a Shrinkwrap Modifier

The UV sphere is wrapped around the cone

Figure 12.98

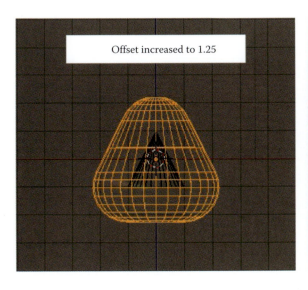

Offset increased to 1.25

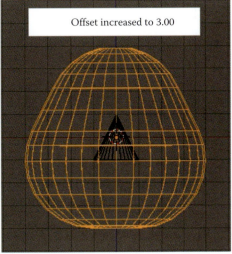

Offset increased to 3.00

Figure 12.99

12.5.9 Simple Deform Modifiers

The "Simple Deform" modifier deforms a mesh by changing values in the modifier and having a second object with an influence. To see this modifier in action, add a UV sphere in the default scene with a scaled down cube located in the center of the sphere (Figure 12.100). Switch to "Wireframe" display mode and add the simple "Deform" modifier to the UV sphere with "Cube" entered as the origin (Figure 12.101). Drag the "Limits" slider to see the change to the sphere; select the cube with the RMB and manipulate it on an axis to deform the sphere (Figure 12.102).

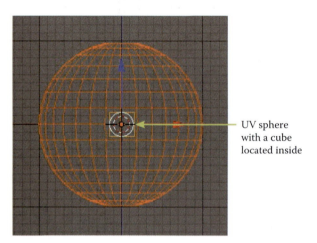

UV sphere with a cube located inside

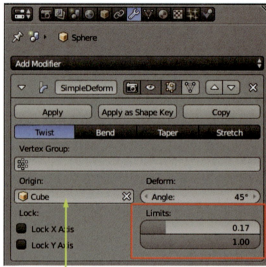

Enter "Cube" as the origin

Figure 12.100

Figure 12.101

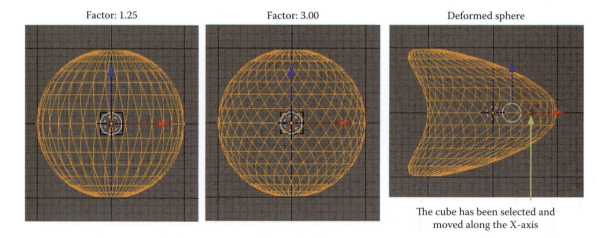

Factor: 1.25

Factor: 3.00

Deformed sphere

The cube has been selected and moved along the X-axis

Figure 12.102

12.5.10 Smooth Modifiers

The "Smooth" modifier smooths the mesh object by softening the angles between adjacent faces; this shrinks the size of the original object at the same time. Note the smoothing effect is only applied to how the objects surfaces are drawn in the 3D window. In smoothing, no additional vertices, edges, or faces are added to the mesh object. The modifier is based on the "Smooth" function in the tools panel.

The modifier panel in Figure 12.103 includes the following buttons:

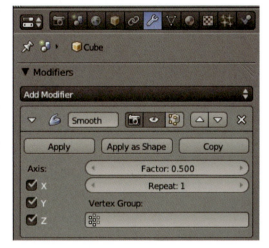

- **X, Y, Z**. Specifies along which axis the modifier will be applied.
- **Factor**. Defines the amount of smoothing. Lower or negative values can be used but can deform the mesh object.
- **Repeat**. Specifies the number of smoothing iterations.
- **Vertex group**. Vertex group named to specify which vertices are affected (if novertex group is specified, the whole object is affected).

In applying the "Factor" and "Repeat" values, the logic of the operation is to first set a value (the Factor) then perform the calculation a number of times to achieve the desired

Figure 12.103

smoothing effect. In the last two images of Figure 12.104, a Factor value of 2.00 has been set; the calculation has been performed once (Repeat: 1) then performed a second time (Repeat: 2).

Factor: 0.500, Repeat: 1 Factor: 2.00, Repeat: 1 Factor: 2.00, Repeat: 2

Figure 12.104

Note an object should have a reasonable number of faces before the modifier is effective. For example, the default cube object with six faces will merely shrink in size as "Repeats" are applied with a "Factor" value of 1.000. Subdividing the cube three or four times will show a completely different effect.

12.5.11 Laplacian Smooth Modifier

The "Laplacian Smooth" modifier is similar to the "Smooth" modifier 12.5.10 except that it does not use the same calculation as the "Smooth" function in the tools panel. It uses the mathematical operator "Laplace" in the calculation for drawing the surface of the mesh (http://en.wikipedia.org/wiki/Laplace_transform). Again, no additional vertices, edges,

Figure 12.105

or faces are created. As well as smoothing angles between adjacent surface faces it also allows smoothing of edges. Edges are smoothed by applying the "Border" value.

To demonstrate, use the default cube object with its surface subdivided three or four times in "Edit" mode but remember the modifier only works in "Object" mode.

In the modifier panel (Figure 12.105) the default settings are Lambda; Factor: 0.010 and Lambda; Border: 0.010 and a calculation has been made once (Repeat 1). Even with the surface of the cube subdivided you will find it difficult to see the slight smoothing that has been applied. To see a more pronounced smoothing set the "Factor" value to 1.000 and the "Border" value to 0.000. With these values smoothing is applied to the surface only. Observe the effect with "Repeat" values of 1, 2, and 3 (Figure 12.106).

To demonstrate the effect of applying the "Border" value, in "Edit" mode, remove vertices as shown in Figure 12.107. Set "Factor" value

The difference when "Factor 1" is applied to the "Cube" object

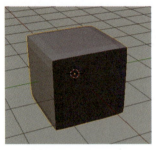 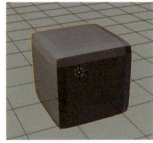 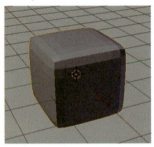

Figure 12.106

Factor: 1, Repeat: 1   Repeat: 2   Repeat: 3

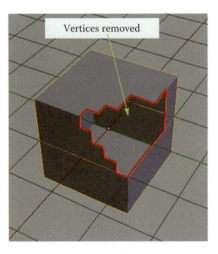 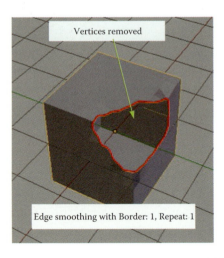

Figure 12.107   Figure 12.108

to 0.000 and "Border" value to 1.000. Observe the smoothing effect on the raw edge of surface around the gap where vertices were removed with "Repeat" values. Remember that the smoothing effect can be controlled to apply to all or any of the X-, Y-, and Z-axis and it may be applied to a selected "Vertex Group" (Figures 12.107 and 12.108).

12.5.12 Wave Modifiers

The "Wave" modifier applies a deformation in the form of a wave. To demonstrate, we will apply the modifier to a plane. In the default Blender scene, delete the cube and add a plane. Scale the plane up (the S key + 6), tab into "Edit" mode, and subdivide the plane by clicking "Subdivide" in the tools panel five times. Tab back to object mode.

Lesson 08
08-09
Wave Modifier

Go to the "Properties" window, "Object Modifiers" button and click "Add Modifier" to open the drop down selection menu. Select "Wave." In the 3D window, you immediately see the plane deform; it is pulled up in the middle and punched in at the top of the bulge (Figure 12.109). The "Wave" modifier has been applied on both the X- and Y-axis. In the

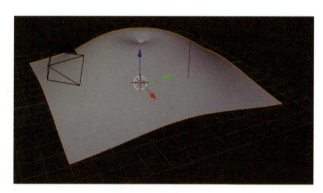

Figure 12.109

Wave form control value

Figure 12.110

"Modifiers" tab you see "X," "Y," and "Cyclic" ticked (Figure 12.110). "X" and "Y" refer to the axis and "Cyclic" means that an animation of the wave will repeat over and over.

With your cursor in the 3D window, press Alt + the A key to see the animation play. Press Esc to stop. Untick the "X" axis in the "Modifiers" tab and play again—a wave along the Y-axis results. At the bottom of the "Modifiers" tab, change "Speed" to 0.09, "Width" to 1.08, and "Height" to 0.34 (Figure 12.111). Play the animation again. You can change these values to whatever you want; in fact, go ahead and play around with different values to see what happens. It's the only way to get the idea.

Figure 12.111

Properties window—object modifiers button

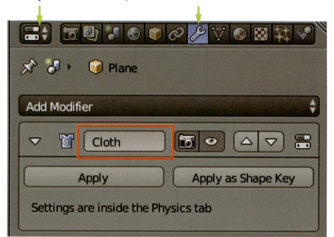

Figure 12.112

Properties window—Physics buttons

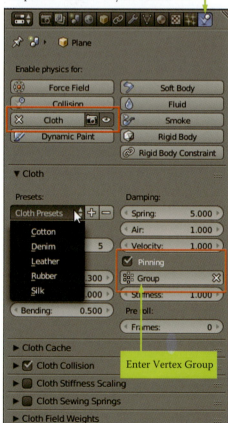

Enter Vertex Group

Figure 12.113

12.6 Modifiers for Simulating

12.6.1 Cloth and Collision Modifiers

The "Cloth" modifier allows a mesh object to be animated to exhibit the characteristics of a cloth material or fabric. To demonstrate the application of the modifier, follow this brief tutorial.

In a new scene delete the default cube and add a plane object. Scale the plane up four times and in "Edit" mode subdivide four times. A reasonable number of subdivisions are required to produce a good effect. With the plane selected in the 3D window, in "Object" mode, go to the "Properties" window, "Object Modifiers" button and add a "Cloth" modifier (Figure 12.112).

Note: The "Cloth" modifier controls are located in the "Properties" window, "Physics" buttons. Adding a "Cloth" modifier from the modifiers selection menu opens the "Cloth" tab in the "Physics" buttons therefore you may go directly to the "Physics" buttons and enable physics for "Cloth" (Figure 12.113).

With your cursor in the 3D window, press Alt+ the A key to play an animation. At this stage, the animation will simply show the plane descending and disappearing out of view. Press Esc to end the animation. If you look in the "Properties" window, "Scene" tab, you will see that a gravitational effect is applied (the "Gravity" box is ticked); therefore, the plane descends due to this force.

In the "Physics" buttons note that "Cloth Presets" is applied under the "Presets" tab. There is a drop down selection menu here for a variety of material types. Leave the preset as the default setting. Also note that there is no tick in the "Pinning" box, therefore this property is not activated. "Pinning" refers to pinning the cloth in place such as pinning to a notice board or pegging to a clothesline.

To "Pin" the "Cloth" (the plane), in the 3D window with the "Plane" selected, tab into "Edit" mode, deselect all the vertices, and then select only the two vertices on the rear

corners of the mesh. Go to the "Properties" window, "Object Data" button—"Vertex Groups" tab and click on the + sign to add a "Vertex Group." With the two vertices selected press "Assign," which assigns the two vertices to the group (Figure 12.114). Note that Blender has named the "Vertex Group," "Group." You can of course change this name if you wish. Tab back to "Object" mode, go to the "Physics" buttons and tick "Pinning" in the "Cloth" tab, then click on the vertex group panel just below "Pinning" and click and select "Group" to select the vertex group (Figure 12.115). In the 3D window, press Alt + the A key to play the animation again. Observe that the plane (cloth) falls away as if pinned in place and held by its two corners (Figure 12.116). Press Esc to stop the animation. Change the cloth "Presets" and replay the animation to see the different characteristics of the materials.

The cloth plane can be made to interact with other objects in the scene. Add a UV sphere and position it below the plane as shown in Figure 12.117. With the sphere selected, go to the "Properties" window, "Object Modifiers" button and add a "Collision" modifier. Replay the animation and you will

Figure 12.114

Figure 12.115

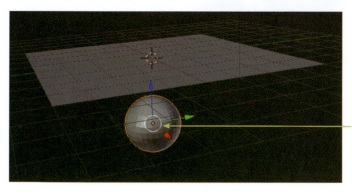

The two rear corners appear to be pinned in place, and the rest of the cloth falls away

Figure 12.116

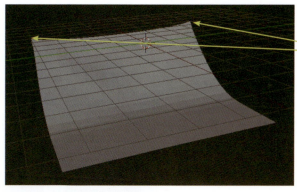

The UV sphere is selected in the 3D view as indicated by the manipulation widget

Figure 12.117

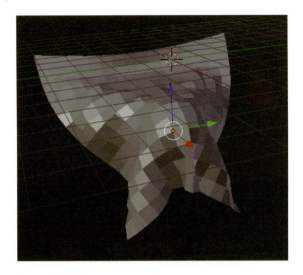

Figure 12.118

see the cloth plane fall and drape over the sphere (Figure 12.118).

Adding modifiers to objects introduces data in the "Physics" button, which controls how the objects react and interact. It is beyond the scope of this basic demonstration to explain all the settings. Experiment with the settings and record your findings to become proficient in the use of these modifiers.

12.6.2 Dynamic Paint Modifier
12.6.2.1 The Modifier

"Dynamic Painting" is the process of adding material color and deformation effects to the surface of a mesh object. With the "Dynamic Paint" modifier you use one object in a scene (the brush) to paint or deform the mesh surface of another object (the canvas). Although "Dynamic Paint" is listed in the "Properties" window, "Modifier" button, "Modifier" selection menu the controls are in the "Physics" buttons. Selecting the modifier from the modifiers selection menu adds the controls panel in the physics buttons.

12.6.2.2 Painting

To demonstrate "Dynamic Painting," delete the "Cube" object from the default Blender scene and add a "Plane" and a "UV Sphere." Scale the "Plane" up six times and in "Edit" mode subdivide six times (Figure 12.119).

With the "Plane" selected in "Object" mode go to the "Properties" window, "Physics" buttons and click on "Dynamic Paint." In the "Dynamic Paint" tab note that by default "Canvas" is active (Figure 12.120). Click "Add Canvas." We will be painting on the "Plane" therefore it

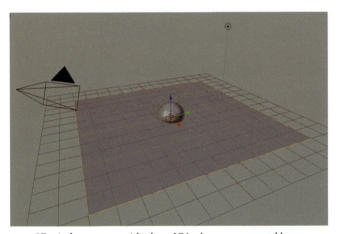

3D window—scene with plane, UV sphere, camera, and lamp

Figure 12.119

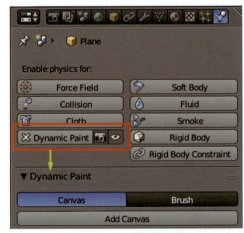

With Plane selected click "Add Canvas"

Figure 12.120

12. Modifiers

will be our canvas. Notice that in the "Physics" buttons, "Dynamic Paint Advanced" tab, the surface type is "Paint." To enable the paint application to render click the plus sign next to the "Paintmap Layer" button in the "Dynamic Paint Output" tab (Figure 12.121).

Still with the "Plane" selected, add a material. In the "Materials" buttons, "Options" tab check (tick) "Vertex Color Paint." This is also required to enable rendering.

Deselect the "Plane" in the 3D window and select the "UV Sphere." In the "Physics" buttons click on "Dynamic Paint," click "Brush" then "Add Brush." The "UV Sphere" will be the object with which we will paint. Note the blue color bar in the "Dynamic Paint" tab. This is a color picker where you may select your paint material color. Blue is the default color. In the 3D window, you will see the default blue appearing where the surface of the sphere intersects with the plane (Figure 12.122).

Dynamic painting is performed when an animation of the scene is running in the "Timeline" window. Change the 3D window to "Top Orthographic" view.

Click the plus sign here (changes to minus as shown) to enable rendering

Figure 12.121

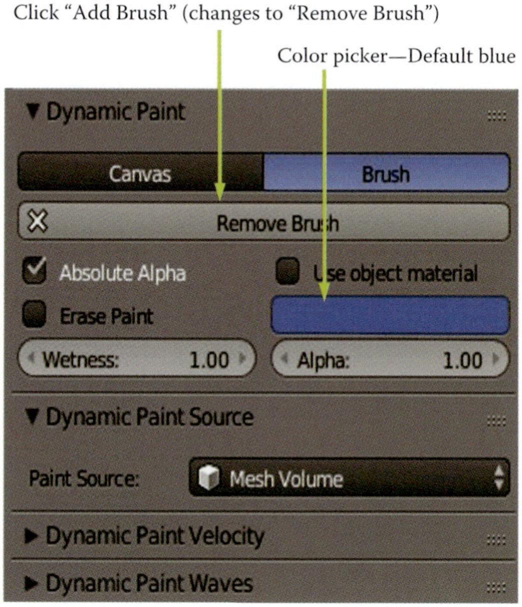

Click "Add Brush" (changes to "Remove Brush")

Color picker—Default blue

Figure 12.122

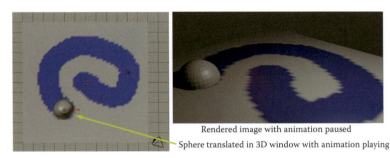

Rendered image with animation paused

Sphere translated in 3D window with animation playing

Figure 12.123

The application of material color from "Brush" takes place at the intersection of its surface with the "Canvas." Moving the sphere in "Top Orthographic" view limits the movement to the XY plane. To paint press "Alt + A key" or click on the "Play" button in the "Timeline" window then drag the sphere (G key—move mouse). As the "Brush" is moved material color is applied to the canvas as long as the animation plays. Remember the default animation in the "Timeline" window is set at 250 frames and the default frame rate is 24 frames per second this gives approximately 10.4 s of animation. You may increase the time for painting by increasing the "End" value in the "Timeline" window header. Once the animation reaches the end the canvas is wiped clean. Before the end of the animation, pause the animation (Figure 12.123). Render an image.

The "Dynamic Paint," "Physics" buttons allow a variety of paint application effects. You will have to experiment with the settings and record your findings but to get you started try the following.

Tip: The simple "Plane–Sphere" scene arrangement will provide a base for experimenting but it is tedious to restart the animation play, select and grab the sphere each time you try a new setting. With the scene in "User Perspective" view and the "Sphere" in grab mode, the paint application stops when the "Sphere" goes above or below the surface of the "Plane." This has the potential for an animation effect but to make life a little easier set up a simple animation to have the sphere move across the surface of the plane as the timeline animation plays. You can then change "Dynamic Paint" settings and simply press "Alt + A key" to see results.

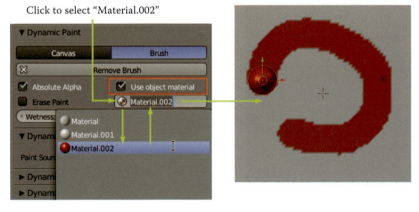

Figure 12.124

The alternative to using the brush color bar picker is to use the material color of the "Brush" object. Add a material to the sphere then in the "Physics" buttons, "Dynamic Paint" tab check (tick) "Use object material." The default blue is replaced by a button with a sphere icon. Click on the button and select the material you have just added to the sphere (Figure 12.124).

The "Physics" buttons, "Dynamic Paint Source" tab is a particular area of interest (Figures 12.125 and 12.126).

Click to show Paint Source options

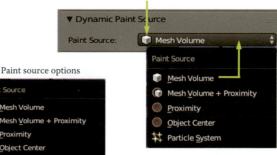

Figure 12.125

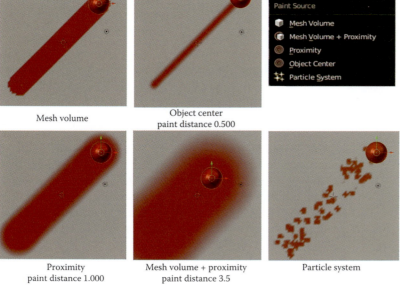

Mesh volume

Object center
paint distance 0.500

Paint source options

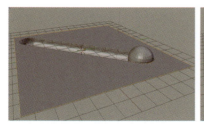

Proximity
paint distance 1.000

Mesh volume + proximity
paint distance 3.5

Particle system

Figure 12.126

12.6.2.3 Deforming

The "Dynamic Paint" tools may also be used to deform the surface of a mesh object.

Use the same "Plane–Sphere" scene arrangement. Even better use the scene with the sphere animated on the surface of the plane.

With the "Plane" selected, in the "Properties" window, "Physics" buttons—"Dynamic Paint," "Dynamic Paint Advanced" tab change the "Surface Type" to "Displace" (Figure 12.127). Animate the scene to see the sphere deform the plane. With the default settings the sphere gouges a furrow in the surface of the plane (Figure 12.128).

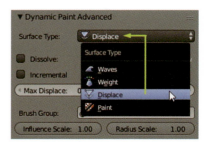

Figure 12.127

Vertices displaced—gouged furrow

Vertices displaced—welt created

Figure 12.128

Select the "Plane" in the 3D window, tab to "Edit" mode and in the "Tools" panel (T key to display), "Shading/UVs" tab, "Shading"—"Normals" click on "Flip Direction." Replay the animation to see the sphere create a welt on the surface of the plane. The deformation takes place in the direction of the normal to the plane (at right angles to the surface).

Experiment with the "Max Displace" and "Displace Factor" settings in the "Dynamic Paint Advanced" tab.

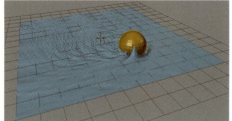

Waves created as sphere is translated

Figure 12.129

12.6.2.4 Waves

Create wave effects on the surface by changing the "Dynamic Paint Advanced" "Surface Type" to "Waves." With the sphere animated to move on the surface of the plane the sphere appears to plough through water (Figure 12.129).

12.6.3 Explode Modifier

The "Explode" modifier makes a mesh object fly apart or explode. Before you can apply an "Explode" modifier, you must apply an "Emitter Particle System." If you are working methodically through this manual, you haven't learned to apply an "Emitter Particle System" at this point, so maybe put this on hold until that information is attained. I will write the procedure now since it is such a neat modifier—bookmark this page and make sure you return to it later.

In the 3D window, delete the cube and add a "UV Sphere." Leave the default number of segments and rings and zoom in on the sphere. With the sphere selected, go to the "Properties" window, "Particles" button and in the panel click on the "New" to add a particle system (Figure 12.130). The "Particle System" controls display (Figure 12.131). In the "Emission" tab, change the "Number" value to 100 and the "Lifetime" value to 250. In the "Properties" window—"Scene" button—"Gravity" tab, untick "Gravity" (Figure 12.131). In the "Properties" window—"Object Modifiers"

Properties window—Particles button

Figure 12.130

button, click "Add Modifier" (you will see that there is already a "Particle System" modifier applied) and select "Explode." With your cursor in the 3D window, press Alt + the A key to see the sphere fly apart (Figure 12.132).

12.6.4 Fluid Simulation Modifier

For fluid simulation, see Chapter 17.

12.6.5 Ocean Modifier

The "Ocean" modifier creates an animated ocean topography from a "Plane" object. This modifier is sometimes referred to as the "Ocean Simulator." To demonstrate its application, perform the following procedure remembering this is a basic introduction. To realize the full

Properties window—particle system buttons ⟶

Properties window—scene buttons

Untick "Gravity"

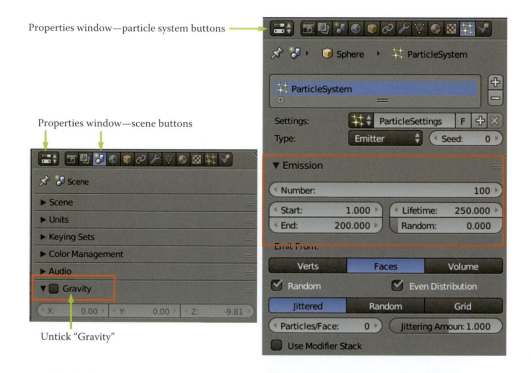

Figure 12.131

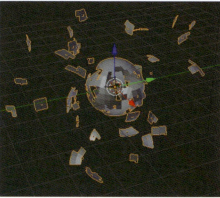

Figure 12.132

potential of the "Ocean" modifier it has to be used in conjunction with material settings and lighting effects. Instruction for this can be found in video tutorials on the Internet.

12.6.5.1 Set the Scene

In the default Blender scene delete the "Cube" object and add a "Plane" object.

Leave everything as presented by default except the location and orientation of the "Camera." The scene can be arranged however you like but in order to see the demonstration as depicted make the following adjustments to the location and rotation of the "Camera."

Select the "Camera" and with the mouse cursor in the 3D window press the N Key to display the object properties panel. Change the Z location value to: Z: 1.0442. This lowers the "Camera" in the scene to a position closer to the midplane. Change the "Camera" rotation values to X: 82.849, Y: −3.441, and Z: 51.073 (Figure 12.133).

Deselect the "Camera" and select the "Plane."

In the "Properties" window, "Modifier" buttons, click "Add Modifier" and select the "Ocean" modifier in the selection panel that displays (Figure 12.134).

In the 3D window, you will immediately see that the "Plane" object is expanded beyond the view of the 3D window (Figure 12.135). The "Plane" has in fact been converted into an "ocean" topography.

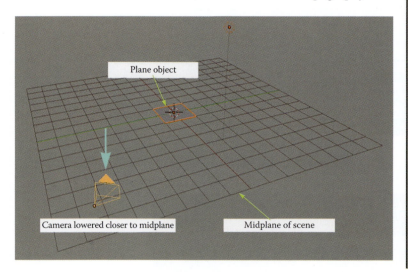

Figure 12.133

Figure 12.134

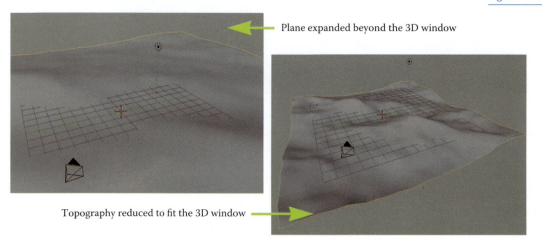

Plane expanded beyond the 3D window

Topography reduced to fit the 3D window

Figure 12.135

In the "Properties" window, "Ocean Modifier" panel you will see buttons and sliders for adjusting the display of the ocean topography. To adjust the topography to coincide with the demonstration click on the "Size" panel, press delete and type the new value 0.42. This reduces the ocean topography to fit within the 3D window view (Figure 12.135).

What you see in fact is the "Plane" object deformed to represent the surface of the ocean. At this stage, it is deformed using the default values in the "Ocean" modifier panel except for the "Size" value. The modifier panel contains buttons and sliders for adjusting the ocean topography to suit your particular needs. We will leave you to research and experiment with these values since this is merely an introduction.

12.6.5.2 Animating the Scene

At the bottom of the default Blender screen is the "Timeline" window, which is a graphical representation of an animation sequence. Note the vertical green line cursor located at frame number 1. In the "Properties" window, "Ocean Modifier" panel you will see a "Time" button/slider with the value 1.00 set.

You are therefore at frame one of the animation at the start time 1.00 s. If you want to be pedantic you could set the start time to 0.000 s.

Right click on the "Time" slider and select "Insert Keyframe." The "Time" slider turns yellow and you see a vertical yellow line displayed in the "Timeline" window at frame one, indicating that a "Keyframe" has been set. Move the timeline cursor (vertical green line) to frame 250 (250 is the number of frames in the default animation). In the "Time" slider panel change the value to 5.00 (5 s). This means that the 250 frames will play in 5 s. With 5.00 set right click on the "Time" panel and again select "Insert Keyframe" to place a second "Keyframe" at the end of the 250-frame animation (Figure 12.136).

In the "Timeline" window press the "Play" button to see the ocean animated.

Change to "Camera" view to see the ocean waves rise and fall as if viewed from a small boat or raft. Add a material color to the "Plane" object now the ocean for a more realistic effect. Experiment with the different settings in the "Ocean" modifier panel for even more realistic effects. Add material and texture and play with lamps and lighting for more effect. The effects are limitless (Figure 12.137).

Figure 12.136

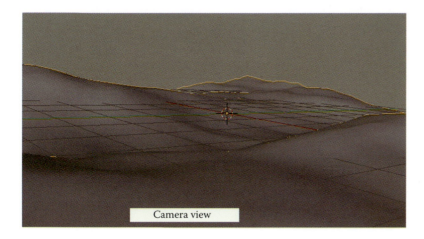

Camera view

Figure 12.137

Note: With a texture added to the "Plane" rendering each frame takes a considerable time, therefore, to see an animation play you will have to render an animation sequence.

12.6.6 Particle Instance Modifier

The "Particle Instance" modifier allows you to duplicate an object and position the duplicates to mimic the position and number of particles emitted from a particle system.

As always, an example is a good way to explain this type of application. Before you begin, be familiar with particle systems as described in Chapter 13. In a new scene, delete the default cube and add a plane object. Deselect the plane and add a UV sphere—both the plane and the sphere will be located at the center of the world. Go to the "Scene" button in the properties window and untick "Gravity" (Figure 12.138). This is done so that particles emitted from an object will not be subject to a gravitational force. With the "Plane" selected in the 3D window, add a particle system. In the "Properties" window, "Particles" buttons click "New." Use the default system and change the following settings (Figure 12.139):

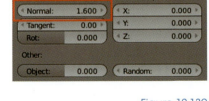

Remove the tick

Figure 12.138

Figure 12.139

- **"Emission" tab**
  - Number: 5 (number of particles emitted)
  - Lifetime: 250 (length of the default animation in frames)
  - Emit from: Verts (particles will emit from the vertices)
- **"Velocity" tab**
  - Normal: 1.600 (gives the particles a starting velocity)

Properties window—Modifiers buttons

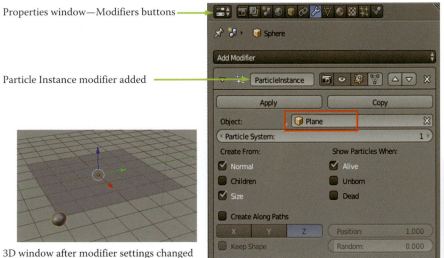

Particle Instance modifier added

3D window after modifier settings changed

Figure 12.140

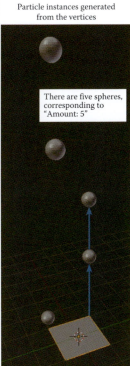

Particle instances generated from the vertices

There are five spheres, corresponding to "Amount: 5"

Figure 12.143

With the UV sphere selected in the 3D window, add a "Particle Instance" modifier. Click in the "Object" panel (orange cube icon) and select "Plane." The plane in the 3D window is surrounded by spheres. In the "Create From:" and "Show Particles When:" columns, tick the boxes as shown in Figure 12.140. We only want to show objects associated with live particles and we want to control the size of the objects by adjusting the size of the particles. In the 3D window all but one very tiny sphere disappeared.

Go back to the plane's particle system (select the plane) and in the "Physics" tab, set "Size: 0.300" (Figure 12.141). This controls the size of the object instances in the 3D window. Press Alt+ the A key with the cursor in the 3D window to animate the generation of particles and duplicates of the sphere. You will see that the spheres are being generated from the corners of the plane (vertices) in a random order (Figure 12.143). In the plane's "Particle System"—"Emission" tab, "Random" is ticked (Figure 12.142).

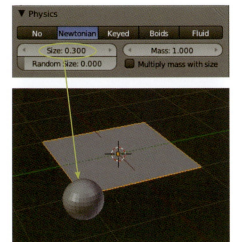

Figure 12.141

Figure 12.142

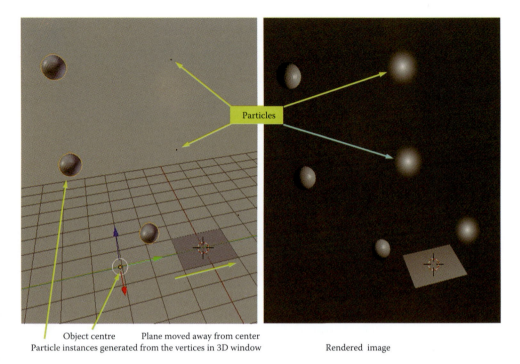

Object centre   Plane moved away from center

Particle instances generated from the vertices in 3D window   Rendered image

Figure 12.144

Allow the 250-frame animation to play then press Esc. You can use the up/down and left/right arrow keys to move through the animation frame by frame to see the sphere duplications; you can also render an image at any stage to see the result (Figure 12.144). You will probably have to reposition the camera to get a good view.

Finally, while at frame 1, select the plane and drag it away from the center of the scene. Step through the animation again. The spheres are generated, mimicking the position of the plane's vertices (Figure 12.144). If you render an image (press F12), you will see the particles rendered as halos as well as the sphere duplicates.

This example has demonstrated that you can duplicate objects using a particle system and control the effect with the particle system. As always, there are plenty of controls with which you can experiment. You will find detailed tutorials on the Internet describing specific applications of the particle instance modifier (see the Bibliography section).

12.6.7 Smoke Modifier

See Chapter 18 for Smoke Simulation.

The "Smoke" modifier adds a smoke and fire simulation to your scene such as flame and smoke from a fire or just smoke from a chimney. The following procedures for adding smoke are basic examples. Experimentation will be required to fully understand the application of this modifier.

In Blender, smoke is emitted from an object (the Flow Object) into a defined volume of space (the Domain). In the later versions of Blender, there is the option to emit smoke from a "Mesh" or from "Particles." Particles are described in Chapter 13 and their movement can be affected by force fields; therefore, using particles to emit smoke gives flexibility to smoke generation and how it displays and animates.

To demonstrate the smoke modifier we will begin with the basics and have the smoke emitted from a mesh object.

Having said the above it must be noted that adding a "Smoke Modifier" to an object in a Blender scene simply activates the "Smoke Physics." Controls for generating smoke and fire are contained in the "Properties" window, "Physics" buttons.

12.6.7.1 The Quick Method

This example will use the "Quick Smoke" and "Fire" generation method in Blender. It will allow you to see the basics of what can be achieved. It is recommended that you use this procedure as a starting point only and then take time to fully analyze smoke generation as outlined in the following procedures.

Select the default "Cube" object in the 3D window. Press the "Space" bar to open the search feature in Blender and type "Quick." You will be presented with the options, "Quick Smoke," "Quick Fur," "Quick Explode," and "Quick Fluid." Select the "Quick Smoke" option.

The default cube will display in "Wireframe" mode and be surrounded by an orange cuboid. The orange outline is the "Domain," which is defining the cubic volume of 3D space in which smoke will be generated. The "Cube" inside the "Domain" is the "Flow" object (Emitter) for smoke generation. In the "Tool Panel" at the lower left of the screen the "Quick Smoke" tab is displayed with a drop down selection menu displaying "Smoke." Change "Smoke" to "Smoke + Fire" and check (tick) "Render Smoke Object." The smoke emitter object will not render if this is unchecked.

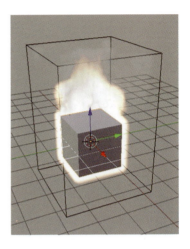

Figure 12.145

In the "Timeline" window press the "Play" button to set the cube on fire. Press the "Pause" button at frame 40 and render (F12) to see an image of the burning cube (Figure 12.145).

Make note that in the "Physics," "Smoke" tab with the "Flow" object selected the "Flow Source" is the default "Mesh" option.

12.6.7.2 The Long Way

The quick method is the freeway to smoke generation, which is the quick and easy method. It automatically sets up Blender to perform a smoke and fire generation from an object in

the 3D window and can be used as a starting point for a more advanced exercise. You must, however, take the long and winding road to fully understand the procedure and take advantage of this feature (see Chapter 18—Smoke Simulation).

12.6.8 Soft Body Modifiers

The "Soft Body" modifier in some respects is similar to the "Cloth" modifier in that it allows the animation of a deformation of a mesh object. To demonstrate this modifier, use a UV sphere positioned above a plane. Scale the default plane up four times and, in edit mode, subdivide it four times (Figure 12.146).

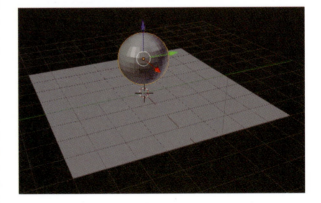

Figure 12.146

In the 3D window, select the "UV Sphere," tab into edit mode, and with all the vertices selected create a vertex group ("Properties" window, "Object Data" button, "Vertex Groups" tab—click on the + (plus) sign—click "Assign"). Set the "Weight" value to 0.000, which means that the vertices will not be anchored and will be able to fall under the influence of the "Gravity" setting in the "Scene" tab (Figure 12.147).

Figure 12.147

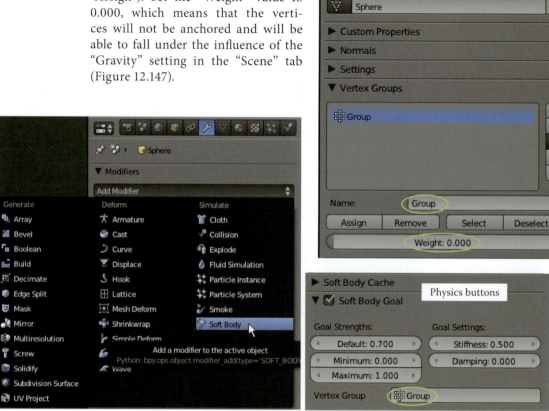

Figure 12.148

Add a "Soft Body" modifier to the sphere and in the "Physics" tab—"Soft Body Goal" tab—"Vertex Group," enter "Group" (Figure 12.148). Pressing Alt + the A key in the 3D window will play an animation of the sphere falling through the plane. Deselect the sphere, select the plane, and add a "Collision" modifier (Figure 12.149). When the animation is played, the sphere now descends and deforms as it comes in contact with the plane, eventually becoming a flat blob on the surface of the plane (Figure 12.150).

12. Modifiers

Figure 12.149

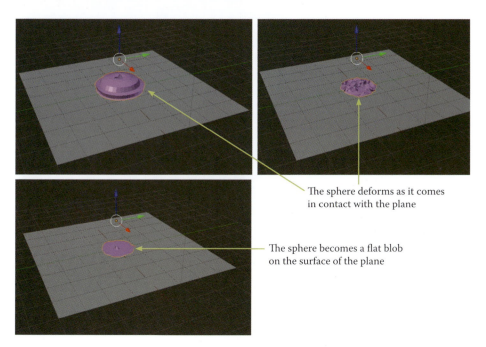

The sphere deforms as it comes in contact with the plane

The sphere becomes a flat blob on the surface of the plane

Figure 12.150

13

Particle Systems

13.1 Overview

Particle systems are used to simulate large amounts of small moving objects, creating effects such as fire, dust, clouds, smoke, or fur, grass, and other strand-based objects. In Blender "Particles" are points on the computer screen seen initially as small black dots being emitted from an object which render as fuzzy points of light (a light point with a halo effect). To emit particles from an object a "Particle System" is assigned (added) to the object then an animation sequence is run.

Lesson 10
10-01
Basic Blender
Particles—Part 1

Adding a "Particle System" to an object creates a system ready to run with default settings. The default settings are altered to change the way particles display and with multiple particles emitted, to create the desired effects.

Lesson 10
10-02
Basic Blender
Particles—Part 2

Particles are created by adding a "Particle System" to an object, which has been selected in the 3D window. The default settings in a new "Particle System" display an array of particles when an animation is played in the "Timeline" window. The animation is automatically created when the system is added.

Lesson 10
10-07
Static Particles

The best way to see how this is accomplished is to follow a few simple instructions and run the default "Particle System."

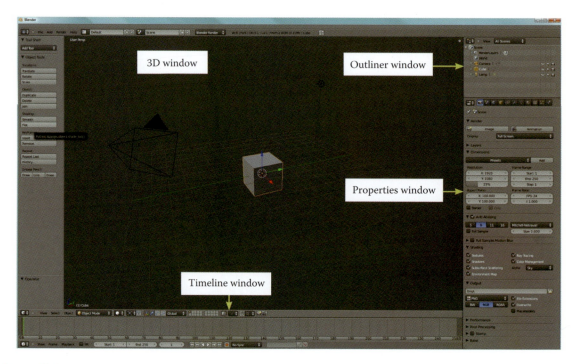

3D window

Outliner window

Properties window

Timeline window

Figure 13.1

Before setting up a system recap on the screen arrangement (Figure 13.1) and in particular the "Properties" window that contains the controls for manipulating the display in the 3D window. You also need to know how to play an animation in the "Timeline" window.

13.1.1 Nomenclature

When referring to the "Properties" window, "Particles" tab, the nomenclature in Figure 13.2 will be observed.

13.2 Setting Up the Default Particle System

Open Blender, delete the default cube object from the scene, and add a new UV sphere. Particles are emitted from the vertices or faces on the surface of a mesh object. Using a sphere provides a reasonable number of vertices and faces from which to emit particles. Leave the default values for the sphere as they appear in the "Properties" window. With the "Sphere" selected, go to the "Properties" window and click the "Particles" button. Click on "New" to add a particle system (Figure 13.3). The window will open with the "Tabs" (panels) that control the system. This display may appear daunting at first, but Blender has automatically created a default "Particle System" for the "Sphere" (Figure 13.4). A system is created and is unique for the selected object in the 3D window.

The arrangement of the "Tabs" (panels) is purely a matter of convenience. There is no order of priority. With the "Properties" window arranged at the right-hand side (RHS) of

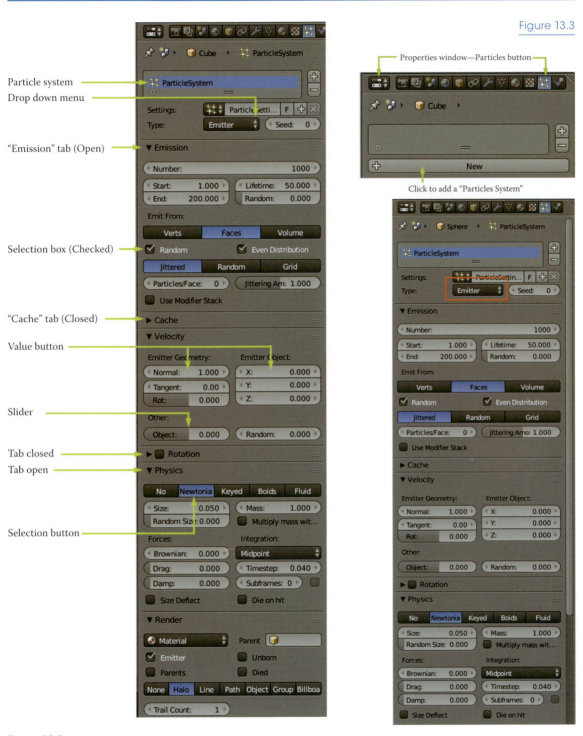

Particle system

Drop down menu

"Emission" tab (Open)

Selection box (Checked)

"Cache" tab (Closed)

Value button

Slider

Tab closed

Tab open

Selection button

Figure 13.2

Figure 13.3

Properties window—Particles button

Click to add a "Particles System"

Figure 13.4

the screen with the tabs in a vertical stack, the "Tabs" (panels) may be moved up or down by LMB click and dragging the dimpled area in the upper RH corner of each tab.

Note: Particles only display in the 3D window when an animation sequence is run by activating "Play" in the "Timeline" window or scrubbing (dragging) the "Timeline" cursor (vertical green line) to a frame in the animation.

Note: It is easier to see particles with the object selected. With the object selected they display as small orange squares. With the object deselected the particles appear as small white specs.

The first panel at the top of the stack is not labeled and unlike the "Tabs" it remains opened. This panel shows the name of the selected object next to the little orange cube icon. Where you see "Particle System" highlighted in blue is the name of the particle system being applied to the selected object (there can be more than one system applied to an object). The settings panel shows the name of the "Settings" data block assigned to the particle system being used. You will then gather that there can be a mix and match of particle systems and settings.

Note the "Type: Emitter." Clicking on the tab where the word "Emitter" is displayed will open a drop down menu with two selection options, "Emitter" and "Hair." Type: "Hair" is a unique system which will be discussed later.

To see the default "Particle System" in action, with the mouse cursor in the 3D window, press Alt + A key or press the play button in the "Timeline" header to run an animation showing particles being generated. Note that the "Timeline" window displayed across the bottom of the screen shows a green line (timeline cursor) moving as the animation plays. With the emitter object selected (the sphere), the animation will play showing particles as small orange squares being emitted and then falling toward the bottom of the screen (Figure 13.5). If the emitter object (the sphere) is not selected, the particles show as small black dots. The animation will play for 250 frames then repeat itself. Press "Esc" to stop the animation. Using the right/left arrows on the keyboard (with the mouse cursor in the 3D window) or by clicking and dragging the green line cursor in the timeline or by LMB clicking on frame 100 in the "Timeline" window, move the animation forward to frame 100; the particles will now be displayed as they occur at frame 100. Render the scene (press F12 or change the 3D window "Viewport Shading" to "Rendered") and you will see the UV sphere with the particles as halos (fuzzy balls of light, merged together) cascading downward (Figure 13.6). Press Esc to cancel the rendered image or return to the 3D window to "Solid Viewport Shading."

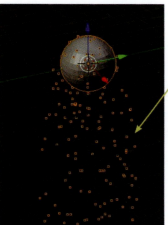

The particles are emitted as orange squares, as seen in the 3D window with the sphere selected

Figure 13.5

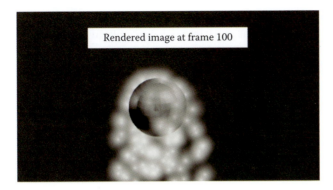

Figure 13.6

Properties window—Scene button

Click to remove the check (tick)

Figure 13.7

Note that particles emit their own light, therefore, it is not necessary to have a lamp in the scene. If the default lamp is deleted from the scene, the image rendered will show the halos and the emitter object illuminated by the light emitted from the particles.

By default, Blender renders an image in the "UV Image Editor" window (see the "Properties" window, "Render" buttons, "Render" tab, "Display" settings for other options).

In essence, the example has demonstrated a particle system being applied. It is now time to progress and discover how to manipulate the system. In the demonstration, the particles emitted from the sphere cascaded downward; this occurred since there is a gravitational effect applied. We will now turn that effect off. Go to the "Properties" window, "Scene" button and remove the tick from the little box in the "Gravity" tab (Figure 13.7). Set the animation in the timeline back to frame 1 and replay the animation (Alt + the A key). This time the particles emitted from the "UV Sphere" disperse in all directions away from the sphere (Figure 13.8). Note that the particles seem to only move for a certain time and disappear before the end of the animation; obviously there is something happening to cause this.

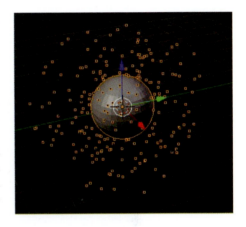

Figure 13.8

13.2.1 The Emissions Tab

Take a look at the "Properties" window with the "Particles" button activated and look at the "Emission" tab (Figure 13.9). You will see the following values: "Amount: 1000," "Start: 1.000," "End: 200.000," and "Lifetime: 50.000." These values mean that 1000 particles will be emitted starting at frame 1 and stopping at frame 200, but each particle will only be visible for 50 frames. The particles disappear after existing for 50 frames. Also look at the "Velocity" tab

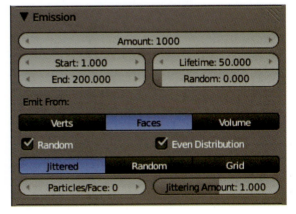

Figure 13.9

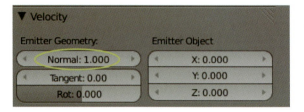

Figure 13.10

and the "Normal: 1.000" value (Figure 13.10). This means that particles are being emitted at a speed of 1 unit per second normal to the surface of the sphere (at 90° to the surface). Increase the "Lifetime" value to 200 and replay the animation. Now particles are displayed for the whole 250-frame animation since particles emitted at frame 200 stay visible until frame 250 (50 frames).

13.2.2 The Velocity Tab

To demonstrate another particle emission control feature, change the "Emitter Geometry Normal" value to 0.000 and the "Emitter Object Y" value to 10.000 in the "Velocity" tab. Replay the animation and you'll see that all the particles emitted move fairly rapidly along the y-axis of the scene (Figure 13.11). You have just told Blender to emit the particles along the Y-axis at 10 units per second instead of emitting them at 1 unit per second at 90° (normal) to the face on the surface of the sphere. Note that "Emit From Faces" in the "Emission" tab is activated (Figure 13.12).

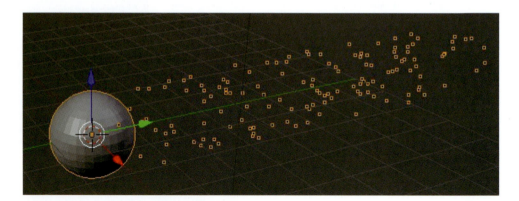

Figure 13.11

Figure 13.12

The forgoing example has demonstrated that a particle system can be controlled by values in the "Particles" buttons tabs.

Let's now look at where and how particles are emitted from an object. In the "Properties" window, "Particles" buttons, "Emission" tab, note the "Emit From": "Verts" (vertices), "Faces," and "Volume." The default value "Faces" is highlighted in blue. To see the effect of these buttons, start with a new Blender scene and delete the default cube. Add a plane object and remove the 3D manipulator widget (removing the widget will let us see more clearly what is happening when particles are emitted). Untick the "Gravity" box in the "Scene" buttons and add a particle system to the plane. Press Alt + the A key and play the animation showing the particle generation. You will see the particles being generated

on the face of the plane object (Figure 13.13). The particles are being generated at an initial velocity of 1 unit per second normal to the face of the plane (at 90° to the surface), which is in accordance with the default values in the "Velocity" tab.

In the "Emission" tab, "Emit From" buttons, select "Verts" (vertices) and replay the animation. You will now see the emission of particles from the four corners of the plane (Figure 13.14). Selecting "Faces" or "Verts" depends on what you want to see in your final render. The different combinations: "Verts," "Faces," "Volume," "Random," "Even Distribution," "Jittered," "Random," "Grid" create many particle emission variations. Experiment with these values and record your findings.

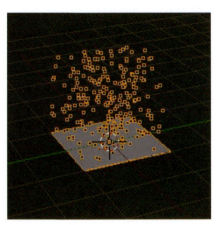

Figure 13.13

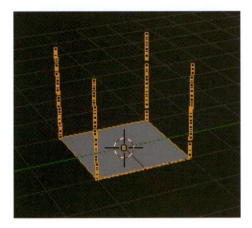

Figure 13.14

We will now investigate particle generation further. Start over with a new Blender scene and delete the default cube object. Add a circle object to the scene and scale it up three times (press the S key + 3). Tab into "Edit" mode and with all vertices selected, press the E key (extrude—**do not move the mouse**), click LMB followed by the S key (scale), and move the mouse toward the center of the circle. This creates a flat ring object with an outer and inner circle of vertices. When you are finished creating the new shape, click LMB (Figure 13.15). With the E key you have extruded (created a new set of vertices) and the S key has allowed you to scale the set of new vertices. Tab back to object mode and add a particle system. Go to the "Properties" window, "Scene" button, untick "Gravity," and play the animation. You will see particles being generated, but some may be moving up and some may

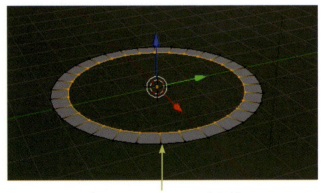

The outer vertices are extruded and scaled down to form the inner ring

Figure 13.15

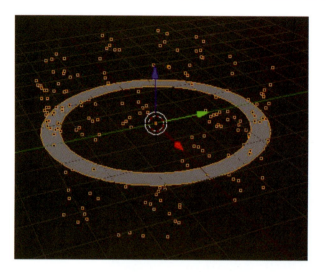

Figure 13.16

be moving down (Figure 13.16). Note that the default "Emission" tab—"Emit From" value is "Faces" and the "Velocity" tab—"Emitter Geometry"—"Normal" value is 1.000. We are therefore emitting particles from the faces of the object at 1 unit per second normal to the ring's faces.

Note: A "Normal" in Blender particles is a straight-line trajectory at 90° to the emitting surface. In complex modeling, this trajectory can be calculated in a positive or negative direction for different points, for example, outward or inward from an objects surface. At times this has to be corrected to direct all "Normals" in the same direction or reverse the direction.

In modeling the circular plane object, some faces may have been assigned a negative "Normal" value and some may have been assigned a positive "Normal" value, hence the movement of the particles in the positive and negative direction. If this occurs, the "Normal" values need to be recalculated to align them in the same direction.

To realign the "Normals," Tab into "Edit" mode and select all the vertices. With the cursor in the 3D window, press Ctrl+ the N key. "Make Normals Consistent" will display in the side panel at the lower LH corner of the screen.

Tab back to "Object" mode and replay the animation. All the particles will move in the same direction but not necessarily upward. Note that if the "Normal" value is changed to −1.000, the particles will move in the opposite direction; set the "Normal" value to +1.000 so the particles will move upward.

We will now look at what is happening when particles are generated. There are many combinations of settings with which to experiment therefore to attempt to introduce some logic we will consider only one scenario.

If you look at the extruded double circle in "Edit" mode you will observe that it is divided into 32 segments, therefore, there are 64 vertices (Figure 13.15).

In the "Properties" window, "Particles" buttons, "Emissions" tab note "Number: 1000" which means that 1000 particles will be generated over 200 frames of the animation. If we change "Emit From" from "Faces" to "Vertices" and untick "Random" Blender will emit 1000 particles from 64 vertices over 200 frames. Since we have unticked "Random" it will generate the vertices progressively around the circle. One thousand particles divided by 64 vertices equates to 15.625 particles per vertex. If you run the animation with "Lifetime" set at 200, you will observe groups of 16 vertices being generated at each vertex around the circle at first from the outer circle then from the inner circle. This produces the spiral

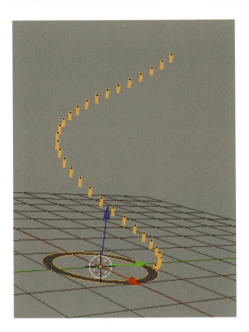

Figure 13.17

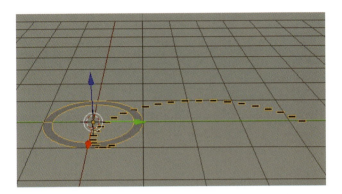

Figure 13.18

effect shown in Figures 13.17 and 3.18. In Figure 3.18, the "Emitter Geometry" normal value is 0.000 and the "Emitter Object" Y value is 1.000.

So far, the particles that have been generated have been displayed as dots or little orange squares in the 3D window and have been rendered as halos. In the "Render" tab, you will see a selection of render options: None, Halo, Line, Path, Object, Group, and Billboard (Figure 13.19). Select the "Object" option and reduce the number of particles in the "Emission" tab "Amount" to 32. Our plane circular ring object was created from a circle with 32 vertices, therefore it has 32 faces. Reducing the particle amount to 32 gives us approximately one particle per face. This is approximate since at this point the generation of the particles follows an animation curve that accelerates and decelerates. Play the animation again to regenerate the particles, then cycle through the animation and at frame 200 you will see 32 particles; however, they are not evenly spaced along the spiral (Figure 13.20). This is showing the influence

Figure 13.19

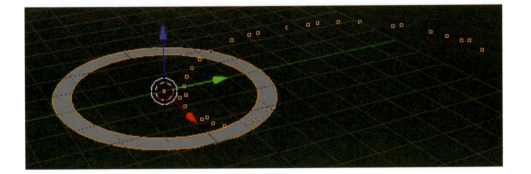

Figure 13.20

of the acceleration change in the generation. We are only concerned with reducing the particle count just now.

Deselect the ring in the 3D window, add a UV sphere object, and note that it is called "Sphere" (see the lower LH corner of the window). Move the sphere to one side away from ring. Deselect the sphere and reselect the ring. In the "Particles" button, "Render" tab, select render type "Object," look for "Dupli Object," click on the orange cube icon and select "Sphere" in the drop down panel that displays. The particles are now displayed in the 3D window as tiny little spheres (Figure 13.21). Go to the "Physics" tab and increase the "Size" value to increase the size of the tiny spheres in the 3D window. Render to see an image of the spheres.

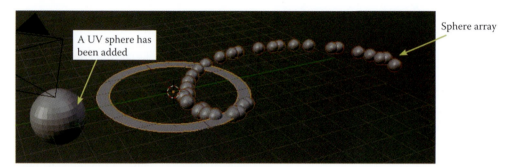

Figure 13.21

Up to now everything created and rendered has been the default dull gray color. Adding a new material color to the sphere will cause the array of spheres to display and render in that material color (Figure 13.22). Adding a material to the ring in the 3D window will cause the particles with a halo value to render in that material color.

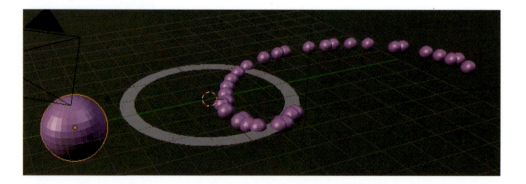

Figure 13.22

This demonstration of particle system applications has only shown the tip of the iceberg. We must now delve into a detailed study of the "Particles" button to ascertain the function of each tab and formulate the logic of the particle systems interface. There are many excellent tutorials available online to complement this study (see Bibliography section), and it is recommended that you attain a full understanding of the buttons to allow for the transition from an operator of the program to a creative artist.

13.3 Particle Settings and Material Influence

We will continue the study of the particle system by examining the particle settings and material influence and seeing how settings are entered to create effects. The possible effects that can be created are endless and only limited by the imagination: particles can be deflected off other objects, blown by the wind, displayed before they are built, and much more. It would be impossible to demonstrate everything and only by experimentation and recording settings for future use will you become proficient. Remember that a particular effect can be saved as a Blender file, which can be imported into a scene in another Blender file. When you create something interesting, it's worth saving and recording for future use. Blender doesn't come prepacked with instant goodies, so the objective for a Blender artist should be to compile an extensive library.

As we have seen, the particle settings are controlled by the sliders and buttons in the "Particle" buttons "Tabs" (Figure 13.23). Blender automatically creates a particle system when the "New" button is pressed. We must modify that system to produce the particular effect that we require. The system is then saved to a cache to be used.

13.4 The Particles Panel

The "Particles" button contains all the options relating to how particles are generated and displayed. To understand how to create specific effects using particles, we examine some of the "Tabs" in more detail.

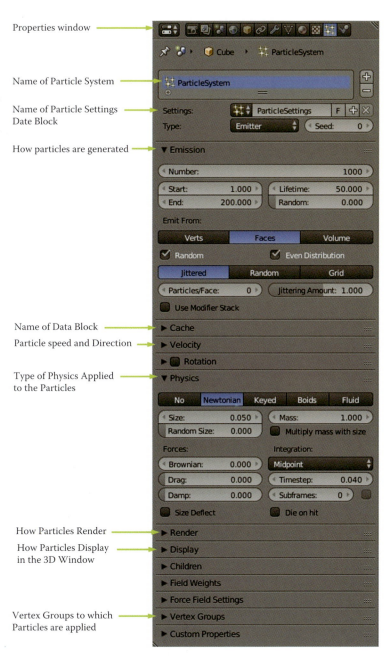

Properties window

Name of Particle System

Name of Particle Settings Date Block

How particles are generated

Name of Data Block

Particle speed and Direction

Type of Physics Applied to the Particles

How Particles Render

How Particles Display in the 3D Window

Vertex Groups to which Particles are applied

Figure 13.23

13.4.1 The Emission Tab

The "Emission" tab controls how particles are emitted (Figure 13.24).

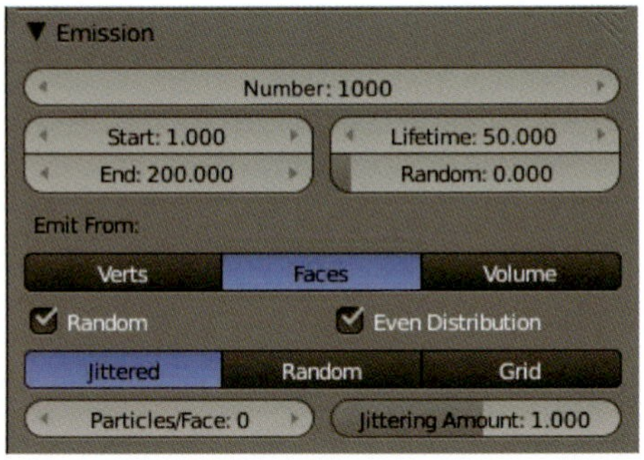

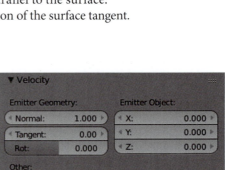

- **Amount.** The number of particles emitted in the animation between the start and the end frame settings.
- **Start.** The frame number in the animation where particles will start to be emitted.
- **End.** The frame number in the animation where particle emission will stop.
- **Lifetime.** How long each particle will be visible (number of frames) in the animation.
- **Random.** Particles are emitted from faces in a random order.
- **Even Distribution.** Distribution from faces based on face areas or edge length.
- **Emit From.** Particles may be emitted from vertices, faces, or the volume. "Faces" is selected in Figure 13.24, as indicated by the blue highlight.

Figure 13.24

The remaining options in the tab control the order of particle generation.

- **Random, Even Distribution; Jittered, Random, Grid; Particles/Face, Jittering Amount.** These options vary depending on which of the "Emit From" options has been selected. Experimentation and recording of results are required to establish combinations for specific applications.

13.4.2 The Velocity Tab

The "Velocity" tab settings control how fast and in what direction particles are emitted from a mesh object (Figure 13.25).

- **Emitter Geometry**
    - Normal: Velocity of the particles normal (at 90°) to the emitting surface.
    - Tangent: Velocity of the particles parallel to the surface.
    - Rotation: The value rotates the direction of the surface tangent.

- **Emitter Object**
    - The velocity of particles along the x, y, and z axes in the scene.
    - Note: All values may be entered as positive or negative, which reverses the direction.

- **Other**
    - Object: The object gives the particles a starting speed and direction.
    - Random: Gives the starting speed direction a random variation.

Figure 13.25

Note: The "Other" values are best demonstrated with particles being displayed as objects. See also the "Render" tab.

13.4.3 The Physics Tab (Not To Be Confused with the "Physics" Buttons)

Physics determine the way particles move and interact with the world around them. Note the selection bar at the top of the "Physics" tab with "Newtonian" highlighted in blue (Figure 13.26). "Newtonian" is the normal particle physics that we will consider at this time. The other options are:

- **No**. Particles stick to their emitter for the whole lifetime.
- **Keyed**. Allows particles to be directed from one emitter to another, setting up a chain of particles moving from one place to the other.
- **Boids**. Allows particles to be given rules of behavior, which allow them to represent flocks, swarms, herds, and schools of various kinds of animals.

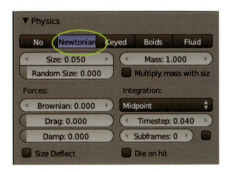

Just for the moment the only setting we need to concern ourselves with in the "Newtonian" system is the "Size" value, which controls the size of the particles as seen in the 3D window and as rendered in an image or movie.

Figure 13.26

13.4.4 The Display Tab

The "Display" tab controls how particles are seen in the 3D window. The options in this tab are useful when multiple particle systems are in play and it is desirable to distinguish between the particles in the different systems. Let's work with our examples and begin by starting a particle system to recap what we learned previously.

13.5 Starting a Particle System

We have already examined the default "Particle System" but to reinforce the procedure carry out the following.

Open Blender with its default scene containing a mesh cube object. Delete the cube and add a UV sphere, keeping the segments at 32 and rings at 16. The number of segments and rings may be altered in the tools panel (the T key toggles between hiding and showing this panel) at the lower left of the screen. With the sphere selected in the 3D window, go to the "Properties" window, "Particles" button and click "New" to add a particle system.

Blender has created a complete particle system that we can modify to produce whatever effect we want. Note the "Timeline" window displayed across the bottom of the screen; the timeline shows a 250-frame animation window as seen by "Start: 1" and "End: 250"

Figure 13.27

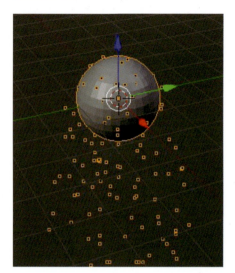

Figure 13.28

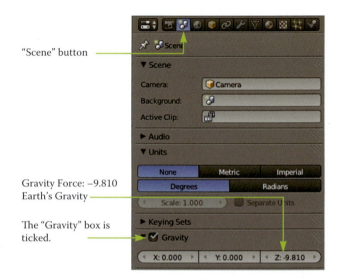

"Scene" button

▼ Scene

Camera: Camera
Background:
Active Clip:

► Audio
▼ Units

Gravity Force: –9.810
Earth's Gravity

The "Gravity" box is
ticked.

► Keying Sets
Gravity

X: 0.000   Y: 0.000   Z: -9.810

Figure 13.29

(Figure 13.27). With your cursor in the 3D window and with the UV sphere selected, press Alt + A key or press the play button in the timeline header to play the animation of particles being generated. The particles emit from the surface of the sphere in a random order and fall toward the bottom of the screen. The animation plays for 250 frames then repeats. Press Esc to cancel the animation.

Click on the green line and drag it over to frame 41 to see the view in Figure 13.28. The particles behave in this manner since there is a gravitational force being applied. Have a look at the "Properties" window, "Scene" button and note the tick in the "Gravity" box (Figure 13.29). Click on the tick to remove it and play the animation again—this time the particles emit from the sphere and float off into space (Figure 13.30). They still emit in a random order from the faces of the sphere. Look at the "Emission" tab and note the values inserted (Figure 13.31). These values tell us that 1000 particles will be generated in the animation starting at frame 1 and ending at frame 200 during the animation and that the animation is 250 frames in length. There is also a "Lifetime" value that tells us that when a particle

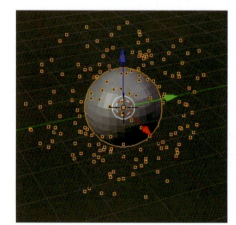

Figure 13.30

is generated, it remains visible for 50 frames. Therefore, a particle generated at frame 200 will remain visible until frame 250.

Note the tick in the box labeled "Random" in the "Particles" button—"Emission" tab. This provides the random order of generation of the particles. Click on the tick to remove it. Play the animation again and press Esc to cancel. The 3D window is in user perspective view, therefore it is difficult to see what has been achieved by removing the "Random" tick. Change the view to top view (number pad 7) and then to front view (number pad 1) (Figure 13.32). With the timeline advanced to frame 41, you will see an ordered array of particles.

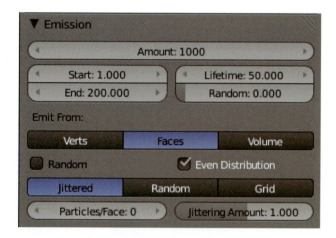

Figure 13.31

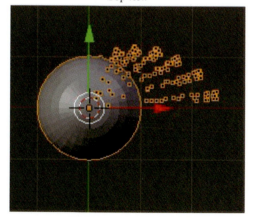

Top view

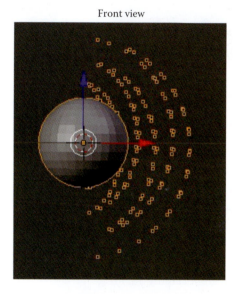

Front view

Figure 13.32

13.6 Material Influence on Particles

Particles emit their own light so it isn't necessary to have lamps in the scene when particles are rendered. To give particles color, you have to add a material to the emitting object. We can render an image at frame 41 of what we have already created by pressing F12 on the keyboard—what we get is a plain gray-and-white picture (Figure 13.33). Press Esc to cancel the image. With the sphere selected in the 3D window, go to the properties window—"Material" button. Press "Add

Figure 13.33

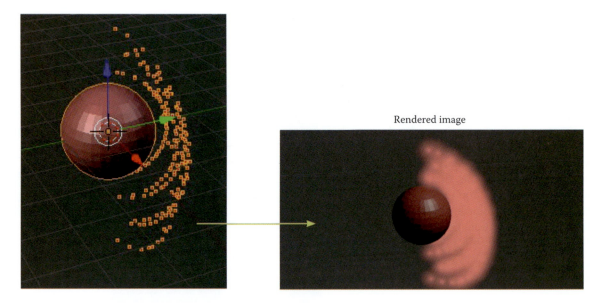

Rendered image

Figure 13.34

New" and click on the diffuse color bar to display the color picker. Select a color (I've chosen red) then render the image again (Figure 13.34).

We see the emitter object (sphere) and the particles rendered in the same color. To advance this subject a little further, go to the "Particles" button and find the "Render" tab. In the "Render" tab, you will see "Halo" highlighted in blue (Figure 13.35). This is telling Blender to render the particles as halos. Since there are a considerable number of particles visible at frame 41, our rendered image shows us a colored blob. Note also the tick in the "Emitter" box; this tells Blender to render the emitter object in the image. Click in the box to remove the tick. Go back to the "Material" button and find the "Transparency" tab. Click and add a tick in the "Transparency" box. Reduce the "Alpha" value to 0.050 and render again: now only the particles are rendered and they are transparent (Figure 13.36).

Figure 13.35

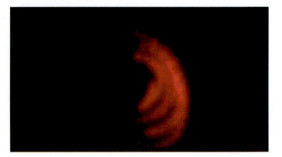

Figure 13.36

13. Particle Systems

This has demonstrated some of the effects of materials on particles. There are many more combinations to play with. We will have a look at adding halo effects to particles and at the same time introduce a few more tricks to give you the feel for the versatility of the particle system.

Open a new Blender scene, delete the cube, and add a plane object. Leave the "Gravity" box in the "Scene" button ticked to maintain a gravity effect. With the plane selected, go to the "Properties" window, "Particles" button and add a particle system. In the "Emission" tab, change "Amount: 61" and "Lifetime: 200" (Figure 13.37). In the "Velocity" tab, change "Normal: 7.500" and "Emitter Object Y: 0.990." At the bottom of the "Velocity" tab set "Random: 2." We are decreasing the amount of particles so we don't flood the scene, but changing the "Lifetime" value makes the particles visible longer in the animation. We still have gravity working, but with normal velocity at 7.500 the particles will project up before descending. Setting "Emitter Object Y: 0.990" gives the particles a slight horizontal velocity along the *y*-axis, making them move in an arc.

Now let's jazz the particles up a bit. With the plane still selected, go to the "Material" button and add a new material. Just above the "Preview" tab, change to a halo material ("Halo" will become highlighted in blue). In the "Halo" tab that displays click on the color bar and select a nice bright yellow. Change the halo size to 0.700 and tick "Rings" and "Star Tips" (Figure 13.38). Press Alt + the A key and run the animation. Press Esc to exit, then cycle the animation to frame 41 and render the image (Figure 13.39).

Figure 13.37

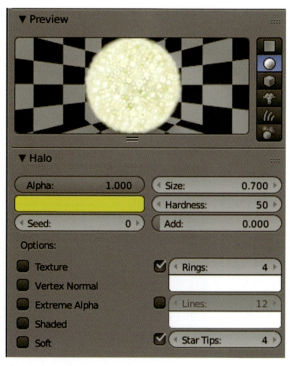

Figure 13.38

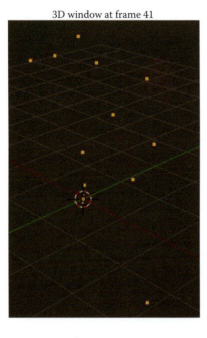

3D window at frame 41

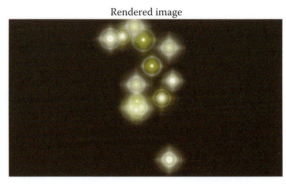

Rendered image

Figure 13.39

Experiment with rings, lines, stars, and halo size. For example, in the "Material" buttons "Halo" tab untick "Rings" and "Star tips" to change the particle render back to a plain halo. Set the halo size to 4 so that the image fills the camera view. In the "Halo" tab, decrease the "Alpha" value to 0.100 to give the halo a transparent look; this should produce something that looks like a cloud of smoke. If you place an object in the scene (in this case, a monkey object) and position it where the particles are at frame 41, the object renders in the smoke cloud (Figure 13.40). There are many combinations, all producing different effects, so make sure you experiment and record your results.

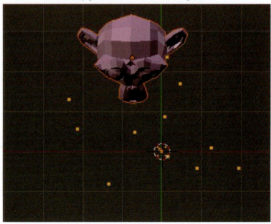

Monkey positioned behind the particles

Rendered image

Figure 13.40

13.7 Particle Interaction

Particles can interact with other objects and be affected by forces like wind. Particles can bounce off other objects and act like sparks or droplets. To show how these features work, set up a scene with a sphere positioned above a plane as shown in Figure 13.41 (the plane is scaled up three times). With the sphere selected, go to the "Properties window", "Particles" button and add a particle system. In the "Emission" tab, set the "End" value to 100 and in the "Velocity" tab, set the "Emitter Object: Z" value to −3.000 (Figure 13.42). With your cursor in the 3D window, press Alt + the A key to play the animation of the particle generation—you will see the particles fall and pass through the plane, as in Figure 13.43.

The next step is to stop the particles from falling through the plane. Select the plane and go to the "Properties" window, "Physics"

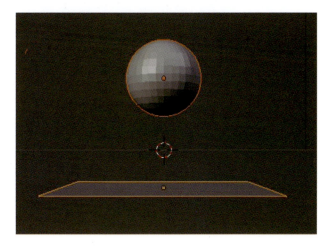

Figure 13.41

Figure 13.42

Figure 13.43

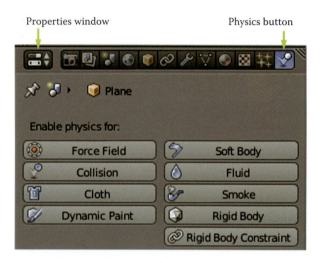

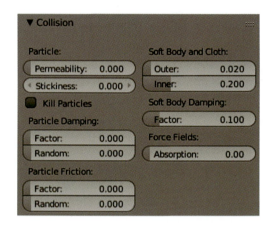

Figure 13.44   Figure 13.45

button (Figure 13.44). Select "Collision" and press Alt + the A key again to replay the animation (remember you must be at frame 1 before you replay); you will now see the particles bounce up from the surface of the plane (Figure 13.45).

Tip: Shift select the sphere and the plane to see the particles better.

By increasing the "Particle Damping: Factor" value in the "Collision" tab to 1.000, the particles will land on the plane but they will no longer bounce; they will just slide off the surface. By experimenting with other particle and collision settings and by applying materials with halos, line, and stars, you can simulate sparks bouncing with high-quality results.

13.8 Wind Force

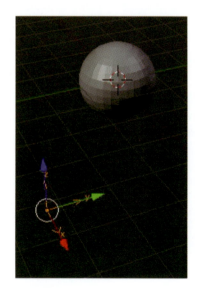

Figure 13.46

Blender allows particles to be influenced by a simulated wind force. To create a wind effect, you have to place an object in the scene and assign a wind force to it. An object called an empty is great for this since it doesn't render. Begin by opening a new scene, deleting the cube, and replacing it with a UV sphere. Add a particle system to the sphere and leave the default settings. Add an empty to the scene, select the empty by clicking RMB, and position it just below the sphere off to one side, as shown in Figure 13.46.

The sphere will emit particles that will fall downward since the "Gravity" box is ticked in the "Scene" tab. With the empty selected in the 3D window, go to the "Properties" window, "Physics" button and click on the "Force Fields" button. Select "Wind" from the "Type" drop down

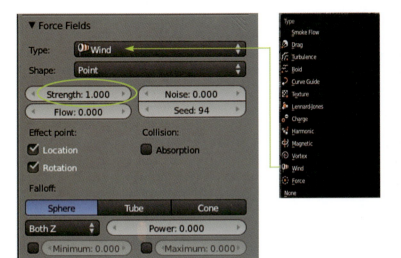

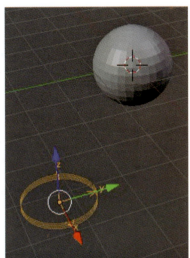

Figure 13.47

Figure 13.48

selection menu (Figure 13.47). You will see the wind force field in the 3D window attached to the empty object (Figure 13.48). The wind force is acting along the z-axis of the empty object at a strength of 1.000. We want the wind to blow the particles falling from the sphere along the global y-axis. With the empty selected, rotate it about the x-axis so that the empty local z-axis points in the same direction as the global y-axis. Increase the "Strength" value to 10 and play the animation to see the sphere's particles being blown (Figure 13.49). Wind strength is able to be animated, which creates a realistic wind effect.

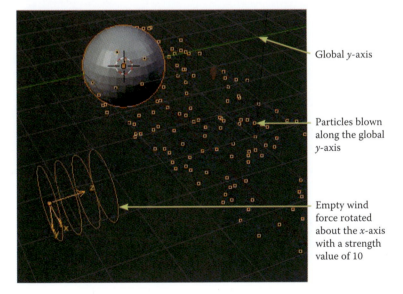

Global y-axis

Particles blown along the global y-axis

Empty wind force rotated about the x-axis with a strength value of 10

Figure 13.49

13.9 Sample Particle Settings

The following are some sample settings for various uses. Follow the settings carefully otherwise you will not get the results as demonstrated. Settings can be tweaked to produce whatever results you want and only by experimentation will you discover what can be achieved. Remember to record settings for future use when you discover something especially neat.

13.9.1 Snow Effect

In a new scene, delete the cube and add a plane. Scale the plane up five times and subdivide the surface four times. Position the plane at the top of the screen above the camera out of camera view—the plane is there to emit particles, not to be included in the rendered image or movie. Go to the "Properties" window, "Scene" button and set "Gravity Z: −0.210." This is a low value since we want our snow to float down gently. Remember, if there are other objects in the scene that are affected by gravity, they will also float.

Add a particle system to the plane. In the "Emission" tab, set "Lifetime: 200" and in the "Velocity" tab set "Normal: 0.010" and "Random: 0.320." We want the particles to display for a fair amount of time, not go careering off at a 100 miles an hour. In the "Material" button, add a material (white is appropriate) and set it as "Halo." Set the halo size to 0.050 to make small snowflakes. Run the animation to generate particles then advance the animation to about frame 230 and render an image (Figure 13.50).

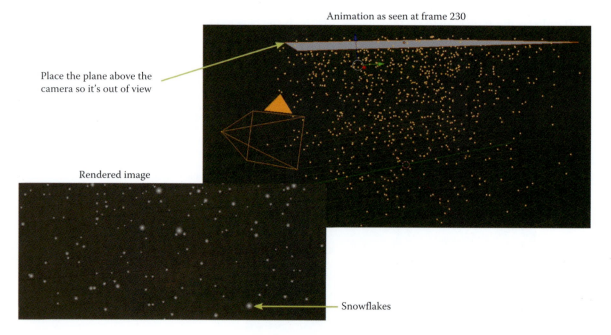

Animation as seen at frame 230

Place the plane above the camera so it's out of view

Rendered image

Snowflakes

Figure 13.50

13.9.2 Fire

In a new scene, delete the cube and add a UV sphere. Add a material, make it a halo type, and use the color picker to change it to a yellow color. Set the halo size to 0.300. In the "Scene" button, untick the "Gravity" box. Add a particle system to the sphere and in the "Velocity" tab set "Normal: 0.000" and the "Emitter Object Z: 2.870." In the 3D window, move the sphere down the z-axis slightly to position it at the bottom of the camera view. Run the animation then cycle forward through the frames and render an image (Figure 13.51).

Lesson 10
10-05
Fire Particles

Lesson 10
10-06
Fire Simulation

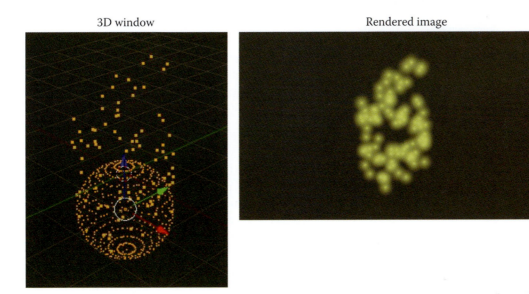

3D window   Rendered image

Figure 13.51

Tip: Remember the "Quick Smoke" modifier in the modifiers section.

Go back and take another look and find the "Fire" and "Smoke + Fire" options in the "Tools Panel" under "Smoke Style."

13.9.3 Simple Fireworks

Create a new scene, delete the default cube, and add a scaled down UV sphere. Position the sphere at the top of the camera view (Figure 13.52). In the "Material" button, add a material, make it a halo type, and change the color to yellow and the halo size to 0.100. In the "Particles" button, add a particle system. In the "Emission" tab, change "Lifetime: 100," "Start: 50," and "End: 51." In the "Velocity" tab, set "Normal: 2.000." Run the animation and then

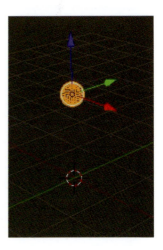

Figure 13.52

3D window

Camera view

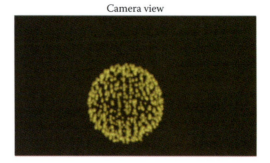

Figure 13.54

Figure 13.53

advance to frame 67 (Figure 13.53). In the "Particles" button, "Render" tab, untick "Emitter," and render the scene (Figure 13.54). Add several different sized spheres to the scene with different colors located slightly apart and repeat the setup for each with different normal values.

13.10 Keyed Particle Systems

So far we have looked at particle systems of "Type: Emitter" with "Newtonian" physics. We will now consider "Type: Emitter" with "Keyed" physics, which we call keyed particles. "Keyed" physics is a way of controlling the movement of particles by directing them from the original emitter object to a second target object and onto a third and subsequent objects. The flow of particles may be used as an animation or used to create a static image. The following procedure for setting up a keyed system will demonstrate the principles involved.

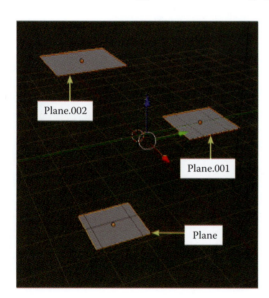

Open a new scene in Blender and delete the default cube. Add three separate plane objects and position them as shown in Figure 13.55. A simple way to do this is to add one plane, then with the plane selected, press Shift+ the D key to duplicate it. The new plane will be in grab mode (you'll see a white outline). Note that the first plane was named "Plane" by Blender (you can see the names at the lower left of the screen when an object is selected). The second plane is named "Plane.001" and the third "Plane.002." Arrange the planes in the 3D window in order of name—it will help later on.

Note: You can go to the properties window— "Object Data" button and edit the name in the "Name" box at the top of the window (Figure 13.56). You could use any name you like; however, since the planes are all identical, it's probably best to stay with the "Plane" names.

Figure 13.55

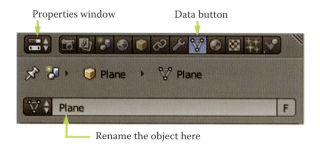

Properties window   Data button

Rename the object here

Figure 13.56

Click to Add a Particle System

Figure 13.57

Select "Plane" and in the "Properties" window, "Particles" button, click on "New" to add a particle system (Figure 13.57). In the "Particle System" buttons go to the "Physics" tab and click on the type "Keyed" option (Figure 13.58). Still in the "Physics" tab click on the plus sign next to the "Keys" panel (Figure 13.59). Clicking the plus sign enters a target channel and in this case, Blender inserts the name "Particle System," which is the particle system that has been assigned to the object named "Plane."

The "Keys" panel is where the targets for the particles are set up. In entering "Particle System" as the target name for particles being emitted from the object "Plane" it could be construed as saying, "Hey you particles, assemble here at the starting point until you are told where to go."

Note the panel just below the "Key" panel with a small orange cube displayed.

Leave this empty for the time being.

Deselect "Plane" in the 3D window and select "Plane.001." Repeat the procedure for adding a "Keyed" type particle system except there is no need to enter anything in the "Physics" tab, "Keys" panel. Just click "Physics," "Keyed."

Tip: When you select "Plane.001," all the buttons in the "Particles" tab may appear to disappear. Drag up the scroll bar at the RHS of the window to reveal the "New" button to add a new system.

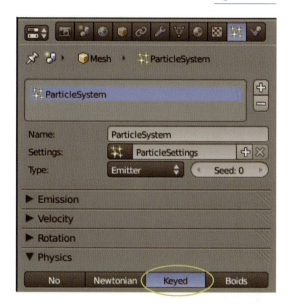

Figure 13.58

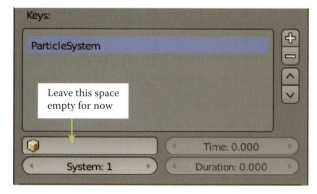

Leave this space empty for now

Figure 13.59

Do the same for "Plane.002."

OK! We have "Plane," "Plane.001," and "Plane.002" each with a "Keyed" type particle system and we have told the particles generated from "Plane" to assemble.

Select "Plane" in the 3D window and in the "Properties" window, "Particles" button, "Physics" tab click in the plus sign next to the "Keys" panel again. Blender enters a new channel and again inserts the name "Particle System." Now click on the panel with the little orange cube displayed and in the drop down menu that displays click on "Plane.001." Blender amends the name in the second channel to "Plane.001: ParticleSystem." This is telling the particles emitted from "Plane" to go to "Plane.001" (Figure 13.60).

Still with "Plane" selected in the 3D window repeat the process and this time select "Plane.002" as the target. Hit Alt + the A key to see the animation (Figure 13.61). Remember that all the rules for number of particles, lifetime, start, end, and normal velocity apply.

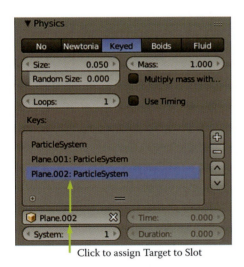

Click to assign Target to Slot

Figure 13.60

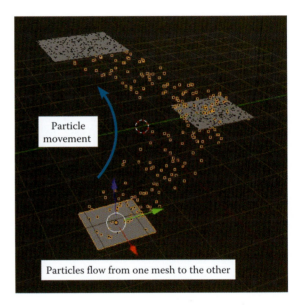

Particles flow from one mesh to the other

Figure 13.61

13.11 Boids Particle Systems

Boids particle systems are used to simulate flocks, swarms, herds, and schools of various kinds of animals or anything that acts with similar behavior. Boids particle systems are of "Type: Emitter" but have "Boids" physics applied. "Boids" particles in one particle system can react to particles in another system or they can react to particles within their own system. Boids are given rules of behavior, which are listed in a stack. The rules at the top of the stack take precedence over rules lower down in the stack, but the stack is able to be rearranged once it is written. Since only a certain amount of information is able to be evaluated if the memory capacity is exceeded, rules lower down the stack are ignored. The procedure for setting up "Boids" particle systems will be demonstrated with the following examples.

13.11.1 Example: A Flock of Birds

Since we're still working with the basics, our particles will *act* like a flock of birds but won't actually look like birds. Open a new Blender scene and stick with the default cube: this will be our particle emitter. In the properties window—"Particles" button, add a new particle system. Leave all the button settings as their default values, except for the following:

- **"Emission" tab**
  - Number: 30 (we'll have a small flock)
  - Lifetime: 250 (the default animation length in the timeline)

- **"Physics" tab**
  - Select "Boids"

- **"Boid Brain" tab**
  - With "Separate" highlighted, hit the minus sign to delete it. Click on the plus sign at the RH side of the window to display a selection drop down menu for boids rules and select "Follow Leader." Click on the up arrow below the minus sign to move "Follow Leader" to the top of the stack.

We have told the particles to follow the leader while flocking together. We will now give the particles a leader to follow. Deselect the cube in the 3D window (press the A key) and add an empty; an empty is a location point that can be animated to move in the scene but does not render. Grab the empty and move it to the side (Figure 13.62). Deselect the empty and select the cube. Go back to the "Boid Brain" tab and make sure "Follow Leader" is highlighted. Below the stack window you will see an empty box with a little cube in it. Click in this box and select "Empty" from the drop down menu that displays (Figure 13.63). We have told the particles to follow the empty. Animate the empty to move across the screen (see Chapter 9 for a refresher on animation). When the animation is

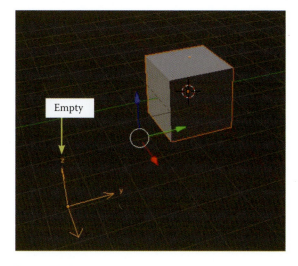

Figure 13.62

Figure 13.63

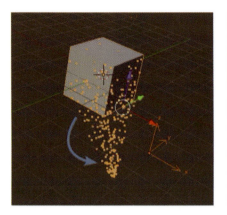
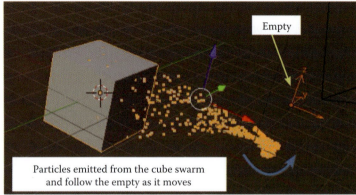

Particles emitted from the cube swarm
and follow the empty as it moves

Figure 13.64

played, select the cube in the 3D window. Particles are emitted from the cube, head toward the empty, and attempt to follow it as it moves across the screen (Figure 13.64). Having the cube selected displays the particles as little orange squares; if it isn't selected, all you get are black dots, which are hard to see.

Note: With a high particle amount, Blender may crash due to overload when calculating data. This of course depends on the capability of your computer.

13.11.2 Example: Directing Movement

In this example, I will demonstrate how to direct particles to move from one object to another. Start a new scene and add a second cube object by pressing Shift + the D key. Note that the default cube is named "Cube" (see the lower left side of the 3D window) and the new cube is named "Cube.001." Position the Cubes as shown in Figure 13.65, scaling the new cube down.

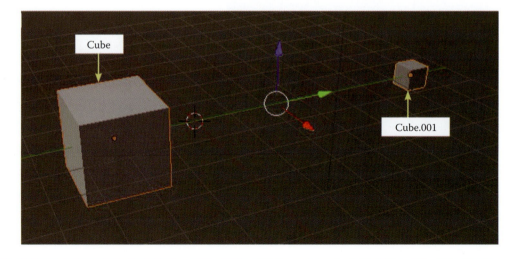

Figure 13.65

Select the original cube and add a particle system with "Boids" physics. In the "Emission" tab, reduce the "Number" value to 10 and set the "Lifetime" value to 1500; we want to keep the number of particles low and have them visible for a fair amount of time in the animation. Go to the "Timeline" window and set the animation "End" value to 1500 frames.

Now let's display the particles in a different way. In the "Particles" button—"Display" tab, select "Cross" and set the "Draw Size" value to 10 px; you will see a cross appear on the cube. In the "Boid Brain" tab, remove "Separate" and "Flock" and add "Goal." Click in the "Object" box below the rule window and select "Cube.001"—this tells the particles emitted from the original cube to go and find the target. Play the animation to see the result: crosses emitted from "Cube" migrate across to and accumulate on the target (Figure 13.66). Remember that the location of either or both of the cubes in the scene may be animated at the same time. Animating the target cube can cause the particles confusion. They may head over to where the target cube was originally located, have a think, then chase the target. Some particles may take off in a completely different direction but in letting the animation play on they will eventually find out they have made a mistake and discover where they should be going.

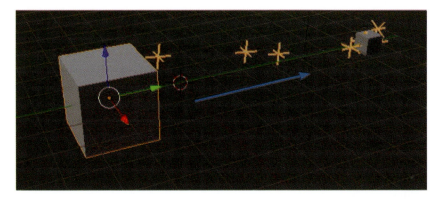

Figure 13.66

13.11.3 Example: Prey/Predator Relationship

Boids particles will not only act like swarms or flocks in their movement; they can also be made to react to one another. An example would be one flock of birds chasing off another flock. Let's set up an example in a new Blender scene with two cubes, as shown in Figure 13.67. Make the larger cube two times bigger than the smaller cube and position the cubes four Blender units apart. The small cube will emit predator particles, which will attack prey particles emitted from the large cube.

Predator particles. Select the small cube in the 3D window and add a particle system in the "Properties" window, "Particles" tab. Change the following settings:

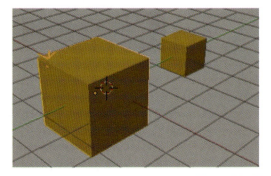

Figure 13.67

- **"Emissions" tab**
  - Number: 100 (the larger number becomes the aggressor)

- Lifetime: 1500 (allows the particles to be visible for the duration of the animation)

- **"Display" tab (way down the bottom)**
  - Select "Point" and set the "Draw Size" value at 3 px

- **"Physics" tab**
  - Select "Boids"
  - Size: 0.030
  - Max. Air Speed: 10.000 (the "Air Speed" value range is 0–100. The value 10 gives an advantage over the slower "Prey" particles which will have a value of 1)

- **"Boids Brain" tab**
  - The default "Separate" and "Flock" rules are applied. Add a "Fight" rule (click the plus sign and select "Fight") and move it to the top of the stack (click ^ twice)

Prey particles. Select the large cube in the 3D window, add a particle system. Change the following settings:

- **"Emissions" tab**
  - Number: 10
  - Lifetime: 1500

- **"Display" tab**
  - Select "Cross" and set the "Draw Size" value at 10 px

- **"Physics" tab**
  - Select "Boids"
  - Size: 0.030
  - Max. Air Speed: 1.000 (combined with its size this makes the Prey bigger and slower)

- **"Relations":** Click the plus sign then click on the target selection box (orange cube icon) and select "Cube.001" (the smaller cube in the 3D window). "Cube: Particle System" displays in the window. Select "Enemy"

- **"Boids Brain" tab**
  - The default "Separate" and "Flock" rules are applied. Delete the "Flock" rule, add an "Avoid" rule and move it to the top of the stack.

Go back and select the predator (Cube.001) and repeat the "Relations" setup, this time selecting "Cube" as the target and selecting "Enemy" (you cannot set up "Relations" until the other object has a particle system). In the "Physics" tab, with the larger cube selected, change to Newtonian physics then tick in the "Die on hit" box. Change back to "Boids"

physics. In the "Timeline" window change the "End" value to 1500. You may have to zoom out in the window. Changing to "Wireframe" display mode in the 3D window gives a better view of the particle swarms. Shift select both cubes in the 3D window and play the animation to see the result; selecting both cubes draws orange lines around the particles and makes them more visible. The cross particles emitted from the large cube are attacked by the swarm of small particles from the small cube and the cross particles die when they are hit (Figure 13.68).

For simplicity, we are showing only dots and crosses as seen in the 3D window. A render could show anything you wish by choosing "Object" in the "Render" tab and assigning a preconstructed mesh object. A complex single frame can take a while to render and a complex animation can take an eternity.

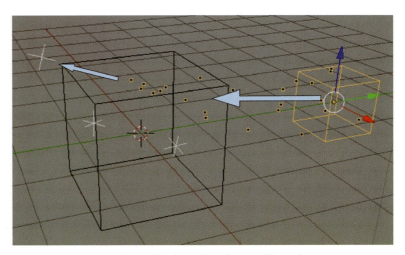

Predators (Dots) attacking the Prey (Crosses)

Predator particles shown as dots are emitted from the smaller cube. The predators attack the prey particles shown as crosses which are emitted from the larger cube. The prey dies when the predator strikes (Extinguish from the scene).

Figure 13.68

13.11.4 Example: Follow Terrain

Boids particles can be made to emulate herds of animals or a swarm of insects following a terrain. Set up a new Blender scene, as shown in Figure 13.69. The cube object is the default cube and will act as a target to which the particles will be directed. The other two objects in the scene are two planes with one being scaled up and shaped to act as our terrain.

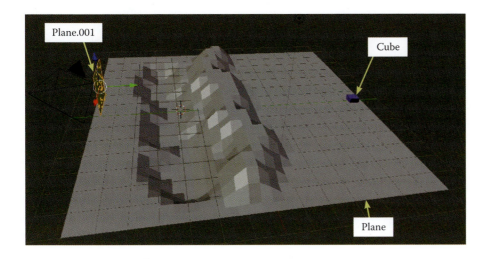

Figure 13.69

To create the terrain, add a "Plane." Scale the plane up five or six times, tab into "Edit" mode, and subdivide five times. Deselect all the vertices and press the C key for circle select mode. Click, hold, and drag the LMB, selecting a row of vertices from one side of the plane to the other. Press Esc to cancel the circle select. In the 3D window header, turn on proportional editing. Click on the blue arrow of the manipulation widget and drag down to form a ditch in the terrain. Repeat the procedure to form a rise along the side of the ditch.

With the scene assembled, select the objects as listed and perform the following setup in the properties window:

- Select "Plane.001" (the small plane rotated, which will act as our emitter).
- Add a particle system and in the "Physics" tab, select type "Boids"; untick "Allow Flight" and tick "Allow Land." Reduce "Max Land Speed" to 0.596 and check that "Jump Speed" is 0.000.
- In the "Emission" tab, change the values to "Number: 100" and "Lifetime: 1500" and change the animation length in the timeline to 1500 frames.
- In the "Boid Brain" tab, add a "Goal" rule, move it to the top of the stack, and select "Cube" as the goal.
- In the "Display" tab select "Point" and set "Draw Size" to 2 px.
- Select "Plane" (the terrain).
- In the properties window—"Physics" button, click the "Collision" tab.
- The cube (target) requires no action other than to scale it down a bit.

Select "Plane.001" and play the animation; the particles emitted follow the contour of the terrain as they move to the target (Figure 13.70).

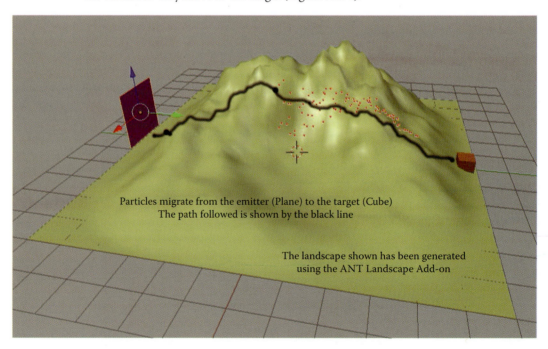

Particles migrate from the emitter (Plane) to the target (Cube)
The path followed is shown by the black line

The landscape shown has been generated
using the ANT Landscape Add-on

Figure 13.70

Tip: Instead of creating a landscape as described above you may use one of Blender's Add-ons. In the "User Preference" window, click "Add-ons" at the top of the window then click the "Add Mesh" category (LH side of window) and find the "Add Mesh: ANT Landscape" add-on. Click the little button at the far right of the add-on to activate it. In the 3D window press "Shift + A key"—Add Mesh and select "Landscape." The terrain shown in the second part of Figure 13.70 will be added to your scene. Scale up to suite.

13.12 Hair Particle Systems

The previous pages describing particles have introduced particles of "Type: Emitter" with physics types "No," "Newtonian," "Keyed," and "Boids." We will now take a look at particles of "Type: Hair," where particles are rendered as strands and may be edited in the 3D window. Hair type particles may be used to represent such things as grass, fur, hair, or anything that has a surface with fibrous strands.

We will perform a quick demonstration to show what is meant by hair particles. In the 3D window, delete the default cube object, add a plane, and zoom in a bit. With the plane selected, go to the "Properties" window, "Particles" button and click on the "New" to add a particle system (Figure 13.71). At the top of the "Particles" window, click on the drop down menu that says "Type: Emitter" and select "Hair." The plane in the 3D window will show long strands sticking up from the surface of the plane. Go to the "Hair Length" value in the "Emission" tab and decrease the default value to see the length of the strands shorten—we now have a hairy plane (Figure 13.72).

Let's proceed with something a little more exciting. Start a new Blender scene, delete the cube, and add a monkey. If we add a hair particle system, we will get a hairy-headed monkey with hair sticking out in every

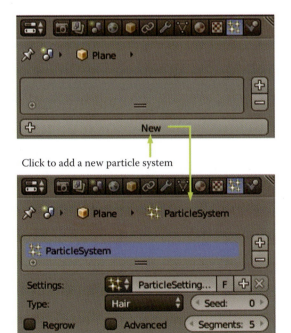

Click to add a new particle system

Figure 13.71

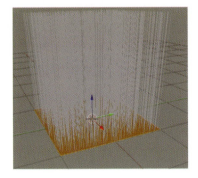

Figure 13.72

direction; however, let's try for a more clean-cut look with some hair on the head and a beard. Press the number pad 7 key to access a top view, looking down on the monkey's head. We will designate where we want the hair to grow by selecting a bunch of vertices; this bunch is called a vertex group. Tab into edit mode, zoom in so you can see what you are doing, and in the 3D window header make sure the "Limit Selection to Visible" button is set to only allow selection of vertices that are visible (Figure 13.73).

Limit selection to visible

Figure 13.73

Press the A key to deselect all the vertices, then select a group on the top of the monkey's head (Figure 13.74). You can do this by pressing Shift + the RMB on the individual vertices, by pressing the B key and the LMB to drag a box over the vertices, or by pressing the C key and the LMB to drag the circle to select (scroll the MMB to change the circle size and press Esc to cancel when your selection is finished). Leave the vertices selected and click on the "Data" button in the properties window. In the "Vertex Groups" tab, click on the plus sign to add a vertex group. A vertex group named "Group" is added, named "Group" which is highlighted in blue. Double click on the highlight and rename the group "Hair."

In the name box, click on "Group" and delete it (Blender names every new vertex group "Group"). Type in "Hair" and press Enter to rename the group (Figure 13.75). We still have our vertices selected in the 3D window. In the "Vertex Groups" tab, just below "Name" click on the "Assign" button—this assigns the selected vertices to the vertex group named "Hair."

So far, there is a head and we have nominated an area on the head by selecting a group of vertices. We do not have hair. Go to the "Particles" button and click on "New" to add a particle system. Change "Type: Emitter" to "Type: Hair" (Figure 13.76). Still, nothing happens because we are in edit mode. Note that Blender has named the particle system "Particle System." Tab to object mode in the 3D window and you should see plenty

Top view of the monkey head
with the vertices selected

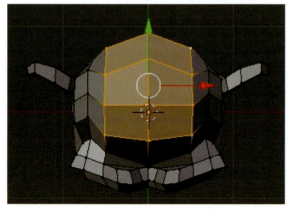

Double click to rename the vertex group

Figure 13.74

Figure 13.75

13. Particle Systems

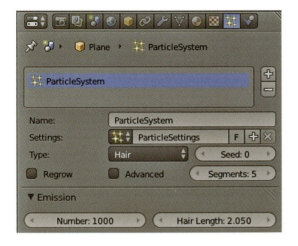

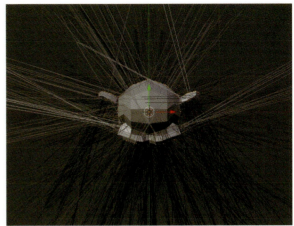

Figure 13.76

Figure 13.77

of hair (Figure 13.77). In fact, there is hair everywhere. To correct this look, start in the "Hair Length" box in the "Emission" tab and decrease the value until the hair strands look reasonable; say, about 0.820. Next, while still in the "Particles" button, go down to the "Vertex Groups" tab and in the box next to "Density" click and select "Hair" (Figure 13.78). We now have hair only on the area we selected. Press Num Pad 3 to get a side view—what a scrawny bunch of hair (Figure 13.79)! To fix the scrawny look, go to the "Children" tab and click on "Simple"—now we have a bushy, Mohawk hairdo (Figure 13.79, right).

We will continue and add a beard as promised. To make the process interesting but hopefully not difficult to understand, I will vary the procedure just a little. We previously selected a bunch of vertices, created a vertex group, named it, and then assigned the selected vertices to the group.

Figure 13.78

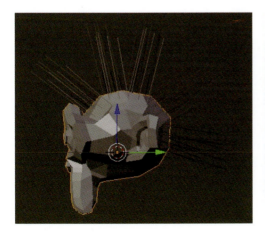

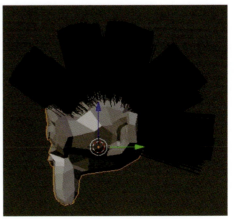

Figure 13.79

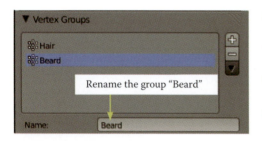

▼ Vertex Groups

⊞ Hair
⊞ Beard

Rename the group "Beard"

Name: Beard

Figure 13.80

Figure 13.81

Figure 13.82

Let's create a new vertex group first this time. With the "Monkey" selected in "Object" mode in the 3D window, go to "Properties" window, "Data" button and click on the plus sign in the "Vertex Groups" tab to add a new vertex group. Blender again names the new group "Group." Rename this to "Beard" as we did before for the hair (Figure 13.80). Now we need to select the vertices to assign them to the new group. We could use the procedures as outlined previously, but let's do it a different way.

First tab into edit mode and deselect all the vertices. In the 3D window header, change to weight paint mode. Our monkey turns blue in the 3D window, which shows that no vertices are selected. Note that "Beard" is highlighted in blue in the "Vertex Groups" tab. Click on "Hair." If you look closely amongst all that black hair (it may help to rotate the view), you will see a red scalp; this is showing the area that was previously selected by individual vertices. Tab to edit mode and click on "Select" in the "Vertex Groups" tab and you'll see the vertices that were painted.

Press the A key in the 3D window to deselect and click on "Beard" again in the "Data button"—"Vertex Groups" tab. Tab to weight paint mode in the 3D widow and look at the tools panel at the left-hand side of the screen. In the "Brush" tab, drag the "Strength" slider all the way to the right so the value is 1.000 (Figure 13.81). In the 3D window, click LMB, hold and drag the circle that appears as the mouse cursor over the monkey's chin—you will see the color change as you drag. Keep dragging until the chin is all red, which means that you have selected this area as the new vertex group for the beard (Figure 13.82). Tab to edit mode, make sure all vertices area deselected, then in the "Vertex Groups" tab click on "Assign" to assign the painted vertices to the beard vertex group. Click "Select" to see them.

With the painted vertices selected go to the "Particles" button and add a new particle system (click on the plus sign next to where you see "ParticleSystem" in blue). Note that Blender names this system "Particle System 2." Select "Type: Hair," decrease the "Hair Length" value in the "Emission" tab to 0.290, and go down to the "Vertex Groups" tab, click in the "Density" box, and select "Beard." In the "Render" tab click "Path." Tab to "Weigh Paint" mode in the 3d window. We now have scrawny hair on the monkey's chin. Go to the "Children" tab and click "Simple" for a hairy monkey (Figure 13.83). It doesn't matter in which order you do it, the procedure is the same: select

Figure 13.83

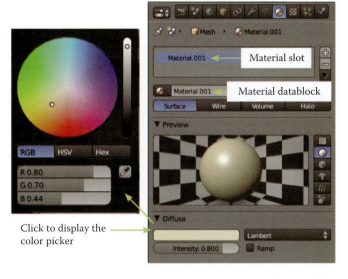

Click to display the color picker

Material slot

Material datablock

Figure 13.84

vertices to define the area, create a vertex group, assign vertices to the vertex group, create a hair particle system, and assign it to the vertex group.

A gray monkey with a black beard and hair in the 3D window is fine, but it isn't all that exciting in a render—let's jazz it up a bit. Select the monkey in object mode in the 3D window and go to the "Properties" window, "Material" button. Click on "New" to add a material. Click in the diffuse color bar and select a color for the monkey with the color picker that displays (Figure 13.84). To start with, this color will be applied to the monkey: his skin. At the top of the "Material" window, note that "Material.001" is highlighted in blue and just below that "Material.001" is listed again. The blue highlighted "Material.001" is a material slot and the lower "Material.001" is a material data block. In the "Material" window's "Unique Datablock ID Name," click on "Material.001," and delete and rename it "Skin" (Figure 13.85). Click on the plus sign to add a new slot add a material and name the slot "Hair." Repeat the process again, click "New" and rename it "Beard." There are now three material slots, each with a separate data block. You have to add a material to the slot before they can be renamed.

Go to the "Particles" button and at the top, you will see "Particle System" and "Particle System 2." Remember that the first system is for the hair and the second is for the beard. Select "Particle System" (hair) and in the "Render" tab, immediately below the tab heading you will see "Skin." Click and select "Hair." The hair in the 3D windows displays in the chosen color.

Now do the same for "Particle System 2," selecting "Beard" (Figure 13.86). The beard and hair look strange, but at least

Click—Delete—Rename "Skin"

Figure 13.85

Click to select material

Figure 13.86

Figure 13.87

the colors are pretty (Figure 13.87). As always, there is much more to play with in Blender; try the hair tutorials at www.blendercookie.com.

13.12.1 Final Note

Adding hair to an object can add an awful lot of vertices, which when rendering can take an awful lot of time and may even cause your computer to stall out. If you are not doing anything serious and have a slow machine to start with, keep the number of strands low.

13.13 The Assignment Tab

When a particle system is first added to a scene by clicking on the plus sign, Blender introduces a block of data to the scene that comprises a default particle system. Blender names this data block "Particle Settings," as seen in the "Settings" panel. The data block named "Particle Settings" is automatically linked to the default particle system that is named "Particle System." "Particle System" is placed in the assignment panel where it is assigned to an object in the 3D window. This explanation may be viewed in Figure 13.88. There is no "Assignment" tab or "Assignment" panel as such, but for the purpose of this discussion, we will consider the area marked in green as the "Assignment" tab and the panel displaying "Particle System" highlighted in blue as the assignment panel.

In the "Assignment" tab, there is a "Type" drop down menu that displays the options "Emitter" and "Hair." "Type: Emitter" is the default selection, which means that with the particle system assigned to an object in the scene, that object becomes the emitter of the

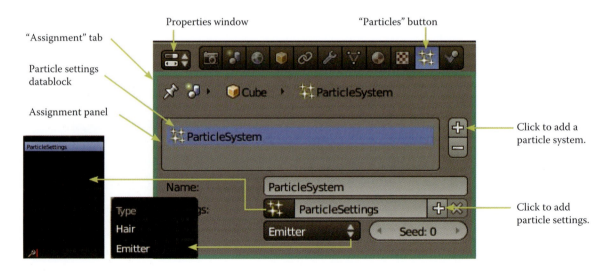

Figure 13.88

particles. In either case, the object becomes an emitter with a particle system assigned. "Type: Hair" may be viewed as a specialized static emitter.

Note that the names "Particle Settings" and "Particle Systems" may be renamed by clicking in the panels, deleting the name, and retyping a new name. This is useful when there are multiple objects, data blocks, and particle systems. Multiple objects in the 3D window can each have a different particle system assigned, and each object may have more than one particle system.

When a new particle system data block is added to the scene, Blender creates a new name for the data block. The default particle settings data block is named "Particle Settings" as previously stated. When a second data block is added, it is named "Particle Settings.001," a third would be named "Particle Settings.002," etc. Renaming data blocks to something more relevant to objects in the scene would be an advantage. When new data blocks are created, they are stored in a cache for reuse by other particle systems.

When a new particle system is added to the scene, Blender assigns that system to the object that is selected in the 3D window. If no objects are selected, the new particle system is assigned to the last object that was introduced to the scene. Particle systems added to a scene initially have the default "Particle Settings" data block linked and a new name applied as described previously. At this point, the data block settings may be altered to create a new unique data block or a previously created data block may be selected and linked to the new particle system. Clicking on the icon in front of the "Particle Settings" panel reveals a drop down menu showing the cache mentioned previously with data blocks for selection.

The foregoing statements may seem confusing and not easily related to what has been labeled the "Assignment" tab. The following exercise will attempt to clarify the statements and at the same time demonstrate the application of particle systems in practical terms.

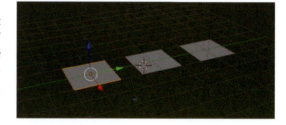

Figure 13.89

13.13.1 Practical Exercise

Open a new scene in Blender and delete the cube from the 3D window. Add three separate plane objects and position them at the center of the scene so that they are all visible in camera view and an image containing all three may be rendered (Figure 13.89). Add a diffuse material color to each of the planes—let's make them red, green, and blue (the colors do not have to be accurate). Turn off the "Gravity" setting in the "Scene" tab and turn off the 3D manipulator widget in the 3D window (Figure 13.90). At this time, the three

Click to untick and remove the effects of gravity

Click in the 3D window header to turn the widget off

Figure 13.90

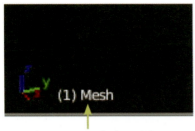

Object name in the lower left
corner of the 3D window

Figure 13.91

Figure 13.92

plane objects have been named "Plane," "Plane.001," and "Plane.002" by Blender, as seen in the lower LH corner of the 3D window when each is selected (Figure 13.91). This naming is not all that relevant to what we have in the scene, so we will rename the objects.

In the 3D window, select the red plane and go to the properties window—"Object" button. At the top of the window you will see "Plane" in the unique data block ID name panel (Figure 13.92). Click on the name to highlight it, hit delete, type in "RedPlane," and press Enter. Select the green plane in the 3D window and rename it "GreenPlane," and then similarly for the blue plane.

We will now add particle systems to the planes. Select the red plane and click on the "Particles" button in the properties window. Click on "New" to add a particle system. The particle system panel displays with all the tabs and buttons for controlling the settings and has been set up with default values. Leave all the values as is except for the "Lifetime" value in the "Emission" tab—change this value from the default 50 frames to 200 frames (Figure 13.93). This will give us a better view of particles being generated. Do the same for the other two planes and in addition change the "Number" value in

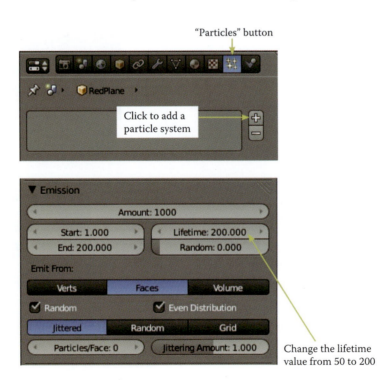

Figure 13.93

13. Particle Systems

the "Emission" tab to 100 for the green plane and 10 for the blue plane. Shift select all three planes in the 3D window and hit Alt + the A key to play the animation of particles being generated. Cycle through the animation in the timeline window to frame 180 and observe the particles (Figure 13.94). We have three different planes with three different particle systems—red plane: 1000 particles, green plane: 100 particles, and blue plane: 10 particles.

In the 3D window select each plane separately and note in the "Properties" window, "Particles" button, "Assignment" tab, the names that display in the "Name" and "Settings" panels (Figure 13.95).

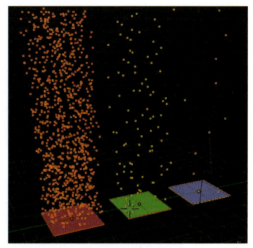

The number of particles emitted from each plane object shows the different systems

Figure 13.94

- **Red plane**
  - Name: Particle System
  - Settings: Particle Settings

- **Green plane**
  - Name: Particle System
  - Settings: Particle Settings.001

- **Blue plane**
  - Name: Particle System
  - Settings: Particle Settings.002

We previously stated that we have three separate particle systems; however, now we see that the three names are all "Particle System," but each one has a different "Settings" name. It's probably a good idea to do some renaming. Change the names to the following:

Figure 13.95

- **Red plane**
  - Name: RedPSystem
  - Settings: RedPSettings

- **Green plane**
  - Name: GreenPSystem
  - Settings: GreenPSettings

- **Blue plane**
  - Name: BluePSystem
  - Settings: BluePSettings

We should be able to see where we are now. To continue, in the 3D window select the green plane—we are going to reassign some settings. In the properties window—"Particles" button, "Assignment" tab, click on the button just in front of the name panel and next to

Click to reveal the
drop-down menu

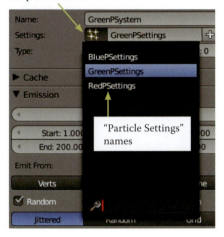

Figure 13.96

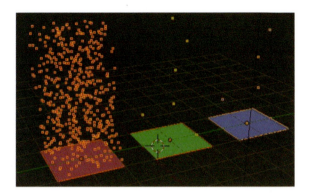

Figure 13.97

"Settings." The drop down menu that displays has the names of the three particle settings data blocks (Figure 13.96). Whenever a new group of particle settings is created, Blender puts it into a cache for reuse. You can see these data blocks in the "Outliner" window in data block mode. The green plane is selected, so in the data block drop down menu click on "BluePSettings." We now have the BluePSettings assigned to the GreenPSystem. If you replay the particle generation animation, the green and blue planes generate the same number of particles (Figure 13.97). Note that in the "Settings" panel for the green and the blue planes, a number 2 has appeared; this tells us that "BluePSettings" is being used by two systems. The color of the particles is controlled by the color of the plane object and the number of particles emitted is set by the particle system settings.

Figure 13.98

Note: Shift select all three planes when replaying the animation to make the particles visible in the 3D window. If a plane is not selected, the particles appear as tiny black dots.

I have demonstrated that you can select any data block of settings and assign it to any particle system. Continue by clicking on the number 2, which makes the data block a single user. Blender does this by leaving the original as it is and creating a new data block; however, the new data block is identical to the original. You can see that the settings name is now "BluePSettings.001" (Figure 13.98), but let's change some data in this new data block. Find the "Render" tab in the "Particles" window (scroll down a bit). In the bar containing the render type selection, click on "Object" (Figure 13.99). In the 3D window, add a UV sphere to the scene and give it a yellow diffuse color. Note that Blender has named the sphere "Sphere." Make sure it is off to one side in the scene away from the planes.

Click on "Object."

Figure 13.99

Figure 13.100

Reselect the green plane in the 3D window and then go back to the "Particles" button in the properties window. Check that you still have "GreenPSystem" and "BluePSettings.001." Now go back to the "Render" tab for "BluePSettings.001" and where it says "Dupli Object" click on the little cube icon and then click on "Sphere" in the drop down menu—we are telling Blender to display and render the particles as spheres (Figure 13.100). Scroll up to the "Physics" tab and slightly increase the "Size" value; you will see a sphere appear on the green plane. Play the particle generation animation and you will see yellow spheres being generated (Figure 13.101).

With the green plane selected, click on the plus sign to add a particle system in the "Properties" window, "Particles" button, "Assignment" tab. You will see a new particle system highlighted in blue named "Particle System 2" with particle settings named "Particle Settings" (Figure 13.102)—this has created a new particle system. With the green plane

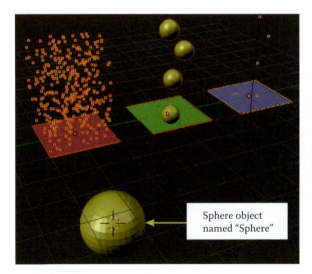

Sphere object named "Sphere"

Figure 13.101

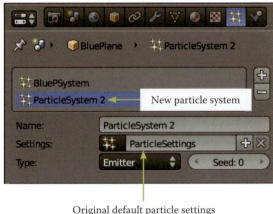

New particle system

Original default particle settings

Figure 13.102

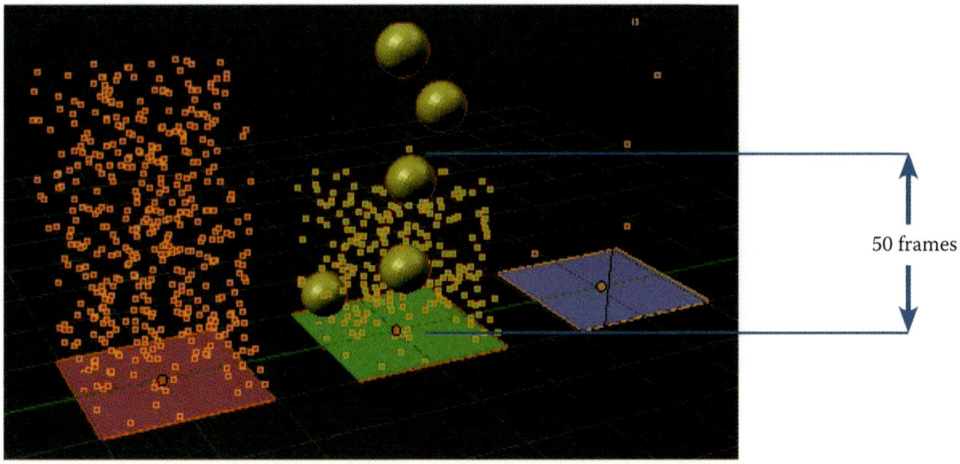

50 frames

Figure 13.103

selected in the 3D window, play the animation again. The green plane now emits yellow spheres and original particles together (Figure 13.103). The original particles only display for a short while since the "Lifetime" value is 50 frames. We have two separate particle systems with separate setting data blocks assigned to the same object. The best way to get the hang of all this is play, play, and more play.

13.14 Fluid Particles

Fluid particles allow you to simulate liquids. This is completely different to "Fluid Simulation" which is covered in Chapter 17.

The following demonstration will introduce you to "Fluid Particles" but there are so many different effects that can be created with the settings, it will be up to you to have a play and discover them for yourself.

In this demonstration, we will simply have an object emit particles, which act as a fluid substance, and have them flow down a trough into a container. To accomplish this we require an "Emitter" object to generate the "Particles," a "Dupli object" to give the particles form, and two "Obstacle" objects, which will be the trough and the container, a cup.

To begin, start with a new default Blender scene, delete the default "Cube" object and add and arrange the objects shown in Figure 13.104. Provided you have saved a Blender (.blend) file which contains the "Cup" and the "Trough" you can **Append** these objects to the new scene. If not, review Section 3.31 for the construction of the "Cup" and Section 3.32.1 Method 2 for the "Trough." Note: The trough construction used is Method 2. Reposition the "Camera" to have the "Trough" and the "Cup" in "Camera View" so they will display in a rendered image.

With the scene arranged complete the settings for the objects as per the following instruction. There is no particular order for doing this so we will work from the simplest

IcoSphere (Dupli object) parked out of " Camera" view.

Camera (Positioned to capture the trough and the Cup in "Camera" view)

Lamp

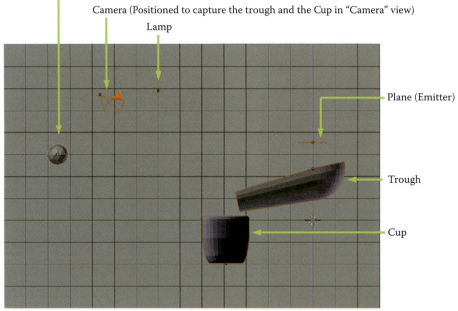

Plane (Emitter)

Trough

Cup

3D window—Scene Arrangement

Figure 13.104

to the more complex. Have each object selected, in turn, in the 3D window then follow the instructions.

Dupli Object The particles emitted in the scene will be duplications of the "IcoSphere" object. Add a bright material color to the "IcoSphere" and have it parked off to one side in the scene out of camera view.

Cup The "Cup" is a "Collision" object in the demonstration in that it reacts with the "Fluid Particles." In the "Properties" window, "Physics" button, click on "Collision" to display the "Collision" tab. Leave the default values in place (Figure 13.105). In the "Properties" window, "Modifier" button, add a "Subdivision Surface" modifier with the "Subdivisions View" value set to 2.000.

Trough The "Trough" is also a "Collision" object. Repeat the previous set up, including the "Subdivision

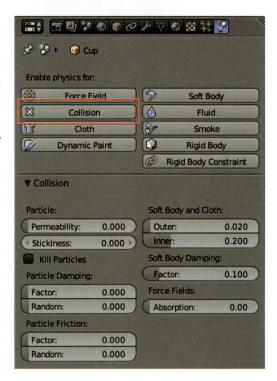

Figure 13.105

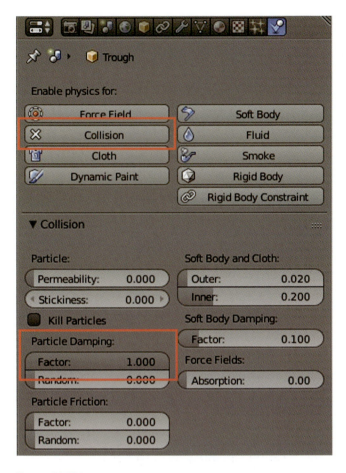

Figure 13.106

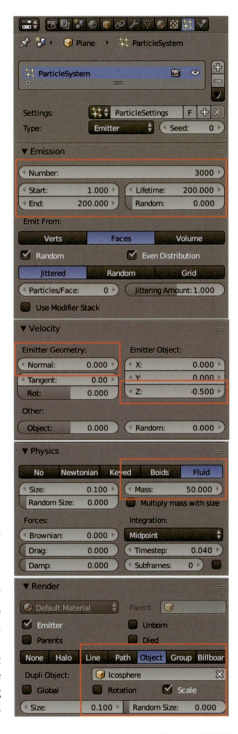

Surface" modifier, but set the "Particle Damping, Factor" value to 1.000 (Figure 13.106).

Emitter

The "Plane" is the object that will emit particles. In the "Properties" window, "Particles" button click on "New" to add a "Particle System." Change the default settings as shown in Figure 13.107.

You will have to experiment with different settings to determine the effects that can be created but to start you off and see something similar to that shown in the diagram provided take note of the following tab settings.

Figure 13.107

Emission

Number 3000 = The number of particles generated during the animation. The animation is the default 250 frames.

Lifetime 200 allows the particles to display for the full length of the animation.

Velocity

The "Emitter Geometry," "Normal" value is set at 0.000 and instead the "Emitter Object" Z: value is set at −0.500 (minus). With the default "Normal" value 1.000 the particles fly off the plane.

Physics

Physics is set to "Fluid."

Mass is set at 50.000 to slow down particle bouncing.

Render

Render is set to "Object" with the "Dupli Object," "IcoSphere" selected.

Size: 0.100 determines the size of the duplicated object in the 3D window.

With the settings in place go ahead and press the "Play" button in the "Timeline" window header to see "Fluid Particles" fall from the plane and slide down the trough into the cup. Figure 13.108 shows the animation paused at Frame 153.

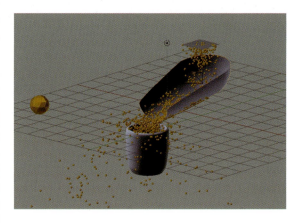

Note: Adding "Subdivision Surface" modifiers to the trough and the cup helps prevent particle surface breakthrough with collision objects but you will observe that the "Dupli Objects" sit half-and-half out on the surface of the trough. If this is not acceptable, one solution is to create a collision object with an inner and outer surface. The cup has been constructed in this way.

Figure 13.108

As previously stated you will have to play with the settings to determine the variations on the fluid particle effects.

14

Child/Parent Relationships and Constraints

14.1 Child/Parent Relationships

Child/parent relationships are used when there are several parts connected together but each part is required to move independently. Examples include a robot arm or a humanoid limb: the components of the arm move, but are connected to the body. The hand is a child of the forearm, the forearm is a child of the bicep, and the bicep is a child of the body—they are all linked together but move separately in their own way.

We will demonstrate the application of this in Blender by connecting several scaled cubes together. Start with the default Blender scene, scale the cube as shown in Figure 14.1, then tab to edit mode, and shift the vertices, positioning the center toward one end. Duplicate the scaled cube twice (press Shift + the D key twice) (Figure 14.2).

Lesson 11
11-01
Relationship
Constraints
Child-Of

Lesson 11
11-02
Relationship
Constraints Floor
Follow Path

Figure 14.1

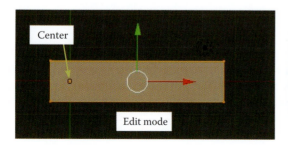

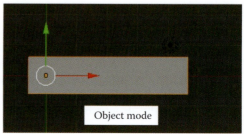

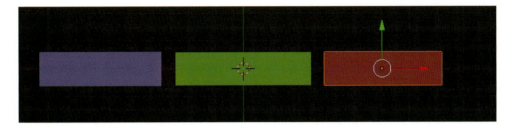

Figure 14.2

Shift each cube and overlap the ends (Figure 14.3). Create the child/parent relationship by first selecting the red cube, then shift selecting the green cube, then pressing Ctrl + the P key, and selecting "Object" in the "Set Parent To" panel that displays (Figure 14.4). Deselect then repeat the process for the green and blue cubes. The first object selected is always the child of the second object selected. Therefore, in Figure 14.4 red is the child of green, which in turn is the child of blue.

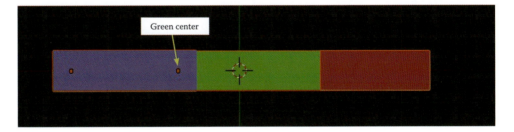

Figure 14.3

To see the relationship in action, select the red cube and rotate it. Select the green cube and rotate it, and you'll see that the red cube will follow. Select the blue cube and rotate it, and both the red and green cubes will follow. You can add a child/parent relationship to any object in Blender. For instance, a camera can be parented to another object so that when the object moves, the camera moves with it.

Figure 14.4

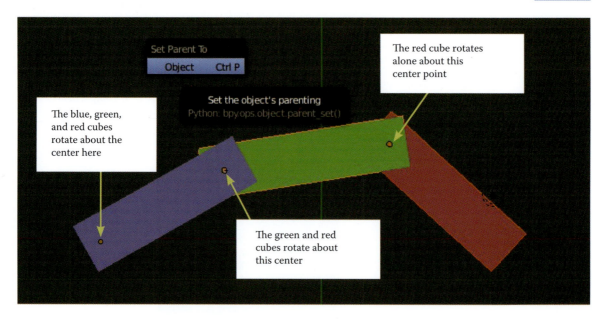

14.2 Introduction to Constraints

Constraints are object features that define spatial relationships between objects. They are the standard method for controlling characters among all 3D animation packages that still implement a more traditional approach to digital character animation. In Blender, "Constraints" can be associated with objects; note however, that not all constraints work with all objects. Constraints are associated with an object by selecting the object in the 3D window then clicking on

Figure 14.5

"Add Constraint" in the "Properties" window, "Object Constraints" button, and selecting the constraint from the drop down menu that displays (Figure 14.5). In many cases, a control object will be required to make the constraint function. There are control values to be inserted to regulate the function.

The following pages in this chapter contain a brief description of constraint functions. Most constraints are self-explanatory, therefore a detailed explanation will only be given for a few common constraints or where it is not self-evident.

14.2.1 Constraint Stacks

It should be noted that in some cases it is appropriate to apply more than one constraint to an object. When this is done, the constraints are placed in a stack in order of priority and the priority can be changed by moving a constraint up or down in the stack (Figure 14.6).

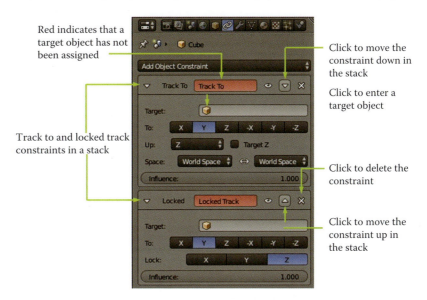

Red indicates that a target object has not been assigned

Click to move the constraint down in the stack

Click to enter a target object

Track to and locked track constraints in a stack

Click to delete the constraint

Click to move the constraint up in the stack

Figure 14.6

Lesson 11
11-03
Transform
Constraints
Copy Rot. Gears

Lesson 11
11-05
Constraints
Transformation
Microscopic

14.3 Transform Constraints

Here is a list of the transform constraints available in Blender and their functions:

- **Copy location:** Forces the object with the constraint added to take up the location of the target object.
- **Copy rotation:** Forces the object with the constraint added to copy the rotation of the target object. When the target rotates, the object rotates.
- **Copy scale:** Forces the object with the constraint added to copy the scale of the target object.
- **Copy transforms:** Similar to the copy location constraint.
- **Limit distance:** Constrains the object to remain within a set distance from the target object. The distance is a spherical field surrounding the target and the object is constrained within or outside the spherical field.
- **Limit location:** Constrains the object's location between a minimum and maximum distance on a specific axis. The distance is relative to either the world center or a parented object.
- **Limit rotation:** Constrains an object's rotation about a specific axis between limits.
- **Limit scale:** Constrains the scale of an object between limits on a specified axis.
- **Maintain volume:** Constrains the dimensions of a side on a specified axis.
- **Transformation:** See Section 14.3.1.

14.2.1 Constraint Stacks

It should be noted that in some cases it is appropriate to apply more than one constraint to an object. When this is done, the constraints are placed in a stack in order of priority and the priority can be changed by moving a constraint up or down in the stack (Figure 14.6).

Red indicates that a target object has not been assigned

Click to move the constraint down in the stack

Click to enter a target object

Track to and locked track constraints in a stack

Click to delete the constraint

Click to move the constraint up in the stack

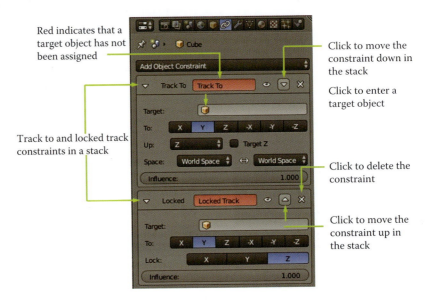

Figure 14.6

Lesson 11
11-03
Transform
Constraints
Copy Rot. Gears

Lesson 11
11-05
Constraints
Transformation
Microscopic

14.3 Transform Constraints

Here is a list of the transform constraints available in Blender and their functions:

- **Copy location:** Forces the object with the constraint added to take up the location of the target object.
- **Copy rotation:** Forces the object with the constraint added to copy the rotation of the target object. When the target rotates, the object rotates.
- **Copy scale:** Forces the object with the constraint added to copy the scale of the target object.
- **Copy transforms:** Similar to the copy location constraint.
- **Limit distance:** Constrains the object to remain within a set distance from the target object. The distance is a spherical field surrounding the target and the object is constrained within or outside the spherical field.
- **Limit location:** Constrains the object's location between a minimum and maximum distance on a specific axis. The distance is relative to either the world center or a parented object.
- **Limit rotation:** Constrains an object's rotation about a specific axis between limits.
- **Limit scale:** Constrains the scale of an object between limits on a specified axis.
- **Maintain volume:** Constrains the dimensions of a side on a specified axis.
- **Transformation:** See Section 14.3.1.

14. Child/Parent Relationships and Constraints

14.3.1 The Transformation Constraint

The "Transformation" constraint allows you to control the location, rotation, and scale of an object or part of an object by adjusting the location, rotation, or scale of another object. The object to be controlled is termed the "source" and has the constraint applied to it while the other object (the controlling object) is termed the "target object." The transforma-

Lesson 11
11-03
Transform
Constraints
Copy Rot. Gears

tion constraint is more complex and versatile than the other transform constraints. The location, rotation, or scale of the target object can be set to affect the location, rotation, or scale of the source object with the constraint applied. The location, rotation, or scale values in either case can be set to operate within a specific range.

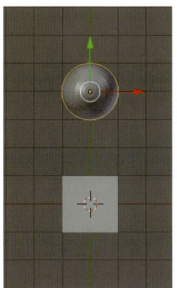

Figure 14.7

To demonstrate this constraint, add a UV sphere to the default scene and move it four Blender units along the Y-axis (Figure 14.7). Place the 3D window in top orthographic view (number pad 7—number pad 5). Select the cube and go to the "Properties" window, "Constraints" button, click "Add Constraint," and select "Transformation" from the drop down menu (Figure 14.8). In the constraint panel, set the values as shown in Figure 14.9. The location of the source (in this case, the UV sphere) is set to operate on the X-axis between 0.000 and 2.000

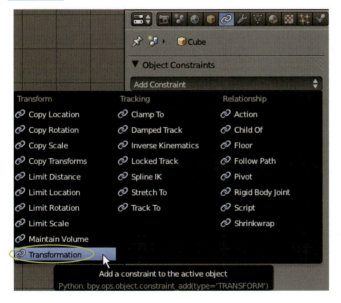

Figure 14.8

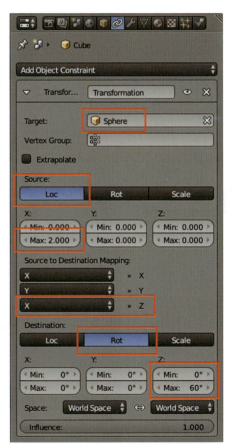

Figure 14.9

Blender units. Note that the X-axis of the source is set to affect the Z-axis of the destination. The destination (the cube) will rotate about the Z-axis from 0.000° to 60.000°.

By translating the sphere along the X-axis between 0.000 and 2.000 Blender units, the cube rotates about the Z-axis between 0.000° and 60.000° (Figure 14.10). The control transformation of the sphere and the rotation of the cube only take effect within the set limits. By adding additional transformation constraints and setting different parameters such as the scale of the sphere to affect the translation of the cube, multiple transformation controls can be established. Adding constraints places them in a stack and the position in the stack may be adjusted.

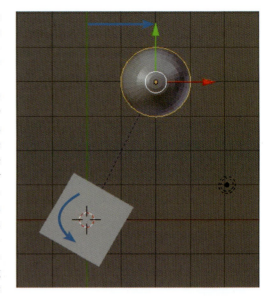

Figure 14.10

Lesson 11
11-04
Constraints
Pivot Track to
Dump Truck

Lesson 11
11-06
Constraints
Loaded Track
Drive Train

14.4 Tracking Constraints

Here is a list of the "Tracking" constraints available in Blender and their functions:

- **Clamp To:** Clamps or locks the position of the object to a target curve.
- **Damped track:** Constrains one local axis of the object to always point toward the target object (Figure 14.11).

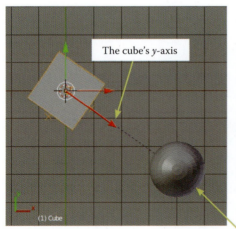

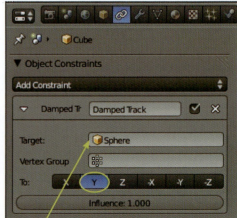

The cube's y-axis is constrained to always point toward the sphere

Sphere target

Figure 14.11

- **Inverse kinematics:** Can only be applied to bones (see Chapter 15 on armatures).
- **Locked track:** Similar to a damped track constraint with more axis control.
- **Spline IK:** Can only be applied to bones (see Chapter 15 on armatures).
- **Stretch To:** Stretches the object toward the target object or compresses the object away from the target object.
- **Track To:** Causes the object to always point toward the target object no matter where either the object or the target is positioned. For example, you can track

Lesson 11
11-07
Constraint
Controls
Windmill

a camera to follow an object that is animated to move. Start with the default blender scene in top view (number pad 7—number pad 5). Select the camera and press Alt + the R key to clear the rotation and align the camera axis with the world axis. With the camera still selected, go to the "Properties" window, "Object Constraints" button, click "Add Constraint," and select "Track To" (Figure 14.12). Enter the cube as the target object, and set "Axis To = –Z" and "Axis Up = Y" to orientate the camera in the world. The camera will now point at the cube when the camera or the cube is moved, and during an animation playback (Figure 14.13).

A track to constraint has been added to the camera

The cube is the target object

Axis values

Figure 14.12

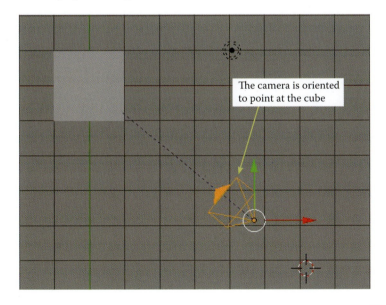

The camera is oriented to point at the cube

Figure 14.13

14.5 Relationship Constraints

Lesson 04
04-03
Parenting
Objects

Lesson 11
11-02
Relationship
Constraints Floor
Follow Path

Lesson 06
06-12
Lamp
Constraints and
Parenting

Here is a list of the "Relationship" constraints available in Blender and their functions:

- **Action:** See Section 14.5.1.
- **Child of:** See Section 14.1.
- **Floor:** Allows the target object to obstruct the movement of the object. For example, a sphere animated to descend in a scene will not pass through a plane that has been set as a target object.
- **Follow path:** Causes the object to be animated to follow a curve path nominated as the target. This constraint also has the feature to follow the curve, which means that the object will rotate and bank as it follows the curve. This constraint can also be employed to duplicate objects along a curve path. (See Sections 14.6 through 14.8.)
- **Pivot:** Causes the object to leapfrog to the opposite side of the target object along an axis between the object and the target centers. The location can be offset on either side of the axis by inserting offset values.
- **Rigid body joint:** See Section 14.5.3.
- **Shrinkwrap:** See Section 14.5.2.

14.5.1 The Action Constraint

An "Action" constraint allows you to control the action of one object by manipulating the action of another. For the purpose of this explanation, consider an action to mean a translation, rotation, or scale of an object in an animation. We will use the translation of a sphere to control the translation of a cube.

Set up a scene as shown in Figure 14.14. The object to which the constraint is applied is called the owner. This is the object that will be controlled; in this case, it's the cube.

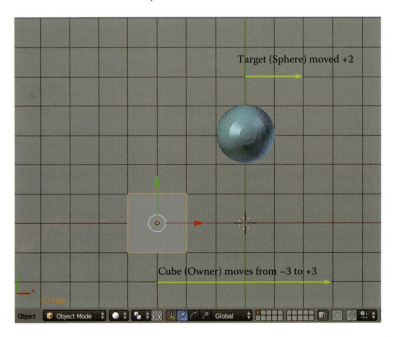

Target (Sphere) moved +2

Cube (Owner) moves from −3 to +3

Object   Object Mode   Global

Figure 14.14

14. Child/Parent Relationships and Constraints

The controlling object (the sphere) is the target. Set up an animation of the cube to translate along the X-axis from −3 grid units at frame 1.00 to +3 grid units at frame 100.00. (See Chapter 9 for a refresher on animation basics.)

With the animation of the cube created, select the cube in the 3D window and add an action constraint by going to the "Properties" window, "Object Constraints" button, clicking on "Add Constraint," and selecting "Action" from the drop down menu. Set the values in the action constraint panel as shown in Figure 14.15.

- **Target:** The controlling object (sphere).
- **Action:** The animation of the cube ("CubeAction").
- **Translation:** "Location X," movement along the X-axis.
- **Action length:** The animation length, frame 1–100.
- **Target range:** The translation range in Blender grid units of the target (sphere) that will control the movement of the cube. In other words, moving the sphere along the X-axis from its original location two Blender units will move the cube from its location at frame 1 to its location at frame 100 (Figure 14.16). Note that the "Target Range" values (movement of the sphere) must be in the positive direction (0.00–2.00).

Figure 14.15

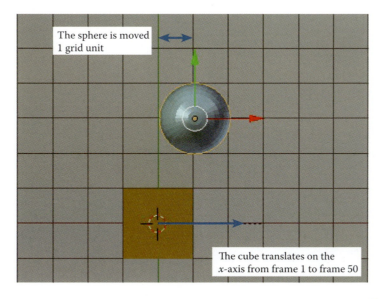

Figure 14.16

Note: On applying the constraint values, the owner (cube) may require repositioning to the start of the animation path.

This is a basic introduction to the action constraint. For a more detailed explanation, refer to the *Blender Manual* at https://www.blender.org/manual/.

14.5.2 The Shrinkwrap Constraint

The "Shrinkwrap" constraint could be more aptly named the mesh surface lock since the constraint locks an object to the surface of another mesh object that's set as the target. Do not confuse this constraint with the "Shrinkwrap" modifier. To demonstrate how the constraint operates, follow these procedures. In the default Blender scene in top orthographic view, add a UV sphere, scale the cube up, and arrange the objects as shown in Figure 14.17. Select the sphere and in the "Properties" window, "Object Constraints" button, add a "Shrinkwrap" constraint (Figure 14.18). In the "Object Constraints" tab, click on the "Target" selection bar and select "Cube" as the target (Figure 14.19). The sphere relocates, positioning its center on the surface of the cube (Figure 14.20).

Note: In the "Object Constraints" tab, the "Shrinkwrap Type" is "Nearest Surface Point." The sphere has therefore located at the nearest point on the surface of the cube (the target).

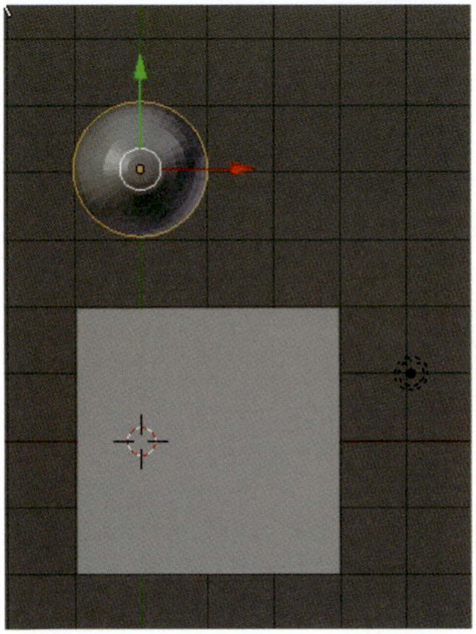

Figure 14.17

Figure 14.18

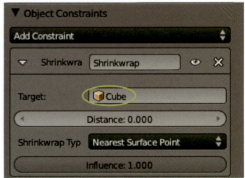

Figure 14.19

In the "Object Constraints" tab, change the "Shrinkwrap Type" to "Nearest Vertex" (Figure 14.21). With this option, the sphere relocates to the nearest vertex on the target object. If the "Shrinkwrap Type: Project" option is selected, the sphere will revert to its original location ("Project'" means to project an axis to the surface). In our setup, the sphere's axes are represented by the RGB arrows of the transformation widget. By default, the axes are the global axes of the imaginary 3D world and with the sphere located in its original position you see that neither of these axes is directed toward a surface on the cube.

Note that the direction of the widget arrows represents the positive direction. With "Shrinkwrap Type: Project" selected, "Axis X," "Axis Y," and "Axis Z" buttons are present in the "Properties" window, "Object Constraints" tab. Check the "Axis X" button. In order to project an axis toward a surface of the cube, we must rotate the sphere's local axes. To do this, with the sphere selected, press the N key with the mouse cursor in the 3D window to display the numeric panel. In the "Transformation Orientation" tab, click on the "Transform" selection drop down menu and select "Local" (Figure 14.22). Rotate the sphere until the X-axis points at the cube (Figure 14.23).

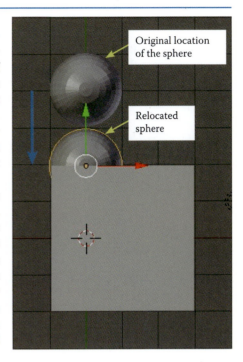

Original location of the sphere

Relocated sphere

Figure 14.20

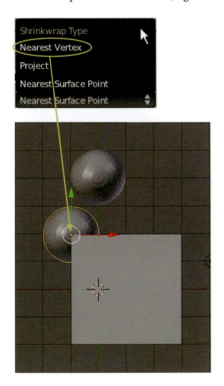

Figure 14.21

Change to "Local"

Figure 14.22

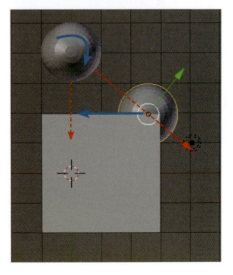

Figure 14.23

As soon as the axis projects to a surface on the cube, the sphere is located on the surface. By slowly rotating the sphere, you will see it move along the surface as the direction of the axis changes. In the "Object Constraints" panel, the "Distance" and "Influence" sliders affect how far the sphere is located between its original position and the surface of the cube. By checking "Axis X" and "Axis Y," the projection line is at 45° between the axes.

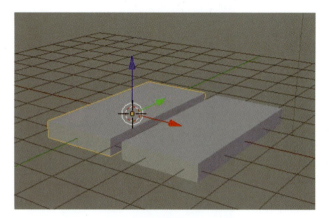

Figure 14.24

Tick "Display Pivot"

Figure 14.25

14.5.3 The Rigid Body Joint Constraint

The "Rigid Body" joint is used to constrain the movement of objects in the Blender game engine (see Chapter 19 for more on the game engine). It is not intended to be used for the manipulation of objects in the 3D window or in an animation. To provide an insight into the use of this constraint, we will demonstrate a simple hinge constraint. In the game engine, a hinged object such as a door would require a force to open and close it. To make our demonstration as simple as possible, we will hinge a trapdoor and use the default gravity force in Blender.

In the "Properties" window, "Scene" button, ensure that "Gravity" is checked in the "Gravity" tab. Set up a scene as shown in Figure 14.24 by scaling the default cube object and then duplicating and transposing the duplication (see Chapter 3 for a refresher). By duplicating the cube, you will have one cube named "Cube" and another named "Cube.001."

Select "Cube" in the 3D window, then in the "Properties" window, "Object Constraints" button click on "Add Constraint" and select "Rigid Body Joint." Note that the constraint type is highlighted in red, indicating that although a constraint has been added, it is not active (Figure 14.25). To activate the constraint, click in the "Target" selection bar and select "Cube.001"—this links the owner of the constraint to a fixed object in the scene (i.e., "Cube.001"). The constraint panel that displays will have "Pivot Type: Ball" selected, so change this to "Hinge." Check "Display Pivot" to display the hinge pivot axes in the 3D window. To see the axes more clearly, rotate the screen, turn off the manipulation widget, change to "Wireframe" viewport shading, and zoom in on the window

(Figure 14.26). You should now see *px*, *py*, and *pz* hinge pivot axes displayed as broken orange lines; the length of the lines are proportional to the sides of the cube sides.

The object will only pivot about the *px*-axis when using the "Hinge" type constraint. We want "Cube" to pivot on a hinge located between the two cubes at the lower edges. It is important to note that before you adjust the location and orientation of the pivot, it is essential to press Ctrl + the A key and select "Rotation & Scale" to apply the pivot scale and rotation (Figure 14.27). Failing to do this results in the pivot working off some ghost location.

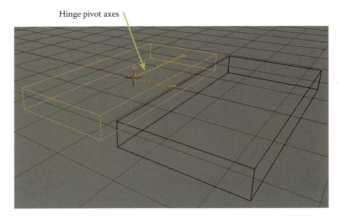

Hinge pivot axes

Figure 14.26

Note: Upon selecting "Rotation & Scale," the axes lines are scaled in proportion to the original default Blender cube (Figure 14.28).

Figure 14.27

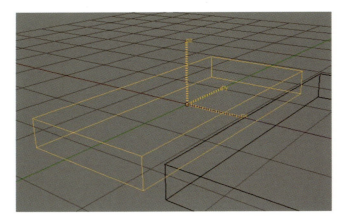

Figure 14.28

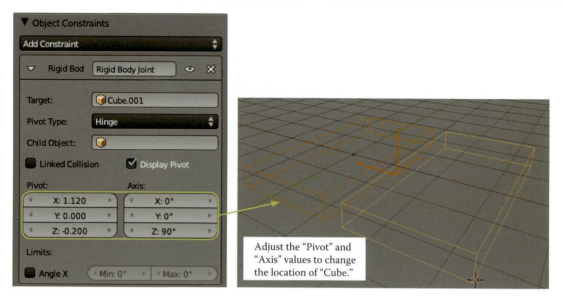

Figure 14.29

Adjust the location and orientation of the pivot by first rotating the pivot axes. In the constraint panel, enter "Z: 90" in the "Axis" bar. Next adjust the "X" and "Z" values in the "Pivot" bar, which locates the *px*-axis as shown in Figure 14.29. The foregoing has set the scene to allow "Cube" to pivot down on the *px*-axis (Figure 14.30). We now have to enter the Blender game engine. Change the Blender screen from the default to the "Game Logic" arrangement and change "Blender Render" to "Blender Game" in the info window header. Zoom in and change the 3D window from "Top" orthographic to "Right" orthographic view. In the properties window—"Physics" button, select "Physics Type: Rigid Body" and check that "Actor" is ticked (Figure 14.31). Place the cursor in the 3D window and press the P key to see "Cube" swing down on the pivot (Figure 14.32). Press Esc to cancel.

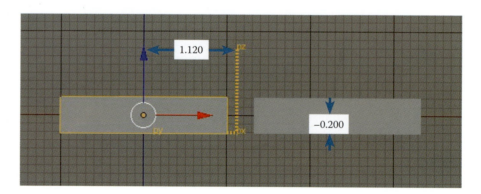

Figure 14.30

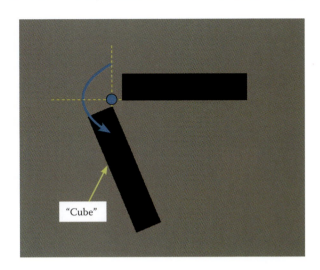

"Physics" tab

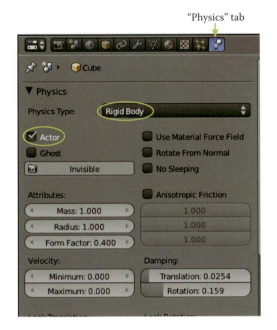

"Cube"

Figure 14.32

Figure 14.31

14.6 Duplicating along Curves

The "Follow Path" constraint can be used to duplicate an object along a curve. For example, start with the default scene with the cube object selected, add a "Bezier" curve to the scene, and shape it in edit mode as shown in Figure 14.33. Select the cube and scale it down very small. In the "Properties" window, "Object Constraints" button, press "Add Constraint," and select "Follow Path." In the "Object Constraints" panel, set the target object as "BezierCurve" (Figure 14.34). In the

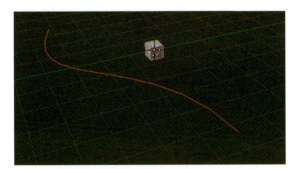

Default scene with a cube and Bezier curve

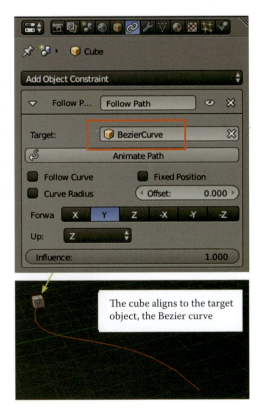

The cube aligns to the target object, the Bezier curve

Figure 14.33

Figure 14.34

Figure 14.35

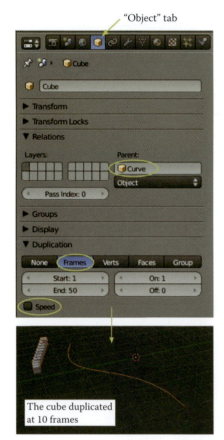

"Object" tab

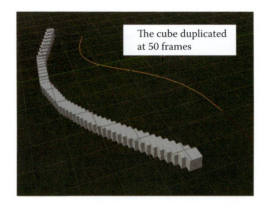

The cube duplicated at 50 frames

Figure 14.36

"Properties" window, "Object" button, "Relations" tab, select "Parent: Curve" and in the "Duplication" tab, select "Frames" and untick "Speed" (Figure 14.35). You may want to scale and reposition the cube at this point. Changing the "End" value will produce a different array of cubes (Figure 14.36).

14.7 Extruding along Curves

A shape can be extruded along a curve to produce a different shape. For example, start with the default Blender scene and delete the cube object. Add a "Bezier" curve and scale it up along the X-axis. For simplicity, put the window into top view (number pad 7— number pad 5). The curve may be scaled and shaped in edit mode to produce a shape for your extrusion to follow.

Deselect the curve and add a "Bezier" or "NURBS" circle; the circle may be shaped in edit mode to produce a cross section shape for your extrusion. Scale the circle way down (Figure 14.37). Deselect the circle and

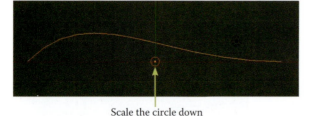

Scale the circle down

Figure 14.37

Figure 14.38

select the curve. In the "Properties" window, "Data" button, "Geometry" tab, enter "Bezier" or "Nurbs" circle in the "Bevel Object" data panel and adjust the scale as required (Figure 14.38).

14.8 The Follow Path Constraint

The "Follow Path" constraint causes an object in an animation to follow a path that has been set as the target. This constraint is combined with the follow curve constraint that, when set, causes the object to rotate and bank as it follows the path. The follow path constraint can also be used to duplicate objects along a path and to extrude an object along a path. In an animation, the motion of the object is set by inserting key frames (see Chapter 9 for a refresher). When using the follow path constraint, the key frames are set in the "Properties" window, "Data" button, "Path Animation" tab. As always, an example is the best way to demonstrate the process.

14.8.1 Scene Setup

Start with the default Blender scene with the default cube object selected and perform the following actions. Press number pad 7 followed by number pad 5 to place the 3D window in top orthographic view. With the cube selected, press the S key, type 0.5, and press Enter to scale the cube down to half its original size. Deselect the cube with the A key and press Shift + the A key—"Add"—"Curve"—"Path." A curve path is added to the scene, which is four Blender grid units long. With the curve path selected press the S key + 5 and then Enter to scale the path up to 20 units long (Figure 14.39). How you scale your object and

Figure 14.39

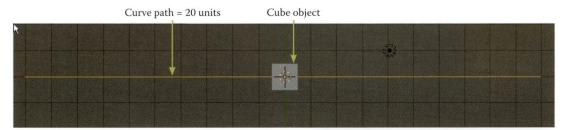

Curve path = 20 units Cube object

set the path length and shape will depend on what you are attempting to achieve in your animation. Here we are merely creating a path that will have some relevance to the values that will be added in our demonstration.

14.8.2 Add a Constraint

Deselect the curve path and select the cube object. Go to the "Properties" window, "Object Constraints" button, "Add Constraint," and select "Follow Path" to assign the follow path constraint and display the constraint panel (Figure 14.40). In the panel, click on the little cube icon in the "Target" bar and then click on "NurbsPath" in the drop down selection menu that displays—this assigns

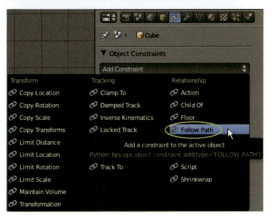

Figure 14.40

Set "NurbsPath" as the target object.

Figure 14.41

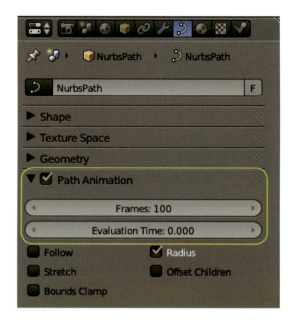

Figure 14.42

the target object (Figure 14.41). At this point, the cube moves to the LH end of the path. Deselect the cube.

In earlier versions of Blender, pressing Alt + the A key would play an animation showing the cube moving along the path; however, in the latest version key frames have to be manually inserted. Key frames are inserted by manipulating values in the path's "Path Animation" tab, and then they are displayed in the timeline window at the bottom of the screen. Therefore, select the curve path in the 3D window then go to the "Properties" window, "Data" button, "Path Animation" tab. Make sure "Path Animation" is checked in the tab and note the values "Frames: 100" and "Evaluation Time: 0.000" (Figure 14.42). Consider the "Frames: 100" value to mean that the curve path length in the 3D window is divided into 100 intervals. Consider the "Evaluation Time" value to mean the interval at which the linked object is residing along the curve path at a given time. The default range is 0.00–100.00. If the number of intervals (frames) is increased, adjust the evaluation time range accordingly. With the cube at the start of the path, the "Evaluation Time" value is 0.000. By default, the "Timeline" window shows a 250-frame animation timeline with values "Start: 1" and "End: 250" and the vertical green cursor at frame 1 (Figure 14.43).

The curve path and the animation timeline are two separate identities. The object's movement along the path may coincide with the timeline, but not necessarily. To demonstrate this we will set the object to move along the path midway in the animation. In the timeline window, move the cursor to frame 25. In the "Properties" window, "Data" button, "Path Animation" tab, click RMB on the "Evaluation Time" bar and then select "Insert Keyframe" (Figure 14.44). The bar will turn yellow and a vertical yellow line is added in the "Timeline" window under the green cursor to show that a key frame has been set at frame 25. In the "Timeline" window, move the green cursor to frame 125. In the "Properties"

Figure 14.43

Timeline window

Green cursor at frame 1

Figure 14.44

window, "Data" button, "Path Animation" tab, change the "Evaluation Time" value to 100. The cube moves along the path as you drag the mouse. At "Evaluation Time: 100," the cube is at the end of the path. Repeat the process for adding a key frame.

14.8.3 Timeline Animation Play Control Buttons

In the "Timeline" window, return to frame 1 and play the animation (press Esc to stop the animation). Consult Figure 14.45 for an explanation of the "Timeline" animation control buttons. The animation plays but the cube remains stationary until frame 25, then it moves along the path and reaches the end at frame 125. The animation continues to play in the timeline until frame 250. In the 3D window, carefully observe the motion of the cube as it moves along the path. At the start, there is a definite acceleration followed by a constant velocity then a deceleration as the cube approaches the end of the path. We can see a graphical representation of this movement in the "Graph Editor" window. Divide the 3D window in two and change one-half to the "Graph Editor" window; you will probably have to zoom in on the window (press the number pad—key several times or scroll the MMB) and also drag the window to centralize the graph (hold and drag the MMB).

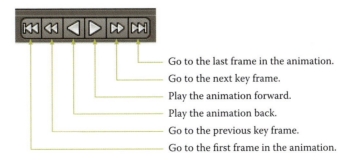

Go to the last frame in the animation.

Go to the next key frame.

Play the animation forward.

Play the animation back.

Go to the previous key frame.

Go to the first frame in the animation.

Figure 14.45

14.8 The Follow Path Constraint

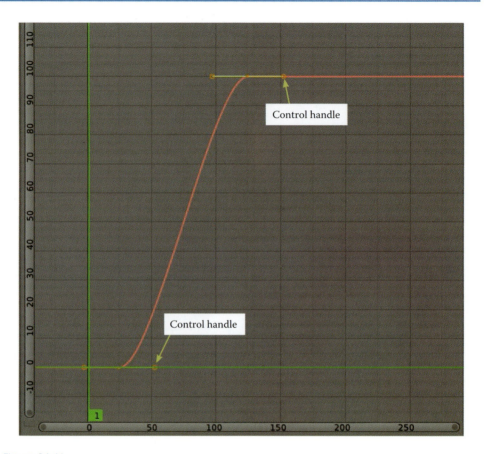

Figure 14.46

Scale the graph horizontally and vertically by holding Ctrl + the MMB and dragging the mouse (Figure 14.46).

The "Graph Editor" window shows the frames of the "Timeline" window across the bottom and the curve path length (intervals) vertically up the LHS. The green horizontal and vertical lines are cursors: the vertical green cursor represents the position of the cube. Click, hold, and drag the vertical line until it's at frame 125; you can see the cube is now at interval 100 of the curve path length (which is the end of the animation). The graph shows a "Bezier" curve with control handles at frame 25 and frame 125. With the cursor located at frame 70, change the "Evaluation Time" value to 30, and note that the cube relocates to interval 30 along the path. Add a key frame and you'll see that a third control handle is added to the graph in the "Graph Editor" window (Figure 14.47). If the animation is played at this point, the cube appears to move in the animation as it moved previously. There is no perceivable change to the movement, but since the shape of the graph is slightly different, there is in fact a change of velocity.

In the "Graph Editor" window, the graph is in edit mode with all the control handles selected. Press the A key to deselect the handles, click the RMB on the new middle handle,

14. Child/Parent Relationships and Constraints

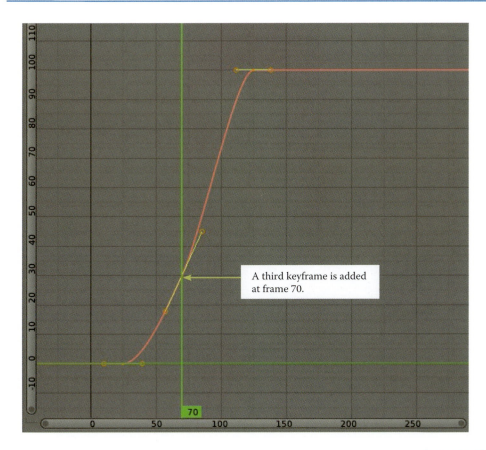

A third keyframe is added at frame 70.

Figure 14.47

then click the RMB again on the upper end of the handle. Press the G key and drag the handle until it is horizontal (Figure 14.48). Play the animation from frame 1 and you will observe that the cube will stop momentarily at frame 70 with the cube 30 intervals along the path, then continue on to the end. By dragging and rotating the middle control handle, you can control how the cube moves along the path. Note that as you reposition the control handle, the key frame in the "Timeline" window repositions.

This demonstration has employed a straight-line path in the 3D window, but the path can be shaped into a curve and extruded. You may add key frames as required and in doing so add control handles to the graph in the "Graph Editor" window. Manipulating the control handles allows control over how your object moves at intervals along the path. You can therefore set the movement of an object to decelerate into a curve and accelerate out of a curve, giving it an extremely realistic motion. With the cube selected in the 3D window, check "Follow Curve" in the "Object Constraints" panel. With the curve path reshaped (reposition the curve path's control handles in the 3D window), the object following the curve path will be aligned to the path (Figure 14.49).

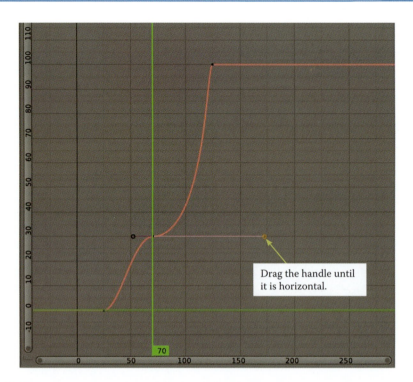

Figure 14.48

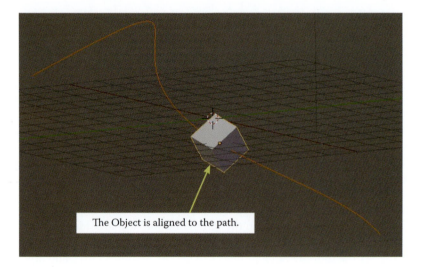

Figure 14.49

14. Child/Parent Relationships and Constraints

15

Armatures

15.1 Adding an Armature

In Blender, "Armature" refers to an object type that is used to deform a mesh. Think of your finger and the skin covering it and the bones inside. The skin would be the mesh and the bones are the armature; when the bone moves, the skin moves with it.

To begin the instruction on armatures, start with the default Blender scene, delete the cube object, and add an armature object (press Shift + the A Key—"Armature"—"Single Bone"). Zoom in (with the number pad + key) and press number pad 1 then number pad 5 to get the front orthographic view.

15.2 Single Bone Armatures

What you see is a single bone armature (Figure 15.1). Armatures can, and usually do, comprise multiple bones, but before we complicate anything we should start with an understanding of bone manipulation. The default single bone armature is displayed in type "Octahedral" (due to the object having eight surfaces): it appears as two four-sided pyramids conjoined at the base with spheres at the apexes. For the purpose of the demonstration, we will name the parts of the armature tip, body, and base.

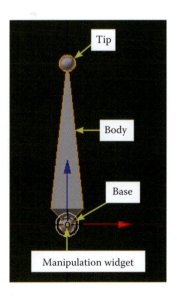

Figure 15.1

Note: Although the armature is an object in Blender, it is not a mesh object. Its shape cannot be edited other than scaling it larger or smaller. It can be rotated and translated. It has a center like any other object, which may be repositioned, but for use in a multibone armature it is best to maintain the center at the apex of the lower (smaller) pyramid in the center of the sphere. With the manipulation widget turned on, the widget is also positioned at the center.

15.2.1 Adding Additional Single Bone Armatures

A single bone armature was added to the scene by pressing Shift + A key and selecting "Add"—"Armature"—"Single Bone." It is positioned at the location of the 3D cursor in the 3D window. The armature is entered in "Object" mode. It may be stating the obvious but what you have added to the scene is an "Armature" comprising one single bone. Note the name "Armature" in the "Outliner" window. Click on the little plus sign to open the file tree and the headings "Armature" and "Pose." Click the plus sign next to the second "Armature" entry and you will see "Bone." These entries say there is one armature comprising one bone (Figure 15.2). Deselect the "Armature" in the 3D window.

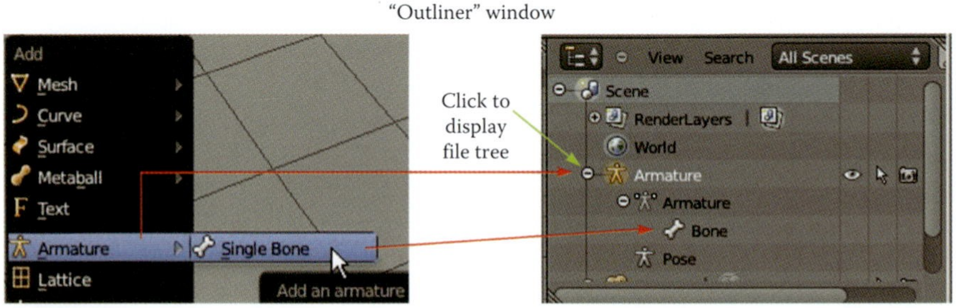

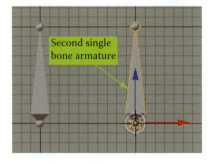

Figure 15.2

Figure 15.3

If you relocate the 3D cursor and repeat the process you add a second single bone armature (Figure 15.3). Note the new name "Armature.001" in the "Outliner" window and the subentries "Armature.001" and "Bone" (Figure 15.5).

If you select either armature in the 3D window and press Shift + D key (Duplicate) and translate (drag the mouse) you create a third single bone armature (Figure 15.4). The name in the "Outliner" window for this armature is "Armature.002" (Figure 15.5).

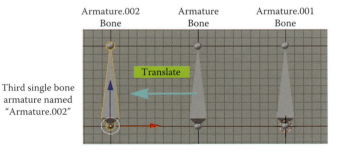

Figure 15.4

15. Armatures

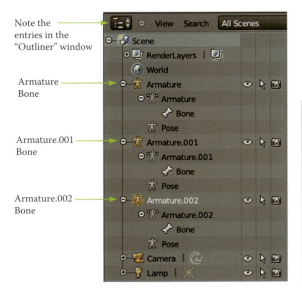

Note the entries in the "Outliner" window

Armature — Bone

Armature.001 — Bone

Armature.002 — Bone

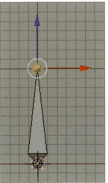

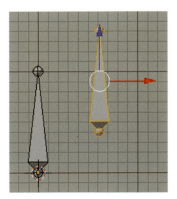

Figure 15.5

Figure 15.6

Note the entries in the "Outliner" window. There are three separate single bone armatures. All three armatures are independent of each other.

Select one of the three armatures, say "Armature.002" and tab into "Edit" mode. In "Edit" mode only the tip of the armature is selected (Figure 15.6 LH). Press A key twice or RMB click on the body of the armature to select the whole armature.

Note **you are in "Edit" mode**. Press Shift + D key (Duplicate) and drag the mouse to reveal a new bone (Figure 15.6 RH). The point here is that it is a new bone that is part of "Armature.002," not a new armature. If you select the original armature "Bone" and tab to "Object" mode both bones will be selected. Translating the original will cause the new bone to follow (Figure 15.7). There is no link shown between the two but they are connected. In the "Outliner" window you will see "Bone.001" entered under "Armature.002".

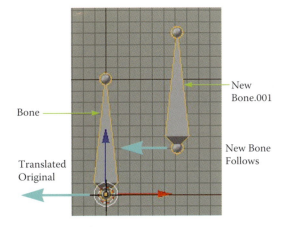

New Bone.001

Bone

New Bone Follows

Translated Original

Figure 15.7

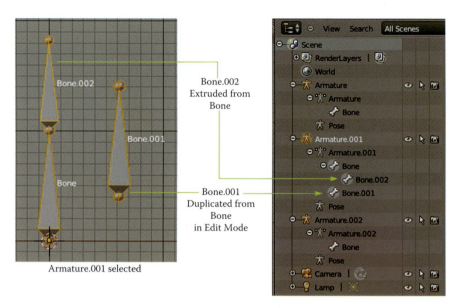

Figure 15.8

Bone.002
Extruded from
Bone

Bone.001
Duplicated from
Bone
in Edit Mode

Armature.001 selected

In "Edit" mode, press the A key to deselect then RMB click on the tip to select the tip of "Bone." Press E key (Extrude) and drag the mouse you extrude a new bone from the tip of the original. This is a new bone that is part of the armature not a new armature. Note the entries in the "Outliner" window. You now have subentry "Bone.002" under "Bone" (Figure 15.8).

If you go to the "Properties" window, "Object Data" button, "Display" tab, and tick "Names" the individual bone names will display in the 3D window.

Select "Pose" mode in the 3D window header. Any bone may be selected then rotated, translated, or scaled independently to enable posing for a still image or for animating. Tab will take you back to "Edit" mode and all bones are displayed in their original positions prior to posing. Observe that Bone.002 follows Bone when it is rotated but Bone.001 remains stationary. In the "Outliner" window under "Pose" for the "Armature" see that Bone.002 is subentered under Bone while Bone.001 is a separate Pose entry. In other words, Bone.002 moves with Bone but Bone.001 will not.

If you require Bone.001 to rotate with Bone go to "Edit" mode, select Bone.001 then shift select Bone and press Ctrl + P key. From the "Make Parent" panel that displays select "Keep Offset." You have told Blender to make Bone the parent of Bone.001 but to leave Bone.001 where it is. If you select the "Connect" option Bone.001 will be moved and connected to Bone. The shift select order is critical since you are telling Blender to make the last bone selected the parent of the first. Play around with this concept noting the order of entries in the "Outliner" window.

You are now set to continue reading and encounter Section 15.4."

15.3 Armature Display Types

The default armature display type is octahedral but there are four alternative display types: stick, b-bone, envelope, and wire (Figure 15.9). The wire display option appears much the same as stick. With the armature bone selected, see the "Properties" window, "Object Data" button, "Display" tab to choose these options (Figure 15.10). Which display type is used

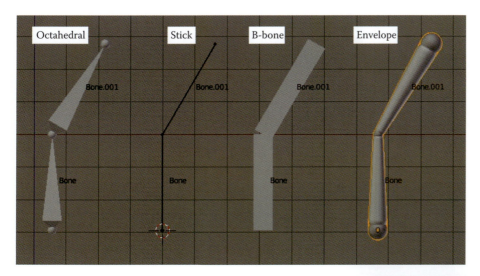

Figure 15.9

depends on what you are doing with the armature. I won't go into the different uses at this time but since the basic function of an armature is to deform a mesh object, we need to understand how this happens.

15.3.1 Basic Procedure

The basic procedure for deforming a mesh object with an armature is to apply an armature modifier to the object and then, in the modifier, name the armature that will do the deformation. It doesn't matter which armature display type is used; each armature has a field of influence in which mesh vertices must reside in order to be influenced.

Change the armature display type to "Envelope" and you will see a shape like a cylinder with a sphere at each end (Figure 15.11). Tab into edit mode, and you will see the field of influence surrounding the armature (you can only see this in envelope display type in edit mode). In edit mode, you can select the whole armature or the spheres at either end separately, then translate them.

To reshape the field of influence to encompass vertices in a mesh, have the armature displayed as "Envelope" in "Edit" mode. Here you can select either the head or the tail of a bone, then in the "Properties" window, "Bone" button, "Deform" tab adjust "Envelope—Distance" or "Radius—Head or Tail."

Just file this information in your memory bank for the time being and go back to the default single bone armature in octahedral display type in object mode. Tab into

Figure 15.10

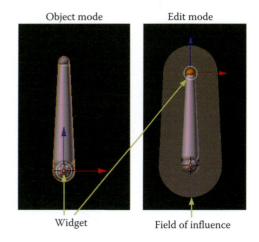

Figure 15.11

With the widget off, the tip is orange

Edit mode

Figure 15.12

edit mode and select the tip—now the widget is located at the tip, which shows that the tip of the armature is selected (Figure 15.12). Turn the widget off and you'll see that the sphere at the tip is orange; having the widget on just makes it easier to see for demonstration purposes. With the widget on you can translate the tip in the 3D window, which also changes the length of the armature. The rotate and scale functions of the widget have no effect.

15.4 Multibone Armatures

Turn the widget off but leave the tip selected. Now press the E key (extrude) and drag the mouse; you will see a new bone being extruded from the tip (Figure 15.13). Select the tip of the new bone, press the E key, and drag the mouse and a new bone is extruded. Select the base of the original bone and repeat the process, creating a multibone armature (Figure 15.14).

New bones extruded from the tip

New bone extruded from the base

Figure 15.13

Figure 15.14

15. Armatures

15.5 Deforming a Mesh Object

So far, I have demonstrated the very basics of what an armature is and how to expand a single bone into a multibone armature. It's time to see how to deform a mesh. To demonstrate the armature principle in Blender, we will make something akin to a finger on your hand and make it deform with an armature.

Start with the default Blender scene, delete the cube, and add a mesh circle. In the tool shelf (the panel at the lower LHS of the 3D window) tab named "Add Circle," reduce the number of vertices from 32 to 8. When creating a mesh for use with armatures, use as few vertices as possible. A high number of vertices will give you a better surface look and a better render, but too many vertices will slow down the computer considerably in an animation.

> Note: When you add a primitive to a scene, it is in object mode and the tool panel at the lower left of the screen provides the facility to edit the size and vertex count. If you tab to "Edit" mode then tab back to "Object" mode the tool panel no longer has this feature.
>
> If you want to alter the vertex count again press the space bar to display the search panel and type "Add Circle." Select this option from the menu that displays. The "Add Circle" tab is reinstated in the "Tool Panel."

Tab into edit mode and extrude the circle on the z-axis to produce a cylinder. With the top ring of vertices selected, extrude the shape again. With the third ring selected, press the S key and move the cursor in toward the center of the cylinder. Continue on extruding and scaling until you get a shape like the one in Figure 15.15 (left). The finger will only have two parts, with a joint in the middle. The vertices close together in the middle of the mesh are where the joint will be; they act like a concertina hose on a vacuum cleaner, allowing the mesh to bend. With the mesh selected, tab into object mode and place the 3D cursor as shown in Figure 15.15 (right).

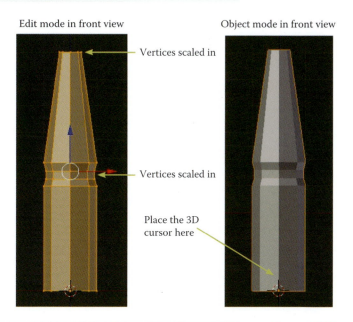

Edit mode in front view · Object mode in front view

Vertices scaled in

Vertices scaled in

Place the 3D cursor here

Figure 15.15

> Note: For the purpose of the demonstration, leave the default circle object with the default radius of 1.000 Blender grid units. If the circle is scaled, the finger mesh vertices may fall outside the armature's field of influence, producing some unexpected results.

Properties window—Object data button

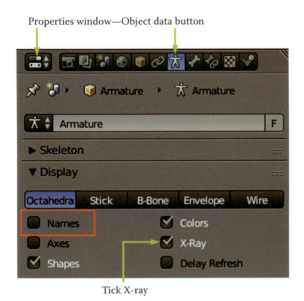

Tick X-ray

Figure 15.16

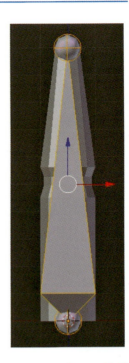

Figure 15.17   Figure 15.18

Figure 15.19

Deselect the mesh finger with the A key and add a single bone armature as previously described. Since the cursor was placed at the base of the finger on the centerline, you probably won't see the armature. Go to the "Properties" window, "Data" button, "Display" tab, and tick "X-Ray" (Figure 15.16). This makes the armature visible in object mode in solid display. It actually makes the armature display on top of the mesh. With the armature selected, tab to edit mode, select the tip of the bone, and drag it up to the middle of the bend point of the finger. Press the E key and extrude the bone, which creates a second bone, up to the top of the mesh finger (Figure 15.17). In the "Properties" window, "Object Data" button, "Display" tab, tick "Names" to show the names of the bones in the 3D window (Figure 15.16). The names will be "Bone" and "Bone.001." Press the A key to deselect the armature bones and change to "Object" mode.

15.5.1 Alternative Method for Creating a Multibone Armature

There is an alternative method for creating a multibone armature. With a single bone armature added, tab to "Edit" mode and drag the tip up to the top of the finger (Figure 15.18). Make sure you have the body of the bone selected (right click on the body), go to the tool shelf at the left of the screen, and click "Subdivide" (Figure 15.19). Successive clicks will subdivide the bone and create a multibone armature.

15.6 Armature Modifiers

We will now add an armature modifier to the finger mesh object. Deselect the armature and select the finger in object mode. In the "Properties" window, "Object Modifiers" button, click "Add Modifier" and select "Armature" (Figure 15.20). Click in the "Object" panel and select "Armature" (Blender named your armature "Armature") (Figure 15.21). In the modifier panel check "Vertex groups" and "Bone Envelope" under the "Bind To"

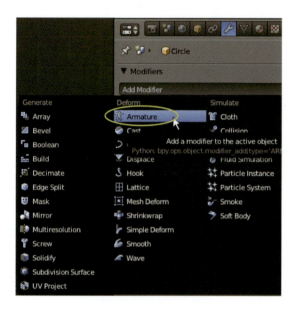

Figure 15.20

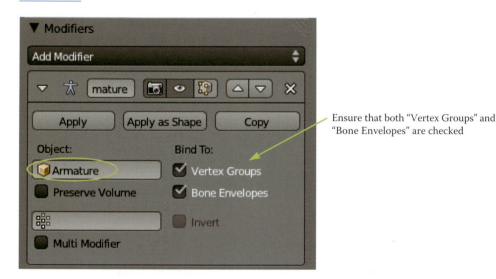

Ensure that both "Vertex Groups" and "Bone Envelopes" are checked

Figure 15.21

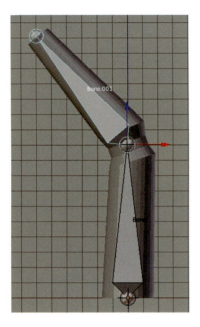

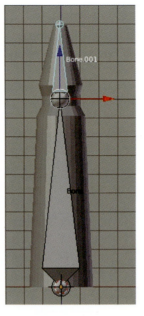

Figure 15.22

Figure 15.23

heading. It is time to test the deformation process. In the 3D window, deselect the finger and select the armature. (Depending on how you positioned the armature in the finger, you may have difficulty selecting. If this is the case, go to the "Outliner" window at the upper right of the screen and click on "Armature" in the display.) With the armature selected, change from "Object" mode to "Pose" mode in the 3D window header—select "Bone.001" (RMB click), which will be highlighted in blue. Press the R key and rotate the bone and you'll see the top of the finger rotate with the bone (Figure 15.22). Next, select a bone and press the S key to scale (Figure 15.23). Then, change the armature to envelope display (Figure 15.24).

The foregoing has demonstrated how to deform a mesh object using armatures and the armature modifier. The ultimate use of armatures is in character animation, which involves rigging a mesh (the character) with a multiboned armature and then animating the movement of the armature to simulate the character's movement. Rigging a character can be a tedious and sometimes complicated process. Blender has a ready-made humanoid armature rig stowed away in the user preferences window.

Rotated bone in envelope display

Scaled bone in envelope display

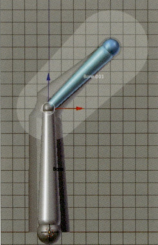

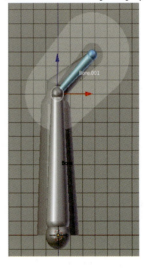

Figure 15.24

15.7 Humanoid Armatures

In the "User Preferences" window of a new scene ("Info" window header, "File," "User Preferences"), click on "Add-ons" at the top of the window. In the panel at the LHS, click "Rigging" and you will have a single-line entry named "Rigging Rigify." Tick the little box at the end of the line. Close the "User Preferences" window and go back to the 3D window and press Shift + the A key. Select "Armature" and you will see that "Human (Meta Rig)" and "Pitchapoy (Meta Rig) have been added to the selection options. Click on the "Human (Meta Rig)" entry and a multiboned humanoid armature is introduced to the scene. On my computer it is entered rather small. If this is the same for you, zoom in or scale the rig up. Pan the window around and have a good look at the rig. If you go into pose mode and select individual bones, you will be able to move them about to create different poses (Figure 15.25). The "Pitchapoy (Meta Rig)" is a little more advanced option.

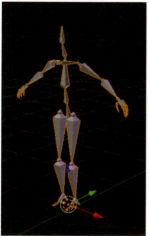 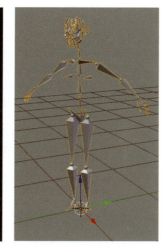

| Blend rig—Object mode | Blend rig—Pose mode | Pitchapoy rig—Object mode |

Figure 15.25

It may be a little ambitious at this stage to construct a model of a human figure and rig it for animation. Of course, you could use the Make Human program (www.makehuman.org/) to create a figure then import it into Blender and rig for animation, but unless you have a reasonable computer you may be disappointed. Make Human models have a pretty high vertex count so there is a lot of stuff to move about in an animation. You would also have to study Section 15.12 in detail. What we have covered so far is the very basics; while on the subject of armatures, let's demonstrate a few more basics.

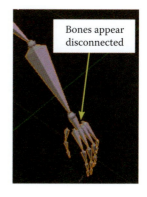

Bones appear disconnected

Figure 15.26

15.8 Disconnected Bones

You may have noticed that in the humanoid armature, some of the bones appear to be disconnected because they are separated from adjoining bones (Figure 15.26). To demonstrate how this occurs, follow this procedure. In a new scene, add a single

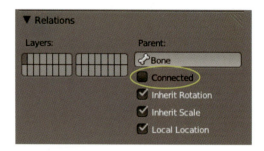

Figure 15.27

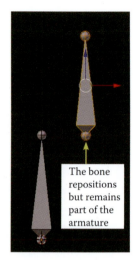

The bone repositions but remains part of the armature

Figure 15.28

bone armature, tab into edit mode, select the tip if it is not already selected, and extrude another bone. Select the body of the new bone and, in the "Properties" window, "Bone" button, "Relations" tab, untick "Connected" (Figure 15.27). The new bone may now be translated (use the G key to grab) and repositioned away from the original bone. It remains part of the armature (Figure 15.28) as seen by the dotted line connecting its base to the tip of the first bone. If "Connected" is reticked, the new bone will be repositioned with its base connected to the original bone.

In the previous examples of deforming a mesh with an armature, the mesh vertices had to be located within the field of influence of the armature. An alternative to this is to manually nominate which vertices will be affected by the armature. There are basically two methods:

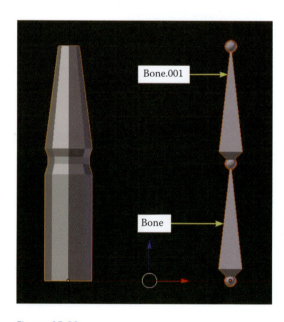

Figure 15.29

1. Select and assign vertices to a vertex group and nominate the control armature bone.
2. Perform the same operation using Blender's weight paint tool.

15.8.1 Method 1: Manually Assign Vertices

In a new scene, construct a finger as previously described. Add a two-bone armature as before, but position it as shown in Figure 15.29. Select the armature and in the "Properties" window, "Object Data" button, "Display" tab, tick "Names" to show the bones named "Bone" and "Bone.001." Deselect the armature. Select the finger, tab into edit mode, and press the A key to deselect the vertices. In the "Properties" window, "Object Data" button, "Vertex Groups" tab, click the + sign to add a new vertex group; a vertex group is added and named "Group" (Figure 15.30). The aim here is to select vertices and add them to the vertex group. The movement of the group is to be controlled by a bone in the armature. By renaming "Group" to "Bone.001," the vertex group will

Click the + sign to add a group

Figure 15.30

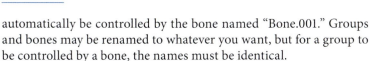

Figure 15.32

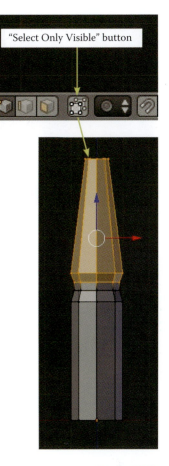

"Select Only Visible" button

Python: bpy.ops.object.vertex_group_add()

Figure 15.31

automatically be controlled by the bone named "Bone.001." Groups and bones may be renamed to whatever you want, but for a group to be controlled by a bone, the names must be identical.

In the 3D window, select the vertices in the upper part of the finger (press the B key—drag a rectangle). Make sure you have the "Select Only Visible" button turned off in the 3D window header or you will only be selecting the front vertices of the finger (Figure 15.31). In the "Vertex Groups" tab, click "Assign" to assign the selected vertices to the group. Check out the assignment by alternately clicking on "Deselect" and "Select" in the tab (Figure 15.32).

Tab into object mode and deselect the finger with the A key. Select the armature and change to pose mode. Select "Bone.001" and press the R key to rotate (Figure 15.33). Nothing happens because we haven't applied an armature modifier to the finger. Go back and

The armature is rotated but nothing happens to the finger

Figure 15.33

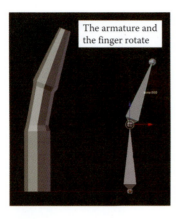

The armature and the finger rotate

Figure 15.34

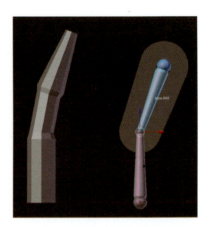

Figure 15.35

Figure 15.36

select the finger and in the "Properties" window, "Object Modifiers" button, click "Add Modifier" and select "Armature." In the armature "Object" panel, click and select "Armature." Deselect the finger and select the armature in pose mode. Select "Bone.001" and rotate it—the upper part of the finger will now deform as the bone is rotated (Figure 15.34). Since the armature is located well away from the finger, the field of influence of the armature is not enforced (Figure 15.35).

15.8.2 Method 2: Weight Paint

Instead of selecting vertices, Blender has a painting method that selects and assigns vertices to a group, automatically linking them to an armature bone. The paint method allows a graduated weight to be given to vertices that dictates how much influence the armature bone will have over the deformation of the mesh.

To begin, set up a new scene the same way you did for Method 1. Select the finger in object mode and add an armature modifier in the properties window. Don't forget to enter "Armature" in the "Object" panel. Select the armature and enter pose mode. In the "Properties" window, "Object Data" button, a "Display" tab, tick "Names" to display the bone names in the 3D window; the names should be "Bone" and "Bone.001" as before. Select "Bone.001" and right click the finger to select it. With the finger selected, go to the 3D window header and change from object mode to "Weight Paint" mode (Figure 15.36). The finger displays in blue, which indicates that no vertices are selected (Figure 15.37).

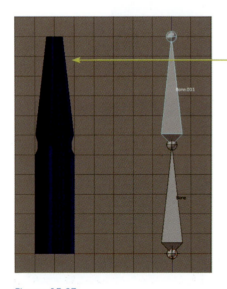

The finger is blue because no vertices are selected

Figure 15.37

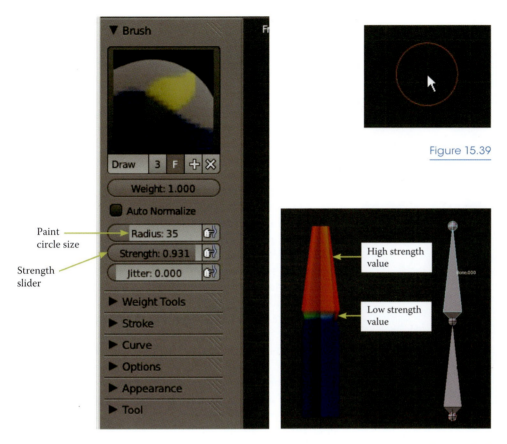

Paint
circle size

Strength
slider

Figure 15.39

High strength
value

Low strength
value

Figure 15.38

Figure 15.40

In the panel at the LHS of the window, make sure the "Strength" slider is set to 1.000 (Figure 15.38). We are about to paint over the finger mesh to select vertices, and by setting the strength to a high value we are telling Blender that the selected vertices are to be rigorously controlled by "Bone.001." In weight paint mode, the cursor in the 3D window has a circle attached to it (Figure 15.39). The size of the circle is the size of the paint tool, which can be altered in the panel at the left. We want the upper part of the finger to be transformed by "Bone.001" so click, hold, and drag the cursor circle over the top part of the finger. The part of the finger painted turns red, which indicates a rigorous control (Figure 15.40). Altering the "Strength" value changes the control strength and will display as some other color.

Turn the mesh around and make sure the vertices on the backside of the finger are painted (pan the 3D view around). Having painted the finger, note that in the "Properties" window, "Object Data" button, "Vertex Groups" tab a vertex group has been created and named "Bone.001." Selecting "Bone.001" in pose mode and translating it will move the top part of the finger.

Select the vertices at the tip only

Figure 15.41

15.9 Vertex Groups or Field of Influence

Having described the deformation of a mesh by employing vertex groups and field of influence, the question arises as to which is being employed when the armature is located inside the mesh. If we follow the preceding examples by either selecting vertices or weight painting, we assign vertices to a vertex group. It is unclear whether the vertex group or the field of influence is controlling the deformation of the mesh. If the armature is moved away from the mesh posing, the bone will still cause a deformation; therefore, the vertex group is in control. However, when the armature is inside the mesh, is it the field of influence or the vertex group?

Follow this example to clarify this dilemma. Create the same scene as in Methods 1 and 2 (see Sections 15.8.1 and 15.8.2), select only the vertices at the tip of the finger, and assign them to a vertex group (Figure 15.41). Name the group Bone.001. Make sure you have added an armature modifier to the finger and have assigned "Armature" in the "Object" panel. Rotate "Bone.001" in pose mode and the whole top of the finger deforms. Place the armature in "Object" mode and move it away from the finger. Rotate the bone again and only the tip of the finger deforms—this only proves that both the vertex group and the field of influence are active.

Place the armature back inside the finger. Select the finger and take a look at the armature modifier. Under the heading "Bind To" there are the two boxes labeled "Vertex Group" and "Bone Envelope." Untick "Bone Envelope"; rotating the bone now only deforms the tip of the finger (Figure 15.42). Obviously you have turned the field of influence off, so herein lies the control for selecting either the field of influence or the vertex group.

Figure 15.42

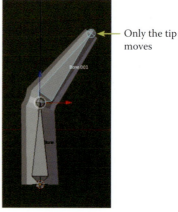

Only the tip moves

Another way of negating the field of influence is to set the "Distance" and "Weight" values to 0.000 in the "Properties" window, "Bone" button, "Deform" tab (Figure 15.43).

15.10 Inverse Kinematics

The "IK" solver constraint is a wonderful tool for animators. IK is the opposite of FK, or forward kinematics, and both IK and FK are ways of controlling the posing and animation of a chain of bones. With FK, you have to rotate the chain of bones one by one to pose it for animation; this is a tedious process but gives you full control. With IK, dragging the end of the chain will result in the chain following the selected bone.

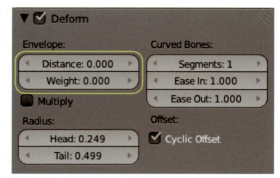

Figure 15.43

An example would be to create a chain of bones as shown in Figure 15.44. With the chain (armature) selected, go into pose mode, select the last bone in the chain, and in the "Properties" window, "Bone Constraints" button, click on "Add Bone Constraint" and select "Inverse Kinematics" (Figure 15.45). In the 3D window in pose mode, with the end

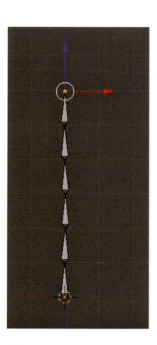

Figure 15.44

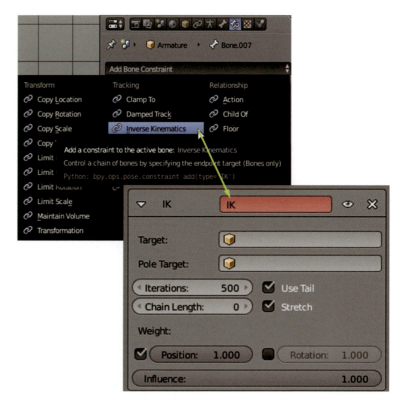

Figure 15.45

bone still selected, press the G key and move the bone (Figure 15.46). Even in this single constraint, there are plenty of settings to play with.

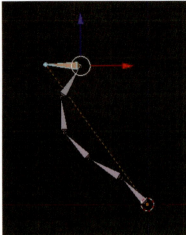

Figure 15.46

15.11 IK Constraint

The IK Constraint forces a multibone armature to follow the shape of a curve. With the armature constrained to the curve, the curve is then manipulated to adjust the shape of the armature and in turn any mesh assigned to the armature. To demonstrate we will create a multibone armature and constrain it to a "Bezier" curve (Figure 15.47).

In the default 3D window delete the cube and add a "Bezier" curve. Leave the 3D window view as "User Perspective." The "Bezier" curve is displayed with the curve shape in "Top" view. If you were to view the 3D window in "Front" view all you would see is a straight line. Scale the curve up four times (S key—4—Enter). Deselect the curve (A key) and add a single bone armature. Scale the armature up four times. Tab into "Edit" mode and select the body of the armature. In the tool shelf click "Subdivide" twice to produce an armature with four bones. Note the location of the armature in the "Top" view. Both the origin of the armature and the center of the "Bezier" curve are located at the center of the scene (Figure 15.48).

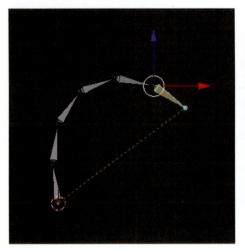

Figure 15.47

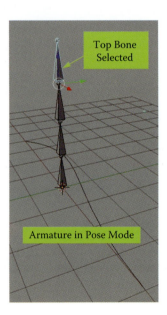

Figure 15.48

With the armature selected, in the 3D window header change from "Edit" mode to "Pose" mode. The outline of the armature will be displayed in blue. Deselect the armature (A key) and select the top bone in the armature (RMB Click).

When selecting the top bone a "Bone Constraints" button displays in the "Properties" window. LMB click this button, click "Add Constraint" and select "Spline IK" in the drop down menu (Figure 15.49).

The constraint panel will display in the "Properties" window. In the

Bone Constraint buttons

Figure 15.49

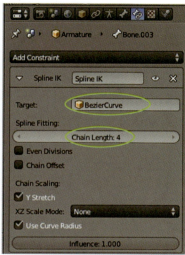

Figure 15.50

panel change the "Spline Fittings: Chain Length" value to 4 (the number of bones in the armature). In the "Target" panel LMB click on the cube icon and select "Bezier Curve" from the drop down. This enters the curve as the target. In selecting the target the armature is relocated in the 3D window and shaped (constrained) to the curve. Note the direction of the bones (Figures 15.50 and 15.51).

The armature bones are arranged in accordance with the direction of the curve. If the curve were being used as an animation path the movement along the path would be in a specific direction. To see the direction of the curve, select the "Bezier" curve (if the armature obstructs the curve in the 3D window selection may be made in the "Outliner"

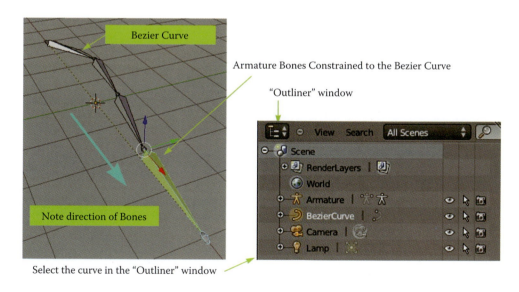

Bezier Curve

Note direction of Bones

Armature Bones Constrained to the Bezier Curve

"Outliner" window

Select the curve in the "Outliner" window

Figure 15.51

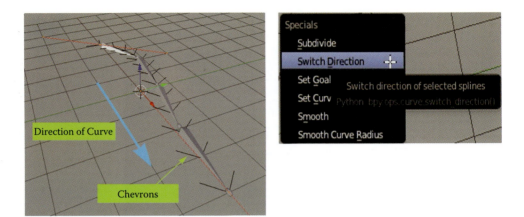

Figure 15.52

window) and "Tab" into "Edit" mode. You will see chevrons spaced along the curve pointing the direction. The direction may be reversed by pressing the W key to display the "Specials" menu and selecting "Switch Direction." In doing this the chevrons are reversed and so are the bones in the armature (Figure 15.52).

With the armature constrained to the curve the armature may be posed by selecting the control handles on the "Bezier Curve." The curve can be subdivided in "Edit" mode to add additional control handles and facilitate more control over the posing. Remember the practical use of the armature is to control the shape and movement of a mesh object, which is assigned to the armature (Figure 15.53).

"Hooks" may be assigned to the control handles of the curve, which give you a nonrenderable object with which to translate and pose the armature.

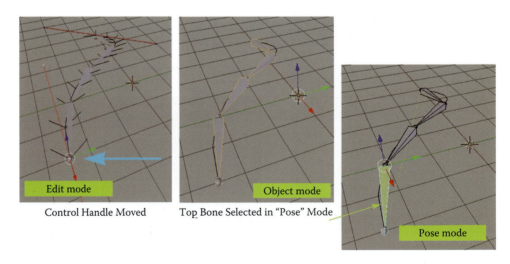

Control Handle Moved   Top Bone Selected in "Pose" Mode

Figure 15.53

To add a "Hook" to a control handle place the curve in "Edit" mode and ensure everything is deselected. Select a control handle (RMB Click) and press "Ctrl + H key and select "Hook to New Object" in the drop down menu that displays. A "Hook" is displayed in the form of a 3D cross (Figures 15.54 and 15.55).

To display the "Hook" in a different format go to the "Outliner" window and open up the file tree under the "Bezier" curve until you find "Empty." Click on "Empty" (LMB) to select it (Figure 15.56).

Figure 15.54

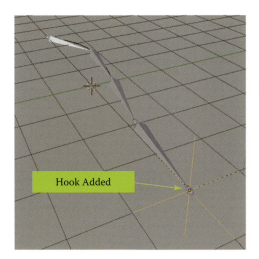

Hook Added

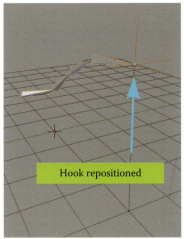

Hook repositioned

Figure 15.55

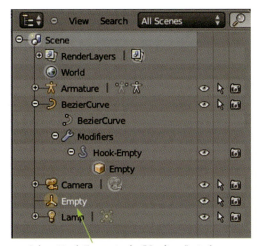

Select Hook Empty in the "Outliner" window

Figure 15.56

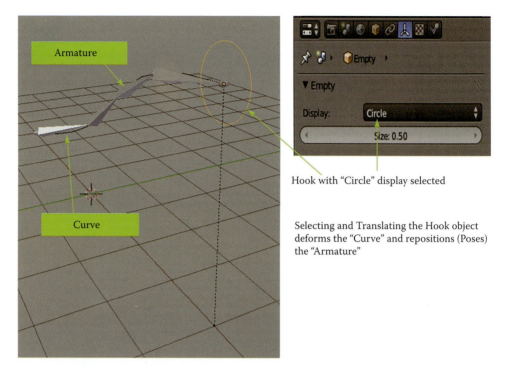

Figure 15.57

Hook with "Circle" display selected

Selecting and Translating the Hook object deforms the "Curve" and repositions (Poses) the "Armature"

In the "Properties" window, "Object Data" button the "Empty" tab will display with a "Display" drop down selection menu. You select a different display format from this menu (Figure 15.57).

Another method of introducing nonrenderable objects to allow curve manipulation, when you have an armature constrained to the curve, is to add single bones. You then parent the bone to the "Hook."

15.12 Character Rigging

15.12.1 Rigging the Character

The basic concept of animating a figure or character is first model a mesh figure or character and second rig an armature (skeleton) inside the mesh which is then posed and animated on a timeline to produce simulated movement. The mesh is linked to the armature so that it follows the movement of the armature.

15.12.2 The Human Figure

Constructing a model of a character or figure can be a lengthy process depending on the detail employed. To jump right in and save time we will use a ready-built human figure. There are several websites where you can download pre-built models some of which are pre-rigged. To understand the rigging process you should begin with a simple "Low Poly" mesh model. "Low Poly" means a mesh model with a minimum number of vertices, edges, and faces. You could start from scratch and build your own model or there are applications for creating human figures. I suggest you choose the first option and download a pre-built

model. One may be obtained from the "BlendSwap" site: (Note: You have to register to download files.)

www.blendswap.com/blends/view/55698

"55698" refers to a Blender (.blend) file named "Basemesh." Clicking "Download" on the site and accepting the agreement saves a compressed (.zip) file named: "55698_basemesh_blend. zip" to your hard drive. Make note of the location where it is saved. Using "Win Zip" or "Win Rar" extract the contents to a folder. You will have two files: Basemesh.blend and BLENDERSWAP_LICENSE.

The Blender file contains a "Low Poly Character" model of a male human figure. This file is supplied by "tweediez" and is released under Creative Commons Attribution 3.0

Open the file in Blender and immediately save a copy by pressing "File—Save As" in the "Info" window header. Give the copy a new name. By doing this you retain the original file for future use.

Figure 15.58

The downloaded file opens a scene with a mesh model of a human figure in "Object" mode. The mesh figure is low poly, which means it has a minimal number of vertices, faces, and edges thus minimizing the number of calculations that have to be performed in posing the mesh during animation and, therefore, minimizing computer processor power (Figure 15.58).

Select "Front Orthographic" view (Num Pad 1). Press "Tab" to enter "Edit" mode and you will observe that the mesh is displayed on one side of the figure only. You will note that some vertices are selected around the midriff. These are selected simply because they were selected when the file was saved. Press A key to deselect these vertices. Go to the "Properties" window, "Modifier" button and you will see that the mesh has been constructed using the "Mirror" modifier (Figure 15.59).

Properties window—Modifier buttons

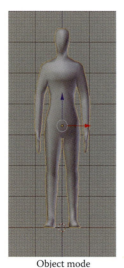
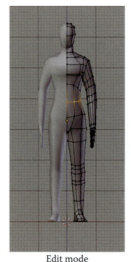

Click to apply the modifier

Object mode   Edit mode

Figure 15.59

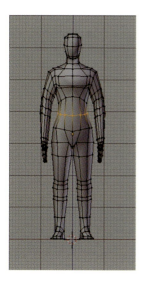

Figure 15.60

The mesh figure is presented this way so that you can modify the mesh and reshape it to whatever you wish. When reshaping by selecting and moving vertices on the mesh side the shape is mirrored on the opposite side. For the purpose of this exercise we will leave the figure as it is presented (Figure 15.60).

After reshaping the mesh you then "Apply" the modifier in "Object" mode. In "Edit" mode the mesh displays on both sides of the figure. In our case we simply apply the modifier without reshaping.

15.12.3 Centering the Cursor

With the mirror modifier applied "Tab" to "Object" mode in "Front Orthographic" view. This presents the figure face on with the objects center located at the center of the scene 3.300 Blender units on the Z-axis. Make sure you have the 3D window cursor located at the center of the scene also (press "Shift" + S key to display the "Snap" menu and select "Cursor to Center") (Figure 15.61). The 3D cursor will be located at the center of the scene midway between the feet.

Deselect the figure (press A key).

Figure 15.61

Tip: In following this demonstration save the Blender file repeatedly at each stage of the exercise. If you get off track further along it will be frustrating to have to repeat the entire procedure over. If you have to repeat the consolation is that repeating consolidates the learning process. I do it often.

15.12.4 Creating the Armature

Perhaps we should begin with some definition (Figure 15.62).

In creating a skeleton for a mesh figure you begin by adding an "Armature"—"Single Bone" and then duplicating or extruding the single bone forming a multibone armature

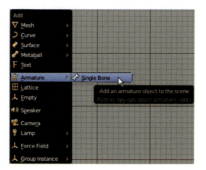

Figure 15.62

which is the skeleton. The skeleton will deform the mesh figure. Other single bones (single bone armatures) are also added as control bones which are used to move or control movement of the skeleton and the mesh figure. The whole kit and caboodle is what we will call the "Armature Rig."

Make sure the figure is deselected then press "Shift" + A key to add an "Armature"— "Single Bone" to the scene. The bone is entered at the location of the 3D cursor in the 3D window, which is at the center of the scene. This single bone will be the "Root Bone" which will be used to move the character around in the scene. It will be a "Control Bone." Control bones are used to move the armature bones, which control the mesh figure in posing. The "Root Bone" will be used to move the mesh figure about in the scene (Figure 15.63).

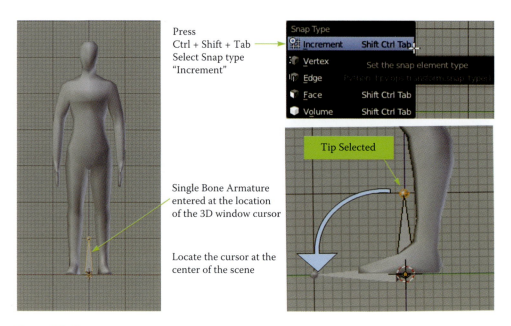

Press Ctrl + Shift + Tab → Select Snap type "Increment"

Single Bone Armature entered at the location of the 3D window cursor

Locate the cursor at the center of the scene

Figure 15.63

With the bone selected in "Object" mode "Tab" to "Edit" mode. The "Tip" of the bone will be selected as shown by the orange outline. The bone is orientated vertically with its tip at the top and with the base of the bone accurately located at the center of the scene. We want the bone to lay flat along the ground plane of the scene on the Y-axis. Change the 3D window to "Right Orthographic" view (Num Pad 3). To lay the bone flat and accurately position it on the Y-axis we will use "Increment Snapping." Press Ctrl + Shift + Tab and select "Snap Type – Increment." With the bone tip still selected press G key (Grab), hold "Ctrl" and drag the mouse pulling the tip down flat along the ground plane. As you drag, the bone tip will jump from one grid intersection to the next and finally locate precisely on the midplane Y-axis (green line). Release "Ctrl" and LMB click to release grab.

15.12.5 Bone Naming

We have one single bone of the "Armature Rig" in place. At this point it is very important to begin naming the bones in the "Rig." Blender will automatically give the bones' names but they will be named Bone, Bone.001, Bone.002, etc. This is fine for very simple armatures where it is obvious which bone is which but for complex armatures it is essential you name the bones with distinguishable names. What you will be doing is renaming Blender's default names.

Start with the single bone and name it "Armature_Root." There are two ways to do this.

You can rename bones in the "Outliner" window. In this instance open up the file tree under "Armature" until you come to "Bone." Press "Ctrl" and LMB click on "Bone" (the name is highlighted), press "Delete" and type "Armature_Root," press "Enter" (Figure 15.64).

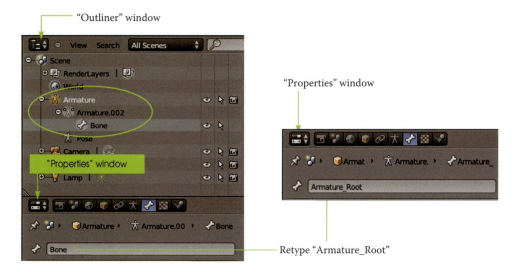

Figure 15.64

In the "Properties" window, with the body of the bone selected in "Edit" mode, click the "Bone" button. Click LMB on the name "Bone," in the name panel (Bone is highlighted), press "Delete," retype "Armature_Root" as the new name and press "Enter."

Either of the methods, "Properties" window or "Outliner" window, will automatically update the name in both windows.

When naming bones in a "Rig" set a convention and maintain it throughout the naming process. In the process of this exercise we will demonstrate a convention as an example. You may name bones anything you like but make sure they are meaningful. Obscure names in a complicated "Rig" will be difficult to find.

15.12.6 Adding More Bones

We will now add a second bone to the "Rig." Select the body of the "Armature_Root" bone in "Edit" mode then press Shift + D key (Duplicate). Drag the mouse and move the

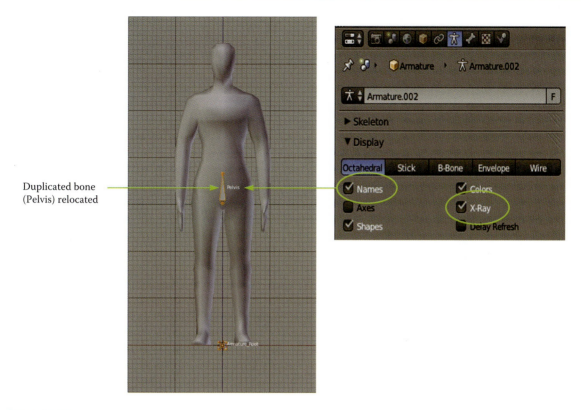

Duplicated bone
(Pelvis) relocated

Figure 15.65

duplicated bone up to the pelvic area of the figure, rotate and position as shown in the diagram by selecting the body of the bone or by selecting the tip or the base. The tip should be positioned in line with the belly button. Switch between "Front Orthographic" and "Right Orthographic" views to orientate the bone (Figure 15.65).

15.12.7 X-Ray

To enable you to see bones inside the mesh figure go to the "Properties" window, "Object data" button, "Display" tab, and tick "X-Ray" (Figure 15.65).

We duplicated the "Armature_Root" bone in "Edit" mode because we want this second bone linked to the "Armature_Root" bone and to be part of the "Rig." Duplicating in "Object" mode would cause the new bone to be an independent "Armature" not connected to the "Rig." Name the new bone "Pelvis." In the "Properties" window, "Bone" button. In the "Object Data" button, "Display" tab tick "Names" to display the bone names in the 3D window. You can now extrude bones to form the remainder of spine. In "Edit" mode select the tip of "Pelvis," press E key then Z, and drag the mouse to extrude a new bone (E key—extrude, Z key confines the extrusion to the Z-axis). Repeat the process for each new bone. Side view allows you to position bones to shape the spline. In front view the

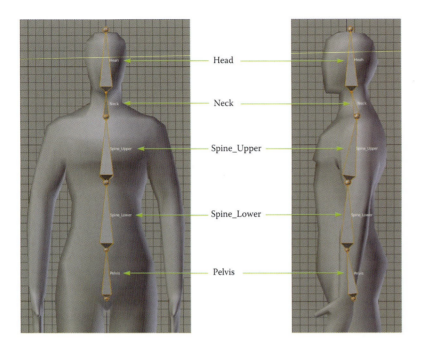

Head

Neck

Spine_Upper

Spine_Lower

Pelvis

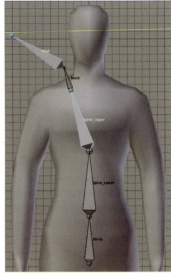

Figure 15.67

Figure 15.66

bones follow the centerline of the figure. For the head bone restrain the extrusion to the Z-axis by pressing E key + Z key (Figure 15.66).

> Note: In "Edit" mode you may select the tip or the base of any bone to adjust its position and alignment.

Position the bones as shown in the front and side view diagrams and name them as shown. You can name the bones anything you like as long as they are meaningful and relevant to the figure you are working on. Obviously, there are many more bones in a human skeleton than shown in the diagrams. In creating an armature for animation it is good practice to minimize the number of bones, which saves computer power in the animation process and uncomplicates the naming process. The more bones you have in a "Rig," the more flexible posing will be therefore you have to work out a compromise (Figure 15.67).

3D window header

Figure 15.68

With all the bones in the "Rig" selected in "Edit" mode, select "Pose" mode in the 3D window header. Select and rotate individual bones to see how bones are parented.

When you tab back to "Edit" mode the bones are arranged as they were before you did any posing. In "Pose" mode press "Alt" + G key followed by "Alt" + R key to return bones to their original pose location (Figure 15.68).

Note: When you create bones in "Edit" mode pressing "Tab" will toggle you between "Edit" mode and "Object" mode. With only one bone selected in "Edit" mode pressing Tab will toggle to "Object" mode with all bones selected.

Note: If you have all bones selected (the complete "Armature") in "Edit" mode and toggle to "Object" mode then deselect the "Armature." You will have to reselect the "Armature" in the "Outliner" window. RMB clicking on the "Armature" in the 3D window selects the mesh figure.

Note: When you select all the bones in "Edit" mode then change to "Pose" mode in the 3D window header pressing "Tab" will toggle between "Pose" mode and "Edit" mode. To reverse the toggle process simply select "Object" mode in the 3D window header.

You may continue and create bones for the arms and legs. Remember we want the arm and leg bones to be part of the armature therefore duplicating and extruding will take place in "Edit" mode.

15.12.8 Creating Arm Bones

See Figure 15.69.

To create the arm bones begin by selecting the body of the bone named "Spine_Upper" in "Edit" mode. Change to "Front Orthographic" view. Press Shift + D key (Duplicate) then drag the mouse and reposition the new bone as shown. Name this bone "Shoulder.L." Make particular note of this naming convention with the ".L" suffix, which denotes a bone on the figure's LHS. Note the figures LHS is on our RHS. Also note the dotted line between the base of "Shoulder.L" and the base of "Spine_Upper." This shows that the two bones are connected (parented) even though they are displaced from each other. If you have the manipulation widget turned on it may obstruct the names in the 3D window so it may be advantageous to

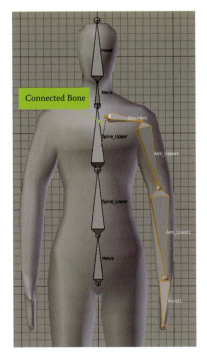
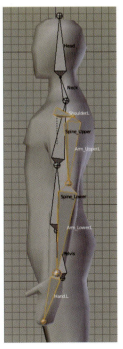

Figure 15.69

Figure 15.70

turn it off. In creating bones for the arms and legs we will duplicate and extrude bones on the LHS of the figure only. Blender has the ability to mirror bones to the opposite side (Figure 15.70).

In "Edit" mode select bone "Shoulder.L." We will not be using the X-axis mirror function so make sure it is unticked in the "Tool Panel," "Options" tab, "Armature Options" panel. Instead of mirroring the bone go ahead and extrude the upper arm, lower arm, and hand bones. You have to rename them at this stage. Name them as shown in the diagram. Use the side view to position the bones within the arms of the figure. When positioning the arm bones it is not important that the edge of a bone may be outside the mesh. The important thing is to have the tips and tails located at the limb joints, that is, elbow and wrist. When the bones are in place and named we can mirror them to the other side of the figure.

15.12.9 Mirror Pivot Point

To mirror we must tell Blender to mirror about a designated pivot point. Make note that our figure is presented with its left right orientation on the X-axis of the scene. The centerline of

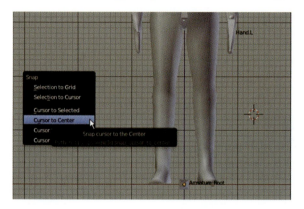

Figure 15.71

the "Armature Rig" is on the vertical Z-axis with its center of origin at the intersection of the X- and Z-axis (the center of the scene). In our case we will mirror about the 3D window cursor (not the mouse cursor); therefore, we have to position the cursor at the center of origin of the armature (center of the scene). Since we have established that this center of origin is at the center of the scene we can use Blenders snap function to position the 3D window cursor. Change from "Edit" to "Object" mode. In following this example the 3D window cursor is already located where we want it, so to prove a point click LMB somewhere in the 3D window which relocates the cursor. Press "Shift" + S key and select "Cursor to Center." The cursor moves to the center of the scene. We have established our point of rotation for mirroring (Figure 15.71).

We now have to tell blender to mirror about this point. In "Object" mode and in the 3D window header click on the "Pivot Point" drop down and select "3D Cursor" (Figure 15.72).

15.12.10 Mirror the Bones

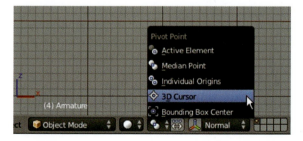

Figure 15.72

Change back to "Edit" mode. Once you have all the arm bones in position "Box Select" (B key—LMB click—Drag rectangle) all the arm bones then press "Shift" + D key (Duplicate) and press "Enter" (Figure 15.73).

This duplicates the bones and leaves them positioned exactly in the same position as the original. In the 3D window header click "Armature," "Mirror," and select "X-Local" to mirror them on the RHS. Press "Enter" (Figure 15.74).

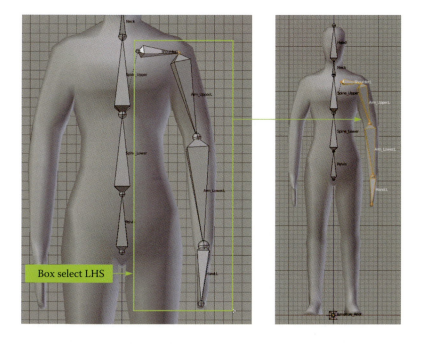

Box select LHS

Figure 15.73

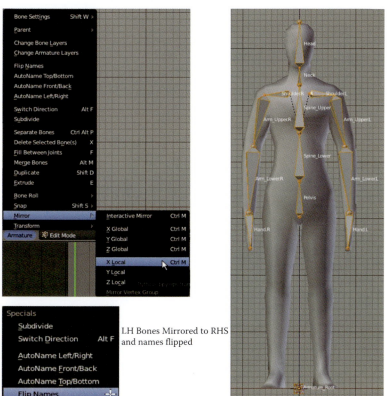

LH Bones Mirrored to RHS
and names flipped

Figure 15.74

With the RHS bones selected press W key (Specials Menu) and select "Flip Names." The bones are automatically named for the RHS.

15.12.11 Alternative Mirror Method

The alternative method for mirroring bones is as follows. It will probably appear that there is little advantage in either method since we are mirroring only four bones. The disadvantage of this alternative method is that the connection for automatic naming of bones for the opposite side is broken. This doesn't matter with only four bones being mirrored since it is easy to manually rename the bones but with many bones, which would be the case if all the finger bones were extruded, you would have a tedious manual renaming process.

15.12.12 Make Sure You Are in "Edit" Mode

To follow this alternative you will have to go back a few steps in the Blender file. Press "Ctrl" + Z key (Undo) and go back to the point where the arm bone "Shoulder.L" has just been created and positioned. Select bone "Shoulder.L." Press "Shift" + D key then press "Enter." This duplicates the bone and leaves it exactly in the same position as the original. In the 3D window header click "Armature" then "Mirror" and select "X-Local." Click LMB. The bone is mirrored on the RHS of the armature. Note the name of the mirrored bone, "Shoulder.L.001." With the bone selected press W key (Specials Menu) and select "Flip Names" to rename the bone "Shoulder.R."

You can now extrude the arm bones. Having established a right-hand–left-hand convention in relation to the armature by setting the shoulder bones we can use the X-axis mirror function in the "Armature Options" in the "Tool Panel."

Tick the "X-Axis Mirror" box. You may now select the tip of the LH shoulder bone and extrude the arm bones. The extrusions will be mirrored on the RHS. To set the bones accurately within the figure's mesh you have to position the bones in front view and side views.

Observe that the bones are being named "Shoulder.L.001," "Shoulder.L.002," etc., which means that with many bones you would have a lot of renaming to do.

15.12.13 Adding the Leg Bones

To add leg bones for the figure repeat the process used for the arms this time duplicating the bone named "Pelvis" in "Edit" mode and repositioning as shown. Extrude and rename the leg and foot bones, etc. Use the "Right Orthographic" view to extrude the foot and toe then in "Front Orthographic" view tilt the scene forward (Press Num Pad 2). The feet are splayed outward slightly. When mirroring ensure that you have the 3D window cursor at the center of the scene (Figure 15.75).

With all the spine, arm, and leg bones in position you have constructed the basis of the Deform Armature Rig.

15.12.14 Assigning the Rig to the Figure

At this point, although the "Armature Rig" is incomplete, we will assign it to the mesh figure. This is the process of linking "Vertex Groups" (groups of vertices) on the figures mesh surface to individual bones. Blender has an automated process for doing this. The bones will then control the posing or posturing of the mesh.

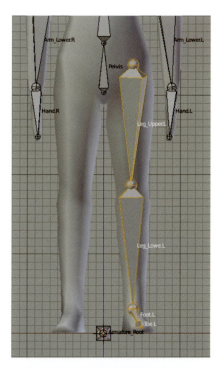

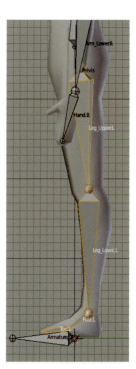

Extrude and align the Leg Bones

Leg Bones Mirrored and
Names flipped

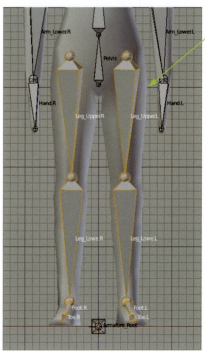

Align the Foot Bones

Figure 15.75

Click to remove the tick

Figure 15.76

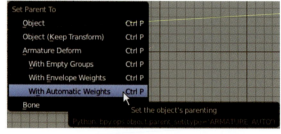

Figure 15.77

Before engaging the automated process we need to exclude the "Root_Bone." This bone is a control bone for moving the figure around in the scene and is not a posing bone. Posing is the process of posturing the figure.

In "Edit" mode select "Armature_Root." In the "Properties" window, "Bone" button, "Deform" tab click on the "Deform" button to remove the tick. This tells Blender that we do not want "Armature_Root" to be part of the deforming rig. Deselect the bone and change to "Object" mode. Deselect the armature rig (Figure 15.76).

Select the mesh figure then "shift" select the "Armature Rig." With the mouse cursor in the 3D window press "Ctrl" + P key to display the "Set Parent To" menu and select the "With Automatic Weights" option (Figure 15.77).

You may now go into "Pose" mode and select and rotate individual bones to pose the figure.

> Note: After posing, in "Pose" mode bones will be returned to their original positions (Reset), individually by selecting each bone or collectivity by selecting all bones and pressing "Alt" + R key (Reset rotation) and "Alt" + G key (Reset Location—Resets Grab).

15.12.15 Vertex Groups

With the mesh selected in "Object" mode go to the "Properties" window, "Modifier" button and you will see that an "Armature" modifier has been added. In the "Object data" button, "Vertex Groups" tab observe that vertex groups have been assigned for each of the bones in the armature. There is a scroll bar at the RHS of the "Vertex Group" panel (Figures 15.78 and 15.79).

In posing the figure you may see that some of the mesh is not deforming correctly. This can be corrected by selecting the appropriate vertex group and using Blender's "Weigh Paint" tool to clean up the connections between the mesh and the vertex groups. To understand how to do this refer to the section on "Weight Painting."

Even with the mesh correctly assigned to the vertex groups there are some issues still to be resolved. For example, when "Spine_Upper" is selected and rotated in "Front

Figure 15.78

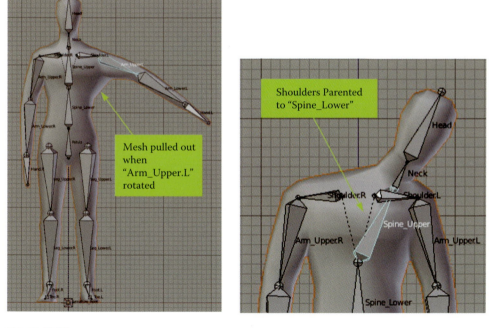

Figure 15.79

Shoulders Parented to "Spine_Lower"

Mesh pulled out when "Arm_Upper.L" rotated

Figure 15.80

Orthographic" view it will be observed that the neck and head of the figure move from side to side across the shoulders instead of the head tilting from side to side on the neck. This is corrected by changing where the shoulder bones are parented. The shoulder bones are currently parented to the tip of "Spine_Lower" because "Shoulder.L" was duplicated from "Spine_Upper" which is parented to the tip of "Spine_Lower." The shoulder bones should be parented to the tip of "Spine_Upper" (Figure 15.80).

Figure 15.81

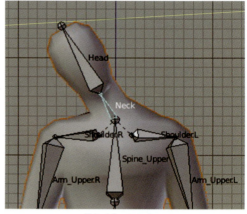

"Neck" rotated

Figure 15.83

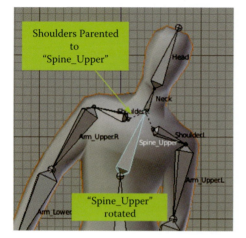

Figure 15.82

In "Edit" mode "Shift" select both shoulder bones and "Shift" select "Spine_Upper." Press Ctrl + P key (Parent) and select the "Keep Offset" option (Figure 15.81).

If you accidentally select the "Connected" option the shoulder bones will be parented to the "Spine" but they will be located as if extruded from the tip of "Upper_Spine" (Figures 15.82 and 15.83).

15.12.16 Parenting Legs

The next issue is that the legs have to be parented to the "Pelvis." In "Edit" mode "Shift" select both "Leg_Upper.L" and "Leg_Upper.R" and "Pelvis." Press Ctrl + P key and select the "Keep Offset" option.

If you rotate "Pelvis" at this stage you will probably find that the whole figure rotates about the 3D window cursor which is still located at the center of the scene. The pivot point for rotation is still set to the 3D window cursor in the header. Change the pivot rotation to "Individual Origins" which in this case means the base of "Pelvis." The whole figure continues to rotate when "Pelvis" is rotated.

The Rig is beginning to take shape but obviously there is more work to do.

15.12.17 Inverse Kinematics

At this stage the only option for posing the figure is by selecting and manipulating individual bones in "Pose" mode. As you can imagine this would be a very tedious process. Fortunately, the process is simplified by employing Blender's "IK."

"IK" sets up a chain link between strings of bones such that by selecting and translating the lead bone or a target bone, the bones in the chain will follow.

15.12.18 IK Chains for the Arms

IK in Blender may be applied in two ways. The easy way and the better way. The easy way is an automatic process which is great for a quick demonstration to see how a chain will react but it does produce some erratic movements which are not realistic (Figure 15.84).

Figure 15.84

15.12.19 The Easy Way

The easy way should be regarded as a temporary method which can be turned on and off. In "Pose" mode go to the "Toolbar" at the LHS of the 3D window and tick the "Auto IK" button. To see the effect grab a hand bone and move it about. The arms will follow the hand but you will probably produce some wacky results. When finished trying this out untick "Auto IK" in the "Tool Panel" then press the A key twice to select all the bones. Press "Alt" + R key followed by "Alt" + G key to return the bones to the original pose position (Figure 15.85).

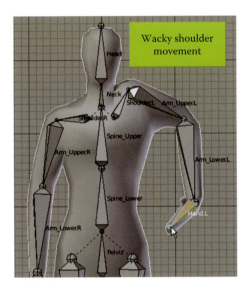

Figure 15.85

15.12.20 The Better Way

The better way is to create a real IK chain, which is manipulated by a "Target" bone. For the arms the target bones will be extruded from the tips of the "Arm_Lower" bones. Make sure you are in "Edit" mode. Before you extrude turn on "X-axis Mirror" in the "Tool Panel" to allow extrusion of bones on both sides of the figure simultaneously. In "Edit" mode, in "Right Orthographic" view, select the tip of "Arm_Lower.L," press E key (Extrude) and drag the mouse to extrude a new bone. With "X-axis Mirror" on, a new bone will be extruded from the tip of "Arm_Lower.R" at the same time. Turn "X-axis Mirror" off. Select each of the new bones in turn (separately) and press Alt + P key and select the "Clear Parent" option. The new bones are now independent of the rig and set

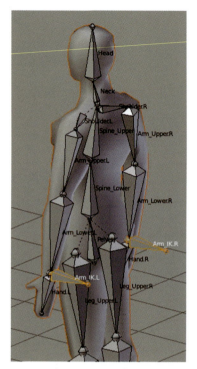

Figure 15.86

to be employed as control bones similar to the "Armature_Root" bone. Rename the new bones "Arm_IK.L" and "Arm_IK.R" (Figure 15.86).

In "Pose" mode select "Arm_Lower.L" and in the "Properties" window, "Bone Constraint" button, click "Add Constraint," and select "Inverse Kinematics" under "Tracking." With a constraint added the bone will be displayed in an olive green color. In the "Constraints" panel set "Arm_IK.L" as the target. To do this first set "Armature" then set the target bone (Figure 15.87). (Tip: Wait for the little "Bone" icon to appear before attempting to select the target bone.)

At this stage grabbing the target bone and moving it rotates the whole figure since the chain length is zero which means the IK chain extends right back to the "Pelvis" bone. To correct this change the chain length to 2 (1 sets the chain to itself, 2 sets it to "Arm_Upper.L") (Figure 15.88).

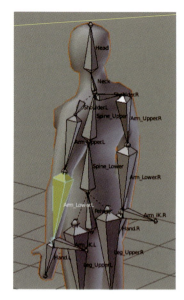

Figure 15.88

Note: When the constraint is added the bone is highlighted (olive green).

Figure 15.87

Repeat the process for the other side of the rig.

The control bones can be selected and translated moving the arms only but there is still some weird movement with respect to the elbows.

Just to make you aware there is a feature called "Pole Target" in the "IK Constraint," which would be used to restrict the movement of the elbows. This process is a little difficult to understand so in the meantime will use another set of target bones.

Extrude control bones from the tip of "Arm_Upper.L" and "Arm_Upper.R" (at the elbows) with "X-axis mirror" turned on. Turn "X-axis mirror" off after extruding.

Select each of the new bones individually and press "Alt" + P key and select "Clear Parent."

Move the bones back per diagram and rename them "Elbo_IK.L" and "Elbo_IK.R," respectively (Figure 15.89).

15.12.21 IK Target Quick Method

There is a quick method for setting the IK. Select the target bone, say "Elbow_IK.L" shift select "Arm_Upper.L" and hit Shift + I key. Select "To Active Bone." In "Properties" window set the chain length to 1. Repeat on opposite side of the figure with "Elbow_IK.R" and "Arm_Upper.R."

When the arms are posed by grabbing "Arm_IK.L or R" the erratic elbow positioning can be corrected by translating the elbow control control bones "Elbow_IK.L or R."

Note: Remember that after posing, in "Pose" mode bones may be returned to their original positions (Reset), individually by selecting each bone or collectivity by selecting all bones and pressing Alt + R key (Reset rotation) and Alt + G key (Reset Location—Resets Grab).

15.12.22 IK Chains for the Legs

Control bones and IK chains are set for the legs similar to the arms. The control bones are extruded at the knees and the ankle (Figure 15.90).

Extrude control bones from the ankles. Remove parenting but leave the new bones in position. Clear parenting and rename. Use the quick method to set up the IK with chain length 2 (up to the hips) by selecting the control bone and shift selecting "Leg_Lower.L and R," press Shift + I key, select "Add Constraint."

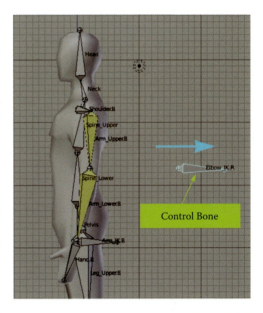

Figure 15.89

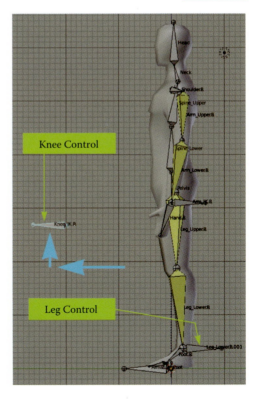

Figure 15.90

Extrude control bones from the knees in "Edit" mode (the tip of "Leg_Upper.L and R"). Name the controls "Knee_IK.L and R." Remove parenting (select each control bone and press Alt + P key and select "Clear Parent"). Locate the control bones forward of the knee as shown in the diagram. I have set my knee control bones forward and above the knee line since it appears to let the knee be raised higher before it starts to roll over sideways (Figure 15.91).

If the knee does roll sideways translating the control bones sideways will let you correct this action.

Use the quick method to set the IK chain to "Leg_Upper" with chain length 1 (up to the hips).

Figure 15.91

Note: In renaming bones Blender has a copy and paste function. With a bone selected, hover the mouse cursor over the name panel and press Ctrl + C key (copy) then select a new bone and hover over it's name panel and press Ctrl + V key (paste).

The rig is reaching the stage where it is functional but there are still a few controls to add.

In some instances such as rotating the hips from side to side you may not want the feet to lift off the ground.

15.12.23 Pinning the Feet to the Ground

To fix the feet to ground, select a foot bone ("Foot.L" or "Foot.R"). In the "Properties" window, "Bone" button, "Relations" tab there are buttons that determine if the bone is connected, if it inherits rotation from the parent, or if it inherits scale and location from the parent. Turn off "Inherit Rotation." The foot remains on the ground when the hips are moved (Figure 15.92).

15.12.24 Controlling Hips and Torso

Maybe you want to move the hips leaving the torso in place. At this stage, when you rotate the "Pelvis" bone the legs and the "Spine_Lower" (torso) bone follow. To allow the "Pelvis" bone to move without moving "Spine_Lower" we will create

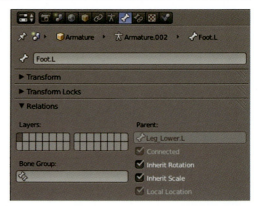

Figure 15.92

Figure 15.93

a new control bone. Remember this is a control bone for moving things as opposed to a deformation bone, which changes the shape of the mesh (Figure 15.93).

Note: All control IK bones should be selected and the "Deform" option in the "Properties" window, "Bone" button, "Deform" tab should be disabled. This has not caused a problem since we assigned the rig to the mesh using automatic weights prior to introducing any controls. If the rig were to be created including controls prior to assigning the rig to the mesh using Blenders automated system then vertex groups would be created for the control bones.

To continue creating our new control, in "Edit" mode, select "Pelvis." We are about to introduce a hip swing control and to do this we want a bone orientated to swing as shown in the diagram (Figure 15.94).

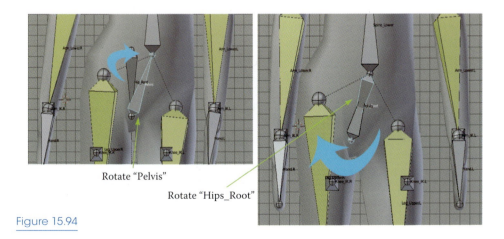

Rotate "Pelvis"

Rotate "Hips_Root"

Figure 15.94

Press Shift + D key + Enter to duplicate "Pelvis." Press W key for the "Specials" menu and select "Switch Direction." Alternatively, you can press Alt + F key to change the direction. Name the new bone "Hips_Root." Parent "Hips_Root" to "Pelvis." Select "Pelvis," shift select "Hips_Root," press Ctrl + P key and select "Connected." "Pelvis" will now follow "Hips_Root," therefore, by selecting "Hips_Root" and rotating it the hips will swing from side to side. By selecting "Pelvis" and rotating the hips swivel up and down. You will have to experiment to see what is meant.

You will observe that in swinging the hips the whole body tilts which is not desirable. To correct this select "Spine_Lower" and turn off "Inherit Rotation" in the "Properties" window, "Bone" button, "Relations" tab.

That cancels the body rotation when the hips rotate but maybe you want a little bit of body rotation to make the movement realistic.

Shift select "Pelvis" then "Spine_Lower." Press Ctrl + Shift + C key and choose the "Copy Rotation" option. Wow! Some weird stuff just happened.

In the "Bone Constraints" panel set "Space" to "Local Space" and "Local Space."

You will observe that "Pelvis" and "Spine_Lower" rotate in opposite directions since their rotation axes are different. In edit mode with "Spine_Lower" selected, in the "Properties" window, "Armature" button, "Display" tab, tick "Axis" to display the bone axis in the 3d window. Note the bone axes are different.

If axes are pointing in the wrong direction use the "Roll" tool to rotate the bones. To rotate the bone press Ctrl + R key and drag the mouse. To rotate a specific number of degrees press Ctrl + R key and type the number of degrees.

To correct, in "Edit" mode, select all bones and press Ctrl + N key and select "Recalculate" on "X-axis."

15.12.25 Pinning the Hands

Pinning means fixing in place. Sometimes you will want the character's hands to move when the body moves. Sometimes you will want the hands to remain stationary when the character moves. How the hands move and when they move will depend on which bone they are parented to.

For example, in "Edit" mode, select "Arm_IK.L" + "Hip_Root," press Ctrl + P, and select "Keep Offset" to parent the LH control bone to the pelvis rotation bone. Repeat for "Hand_IK.R." When "Hip_Root" is rotated the hands will follow but as you will observe the action is not quite right. Undo the parenting by selecting the hand control bone (Arm_IK.L) in "Edit" mode and pressing Alt + P key and selecting "Clear Parent."

Parent the hand control bone to "Spine_Upper" and you will have a better action.

As previously stated, sometimes you will want the hands to remain in position when the body moves. To let you quickly select which action you want a slider can be created in the 3D window properties panel.

Before creating the slider go back and remove the parenting by selecting the hand control bones and pressing Alt + P key (in "Edit" mode) and selecting "Clear Parenting."

Instead of parenting the control bones we will use a constraint. By using a constraint, in the "Properties" window, "Constraint" panel, an "Influence" slider value is introduced that determines how much the constraint affects the constraint action. The value range is 0–1.000 (maximum) so in effect you can turn the effect of the constraint on or off. When

posing the character it is not convenient to be switching from the 3D window to the "Properties" window to control the constraint panel slider.

In "Pose" mode select the hand control bone, "Arm_IK.L." Go to the "Properties" window, "Bone Constraints" button, and click on "Add Constraint." Select "Child of Constraint." In the constraint panel set "Target" as "Armature" and "Bone" as "Hips_Root" and click "Set Inverse." (Note: In the bone selection drop down scroll MMB to display bones.) This has made "Arm_IK.L" a child of "Hips_Root," therefore, when "Hips_Root" moves, "Arm_IK.L" moves and since "Arm_IK.L" is the target of the "IK" constraint placed on "Arm_Lower" the LH arm of the figure moves (Figure 15.95).

Repeat for "Arm_IK.R."

At this point whether the hands follow when the hips are rotated will depend on the value set in the "Constraint" panel "Influence Slider." If the influence value = 1.000 the hands will follow, when the value = 0.000 they will not. The "Constraint" panel is not always displayed when posing, therefore, it is not the most convenient place to have a slider control. We will create a slider in a better location.

To start we will set up a "Property" for the pelvis rotation bone. Select "Hips_Root." In the "Properties" window, "Bone" button, "Custom Properties" tab, click "Add" (Figure 15.96).

In the "Properties" panel click "Edit."

In the "Name" panel enter "Hands_Follow." Press "OK."

We now have a value but it doesn't do anything. Leave it there for the time being.

Go back to the "Hands_IK.L," "Bone Constraint" panel. On the "Influence" slider, R click "Add Driver" (the panel turns purple) (Figure 15.97).

Figure 15.95

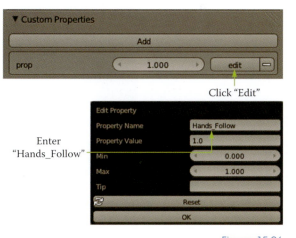

Figure 15.96

Figure 15.97

15.12.26 Adding Drivers

Drivers in general terms are values that are used to control other values or actions that control other actions.

Open the "Graph Editor" window and change from "F-Curve editor" mode to "Drivers" mode. You will see a list of drivers (at this stage only one) and graph line. Select the driver then press N key to display the driver properties panel (Figures 15.98 and 15.99).

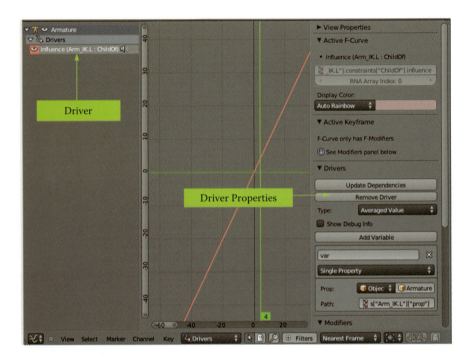

Figure 15.98

In the "Driver Properties" panel, in the "Drivers" tab, change "Type," "Scripted Expression" to "Average Value." You may ignore the error message that displays. Change "Transform Channel" to "Single Property." In the "Properties" panel set "Object" then "Armature."

In the "Path" panel that displays we need to enter the data path of the "Custom Property" previously created. With the "Hips_Root" selected, in the "Properties" window "Bone" panel R click on the "prop" value and select "Copy Data Path." In the "Graph Editor" window, with the "Arm_IK.L" driver selected, hover the mouse over the "Properties," "Driver Path" panel, and press Ctrl + V key to paste the path data in.

In 3D window press N key to display the "Properties" panel. You can now control the "Bone Constraint" influence value from the "Properties" panel slider (Figure 15.100). (Only on the LHS at this stage.)

Select the "Arm_IK.R." The "Graph Editor" window will display the driver for this bone. Hover the mouse pointer over the "Properties," "Driver Path" panel, and press Ctrl + V key to paste in the same data path. Press "Update Dependencies" to correct the error that displays.

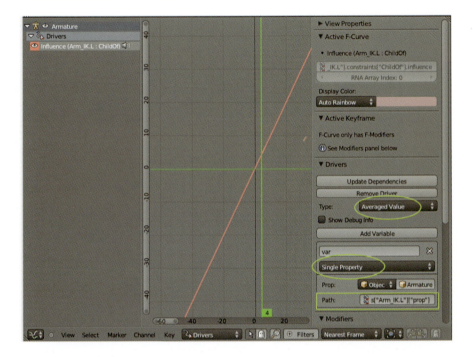

Figure 15.99

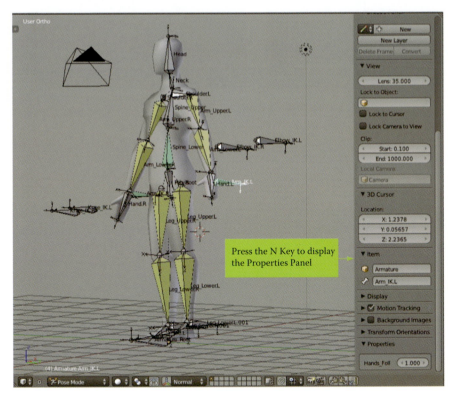

Figure 15.100

With "Hips_Root" selected in "Pose" mode the "Properties"—"Hands_Follow" slider in the 3D window "Properties" panel now controls the constraint for both bones (Figure 15.101).

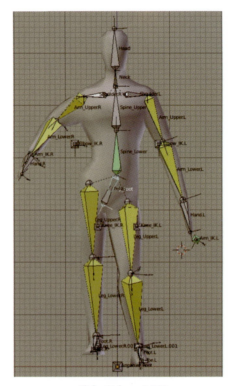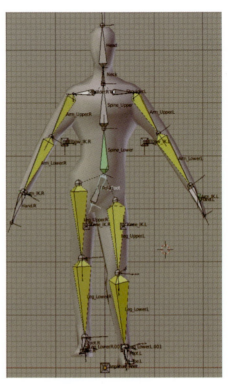

Slider Value = 1.000
Hands Follow Rotation

Slider Value = 0.000
Hands remain Stationary

Figure 15.101

15.12.27 Correcting Erratic Hand Movement

When the hands are fixed in position and the body of the figure is moved you will see that there is some erratic hand movement taking place as they attempt to follow the IK chain. To correct this, select each hand bone in "Edit" mode and in the "Properties" window, "Bone" button, "Relations" tab turn off "Inherit Rotation." The hands will stay in place unless the body of the figure is moved beyond the limits of the IK.

15.12.28 Head Rotation Tweak

Finally, there is just a small tweak to enhance the rotation of the head. Select "Neck" in "Edit" mode and in the "Properties" window, "Bone" button, "Relations" tab turn off "Inherit Rotation." Change to "Pose" mode, select "Neck" and shift select "Head."

In the 3D window header click on "Pose" then "Constraints" and select "Add (With Targets)." In the "Properties" window, "Bone Constraints," in the constraint panel tick "Offset" and change "Space" to "Local Space" and "Local Space." Adjust the axes of the head and neck bones to be the same if they are out of alignment.

15.12.29 Translating the Rig

Finally, in order to move the rig about in the scene, parent the "Hips_Root" bone to the "Root_Bone." Select "Hips_Root" then shift select "Hips_Root." Press Ctrl + P key and select "Keep Offset." Now shift select all the IK control bones and finally shift select the "Root_Bone." Press Ctrl + P key and select "Keep Offset." When you select the "Root_Bone" and translate the whole rig and the figure is moved together (Figure 15.102).

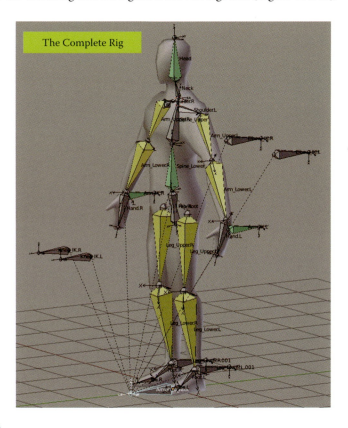

Figure 15.102

This has been an introduction to the basics of character rigging. It is one way of doing it and by no means necessarily the best way. That will depend on your character and what you want to achieve. There are many details not covered in this example, therefore, it is up to you to research and experiment to determine what suits your needs. I hope the exercise has whetted your appetite for what is a fascinating part of Blender.

16

Shape Key and Action Editors

16.1 Introduction

Lesson 07
07-08
Shape Key
Animation

The "Shape Key" and "Action Editors" provide methods of animating shapes and objects. The "Shape Key" editor allows you to control the animation of vertices or groups of vertices, while the "Action Editor" allows you to set up an animation of an object's movement and scale. Both editors are located in the "Dope Sheet" window.

To demonstrate the methods, start with the default Blender scene, delete the cube, and add a simple plane object with four vertices. Go into top view (number pad 7—number pad 5) and zoom in on the view with the number pad + key. Split the 3D window horizontally into two windows and change the bottom one to the "Dope Sheet" window.

16.2 Shape Key Editor

In the "Dope Sheet" window, click on the drop down in the header where it says "Dope Sheet" and select "Shape Key Editor" (Figure 16.1).

With the "Shape Key Editor" editor selected, the window has become an animation timeline with frame numbers in the horizontal bar at the bottom of the window. There is also a vertical green line in the window, which is a "Timeline Cursor" (Figure 16.2).

In the "Shape Key Editor," we will add a "Key Slider" which will allow us to control the shape of an object in the 3D window by moving vertices on the mesh surface of the object.

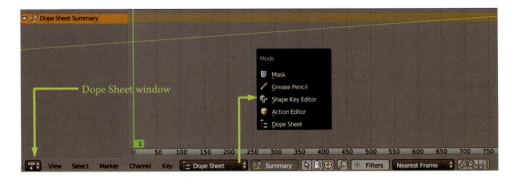

Figure 16.1

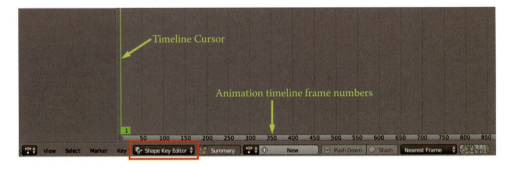

Figure 16.2

The movement of the vertices will be set within limits. By moving the vertices to different positions, within the limits, at different frames in the animation timeline we will create an animation of the change in shape of the object.

16.2.1 Add a Key Slider

Select the plane in the 3D window. In the "Properties" window, "Object Data" button, "Shape Keys" tab click on the plus sign. The tab expands, showing a "Basis Key" inserted. Additionally, a "Dope Sheet Summary" line is added in the "Shape Key Editor" window (Figure 16.3).

Click on the plus sign again and "Key 1" will be added (Figure 16.4). Note that in the "Dope Sheet Summary," "Key 1" is also displayed.

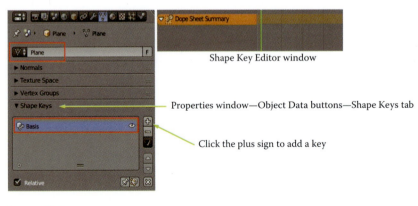

Shape Key Editor window

Properties window—Object Data buttons—Shape Keys tab

Click the plus sign to add a key

Figure 16.3

Click the plus sign to add a key

Figure 16.4

16.2.2 Set Limits of Movement

With the cursor in the 3D window, Tab to edit mode. Deselect all the vertices with the A key. Select one of the vertices and drag it (press the G key and drag the mouse) to where you want it to move (Figure 16.5) then Tab back to "Object" mode—the plane reverts to its original shape. Moving the vertices in edit mode has set the limits for the movement.

16.2.3 Inserting a Keyframe at Frame 1

In the "Properties" window, "Object Data" button, "Shape Keys" tab, changing the "Relative Value" by moving the slider at the bottom of the panel, changes the shape of the plane in the 3D window (Figure 16.6). You can also change the shape by moving the slider next to "Key 1" in the "Dope Sheet Summary," "Shape Key Editor"

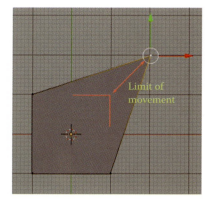

Limit of movement

Figure 16.5

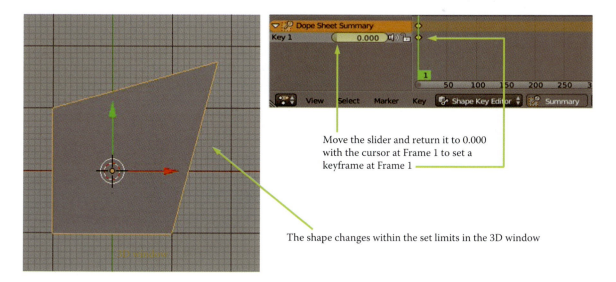

Move the slider and return it to 0.000 with the cursor at Frame 1 to set a keyframe at Frame 1

The shape changes within the set limits in the 3D window

Figure 16.6

(move the slider then return it to value 0.000); by doing so, a keyframe is automatically inserted at the frame where the cursor is located (Frame 1). The keyframe is indicated by the yellow diamond shapes (Figure 16.6). Since the slider was returned to 0.000 at frame 1, the keyframe locates the selected vertex at its origination position.

> Note: The slider moves the selected vertex only within the limits that were set. The slider value is from 0.000 to 1.000 that is from the initial position to the maximum limit of the movement.

16.2.4 Inserting a Second Keyframe

To insert a second keyframe move the green line cursor in the "Shapes Key Editor" window to another frame (Frame 49). Move Key 1 slider until the vertex in the 3D window is where you want it (0.750) (Figure 16.7).

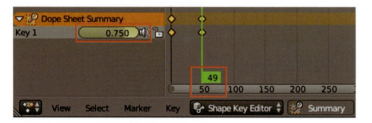

Figure 16.7

16.2.5 Moving Other Vertices in the Animation

Move the cursor to Frame 1. In the "Properties" window, "Object Data" button, "Shape Key" tab, click on the plus sign again to add "Key 2" (Figure 16.8). In the 3D window, tab to edit mode, select a different vertex, and move it somewhere to set the limit of movement. Tab back to object mode and you'll notice that "Key 2" has been added to the "Dope Sheet Summary" (Figure 16.9). Repeat the keyframing process using Key 2.

In the 3D window, tab to Edit mode, select a different vertex, grab and move it to set limits then Tab back to Object mode. Move and reposition Key 2 back to 0.000 to set a "Keyframe" at frame 1. Move the green line cursor to a different frame (frame 97) and move the Key 2 slider (0.431) to set a new keyframe (Figure 16.9).

Click the plus sign to add key 2

Figure 16.8

Figure 16.9

Scrub the timeline (drag the green line) to see the animation. You can also press Alt + the A key with the cursor in the 3D window to play the animation, and Esc to stop (Figure 16.10).

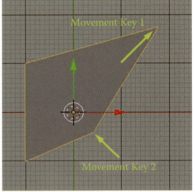

Note: The demonstration has only included two single vertices. You can set limits of movement for multiple vertices or "Vertex Groups" to be controlled by a single Key.

16.3 Action Editor

Figure 16.10

To demonstrate the action editor, begin with the same setup as you used for the shape key editor, except this time select "Action Editor" mode in the dope sheet window. Select the plane in the 3D window in object mode and insert a key frame (with the I key) and select "LocRotScale."

In the "Dope Sheet Action Editor," you will see the key frame displayed in the upper LHS of the window. Clicking on the little triangle in front of "LocRotScale" expands the key frame to show the individual components (Figure 16.11). In the action editor window header, click on "View" and check (tick) "Show Sliders;" there are now value sliders in each

Figure 16.11

component of the key frame (Figure 16.12). By repositioning the cursor in the "Action Editor" to a new frame and moving the sliders, you can manipulate the plane in the 3D window (Figure 16.13). When the slider value changes, key frames are inserted, which produce an animation. As I mentioned previously, you can scrub the animation or press Alt + the A key to play it.

Figure 16.12

The "X Location" slider is set at 2 in the action editor

Keyframes are automatically inserted at a new frame when a slider value is changed

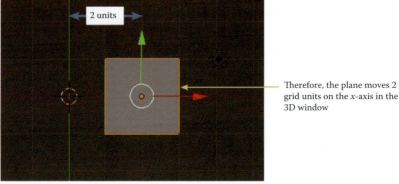

2 units

Therefore, the plane moves 2 grid units on the x-axis in the 3D window

Figure 16.13

16. Shape Key and Action Editors

Click "View"—"Show Sliders" in the window header if the sliders are not displayed by default.

16.4 Shape Keys and Action Editor in Practice

The foregoing examples using a plane object will give you the fundamentals for these tools but they are not very exciting and you could be left wondering what to do with them in some practical application. To expand on the topics perform the following exercise.

In a new Blender scene delete the cube and add a "Monkey" object. Place the scene in "Front Orthographic" view and zoom in to fill the 3D window with the monkey's head. Tab to "Edit" mode and select the vertices in the face as shown in Figure 16.14.

Divide the 3D window as we did previously and make one-half the "Dope Sheet" window. Change the mode to the "Shape Key Editor." In the 3D window position, "Monkey" to have his/her mouth visible (Figure 16.15). Tab to "Object" mode.

In the "Properties" window, "Object data" button, "Shape Key" tab click on the plus sign to add a "Basis" key, which places a "Dope Sheet Summary" in the "Dope Sheet," "Shape Key Editor" window. Click the plus sign again to insert "Key 1."

We are about to make Monkey speak. In the 3D window change to "Right Orthographic" view (side view Num Pad 3). Tab to "Edit" mode. Use the widget and move the selected vertices to the left making monkey's lips protrude slightly (Figure 16.16). Change to "Front Orthographic" view (Num Pad 1). Scale the selected

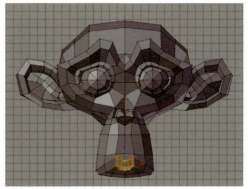

Select vertices for the mouth as shown

Figure 16.14

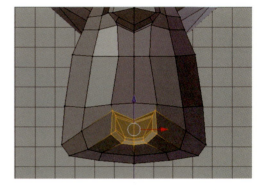

Figure 16.15

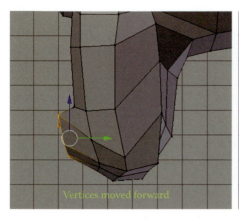
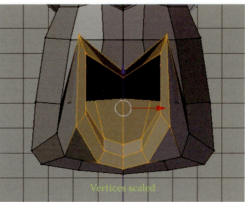

Vertices moved forward

Vertices scaled

Figure 16.16

vertices up on the Z-axis and a little bit on the X-axis. Using the widget move the vertices up (Figure 16.16). Tab to "Object" mode. The vertices revert to their original location.

Keyframe inserted in timeline at Frame 1—slider 0.000 means no displacement

Figure 16.17

Dope Sheet Window—shape Key Editor mode

Keyframe inserted at Frame 10—slider value 1.000 means maximum displacement

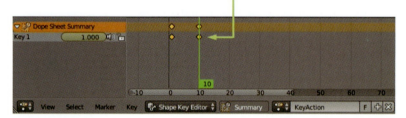

Figure 16.18

In performing the scaling and location operations, you have set the limits of movement for Key 1 for each of the vertices that was selected. Move the Key 1 slider and see the monkey's mouth move. Remember, moving the slider insert a keyframe at

Figure 16.19

the frame number in the animation timeline where the timeline cursor is positioned (Frame 1) (Figure 16.17). If you don't want monkey to start laughing at the start of the animation move the cursor down the track in the timeline. Also remember that by default Blender has a 250-frame animation set in the "Timeline" window. If you place the "Shape Key Editor" cursor beyond this it will have no effect unless you change the "End Frame" value in the "Timeline" window header.

Place a series of keyframes in the animation. Move the cursor to Frame 10 and move the Key slider leaving it in position (Figures 16.18 and 16.19). This inserts a keyframe at frame 10. Move the cursor to frame 20—move the slider. Move the cursor to frame 30—move the slider, etc. (Figure 16.20). Go back to Frame 1 and play the animation. Monkey's mouth moves as the animation plays.

Keyframes at 10 frame intervals up to Frame 50

Slider values are different for each keyframe
At frame 1 and 50 slider value is 0.000

Figure 16.20

Change the "Dope Sheet" window to "Action Editor" mode. Zoom out on the 3D window. With the cursor at Frame 1, press I key and select "LocRotScale" to place action keyframes (Figure 16.21). Move the cursor to Frame 50 to coincide with the "Shape Key" animation and move the "Z Euler Rotation slider to 45° (rotation in Blender is measured in Euler units).

Press I key on keyboard to place action keyframes at Frame 1

Z Euler rotation controls rotation on the vertical Z-axis

Figure 16.21

Place the 3D window in "Camera" view and play the animation. Monkey's mouth moves as he turns to face the camera.

This has been a very simple practical demonstration so use your imagination and experiment, experiment, experiment!

17

Fluid Simulation

17.1 Introduction to Fluid Simulation

Fluid simulation physics provides a means of simulating fluid flow. In this discussion, we will consider two scenarios. The first scenario is animating a volume of fluid such as a droplet of water or larger single volume, which is initially suspended in space and allowed to drop into a container or onto a surface. The second scenario is animating a stream of fluid such as fluid running from a tap or out of a container in a controlled flow. The latter scenario will provide a recap on the former one.

For detailed procedures, see the *Blender Manual*, which is obtainable at http://www.blender.org/manual/physics/fluid/index.html

17.2 Basic Setup (Scenario 1)

The setup in Figure 17.1 represents a basic 3D window scene in "Wireframe" mode, constructed for a fluid simulation. As with all Blender scenes, there must be a light to provide illumination and a camera before anything can be rendered. The scene has been constructed with a fluid object (a default sphere with 32 segments and rings), a domain cube (the default cube scaled up), and an obstacle object (a cup). The extrusion of the cup is described in Chapter 3, Section 3.32

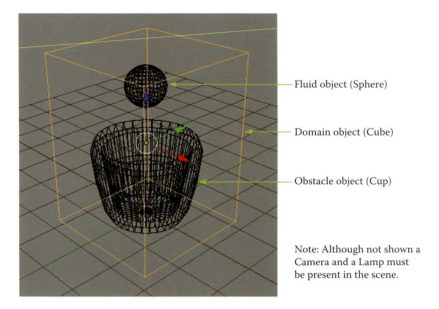

Fluid object (Sphere)

Domain object (Cube)

Obstacle object (Cup)

Note: Although not shown a
Camera and a Lamp must
be present in the scene.

Figure 17.1

Note: Providing you have saved a Blender file containing the extruded cup you will be able to append the cup into a new Blender scene.

In the scene, a volume of liquid (the fluid object) is suspended in space and it will be released and then dropped into a cup (the obstacle object). The falling fluid (fluid simulation) takes place within the confines of the "Domain"—the domain is a segment of space defined by a cubic volume (in this case, the cube). There must be a domain for a simulation to take place and all objects participating in the simulation must be within the domain. Any object partially outside of the domain will not function.

In this simulation, the fluid is represented by a "Sphere" object positioned somewhere toward the top of the domain and immediately above the cup. The size of the sphere relative to the domain and to the other objects within the domain determines the volume of the fluid; for instance, a large sphere relative to the domain and the cup produces a large fluid volume.

The cup is an obstacle that obstructs the movement of the fluid. In this example, the fluid is simply falling in space until it is obstructed by the cup. If the cup did not exist, the fluid would fall until it reached the bottom of the domain and then it would come to rest as if enclosed in a transparent rectangular container, which is defined by the shape of the domain. With the objects placed in the scene, nothing will happen until all the objects have values assigned. This sets up the simulation.

17.2.1 Domain Object Setup

In this scenario, the domain is a cube that has been scaled to enclose the sphere and the cup.

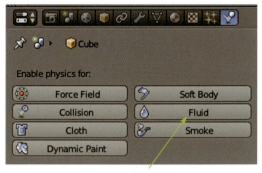

Select "Fluid"

Figure 17.2

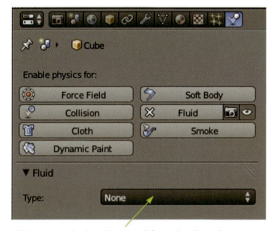

Click here and select "Domain" from the drop-down menu

Figure 17.3

To assign fluid simulation values to the domain, first select the cube in the 3D window. Go to the "Properties" window, "Physics" button, and click on "Fluid" (Figure 17.2) to display the "Fluid" tab (Figure 17.3). Click on the "Type" drop down selection menu where you see type "None" and in the menu select "Domain." The "Domain, Fluid" tabs will display (Figure 17.4). While discussing this first scenario of fluid simulation, default values will be used, with one exception: in the "Fluid" tab, "Time" setting change the "End" value to 0.600, which reduces the bake time to something more reasonable for a demonstration.

Baking is similar to rendering images for an animated movie; it's the process of simulating a fluid flow and can take a considerable time depending on the complexity of the simulation setup. When baking, Blender looks at the "Start" and "End" values set in the "Fluid" tab, calculates the time period, and then computes how the volume of fluid would react to the environment during that time. In our example, the time period is 0.60 seconds. The "Start" and "End" values have nothing to do with how many frames will be produced in the animation of the fluid flow, but instead are concerned with the physical force and the fluid viscosity—in other words, how the fluid will react to its environment in the given time period.

In the "Properties" window, "Render" button, "Dimensions" tab, the default animation length is set at 250 frames (Start frame: 1—End Frame: 250) and the animation will display at the "Frame Rate" of 24 frames per second. The animation frame range is also displayed in the "Timeline" window. These values produce an animation of approximately 10 seconds. Thus, the behavior of the volume of fluid in this scenario over

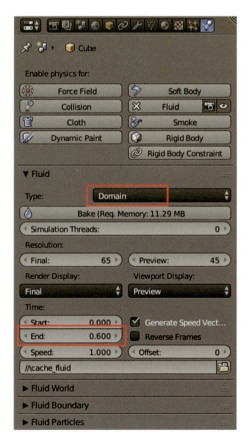

Figure 17.4

0.60 seconds will be spread over the animation time of 10 seconds. Imagine dumping a cup of water and observing its action over 0.60 seconds then stretching that behavior over 10 seconds—a slow motion effect will result. Therefore, a 0.60-second bake will suffice to demonstrate simulating a fluid flow, even though it does not produce a real-time animation.

What is real-time animation? Real-time animation with respect to fluid flow is an animation that shows precisely how the fluid reacts in real time as opposed to our slow motion effect. If you are interested in real time, set the "Start" and "End" values in the "Fluid" tab to match the length of the animation. For example, with the default animation of 250 frames at 24 frames per second equaling approximately 10 seconds, you would set the time values to provide a 10-second period. Be warned: there will be a long wait while your Blender bakes. Varying the "Start" and "End" values of the fluid action, therefore, affects how the behavior of the fluid is seen in the final animation. For now, leave all the values in the "Physics," "Domain Fluid" tab set per the defaults, except for the "End" time setting.

One last point in the domain settings: note the directory name at the bottom of the "Fluid" tab. This gives the location of where the bake files will be saved, but you may change this to whatever you wish. I have already noted that baking takes a long time and with that comes a lot of files. If a simulation is rebaked, the files are overwritten, but after messing about with some trial and error in the learning process, you will still accumulate a whole slew of files.

17.2.2 Fluid Object Setup

In this scenario, the fluid is represented by a "Sphere" that has been placed in the domain immediately above the cup. As I said before, the size of the sphere relative to the domain and the cup determines the volume of the fluid in the simulation. For this demonstration, make sure the sphere is much smaller than the cup, otherwise, you'll have some mopping up to do. Select the sphere in the 3D window, go to the "Properties" window, "Physics" button, and click on "Fluid." In the "Fluid" tab select type "Fluid" in the drop down menu (Figure 17.5). You can leave the settings as they are, but it is worth noting that the "Initial Velocity" values will give your fluid a kick start in whatever direction you set. We will be using the default "Gravity" force setting in the "Properties" window, "Scene" button, "Gravity" tab (Z: −9.81 Earth's gravity).

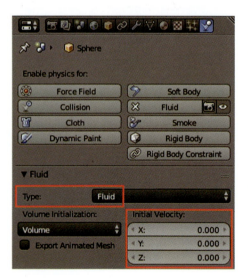

Figure 17.5

Note: In performing the fluid set up remember to continually save your setting in a new Blender **file**. This allows you to correct mistakes or change settings as you progress.

17.2.3 Obstacle Object Setup

In this scenario, the obstacle to the fluid flow will be the cup. The construction of the cup has been described in Chapter 3, Section 3.32.

With the cup selected in the 3D window, go to the "Properties" window, "Physics" button, and click on "Fluid." In the "Fluid" tab select type "Obstacle" (Figure 17.6). Change

the "Volume Initialization" from "Volume" to "Shell"—with "Volume," Blender considers the shape to be solid with no interior. Now that all the objects required for the simulation have settings assigned, the fluid simulation setup is complete and ready to be baked.

17.2.4 Baking

In the 3D window in "Wireframe" mode, select the domain cube. The "Domain" "Physics" properties tabs will be displayed with the values that were previously set. Make note that baking a simulation can take a long time depending on the complexity of the simulation, the resolution, the length of the animation, and the speed of the computer. For the purpose of this scenario the default value has been used (250 frames in the animation "Timeline" window). At a display rate of 24 frames per second, this will produce an animation lasting approximately 10 seconds.

In the "Properties" window, "Physics" button, "Fluid" tab, with the domain object (the cube) selected in the 3D window, click on the "Bake" button (Figure 17.7). The bake progress can be observed at the top of the 3D window in the fluid simulation progress bar; the bar only appears when you bake and will be located in the "Info" window header adjacent to "Blender Render." If you want to cancel a bake, click on the cross next to the bar. The bake takes a considerable time; it is akin to creating an image for each frame of an animation, so be prepared to sit back and wait a while. In this scenario, the bake should take about 30 seconds.

Figure 17.6

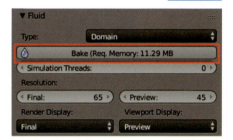

Figure 17.7

Note: If the demonstration does not perform as described you have probably made an error in the setup. Check your settings and change values accordingly, BUT Note; having changed a setting you will have to REBAKE the simulation to overwrite the data in the cache file. Simply changing settings will not correct the action.

Note what happens in the 3D window. The domain has changed into a blob that attaches itself to the sphere fluid object (Figure 17.8). When the bake is completed, change to "Solid Viewport Shading" mode and press Alt + the A key to view the animation of the simulation. The blob descends, deforming as it goes, and splashes into the cup. If the bake is not performing as expected, it can be terminated by pressing the Esc key or the cancel button in the header and settings

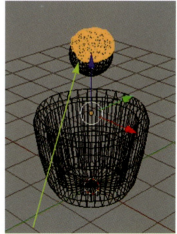

Orange blob attached to "Sphere" (Wireframe mode)

Figure 17.8

can be adjusted to correct the action. To rebake the simulation, select the domain (which is now the blob attached to the sphere) and press "Bake" again in the "Domain," "Fluid" tab. When a simulation is baked, it is similar to rendering files for an animation sequence. Files are created and saved to a folder on the computer's hard drive (refer to https://www.blender.org/manual/physics/fluid/domain.html).

The path to the folder where the baked files are saved can be seen in the "Fluid: Domain" tab (Figure 17.9). The path shown (//\cache_fluid) indicates that the bake files have been saved to a subfolder within the folder where the Blender (.blend) file for the fluid simulation is saved.

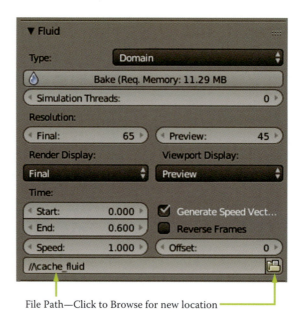

File Path—Click to Browse for new location

Figure 17.9

The folder for the storage of bake files can be changed to any folder you wish by clicking on the file browser icon and navigating to a folder in the "File Browser" window (see the navigation section in Chapter 2 for a refresher). If the bake is executed without altering the path, the bake file will be saved in the default folder. When a simulation is baked without altering the destination folder, any existing bake file is overwritten. To delete a bake file, select the storage folder and delete the files or shred the folder.

17.3 Basic Setup (Scenario 2)

Note: Before setting up a new "Fluid Simulation" clear the data from the "Cache" file or set a new location for saving the "Bake." If data exist in the "Cache" when a new "Domain" is created Blender will attempt to use the existing data.

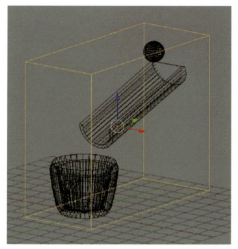

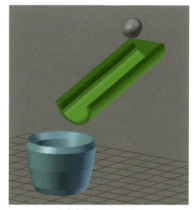

Figure 17.10

Wireframe mode

Solid display mode

Figure 17.11

The setup in Figure 17.10 is a basic scene configuration to demonstrate a fluid simulation in accordance with Scenario 2. The camera and light are not shown but they must exist in the scene. In this scenario, the fluid will flow in a stream from the inflow object sphere, down the obstacle object trough, and into the obstacle object cup. All objects participating in the simulation must be within the confines of the domain. Figure 17.11 shows the arrangement in "Solid Viewport Shading" mode with material color applied to the trough and the cup.

17.3.1 Domain Object Setup

You'll notice that the domain cube has been scaled to confine the participating objects in a restricted volume of space (Figure 17.12). The procedure for assigning the cube as the domain and setting its values is identical to that of Scenario 1, with the exception that

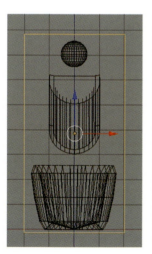
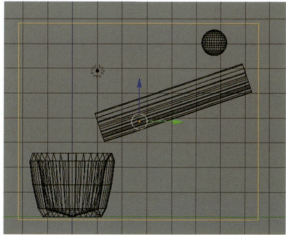

Figure 17.12

Figure 17.13

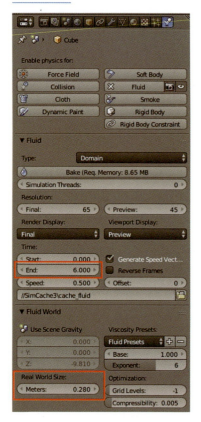

Figure 17.14

the "End" time value has been changed to 6.00 in the "Fluid" tab and the "Real-World Size" has been set at 0.280 m in the "Domain," "Physics," "Fluid World" tab (Figure 17.13).

When setting up this fluid simulation, the length of the final animation in real time and the physical size of the scene in real terms must be considered. The Blender scene viewed on the computer screen is seen in Blender units and an animation is measured in the number of frames viewed at a set frame rate.

17.3.1.1 Length of the Animation

In the "Properties" window, "Render" button, "Dimensions" tab (Figure 17.14) change the "End Frame to 144. In this simulation, the animation will be 144 frames long, viewed at 24 frames per second. One hundred and forty-four frames at 24 frames per second produces an animation of 6 seconds duration. Setting "Start" at 0.00 and "End" at 6.00 in the "Physics," "Fluid" tab computes the action of the fluid over a 6-second time period, that is, over the length of the animation—this produces a real-time animation. If, for example, the "End" value was set at 4.00 seconds, then how the fluid behaved in 4.00 seconds would be spread over the 6.00 seconds of animation (in other words, it would be slowed down).

17.3.1.2 Physical Size of the Scene

In setting the size of a "Domain" the "Real-World Size" has to be considered. The Blender, scene with respect to the size of objects and their position relative to each other, is measured in Blender units (the grid units). These units are purely arbitrator and are mainly used for scaling one object against another but with respect to fluid simulation a "Real-World Size" is set for the grid. For simplicity this was not considered in Scenario 1.

To understand this concept, look at the default Blender scene with the "Cube" object. Go into "Top Orthographic" view. The default cube is scaled at one Blender unit (press N key to display the "Object Properties Panel" and note the "Scale" value in the "Transform" tab). The cube in the 3D window is displayed with its sides, two grid units by two grid units. When the cube is employed as a "Domain" in "Fluid Physics" consideration has to be given as to what this size represents in "Real-World" terms.

If you want to create a "Domain" to encompass a cup or a mug of coffee, this might be 10 cm^2 (0.1 m), while a swimming pool might be 10 m^2 (10.0 m). Obviously, given the same fluid input flow rate the swimming pool is going to take a lot longer to fill than the cup. *Put this on hold for the time being but make a mental note that our cup used in this scenario will be considered to be 10 cm diameter.*

In regards to the size of the scene, start with the diameter of the cup 10 units and make the horizontal length of the trough extending past the edge of the cup 18 units. We then require a domain length a little over 28 units say 30 units. Since we consider the diameter of the cup in "Real-World" terms to be 10 cm the "Real-World Size" value in the "Fluid World" tab is set at 30 cm (0.300 M = 30 cm), which is the longest side of the domain (Figure 17.12).

> Note: The default "Real-World Size" in the default Blender scene for an object used as a "Domain" is 0.500 m.

The actual physical size of the cup and trough objects is irrelevant. The main thing is that they are constructed in the correct proportion to one and other. By setting a "Real-World" size for the surrounding "Domain" the proportional physical size of the objects within the "Domain" is established.

One more setting in the "Domain." In the "Fluid World" tab, "Viscosity Presets" click on the selection menu and select "Water."

17.3.2 Fluid Object Setup

In this scenario, there is no fluid object; instead, we use an inflow object (the sphere) to provide a continuous flow of fluid.

17.3.3 Inflow Object Setup

Make particular note of the scale of the inflow object relative to the obstacle objects; the scale of the inflow object determines the physical volume of the fluid in the scene (Figure 17.15). If the inflow object is too large, the volume of fluid will spill over the sides of the trough and cup.

With the inflow object (Sphere) selected in the 3D window, go to the "Properties" window, "Physics" button, "Fluid" tab. Since the "Domain" object has been previously set, the "Fluid" tab, "Type" option should already be available. Select "Inflow" to display the inflow options (Figure 17.16). To give the fluid a small amount of momentum, set the "Z" initial velocity at 0.20. In doing this, the fluid will move before the acceleration due to the effects of gravity. Leaving the "Z" velocity at 0 produces a rather sluggish fluid flow.

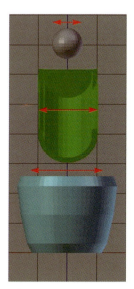

Figure 17.15

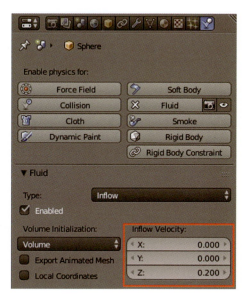

Figure 17.16

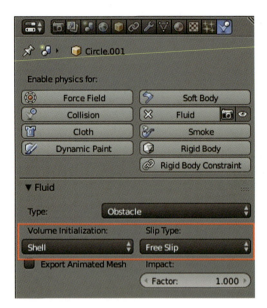

Figure 17.17

Figure 17.18

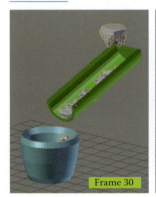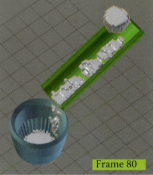

Figure 17.19

17.3.4 Obstacle Object Setup (Trough)

With the trough selected in the 3D window, go to the "Fluid" button, "Fluid" tab, and select "Obstacle" (Figure 17.17). Set the "Volume Initialization" option to "Shell" and the "Slip Type" to "Free Slip." The "Volume Initialization" and "Shell" options initialize a thin layer for all the faces of the mesh, which prevents fluid breakthrough. The "Free" option allows fluid movement along the obstacle. For other options, see the *Blender Manual*.

17.3.5 Obstacle Object Setup (Cup)

The model of the cup is identical to that used in the first scenario. Set the value options the same as for the trough obstacle object, except set the "Volume Initialization" option to "Shell" and the "Slip Type" to "Partial Slip" (Figure 17.18).

All objects included in the simulation have been assigned and the process can be baked, so you can now follow the procedure as outlined in the first scenario (select the "domain" and press "Bake").

Note: The "Bake" will take considerably longer than Scenario 1.

Note: In playing the animation, fluid is seen breaking through the trough and cup. Applying a subdivision surface modifier to the trough and cup mesh and increasing the "Domain," "Physics," "Resolution"—"Final" value in the— "Fluid" tab will resolve this. After changing values clear the "Cache" and "Bake" again. Note: Increasing the "Resolution" increases the "Bake" time.

The bake process takes a fair while and no action is observed in the 3D window other than the small bake progress bar at the top of the screen. When the bake has completed, the progress bar disappears. Play the animation or step through the animation in the timeline to see the result (Figure 17.19).

17.3.6 Outflow Object

An outflow object is used to limit the buildup of fluid to a certain level within the confines of the domain (Figure 17.20). The outflow would be used if you wanted the fluid to overflow from the cup and you only wanted the fluid level in the domain to reach a certain level.

17.3.7 Fluid Material Color

To add a material color to your fluid, select the "Domain" (the cube shown attached to the "Inflow" object sphere as a blob). In the "Properties" window, "Material" button, select a diffuse material. The fluid will display in the color of your choice.

17.4 Fluid Simulation with Particle Objects

So far, "Domain, Obstacle, Inflow, and Outflow" objects have been considered. Now let's consider the application of "Particle" objects.

> Note: This is a completely different method to "Particle Fluid Physics."

Particles can be used here to provide effects to the "Fluid." In chapter on "Particles," we discovered that particles will render with a "Halo" effect. We can mix particles in with the fluid adding a halo effect to the fluid.

Start with the fluid system that you used in the second scenario. Add a sphere to the scene and position it within the confines of the domain, as shown in Figure 17.21. With the new sphere selected in the 3D window, go to the "Properties" window, "Physics" button, "Fluid" tab, select "Type: Particle," and tick "Tracer" (Figure 17.22). Set the "Influence" size to 1.000 and the "Alpha" value to 1.000. Set the "SimCache" file path the same as the "Domain" "SimCache" file path.

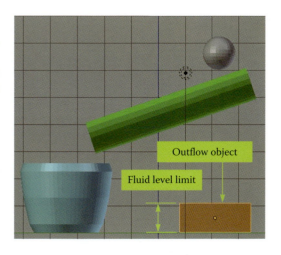

Figure 17.20

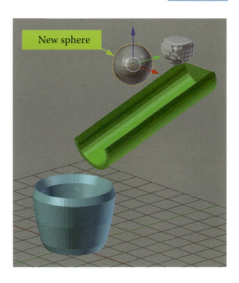

Figure 17.21

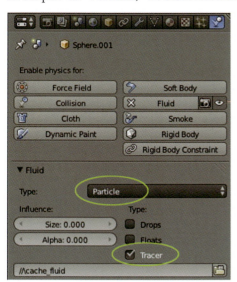

Figure 17.22

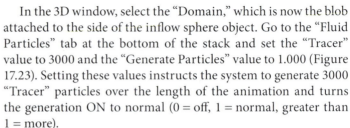

Figure 17.23

In the 3D window, select the "Domain," which is now the blob attached to the side of the inflow sphere object. Go to the "Fluid Particles" tab at the bottom of the stack and set the "Tracer" value to 3000 and the "Generate Particles" value to 1.000 (Figure 17.23). Setting these values instructs the system to generate 3000 "Tracer" particles over the length of the animation and turns the generation ON to normal (0 = off, 1 = normal, greater than 1 = more).

In the "Fluid" tab under "Type: Domain," click on "Bake." The system will now rebake the simulation, taking as long as it did the first time. More if you have increases, the "Resolution—Final" value. Note that there are dots distributed randomly among the fluid as the fluid is being generated; these dots are the particles and will show as halos when rendered (Figure 17.24). In Figure 17.25, a material color and a spotlight have been added.

Note: The domain has been moved to level 2, therefore only the particle halos render.

17.5 Fluid Simulation with Control Objects

Control objects are placed in the scene within the domain to influence the flow of fluid. In Figure 17.26, a domain has been set up containing an inflow cube object and an outflow cylinder object. The inflow provides a continuous flow of fluid, which simply accumulates on the floor of the domain until it reaches the level of the outflow object.

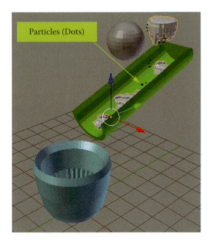

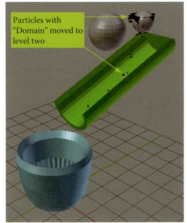

Figure 17.24

Figure 17.25

Scene at frame 80 without the control object

Figure 17.26

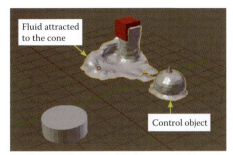

Scene at frame 80 with the control object

Figure 17.27

In Figure 17.27, a cone object has been added to the domain as a control object. With the control cone added, the fluid flows toward the cone before seeking the outflow object. By placing control objects within the domain, the flow of fluid can be directed.

17.6 Summary

The foregoing examples are but the tip of another iceberg. The examples will at least familiarize you with the interface that drives fluid simulation but there is much more to learn and by experimenting with the settings you will discover the versatility of this subject.

18

Smoke Simulation

18.1 Smoke Generation

Chapter 12, Section 12.6.7 demonstrated the "Quick Smoke" method in Blender. To assist you in understanding how to develop smoke and fire generation the following examples are provided.

Lesson 10
10-04
Smoke
Simulation

In the examples, we will attempt to reduce everything to the basics and use as many default settings as possible. We will not attempt to produce an advanced video demonstration but hopefully by understanding the logic of the interface you will be able to experiment and find your way through the tutorials provided on the Internet.

18.2 Creating Smoke from Scratch

The following procedure will create a smoke simulation from basic principles. Smoke can be generated using a mesh object in a scene as an emitter or by using an object as a particle emitter where smoke is generated from the particles. Particles are provided with a vast array of control therefore giving great flexibility to smoke generation. We will start by using a mesh object as the emitter.

There are basically only two objects required in a scene for a smoke simulation, a "Domain" and an "Emitter." This is similar to the principals for setting up "Fluid Simulation."

18.3 Create a Domain

Whether you emit smoke from a mesh object or from particles you have to define a volume of space in which the smoke simulation takes place. In Blender physics this volumetric space is called the "Domain." Use a "Cube" object. Note that if you use the default cube in the 3D view this cube has a default "Material" and "Texture" already applied. A new cube object introduced to the scene will not have material or texture. In this demonstration use the default cube and leave it located at the center of the scene. With the cube selected press the S Key + Z Key + 1.5 then "Enter" to scale the cube up 1.5 times on the Z-axis. With the "Cube" selected go to the "Properties" window, "Physics" button, and enable physics for "Smoke" (Figure 18.1).

In the Smoke tab click "Domain." The cube changes from a solid object to an orange outline, which indicates that the cube is now a "Domain" in Blender physics. Deselect the domain cube (A Key) (Figures 18.2 and 18.3).

Figure 18.1

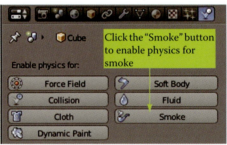

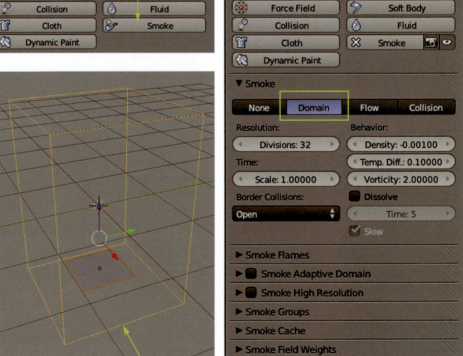

Figure 18.2

Domain

Figure 18.3

18.4 Smoke from a Mesh Object

In the "Quick Smoke" method, demonstrated in Section 12.6.7 "Smoke Modifier," smoke and fire were generated from the surface of the emitter object. This method generates smoke only from the surface of a mesh object. The following methods will expand on that procedure.

18.5 Flow Object

A "Flow" object is the smoke emitter, the object from which smoke emanates. Add a "Plane" object to the scene, scale it down slightly, and locate it within the "Domain" toward the bottom (Figure 18.4). Note that in the 3D window, the cursor has not been moved in the scene; therefore, it is located at the center of the scene. When you add an object to the scene it is located at the position of the 3D window cursor (Figure 18.4).

Make sure the "Plane" is totally inside the domain (check in "Front Orthographic" view). In the "Properties" window, "Physics" button, enable physics for "Smoke," and click on "Flow" to set the plane as the smoke emitter (Figure 18.5).

By default the "Flow Source" is "Mesh." This defines that the smoke will be emitted from the surface or surfaces of the mesh object.

To see smoke being generated press the "Play" button in the "Timeline" window or press "Alt + A key" with the mouse cursor in the 3D window. Smoke will issue from the plane and rise in a column toward the

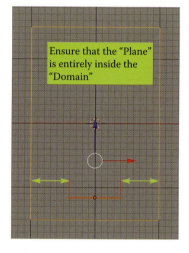

Ensure that the "Plane" is entirely inside the "Domain"

Figure 18.4

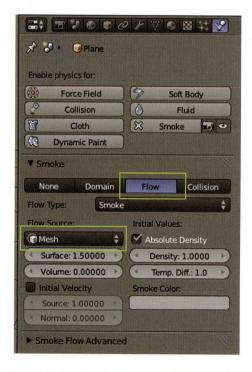

Figure 18.5

Figure 18.6

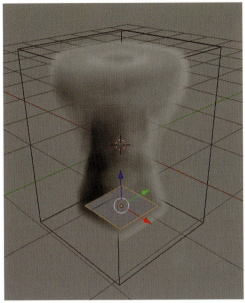

Smoke generation with the animation
paused at frame 93

top of the "Domain" cube. This simulation will play for the default 250 frames as set in the "Timeline" window and then repeat. Press "Esc" to quit or press the "pause" button in the "Timeline" window and then the "Return to Start" button (Figure 18.6).

Having quit the smoke generation you may play again to regenerate the smoke and press the "Pause" button at any time within the 250 frames to see a still view of the smoke. Note you are not able to scrub through an animation in the "Timeline" window. Animation frames have not been created. If you drag the mouse slowly, moving the "Timeline" window cursor, smoke is recreated. This is the same as using the "Play" button but there is no animation produced.

18.6 Rendering

With the smoke generation paused at a frame in the timeline, rendering an image will result in an image of the original solid cube object used for the "Domain," in the default gray color. To render showing the smoke, settings must be made to the material and texture of the domain cube.

> Note: In using the default Blender "Cube" object as presented in the 3D window the cube has a material and a texture applied by default. If you have introduced a new cube object to the scene you will have to apply a material and a texture manually.

18.7 Domain Settings for Rendering

How smoke displays in the 3D window and how it renders in an image or animation depends on "Texture" settings. Before you can have a "Texture" you must have a "Material" (color) applied.

18.8 Material Buttons

Select the "Domain" cube object in the 3D window then in the "Properties" window, "Material" button, change the material type from "Surface" to "Volume." In the "Density" tab that displays set the "Density" value to 0.000. Failing to set "Density" to 0.000 will result in the entire "Domain" being filled with smoke (Figure 18.7).

With the "Domain" selected in the 3D window, in the "Properties" window, "Texture" buttons, change the texture

Figure 18.7

Figure 18.9

Figure 18.8

type to "Voxel Data" (Figure 18.8). In the texture "Voxel Data" tab set the "Domain Object" as the "Domain" cube (click on the orange cube icon and select "Cube" in the drop down window).

In the "Influence" tab check (tick) the "Density" button and leave the value as 1.000. Uncheck "Emission Color" in the second column.

The render at this time produces an image of the frame in the animation where you paused the smoke generation. The render will show a gray plane with gray smoke against a gray background. This may be difficult to see with the default settings (Figure 18.9).

To show smoke with the "Emission" color, check "Emission" in first column of the "Texture" buttons, "Influence" tab (Figure 18.8). In the "Material" buttons, "Shading" tab, click on the "Transmission Color" bar and in the color picker that displays select a color.

With the settings so far you can replay the smoke generation from the beginning, pausing at a frame to render a still image. In the 3D window in "Solid Viewport Shading" you will see the smoke generated as gray smoke. In a rendered image or in "Rendered Viewport Shading" the smoke displays in color.

Note: If the smoke is generated while the 3D window is in "Rendered Viewport Shading" mode you will not see smoke until the generation process is paused.

You can render an animation preview in the form of a series of still images, which can be played back.

Go to the "Properties" window, "Render" buttons. In the "Dimensions" tab you can set the number of frames for the preview in the "Frame Range" settings but you will always have to begin at Frame 1. In the "Output" tab set the folder where you want the images stored. The default location is in the "/tmp\" folder. Set the type of image you require. The default image type is "PNG." In the "Render" tab press the "Animation" button and sit back and wait. With the simplest settings on an old computer it can take time to generate an image. You will see a progress report at the upper LHS of the 3D window. Once all the images (frames) are generated press the "Play" button in the "Render" tab (Figure 18.10).

If you want to render a movie file for the smoke generation begin by setting the file type in the "Output" tab. For example, change PNG to MPEG. Set the location of the output folder. In the "Dimensions" tab choose a render "Preset," say TV Pal 16.9 (European & Australia) or TV NTSC 16.9 (USA). This will automatically change the "Frame Rate" to suit. Once again press the "Animation" button and be prepared to wait (Figures 18.11 and 18.12).

Figure 18.10

Figure 18.11

Figure 18.12

18.9 Smoke Generation Settings

At this stage the smoke generation has used the "Flow Source," "Mesh" option in the "Flow" object, "Physics" buttons, "Smoke" tab, and default generation settings. Changing default settings will affect how the smoke is generated and adding a single or multiple "Force field" objects to the scene will influence the smoke generation. It is recommended that you study some of the video tutorials available on the Internet to learn about settings for various effects (Figure 18.13).

To make the smoke more attractive, with the "Flow" object (plane) selected, click on the "Smoke Color" picker in the "Physics" buttons, "Smoke" tab. Regenerate the smoke by replaying the animation in the "Timeline" window. To render an image showing the color, select the "Domain" and check "Emission" in the "Texture" buttons, "Influence" tab under "Volume" just below the "Density" slider (Figure 18.14).

Figure 18.13

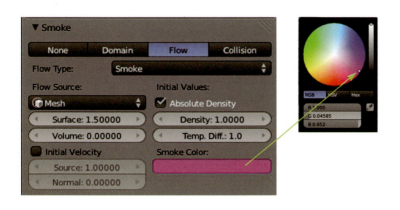 

Rendered image with colored smoke

Figure 18.14

Note: With the "Domain" selected and the "Physics" buttons opened, clicking the "Texture" button opens the "Texture" buttons with the "Other Texture Data" option active (NO Texture buttons show). Required to select the "Materials Texture" option to see the "Texture" buttons.

Figure 18.15

Camera repositioned closer to the smoke and a "Sun" lamp added

Figure 18.16

You can improve your rendered image by simply adding a "Lamp" or several lamps to the scene and repositioning the camera to concentrate on the smoke generation within the "Domain" (Figure 18.15).

Note: An animation sequence is not saved in the "Timeline" window. You cannot scrub (drag the timeline cursor) to see the smoke generation. You have to replay the generation sequence and pause at the required frame.

We will not attempt to demonstrate all the settings in the various tabs but will move on to the "Flow Source," "Particle System" option for smoke generation.

18.10 Using Particles

The difference between using the "Flow Source," "Mesh" and the "Flow Source," "Particle System" setting is that smoke is emitted from the particles rather than the object itself. A "Particle System" is applied to the "Flow" (Emitter) object. All the control over the number of particles and the way in which they are emitted and influenced by "Force Fields" may be utilized.

In a new default Blender scene delete the "Cube" object then add a new "Cube." In doing this we are starting from bare bones and will have to create all the settings that are required.

Scale the "Cube" object to be used as the "Domain" then add a "Plane" object and position as "Flow" (the Emitter) the same as in the previous example. You can change from "Solid" display to "Wireframe" display do allow you to see the placement of the plane inside the cube before applying the "Physics," "Smoke" settings to the cube. Change back to "Solid" display, select the "Cube" and activate the "Physics" buttons selecting "Smoke" and then the "Domain" option in the "Smoke" tab. For the moment do not activate the "Physics" buttons for the "Plane." Make sure the "Plane" is entirely within the "Domain."

Select the "Plane," go to the "Properties" window, "Particle" buttons, and add a new "Particle System" ("Particles" are discussed in detail in Chapter 13).

Change the following settings in the "Particle" buttons tabs. Emissions tab: Number: 5 (Default is 1000), Lifetime: 250. These values will allow you to see what happens to a minimal sample of particles and keep them displayed during the default 250-frame animation in the "Timeline" window (Figure 18.16).

Still in the "Particle" buttons go to the "Field Weights" tab and reduce the "Gravity" setting to 0.000. Particles are influenced by the gravity setting in the "Properties" window, "Scene" buttons, "Gravity"

tab. The "Gravity" setting could be turned off here but if there were other objects in the scene that required the influence of gravity they would also be effected. Reducing the setting in the "Field Weights" tab, therefore, allow you to negate the influence of gravity as applied to the particles only (Figure 18.17).

Note: In the "Emission" tab, "Emit From" has the "Faces" option selected meaning that the particles will be emitted from the emitter objects faces. You can select "Vertices" in which case particles would be emitted from the object's vertices.

Figure 18.17

Playing the animation in the "Timeline" window will show the five particles emit from the plane and rise in the 3D window. Press "Esc" to quit the animation.

To see the effect of a "Force Field" introduced to the scene deselect the "Plane" and add a "Force Field," "Vortex" (press Alt + A Key—select, Force Field—then, Vortex) (Figure 18.18).

With the "Vortex" selected, in the "Properties" window, "Physics" buttons, "Force Fields" tab, change the "Strength" value to 3.000. Replay the animation and see the particles rise until they reach the vortex where they are swirled about. You can see this effect better with the "Plane" selected (Figure 18.19).

Having set up the particle system on the "Plane," with the plane selected activate the "Physics" buttons, "Smoke," and select "Flow." In the "Smoke" tab change the "Flow Source" from "Mesh" to "Particle

Figure 18.18

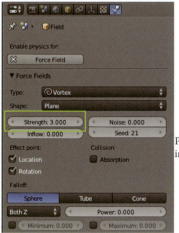

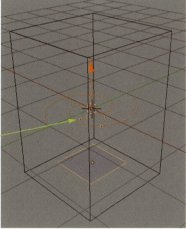

Particles caught in the vortex

Figure 18.19

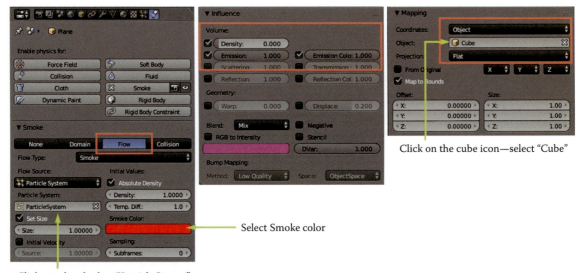

Click on the cube icon—select "Cube"

Select Smoke color

Click panel and select "Particle System"

Figure 18.20

System" then in the "Particle System" window just below "flow Source," enter "Particle System." In the "Smoke Color" picker select a nice bright color. Replaying the animation will show the swirling particles emitting smoke and the smoke continuing to rise in the domain. Pause the animation when a quantity of smoke has accumulated in the "Domain" (Figures 18.20 and 18.21).

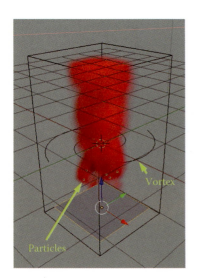

Vortex

Particles

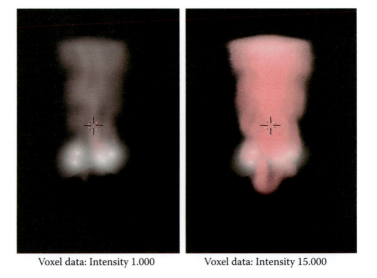

Voxel data: Intensity 1.000   Voxel data: Intensity 15.000

Figure 18.21

Figure 18.22

To render an image showing the smoke with color, select the "Domain" and add a "Volume" material and a "Voxel Data" texture as we did previously. In the "texture" buttons, "Influence" tab check "Density" and "Emission" (just below density) leaving the default 1.000 values. Leave "Emission Color" checked.

Do not forget to set "Density" to 0.000 in the "Material" button, "Density" tab.

In the "Texture" buttons, "Mapping" tab set "Coordinates" to "Object" then in the "Object" panel click on the cube icon and select the "Domain" (cube).

Rendering an image will show the colored smoke a dark plane and the particles as halos. Select the plane and in the "Particles" buttons, "Render" tab, uncheck "Emitter," and set the render display type as "None." Render again to see smoke only. You can add more lamps to the scene and increase their energy settings to enhance the image and you can move the camera in toward the domain to concentrate on the smoke. You can also darken the "Horizon" color in the "Properties" window, "World" buttons, "World" tab (Figure 18.22).

Everything prior to this has involved smoke generation only but there is also fire as was seen in the "Quick Smoke" method.

18.11 Fire

Fire is added to a smoke generation by adding a second "Texture" channel to the "Domain." To demonstrate "Fire" continue by setting the number of particles emitted by the plane to the default 1000. Also uncheck "Emitter" and set the display to "None" in the "Render" tab so that the particles will not render. Rendering the particles as "Halos" will distract from the fire simulation.

With the "Emitter" selected, in the "Physics" buttons, "Smoke" tab set the "Flow Type" to "Type" to "Fire + Smoke" (Figure 18.23).

Select the "Domain" and go to the "Properties" window, "Texture" buttons. On my machine the texture buttons will not display until I have first selected the material buttons. Select a new "Texture" channel and click the "New" button to add a new texture.

Lesson 10
10-06
Fire Simulation

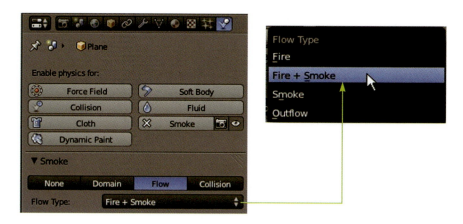

Figure 18.23

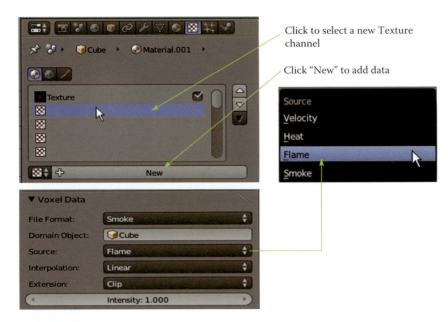

Click to select a new Texture channel

Click "New" to add data

Figure 18.24

Change the type to "Voxel Data" and set the "Domain Object" in the "Voxel Data" tab as "Cube." Change the "Source" to "Flame" (Figure 18.24).

Figure 18.25

In the "Influence" tab check "Density" and "Emission." Leave the "Emission Color" checked (Figure 18.25).

18.12 Color Ramp

The flame color is produced by introducing a graded texture color. Still in the "Domain," "Texture" buttons go to the "Colors" tab and check "Ramp." Set the color ramp as shown in the diagram (see Section 4.10) (Figure 18.26).

Click to add Color channel

Color channel—click to select

Dotted line indicates selected channel. Click and drag to reposition

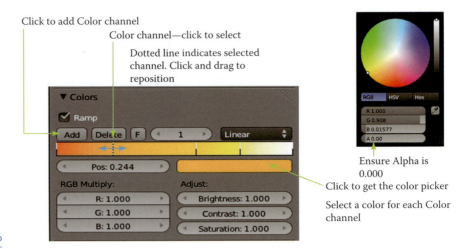

Ensure Alpha is 0.000

Click to get the color picker

Select a color for each Color channel

Figure 18.26

Regenerate the smoke, pause the animation, and render an image.

Don't forget to reset the "Mapping Coordinates," "Coordinates: Object," "Object: Cube" (Figures 18.27 through 18.29).

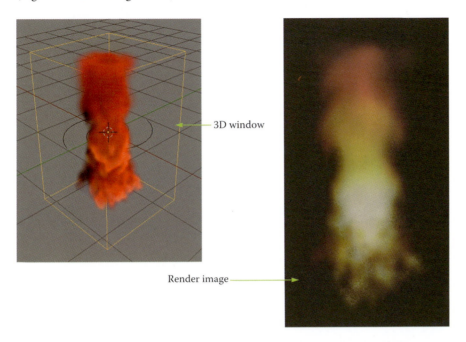

— 3D window

Render image ——

Figure 18.27

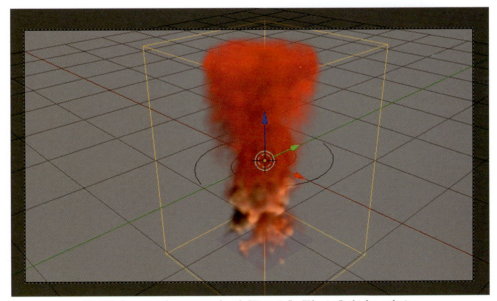

3D Window—smoke generated with "Domain"—"Physics"—high resolution

Figure 18.28

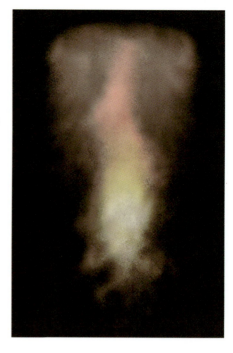

Rendered image of high resolution smoke generated with a "Sun" lamp added to the scene directed at the smoke

Lamp energy setting 3.000

The camera has been repositioned to focus on the smoke

Figure 18.29

18.13 Summary

Understanding the Blender interface with respect to Smoke Generation will place you in a better position to decipher video tutorials on the Internet, which detail procedures for specific effects. This is a reasonably complex topic and you will no doubt have specific requirements when creating a scene in an animation. When you find something of interest, record your findings, and if possible create and save a Blender file for future use. Remember you can "Append" to a new Blender scene.

19

Nodes

19.1 Introduction to Nodes

The Blender node system is a graphical display used to enter data to create materials (colors) and textures, and applying them to objects in a scene. The method is also used for assembling and enhancing images or movies.

This system employs data entry windows called "Nodes" which are arranged and linked together combining data from one node with another. The data is outputted and applied to an object which has been selected in the 3D window.

Consider "Nodes" as tools which are preassembled blocks of code for making objects display, in a prescribed way, in the 3D window.

Before you can use "Nodes" you have to activate the system and know how to introduce nodes, arrange them, and link them together.

To work through the examples in this chapter arrange the screen as shown in Figure 19.1.

Note: How you see the results of applying nodes in the "Camera View—Rendered Viewport Shading" mode depends to a great extent on the lighting arrangement in the scene.

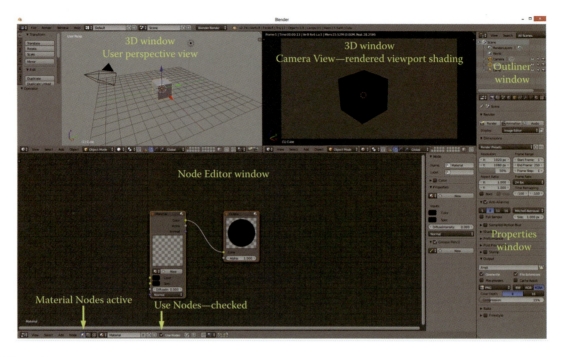

Figure 19.1

Nodes are accessed in the "Node Editor" window and are available in three categories: Material Nodes, Texture Nodes, and Compositing Nodes. By default the "Material Nodes" option is active in the "Node Editor" window. The different categories are selected in the "Node Editor" window header. With the default cube selected, the "Material Node" button active and the "Use Nodes" button checked two nodes display in the "Node Editor" window (Figure 19.1).

Note: In this chapter, "Nodes" will be discussed in relation to the "Blender Internal" rendering system. Nodes in the "Cycles Rendering" system are more extensive although the operation and arrangement are similar.

Note: In the "Blender Internal," rendering system nodes can only be used in conjunction with an object which is selected in the 3D window and which has a material applied.

As an introduction to the node system follow this demonstration.

Begin with the default Blender scene containing a "Cube" object (Figure 19.1). By default the cube is selected and it has a material pre-applied. In the "Properties" window, "Material" buttons you will see the "Properties" tabs displayed (Figure 19.2). Click on the "Browse Material to be Linked" button to display the "Material Cache" and observe the

"Material" named "Material" as the single entry in the cache. Delete the default cube and add a new cube. The "Properties" window, "Materials" buttons will now only show the "New" button. Open the material cache again and observe that "Material" remains the single entry. Obviously, Blender needs to have something to show you in the 3D window so it uses "Material" as a default display material.

Make sure the cube is selected in the 3D window. To activate the node system you have to check (tick) "Use Nodes" in the "Node editor" window header. It's not there.

It was previously stated that you must have an object selected with a material applied. We have a new cube selected but no material has been applied. To apply a material either click on "New" in the "Properties" window, "Materials" buttons or "New" in the "Node Editor" window header.

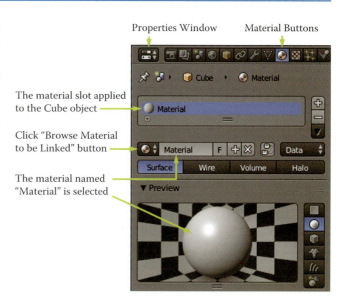

Properties Window   Material Buttons

The material slot applied to the Cube object

Click "Browse Material to be Linked" button

The material named "Material" is selected

Figure 19.2

Clicking "New" has introduced a new material named "Material.001." You see this in the "Properties" window and in the "Node Editor" header. There are now two entries in the material cache. Now check (tick) the "Use Nodes" box, which has displayed in the "Node Editor" window header. Two nodes display in the "Node Editor" window: Material and Output. They are linked together by a curved line (zoom in to enlarge). Both nodes are selected as shown by the orange and red outlines (Figure 19.3).

For the time being disregard the contents of the nodes.

Press A key with the cursor in the "Node editor" window to deselect. Right click on the "Output" node to select it and X key to delete. Do the same with the "Material" node. In the window header click on "Add"— "Input" and select "Material." The "material" node is reinstated in the window where the mouse cursor is located. Drag the mouse to position the node in the window. Repeat the process this time selecting "Output"—"Output."

Figure 19.3

Note: You may also press Shift + A key to open the selection menu in the window. With the mouse cursor located in the center of the window the "Add" selection menu will display at that location and when you click to add a "Node," the "Node" is also entered at that location.

With both nodes in the window press A key to deselect them. Left mouse click on the yellow "Color" dot (socket) on the upper RHS of the "Material" node, hold and drag over to the yellow "Color" dot (socket) on the LH edge of the "Output" node to reconnect them.

This has demonstrated how you add nodes, position them in the window, and connect them together.

To disconnect nodes click on the socket at the RH end of the connecting line, hold and drag away from the socket.

19.1.1 Resizing Nodes

Placing the mouse cursor on either edge of a node changes the cursor to a double-headed arrow. Click and drag the arrow to resize the node panel.

Note: Nodes are selected and deselected like any other object.

19.1.2 Expanding and Collapsing Nodes

Besides changing the size of a node panel, you can also expand and collapse it to save space on the screen. Simply click on the small triangle in the upper left of the node panel (Figure 19.4).

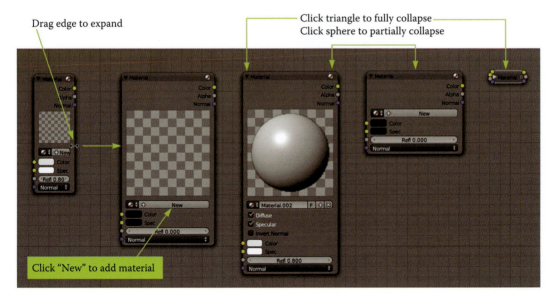

Figure 19.4

19.1.3 Moving and Arranging Nodes

Click and hold anywhere in the node panel **header** and drag the mouse to move the node.

19.1.4 Zoom Window

Scrolling the mouse wheel or pressing the number pad + and keys will zoom in and out in the "Node Editor" window. Click and hold the MMB to pan the window.

19.1.5 Connecting and Disconnecting Nodes

To reinforce this procedure, see that the material node is connected to the output node by a curved line between the two yellow "Color" sockets (Figure 19.5). Click and hold on the output node's yellow socket and drag your mouse away from the socket; release the hold, and you will have disconnected the nodes (the connecting line disappears). Click and hold on the material node's yellow socket, drag the mouse to the output node's yellow socket, and release the hold to reconnect the nodes. In general, sockets should be connected yellow to yellow, gray to gray, and blue to blue. This connection sequence is a generalization. Yellow sockets are for color, which is expressed in numeric terms such as the RGB values. Gray sockets are also for numeric values therefore there are occasions when yellow and gray sockets are connected. Blue sockets, which may appear purple, are for vector values such as x, y, z coordinates.

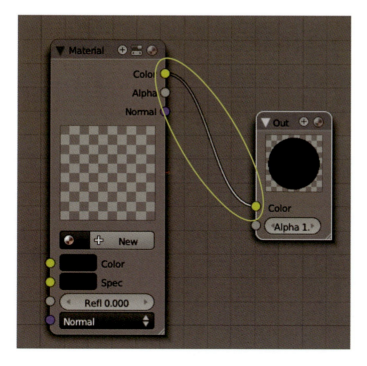

Figure 19.5

19.2 Material Nodes

Material node arrangements are for creating materials and once a material is created, it is saved for future use in the Blender file. You can use any object that is selected in the 3D window in conjunction with the "Node Editor" when dealing with material nodes.

We will work through a simple exercise and create a material using nodes. Start with the default Blender scene with the default cube object selected. The cube will have the default material applied to it, as seen in the "Properties" window, "Material" button, the material displays as the default gray color. At this point, it is worth taking a look at what we have in terms of the material. Look at the "Properties" window, "Material" button. The preview tab shows a sphere with the gray color and a material named "Material" is selected and assigned to the material slot (Figure 19.6). The material slot is linked to the selected cube object in the 3D window, which renders as the gray color. Clicking on the "Browse Material to be Linked" button shows the material cache with the material named "Material" stored in it.

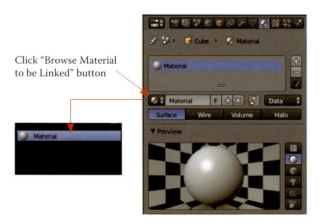

Click "Browse Material to be Linked" button

19.2.1 What Is a Material?

A material in Blender is data that tells the program to display the surface of an object in a certain way (i.e., gray in color, reflecting a certain color under a light source, having bumps or spots, etc.). The data is grouped together in a block called a "Datablock."

Figure 19.6

19.2.2 Data Blocks

If you change the 3D window to the "Outliner" window in "Datablocks" mode, you will see the "Materials" data block as one of the entries (Figure 19.7). Click on the plus sign next

Figure 19.7

to "Materials" to see the datablock for the material named "Material." Note that Blender's default screen arrangement has an "Outliner" window in the upper RHS of the screen—as mentioned before, this window is an abridged version of the full "Outliner" window. It's worth mentioning here that you can change the name of the material in the name slot in the data block. Just click in the slot, delete, and retype a new name and the name change will be reflected in the "Properties" window, "Material" button. This is very useful when creating multiple materials.

Change the "Outliner" window to the 3D window to get us back to square one. Make sure the cube is selected and make note that Blender has assigned the material named "Material" to the cube (material nodes will not work unless a material has been assigned to the selected object). Change the 3D window to the "Node Editor" window and you will get a blank window. At the start of this chapter, I said that nodes were accessed through the node editor window. By default, "Material" nodes mode is selected but to activate the nodes you must check (tick) the "Use Nodes" box in the window header. The "Material" node shows a blank chequerboard preview panel, the "Output" node shows a black circle, and in the "Properties" window, "Material" button, "Preview" tab, you should see the same black circle.

Note: When using "Nodes" the "Properties" window, "Materials" buttons are reduced.

If you click on the "Browse Material to be Linked" button you will see that the default material named "Material" is still the only thing in the cache but it is now showing a black circle; note that "Material" is still shown selected and placed in the material slot. If you render an image (by pressing F12) all you get is a black profile of the cube. Consider activating "Use Nodes" as taking over the material creation process and at this stage we have not created any new material. In the "Material" node, click on "New," the material node expands and the "Color" and "Spec" color selection bars show white. If you click on either "Color" bar, you will see RGB values of 0.800 (gray) and the "Spec" bar shows RGB values of 1.000 (white)—this is why you see gray spheres in all the preview windows. Render an image (F12) and you should see a gray cube.

Note that in the "Material" button, "Material" is still showing as selected and in the material slot. Click on the "Browse Material to be Linked" button and you will now see two materials: "Material" and "Material.001." Clicking on "New" in the material node has created a new material; since "Material" and "Material.001" are identical, you can only render a gray cube.

Click on the color selection bar in the material node and pick a new color. All the previews display the new color, but in the 3D window the cube is still gray. Note that in the material node the name of the material is showing "Material.001," which shows that the node is editing "Material.001." Untick "Use Nodes" in the header, go to the "Material" button in the "Properties" window, click the "Browse Material to be Linked" button and select "Material.001" from the "material Cache." This places "Material.001" in the material slot and assigns it to the cube in the 3D window. The cube will now display the color you choose.

This has been the very basics of using material nodes; there is much more. Clicking on "Add" in the node editor window header or pressing Shift + A key with the cursor in the

"Node Editor" window reveals a pop-up selection menu with several categories of node types. Each category has individual node type options. It is not possible to demonstrate all of the node combinations, but the following examples will give you the idea. Remember, when you create a node arrangement that produces a desired result, create a node group, and save the .blend file for future use. The node group can be appended to any new Blender scene and applied to any object in the scene. Therefore, it's possible to create a single .blend file containing many node groups for future appending.

19.2.3 Example 1: Creating a Node Arrangement

In this example, we will combine a material color with texture color. This means that we will select a color from Blender's inbuilt color system then select an inbuilt Blender procedural texture and combine the colors from the texture with the plain color.

To follow the example set up the scene as follows so that the results will match the procedure. There are many possible variations with only slight deviations in scene setup and values so as far as possible be precise. In the end, you will have to experiment and record results that you find useful but for now we are attempting to get you started and understanding the methods.

19.2.3.1 Set Up the Scene

With the screen arrangement as shown in Figure 19.1 set up the scene as shown in Figure 19.8. This shows the scene in the 3D window and in "Camera" view with "Rendered Viewport Shading." The default cube has been replaced with a UV sphere, which has been smoothed and scaled down on its Z-axis to form a disc. The disc is scaled up to fill the camera view. The default single spot lamp has been replaced with a "Hemi" lamp to improve lighting.

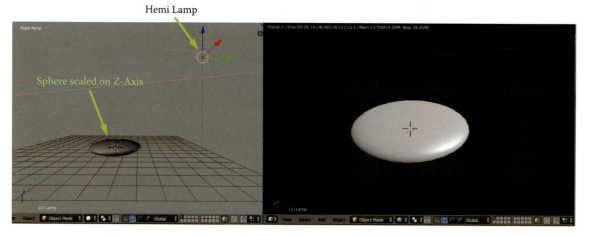

Figure 19.8

With the disc (UV sphere) selected add a material in the "Properties" window "Material" buttons by clicking on "New." Blender default gray color will be applied. It is important to add the material since "Material Nodes" will not work unless this is done.

In the "Node Editor" window header with "material" nodes active tick "Use Nodes." By default a "Material" node and an "Output" node will display.

19.2.3.2 Set Up the Material Node

In the "Material" node click "New" and then click on the "Color" bar to display a color picker. Set the RGB values to R: 0.800, G: 0.060, and B: 0.400 (a nice red color). You may choose any color you like but by setting the values exactly, hopefully you will reproduce the outputs show in the example figures.

With the node's RGB values set the "Output" node displays the color and it is also shown on the selected object in the 3D window.

> Note: If the material does not display immediately, deselect then reselect the object in the 3D window. This causes the program to reevaluate the settings.

19.2.3.3 Add a Texture Node

With the mouse cursor in the "Node editor" window press Shift + A key and select "Input"—"Texture" to add a "Texture" node. Reposition and resize the new node. This new node has no texture assigned.

With the "Texture" node selected (right click to select) go to the "Properties" window, "Texture" buttons—Click "New," and change the texture "Type" to "Magic."

(By default Blender has a texture datablock named "Tex" in the cache. Clicking "New" introduces a second texture datablock named "Texture.")

In the "Node Editor" window, in the "Texture" node click on the texture icon and from the menu that displays select "Texture." This assigns the texture from the "Properties" window to the texture node.

To tidy up go back to the "Properties" window, "Texture" buttons, and click on X to unlink the texture datablock.

19.2.3.4 Add a "Vector—Mapping" and "Color—Mix RGB" Node

With the mouse cursor in the "Node Editor" window press Shift + A and select the node types to add them to the window. Position them as shown in Figure 19.9.

19.2.3.5 Link the Nodes

Link all the nodes together as shown (Figure 19.9).

With the links complete the color from the texture assigned to the "Texture" node is combined in a 50:50 ratio per the 0.500 setting in the "Mix" node and displayed in the "Output" node. The combined colors are in turn assigned to the selected object in the 3D window. Rendering an image (press F12) shows the result. Alternatively change the 3D window display mode to "Rendered."

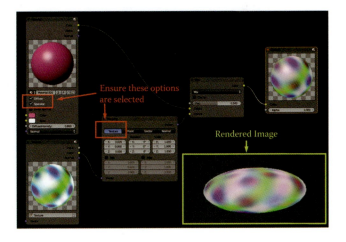

Figure 19.9

At this stage the "Mapping" node does nothing since all its values are default values. Ensure the "Texture" option is highlighted in the "Mapping" node.

To see an example of changing a value in the "Mapping" node change the Y scale value to 9.000 and the Z scale value to 24 and render an image (Figures 19.10 and 19.11).

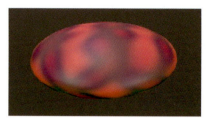

Figure 19.10

Figure 19.11

The "Mix" node has a drop down selection menu where you can change the type of mix. Experiment with the different settings to see the results (Figures 19.12 and 19.13).

Mix changed to Divide

Mix changed to Linear Light

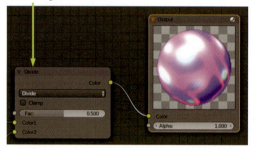

Figure 19.12

Figure 19.13

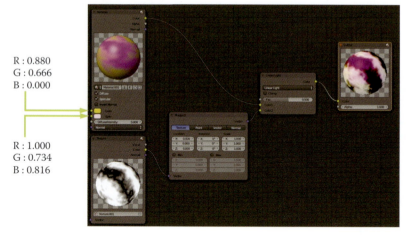

R : 0.880
G : 0.666
B : 0.000

R : 1.000
G : 0.734
B : 0.816

Figure 19.14

19.2.4 Example 2: Variation

Figure 19.14 shows another variation on Example 1, this time with a marble texture (Figure 19.15). Figure 19.16 shows the rendered image.

19.2.5 Example 3: Variation

Figure 19.17 shows two RGB inputs connected to a "Mix" panel with a "ColorRamp" panel applied. Note that the

Figure 19.15

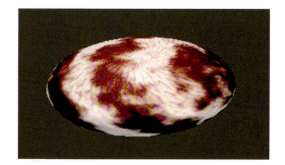

Figure 19.16

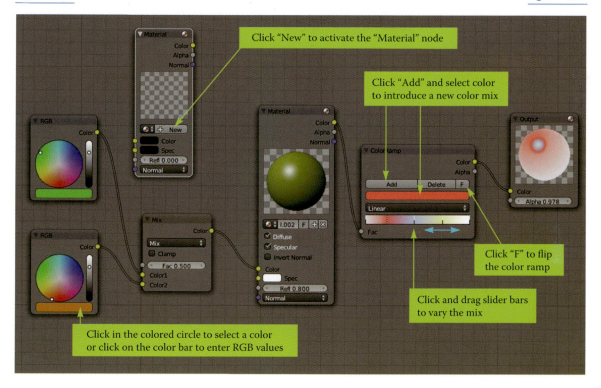

Figure 19.17

three examples shown so far simply create a material and apply it to a selected object in the 3D window.

19.2.6 Example 4: Nodes with Objects

This example demonstrates the use of material nodes in combination with other objects in the scene. The objective here is to create a simple graduated material. First, we have to

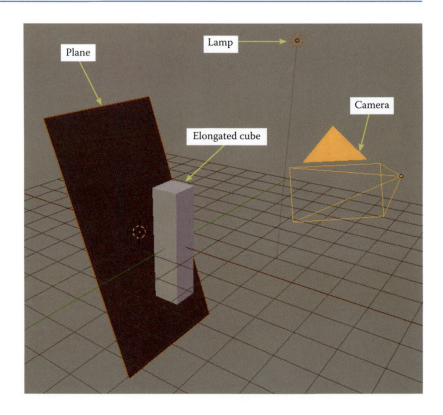

Figure 19.18

set up the scene as shown in Figure 19.18; the default cube has been elongated into a vertical column, and a simple plane object has been added to the scene, scaled up, and posi-

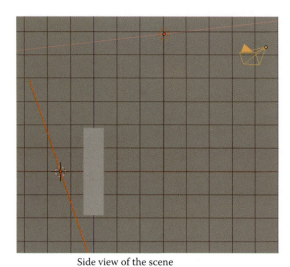

Side view of the scene

Figure 19.19

tioned behind the elongated cube, forming a backdrop in the camera view (Figure 19.19). Make sure the lamp is positioned on the camera side of the plane. Select the plane in the 3D window and assign the default material and a marble texture to it in the "Properties" window, "Material" button. Deselect the plane then select the elongated cube. In the "Properties" window, "Material" button, "Diffuse" tab, pick a diffuse color, and in the "Specular" tab, pick a specular color. In the "Transparency" tab, tick "Transparency" and change the "Alpha" value to 0.000. While still in the "Transparency" tab, click "Raytrace" and set the "IOR" value to 1.2. In the "Properties" window, "Render" button, "Shading" tab, untick "Shadows." The diffuse and specular colors can be anything you want. Obviously, "Transparency" makes the cube transparent; with the "Alpha" value at 0.000, it is fully transparent. The "IOR" value is an angular index of refraction for raytraced refraction; the value of 1.200 makes the cube

appear to look something like glass. Only by experimenting with different values will you understand how to achieve the outcome you want.

Make sure the cube is selected in the 3D window and then in the "Node Editor" window, "Material Shader" nodes mode, tick "Use Nodes," and set up the arrangement shown in Figure 19.20. Note that the "Separate R" node in the figure is actually "Separate RGB" and the "Extend" node is "Extended Material" (drag the sides of the node to reveal the full names). Note also all the unconnected sockets on the extended material node. The rule here is that an unconnected input socket will relay the value in its adjacent panel to the output. If an input node is connected then that node overrides the value. For example, "DiffuseIntensity 0.800" is the value used since there is no input connected to the socket.

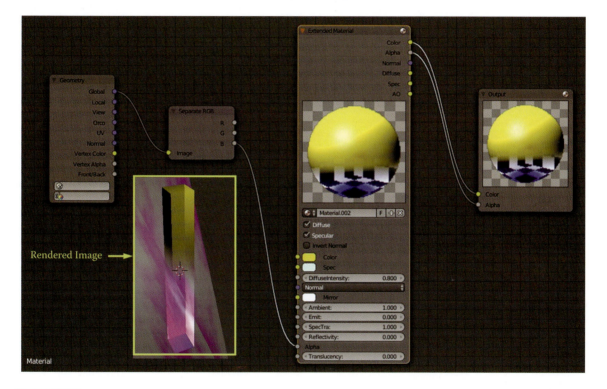

Figure 19.20

Note: Before entering the Diffuse and specular values in the "Extended Materials" node click "New."

It's worth remembering that in any scene, the lamp or number of lamps, the type of lamp, the energy settings, and color of the lamp light can have a dramatic effect on the rendered image. Something else to note in this example is that the rule of connecting like-colored sockets has been broken: the blue "Global" socket on the geometry node is connected to the yellow "Image" socket on the "Separate RGB" node.

"Separate RGB" tells Blender to separate the RGB values; it is being used to separate the coordinates that are vector values. RGB in this case represents *x, y, z* coordinate values that are fed to the "Alpha" value in the "Extended Material" node. "B" corresponds to the *z* value, or the vertical coordinate. Therefore, we are applying the material to a vertical cube column. The value is fed into the "Alpha" socket on the extended material node, which is the value that controls transparency. "Geometry"—"Global" is telling Blender to use global coordinates. The combination is telling Blender to apply the diffuse color and the transparency to the elongated cube on the *z*-axis.

We have "Ray Tracing" applied and we have given the elongated cube the characteristics of glass. The cube is therefore refracting the light reflected from the backdrop in the scene (the plane); Figure 19.20 shows the application. To see the rendered effect, render an image (F12) or change the 3D window to "Rendered" display mode with the window in "Camera" view. This example shows how you can mix and match nodes, lamp settings, and objects in the scene to produce stunning effects. Bear in mind that in this type of setup, the proximity of objects in the scene, the position of the lamp and its settings, the number of lamps, and the color and type of texture, all have an effect on the rendered output. When following this example, you probably won't produce the same image as shown.

19.3 Texture Nodes

Texture nodes allow you to create textures and apply them to a selected object in the 3D window. As far as adding nodes to the node editor, manipulating them, and connecting them, the process is the same as for material nodes. However, activating the node editor in texture mode is slightly different.

Start a new Blender scene and delete the default cube object. Add a simple plane object and scale it up a bit; a plane will provide a nice flat surface on which to place the texture. In the "Properties" window, "Material" button, click "New" to add the default material. As with material nodes, texture nodes cannot be activated unless a material has been applied to the selected object. Change the 3D window to node editor and note that the "Material Shader" node option in the header is selected by default. Change this to "Texture" node mode and click on "New" in the "Properties" window, "Textures" button. Now tick "Use Nodes."

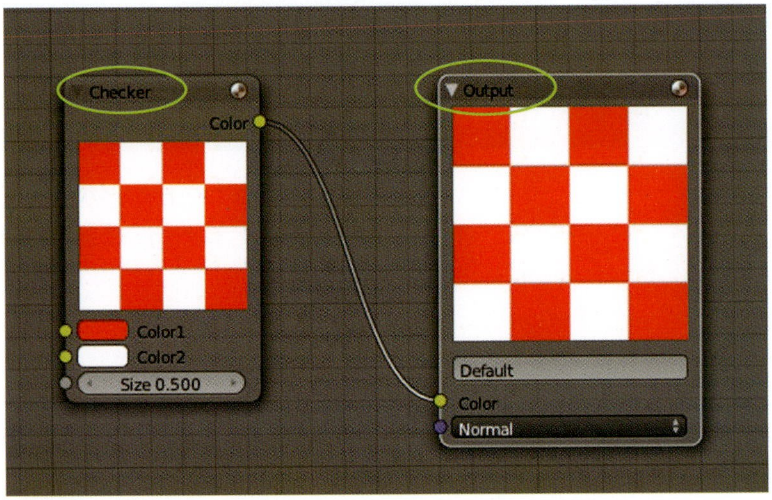

Two nodes appear in the editor window: "Checker" and "Output" (Figure 19.21). In all texture node arrangements, there must be an output node. If you render an image (F12), you will see the checker texture applied to the plane object, which is selected in the 3D window (Figure 19.22).

Figure 19.21

Rendered image

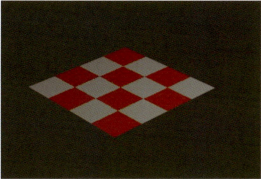

Figure 19.22

Note: To get the texture displayed as shown in Figure 19.22, in the "Properties" window, "Texture" buttons, "Mapping" tab change the Mapping Coordinates to "Generated."

In the "Properties" window, "Textures" buttons, you will see that a texture named "Texture" is selected and placed in the texture slot. Click on the "Browse Texture to be Linked" button and see that there are two textures in the cache: "Tex" and "Texture." "Texture" is the new texture you have just created using nodes and "Tex" is Blender's hidden default texture data block. As with everything else in Blender, entering data for a new material or texture is in fact modifying something that already exists.

At this stage, you have "Use Nodes" active so the node editor is applying the new texture to the object. If you untick "Use Nodes," a render will only show the plane object as having the default gray material color. In the "Properties" window, "Textures" button, click on the "F" next to "Texture" to save the texture data block. A "2" appears, indicating that there are two users of the data, so click on the "2" to make a single user. The "2" disappears and if you look in the cache (click the "Browse texture to be linked" data button), you will see "Tex," "F Tex," and "Texture.001." "Tex" just renders a gray plane while "F Tex" and "Texture.001" displays the texture in the node editor. You still have to tick "Use Nodes" to render the checker texture to the object.

This has demonstrated the basic application of "Texture" nodes. There are many combinations of node arrangements that will produce many textures. The following examples will show simple arrangements. Note that complicated node arrangements consume computer power and unless you are working on a powerful machine, rendering an image will take forever or will just never happen.

19.3.1 Example 1

In Figure 19.23, an image has been loaded into the "Image" node and mixed with a "Wood"

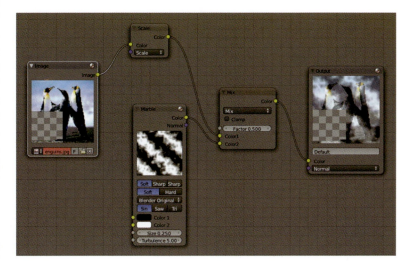

Figure 19.23

Rendered image

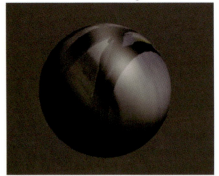

Figure 19.24

texture node. The "Scale" node resizes the image and the texture created is mapped onto a sphere object selected in the 3D window. Figure 19.24 shows the rendered image.

19.3.2 Example 2

In Figure 19.25, the "Compose RGB" node creates a color and the "Mix" node combines the color with an image from the "Image" node to produce a texture, as seen in the "Output" node. The texture is applied to a plane object selected in the 3D window (Figure 19.26 shows the rendered image).

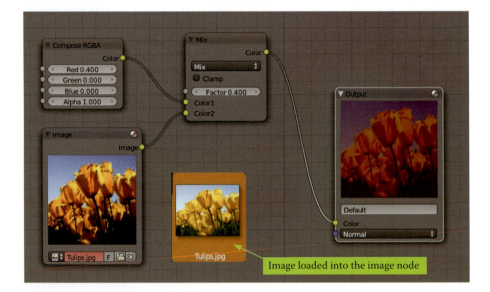

Figure 19.25

Image loaded into the image node

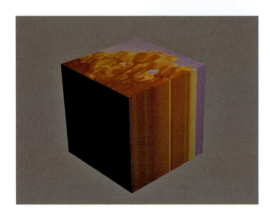

Figure 19.26

19.4 Compositing Nodes

Compositing nodes (or composite, for short) allow you to create and enhance an image. The contents of the Blender scene can be the basis for the image or an image already saved on the hard drive can be used. A presaved image can be combined with other images or the Blender scene to create a new image. Unlike material and texture nodes, it is not necessary to have an object selected in the 3D window or to have a material applied to an object. Of course by default, any object added to a scene has the default material added to it even though this does not display in the properties window until the "New" button is pressed.

To demonstrate the activation of the "Compositing Node Editor," start with a new Blender scene and delete the default cube. Add a "Monkey" object and deselect the object in the 3D window. Change the 3D window to "Node Editor" and select the "Compositing" mode in the window header. Tick "Use Nodes" and two nodes will display in the window: "Render Layers" and "Composite" (Figure 19.27). Render an image (F12) to create a picture of the camera view with the monkey (Figure 19.27 inset). Remember that the "Monkey" is not selected in the 3D window and no material has been applied. Through the "Render Layer" and "Composite" nodes, Blender is rendering an image of the camera view in the scene. Rendering places the image of the camera view into the "Render Layers" node (Figure 19.28). Note that for Blender to render an image, there must be a "Compositing" node in the "Node Editor." The following are two examples of simple "Compositing" node arrangements.

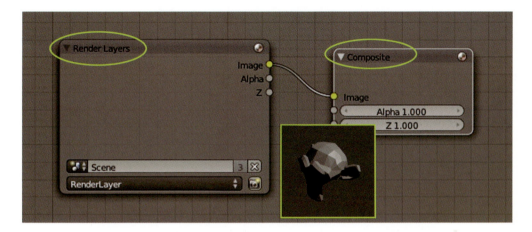

Figure 19.27

Figure 19.28

19.4.1 Example 1

When activating "Composite" nodes as previously described, the 3D camera view is introduced to the "Render Layers" node and the "Composite" node. Click on "Add" in the node editor window header and select "Input"—"Image" node and then a "Color–Mix" node. Connect the nodes as shown in Figure 19.29. In the "Image" node, click on "Open" to open the file browser then navigate to an image stored on your hard drive. Select the image then click on "Open Image."

With the nodes linked, the 3D camera view and the new image are combined. Adjust the values in the "Mix" and "Composite" nodes as shown in Figure 19.29. Press F12 to render the combined image.

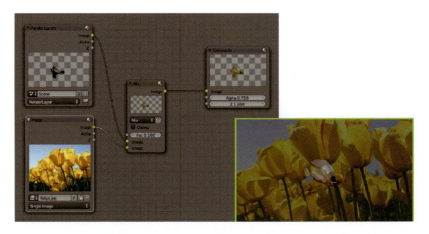

Figure 19.29

> Note: The combined image does not display in the 3D window in "Rendered Viewport Shading" mode.

19.4.2 Example 2

By entering an "Image" node, a "Color Balance" node, and a "Composite" node, the color of a rendered image can be adjusted to produce a variety of effects. Figure 19.30 shows an

Figure 19.30

Adjust slider positions and pick colors to vary the effect

example. The effects are limitless (Figure 19.31), as you will discover by experimenting with combinations of values in the color balance and composite nodes.

19.5 Node Groups

The foregoing are very simple examples of node arrangements. It is obvious that with more nodes added the arrangement would take considerable space in the window. To save space, several nodes may be grouped together into a single panel. The group panel may be expanded and collapsed.

Figure 19.31

To demonstrate grouping, in the arrangement created in "Example 1," Section 19.2.3, select the "Mapping" node and the "Mix RGB" node. To select the nodes press the B key (Box select) and drag a rectangle around the nodes or shift select the nodes. Press Ctrl + the G key. The "Node editor" window changes displaying the components of the node group (Figure 19.32).

Note: You cannot include a "Render Layers" node in a group.

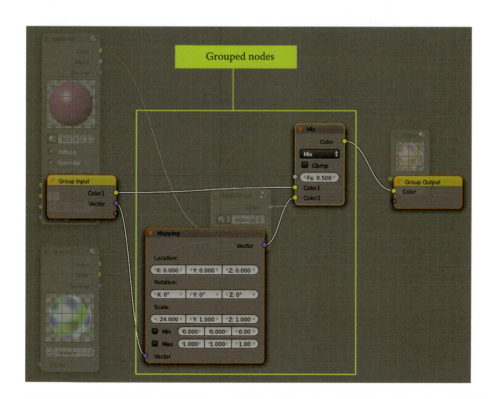

Figure 19.32

Press the "Tab" key to see the group minimized in the overall arrangement of the nodes (Figure 19.33). Selecting the group and pressing Alt + the G key ungroups the selection, and pressing "Tab" toggles between expanding and collapsing the group.

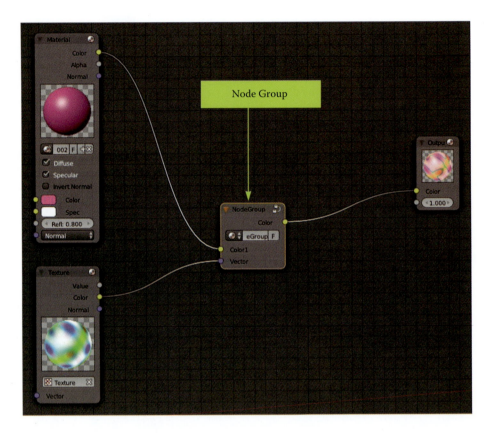

Figure 19.33

Grouping nodes provides a means of saving a particular node combination and thus the means of creating an effect and then appending this for use in other Blender files. In this way, you can build a library of node combinations for reuse. Once a node group is created, you can select it and then add, remove, link and unlink, and move nodes around within the group—in other words, you can edit the group. When you have finished editing a group, press Tab to collapse it and the A key to deselect it. You can now add more nodes to the screen.

19.5.1 Naming Node Groups

You may wish to change the names of the node groups to something more meaningful, which you can do in the "Outliner" window. Blender's default scene opens with an "Outliner" window in the upper RHS of the screen, but this is an abridged version of the full window. Divide one of your larger windows in two and change one part to the "Outliner" window—it should display in "All Scenes" mode. Change this to "Datablock" mode. Data blocks mode shows entries for everything in your scene. Scroll down and

find "Node Groups," if you have just created a node group, you will find it as a subentry (Figure 19.7). Expand the subentry and change the name of the group in the "Name" panel. A name change here will be reflected in the node editor window.

19.6 Saving and Appending Node Groups

When a "Node Group" is created in Blender it is retained when the file is saved and by default is simply named "Group." You may rename the group to something meaningful. Creating a "Node Group" also creates a folder in the Blender file which is named "Node Tree." The group is saved into this folder. The node group is therefore available to be imported or appended to another Blender file and applied to an object.

Note: If the "Group" is "Imported" and it's properties are altered then the properties of the original group are also altered. By "Appending" the group properties may be altered without affecting the original group.

To "Append" a node group click on "File" in the "Info" window header and select "Append." This opens a file browser where you navigate and select your group. Find the .blend file which contains the node group and search for the folder named "Node Tree." Click on the node group name in this folder then click "Append from Library" in the upper RH corner of the "File Browser" window.

When you perform the "Append" operation you may or may not have an object selected in your scene. Appending does not automatically apply the "Node Group" to a selected object.

To apply the "Node Group" to an object have the object selected in the 3D window then in the "Node Editor" window header click "Add"—"Group"—"Group Name" (Figure 19.34). The properties of the "Node Group" are applied to the selected object. When the "Node Group" is entered in the "Node editor" window it is minimized. Press

Click Add—Group—select "Node Group"

Figure 19.34

Tab to expand and reveal the contents of the node. The contents are revealed in a transparent window overlaid on the "Node Editor" window (Figure 19.35).

Node Group expanded—Overlaid on the Node Editor Window

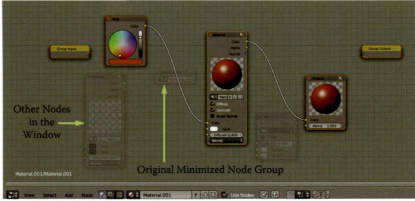

Other Nodes in the Window

Original Minimized Node Group

To expand the Node Group select the minimized version and press Tab

Figure 19.35

Note: Be aware that a "Node Group" created when "Cycles Render" is employed will not work with the "Blender Internal" render engine and vice versa. This is the case unless the group has been specifically designed to work in both engines.

19.7 Summary

This introduction to Nodes has looked at the tip of the iceberg. The combination of nodes is endless. With trial and error you will become familiar with the system and build up a library to suit your needs. With the introduction of the "Cycles Render Engine" comes a whole new selection of nodes with even more variation.

20

Cycles Render

In the previous discussion on rendering and render settings (Chapter 8) we limited the subject to the use of the Blender internal render engine. There are external render engines that can be used to render Blender files but Blender incorporates "Cycles Render."

The "Cycles Render" engine is a ray tracing-based engine with support for interactive rendering. It incorporates a shading node system, a different material and texture workflow and it utilizes GPU (graphics processing unit) acceleration.

To simplify this definition of "Cycles," consider it as a rendering process that allows you to see the render as you manipulate and edit the scene in the 3D window.

There are fantastic video tutorials on the Internet describing how to drive "Cycles" but before you can drive you have to know how to start the engine, the "Blender Cycles Render Engine."

20.1 PC Specifications for Cycles

Before attempting to use "Cycles," be aware that you will require a reasonable computer processor and possibly a graphics card which meets the specifications to handle this advanced process (refer to the Blender Wiki—Hardware Requirements).

The minimum requirements are the following:

- Processor: 1 GHz, single core
- Memory: 512 MB RAM
- Graphics Card: Open GL with 64 MB video RAM
- Display: 1024 × 768 px, 16-bit color
- Input: Two-button mouse

The recommended requirements are:

- Processor: 2 GHz, dual core
- Memory: 2 GB RAM
- Graphics card: Open GL with 256 or 512 MB video RAM and CUDA
- Display: 1920 × 1200 px, 24-bit color
- Input: Two-button mouse

The production standard requirements are:

- Processor: 2 GHz, multi-core (64-bit)
- Memory: 8–16 GB RAM
- Graphics card: Open GL with 1 GB video RAM, ATI FireGL or NVIDIA Quadro
- Display: 1920 × 1200 px, 24-bit color
- Input: Two-button mouse and graphics tablet

In essence, to fully utilize "Cycles" you need a fast processor, heaps of memory (RAM), and a graphics card with Open GL (graphics card with built-in memory and CUDA [Computer Unified Device Architecture] enabled).

Note: Cycles rendering is activated from the main Blender interface but CUDA and GPU acceleration require a secondary activation similar to an Add-on.

If you are new to Blender these terminologies and specifications may be slightly on the technical side but just be aware that, to utilize the full effects of "Cycles" your computer has to meet the requirements. The following will show you how to activate "Cycles" and discover if your system is up to speed.

20.2 Start Cycles

Start by setting up a scene in the 3D window as shown in the diagram (Figure 20.1). This will give us something to work with.

In the "Info" window header click on the drop down selection button next to "Blender Render" (Figure 20.2—"Blender Render" indicates that Blender's internal render engine is selected and an image of the 3D window can be rendered by pressing F12 on the keyboard). From the drop down select "Cycles Render." You will note that some of the

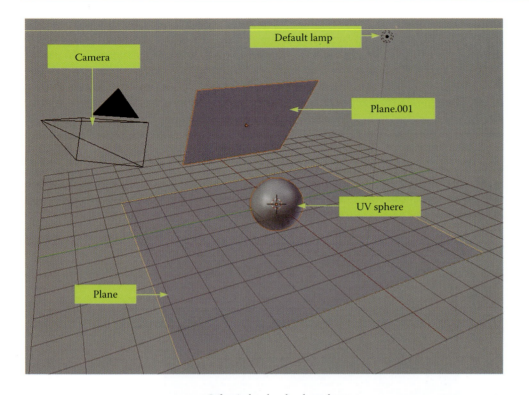

Figure 20.1

Info window header drop-down

Viewport Shading

Figure 20.2

options in the "Properties" window change. Leave all the settings just as they are for this demonstration.

In the 3D window header set the "Viewport Shading" to "Rendered" (Figure 20.2). The 3D window will change showing the objects with a gray background which appears as if you had rendered an image. This is exactly what has taken place. If you rotate the scene in the 3D window you will see the objects being re-rendered as you rotate. Unless you have a reasonably fast processor the render will be very blocky and grainy and can take a considerable time.

Cycles rendering is a continuous process that re-renders at each change in the 3D window scene. The longer you wait the clearer the render becomes, up to a point. You wouldn't want your computer stuck in an infinite rendering loop so Blender incorporates

a time-out setting to limit the render. When the scene is changed, for example, rotated, the "Cycles Render" is activated. At the top of the 3D window you will see a progress display giving the elapsed time and the number of render passes. The default is 10 passes. In the "Properties" window, "Render" buttons, "Sampling" tab see "Samples: Render 10—Preview 10." These are the default settings for the render. They can be increased to produce a better render, bearing in mind that an increase in passes incurs an increase in time. On my old machine, with the **default Blender scene** containing the single "Cube" object the elapsed time for 10 passes is 0.50.94 s. With the scene as shown in the diagram the time is 01.27.96 which demonstrates that the content of the scene significantly affects the render time.

The 3D window view is very dark (Figure 20.3) since the default lamp provides only a limited illumination. Additional lamps will improve the illumination but in Cycles you can use objects as a light source. More on that later.

Figure 20.3

What to expect from cycles will depend on your computer and operating system, your display adapter (graphics card), and the drivers (software) that have been installed for the card.

Before proceeding it would help to understand some terms.

- **NVIDIA graphics:** NIVIDIA is one of many suppliers of graphics chipsets used in graphics cards. At the time of writing Blender is configured to use NVIDIA with Open GL and CUDA enabled for GPU rendering.
- **Open GL** is a set of graphics standards used worldwide that is designed to give maximum performance on the GPU.
- **GPU** is the processing device built into the graphics card that performs computations in parallel with the computers central processing unit (CPU).
- **CUDA**™ is a parallel computing platform and programming model that enables dramatic increase in computing performance by harnessing the power of the GPU.

In summary, the GPU performs computations in conjunction with the CPU, which significantly speeds up the changing graphics display that is required for "**On the Fly**" graphics rendering. BUT! Whether the GPU is faster than the CPU depends on your computer configuration. It could be your CPU is faster for some aspects of the process.

Another factor in this technicality is the "Compute Capability" rating of your graphics card. Cards are rated through a range something like 1.1–3.0. At the time of writing Blender only supports graphics cards rated at 1.3 and above for GPU processing (rendering), so again, unless your system meets the requirements you will not realize the full capability of "Cycles."

OK! We have turned on "Cycles" and have a display in the screen but at this point the CUDA architecture and GPU processor are not activated. As previously stated CUDA and GPU require a secondary activation.

Also be aware that what you see in the Blender controls will depend on your system configuration. Blender takes a look at your system and displays controls accordingly.

In the "Info" winder header click on "File" and open the "User Preferences" window. Select "System" from the options at the top of the window. At the lower LHS of the window see "Computer Device" (Figure 20.4).

If you do not have a NVIDIA graphics chipset or your drivers for the card are outdated then you will see the display as shown above (Figure 20.5). CPU will be the only option in the selection panel. This means that Blender only recognizes the CPU and, therefore, the "Cycles" rendering process will be performed entirely by the CPU.

Figure 20.4

Provided you do have the correct graphics chipset and you update the drivers for your card, the display will be in Figure 20.6.

With the option "CUDA" displayed click on it to activate CUDA and the display will change showing the name of your

Figure 20.5

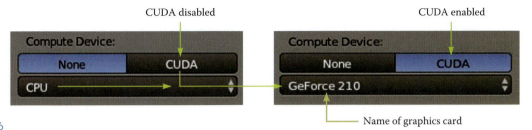

CUDA disabled   CUDA enabled

Name of graphics card

Figure 20.6

graphics card. At this stage, even if your graphics card has CUDA enabled it still may not be capable of GPU rendering.

GPU rendering is faster but "Cycles" can be demonstrated without it.

Go to the "Properties" window, "Render" buttons, "Render" tab, and click on the "Device" selection drop down (Figure 20.7) which shows CPU. In the selection drop down select "GPU Compute." If your graphics card is OK it will be accepted if not an error message displays at the top of the 3D window, which states that "CUDA device supported only with compute capability 1.3 or up, found 1.2." The 1.2 is the rating of my NVIDIA GeForce 210 card.

Figure 20.7

Graphics cards have a "Compute Capability" rating and Blender only accepts ratings above 1.3. The "**found 1.2**" or similar is the rating of your card. If your card is not accepted change the setting back to CPU and continue. If your card is accepted all well and good.

Let's continue.

Select the plane (Plane.001) object as shown in the diagram by RMB click. There is no orange outline to indicate that this plane is selected, however, you will see "Plane.001" in white lettering in the "Outliner" window (Figure 20.8).

Go to "Properties" window, "Material" buttons. Note, when the "New" button is pressed the materials buttons have changed from what they were with the default Blender internal render (Figure 20.9).

Cycles uses a different system.

In the "Surface" tab click on the "Color" bar and in the color picker that displays, select a bright yellow color. In the "Roughness" bar change the value to 1.000. In "Surface" bar where you see "Diffuse BSDF" click and select "Emission" (Figure 20.10). This changes the plane into a light source.

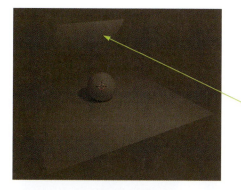

Figure 20.8

Click and change Diffuse BSDF to Emission

Figure 20.9

Figure 20.10

The Plane is acting as a light emitter illuminating the scene

Figure 20.11

Each time you manipulate something in the 3D window "Cycles" commences to re-render the scene. How long this takes and how effective this is will depend on the speed of your processor.

Figure 20.11 shows the 3D window in "Rendered Viewport Shading" mode with "Cycles Render" activated. The computer being used has limited memory, a slow processor, and no memory on the graphics card.

Besides employing the controls in the "Properties" window, "Cycles Rendering" is also used in conjunction with the Blender "Node Editing" system as discussed in Chapter 19. To demonstrate this, place the **default 3D window** in "Cycles Render" mode with "Viewport Shading—Rendered." Change the "Timeline" window to the "Node Editor" window. Click on the "Material" button in the "Properties" window. At this point you have the gray cube in the 3D window and nothing in the "Node editor" window.

In the "Properties" window, "Surface" tab click on "Use Nodes" (Figure 20.12). Zoom in on the "Node Editor" window to see the nodes that have displayed.

Figure 20.12

Note: We are working with the "Materials" buttons in the "Properties" window, therefore, the "Material Node" button in the "Node Editor" window is active (Figure 20.13). Clicking "Use Nodes" in the "Properties" window, "Materials" buttons, "Surface" tab is the same as checking (ticking) the "Use Nodes" button in the "Node Editor" window header.

Note: When changing to "Cycles Render" with the default cube in the default scene the "Properties" window, "Material" buttons, "Tabs" are displayed and you click "Use Nodes" to show the default material nodes in the "Node editor" window. Alternatively, you can check the "Use Nodes" button in the "Node editor" window header. When you add a new object to a scene the "Properties" window, "Material" buttons only show the "New" button. Click "New" to open the tabs. "Use Nodes" is automatically activated and nodes are displayed in the "Node editor" window. The default nodes are "Diffuse BSDF" and "Material Output."

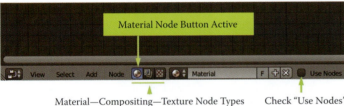

Material Node Button Active

View   Select   Add   Node   Material   F   Use Nodes

Material—Compositing—Texture Node Types   Check "Use Nodes"

Figure 20.13

The "Diffuse BSDF" node is a replica of the "Surface" tab in the "Properties" window and note, this node is linked to the "Surface" input on the "Material Output" node. In other words, the diffuse color is being mapped to the surface of the selected cube object. Clicking on the color bar in the "Diffuse BSDF" node displays a color picker where a new color may be selected, the same as in the "Properties" window (Figure 20.14). This demonstrates that "Nodes Editing" and "Cycles Rendering" are used in conjunction with each other.

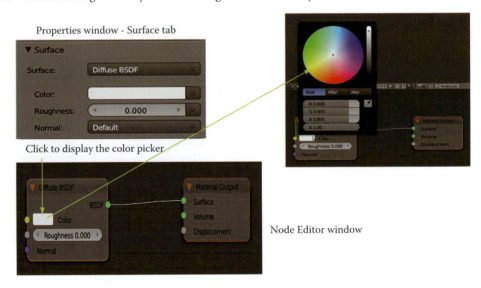

Properties window - Surface tab

Click to display the color picker

Node Editor window

Figure 20.14

20.3 Cycles in Perspective

To place "Cycles Render" in perspective and demonstrate its practical application work through the following demonstration which will show you how to create and illuminate a scene.

Set the scene: Arrange a sphere, a monkey, and a plane in a new Blender scene as shown (Figure 20.15). The sphere and the monkey have smooth shading applied and the plane has been extruded to give it thickness.

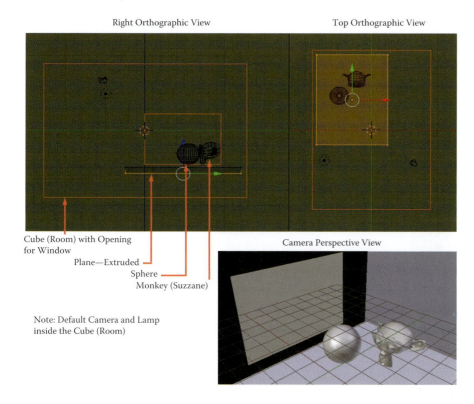

Right Orthographic View   Top Orthographic View

Cube (Room) with Opening
for Window

Plane—Extruded

Sphere

Monkey (Suzzane)

Camera Perspective View

Note: Default Camera and Lamp
inside the Cube (Room)

Figure 20.15

The scene will eventually show the objects inside a room. The room is simply a cube, scaled and positioned as shown with an opening in one side representing a window.

The camera and single spot lamp are inside the cube and the other objects are positioned to be in Camera View.

With the 3D window in "Solid Viewport Shading" mode all you see is the cube. To see objects inside the room change the 3D window to "Wireframe Viewport Shading."

At this stage the scene is illuminated by the default spot lamp, which is inside the room. Pressing F12 renders an image of the camera view in the diagram.

Arrange the screen: Divide the 3D window into three separate windows as shown in Figure 20.16.

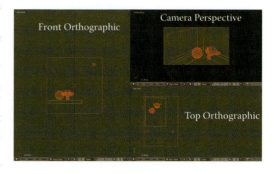

Figure 20.16

Figure 20.18

More set up stuff: Before adding anything further, select the cube and press the H key to hide it from view. You unhide it by pressing Alt + H key. Hiding the room allows you to work in "Solid Viewport Shading" mode.

Figure 20.17

In the "Info" window header change "Blender Render" to "Cycles Render" (Figure 20.17) and change the "Camera Perspective" view to "Rendered Viewport Shading" (Figure 20.18). This will allow us to see rendered results as we progress. If you have GPU rendering available and it is faster than CPU rendering it's time to turn it on. In either case go to the "Properties" window, "Render" buttons, "Sampling" tab, and change both the "Render" and "Preview" values to 50 (Figure 20.19). The default is 10 which doesn't allow a fantastic result.

> Note: At this stage rendering times should be fairly quick but as data is added to the scene it will slow down. It is not, therefore, advisable to have the render passes set too high when work is in progress.

Figure 20.19

Time to add material: Select the monkey in the 3D window. Note that monkey is named "Suzanne" as you can see in the lower LH corner of the 3D window and in the "Outliner" window.

In the "Properties" window, "Material" buttons, click on the "New" button. As previously explained the materials buttons for "Cycles Render" are completely different to "Blender Render" (Figure 20.20).

The default settings show "Surface: Diffuse BSDF," which is one of 19 material "Shader" types available (Figure 20.21). The "Color" (the white color bar/picker) is showing Blender's default gray, RGB 0.800. Click on the "Surface" button and select "Glass BSDF." This gives Suzanne a gray glass-like effect. You can change the color if you wish. The effects of the "Surface Shader" and color are immediately seen in the "Camera" view (Figure 20.22).

Remember the application of "Materials" using "Cycles Render"

Figure 20.20

Figure 20.21

is using the Blender "Nodes" system but instead of using the "Node Editor" window, buttons are provided in the "Cycles Material" buttons. You may use the buttons, the "Node Editor" window, or the "Node System."

Note: Adding, manipulating, and connecting nodes when using "Cycles Render" is the same as when using "Blender Render." The difference is that in "Cycles Render" there are more node options to choose.

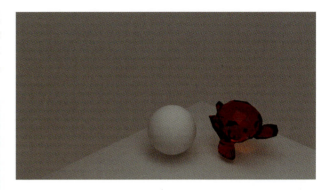

Figure 20.22

Note: Node Groups "Appended" which were created by using "Blender Render" will not work when using "Cycles Render" unless they are specifically designed to do so.

Deselect Suzanne and select the sphere. Add a material this time select a nice bright color and select the "Glossy BSDF Surface Shader." You can of course experiment with the colors and shaders to see the different effects.

Select the extruded plane. Add a material. This time we will combine two different shader options. Select the "Mix Shader" option in the "Surface" shader selection menu. You are presented with a "Surface" tab containing two separate shader selection buttons (Figure 20.23). The "Fac: (Factor)" slider allows you to adjust the proportion of how the two shaders are mixed. The default value is 0.500 means 50-50.

Figure 20.23

In the first shader selection choose "Diffuse BSDF" and the second choose "Glossy BSDF." The default color values in both are the gray color RGB 0.800. The difference is the first is a flat diffuse material and second is a glossy material. They are being mixed together in a ratio of 50:50.

We will now introduce a "Texture" into the mix. Click on the button at the end of the "Diffuse BSDF" color bar. Select "Image Texture" from the menu (Figure 20.24). The color changes to "Image Texture." Click on the "Open" button, which opens the "File Browser" window where you navigate to an image saved on your computer. Having selected an image click on the "Vector" button and select "Texture Coordinate—Generated" to map the image properly. Remember the

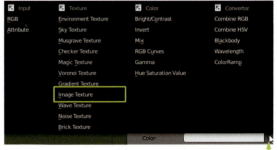

Click button to add texture

Figure 20.24

Figure 20.25

Click to display the selection menu ─────

Figure 20.26

Plane scaled and positioned out of Camera View

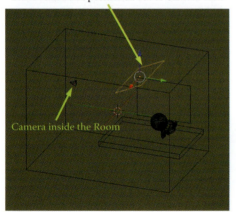

Camera inside the Room

Figure 20.27

image texture is being mixed with the "Glossy Diffuse BSDF" gray material. Adjust the "Fac: Value" to see the difference when the proportion of the mix is changed.

You will see in the "Rendered Viewport Shading," "Camera View" that we are slowly getting the picture (Figure 20.25).

Introduce sky lighting: Up to now we have been reliant on that default single point lamp for illumination. We will lighten the scene with "Sky Light."

In the "Properties" window, "World" buttons, "Surface" tab, click "Use Nodes." At the end of the "Color" bar, click on the button and select "Sky Texture" from the menu (Figure 20.26). Vola! We have blue sky in the background. In the "Color" bar you will see "Sky Texture." Click, hold, and drag the mouse on the "Sphere" (Sky Ball) to adjust shadow effect in the scene. You may also adjust the "Turbidity" value between 1.00 and 10.00 for a variation. The "Strength" value also changes the sky effect. Sky lighting has set the lighting for outdoors. It is time to go indoors.

Reinstate the room: Press Alt + H key to bring back the hidden cube (Room). The rendered scene reverts to being illuminated by the single point lamp which was positioned inside the room. With the top and side "Orthographic" windows in "Solid Display" mode all you see is the outside of the room. Change a view to "Wireframe" display mode to see what's inside. Select and delete the point lamp. The rendered window turns black; no light inside the room.

Add an object light: Instead of the point lamp we will introduce an object to act as a light source. Add a plane and position as shown in Figure 20.27. In the "Properties" window, "Material" buttons, click "New" to add a material. Select "Surface", "Shader" type, "Emission." This makes the plane a light source.

Place the "Camera" view in "Rendered" mode to see the inside of the room illuminated. Don't forget the light "Color" can be changed and the "Strength" value adjusted. The position and scale of the light source affect the rendered view. You may add more than one light source.

Note: A fair amount of data has been added to the scene therefore the render time will have increased.

Let in the light: For effect, add an "Image Texture" to the "World" background. With the outside light strength value in the "Properties" window, "World" buttons, "Surface" tab ramped up light will come streaming in (Figure 20.28).

20.4 Useful Cycles: Add Mist

To reinforce the concept of using the Blender "Node" system in conjunction with "Cycles Render," adding a mist effect is a useful example.

Mystifying: Adding a "Mist" effect to a scene is a way of enhancing an image or animation. I have titled this demonstration "Mystifying" because, without instruction, it is. In the previous demonstration of "Cycles Rendering" we touched on the fact that "Cycles" uses the Blender "Node" system for some application and that buttons for using "Nodes" are included in the "Properties" window. This is not always the case. Sometimes you have to use the "Node Editor" window in conjunction with "Cycles." Applying a "Mist" effect is one such example.

The process involves adding, manipulating, and connecting "Nodes," therefore a visit to Chapter 19 is essential before continuing.

Set up a scene: To demonstrate the "Mist" effect arrange a group of objects in "Camera" view such that some are close to the camera and others are progressively further away (Figure 20.29). Mist or fog usually appears denser in the distance. Arrange the objects on a ground plane and lower the camera closer to the ground. You may add material or texture to the plane and the objects if you wish and add different lamp types for effect. Turn "Cycles Render" on in the "Info" window header.

Add mist: Adding "Mist" in the first instance is somewhat similar to the procedure used when using Blenders internal render system. In the "Properties" window, "Render Layers" buttons, "Passes" tab check "Mist" (Figure 20.30).

Figure 20.28

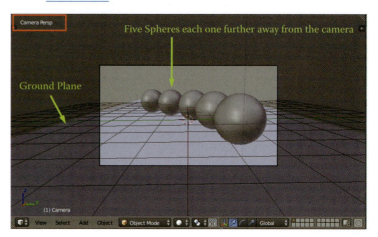

Figure 20.29

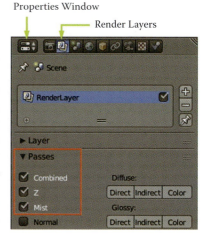

Figure 20.30

Properties Window

World

Figure 20.31

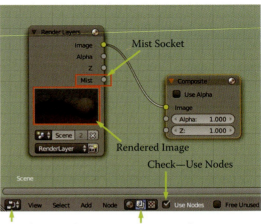

Mist Socket

Rendered Image

Check—Use Nodes

Node Editor Window   Compositing Nodes

Figure 20.32

With "Mist" checked you will find that a "Mist Pass" tab has been added to "World" buttons (Figure 20.31). The tab contains two value sliders. "Start" is the distance in Blender units in front of the camera where the mist begins. "Depth" is the distance beyond the start point where the mist effect is at its maximum density.

At this point you will be disappointed to find that there is no mist in the 3D window when viewed in "Rendered Viewport Shading" mode. Render an image by clicking on "Render" in the "Properties" window, "Render" buttons or by pressing F12. Still no mist!

Node editor: This is where the "Node editor" window comes into play. Open the "Node editor" window. In the window header activate "Compositing" nodes and check the "Use Nodes" button. You will see two nodes: "Render Layers" and "Compositing" (Figure 20.32). In the "render Layers" node note the gray "Mist" socket. This will not be there unless you have checked "Mist" as previously instructed. Note also that the node shows a small replication of your rendered image. This is not displayed unless you have rendered an image.

We are about to use the "Compositing" node system to introduce "Mist" to the rendered image.

Add a "Color"—"Mix" node to the editor and connect as shown (Figure 20.33). Render an image to see the mist. You may click on the lower "Image" color socket in the "Mix" node

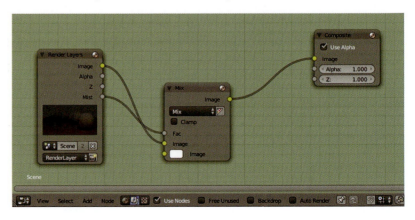

Figure 20.33

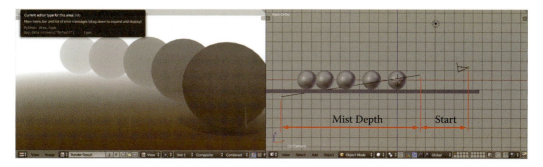

Mist Pass—Start 5.00—Depth 14.40

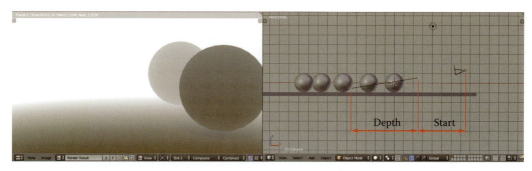

Mist Pass—Start 5.00—Depth 7.20

Figure 20.34

to add color to the mist. Adjust the "Start" and "Depth" values in the "Properties" window, "World" buttons, "Mist Pass" tab (Figure 20.34).

To introduce some further mist effect controls add a "Vector"—"Map Value" node (Figure 20.35). Adjusting the "Offset" and "Size" values varies the mist effect. The "Use Minimum and Maximum" values set limits for the adjustment.

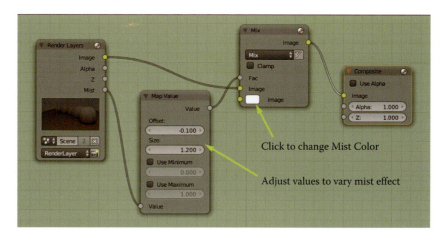

Figure 20.35

20.5 Adding Texture in Cycles

So far, in this chapter, "Material Nodes" and "Compositing Nodes" have been used with "Cycles." Texture has been breezed over except for sneaking in the example of mixing a material with an image texture (20.3 Cycles in Perspective—Time to add a Material). This example used "Material Nodes" and this in fact is where to start.

To demonstrate open a new Blender scene, delete the default cube and add a "UV Sphere" and set "Shading" to smooth in the "Tools Panel." Remember that a new object added to a scene does not have a material applied. Change from "Blender Render" to "Cycles Render." Arrange your screen as shown in Figure 20.36. In the "Properties" window, "Material" buttons, click "New" to add a material and display the material buttons. As we have discovered the buttons in "Cycles" are different than those in "Blender Render." In the "Surface" tab click "Use Nodes."

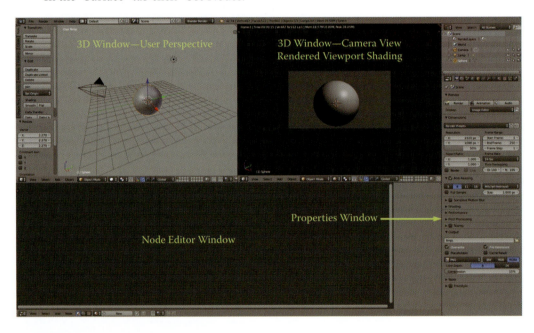

Figure 20.36

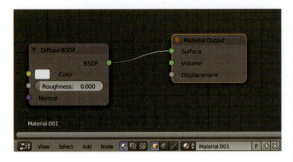

Figure 20.37

At this point we have the default gray (RGB 0.800) material applied to the sphere. You may click on the "Color" bar in the "Material" buttons, "Surface" tab, and select a different color but we will be applying a texture and the texture color will supersede the material. To apply a texture with "Blender Render" active you would go to the "Properties" window, "Texture" buttons but in "Cycles" we stick to the "Material" buttons. You will see in the "Node Editor" window that a "Diffuse BSDF" and a "Material Output" node have been installed and that they are connected (Figure 20.37).

In the "Material" buttons, "Surface" tab, click on the little button at the end of the "Color" bar. The menu that displays has a selection of options which are "Nodes." Click on the "Image Texture" entry (Figure 20.38). The color bar will show "Image Texture" and underneath is the "Open" button which you click to open a file browser, navigate in your system, and select an image for your texture (Figure 20.39). Note that as soon as you select the "Image Texture" option an "Image Texture" node is installed in the "Node Editor" window connected to the "Diffuse BSDF" node (Figure 20.40).

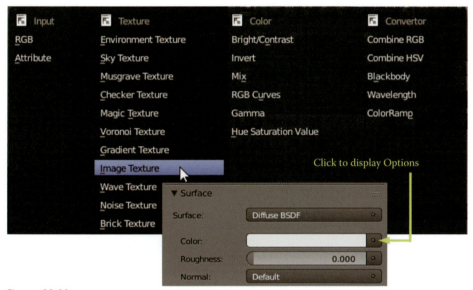

Figure 20.38

OK. Select an image. You will see the name of your image in the "Surface" tab of the "Material" buttons and in the "Image Texture" node in the "Node editor" window. You **do not** see the image displayed as a texture in the 3D window rendered camera view.

Figure 20.39

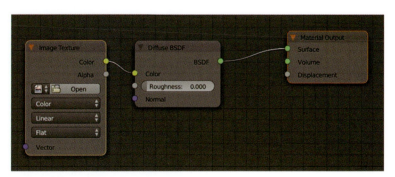

Figure 20.40

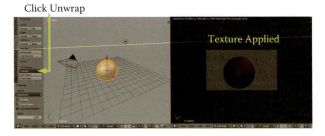

Click Unwrap

Texture Applied

Figure 20.41

To apply (Map) the texture to the sphere, the sphere has to have "UV Unwrapping" applied (Chapter 5). With the sphere selected in the 3D window, Tab to "Edit" mode and in the "Tool Panel," "Shading/ UV" tab, "UVs" tab click "Unwrap" and select "Unwrap" from the options that display. You may select any of the options but for simplicity select "Unwrap." The texture is applied to the sphere and shows in rendered camera view (Figure 20.41).

To adjust how the texture is mapped to the sphere go to the "Properties" window, "Texture" buttons, "Node" tab, and try the different "Vector" mapping methods. Try the "Generated" method. In the "Mapping" tab experiment with the mapping options and slider values to see the effects (Figure 20.42).

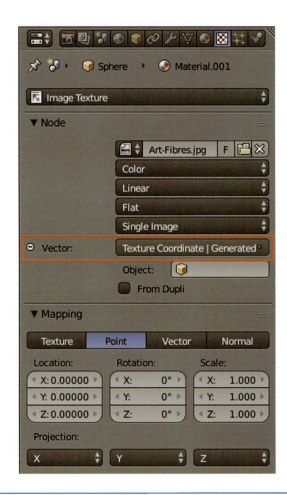

Figure 20.42

21

The Blender Game Engine

21.1 Introduction to the Game Engine

Blender includes the tools to create interactive video games. The program integrates real-time motion with physics and logic blocks, allowing you to turn objects into actors and move them around. This process also incorporates character animation and interactive walk throughs where doors open and close. The game engine is extensive in its application and it is not possible to cover all of its intricacies in this manual. This chapter, as the title states, is an introduction, which will allow you to research and experiment and become proficient. We will begin with a very basic example where an object is designated as an "Actor" and provided with controls to move it in the scene.

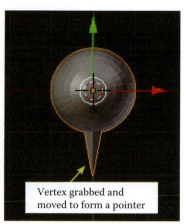

Vertex grabbed and moved to form a pointer

- **Introduce the Actor:** Start with the default Blender scene, delete the cube, and add a UV sphere. Gaming is a form of animation, therefore, as with all animation, it is best to keep animated objects with a low vertex count. To keep things simple, the default UV sphere will suffice. In the 3D window, tab into edit mode with the sphere selected and grab one single vertex on the side and make a pointer, as shown in Figure 21.1. This will provide an indicator showing in which direction you are pointing when moving. The sphere with the pointer will be our actor.

Figure 21.1

Figure 21.2

- **Set the Scene:** Go to the "Info" window header and change the screen arrangement from the "Default" screen to the "Game Logic" screen and change "Blender Render" to "Blender Game" (Figure 21.2). The screen is configured for setting up the game engine with the windows displayed as shown in Figure 21.3
- **Activate the Actor:** With the sphere selected in the 3D window, go to the "Properties" window, "Physics" button and in the "Physics" tab change the "Physics Type" to "Dynamic." Make sure the "Actor" box is checked.

Note: Ticking the "Actor" box assigns the sphere as an actor. If it is not ticked, tick it.

To check if the sphere is behaving itself and is going to cooperate as an actor in this game, set the 3D window to "Front Orthographic" view (Num Pad 1) and with the mouse cursor in the 3D window press the P key. Alternatively in the "Properties" window, "Render" buttons, "Embedded Player" tab click "Start." Either method puts the 3D window into play mode. In "Front Orthographic" view the sphere will descend in the window and disappear out of sight. Press Esc to return the sphere to center stage in the window. You have just proved that the sphere actor is behaving itself; gravity has taken hold of the sphere and caused it to fall. Since there is nothing below the sphere to obstruct its motion,

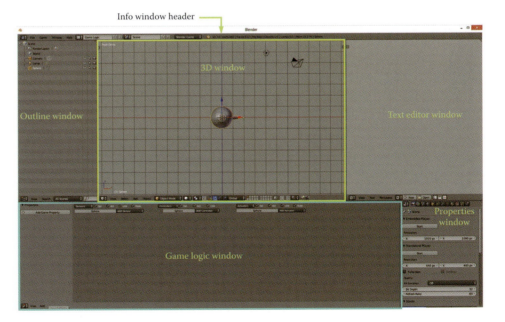

Figure 21.3

it falls to infinity. We had better do something to correct this.

- **Add an obstruction:** Put the 3D window into "Top Orthographic" view and add a plane to the scene. Scale the plane up, go to "User Perspective" view, and move the sphere up above the plane (Figure 21.4). To move to user perspective view press number pad 0 then number pad 5 twice. Press the P key to play and see the sphere descend and sit on the plane (Figure 21.5) then press Esc to go back to "Object" mode. It is time to tell Blender when and how we want our actor to move.

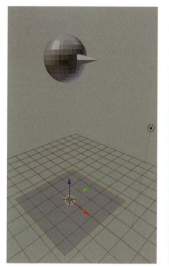

Figure 21.4

Figure 21.5

- **Add movement controls:** With the "Actor" (sphere) selected in the 3D window the "Logic Editor" window at the bottom of the screen will display three logic block selection menus: "Sensors," "Controllers," and "Actuators" (Figure 21.6).
- **The Sensor:** The "Sensor" is the device that triggers an action. Click on the "Add Sensor" drop down menu to see the options. In this case we will use the mouse to signal an action, therefore, select "Mouse" (Figure 21.6). We also have to state which part of the mouse is to be used. In the panel that has displayed, where it

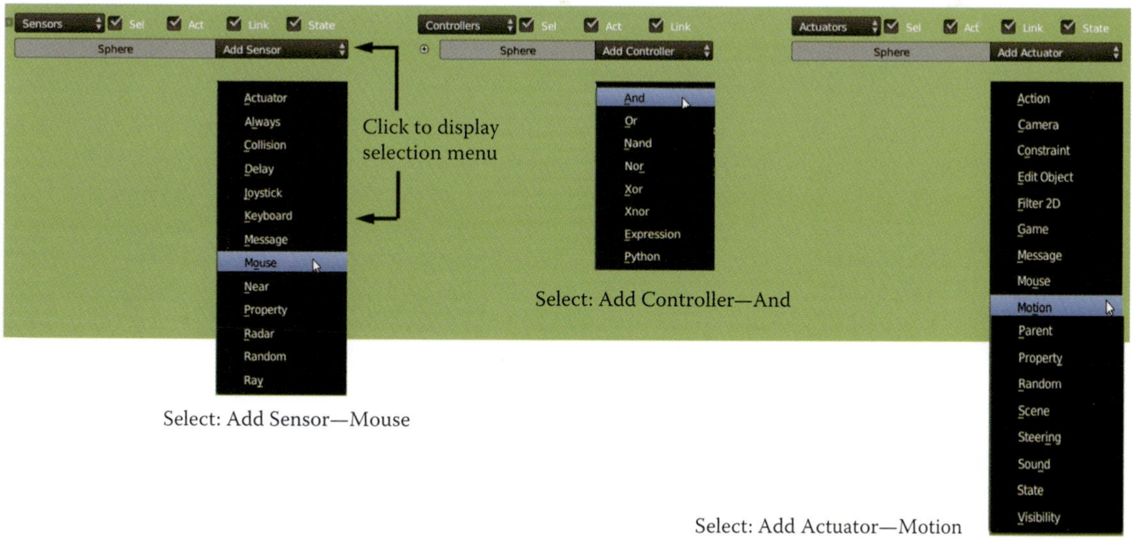

Select: Add Sensor—Mouse

Select: Add Controller—And

Select: Add Actuator—Motion

Figure 21.6

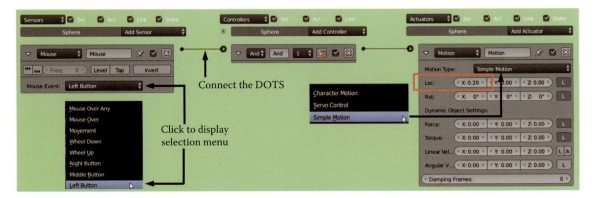

Figure 21.7

says "Mouse Event," click on the selection menu button and select "Left Button" (Figure 21.7).

- **The Controller:** The "Controller" will relay the signal from the "Sensor" to the "Actuator." There are several options for doing this which at this stage will have no meaning whatsoever. In the case in hand click on "Add Controller" and select the option named "And."
- **The Actuator:** The "Actuator" tells the actor what to do and how to do it, so click on "Add Actuator" to see the options. We are about to make our actor move in the scene, therefore, in this case select "Motion" (Figure 21.6). Note that the "Motion Type" is "Simple Motion." There are two alternatives as you can see by clicking on the "Motion Type" button (Figure 21.7).

Note: If, at this point, you only see the three lines: Motion Typ, Loc:, and Rot: in the "Actuator" you have forgotten to set your actor as "Dynamic" in the "Physics" buttons.

Finally, we have to say in what direction and how fast we want the actor to go. Immediately below "Motion Type" you will see "Loc" and "Rot" (Location and Rotation) (Figure 21.7). Adjacent to these entries are three panels for entering values for the X-, Y-, and Z-axis in the 3D window. We will have our actor move in one direction only so in the "Loc" X-axis panel (the first panel adjacent to Loc:) enter 0.200. Note 0.200 is a movement in the positive direction on the X-axis, −0.200 would be in the opposite direction. At each click of the LMB the "Actor" moves 0.200 units. Holding the LMB causes the computer to send repeated signals that produces a continuous movement.

- **Making connections:** Finally! (Yes I know I already said that) but we have to "**Connect the DOTS.**" Click on the small dot next to the "Mouse" sensor panel, hold and drag across to the big dot at the side of the "And" controller panel. Do the same between the "Controller" and the "Actuator" (Figure 21.7).

  We are good to go.

- **Test drive the game:** Time for a test run. Put your mouse cursor in the 3D window and press the P key. The sphere descends and sits on the plane. Give your LMB a click and you will see the sphere move. It may not be in the direction of the pointy bit on the sphere, but that can be adjusted. If you hold the LMB down, the sphere will continue moving, fall off the side of the plane, and disappear into infinity. That's it! Press "Esc" to end the game.

- **Adding more controls:** That was one small step for a gamer, now it's time to add a few more controls. Adding controls (or logic blocks) soon fills up the logic editor window; to save space you can click on the little triangles at the upper LHS of the panels and collapse them. Click again to expand. Add more sensors, controllers, and actuators, as shown in Figure 21.8, paying particular attention to the values in the motion actuators. There are location and rotation values. Do not forget to connect them together.

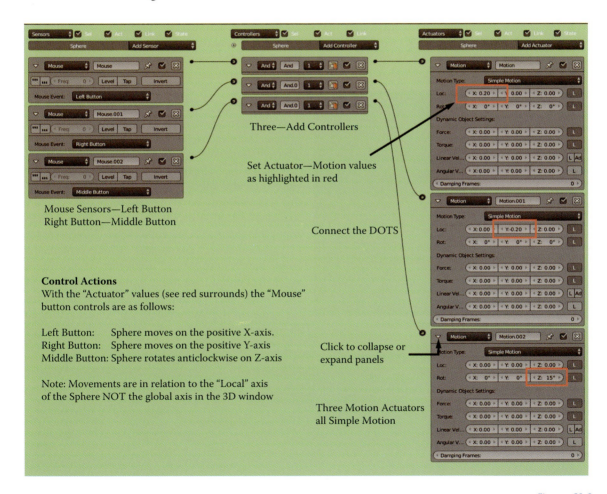

Figure 21.8

With the controls set as shown in Figure 21.8, you can drive the actor around the plane (Figure 21.9). Play with the mouse buttons (MMBs) and you will soon get the hang of it. Note that the sphere only rotates in one direction, but you can add another set of controls to rotate it in the opposite direction. Maybe change the mouse sensor to keyboard and use the A and S keys for rotation. You could also change all the sensor controls to keyboard and use a pattern of keys. This is about as simple as it gets, so it's time to research and experiment further.

- **Adding to the game:** Driving the pointy-nosed sphere around on the surface of the plane is all very well but we can make this more interesting by introducing a second object that is animated to move as we play. The following will give you one idea.

In the 3D window add a "Cube" object and give it a bright "Material Color." Position the cube on the surface of the plane. In the "Properties" window, "Physics" buttons just leave the default "Static" "Physics Type."

For the time being change the "Logic Editor" window to the "Timeline" window. Select the cube in the 3D window and move it to one corner of the plane. Set up a simple animation to have the cube move across the surface diagonal to the opposite corner in say 200 frames (slow movement).

Figure 21.9

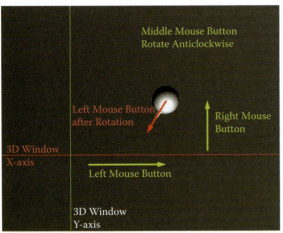

Mouse Button Movement Control

The objective is to have the cube move according to the animation when we play the game of driving the sphere. The objective is being to avoid the cube or to intercept as the case may be.

Change the "Timeline" back to the "Logic Editor." Have the cube selected in the 3D window. In doing this you will only have the "Sensor, Controller, and Actuator" selection panels displaying. These are now applicable to the selected cube. Add a "Mouse sensor," a "And Controller," and, hold it, a "Action Actuator." Leave the "Mouse sensor" with the "Mouse Event" as "Left Button." We want some action from the cube when we press the LMB when we are playing the game. In the "Action Actuator" insert settings as shown in Figure 21.10.

Figure 21.10

With everything in place (don't forget to connect the DOTS) we can play the game. In "Game Play" mode, as soon as we click LMB the sphere will move and at the same time the cube will commence moving across to the opposite corner of the plane. Keep out of it's way or chase it as you will.

21.2 Reinforcing Fundamentals

There hasn't been any shoot em up whiz bang action which you would expect from a computer game. To produce something like that there is a way to go, so to keep your interest we will look at some examples of actions that can be set up in the Game Engine. Having said that there are a few fundamentals that need to be reinforced.

- **Setting the scene in the game engine:** A scene is created in the 3D window. In the previous example, the Blender default screen arrangement was changed to the "Game Logic" screen arrangement.

  You may use this arrangement but it is not necessary that you do so. To gain space on the screen I would suggest the minimal requirement is a screen arrangement containing the 3D window, the "Properties" window, and the "Logic Editor" window. The "Info" window header will remain at the top of the screen and you must change from "Blender Render" to "Blender Game."

  Objects or models are entered into the scene as you would in the default screen arrangement and materials, textures, modifiers, etc., are added per normal. In the Blender Game Engine all objects in the scene must have "Physics" applied. Changing from "Blender Render" to "Blender Game" introduces "Game Physics" in the "Properties" window. In the "Physics" tab note "Physics Type:." "Static" is the default physics type but there are seven alternatives available in the drop down menu (Figure 21.11). For the time being only be concerned with the "Dynamic" option. We will only have objects that move about (dynamic) or objects that do not move about (static).

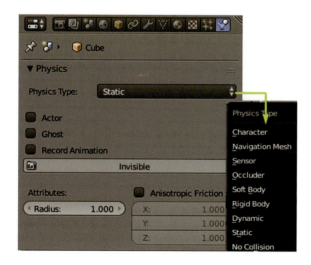

Figure 21.11

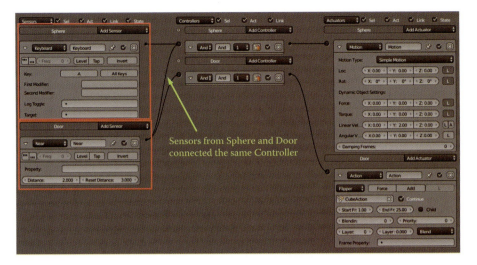

Sensors from Sphere and Door
connected the same Controller

Figure 21.12

- **Logic blocks:** With an object selected in the 3D window we have seen that "Logic Blocks" are entered in the "Logic Editor" window and these blocks are related to the selected object in the 3D window. With more than one object selected (shift select) logic blocks display for all object and are grouped by name (Figure 21.12). Be aware that when linking "Sensors," "Controllers," and "Actuators" you can link from one group to another thus, for example, a "Keyboard" command can send a signal to more than one object's "Actuator."
- **Physics:** Physics in the "Game Engine (Blender Game)" is different to that employed in Blender render. The Physic Types available are listed here with a brief description of their function.

  No collision: Is not affected by the simulation nor affects other objects.

  Static: Participates in the simulation, affecting other objects, but is not affected by it.

  Dynamic: Object that can move besides colliding and being collided with.

  Rigid body: Has rigid-body dynamics which simulates real-world action.

  Soft body: Soft-body dynamics. Simulates cloth, fabric.

  Character controller: Character controller.

  Vehicle controller: Vehicle controller.

  Occluder: Prevents calculation of rendered objects (not their physics, though!).

  Sensor: Detects presence without restitution collisions.

  Navigation mesh: To make pathfinding paths. Useful for Artificial Intelligence.
- **Bounding volume:** Objects (models) in the game engine interact with other objects. In Blender Game physics each object has a "Bounding Volume" which is a volume of space applied to the object, used to calculate its physical contact limits with other objects. This is different to the physical surface volume of the object. To demonstrate we will use the default cube object in the default 3D window.

  Add a plane object to the scene, extrude it slightly on the Z-axis and position as shown in Figure 21.13 the cube.

Have the 3D window in "Blender Game" render mode and apply "Dynamic" physics to the cube and "Static" physics to the plane.

Change to "Wireframe Viewport Shading" mode. Place the 3D Window in "Front Orthographic" view (Num pad 1 Num pad 5). Zoom to get a good view of the cube. Select the cube and rotate 45° (Figure 21.14).

You will see that a dotted circle is displayed inside the cube (Figure 21.14). This is a spherical representation of a "Bounding Volume" which is the outer limit that Blender uses for calculating the contact of the cube with other objects in the scene. Remember the cube has "Physics Type: Dynamic" applied. By rotating the 3D window you will observe that the circle always displays as a circle, which is indicative that it is in fact the periphery of a sphere: "Spherical Bounding Volume."

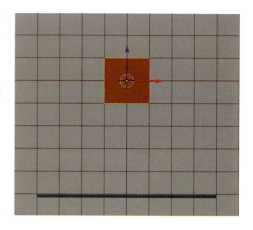

Figure 21.13

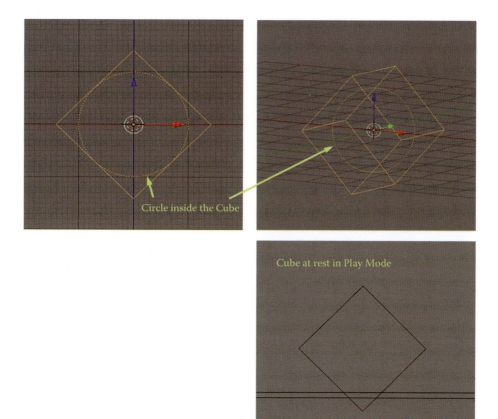

Circle inside the Cube

Cube at rest in Play Mode

Figure 21.14

In the "Properties" window, "Physics" buttons, "Collision Bounds" tab, note that "Bounds: Box" is shown and at this point is grayed out (not active).

Press the P key to play the game and observe that the cube descends and comes to rest on the surface of the plane with the lower edge protruding below the surface. The cube has come to rest with the lower edge of the "Spherical Bounding Volume" in contact with the surface of the plane. Press Esc.

Check (tick) the "Collision Bounds" button in the "Properties" window. This activates the "Bounds" selection menu. The circle inside the cube disappears since "Bounds: Box" is active. The "Box" bounding volume is of the same size as the cube. Without "Collision Bounds" active the default volume is the sphere. "Collision Bounds" overrides the default to whatever "Bounds" volume type is selected. Change "Box" to "Sphere." A sphere displays inside the cube (Figure 21.15). Press the P keys to play and observe the cube descend and sit on the plane as before. Press Esc.

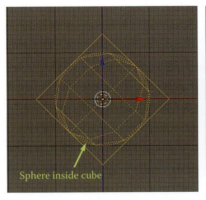
Sphere inside cube

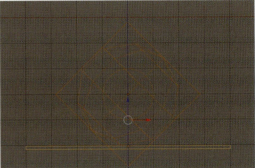
Cube at rest with the scaled volume in contact with plane

Figure 21.15

In the 3D window scale the cube up times 2. In "Wireframe Viewport Shading" mode you will see that the "Bounding Volume" has also been scaled. Play again and observe that the cube comes to rest with scaled volume in contact with the surface.

In the "Properties" window, "Physics" buttons, "Physics" tab, "Attributes" you will find a "Radius" slider with value = 1.000. Play the game with this value at 2.000 and 0.500 and observe how the cube comes to rest. The slider scales the "Bounding Volume" even though the sphere inside the cube stays the same. If you look closely in the cube you will see a circle that changes size when the "Radius" value is changed. The circle represents the limits of the "Spherical Bounding Volume."

A further consideration considering "Bounding Volumes" is location. Revert to the cube at scale 1.000 and the "Attribute" radius = 1.000. In the 3D window with the cube selected tab to "Edit" mode. Using the manipulator widget move the cube's vertices as shown in Figure 21.16. When the game is played the cube is left suspended in midair when the "Bounding Volume" rests on the plane.

- **Mass:** You may adjust the "Mass" of an object under "Attributes." A small object with a greater mass than a larger object with less mass has more effect on impact.

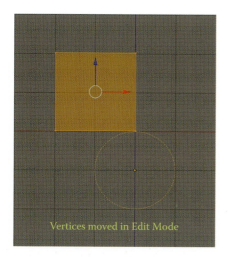
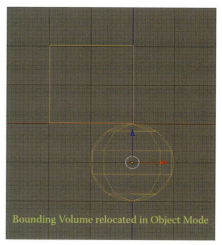

Vertices moved in Edit Mode | Bounding Volume relocated in Object Mode

Figure 21.16

21.3 Examples

Here are the examples promised at the beginning of Section 21.2.

Example 21.1: Automatic Opening Door

In this example, a door will automatically open to allow a vehicle to pass through. The scene arrangement is shown in Figure 21.17.

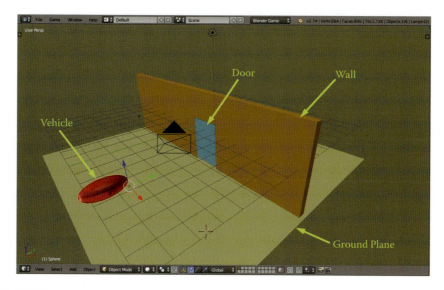

Figure 21.17

Ground—Plane—extruded slightly on the Z-axis—Physics type: Static.

Wall—Cube—scaled, subdivided in "Edit" mode with faces deleted to produce a door opening—Physics type: Static.

Vehicle—Sphere elongated by scaling on the Y-axis—Physics type: Dynamic.

Door—Cube scaled to fit the opening in the wall—Physics type: Dynamic.

Pay particular attention to the "Bounding Volumes" for both the vehicle and the door.

The door's "Bounding Volume" has been reduced in diameter so that it fits inside the surfaces of the wall. It has also been repositioned to make the bottom of the door sit just above the ground plane when in "Game Play" mode.

The center of the vehicle object has been repositioned and the "Bounding Volume" scaled such that the vehicle floats above the plane. Locating the center of the object

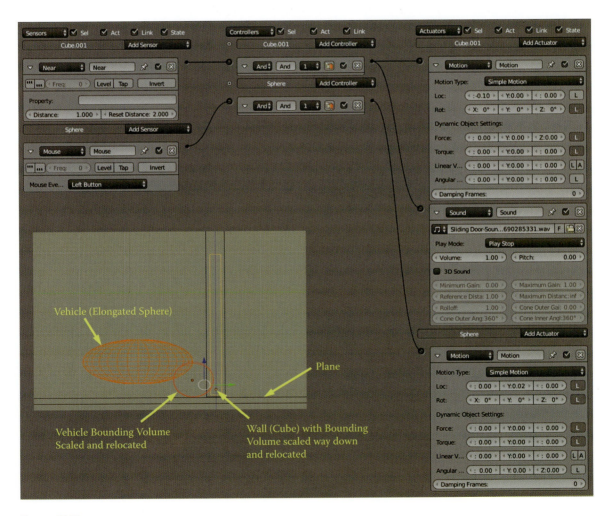

Figure 21.18

at the front of the vehicle ensures that the vehicle's "Bounding Volume" contacts the door's "Bounding Volume" in time for the door to open.

The "Logic Block" arrangement is shown in Figure 21.18. Note that I have not renamed objects to suit the scene. The vehicle is "Sphere" and the door is "Cube.001."

For both the vehicle and the door "Simple Motion" actuators are employed. For the door (Cube.001) the actuator receives a signal via the "And Controller" from a "Near Sensor." The "Near Sensor" sends the signal when something contacts the door's "Bounding Volume." The vehicle (sphere) receives a signal to move from a "Mouse Sensor" with the "LMB" as the trigger. As long as the button is pressed the vehicle moves. Note the motion values and the axis to which they are applied in the "Motion Actuators."

To jazz the game up just a little a "Sound Actuator" is applied to the door. This also receives a signal from the "Near Sensor." A sound file (.wav) which is saved on the hard drive has been entered in the "Sound Actuator."

(SlidingDoor.Soun...690285331.wav)

When the game is played and the door opens, the sound of the door opening is heard.

Example 21.2: Pendulum

The arrangement in Figure 21.19 shows an elongated cube object (pendulum) hinged at one end to a second elongated cube object and supported at the other end by a third cube object. When the supporting cube moves the pendulum swings down striking a sphere, a sound is played.

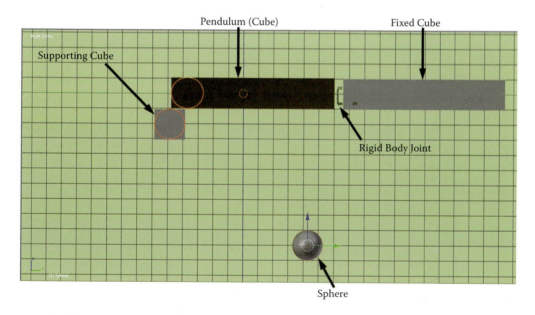

Figure 21.19

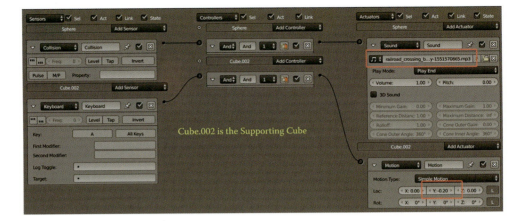

Figure 21.20

The pendulum is hinged as described in Section 14.5.3. The "Logic Block" arrangement is shown in Figure 21.20.

As in the previous example "Bounding Volumes" have to be considered. The "Bounding Volume" of the pendulum has been scaled and located at the LH end of the object such that it is in contact with the "Bounding Volume" of the supporting cube. It is also located at this point to make it contact the sphere's "Bounding Volume" when it swings down after being released.

The supporting cube is caused to move by a "Keyboard Sensor" activated by pressing the A key when the game is played. A "Collision Sensor" assigned to the sphere sends a signal to a "Sound Actuator" playing the sound of railway crossing bells (railroad_crossing_...1551570865.mp3). The sound file is saved on the hard drive.

Example 21.3: Shooting

Every game needs a shooting scene. This is a very simple quick shoot where a cannon is aimed and a cannonball is fired to knock down a wall.

The scene arrangement is shown in Figure 21.21. The scene contains a cannon, a gun platform, a ground plane, and a wall. Oh yes! And a cannonball (sphere).

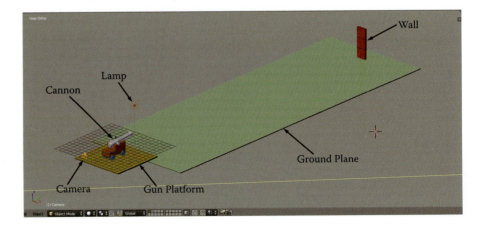

Figure 21.21

The cannon is constructed from a cylinder for the barrel, rotated, scaled, and extruded. The dangerous end is open. The other parts of the cannon are cubes and cylinders scaled and arranged to form a gun carriage. The barrel is located as shown in the diagram then parented to the carriage. When parented in this position it will rotate about its center allowing adjustment for elevation. The cannon is then placed above a plane representing a gun platform (Figure 21.22). A sphere object is the cannonball located inside the barrel (Figure 21.23).

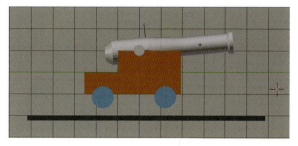

Figure 21.22

A second plane forms the ground plane and positioned way down the end of the scene is a wall consisting of three cubes scaled to produce a thinnish section, which are stacked one on top of the other.

The cannon is aligned to point toward the wall. The camera is positioned to show the view in Figure 21.24.

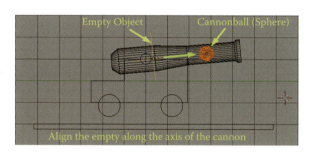

Figure 21.23

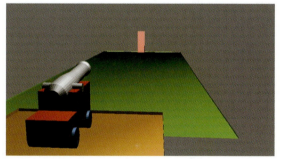

Figure 21.24

Now for the secret weapon, the bit that shoots the cannonball. An "Empty" object is placed inside the barrel of the cannon and rotated to align with the barrel (refer back to Figure 21.23). If the cannon were to be moved about in the game the "Empty" would be parented to the cannon.

With all objects in place it is time to set the "Physics." The scene may be created in "Blender Render" mode but for "Physics" change to "Blender Game" mode. Set physics as follows:

Gun barrel: Physics type—static.
Carriage: Physics type—static.
Cannonball: Physics type—dynamic with the "Attributes Radios" reduced to fit the "Spherical Bounding Volume" well inside the barrel of the cannon.
Gun platform: Physics type—static.
Ground plane: Physics type—static.
Wall blocks: Physics type—rigid body with "Collision Bounds" type "Box."

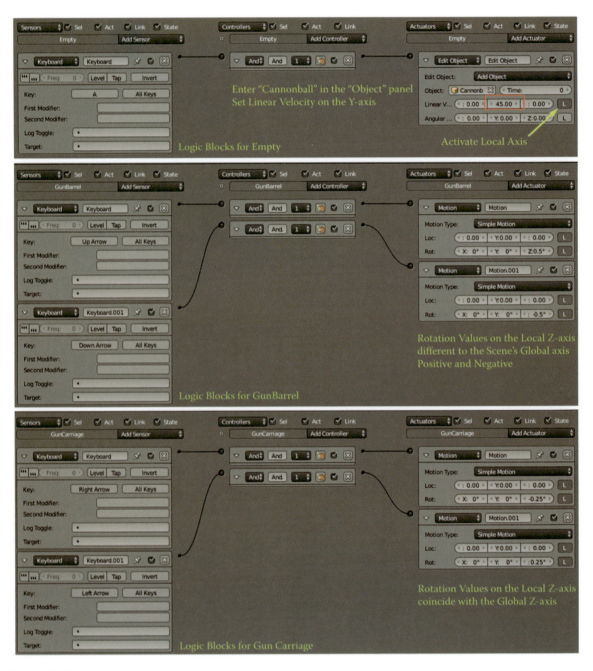

Figure 21.25

Select the "Empty" object and set up "Logic Blocks" as shown in Figure 21.25. Pay particular attention to the "Edit Object Actuator" and the "Linear Velocity" value. The velocity has to be on the correct axis and set the "Transformation Locally" active (click L). In my arrangement, I am firing the cannonball along the Y-axis, which is aligned with the barrel of the cannon. You will have to adjust the velocity value to get the cannonball to hit the wall.

Select the cannonball (sphere) and move it to level 2 in the 3D window. (With the cannonball selected press the M key and click on level 2.)

Select the barrel of the cannon and arrange "Logic Blocks" as shown in Figure 21.25 using the keyboard up and down arrows to elevate and depress the barrel.

Select the gun carriage and arrange logic blocks as shown using the keyboard left right arrows to align the cannon.

With everything set up and with the mouse cursor in the 3D window press the P key to play the game. Pressing the keyboard up and down arrows adjusts the elevation of the gun barrel. Pressing the keyboard left and right arrows turns the cannon. Pressing the A key fires the cannonballs. Repeatedly pressing the A key fires multiple cannonballs.

Example 21.4: Using Python Script

There are many "Logic Block" arrangements that allow a vast variety of actions to be performed but you will inevitably find that it's just not possible to achieve what you want. This is where Python scripting comes into play, if you know how to write Python for Blender or if you know where to find a prewritten script. I will not attempt to instruct you in either of these pursuits but I will show you how Python script is used in the Game Engine.

At the beginning of the chapter we learned how to drive an abject around in the scene. In that exercise simple location values for motion were used, which meant that pressing an MMB or holding an MMB advanced the object at set number of Blender units or fractions of a unit. We could have used a "Linear Velocity" value but that would simply advance the object by that set value. In this example, we will use a Python script designed to accelerate, stop, and reverse an object.

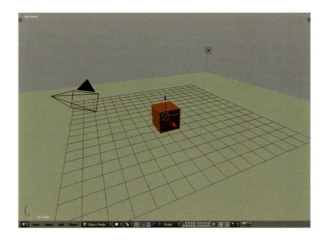

- **Set the scene:** The scene is simply the default cube object sitting on a ground plane. The "Blender Game" physics for the cube is "Type: Static" but with the "Actor" button active (ticked) (Figure 21.26).
- **Logic blocks:** With the cube selected in the 3D window set up logic blocks

Figure 21.26

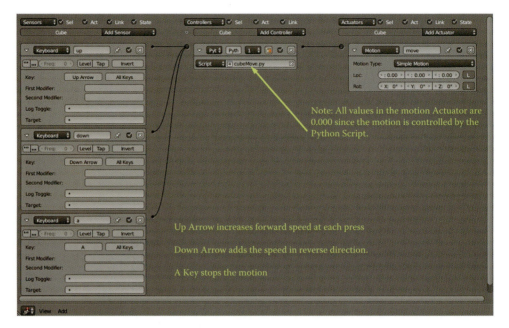

Figure 21.27

as shown in Figure 21.27. In the "Keyboard Sensors" enter the sensor names as shown and use the "Up Arrow," "Down Arrow," and "A Key" as keyboard inputs. The "Controller" is a "Python Controller" and note the name of the script that is entered (cubeMove.py). The "Actuator" is a "Simple Motion" type. Note the values in the "Motion Actuator" are all 0.00.

• **Enter the Python Script:** The particular script used in this example is shown in Figure 21.28. To enter the script have the "Text Editor" window open and in the window header click on the "New" button. This sets the window for entering new material. Blender enters a default name for the text file as "Text." Delete this and enter the name for your "Python script," in this case "cubeMove.py" (the same as that entered in the Python Controller Logic Block). Make sure you add the .py

```
import bge
cont = bge.logic.getCurrentController()
own = cont.owner
move = cont.actuators["move"]
pressup = cont.sensors["up"]
pressdown = cont.sensors["down"]
pressa = cont.sensors["a"]
speed = move.dLoc[1]

if pressup.positive:                    pressup: Forward motion.
    speed = speed + 0.05
    move.dLoc = [0.0, speed, 0.0]
    cont.activate(move)

elif pressdown.positive:                pressdown: Reverse
    speed = speed - 0.05
    move.dLoc = [0.0, speed, 0.0]
    cont.activate(move)

elif pressa.positive:                   pressa: Stop
    speed = 0
    cont.deactivate(move)
    move.dLoc = [0.0, 0.0, 0.0]
```

View   Text   Edit   Format   Templates   cubeMove.py   Run Script   Register

Figure 21.28

21. The Blender Game Engine

suffix, which denotes the text as a "Python script." You will see a red cursor in the upper LH corner of the "Text Editor" window. Type the text or copy and paste the text exactly as shown in Figure 21.28 paying attention to line spacing and indentation. The text must be exact.

If you know the Python language you will understand what the script means but in simplistic terms it reads as follows:

Note: Blender has Python installed as part of the program package or you will have Python installed on your computer. This means that behind the scenes there are a whole host of functions available to be used.

The first three lines of the script call functions from the Python program. The next four lines refer to the "Logic Blocks" that have been set up. The following three blocks of text read as:

If the up arrow is pressed (pressup) add the value of plus 0.05 to speed in the "Motion Actuator." The axis of motion is in the parenthesis, 0.00 being the X-axis, speed the Y-axis followed by 0.00 the Z-axis. The last line says once a signal has been received, keep it moving. For instance, pressing the up arrow causes the cube to move on the Y-axis. The cube continues to move without the key being pressed. Pressing the key a second time increases the speed.

Otherwise, if (elif) the down arrow is pressed (pressdown) add the value of minus 0.05 to speed. With the cube moving on the Y-axis the speed will either be reduced or the motion reversed.

Otherwise (elif) if the A key is pressed the value of speed is zero. The motion stops.

You see that instead of "Actuator Logic Blocks" dictating the motion of the cube it is being controlled by the Python script. Go ahead and alter the arrangement of values in the "move.dLoc" statements to see the results or add additional "elif" blocks and additional keyboard sensors.

These few examples show a minuscule sample of actions that can be arranged in the Game Engine. To be proficient at creating games you will have to create a library of actions, which you then incorporate into your games.

21.4 Game Animation

The "Game Engine Physics" may be used to produce animations by converting the "Game Physics" to "Keyframes" in the "Timeline" window.

A simple example will show several cubes fall and land randomly on a surface in the "Game Engine." The "Game Physics" will then be converted to "Keyframes" producing an animation sequence with "F Curves" which may be used in conjunction with other animation sequences in the default Blender window.

- **Set the window for game:** There is no need to use the "Game Logic" screen layout for this exercise, simply change the engine to use for rendering from "Blender Render" to "Blender Game" (Figure 21.29).

Figure 21.29

Remember that when you activate "Blender Game," the "Properties" window buttons for "Render" and "Physics" change to suit the "Game Engine."

- **Add Objects to the Scene:** Add a plane to the default scene scale it up and extrude it in the Z direction to give it a thickness. Extruding merely gives it some thickness, which allows it to be viewed in a front or side view. Add a material color that enhances the viewing. Select the default cube object and position it above the plane and rotate it with one edge pointing down (Figure 21.30).
- **Add Physics to the Objects:** All objects participating in the scene require physics to be applied. With the cube selected, go to the "Properties" window, "Physics" buttons, "Physics" tab, and change the "Physics Type" from "Static" to "Dynamic" (Figure 21.31). We want the cube to move. Note that the "Actor" button is checked (ticked).

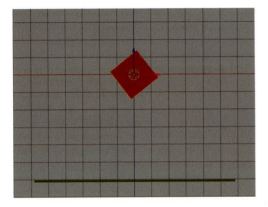

Figure 21.30

Figure 21.31

Note: We are creating an animation using the Blender "Game Engine Physics" without logic blocks and, therefore, have no force effects. The force effecting the movement of the cubes is "Gravity." The gravity settings in the "Game Engine" are found in the "Properties" window, "World" buttons, "Physics" tab. The value 9.80 represents Earth's gravity force.

Select the "Plane" and in the "Physics" buttons check that the "Physics Type" is "Static" and that "Actor" is **NOT** checked. We want the "Plane" to remain stationary.

Note: The default "Lamp" and "Camera" in the scene both have "Static" physics applied.

- **Play the game:** With all objects in position and physics applied the game may be played. If "Blender Game" is activated, pressing the P key will play the game. The cube will descend, due to the gravitational force applied and come to rest on the upper surface of the plane as if the lower edge is stuck into the plane (Figure 21.32). The limit of the spherical bounding volume is resting on the upper surface of the plane. The lowest edge of the cube is below the surface of the plane. Press Esc to return to the 3D view.

    In real life the cube would rotate on the corner and come to rest on its lower flat side.

    To make this occur, change the cube's "Physics Type" from "Dynamic" to "Rigid Body."

    In the "Physics" buttons, "Collisions Bounds" tab, tick the button to enable "Collision Bounds." In the "Bounds" selection note the default selection type is "Box" which is one of seven collision shapes. The default spherical bounding volume has been replaced by a cube of scale equal to the size of the cube object.

    Press the P key again to see the effect. The cube will descend and when the lower edge contacts the plane it falls on to one side and skids to a stop. Press "Esc" to return to the 3D window view.

- **Add more Cubes:** To make things more interesting duplicate the cube, rotate and position as shown in Figure 21.33. Note that in duplicating the cube you have also duplicated it's physics. If you entered a new cube into the scene you would have to add physics to the new cube.

    Press the P key again and see the cubes fall, bounce against each other, and come to rest on the plane (Figure 21.34).

- **Convert game animation to key frame animation:** At this stage we have created an animation which only plays in the "Game Engine." There are no keyframes recorded in the "Timeline" window and there is no "F-Curve" graph in the "Graph editor" window.

It would be nice if we could save this as an "F-Curve" animation for future use. To do this, follow this simple procedure.

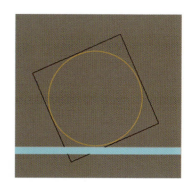

Figure 21.32

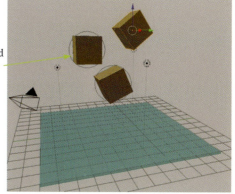

Cubes duplicated and positioned above the Plane

Figure 21.33

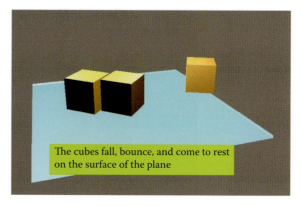

The cubes fall, bounce, and come to rest on the surface of the plane

Figure 21.34

In the "Information" window header click on "Game" and check "Record Animation." Press the P key to play the animation in the "Game Engine" and then hit Esc at the point where you want to stop recording. With the mouse cursor in the 3D window press Alt + A key to display the key-frames in the "Timeline" window. You may play the recorded animation using the "Timeline" window play controls.

You can scrub the "Timeline" window cursor and replicate the movement in the 3D window (Figure 21.35).

Recorded keyframes in the "Timeline" window

Figure 21.35

If you open the "Graph Editor" window in "F-Curve" mode you will see the graphical representation of the recording. Figure 21.36 shows the "F-Curve" for one of the cubes. To see all "F-Curves," shift select the cubes in the 3D window. "F-Curves" may be manipulated to modify the animation.

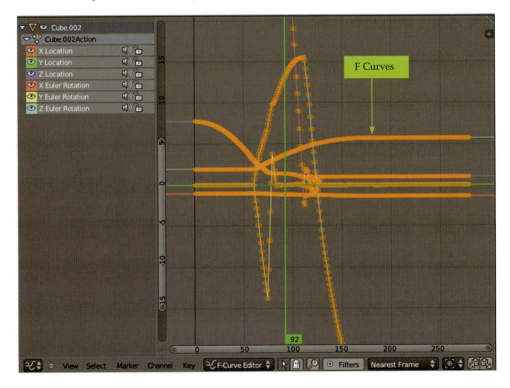

Figure 21.36

Note: Don't forget to cancel the "Record Animation" function in the "Info" window header.

But hey! The recorded animation plays much slower than what you see in the "Game Engine." This is because the Game Engine plays at 60 frames per second while the default frame rate is set at 24 frames per second. To get the F-Curve animation to play the same as the Game Engine, in "Blender Game" mode change the "Animation Frame Rate" in the "Properties" window, "Render" buttons, "Display" tab to 60.

21.5 Rigid Bodies: Dynamics

In the previous example of "Game Animation" we saw how to create an animation in the "Blender Game Engine" using "Game Physics."

"Rigid Bodies—Dynamics" works in a similar way directly in the 3D window with the default "Blender Render" set. This type of simulation animates the motion and interaction of solid objects without deforming them.

To demonstrate using "Rigid Body—Dynamics" we will create a scene where a ball rolls down a plane and demolishes a wall. As in the previous demonstration the force effecting the movement is "Gravity."

- **Set the Scene:** The simplest way to set a scene for "Rigid Body—Dynamics" is in the "Properties" window, "Scene" buttons, click on "Add Rigid Body World" in the "Rigid Body World" tab. This creates a world where every object added into the scene with "Rigid Body" physics applied becomes part of this dynamic world.

  With a new Blender scene opened and with the default "Cube" object selected, go to the "Scene" buttons and press "Add Rigid Body World" (Figure 21.37).

  With the "Cube" object still selected, in the "Properties" window, "Physics" buttons, click on the "Rigid Body" button to enable physics for "Rigid Body" for the cube. The outline of the cube in the 3D window turns green. In the "Rigid Body" tab the physics type is "Active" and "Dynamic" is checked. The physics type options are "Active"

Properties Window—Scene Button

Figure 21.37

Lesson 14
14-01
Rigid
Bodies Part 1

Lesson 14
14-02
Rigid
Bodies Part 2

Lesson 14
14-03
Rigid
Bodies Part 3

Lesson 14
14-04
Rigid Bodies
Part 4-Constraints

Lesson 14
14-05
Rigid
Bodies Part 5

Lesson 14
14-06
Rigid
Bodies Part 6

Lesson 14
14-07
Rigid
Bodies Part 7

and "Passive." In the 3D window "Tools" panel there is an "Add Rigid Body" tab containing a "Rigid Body Type" selection menu with the same two options.

The cube will be an active object in the scene, therefore, we can leave the physics settings as they are and we can leave the cube where it is for the time being.

- **Create a ground plane:** Deselect the cube and add a "Plane" object. The plane will act as a ground plane on which action will take place. Scale the plane up, say 10 times.

  In "Edit" mode extrude the plane on the Z-axis to give it some thickness. Doing this merely makes the plane visible in the 3D window, front or side views.

- **Add Physics to the Objects:** All objects in a scene using "Rigid Body—Dynamics" will have "Rigid Body Physics" applied.

  With the "Plane" selected (orange outline), in the "Physics" buttons, press the "Rigid Body" button. The outline turns green indicating that the plane is part of the "Rigid Body World." The "Physics Type" by default is "Active." Change the type to "Passive." This is fine for the ground plane since it will not be moving in the scene.

- **Bounding volume:** We have seen that in Blender physics interacting objects have a "Bounding Volume." In "Rigid Body—Dynamics" a similar volume is applied which is found in the "Physics" buttons, "Rigid Body collision" tab (Figure 21.38). There are seven "Shape" options, which are self-explanatory except for the default

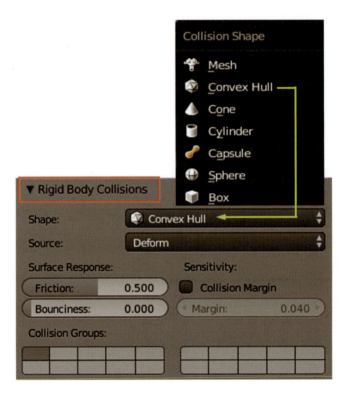

Figure 21.38

option "Convex Hull." A box is a box but if you have an irregular shaped object such as Susan the Monkey "Convex Hull" applies a bounding shape as if you had covered the object in shrink wrapping. The bounding limits are stretched from one high point on the surface to another high point.

- **Build the wall:** Reselect the default "Cube" and position it just above the top surface of the ground plane toward the back of the scene. The wall is constructed from a series of duplicated cubes stacked on top of each other. The "Cube" already has "Rigid Body Physics" applied (green outline).

Note: Before duplicating objects in a scene apply the "Rigid Body Physics" properties otherwise you will have to apply settings individually to each duplication.

With the "Cube" selected, in the "Physics" tab, have "Rigid Body" type "Active" selected and the "Collision" type "Box" would be appropriate.

Go ahead, duplicate, and stack cubes forming the wall. Accuracy of placement isn't necessary (Figure 21.39).

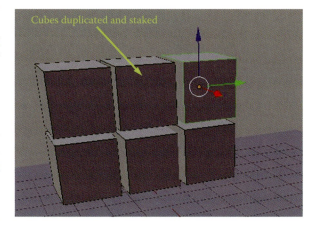

Figure 21.39

- **Making the Ramp:** The "Ramp" is simply a new "Plane" object scaled, rotated, and positioned above the ground plane as shown in Figure 21.40. The angle of the incline is approximately 20°. The "Rigid Body" type for the ramp is "Passive," "Collision Shape" is type "Box."
- **The ball:** The ball is a "UV Sphere" object. "Rigid Body" physics type "Active" with "Collision Shape," "Sphere."

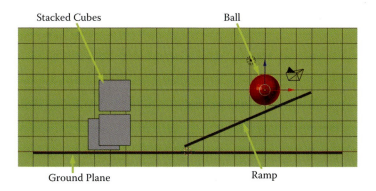

Figure 21.40

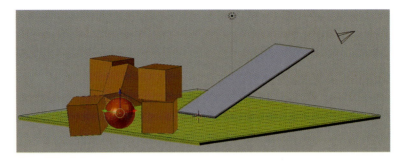

Figure 21.41

- **Play the animation:** With the mouse cursor in the 3D window press Alt + A key. The ball will roll down the ramp and crash into the wall (Figure 21.41). At the same time animation frames are generated in the "Timeline" window. Press Esc to cancel the generation then return to frame 1 and press "Play" to replay the animation or scrub the "Timeline" window cursor. You can also press the "Play" button in the "Timeline" window to see the animation.

This basic example of "Rigid Body Dynamics" is again a tip of an iceberg.

21.6 Making a Stand-Alone Game

The examples included in the chapter have all been played in Blender Game mode within the Blender program. Having created a game you will want to share it with the world and that includes potential users who do not have Blender installed on their computers. To make this possible you convert the game into a "Stand Alone" version of the game. The following procedure explains how this is done.

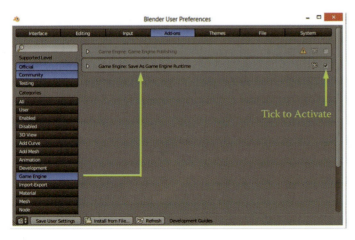

Figure 21.42

The conversion will create all the necessary files required to run the game. You have to create a folder on your computer in which to save these files, so go ahead, make a new folder, and give it the name of your game.

With the Blender program running and the Blender file (.blend) open containing the game, go to the "User Preferences" window and open "Add-ons." Select the "Game Engine" category and activate "Game Engine: Save As Game Engine Runtime" (Figure 21.42). Close the "User Preferences" window. Having activated the "Add-on" you may now go to the "Info" window header, click on "File,"

Name	Date modified	Type	Size
2.74	24/06/2015 4:21 PM	File folder	
avcodec-55.dll	29/07/2014 7:50 PM	Application extens...	16,745 KB
avdevice-55.dll	29/07/2014 7:50 PM	Application extens...	242 KB
avformat-55.dll	29/07/2014 7:50 PM	Application extens...	1,695 KB
avutil-52.dll	29/07/2014 7:50 PM	Application extens...	336 KB
BlendThumb64.dll	29/07/2014 7:44 PM	Application extens...	99 KB
Cannon.exe	24/06/2015 4:25 PM	Application	33,597 KB
libsndfile-1.dll	29/07/2014 7:24 PM	Application extens...	2,320 KB
msvcp120.dll	5/10/2013 7:58 AM	Application extens...	645 KB
msvcr120.dll	5/10/2013 7:58 AM	Application extens...	941 KB
OpenAL32.dll	27/12/2014 2:21 AM	Application extens...	779 KB
OpenColorIO.dll	29/07/2014 7:45 PM	Application extens...	1,193 KB
pthreadVC2.dll	29/07/2014 7:30 PM	Application extens...	241 KB
python34.dll	8/12/2014 4:21 AM	Application extens...	3,939 KB
SDL2.dll	14/11/2014 12:49 ...	Application extens...	1,163 KB
sqlite3.dll	8/12/2014 4:14 AM	Application extens...	658 KB
swscale-2.dll	29/07/2014 7:50 PM	Application extens...	436 KB
vcomp120.dll	5/10/2013 7:58 AM	Application extens...	135 KB

Figure 21.44

Figure 21.43

"Export," and select "Save As Game Engine Runtime" (Figure 21.43). The "File Browser" window opens where you navigate to the new folder you have created then click on "Save As Game Engine Runtime" in the upper right hand corner of the window. The time it takes to create the stand-alone version of the game depends on the complexity of the game.

When finished you will have a folder containing files similar to those shown in Figure 21.44. The subfolder "2.74" at the top of the list is an abbreviated version of "Python" containing python files required to run the game. The file with the Blender icon, for example, **Cannon.exe** is the executable file, which you double click or RMB click and select "Open" to run your game.

BUT! In this method there is a catch. Creating the stand-alone game this way only allows the game file to be played on a computer with the same operating system on which it was created. For example, if your game was created using Blender 2.74, 64 bit on a Windows 64-bit system it will not run on a 32-bit Windows system. To publish for a different operating system you use a different "Add-on" in conjunction with the following method.

As before create a folder into which your game files will be created.

Go to the Blender website and download the ZIP file for the version of the Blender program you intend to publish for. If you have created your game using Windows 64 bit this could be Windows 32 bit or it could be Blender for Mac OSX or the Tarball.bz2 file for either of the GNU/Linux versions. With the file downloaded extract it to a folder.

You are now ready to publish your game. Open the Blender program with your .blend file containing your game. In the "User Preferences" window, "Add-ons" tab, "Game Engine"

category, activate the Add-on "Game Engine: Game Engine Publishing" (Figure 21.45). Close the window. With "Blender Game" render active a "Publishing Info" tab will display in the "Properties" window, "Render" buttons. Enter the information shown in Figure 21.46, working from the top to the bottom, then press "Publish Platforms." When Blender has finished compiling the game your designated folder will contain all the files necessary to run the game on the system you have chosen. The game is played by installing the folder containing the files on the computer then opening the executable file. In my case I named the game "Cannon" and published it to the folder named "StandAloneGame," therefore, I would navigate to that folder and open the file "Cannon.exe" (double click the file or right LMB click and select Open). Remember if the game has been published for Blender/Windows 64 bit then it will only play on the 64-bit system.

Activate "Game Engine: Game Engine Publishing"

Figure 21.45

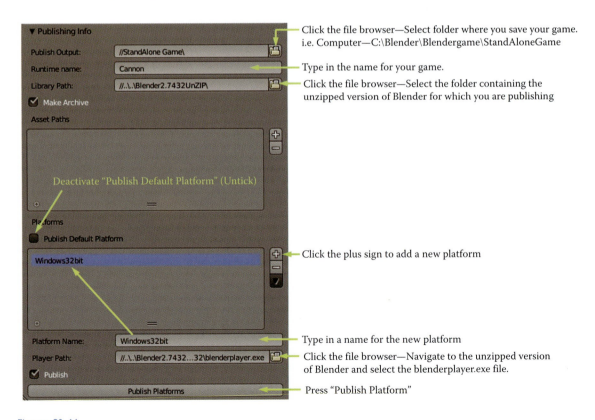

Figure 21.46

Note: You may also run the game from a USB Flash Drive (memory stick).

21.7 Summary

With the preceding examples you have been introduced to the interface for controlling the Blender Game Engine, Game Animation, and Rigid Body—Physics. This should get you started and help you when viewing the many informative video tutorials that are available. As with many things in Blender the Game Engine incorporates techniques that have to be combined to produce a complete game. Research, experiment, and record your findings in a library for future use.

22

The Video Sequence Editor
Making a Movie

22.1 Making a Movie

Movies are made by piecing together video clips, which are short segments of video produced when you render an animation. How to render animation sequences to video has been described in Chapter 8. You can also make use of the Blender's "Scenes" feature as described in Chapter 1. This feature is extremely useful for movie making. When you create an animation sequence in the 3D window the sequence is created in the default "Scene." Adding a new scene to the Blender file by pressing the plus sign to the right of the scene panel gives you options for the new scene. If you were to select "Full Copy" everything in the original scene is copied to the new scene, which is then named Scene.001 (you may rename the scenes to something more meaningful if you wish). Having copied everything to the new scene you can modify the scene. If you have an animation sequence it can be modified. All object models in the original scene are in the new scene and can be modified. By creating new scenes with different animation sequences and rendering the animations to video files you create a series of video sequences, which can be combined and edited into a movie file.

Save the video files to a folder and make note of the location on your computer. I have saved five animation sequences rendered to video. Each animation sequence is from one of the five separate scenes in a single Blender file. The video files are type "AVI JPEG" (.avi).

I have saved these files to "D:\Users\John\MyBlenderMovie\"

Figure 22.1

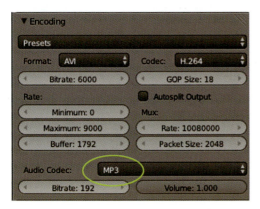

Figure 22.2

22.1.1 Preparation

Open a new Blender file. Leave the cube, lamp, and camera in the default scene.

22.1.2 Set the File Path for Saving

The first step in the movie making process is to set the file path to the location where you want your movie saved and define the video output format.

By default Blender sets the file path to the "temp" (temporary) folder on your hard drive. This can be seen in the "Properties" window, "Render" buttons, "Output" tab. You change this setting by clicking on the "Browse Folder" button and navigating to a new folder in the "File Browser" window that opens. Select the folder then click on the "Accept" button at the top right-hand side (RHS) of the window.

For convenience and simplicity I have set my file path to the same folder where I saved my video files (Figure 22.1).

D:\Users\John\MyBlenderMovie.

22.1.3 Set the Video Format

The next step is to set the movie video output format (file type). In Chapter 8, Section 8.6 video codecs were explained. To demonstrate the movie making process we will use the "H.264" codec from the "Movie" list in the "Properties" window, "Render" buttons, "Output" tab drop down selection menu.

On selecting the "H.264" codec the "Encoding" tab will display immediately below the "Output" tab (Figure 20.4). You will see that a video (movie) file is created in the "AVI" format using the "H.264" codec. Leave all the default values set, except in the "Audio Codec" section change "None" to "MP3" by selecting it in the drop down menu (Figure 22.2).

There are many video and audio codecs to choose from which precludes a detailed explanation from the scope of this book. The use of the different codecs is a complex subject but well worth pursuing if you are keen to enter the video movie making profession. You can start by looking at

https://www.blender.org/manual/render/output/video.html?highlight=video rendering

We will assume you have rendered some animation sequences to video files and have them saved on your computer.

22.2 The Video Editing Screen

Once you have completed the preparation go to the "Info" window header and change the screen display to "Video Editing" (Figures 22.3 and 22.4).

"Info" window header   Click to display options and select "Video Editing"

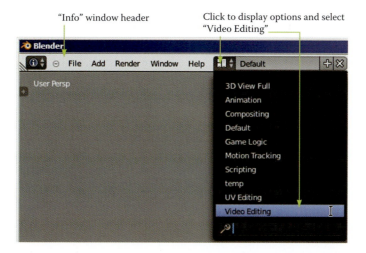

Figure 22.3

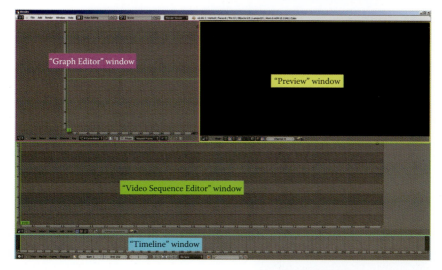

"Graph Editor" window

"Preview" window

"Video Sequence Editor" window

"Timeline" window

Figure 22.4

The "Video Editing" screen contains four windows, the "Preview" window, the "Video Sequence Editor" (VSE) window, the "Timeline" window," and the "Graph Editor" window. In this basic instruction we will be concerned with the first three of the windows only. Note that the "Preview" window is actually a duplication of the "VSE" window, which has been placed in "View" mode (Figure 22.5).

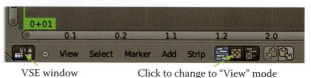

VSE window   Click to change to "View" mode

Figure 22.5

The "Preview" window is where we see the video playing.

The "VSE" window is where we assemble our movie by combining video files (clips), still images, and sound files.

The "Timeline" window allows us to control how the video sequence plays.

On my computer I have saved five video files to the following location on my hard drive:

D:\Users\John\MyBlenderMovie

The video files used are named: sub01.avi, sub02.avi, sub03.avi, sub04.avi, and sub05.avi, which obviously give no indication of the content. In practice, the files would be given meaningful names that would relate to the storyboard showing the intended sequence for the movie.

Note: The "File Browser" window will show your video files in a variety of ways. The default display shows the file name that may or may not give you sufficient information about which file you are seeking. You can change this to display your files as thumbnail images (the first frame of the file) which is a visual reference. Click on the button shown in the diagram (Figures 22.6 and 22.7). Experiment with the other buttons in the header to discover other display options.

Click to display files as thumbnail images

Figure 22.6

Files displayed as thumbnail images

Figure 22.7

       22. The Video Sequence Editor

22.3 Storyboard

A movie is a visual way of telling a story or communicating a message. To effectively piece together a movie you must have at least an idea of how you want to tell your story. In other words you should have a plan or sketch to use as a reference. The plan is called a "Storyboard." It is easy to become submersed in the technical detail of the process and loose the plot.

In the movie in this demonstration a submarine on the surface of the ocean dives underwater and conducts a torpedo attack. The story has been broken down into five parts: submarine on surface, submarine dives, two underwater views, and firing torpedoes. Each part has been constructed as a separate scene in a Blender file, which has been animated then rendered as a video file.

The video files are all rendered from 250 frame animations that when combined equal a movie of 1250 frames. The movie will be rendered for PAL TV, which plays at 24 frames per second; therefore, the movie will play for approximately 52 seconds. It is a long way from being a feature film but will give you the idea.

To demonstrate the process of compiling a movie, follow the procedure as follows. The demonstration will combine the five video files and a sound file.

Sound file? Sound files can be background music, recorded voice, sound effects, in fact anything to enhance the video. For the purpose of the demonstration I have compiled a sound file in ".wav" format. As with video files there are many types of sound files. You are probably familiar with "MP3," "MP4," etc. Blender supports WAV files best although you can enter MP3. For this demonstration I have combined a series of sounds downloaded from "Free Sounds" at www.freesound.org and combined them (Figure 22.8) using "Audacity" (also a free program).

Audio file "Wave" format

Figure 22.8

22.4 Video Sequence Editor

This window is similar to other Blender windows in that it has a "Header" bar (this can be at the top or the bottom depending on the display configuration) and two panels. The main panel provides an area where a graphical representation of the video files being assembled is laid out. This panel is divided horizontally into "Channels." The panel may be resized within the window by clicking and dragging on the edges. You can zoom in and out by using the plus and minus keys on the keyboard and pan the view by clicking, holding, and dragging the MMB. The smaller vertical panel at the RHS provides data relevant to files that have been selected in the window (Figure 22.9).

Information panel with data relating to a selected file

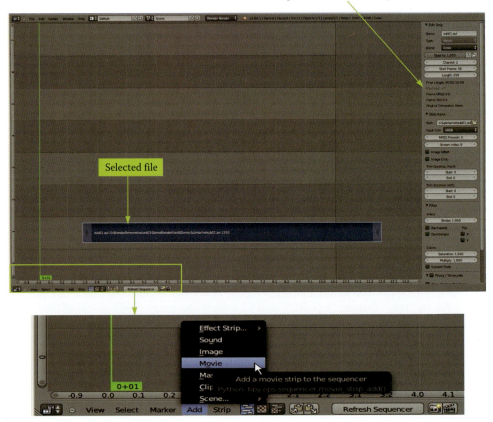

Selected file

Figure 22.9

22.4.1 Placing Video in the VSE

In the header bar, click on "Add" and select "Movie." The screen will change to the "File Browser" window. Navigate to the folder on your hard drive containing your video files. Click on a file to highlight it (orange color) then press "Add Movie Strip" at the upper RHS of the screen.

22.4.2 The Add Button

Take another look at the "Add" button in the VSE window header.

- **Add scene:** Adds a strip containing information about a scene in the Blender file.
- **Add clip:** With the event of "Camera tracking," the "Movie Clip Editor" window has been introduced to Blender. A video file entered in the "Movie Clip Editor" immediately becomes a "Video Clip." It doesn't have to be modified or edited but once it is entered it is a clip which can be added to the VSE and then by using the "Effects Strip—Add" option is able to be superimposed over another video file.

- **Add mask:** If a mask has been created it can be added to the VSE to hide or alter the appearance of parts of the video.
- **Add image:** A still image or a series of images may be inserted into the video much like adding individual frames of an animation.
- **Add sound:** Sound files can be inserted in the VSE to enhance video.
- **Add effects strip:** Effects to provide enhancement, background, and transition.

22.4.3 Selecting and Deselecting Strips

When you have selected a "Movie" file and pressed "Add Movie Strip" the screen display reverts to the Blender "Video Editing" display. In the "VSE" window you will see a blue strip with a white boarder. The white boarder indicates that the strip is selected (Figure 22.10). Press the A key to deselect—RMB click to select. Your video file is contained within the strip. In the information panel at the RHS of the window in the "Edit Strip" tab you see information about the selected video file.

Graduations in seconds and decimal parts of a second

Figure 22.10

22.4.4 Mega Strips

The distinction is made between video file and video strip since more than one video file can be placed in a single strip called a "Mega Strip." Be aware that once files are combined into a "Mega Strip" the information panel no longer gives information about the individual files.

22.4.5 Channels

The strip containing the video file is located within one of the horizontal bands in the VSE window. The bands are called "Channels." Note that the video file that has been entered is in Channel 1. You may move a video file that is selected in the VSE to another channel by changing the channel number in the "Properties" panel, "Edit Strip" tab. Clicking on the triangle at the end of the "Channel" button in the "Edit Strip" tab changes the channel number and relocates the selected video file in the new channel. The video file has been placed horizontally in the channel with the first frame of the clip at the location of the green cursor. By pressing the G Key and dragging the mouse you can relocate the clip horizontally in the channel or vertically to a different channel.

Placing the file horizontally in a VSE window channel is said to be placing the file in the "Video Timeline." The timeline is the graphical representation that dictates which frame of which video file plays at which time. By setting up the timeline you control the sequence of what you see and hear in your final video movie. To produce specific effects you may wish to play video files or parts of a file at prescribed intervals and introduce special transition effects when traversing from one file to another. To control this sequencing an understanding of the "VSE Timeline" graduation is required.

22.4.6 VSE Timeline Graduations

The *graduations* along the lower edge of the VSE window are in seconds and decimal parts of a second. They are approximate only depending on how the graph is scaled and vary depending on the playback frame rate.

Make note that the default playback frame rate is 24 frames per second as shown in the "Properties" window, "Render" buttons, "Dimensions" tab.

A more accurate indicator for positioning is the vertical green line cursor. At frame number 1 the number at the lower end of the cursor showing 0 + 01 indicates that the cursor is at position 0 plus one frame. The VSE window cursor follows the position of the green cursor in the "Timeline" window in the lower part of the screen. In the "Timeline" window the graduations along the timeline are in frames. The "Timeline" window cursor and the "VSE" window cursor are located by default at frame 1, that is, position 0 plus one frame.

Note: When adding video clips to the VSE window they are entered with the beginning of the clip at the position of the green cursor.

To reinforce the correlation between the graduations in the VSE window and "Timeline" window, click and drag the "Timeline" window cursor and position it at frame 34. The VSE window cursor follows and locates at position 1 + 10. 1 times 24 frames per second = 24 frames plus 10 frames equals 34 frames (Figure 22.11).

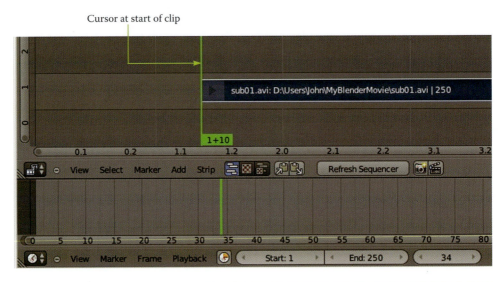

Figure 22.11

22.4.7 Positioning in the Timeline

With the mouse cursor in the VSE window and the video clip selected, press the G key and drag the clip placing the beginning of the clip at frame 34.

In doing this frame 34 becomes the "Start Frame" of the video clip as shown in the properties panel. Observe that in moving the cursor in the VSE window the cursor in the "Timeline" window has followed and is at frame 34.

This is all very elementary but without instruction requires a little time and experimentation to work out. I trust the explanation has helped.

Move the cursors back to the default positions (0 + 01).

With the clip selected and the mouse cursor in the VSE window press G Key and drag the video file to the start at 0 + 01 (frame 1). You will observe that the start position of the file is displayed in white as you drag the file. Note the start frame value changes in the properties panel (Figure 22.12).

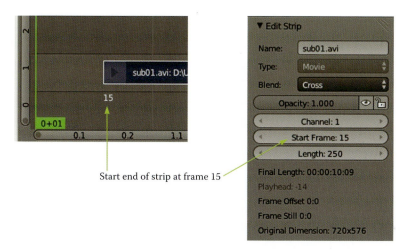

Start end of strip at frame 15

Figure 22.12

22.4.8 Playing the Video File

No matter where the file is located you can view different frames in the file by dragging the cursor along the timeline. You play the file by pressing the "Start" button in the "Timeline" window. Press "Esc Key" to quit or "Pause," "Fast Forward," etc., by using the play controls.

Just to mention some more obvious information about playing consider this: my video file is 250 frames long. With it located with the "Start Frame" at 0 + 01 it will play in its entirety then repeat until I press "Esc." This only occurs since, in the "Timeline" window, "Start: 1" and "End: 250" are set. If "End: 100" was set the file would only play for 100 frames then repeat or if the start frame of the file was positioned on the VSE timeline other than at frame 1 then only part of the file would play.

22.4.9 Adding More Video Files

It is time to add a second video file but before doing so consider scaling and panning the VSE window. With the mouse cursor in the VSE window you can zoom in and out by

pressing the plus and minus keys on the keyboard or by scrolling MMB. In the graduation bar you will observe a panel displayed in a lighter gray color. By clicking LMB and dragging this panel you pan the view left and right. By clicking on either of the dots at each end of the panel and dragging left or right you adjust the scale display. As you do this, the scale values expand and contract accordingly. This is the same as zooming in the VSE window.

OK! Now add the second video file (press Add—Movie—navigate in the "File Browser" window—select, etc.). Zoom out in the window to see the two files. The first file was entered by default in Channel 1; the second file is entered in Channel 2. The files can be moved to different channels as you wish and positioned horizontally.

To have the two video files play end to end as a continuous sequence position the start of the second file horizontally at the end of the first file (they do not have to be in the same channel). With the second file selected press the G Key and drag the mouse. You will see frame numbers display at the beginning and end of each strip, which makes it is easy to align exact frames. You can purposely overlap strips since a file in a higher channel will take precedence over a file in a lower channel when playing (Figure 22.13).

Note: If you shift select multiple video files in the "File Browser" window they will be automatically placed end to end in a single channel.

Sound file   Five video files 250 frames each

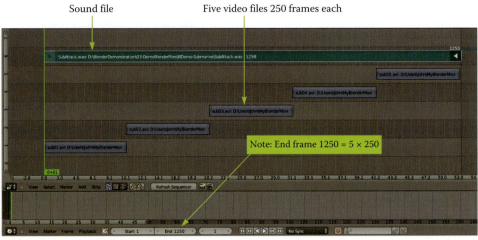

Figure 22.13

VSF window showing the compiled movie

22.4.10 Cutting Video Strips

Another feature to be aware of is the ability to select only part of a video strip for playback. You can cut the strip into segments. There are two ways to do this they are a "Soft Cut" and a "Hard Cut." In either case, first position the green line cursor at the frame where you wish to make the cut. For a "Soft Cut" press the K key. For a "Hard Cut" press Shift + K key. In either case you finish up with two separate segments of clip which you can reposition or

Figure 22.14

move to a different channel in the VSE. The difference is with a "Soft Cut" both segments of the clip retain the data for the other part. With a "Hard Cut" the data is not retained.

The above probably doesn't make a whole lot of sense so have look at Figure 22.14.

> Note: Disregard the clip names at the beginning of each line. Blender automatically assigns names to the parts as they are cut. I have cheated a little in creating a diagram to explain cutting.

I have added a clip named sub01.avi to channel number 1 of the VSE. The clip is sub01. avi is 250 frames long, therefore, it starts at Frame 1 and ends at Frame 250 as you see in the "Timeline" window. In the VSE window timeline this is Start 0 + 01, End 10 + 10. Remember this is with a play rate of 24 frames per second as set in the "Properties" window, "Render" buttons, "Dimension" tab.

i.e. End $10 \times 24 = 240 + 10 = 250$

I have positioned the VSE cursor at 5 + 05 (Frame 125—Half Way). I have pressed the K key (Soft Cut) then RMB clicked on the second half to select it and moved it to channel 3. With the second half selected I have pressed Shift + D to duplicate it and then moved the duplication to channel 5. I then RMB click on the triangle at the beginning of the second half of the clip and drag to Frame 1. This results in reinstating the data for the first half of the clip thus producing a full-length clip again as shown in channel 7. If this were attempted after an initial "Hard Cut" dragging the triangle at the start of the second half produces a blank segment since data has not been retained. When "Hard Cutting" you simply create two bits. "Short Cutting" allows you to shorten a clip while retaining all the data.

Note: Clips or parts of clips are repositioned in channels by changing the channel number in the "Edit Strip" tab in the "Properties" panel at the RHS of the VSE window. You may also RMB click on a strip and G key drag to another channel.

22.4.11 3D Window Scene Background

By selecting (RMB click) a video file strip then a scene strip, then selecting and clicking "Add," "Effect Strip," "Add," the 3D window scene will be superimposed and display as a background to the video file (Figure 22.15).

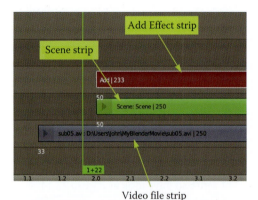

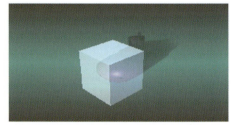

Preview window showing the frame at the location of the cursor

Video file strip

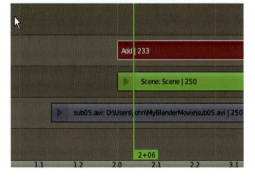

Preview window showing the "Cube" in the default scene added to the view. Note the position of the cursor

Figure 22.15

22.4.12 Adding Sound Files

Sound files such as MP3 and WAVE are entered by selecting "Sound" instead of "Movie" and then manipulated the same as a video file.

With all your strips aligned and edited you can press the "Play" button in the "Timeline" window to preview the final movie.

22.4.13 Rendering the Movie File

When all the specifications have been set for your movie output file it is time to render the final movie.

Open the "Properties" window and click the "Animation" button in the "Render" tab. Be prepared to wait a considerable time. Even a short movie will take a while depending on the speed of your computer. Long movie sequences are often uploaded to websites called "Render Farms" which will perform the render process (at a cost).

Once the render is complete you find the file in the output folder and give it a test run in a media player.

22.5 Summary

The preceding instruction has introduced you to compiling a movie file from a series of video clips and adding sound files. It is fairly obvious that you can introduce clips and arrange them in order along the timeline or rearrange the order. Compiling a movie requires considerable dexterity in order to produce a professional production.

The Blender's VSE allows you to introduce transitional effects between video clips, to render a video file into a series of image files so that you can manipulate images (Frames) within any one clip then render the reconstructed frame back to a video file. Video files can be cut and edited and combined to produce the most sophisticated animated movies.

A more detailed instruction of this is beyond the scope of this publication but for those who are interested it is a subject well worth pursuing.

23

Drivers

23.1 Blender Drivers

Drivers are functions that use properties (values) to affect other properties. To demonstrate this we will use the translate property of a cube object to control the rotation property of a monkey object. Moving the cube in the 3D window will cause the monkey to rotate.

Follow this example:

Open Blender with the default scene containing the cube object. Deselect the cube and add a monkey object. Move the monkey to one side as shown in Figure 23.1.

Split the 3D window in two and make one part the "Graph Editor" window. Change the "Graph Editor" from "F-Curve Editor" mode to "Drivers" mode. With the cursor in this window press N key to display the "Drivers Properties" panel. Expand the "View Properties" tab.

We will set up a driver to cause the monkey to rotate on its Z-axis when the cube is translated on its Y-axis.

With the cursor in the 3D window press the N key to display the "Object Properties Panel." We now have a properties panel in the 3D window and in the "Graph Editor" window. In the 3D window press the T key to close the "Tools" panel and remove clutter from the scene (Figure 23.1).

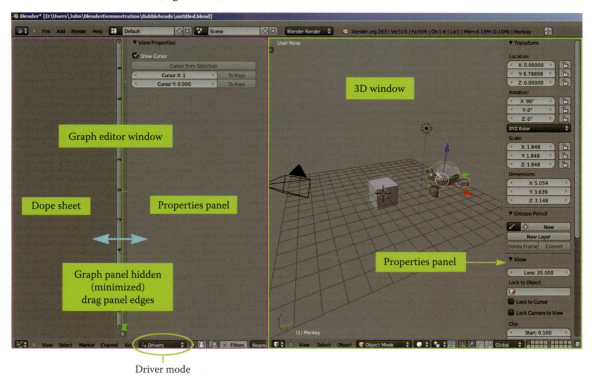

Figure 23.1

With the monkey object selected right click on the Z-axis rotation slider in the 3D window "Properties Panel." Select (click on) "Add Single Driver." The slider will turn purple showing that a driver has been added (Figure 23.2).

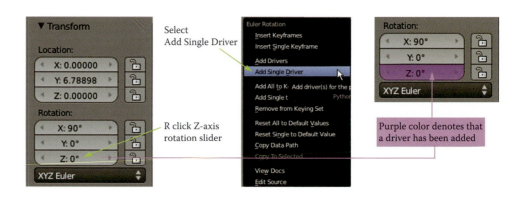

Figure 23.2

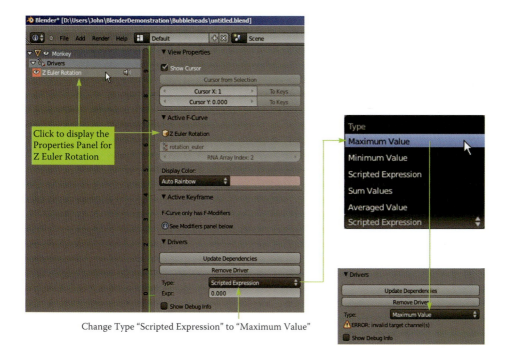

Change Type "Scripted Expression" to "Maximum Value"

Figure 23.3

In the "Graph Editor" window at the upper LHS, you will see that a driver has been added by the insertion of the "Z Euler Rotation" channel. To display the properties left click on the channel.

In the "Properties Panel," "Drivers" tab change "Type" from "Scripted Expression" to "Maximum Value" (Figure 23.3). Note: "ERROR: Invalid target channel(s)" message. **Ignore this for the time being.**

By default, in the "Graph Editor" properties panel a "Variable" (var) datablock is displayed (Figure 23.4).

Figure 23.4

Just below where you see "Transform Channel" click on the little orange cube icon and select "Cube." Change "X Location" to "Y Location." Note: The ERROR message disappears.

Select the cube and translate it along the Y-axis. The monkey rotates on its Z-axis (Figure 23.5).

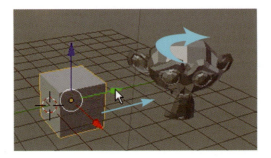

Figure 23.5

23.2 Randomize Object Properties

The following instructions have been transcribed from a video tutorial by David R Miller of Miller Mattson—Marketing Technical and Business Communications. The video is titled: Variations: Blender Drivers for Randomizing and may be viewed at: vimeo.com/40389198. David has combined numerous Blender functions in this very informative and interesting tutorial.

The objective in these instructions is to create a number of similar objects that vary in their characteristics. To be specific, say you want to create a bunch of cubes each of which is slightly different in size, is rotated, and located in different positions in a scene. You do not require any specific differences, in fact you want a random array.

There are several ways in which you could create the array. You could simply duplicate the cube in the 3D window then scale, rotate, translate, and change the material. Keep on doing this until you have sufficient cubes. Or you could use an "Array" modifier.

23.3 The Array Modifier

See Chapter 12, Section 12.4.1.

The "Array" modifier may be used to duplicate an object (Figure 23.6). For example: With the cube selected in the 3D window and a simple array modifier added, with the "Relative Offset" values set at 1.100 on the X-axis and 0.300 on the Y-axis the object is duplicated and positioned as shown in the diagram. This is an array consisting of three objects offset by the "Relative Offset" values. Since an array is considered a single entity it simulates a cuboid. By changing the "Relative Offset" values using different settings for the X, Y, and Z offsets produce different array configurations. Pressing Shift + D key will duplicate the array. Altering the X, Y, and Z offset values within the range 0.001–1.000 produce varying object sizes. Multiple array modifiers may be introduced to separately control the sizes. With an array duplicated it can be manually translated and rotated in the scene. Needless to say this method of producing multiple objects is somewhat tedious.

Properties window—Modifier button

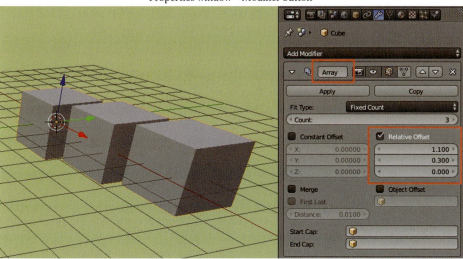

Figure 23.6

23.4 Shapes Keys

Shapes Keys may be set and employed to vary the size of the cube but again this is a lengthy and tedious process (see Chapter 16).

23.5 Randomizing Property Values

The following demonstration will automate the process of creating randomly sized and rotated objects using Blender "Drivers" in conjunction with a "Python" script. The objects will also be translated to different locations in the scene. Python is the programming language of Blender.

23.6 "Python" Script

A "Python" script is a piece of code written in the "Python" computer language and is simply a text file. As part of the demonstration the script shown in Figure 23.7 will be used.

Type the text shown in the diagram into a text editor such as Notepad or Wordpad and save the text file. We will copy and paste this into a Blender file. You can type it directly into the Blender text editor but having it saved as a text file gives you a backup.

```
DriverPye - Notepad
File  Edit  Format  View  Help
import bpy
import random

# Random floating point number between lo and hi

def randf(lo, hi):
    return random.uniform(lo, hi)

# Random integer from lo (inclusive) to hi (inclusive)

def randi(lo, hi):
    return random.randint(lo, hi)

# Random values given mean and standard deviation

def gauss(mean, stdev):
    return random.gauss(mean, stdev)

bpy.app.driver_namespace["randf"] = randf
bpy.app.driver_namespace["randi"] = randi
bpy.app.driver_namespace["gauss"] = gauss
```

Figure 23.7

The "Python" script will be used in conjunction with the Blender "Drivers" function.

In simple terms "Drivers" are functions that affect the attributes or properties of an object. Refer to the demonstration at the beginning of this chapter where the translation of an object controls the rotation of another object. Instead of using the translation of an object we will introduce a "Python" script, which in itself includes functions, which will be made available to a driver function to control the shape and rotation of our objects.

23.7 Register the Script

The first step is to enter and register the "Python" script in a Blender file. This will create a Blender file, which you can save for future use.

Open a new Blender file and open the "Text Editor" window. Create a new "Text Block" by clicking "New" in the text window header or by clicking "Text"—"Create New Text Block."

The default name of the new text block is shown simply as "Text." Rename this to something more significant. Since we are about to work with random properties, may I suggest "ran.py?" Note the suffix ".py" is very important so make sure you include this in the name.

With the text block created go get your "Python" script. That is go to the text file you previously created. Open the file and select (highlight) the text and copy it to the clipboard. Paste the text into the newly created text block in the Blender "Text Editor" (Figure 23.8).

In the "Text Editor" window header click "Run Script" then tick "Register." Run script makes the functions contained in the script available to the driver function. The functions in the "Python" script are the "randf," "randi," and "gauss" functions. "Register" means that the next time you open the Blender file it will run the script and register automatically.

Save the Blender file for future use. Name it "RandomPy.blend." (You can name the file anything you like. Just remember what the name is and where you save it.)

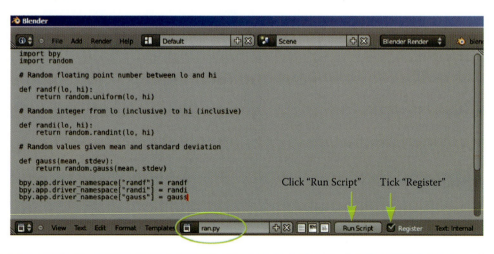

Figure 23.8

562

23. Drivers

Registering the "Python" script makes the "randf," "randi," and "gauss" functions available for use by the Blender Drivers. Either of these functions can be called (entered into Blender) for use by a driver. Saving the "RandomPy.blend" file means you now have a Blender file available for generating random properties. We will demonstrate how the "randf(lo, hi)" part of the "Python" script works. This is the only part being used in this demonstration. Including the "randi (lo, hi)" part and the "gauss (mean, stdev)" parts merely makes them available should you wish to use them in the future. To understand these statements you will have to undertake a study of the Python programming language.

OK! With the "RandomPy.blend" file open you can close the "Text Editor" window and return to the 3D window.

Note: If you have closed the "RandomPy.blend" file and you reopen it at a later date you will see a notice in the "Info" window header stating "Autorun" disabled: Text "ran.py." Click on the "Reload Trusted" button adjacent to this message and select "OK—Revert."

Blender recognizes that you are about to run a "Python" script (.py) and is asking you to confirm that the script is trusted.

You can negate this warning by setting autorun in the "User Preference" window, "File" tab. See "Auto Execution:—AutoRun "Python" Script." Place a check in the button. To make this available for each time you open the file, click "Save User Settings."

With the default cube selected we will add drivers to the x, y, and z rotational properties, which will randomly recalculate these values.

23.8 Set Up the 3D Window

With the mouse cursor in the 3D window press the N key to display the "Properties Panel" at the RHS of the window. Note: This "Properties Panel" as being distinct from the "Properties" window displayed at the RHS of the screen (Figure 23.9).

Also note that some values display in both, that is, in the "Properties Window," "Object buttons," "Transform tab" there are "Location, Rotation, and Scale" sliders. Identical sliders for the same "Transform" properties are displayed in the "Properties" panel of the 3D window.

Split the 3D window in two and change one part to the "Graph Editor" window and change it from "F-Curve" mode to "Driver" mode. With the cursor in the "Graph Editor" window press the N key to display the "Object Properties" panel. The graph part of this window will not be used so you can arrange the

Figure 23.9

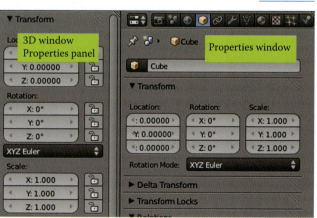

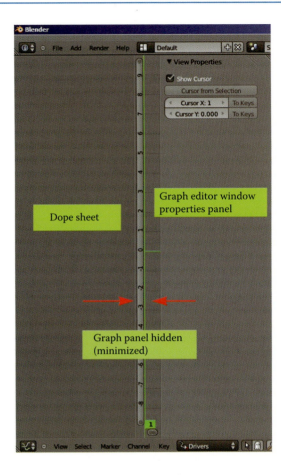

Figure 23.10

window to only show the "Dope Sheet" and the "Properties Panel" (see Figure 23.10). With the mouse cursor in the 3D window press the T key to remove the "Tool" panel to remove clutter.

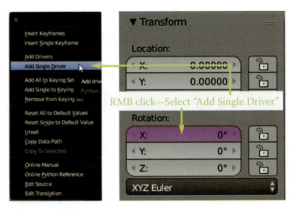

Figure 23.11

- **A point of clarification:** At this point in the demonstration we have three properties panels displayed. We have properties panels in the "Graph Editor" window, the 3D window, and the "Properties" window.

23.9 Rotation Driver Properties

We will begin by setting a driver for the X rotation property of the default cube object in the 3D window. Make sure your object, the cube, is selected in the 3D window. In the "Object Properties" panel of the 3D window, right mouse click on the "X Rotation" slider and select "Add Single Driver" (Figure 23.11).

Note that if you select "Add Drivers" all three x, y, and z channels will have drivers added.

The slider turns purple indicating a driver has been added and the driver channel displays in the "Dope Sheet" in the "Graph Editor" window (Figures 23.12 and 23.13).

At this point all that displays in the "Graph Editor" properties panel is the "View Properties" tab. Minimal information is displayed in the properties panel since the driver channel is not selected. Click on the channel in the dope sheet and more properties display in the panel.

We will explain some of the property values that are shown (Figure 23.14).

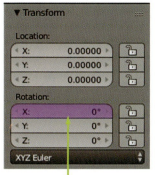

Slider turns purple indicating that a driver has been added

Figure 23.12

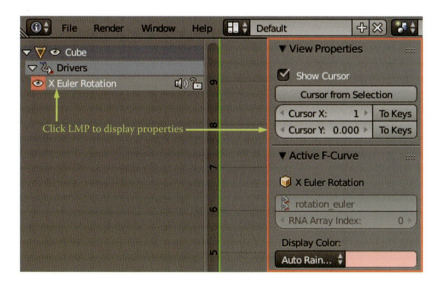

Figure 23.13

- **View properties:** Controls how the driver graph will display in the user interface. The driver graph is only used in an animation, therefore, we are not concerned with it at this time.
- **Active F-Curve:** Shows where the driver data is written.
- **Active keyframe:** Not being used here. This is an animation feature.
- **Drivers:** Where the driver gets its new numbers from when it is reevaluated.
- **Type: Scripted Expression:** Where the driver gets its information. The drop down selection menu provides a choice of options.
- **Max, Min, or Average Values, etc.:** Can be entered manually.

Figure 23.14

Since we are using the "Python" script to generate values Select Type: "Scripted Expression."

Before continuing we will explain a few points:

1. In the "Python" script (see the "Text Editor" window): "def randf(lo, hi):" the script is called to generate a floating point value in a low (lo) and a high (hi) range. Since we are considering the rotation of the object these range values will be expressed in circular measurement.

2. Normally, in layman terms, circular measurement is expressed in degrees of rotation with 360° in a circle. In Blender you can have either "Degrees" or "Radians," depending what units you have chosen in the "Properties Window," "Scene buttons," "Units tab." There are 2π radians in a circle (~2×3.142 radians).

3. In the Blender "Properties" window, "Object" buttons, "Transform" tab you will see a drop down selection panel for "Rotation Mode." These are different combinations of "Euler" rotation values. Euler rotation measurements take into consideration the x-, y-, and z-axis of the object with respect to other sets of axes. For example, the x, y, and z local axis of the object with respect to the x, y, and z global axis of the scene. For our purposes, leave the default "Euler XYZ" combination in place.

4. In Python, circular measurement is expressed in "Radians," therefore, for a circle where there are "2π radians" this may be considered as a range of minus π to plus π. In Python scripting this is written as −pi and pi.

Let's continue:

- **Enter the function:** Since we are using a "Scripted Expression" and calling the "randf" function from the "Python" script, enter the function from the script as "randf(−pi, pi)" and hit "Enter" (Figure 23.15). You enter this in the "Graph Editor" window, "Properties" panel, "Drivers" tab, just below the "Scripted Expression" selection button. **Enter "randf(−pi, pi)" in the Expr: panel** (Figure 23.15).

Note: If you see, "**Error: Python auto execution disabled,**" go to the "User Preferences" window, "File" tab, see "Auto Execution" (lower LH corner), and place a tick in the "AutoRun Python Scripts" box.

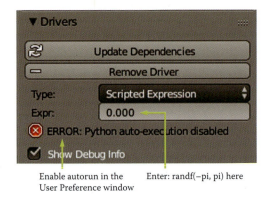

Enable autorun in the   Enter: randf(−pi, pi) here
User Preference window

Figure 23.15

Note: If you see, "**Error: Invalid Python Expression**," go back and check the script in the "Text Editor" window, very carefully. The slightest mistake will result in this error message.

Entering the function is in effect telling Blender to use "randf" expression of our "Python" script with the arguments "−pi" and "pi" to recalculate a random value of rotation about the cubes x-axis within the range minus π to plus π. In other words, pick a rotational value about the x-axis between 0° and 360° since there are 2π radians in a circle (arguments are values that an expression uses in its calculation).

Immediately you enter the expression Blender will reevaluate the x rotation value and you will see the cube in the 3D window rotated. Every time you click "Update Dependencies" the rotation values will be recalculated and the cube randomly rotated.

Note: In the 3D window the cube is rotated at each reevaluation.

In the driver properties panel you can activate the "Show Debug Info" option, which will display values that have been calculated (Figure 23.16).

Figure 23.16

Figure 23.17

You can also see values in the "Graph Editor" window in "Drivers" mode. Click "View"—"Show Sliders" which displays value sliders in the driver channel (Figure 23.17).

The forgoing has set the driver for the x-axis rotation. Repeat the procedure for the y- and z-axis.

With the drivers set for all three axes using the "Scripted Expression," whenever you click "Update Dependencies" all three rotational values are randomly recalculated and the cube in the 3D window rotates. Note: Translating the cube in the 3D window will also Update Dependencies and randomly rotate the cube.

Figure 23.18

Note: When using scripted expressions you can delete the "Variable" datablock in the "Graph Editor" driver properties. You can also delete the driver modifier if it is displayed by default (Figure 23.18).

23.10 Alternative Method for Activating

There is an alternative method for **activating drivers**. First add drivers to the x, y, and z sliders in the 3D window Properties panel, Object button, Transform tab, by right clicking on each of the sliders and selecting "Add Single Driver." This adds a driver to the x, y, and z slider values. Note: You may select "Add Drivers" instead of "Add Single Driver" in which case drivers are automatically added to all three rotation channels. Left click on each of the driver channels in turn and in the "Graph Editor" window, "Properties Panel," "Drivers" tab delete the "Expr." values. In place type the Python expression "randf(−pi, pi)." When done hit "Enter." Note the "randf(−pi, pi)" expression is replaced by a numeric value. Do this for all three sliders. Entries are automatically placed in the "Graph Editor" window (Figure 23.19).

The setup is ready to go by clicking on "Update Dependencies" in the "Graph Editor" properties panel or by translating the cube in the 3D window.

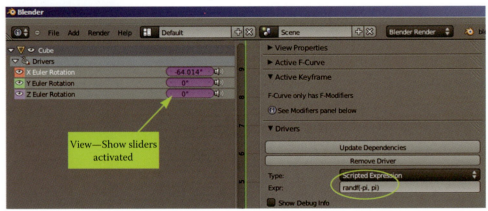

Figure 23.19

23.11 Reevaluating Drivers

With drivers set, in the 3D window solid shading display mode, press G key (grab) drag the mouse and move the object in the 3D window. Blender constantly reevaluates the driver and produces random values for the properties values. Note this will affect any driver that has the

"randf," "randi," or "gauss" Python expression inserted. This is just another method of updating dependencies. This function can be negated by clicking on the camera icon in the driver dope sheet panel adjacent to the driver (mute). You will want to negate this function if you require to manually reposition the cube.

23.12 Scale Properties Driver

We were previously creating rotation drivers. Now we create scale drivers and we set up a process where the X-, Y-, and Z-axis all scale in proportion to each other. To show how this works we will demonstrate a different process for each axis. You may, however, use any one of the processes on each axis.

23.13 X-Axis Scale Driver (Scripted Expression)

Start by adding the X-axis scale driver using the scripted expression with scale values say 0.8–1.2 Blender units. For example, randf(0.8, 1.2) (Figure 23.20).

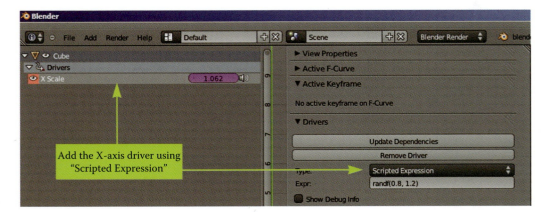

Figure 23.20

This set up is the same as we used for the X-axis rotation with the exception that we insert the values 0.8 and 1.2 instead of −pi and pi.

The x scale value will now be randomly reevaluated between 0.8 and 1.2 Blender units when you click "Update Dependencies." You can set any values you like but don't get carried away.

Figure 23.21

23.14 Y-Axis Scale Driver (Max, Min, Sum, Average Values with Variable)

On the Y-axis scale properties values, right click—"Add Single Driver" but instead of selecting "Scripted Expression" choose "Max, Min, Sum, or Average" driver types. We will use "Average" (Figure 23.21).

Figure 23.22

This is where the "Variable datablock" is used which displayed by default in the "Graph Editor" window "Properties" panel. Note: An error message displays until data is entered in the "Variable datablock" and you click "Update Dependencies" (Figure 23.22).

OK! We are setting up the Y-axis scale driver but we are using the X-axis scale data via the variable data block to control the scaling of the cube on the Y-axis (Figure 23.23).

In referring to the X-axis scale you can use driver variable type "Transform Channel" or "Single Property." "Single Property" is more general purpose and allows the use of any property. "Transform Channel" is more simplified and applies only to transform, rotate, and scale. Since this is what we are interested in we use "Transform Channel."

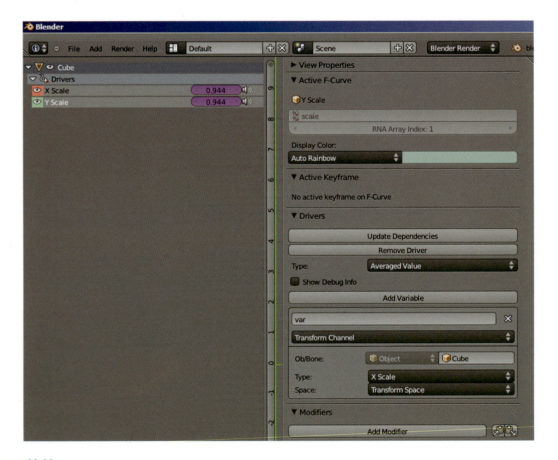

Figure 23.23

Note: Since we are referring to the X-axis scale to control the Y-axis scale we must have the X-axis scale driver in place.

Enter the following in the variable data block. Use: "Transform Channel." Select: "Cube" (the cube object being used) in the "Specific Property I.D." block. Type: "X Scale." Space: "Transform Space" (Figure 23.23).

At this point clicking "Update Dependencies" produces a random scale change along the X-axis of the cube with a corresponding change on the Y-axis.

Note: The Error message previously noted remains displayed until "Update Dependencies" is activated (clicked).

23.15 Z-Axis Scale Driver (Single Property with Variable)

We could repeat the identical process for the Z-axis as was used for the Y-axis. We will, however, demonstrate a variation.

Have the X-axis scale and Y-axis scale drivers installed as previously discussed.

Add a single driver to the Z-axis scale slider.

Instead of selecting "Transform Channel" we will use "Single Property." As stated previously this is a more general expression that allows the selection of any property of the object or *any other object*. We are merely doing this to show how it works.

Note: We did say "of the object or any other object" (see "Drivers" at the beginning of this document).

In this case you can choose what other data block you are referring to, that is, Object (from the drop down menu). Choose specifically "Cube" and its path can be any property of the cube. We are concerned with scale and therefore to get the path hover the cursor over the X scale property value in the 3D window properties panel to see "Object.scale" (the name of the item) (Figure 23.24).

Right click in the X scale property slider—click "Copy Data Path" (copies to the clipboard). Click in the variable path box in the "Graph Editor" properties panel and hit "Ctrl + V" to paste the path into the path box.

"Scale" is entered but the full path is required, therefore, add [0] after "Scale," that is, "Scale[0]" (Figure 23.25).

Figure 23.24

Variable Path Box

Figure 23.25

In this case:

[0] = X-axis
[1] = Y-axis
[2] = Z-axis

See Figure 23.26.

We are, therefore, specifying the X-axis scale by adding [0] (Figure 23.27).

Clicking "Update Dependencies" recalculates random scale values and all axes scale in proportion. Translating the cube in the 3D window does the same thing.

OK! Take a deep breath. We are not finished.

Note: As previously stated, if you take a break and save and close the program, then come back to it later on, you may find an error message in the "Graph Editor" window, "Driver Properties" panel, stating, "ERROR: Python auto execution disabled." There will also be a "Autorun disabled Driver" notification in the "Info" window header. If this occurs click on "Reload Trusted" in the "Info" window header.

Figure 23.26

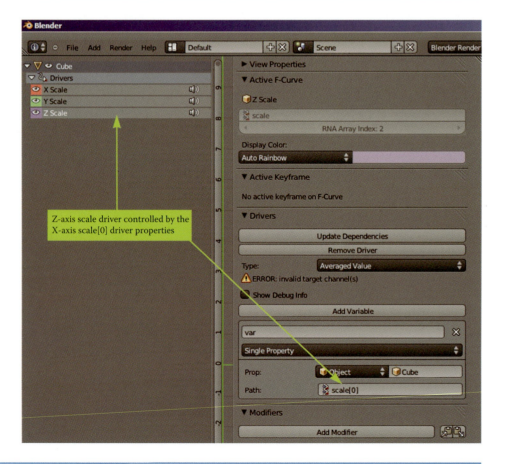

Figure 23.27

23.16 Material Property Drivers

Material properties can be randomized using "Python" script just as we did with the rotation and scale properties. For the rotation we used a value range of " − pi" to "pi" (2π radians in a circle, therefore, −π to +π) and for the scale the range was 0.8–1.2 Blender units.

Just think about the "randf(min value, max value)." What do we use here for material color? Take a look at the diffuse material color sliders in the color picker in the "Properties" window. There are three sliders for the RGB color channels each with a minimum value of 0.000 (black) and a maximum value of 1.000 (white) (Figure 23.28).

The values between these maximum and minimum values produce the spectrum of visible color between white and black. To randomize material within the spectrum all that is required is to use the expression "randf(0.000, 1.000)."

Right click on the diffuse color bar and select "Add Driver." A "Material" drivers channel (tab) is displayed in the "Graph Editor"—"Drivers" mode— "Dope Sheet" panel. Click on the expansion button (triangle) to display the RGB diffuse color drivers (Figure 23.29).

Clicking on each driver entry will display the driver properties where you replace the default value "0.800" with the "randf(0.000, 1.000)" expression. In the variable data block (var) change "Transform Chanel" to "Single Property" and click on the cube icon and select "Cube" as the ID data block. Do this for all three drivers (Figure 23.30).

Clicking "Update Dependencies" or *translating the cube in the 3D window* reevaluates the material values and changes the diffuse color of the cube.

RGB   HSV   Hex

R 0.800
G 0.800
B 0.800

Slider Min. value 0.000
Max. value 1.000

Figure 23.28

Figure 23.29

Figure 23.30

Figure 23.31

23.17 Duplicating the Object

In the preceding sections we have set up drivers to reevaluate the properties of our cube object but at each reevaluation of the cube's properties in the 3D window we only have a single cube located at some place in the scene. Remember, at the beginning of the chapter, we wanted a bunch of cubes scattered about the scene.

All you do is simply duplicate the cube. With the cube selected press Shift + D key to duplicate it. A duplicate is created and placed in grab mode ready to be translated. Drag the mouse to relocate and observe that the original and the duplicate are both reevaluated by the drivers and the properties change.

There are now two cube objects in the scene that are identical and appear to be separate. The duplicate cube (Cube.001) is however linked to the original (Cube) in that it is sharing properties datablocks of the original. If you translate "Cube.001" "Update Dependencies" is activated and the properties of the cube change. If you translate "Cube" the properties of both cubes are changed.

Shift select both cubes and you will see two sets of drivers in the "Graph Editor" window (Figure 23.31).

To make the cubes independent of each other, shift select both—press U key—select "Material + Texture" (Figure 23.32).

In the "Graph Editor" window ensure that the ID block is set as "Cube" for the original and "Cube.001" for the duplicate in all three driver channels (Figure 23.33).

Figure 23.32

Figure 23.33

24

Installing Add-Ons

24.1 Installing

Add-ons are additional Blender functions, hidden away in the "User Preferences" window to prevent cluttering the interface. Add-ons are Python scripts (pieces of code in the Python programming language) that, when activated, provide additional functionality to the Blender program. Blender comes preloaded with a selection of Add-ons, but there are literally hundreds of scripts available for download on the Internet—the Blender website contains a link to the scripts repository where a great number can be found.

When you have downloaded an Add-on (Python script), you have to install it into Blender; the best way to demonstrate this process is to provide an example.

A very interesting Add-on to Blender is a Celtic Knot Generator, which is a script for manipulating a mesh into the shape of a Celtic Knot. This exercise will show you how to download a compressed (.zip) file and extract it to a folder, find a Python script contained in the decompressed file, then install the script into Blender. This is an exercise in manipulating files to add functionality to Blender.

To begin, we will go to the Internet and download a compressed folder (zip file) containing the Python script. You must have a program installed on your computer to unzip: WinZip, WinRar, or 7zip will do the trick.

Before you download, keep in mind where on your hard drive you want to save your download and into which folder you want to unzip it. Windows usually has a default folder

such as "Downloads" or "My Documents" where it saves downloaded files. If you want to download somewhere else or create a new folder, head to the section on navigation and Windows Explorer in Chapter 2. Whatever you do, remember where your files are located; if you have a memory like mine, it's best to create a log file somewhere and remember where you keep it.

24.2 Finding the File

Go online, open a browser window, and search for "Boris The Brave/celtic-knot." You will undoubtedly see the "Blender Artists" website listed with "celtic-knot" referenced (Figure 24.1) and a link to the download page (Figure 24.2).

We are getting close to what we want. Click on the "Download ZIP" link at the bottom of the window (Figure 24.3). Save the file "celtic_knot_master.zip" to a folder on your computer (Figure 24.4).

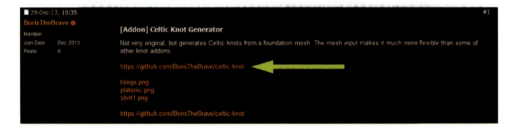

Figure 24.1

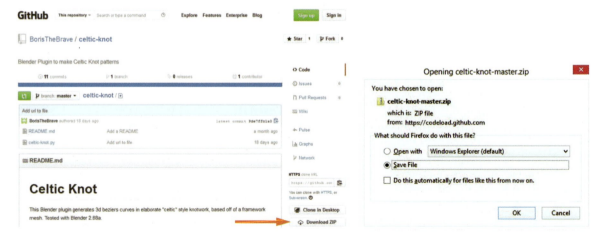

Figure 24.2

Figure 24.3   Figure 24.4

Unzip the file to a folder on your hard drive. You will now have two files, a subfolder named celtic-knot-master containing: "celtic_knot.py" and "README.md."

24.3 Installing the Python Script

Open Blender and change the 3D window to the "User Preferences" window. Click on the "Add-Ons" tab at the top of the window; by default, the tab will display all the Add-ons that have been included with the program. We are going to install the Celtic_knot.py script. Before we install the script, note what scripts are already installed. At the LHS of the window there is a selection list with "All" highlighted in blue. Click on any of the different categories and the list will then only display entries that are relevant to that category. Click on the category "User" and make particular note of the listings. If you haven't installed any scripts there are probably no entries (Figure 24.5).

Look at the lower LHS of the window and click on the "Install from File..." button. This opens a file browser window (Figure 24.6). Navigate to the folder to where you unzipped and find the "Celtic_knot.py" file (the .py suffix denotes something written in the "Python" programming language thus it is a Python script). Select the file (click to highlight) and then click on the "Install from File" button in the upper RH corner of the window. The Add-on is entered under the "All" category in the "User Preferences" window. But HEY! This is the only entry and some of the other category entries are not showing. Close Blender and reopen the program and "Celtic Knot" will be in the "Users" category" and the other categories will display.

At this point we may as well find out how to remove an "Add-on." Click on the little triangle at the LHS of

Figure 24.5

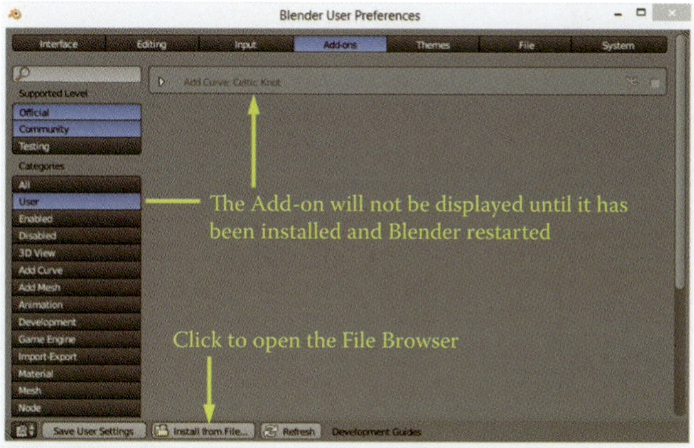

Figure 24.6

Figure 24.7

the "Add-on" line to display the information panel. To remove the "Add-on" click the "Remove" button (Figure 24.7).

24.4 Activating the Script

Although the script has been installed it is not ready to be used. In the "User Preferences" window in the "Add-Ons" section, "Users" category you will see "Add Curve: Celtic Knot" listed. To activate the script you have to click on the "Enable an Add-on" button at the RHS of the listing. This is the little square button at the extreme right of the line. Click to place a tick and close the "User Preferences" window (Figure 24.8).

Figure 24.8

Note: This particular script is designed to affect a mesh object which is selected in the 3D window. For demonstration purposes use the default "Cube" object. Ensure that the cube is selected.

The Python script is automatically installed to Blender. Before activating the script, by way of demonstrating the difference between active and nonactive, perform the following.

In the 3D window, with the default cube selected, press Shift + A key to display the "Add" drop down menu and select "Curve." Note the options available.

Go back to the "User Preferences" window and tick the activation button then return to the 3D window, and repeat the above. Note that "Celtic Knot From Mesh" has been added to the drop down list (Figure 24.9).

Figure 24.9

24.5 Using the Script

With the cube object selected in the 3D window and the Add-on activated select "Celtic Knot From Mesh" in the "Add" drop down. In the 3D window the orange outline of the cube is replaced by red lines wrapped and crossed around the cube (Figure 24.10).

In the "Object Tools" panel to the left of the window the "Celtic Knot" tool tab is displayed containing a series of sliders and buttons (Figure 24.11). Select the "Thickness" slider at the bottom and increase the value slightly (0.12) (Figure 24.12). I will leave it to you to experiment with the other values but note that subdividing the surface of the cube also affects the result. Note also that the knot produced is parented to the Object center. Translating moves the knot away from the cube (Figure 24.13).

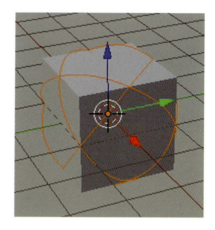

Figure 24.10

I trust the foregoing has demonstrated the versatility and shown the potential power of Blender by installing Add-ons. The manipulation of files and folders is a part of Blender life, so being conversant with your computer file system will add new dimensions to your Blender experience.

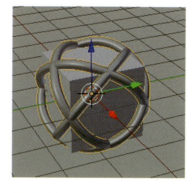

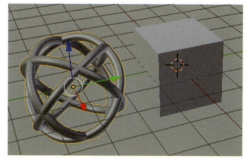

Figure 24.11   Figure 24.12   Figure 24.13

Bibliography

The following websites are recommended for information on Blender:

- Gryllus 3D Design Course: www.gryllus.net/Blender/3D.html
- The Blender Website: www.blender.org
- The Blender Manual: www.blender.org/manual/
- The Blender Wiki: wiki.blender.org
- Blender Nation: www.blendernation.com/

In addition here are a few of the many sites that offer Blender tutorials

- Blender Tutorials: www.blender.org/support/tutorials/
- Blender Cookie: www.cgcookie.com/blender
- Blender Artists: www.blenderartists.org
- Blender Guru: www.blenderguru.com
- Blender 3D Tutorials: www.tutorialized.com
- C G Tutorials: www.cgtutorials.com/c3/Blender

There are many graphics programs which are free to use and websites which are interesting and informative:

- Make Human (Create Figures): www.makehuman.org
- Terragen (Terrain Generator): planetside.co.uk
- Fast Stone Image Viewer: www.fastone.org
- Pov Ray (Create Graphics): www.povray.org
- Lohmuller (Interesting Graphics): www.f-lohmueller.de
- Gimp (Photo Editing): www.gimp.org

Appendix A: Basic Blender Commands

This is a partial list of Blender commands. Please visit www.blender.org for more details.

- **A key.** Deselect the selected or select all.

- **B key.** Box Select; drag a window to select multiple objects or components.

- **C key.** Circle Select; gives you a circle to select multiple objects or components. The circle can be sized by scrolling the mouse wheel. Press Esc to cancel.

- **E key.** Extrude; while in Edit mode, selected vertices, edges, and faces are extruded.

- **G key.** Grab; press the G key and drag the mouse to freely move an object or selected vertices.

- **I key.** Inserts an animation key.

- **M key.** Move; in object mode, it opens the "Move to Layer" option.

- **N key.** Toggles between showing and hiding the numeric data display for the selected object.

- **O key.** While in edit mode, it puts you into proportional vertex editing.

- **P key.** In edit mode, it opens the "Separate" menu in order to separate. In the Game Engine it enters play mode.

- **R key.** Rotate; press the R key and drag the mouse to rotate an object or selected vertices.

- **S key.** Scale; press the S key and drag the mouse to scale an object or selected vertices.

- **T key.** Toggles the tool panel display on off.

- **U key.** In edit mode, it opens the "UV Mapping" menu. In object mode, it opens the "Make Single User" menu.

- **W key.** Opens the "Specials" menu.

- **X key.** Delete key. Deletes a selection.

- **Z key.** Toggles the view between wireframe and solid.

- **Alt + the A key.** Plays an animation in the selected window (your cursor must be in that window for it to play).

- **Alt + the C key.** Opens the "Convert to" menu to convert between a mesh and a curve.

- **Alt + the Z key.** Toggles between a texture view and a shaded view.

- **Arrow keys.** Used to advance frames in an animation: left and right arrows = 1-frame increments, up and down arrows move to the next keyframe.

- **Ctrl + the A key.** After an object has been resized and/or rotated, it opens the "Apply" menu; this can reset the object's data.

- **Ctrl + the J key.** Joins two selected objects.

- **Ctrl + the S key.** Opens the file browser to save a file.

- **Ctrl + the T key.** Displays the "Make Track" menu.

- **Ctrl + the Z key.** The global undo command; with each press, one step will be undone (up to 32 steps are possible by default). If you are in edit mode, it will only undo editing steps on the selected object.

- **Esc.** Cancels an action and ends an animation.

- **F1.** Opens the file browser window.

- **F2.** Saves a file.

- **F3.** Saves a rendered image.

- **F12.** Renders an image.

- **LMB.** Left mouse button. Click to manipulate the 3D manipulator widget, to locate the 3D cursor, to activate functions, to enter values, etc.

- **RMB.** Right mouse button. Click to select.

- **MMB.** Middle mouse button. Click to manipulate specified options.

- **MSW.** Mouse scroll wheel. Zooms in and out and scrolls to expand/contract selection options.

- **NumPad.** Number pad. Controls the view.

  - 7: Top.

  - 1: Front.

- 3: Side.

- 0: Camera.

- 5: Perspective.

- + and – : Zoom in and out and control the affected vertex size in proportional vertex editing.

- **Shift key.** Hold down while clicking the RMB to make multiple selections.

- **Shift + the A key.** Displays the "Add" menu to add objects to the scene such as meshes, cameras, lights, etc.

- **Shift + the D key.** Duplicates or copies selected objects or vertices.

- **Shift + the S key.** Displays the "Snap" menu.

- **Shift + the Space Bar.** Toggles between a view with multiple windows and a full screen view.

- **Shift + RMB.** Selects multiple objects or vertices.

- **Space Bar.** Displays the search window.

- **Tab.** Toggles between edit mode (vertex editing) and object select mode.

Note: The selection menus found in the window headers display shortcut commands for many of the selection options.

Index

I

IK, *see* Inverse kinematics (IK)
Image
    adding, 549
    as background, 167
    as template, 168
    textures, 134
Imperial units, 50
Importing objects, 43–44
Inflow object setup, 453
Info window, 7, 8, 31, 33
Input–Shader, 113, 115
Insert Keyframe, 231
Inset Faces command, 62–63
Installing, 575–576
    Python Script, 577–578
Intensity of color, 107
Interpolation, 186
Interpolation Mode, 202
Intersection, 80, 260–261
Inverse kinematics (IK), 371, 403–404, 422
    armature bones, 405
    Bezier curve, 406
    chains for arms, 423
    chains for legs, 425–426
    constraint, 404
    control handle, 407
    Object Data button, 408
    target quick method, 425

J

Joining meshes, 64
    in Edit Mode, 65
    in object mode, 64–65

K

Keyboard shortcuts, 4, 5
Keyed physics, 340
Keyed particle systems, 340–342; *see also*
    Boids particle systems; Hair particle
    systems
Keyframes, 186, 188, 192, 199, 202, 221
Keying Sets, 212
Knife tool, 81–82

L

Lamp animation options, 210
Lamp settings, 169–171
Laplacian Smooth modifier, 297–299

Lattice modifier, 292–293
Layers, 13–14
Left-hand (LH), 3
Left-hand side (LHS), 7
Left mouse button (LMB), 3, 6
LH, *see* Left-hand (LH)
LHS, *see* Left-hand side (LHS)
Lighting, 169
Limit Selection to Visible function, 54
Linear Extrapolation, 197
Link command, 41–42
LMB, *see* Left mouse button (LMB)
LocRotScale, 189, 191–193
Lofted tunnel, 245–246
Logic blocks, 520
Logic Editor window, 518

M

Make Human program, 43
Making movie, 181
Manipulation Widget, 97
Manually assign vertices, 398–400
Mapping, 147
Mask modifier, 268–269
Mask, adding, 549
Material animation options, 210
Material buttons, 462–464
Material Cache, 125
Material Datablocks, 125
Material nodes, 478; *see also* Compositing
    nodes; Texture nodes
    adding texture node, 481
    Color—Mix RGB node, 481
    creating node arrangement, 480
    data block, 478–480
    linking nodes, 481–482
    material, 478
    nodes with objects, 483–486
    setting up, 480, 481
    variation, 482–483
    vector—mapping node, 481
Materials, 103, 478
    adding new, 105–106
    assigning texture color, 134–135
    buttons, 105
    colors, 105
    Diffuse tab, 106–108
    and GUI, 124–125
    halo settings, 118
    hardness value, 109